A HISTORY OF SPAIN

FOUNDED ON THE

HISTORIA DE ESPAÑA Y DE LA CIVILIZACIÓN ESPAÑOLA

OF RAFAEL ALTAMIRA

BY

CHARLES E. CHAPMAN, Ph.D.

THE FREE PRESS, *New York*

COLLIER-MACMILLAN LIMITED, *London*

865 - חיוב

TO MY SON

SEVILLE DUDLEY CHAPMAN

BORN IN THE CITY WHOSE NAME
HE BEARS

946 CHA

M 29538

Copyright © 1918 by The Macmillan Company

Printed in the United States of America

946

A 25760

For information, address:

THE FREE PRESS
A DIVISION OF THE MACMILLAN COMPANY
60 Fifth Avenue, New York, N.Y. 10011

Collier-Macmillan Canada, Ltd., Toronto, Ontario

First Free Press Paperback Edition 1965

PREFACE

THE present work is an attempt to give in one volume
the main features of Spanish history from the standpoint of
America. It should serve almost equally well for residents
of both the English-speaking and the Spanish American countries, since the underlying idea has been that Americans
generally are concerned with the growth of that Spanish
civilization which was transmitted to the new world. One
of the chief factors in American life today is that of the relations between Anglo-Saxon and Hispanic America. They
are becoming increasingly important. The southern republics themselves are forging ahead; on the other hand
many of them are still dangerously weak, leaving possible
openings for the not unwilling old world powers; and some
of the richest prospective markets of the globe are in those
as yet scantily developed lands. The value of a better
understanding between the peoples of the two Americas,
both for the reasons just named and for many others, scarcely
calls for argument. It is almost equally clear that one of the
essentials to such an understanding is a comprehension of
Spanish civilization, on which that of the Spanish American
peoples so largely depends. That information this volume
aims to provide. It confines itself to the story of the growth
of Spanish civilization in Spain, but its ultimate transfer
to the Americas has been constantly in the writer's mind
in the choice of his material, as will appear from the frequent
allusions in the text. An attempt is made to treat Spanish
institutions not as static (which they never were) but in
process of evolution, from period to period. The development
of Spanish institutions in the colonies and the later independent states, it is hoped, will be the subject of another volume.

Neither story has ever been presented according to the present plan to the American public.

Emphasis here has been placed on the growth of the civilization, or institutions, of Spain rather than on the narrative of political events. The latter appears primarily as a peg on which to hang the former. The volume is topically arranged, so that one may select those phases of development which interest him. Thus one may confine himself to the narrative, or to any one of the institutional topics, social, political, religious, economic, or intellectual. Indeed, the division may be carried even further, so that one may single out institutions within institutions. As regards proportions the principal weight is given to the periods from 1252 to 1808, with over half of the volume devoted to the years 1479 to 1808. The three centuries from the sixteenth to the nineteenth are singled out for emphasis, not only because they were the years of the transmission of Spanish civilization to the Americas, but also because the great body of the Spanish institutions which affected the colonies did so in the form they acquired at that time. To treat Spain's gift to Spanish America as complete by the year 1492 is as incorrect as to say that the English background of United States history is necessary only to the year 1497, when John Cabot sailed along the North American coast, or certainly not later than 1607, when Jamestown was founded. In accord with the primary aim of this work the place of Spain in general European history is given relatively little space. The recital of minor events and the introduction of the names of inconsequential or slightly important persons have been avoided, except in some cases where an enumeration has been made for purposes of illustration or emphasis. For these reasons, together with the fact that the whole account is compressed into a single volume, it is hoped that the book may serve as a class-room text as well as a useful compendium for the general reader.

The writer has been fortunate in that there exists a monumental work in Spanish containing the type of materials which he has wished to present. This is the *Historia de España y de la civilización española*, which has won a world-

wide reputation for its author, Rafael Altamira y Crevea.[1]
Indeed, the present writer makes little claim to originality,
since for the period down to 1808 he has relied almost wholly
on Altamira. Nevertheless, he has made, not a summary,
but rather a selection from the *Historia* (which is some five
times the length of this volume) of such materials as were
appropriate to his point of view. The chapter on the reign
of Charles III has been based largely on the writer's own
account of the diplomacy of that monarch, which lays special
emphasis on the relation of Spain to the American Revolution.[2] For the chapter dealing with Spain in the nineteenth
century the volumes of the *Cambridge modern history* have
been used, together with those on modern Spain by Hume and
Butler Clarke. The last chapter, dealing with present-day
Spain, is mainly the result of the writer's observations during
a two years' residence in that country, 1912 to 1914. In
the course of his stay he visited every part of the peninsula,
but spent most of his time in Seville, wherefore it is quite
possible that his views may have an Andalusian tinge.

In the spelling of proper names the English form has been
adopted if it is of well-established usage. The founder of
the Carlists and Carlism, however, is retained as "Don
Carlos" for obvious reasons of euphony. In all other cases
the Spanish has been preferred. The phrase "the Americas"
is often used as a general term for Spain's overseas colonies.
It may therefore include the Philippines sometimes. The
term "Moslems" has been employed for the Mohammedan
invaders of Spain. The word "Moors" has been avoided, because it is historically inaccurate as a general term for all the
invaders; the Almohades, or Moors, were a branch of the
Berber family, and other Moslem peoples had preceded them
in Spain by upwards of four hundred years. Their influence
both as regards culture and racial traits was far less than that
of the Arabs, who were the most important of the conquering

---

[1] The *Historia*, in four volumes, was first published in the years
1900 to 1911, at Barcelona. It has now reached its third edition, —
1913 to 1914. An excellent bibliography eighty-eight pages in length
with well over a thousand items is to be found in the fourth volume.

[2] *The founding of Spanish California* (The Macmillan Company.
New York. 1916), chap. IX.

races, and this fact, together with their late arrival, should militate against the application of their name to the whole era of Moslem Spain. All of these alien peoples were Mohammedans, which would seem to justify the use of the word "Moslems." The word "lords" in some cases indicates ecclesiastics as well as nobles. "Town" has been employed generally for "*villa*," "*concejo*," "*pueblo*," "*aldea*," and "*ciudad*," except when special attention has been drawn to the different types of municipalities. Spanish institutional terms have been translated or explained at their first use. They also appear in the index.

As on previous occasions, so now, the writer finds himself under obligations to his colleagues in the Department of History of the University of California. Professor Stephens has read much of this manuscript and has made helpful suggestions as to content and style. Professors Bolton and Priestley and Doctor Hackett, of the "Bancroft Library group," have displayed a spirit of coöperation which the writer greatly appreciates. Professor Jaén of the Department of Romance Languages gave an invaluable criticism of the chapter on contemporary Spain. Señor Jesús Yanguas, the Sevillian architect, furnished the lists of men of letters and artists appearing in that chapter. Professor Shepherd of Columbia University kindly consented to allow certain of the maps appearing in his *Historical atlas* to be copied here. Doctors R. G. Cleland, C. L. Goodwin, F. S. Philbrick, and J. A. Robertson have aided me with much valued criticisms. The writer is also grateful to his pupils, the Misses Bepler and Juda, for assistance rendered.

CHARLES E. CHAPMAN.

BERKELEY, January 5, 1918.

CONTENTS

xi

INTRODUCTION

THE fact that this book is in great part a summary, or selection, from one of mine, as is stated in the Preface, makes it almost a duty for me to do what would in any event be a great pleasure in the case of a work by Professor Chapman. I refer to the duty of writing a few paragraphs by way of introduction. But, at the same time, this circumstance causes a certain conflict of feelings in me, since no one, unless it be a pedant, can act so freely in self-criticism as he would if he were dealing with the work of another. Fortunately, Professor Chapman has incorporated much of his own harvest in this volume, and to that I may refer with entire lack of embarrassment.

Obviously, the plan and the labor of condensing all of the material for a history of Spain constitute in themselves a commendable achievement. In fact, there does not exist in any language of the world today a compendium of the history of Spain reduced to one volume which is able to satisfy all of the exigencies of the public at large and the needs of teaching, without an excess of reading and of labor. None of the histories of my country written in English, German, French, or Italian in the nineteenth century can be unqualifiedly recommended. Some, such as that by Hume, entitled *The Spanish people*, display excellent attributes, but these are accompanied by omissions to which modern historiography can no longer consent. As a general rule these histories are altogether too political in character. At other times they offend from an excess of bookish erudition and from a lack of a personal impression of what our people are, as well as from a failure to narrate their story in an interesting way, or indeed, they perpetuate errors and legends, long since discredited, with respect to our past and

xiii

present life. We have some one-volume histories of Spain in Castilian which are to be recommended for the needs of our own secondary schools, but not for those of a foreign country, whose students require another manner of presentation of our history, for they have to apply an interrogatory ideal which is different from ours in their investigation of the deeds of another people, — all the more so if that people, like the Spanish, has mingled in the life of nearly the whole world and been the victim of the calumnies and fanciful whims of historians, politicians, and travellers.

For all of these reasons the work of condensation by Professor Chapman constitutes an important service in itself for the English-speaking public, for it gives in one volume the most substantial features of our history from primitive times to the present moment. Furthermore, there are chapters in his work which belong entirely to him: XXXII, XXXIX, and XL. The reason for departing from my text in Chapter XXXII is given by Professor Chapman in the Preface. As for the other two he was under the unavoidable necessity of constructing them himself. His, for me, very flattering method of procedure, possible down to the year 1808, if indeed it might find a basis for continuation in a chapter of mine in the *Cambridge modern history* (v. X), in my lectures on the history of Spain in the nineteenth century (given at the Ateneo of Madrid, some years ago), in the little manual of the *Historia de la civilización española* (History of Spanish civilization) which goes to the year 1898, and even in the second part of a recent work, *España y el programa americanista* (Spain and the Americanist program), published at Madrid in 1917, nevertheless could not avail itself of a single text, a continuous, systematized account, comprehensive of all the aspects of our national life as in the case of the periods prior to 1808. Moreover, it is better that the chapters referring to the nineteenth century and the present time should be written by a foreign pen, whose master in this instance, as a result of his having lived in Spain, is able to contribute that personal impression of which I have spoken before, an element which if it is at times deceiving in part, through the influence of a too local or regional point of view, is always worth more than that understanding which proceeds only from erudite sources.

I would not be able to say, without failing in sincerity (and therefore in the first duty of historiography), that I share in and subscribe to all the conclusions and generalizations of Professor Chapman about the contemporary history and present condition of Spain. At times my dissent would not be more than one of the mere shade of meaning, perhaps from the form of expression, given to an act which, according as it is presented, is, or is not, exact. But in general I believe that Professor Chapman sees modern Spain correctly, and does us justice in many things in which it is not frequent that we are accorded that consideration. This alone would indeed be a great merit in our eyes and would deserve our applause. The English-speaking public will have a guarantee, through this work, of being able to contemplate a quite faithful portrait of Spain, instead of a caricature drawn in ignorance of the facts or in bad faith. With this noble example of historiographical calm, Professor Chapman amply sustains one of the most sympathetic notes which, with relation to the work of Spain in America, has for some years been characteristic, that which we should indeed call the school of North American historians.

RAFAEL ALTAMIRA.

February, 1918.

A HISTORY OF SPAIN

CHAPTER I

THE INFLUENCE OF GEOGRAPHY ON THE HISTORY OF SPAIN

THE Iberian Peninsula, embracing the modern states of Spain and Portugal, is entirely surrounded by the waters of the Mediterranean Sea and the Atlantic Ocean, except for a strip in the north a little less than three hundred miles in length, which touches the southern border of France. Even at that point Spain is almost completely shut off from the rest of Europe, because of the high range of the Pyrenees Mountains. Portugal, although an independent state and set apart to a certain extent by a mountainous boundary, cannot be said to be geographically distinct from Spain. Indeed, many regions in Spain are quite as separate from each other as is Portugal from the Spanish lands she borders upon. Until the late medieval period, too, the history of Portugal was in the same current as that of the peninsula as a whole. Isolation of the Iberian Peninsula.

The greatest average elevation in Spain is found in the centre, in Castile and Extremadura, whence there is a descent, by great steps as it were, to the east and to the west. On the eastern side the descent is short and rapid to the Mediterranean Sea. On the west, the land falls by longer and more gradual slopes to the Atlantic Ocean, so that central Spain may be said to look geographically toward the west. There is an even more gentle decline from the base of the Pyrenees to the valley of the Guadalquivir, although it is interrupted by plateaus which rise above the general level. All of these gradients are modified greatly by the mountain ranges within the peninsula. The Pyrenean Mountains and plateaus.

MAP OF
SPAIN AND PORTUGAL

SCALE IN MILES

COMPILED BY CHARLES E. CHAPMAN
JANUARY 1918.

To accompany "A HISTORY OF SPAIN" by Charles E. Chapman, January, 1918.

range not only separates France from Spain, but also continues westward under the name Cantabrian Mountains for an even greater distance along the northern coast of the latter country, leaving but little lowland space along the sea, until it reaches Galicia in the extreme northwest. Here it expands until it covers an area embracing northern Portugal as well. At about the point where the Pyrenees proper and the Cantabrian Mountains come together the Iberian, or Celtiberian, range, a series of isolated mountains for the most part, breaks off to the southeast until near the Mediterranean, when it curves to the west, merging with the Penibética range (better known as the Sierra Nevada Mountains, the name of that part of the range lying south of the city of Granada), which moves westward near the southern coast to end in the cape of Tarifa.

Geographical divisions of the peninsula. These mountains divide the peninsula into four regions: the narrow littoral on the northern coast; Aragon, Catalonia, Valencia, Murcia, and most of La Mancha, looking toward the Mediterranean; Almería, Málaga, and part of Granada and Cádiz in the south of Spain; and the vast region comprising the rest of the peninsula. The last-named is subdivided into four principal regions of importance historically. The Carpetana, or Carpeto-Vetónica, range in the north (more often called the Guadarrama Mountains) separates Old Castile from New Castile and Extremadura to the south, and continues into Portugal. The Oretana range crosses the provinces of Cuenca, Toledo, Ciudad Real, Cáceres, and Badajoz, also terminating in Portugal. Finally, the Mariánica range (more popularly known as the Sierra Morena) forms the boundary of Castile and Extremadura with Andalusia. Each of the four subdivisions has a great river valley, these being respectively, from north to south, the Douro, Tagus, Guadiana, and Guadalquivir. Various other sub-sections might be named, but only one is of prime importance, — the valley of the Ebro in Aragon and Catalonia, lying between the Pyrenees and an eastward branch of the Iberian range. Within these regions, embracing parts of several of them, there is another that is especially noteworthy, — that of the vast table-land of central Spain between the Ebro and the Guadalquivir. This is an elevated region, difficult of access from all of the surrounding lands. Geologists have considered it the "permanent nucleus" of the peninsula. It is in turn divided into two table-lands of unequal height by the great Carpeto-Vetónica range. The long coast line of the peninsula, about 2500 miles in length, has also been a factor of no small importance historically. Despite the length of her border along the sea, Spain has, next to Switzerland, the greatest average elevation of any country in Europe, so high are her mountains and table-lands.

These geographical conditions have had important consequences climatically and economically and especially historically. The altitude and irregularity of the land have produced widely separated extremes of temperature, although as a general rule a happy medium is maintained. To geographical causes, also, are due the alternating seasons of rain and drought in most of Spain, especially in Castile, Valencia, and Andalusia, which have to contend, too, with the disadvantages of a smaller annual rainfall than is the lot of most other parts of Europe and with the torrential rains which break the season of drought. When it rains, the water descends in such quantity and with such rapidity from the mountains to the sea that the river beds are often unable to contain it, and dangerous floods result. Furthermore, the sharpness of the slope makes it difficult to utilize these rivers for irrigation or navigation, so swift is the current, and so rapidly do the rivers spend themselves. Finally, the rain is not evenly distributed, and some regions, especially the high plateau country of Castile and La Mancha, are particularly dry and are difficult of cultivation. *Disadvantageous effects of geography.*

On the other hand the geographical conditions of the peninsula have produced distinct benefits to counterbalance the disadvantages. The coastal plains are often very fertile. Especially is this true of the east and south, where the vine and the olive, oranges, rice, and other fruits and vegetables are among the best in the world. The northern coast is of slight value agriculturally, but, thanks to a rain- *Beneficial effects.*

fall which is constant and greater than necessary, is rich pastorally. Here, too, there is a very agreeable climate, due in large measure to a favoring ocean current, which has also been influential in producing the forests in a part of Galicia. These factors have made the northern coast a favorite summer resort for Spaniards and, indeed, for many other Europeans. The mountains in all parts of the peninsula have proved to contain a mineral wealth which many centuries of mining have been unable to exhaust. Some gold and more silver have been found, but metals of use industrially — such, for example, as copper — have been the most abundant. The very difficulties which Spaniards have had to overcome helped to develop virile traits which have made their civilization of more force in the world than might have been expected from a country of such scant wealth and population.[1]

Geographical isolation the cause of Spanish individuality.

The most marked result of these natural conditions has been the isolation, not only of Spain from the rest of the world, but also of the different regions of Spain from one another. Spaniards have therefore developed the conservative clinging to their own institutions and the individuality of an island people. While this has retarded their development into a nation, it has held secure the advances made and has vitalized Spanish civilization. For centuries the most isolated parts were also the most backward, this being especially true of Castile, whereas the more inviting and more easily invaded south and east coasts were the most susceptible to foreign influence and the most advanced intellectually as well as economically. When at length the centre accepted the civilization of the east and south, and by reason of its virility was able to dominate them, it

[1] The first and most important social question in the history of the Spanish people, says Altamira, is that of modifying the physical conditions of the peninsula, as the basis of their national development. They have been able to count on the fertility of some regions, the abundant waters of others at some seasons of the year (most of which is lost in the sea, without being utilized), the wealth of subterranean waters in many localities, and the mineral wealth which lends itself also to industrial development. In other words, the problem is that of correcting the unequal distribution of Spain's resources, rather than of a lack of them.

imposed its law, its customs, and its conservatism upon them, and reached across the seas to the Americas, where a handful of men were able to leave an imperishable legacy of Spanish civilization to a great part of two continents.

Specific facts in Spanish history can also be traced very largely to the effects of geography. The mineral wealth of the peninsula has attracted foreign peoples throughout recorded history, and the fertility of the south and east has also been a potent inducement to an invasion, whether of armies or of capital. The physical features of the peninsula helped these peoples to preserve their racial characteristics, with the result that Spain presents an unusual variety in traits and customs. The fact that the valley of the Guadalquivir descends to the sea before reaching the eastern line of the Portuguese boundary had an influence in bringing about the independence of Portugal, — for while Castile still had to combat the Moslem states Portugal could turn her energies inward. Nevertheless, one must not think that geography has been the only or even the controlling factor in the life and events of the Iberian Peninsula. Others have been equally or more important, — such as those of race and, especially, the vast group of circumstances involving the relations of men and of states which may be given the collective name of history.

Events traceable to geographic conditions.

CHAPTER II

THE EARLY PEOPLES, TO 206 B.C.

Prehistoric Spain. THE Iberian Peninsula has not always had the same form which it now has, or the same plants, animals, or climate which are found there today. For example, it is said that Spain was once united by land with Africa, and also by way of Sicily, which had not yet become an island, with southern Italy, making a great lake of the western Mediterranean. The changes as a result of which the peninsula assumed its present characteristics belong to the field of geology, and need to be mentioned here only as affording some clue to the earliest colonization of the land. In like manner the description of the primitive peoples of Spain belongs more properly to the realm of ethnology. It is worthy of note, however, that there is no proof that the earliest type of man in Europe, the Neanderthal, or Canstadt, man,[1] existed in Spain, and it is believed that the next succeeding type, the Furfooz man, entered at a time when a third type, the Cromagnon, was already there. Evidences of the Cromagnon man are numerous in Spain. Peoples of this type may have been the original settlers of the Iberian Peninsula.[2] Like the Neanderthal and Furfooz men they are described generally as paleolithic men, for their implements were of rough stone. After many thousands of years the neolithic man, or man of the polished stone age, developed

[1] So called from the localities in Germany where bones of men of this type were discovered.
[2] The inhabitants of the Canary Islands, a Spanish group off the northwest coast of Africa, are of this race. They preserved their racial characteristics with great purity until the fifteenth century, since which time more and more intermixture has taken place.

6

in Spain as in other parts of the world. In some respects the neolithic man of Spain differed from the usual European type, but was similar to the neolithic man of Greece. This has caused some writers to argue for a Greek origin of the early Spanish peoples, but others claim that similar manifestations might have developed independently in each region. Neolithic man was succeeded by men of the ages of the metals, — copper, bronze, and iron. The age of iron, at least, coincided with the entry into Spain of peoples who come within the sphere of recorded history. As early as the bronze age a great mixture of races had taken place in Spain, although the brachycephalic successors of the Cromagnon race were perhaps the principal type. These were succeeded by a people who probably arrived in prehistoric times, but later than the other races of those ages — that dolichocephalic group to which has been applied the name Iberians. They were the dominating people at the time of the arrival of the Phœnicians and Greeks.

The early Spanish peoples left no literature which has survived, wherefore dependence has to be placed on foreign writers. No writings prior to the sixth century B.C. which refer to the Iberian Peninsula are extant, and those of that and the next two centuries are too meagre to throw much light on the history or the peoples of the land. These accounts were mainly those of Greeks, with also some from Carthaginians. In the first two centuries B.C. and in the first and succeeding centuries of the Christian era there were more complete accounts, based in part on earlier writings which are no longer available. One of the problems resulting from the paucity of early evidences is that of the determination of Iberian origins. Some hold that the name Iberian should not have an extensive application, asserting that it belongs only to the region of the Ebro (*Iberus*), the name of which river was utilized by the Greek, Scylax, of the sixth century B.C., in order to designate the tribes of that vicinity. Most writers use the term Iberians, however, as a general one for the peoples in Spain at the dawn of recorded history, maintaining that they were akin to the ancient Chaldeans and Assyrians, who came from Asia into northern

*The
Iberians.*

Africa, stopping perhaps to have a share in the origin of the Egyptian people, and entering Spain from the south. According to some authors the modern Basques of northern Spain and the Berbers of northern Africa are descendants of the same people, although there are others who do not agree with this opinion. Some investigators have gone so far as to assert the existence of a great Iberian Empire, extending through northern Africa, Spain, southern France, northern Italy, Corsica, Sicily, and perhaps other lands. This empire, they say, was founded in the fifteenth century B.C., and fought with the Egyptians and Phœnicians for supremacy in the Mediterranean, in alliance, perhaps, with the Hittites of Asia Minor, but was defeated, and fell apart in the twelfth or eleventh century B.C., at which time the Phœnicians entered Spain.

The Celtic invasion. The origin of the Celts is more certain. Unlike the Iberians they were of Indo-European race. In the third century B.C. they occupied a territory embracing the greater part of the lands from the modern Balkan states through northern Italy and France, with extremities in Britain and Spain. They entered the peninsula possibly as early as the sixth century B.C., but certainly not later than the fourth, coming by way of the Pyrenees. It is generally held that they dominated the northwest and west, the regions of modern Galicia and Portugal, leaving the Pyrenees, eastern Spain, and part of the south in full possession of the Iberians. In the centre and along the northern and southern coasts the two races mingled to form the Celtiberians, in which the Iberian element was the more important. These names were not maintained very strictly; rather, the ancient writers were wont to employ group names of smaller subdivisions for these peoples, such as Cantabrians, Turdetanians, and Lusitanians.

Celtiberian civilization. It is not yet possible to distinguish clearly between Iberian and Celtic civilization; in any event it must be remembered that primitive civilizations resemble one another very greatly in their essentials. There was certainly no united Iberian or Celtic nation within historic times; rather, these peoples lived in small groups which were independent and which rarely communicated with one another except for the commerce and wars of neighboring tribes. For purposes of war tribal bodies federated to form a larger union and the names of these confederations are those which appear most frequently in contemporary literature. The Lusitanians, for example, were a federation of thirty tribes, and the Galicians of forty. The social and political organization of these peoples was so similar to others in their stage of culture, the world over, that it need only be indicated briefly. The unit was the gens, made up of a number of families, forming an independent whole and bound together through having the same gods and the same religious practices and by a real or feigned blood relationship. Various gentes united to form a larger unit, the tribe, which was bound by the same ties of religion and blood, although they were less clearly defined. Tribes in turn united, though only temporarily and for military purposes, and the great confederations were the result. In each unit from gens to confederation there was a chief, or monarch, and deliberative assemblies, sometimes aristocratic, and sometimes elective. The institutions of slavery, serfdom, and personal property existed. Nevertheless, in some tribes property was owned in common, and there is reason to believe that this practice was quite extensive. In some respects the tribes varied considerably as regards the stage of culture to which they had attained. Those of the fertile Andalusian country were not only far advanced in agriculture, industry, and commerce, but they also had a literature, which was said to be six thousand years old. This has all been lost, but inscriptions of these and other tribes have survived, although they have yet to be translated. On the other hand the peoples of the centre, west, and north were in a rude state; the Lusitanians of Portugal stood out from the rest in warlike character. Speaking generally, ancient writers ascribed to the Spanish peoples physical endurance, heroic valor, fidelity (even to the point of death), love of liberty, and lack of discipline as salient traits.

The first historic people to establish relations with the Iberian Peninsula were the Phœnicians. Centuries before,

they had formed a confederation of cities in their land,
whence they proceeded to establish commercial relations
with the Mediterranean world. The traditional date for
their entry into Spain is the eleventh century, when they
are believed to have conquered Cádiz. Later they occupied
posts around nearly all of Spain, going even as far as Galicia
in the northwest. They exploited the mineral wealth of
the peninsula, and engaged in commerce, using a system
not unlike that of the British factories of the eighteenth
century in India in their dealings with the natives. Their
settlements were at the same time a market and a fort,
located usually on an island or on an easily defensible prom-
ontory, though near a native town. Many of these
Phœnician factories have been identified, — among others,
those of Seville, Málaga, Algeciras, and the island of Ibiza,
as well as Cádiz, which continued to be the most important
centre. These establishments were in some cases bound
politically to the mother land, but in others they were
private ventures. In either case they were bound by ties
of religion and religious tribute to the cities of Phœnicia.
To the Phœnicians is due the modern name of the greater
part of the peninsula. They called it "Span," or "Spania,"
meaning "hidden (or remote) land." In course of time they
were able to extend their domination inland, introducing
important modifications in the life of the Iberian tribes,
if only through the articles of commerce they brought.

The conquest of Phœnicia by the kings of Assyria and
Chaldea had an effect on far-away Spain. The Phœnician
settlements of the peninsula became independent, but they
began to have ever more extensive relations with the great
Phœnician colony of Carthage on the North African coast.
This city is believed to have acquired the island of Ibiza
in much earlier times, but it was not until the sixth century
B.C. that the Carthaginians entered Spain in force. At
that time the people of Cádiz are said to have been engaged
in a dangerous war with certain native tribes, wherefore
they invited the Carthaginians to help them. The latter
came, and, as has so often occurred in history, took over
for themselves the land which they had entered as allies.

Meanwhile, the Greeks had already been in Spain for *The* some years. Tradition places the first Greek voyage to *Greeks* the Spanish coast in the year 630 B.C. Thereafter there *in Spain.* were commercial voyages by the Greeks to the peninsula, followed in time by the founding of settlements. The principal colonizers were the Phocians, proceeding from their base at Marseilles, where they had established themselves in the seventh century B.C. Their chief post in Spain was at Emporium (on the site of Castellón de Ampurias, in the province of Gerona, Catalonia), and they also had important colonies as far south as the Valencian coast and yet others in Andalusia, Portugal, Galicia, and Asturias. Their advance was resisted by the Phœnicians and their Carthaginian successors, who were able to confine the Greeks to the upper part of the eastern coast as the principal field of their operations. The Greek colonies were usually private ventures, bound to the city-states from which they had proceeded by ties of religion and affection alone. They were also independent of one another. Their manner of entry resembled that already described in the case of the Phœnicians, for they went first to the islands near the coast, and thence to the mainland, where at length they joined with native towns, although having a separate, walled-off district of their own, — comparable to the situation at the present day in certain ports of European nations on the coast of China. Once masters of the coast the Greeks were able to penetrate inland and to introduce Greek goods and Greek influences over a broad area of the peninsula. To them is attributed the introduction of the vine and the olive, which ever since have been an important factor in the economic history of Spain.

The principal objects of the Carthaginians in Spain were *Spain* to develop the rich silver mines of the land and to engage *under the* in commerce. In furtherance of these aims they established *Barcas.* a rigorous military system, putting garrisons in the cities, and insisting on tribute in both soldiers and money. In other respects they left both the Phœnician colonies and the native tribes in full enjoyment of their laws and customs, but founded cities of their own on the model of Carthage.

They did not attempt a thorough conquest of the peninsula until their difficulties with the rising power of Rome pointed out its desirability. In the middle of the third century B.C., Carthage, which had long been the leading power in the western Mediterranean, came into conflict with Rome in the First Punic War. As a result of this war, which ended in 242 B.C., Rome took the place of Carthage in Sicily. It was then that Hamilcar of the great Barca family of Carthage suggested the more thorough occupation of Spain as a counterpoise to the Roman acquisition of Sicily, in the hope that Carthage might eventually engage with success in a new war with Rome. He at length entered Spain with a Carthaginian army in 236 B.C., having also been granted political powers which were so ample that he became practically independent of direction from Carthage. The conquest was not easy, for while many tribes joined with him, others offered a bitter resistance. Hamilcar achieved vast conquests, built many forts, and is traditionally supposed to have founded the city of Barcelona, which bears his family name. He died in battle, and was succeeded by his son-in-law, Hasdrubal. Hasdrubal followed a policy of conciliation and peace, encouraging his soldiers to marry Iberian women, and himself wedding a Spanish princess. He made his capital at Cartagena, building virtually a new city on the site of an older one. This was the principal military and commercial centre in Spain during the remainder of Carthaginian rule. There the Barcas erected great public buildings and palaces, and ruled the country like kings. Hasdrubal was at length assassinated, leaving his command to Hannibal, the son of Hamilcar. Though less than thirty years of age Hannibal was already an experienced soldier and was also an ardent Carthaginian patriot, bitterly hostile to Rome. The time now seemed ripe for the realization of the ambitions of Hamilcar.

Siege of Saguntum.

In order to check the Carthaginian advance the Romans had long since put themselves forward as protectors of the Greek colonies of Spain. Whether Saguntum was included in the treaties they had made or whether it was a Greek city at all is doubted today, but when Hannibal got into a dispute with that city and attacked it Rome claimed that this violated the treaty which had been made by Hasdrubal. It was in the year 219 B.C. that Hannibal laid siege to Saguntum. The Saguntines defended their city with a heroic valor which Spaniards have many times manifested under like circumstances. When resistance seemed hopeless they endeavored to destroy their wealth and take their own lives. Nevertheless, Hannibal contrived to capture many prisoners, who were given to his soldiers as slaves, and to get a vast booty, part of which he forwarded to Carthage. This arrived when the Carthaginians were discussing the question of Saguntum with a Roman embassy, and, coupled with patriotic pride, it caused them to sustain Hannibal and to declare war on Rome in the year 218 B.C.

Hannibal had already organized a great army of over 100,000 men, in great part Spanish troops, and had started by the land route for Italy. His brilliant achievements in Italy, reflecting, though they do, not a little glory on Spain, belong rather to the history of Rome. The Romans had hoped to detain him in Spain, and had sent Gnæus Scipio to accomplish this end. When he arrived in Spain he found that Hannibal had already gone. He remained, however, and with the aid of another army under his brother, Publius Cornelius Scipio, was able to overrun a great part of Catalonia and Valencia. In this campaign the natives followed their traditional practice of allying, some with one side, others with the other. Hannibal's brother Hasdrubal was at length able to turn the tide, defeating the two Scipios in 211 B.C. He then proceeded to the aid of Hannibal in Italy, but his defeat at the battle of the Metaurus was a deathblow to Carthage in the war against Rome. The Romans, meanwhile, renewed the war in Spain, where the youthful Publius Cornelius Scipio, son of the Scipio of the same name who had been killed in Spain, had been placed in command. By reckless daring and good fortune rather than by military skill Scipio won several battles and captured the great city of Cartagena. He ingratiated himself with native tribes by promises to restore their liberty and by several generous acts calculated to please them, — as, for

Expulsion of the Carthaginians by the Romans.

example, his return of a native girl who had been given to him, on learning that she was on the point of being married to a native prince. These practices helped him to win victory after victory, despite several instances of desperate resistance, until at length in 206 B.C. the Carthaginians abandoned the peninsula. It was this same Scipio who later defeated Hannibal at Zama, near Carthage, in 202 B.C., whereby he brought the war to an end and gained for himself the surname Africanus.

Results of Carthaginian occupation. The Carthaginians had been in Spain for over two hundred years, and, as was natural, had influenced the customs of the natives. Nevertheless, their rule was rather a continuation, on a grander scale, of the Phœnician civilization. From the standpoint of race, too, they and their Berber and Numidian allies, who entered with them, were perhaps of the same blood as the primitive Iberians. They had developed far beyond them, however, and their example assisted the native tribesmen to attain to a higher culture than had hitherto been acquired. If Rome was to mould Spanish civilization, it must not be forgotten that the Phœnicians, Greeks, and Carthaginians had already prepared the way.

CHAPTER III

ROMAN SPAIN, 206 B.C. — 409 A.D.

UNDOUBTEDLY the greatest single fact in the history of Spain was the long Roman occupation, lasting more than six centuries. All that Spain is or has done in the world can be traced in greatest measure to the Latin civilization which the organizing genius of Rome was able to graft upon her. Nevertheless, the history of Spain in the Roman period does not differ in its essentials from that of the Roman world at large, wherefore it may be passed over, with only a brief indication of events and conditions in Spain and a bare hint at the workings and content of Latin civilization in general. *Importance of the Roman occupation.*

The Romans had not intended to effect a thorough conquest of Spain, but the inevitable law of expansion forced them to attempt it, unless they wished to surrender what they had gained, leaving themselves once more exposed to danger from that quarter. The more civilized east and south submitted easily to the Roman rule, but the tribes of the centre, north, and west opposed a most vigorous and persistent resistance. The war lasted three centuries, but may be divided into three periods, in each of which the Romans appeared to better advantage than in the preceding, until at length the powerful effects of Roman organization were already making themselves felt over all the land, even before the end of the wars. *The Roman conquest.*

The first of these periods began while the Carthaginians were still in the peninsula, and lasted for upwards of seventy years. This was an era of bitter and often temporarily successful resistance to Rome, — a matter which taxed *The military conquest.*

15

the resources of the Roman Republic heavily. The very lack of union of the Spanish peoples tended to prolong the conflict, since any tribe might make war, then peace, and war again, with the result that no conquests, aside from those in the east and south, were ever secure. The type of warfare was also difficult for the Roman legionaries to cope with, for the Spaniards fought in small groups, taking advantage of their knowledge of the country to cut off detachments or to surprise larger forces when they were not in the best position to fight. These military methods, employed by Spaniards many times in their history, have been given, very appropriately, a Spanish name, — *guerrilla* (little war). Service in Spain came to be the most dreaded of all by the Roman troops, and several times Roman soldiers refused to go to the peninsula, or to fight when they got there, all of which encouraged the Spanish tribes to continue the revolt. The Romans employed harsh methods against those who resisted them, levelling their city walls and towers, selling prisoners of war into slavery, and imposing heavy taxes on conquered towns. They often displayed an almost inhuman brutality and treachery, which probably harmed their cause rather than helped it. Two incidents stand out as the most important in this period, and they illustrate the way in which the Romans conducted the war, — the wars of the Romans against the Lusitanians and against the city of Numantia in the middle years of the second century B.C.

Viriatus.

The Roman leader Galba had been defeated by the Lusitanians, whereupon he resorted to an unworthy stratagem to reduce them. He granted them a favorable peace, and then when they were returning to their homes unprepared for an attack he fell upon them, and mercilessly put them to death. He could not kill them all, however, and a determined few gathered about a shepherd named Viriatus to renew the war. Viriatus was a man of exceptional military talent, and he was able to reconquer a great part of western and central Spain. For eight or nine years he hurled back army after army sent against him, until at length the Roman general Servilianus recognized the independence of the lands in the control of Viriatus. The Roman government disavowed the act of Servilianus, and sent out another general, Cæpio by name, who procured the assassination of Viriatus. Thereafter, the Lusitanians were unable to maintain an effective resistance, and they were obliged to take up their abode in lands where they could be more easily controlled should they again attempt a revolt.

Meanwhile, the wars of Numantia, which date from the year 152 B.C., were still going on. Numantia was a city on the Douro near the present town of Soria, and seems to have been at that time the centre, or capital, of a powerful confederation. Around this city occurred the principal incidents of the war in central Spain, although the fighting went on elsewhere as well. Four times the Roman armies were utterly defeated and obliged to grant peace, but on each occasion their treaties were disavowed by the government or else the Roman generals declined to abide by their own terms. Finally, Rome sent Scipio Æmilianus, her best officer, with a great army to bring the war to an end. This general contrived to reach the walls of Numantia, and was so skilful in his methods that the city was cut off from its water-supply and even from the hope of outside help. The Numantines therefore asked for terms, but the conditions offered were so harsh that they resolved to burn the city and fight to the death. This they did, killing themselves if they did not fall in battle. Thus ended the Numantine wars at a date placed variously from 134 to 132 B.C. The most serious part of the fighting was now over. *The wars of Numantia.*

In the next period, lasting more than a hundred years, there were not a few native revolts against the Romans, but the principal characteristic of the era was the part which Spain played in the domestic strife of the Roman Republic. Spain had already become sufficiently Romanized to be the most important Roman province. When the party of Sulla triumphed over that of Marius in Rome, Sertorius, a partisan of the latter, had to flee from Italy, and made his way to Spain and thence to Africa. In 81 B.C. he returned to Spain, and put himself at the head of what purported to be a revolt against Rome. Part Spanish in blood he was *Sertorius.*

c

able to attract the natives to his standard as well as the Romans in Spain who were opposed to Sulla, and in a short time he became master of most of the peninsula. He was far from desiring a restoration of native independence, however, but wished, through Spain, to overthrow the Sullan party in Rome. The real significance of his revolt was that it facilitated the Romanization of the country, for Sertorius introduced Roman civilization under the guise of a war against the Roman state. His governmental administration was based on that of Rome, and his principal officials were either Romans or part Roman in blood. He also founded schools in which the teachers were Greeks and Romans. It was natural that not a few of the natives should view with displeasure the secondary place allotted to them and their customs and to their hopes of independence. Several of the Roman officers with Sertorius also became discontented, whether through envy or ambition. Thus it was that the famous Roman general Pompey was at length able to gain a victory by treachery which he could not achieve by force of arms. A price was put on Sertorius' head, and he was assassinated in 72 B.C. by some of his companions in arms, as Viriatus had been before him. In the course of the next year Pompey was able to subject the entire region formerly ruled by Sertorius. In the war between Cæsar and Pompey, commencing in 49 B.C., Spain twice served as a battle-ground where Cæsar gained great victories over the partisans of his enemy, at Ilerda (modern Lérida) in 49, and at Munda (near Ronda) in 45 B.C. It is noteworthy that by this time a Cæsar could seek his Roman enemy in Spain, without paying great heed to the native peoples. The north and northwest were not wholly subdued however. This task was left to the victor in the next period of civil strife at Rome, Octavius, who became the Emperor Augustus. His general, Agrippa, finally suppressed the peoples of the northern coasts, just prior to the beginning of the Christian era.

Invasions from Africa.

For another hundred years there were minor uprisings, after which there followed, so far as the internal affairs of the peninsula were concerned, the long Roman peace. On several occasions there were invasions from the outside, once by the Franks in the north, and various times by peoples from Africa. The latter are the more noteworthy. In all, or nearly all, of the wars chronicled thus far troops from northern Africa were engaged, while the same region was a stronghold for pirates who sailed the Spanish coasts. A large body of Berbers successfully invaded the peninsula between 170 and 180 A.D., but they were at length dislodged. This danger from Africa has been one of the permanent factors in the history of Spain, not only at the time of the great Moslem invasion of the eighth century, but also before that and since, down to the present day.

Administratively, Spain was divided into, first two provinces (197 B.C.), then three (probably in 15 or 14 B.C.), and four (216 A.D.), and at length five provinces (under Diocletian),[1] but the principal basis of the Roman conquest and control and the entering wedge for Roman civilization was the city, or town. In the towns there were elements which were of Roman blood, at least in part, as well as the purely indigenous peoples, who sooner or later came under the Roman influence. Rome sent not only armies to conquer the natives but also laborers to work in the mines. Lands, too, were allotted to her veteran soldiers, who often married native women, and brought up their children as Romans. Then there was the natural attraction of the superior Roman civilization, causing it to be imitated, and eventually acquired, by those who were not of Roman blood. The Roman cities were distinguished from one another according to the national elements of which they were formed, and the conquered or allied cities also had their different sets of rights and duties, but in all cases the result was the same, — the acceptance of Roman civilization. In Andalusia and southern Portugal the cities were completely Roman by the end of the first century, and beginning with the second century the rural districts as well gradually

The Romanization of Spain.

[1] As an illustration of the close relationship between Spain and northern Africa it may be mentioned that the diocese of Spain under Diocletian included the province of Mauretania, or northern Africa. A seventh province was formed of the Balearic Islands.

took on a Roman character. Romanization of the east was a little longer delayed, except in the great cities, which were early won over. The centre and north were the most conservatively persistent in their indigenous customs, but even there the cities along the Roman highways imitated more and more the methods of their conquerors. It was the army, especially in the early period, which made this possible. Its camps became cities, just as occurred elsewhere in the empire,[1] and it both maintained peace by force of arms, and ensured it when not engaged in campaigns by the construction of roads and other public works.

The Roman gift to Spain. The gift of Rome to Spain and the world was twofold. In the first place she gave what she herself had originated or brought to a point which was farther advanced than that to which other peoples had attained, and secondly she transmitted the civilization of other peoples with whom her vast conquests had brought her into contact. Rome's own contribution may be summed up in two words, — *law* and *administration*. Through these factors, which had numerous ramifications, Rome gave the conquered peoples peace, so that an advance in wealth and culture also became possible. The details need not be mentioned here, especially since Roman institutions will be discussed later in dealing with the evolution toward national unity between 1252 and 1479. The process of Romanization, however, was a slow one, not only as a result of the native opposition to innovation, but also because Roman ideas themselves were evolving through the centuries, not reaching their highest state, perhaps, until the second century A.D. Spain was especially favored in the legislation of the emperors, several of whom (Trajan, Hadrian, and possibly Theodosius, who were also among the very greatest) were born in the town of Itálica (near Seville), while a fourth, the philosopher Marcus Aurelius, was of Spanish descent.

---

[1] Many of these city camps date from the period of Augustus, whose name appears in most of them, *e.g.*: *Cæsaria Augusta* (Saragossa); *Urbs Septima Legionis* (León); *Asturica Augusta* (Astorga) *Lucas Augusti* (Lugo); *Emerita Augusta* (Mérida); *Pax Augusta* (Badajoz); and *Bracara Augusta* (Braga).

In the third and fourth centuries Spain suffered, like the rest of the empire, from the factors which were bringing about the gradual dissolution of imperial rule. Population declined, in part due to plagues, and taxes increased; luxury and long peace had also softened the people, so that the barbarians from the north of Europe, who had never ceased to press against the Roman borders, found resistance to be less and less effective. Indeed, the invaders were often more welcome than not, so heavy had the weight of the laws become. The dying attempt of Rome to bolster up her outworn administrative system is not a fact, however, to which much space need be given in a history of Spain.

Last years of the Roman rule.

In Spain as elsewhere there were a great many varying grades of society during the period of Roman dominion. There were the aristocratic patricians, the common people, or plebeians, and those held in servitude. Each class had various sub-divisions, differing from one another. Then, too, there were "colleges," or guilds, of men engaged in the same trade, or fraternities of a religious or funerary nature. The difference in classes was accentuated in the closing days of the empire, and hardened into something like a caste system, based on lack of equal opportunity. Artisans, for example, were made subject to their trade in perpetuity; the son of a carpenter had no choice in life but to become a carpenter. Great as was the lack of both liberty and equality it did not nearly approximate what it had been in more primitive times, and it was even less burdensome than it was to be for centuries after the passing of Rome. Indeed, Rome introduced many social principles which tended to make mankind more and more free, and it is these ideas which are at the base of modern social liberty. Most important among them, perhaps, was that of the individualistic tendency of the Roman law. This operated to destroy the bonds which subordinated the individual to the will of a communal group; in particular, it substituted the individual for the family, giving each man the liberty of following his own will, instead of subjecting him forever to the family. The same concept manifested itself in the Roman laws with reference to property. For example,

Society in Roman Spain.

freedom of testament was introduced, releasing property from the fetters by which it formerly had been bound.

Even though Rome for a long time resisted it, she gave Christianity to the world almost as surely as she did her Roman laws, for the very extent and organization of the empire and the Roman tolerance (despite the various persecutions of Christians) furnished the means by which the Christian faith was enabled to gain a foothold. In the fourth century the emperors gave the new religion their active support, and ensured its victory over the opposing faiths. There is a tradition that Saint Paul preached in Spain, but at any rate Christianity certainly existed there in the second century, and in the third there were numerous Christian communities.[1] The church was organized on the basis of the Roman administrative districts, employing also the Roman methods and the Roman law. Thus, through Rome, Spain gained another institution which was to assist in the eventual development of her national unity and to play a vital part in her subsequent history, — that of a common religion. In the fourth century the church began to acquire those privileges which at a later time were to furnish such a problem to the state. It was authorized to receive inheritances; its clergy began to be granted immunities, — exemptions from taxation among others; and it was allowed to have law courts of its own, with jurisdiction over many cases where the church or the clergy were concerned. Church history in Spain during this period centres largely around the first three councils of the Spanish church. The first was held at Iliberis (Elvira) in 306, and declared for the celibacy of the clergy, for up to that time priests had been allowed to marry. The second, held at Saragossa in 380, dealt with heresy. The third took place at Toledo in 400, and was very important, for it unified the doctrine of the Christian communities of Spain on the basis of the Catholic, or Nicene, creed. It was

[1] Spain contributed its share of martyrs during the periods of persecution, especially in the time of Diocletian. San Vicente of Valencia, Santa Eulalia of Mérida, San Severo of Barcelona, Santa Leocadia of Toledo, and Santa Engracia of Saragossa were among those put to death in Diocletian's reign.

at this time, too, that monasteries began to be founded in Spain. The church received no financial aid from the state, but supported itself out of the proceeds of its own wealth and the contributions of the faithful.

As in other parts of the Roman world, so too in Spain, heresies were many and varied at this time. One of the most prominent of them, Priscillianism, originated in Spain, taking its name from its propounder, Priscillian. Priscillian was a Galician, who under the influence of native beliefs set forth a new interpretation of Christianity. He denied the mystery of the Trinity; claimed that the world had been created by the Devil and was ruled by him, asserting that this life was a punishment for souls which had sinned; defended the transmigration of souls; held that wine was not necessary in the celebration of the mass; and maintained that any Christian, whether a priest or not, might celebrate religious sacraments. In addition he propounded much else of a theological character which was not in accord with Catholic Christianity. It was to condemn Priscillianism that the Council of Saragossa was called. Nevertheless, this doctrine found favor even among churchmen of high rank, and Priscillian himself became bishop of Ávila. In the end he and his principal followers were put to death, but it was three centuries before Priscillianism was completely stamped out. In addition to this and other heresies the church had to combat the religions which were already in existence when it entered the field, such as Roman paganism and the indigenous faiths. It was eventually successful, although many survivals of old beliefs were long existent in the rural districts.

The Romans continued the economic development of Spain on a greater scale than their predecessors. Regions which the other peoples had not reached were for the first time benefited by contact with a superior civilization, and the materials which Spain was already able to supply were diversified and improved. Although her wealth in agricultural and pastoral products was very great, it was the mines which yielded the richest profits. It is said that there were forty thousand miners at Cartagena alone in the second

Priscillianism.

Economic development and public works.

century B.C. Commerce grew in proportion to the development of wealth, and was facilitated in various ways, one of which deserves special mention, for its effects were far wider than those of mere commercial exchange. This was the building of public works, and especially of roads, which permitted the peoples of Spain to communicate freely with one another as never before. The roads were so extraordinarily well made that some of them are still in use. The majority date from the period of the empire, being built for military reasons as one of the means of preserving peace. They formed a network, crossing the peninsula in different directions, not two or three roads, but many. The Romans also built magnificent bridges, which, like the roads, still remain in whole or in part. Trade was fostered by the checking of fraud and abuses through the application of the Roman laws of property and of contract.

Intellectual life and the fine arts. In general culture Spain also profited greatly from the Romans, for, if the latter were not innovators outside the fields of law and government, they had taken over much of the philosophy, science, literature, and the arts of Greece, borrowing, too, from other peoples. The Romans had also organized a system of public instruction as a means of disseminating their culture, and this too they gave to Spain. The Spaniards were apt pupils, and produced some of the leading men in Rome in various branches of learning, among whom may be noted the philosopher Seneca, the rhetorician Quintilian, the satirical poet Martial, and the epic poet Lucan. The Spaniards of Cordova were especially prominent in poetry and oratory, going so far as to impose their taste and style of speech on conservative Rome. This shows how thoroughly Romanized certain parts of the peninsula had become. In architecture the Romans had borrowed more from the Etruscans than from the Greeks, getting from them the principle of the vault and the round arch, by means of which they were able to erect great buildings of considerable height. From the Greeks they took over many decorative forms. Massiveness and strength were among the leading characteristics of Roman architecture, and, due to them, many Roman edifices have withstood the ravages of time. Especially notable in Spain are the aqueducts, bridges, theatres, and amphitheatres which have survived, but there are examples, also, of walls, temples, triumphal arches, and tombs, while it is known that there were baths, though none remain. In a wealthy civilization like the Roman it was natural, too, that there should have been a great development of sculpture, painting, and the industrial arts. The Roman type of city, with its forum and with houses presenting a bare exterior and wealth within, was adopted in Spain.

In some of the little practices of daily life the Spanish peoples continued to follow the customs of their ancestors, but in broad externals Spain had become as completely Roman as Rome herself.

CHAPTER IV

VISIGOTHIC SPAIN, 409–713

General
character-
istics
of the
Visigothic
era.

THE Roman influence in Spain did not end, even politically, in the year 409, which marked the first successful
invasion of the peninsula by a Germanic people and the
beginning of the Visigothic era. The Visigoths themselves
did not arrive in that year, and did not establish their rule
over the land until long afterward. Even then, one of the
principal characteristics of the entire era was the persistence of Roman civilization. Nevertheless, in spite of the
fact that the Visigoths left few permanent traces of their
civilization, they were influential for so long a time in the
history of Spain that it is appropriate to give their name to
the period elapsing from the first Germanic invasion to the
beginning of the Moslem conquest. The northern peoples,
of whom the Visigoths were by far the principal element,
reinvigorated the peninsula, both by compelling a return to
a more primitive mode of life, and also by some intermixture
of blood. They introduced legal, political, and religious
principles which served in the end only to strengthen the
Roman civilization by reason of the very combat necessary
to the ultimate Roman success. The victory of the Roman
church came in this era, but that of the Roman law and
government was delayed until the period from the thirteenth
to the close of the fifteenth century.

Coming
of the
Vandals,
Alans, and
Suevians.

In the opening years of the fifth century the Vandals, who
had been in more or less hostile contact with the Romans
during more than two centuries, left their homes within
modern Hungary, and emigrated, men, women, and children,
toward the Rhine. With them went the Alans, and a little

later a group of the Suevians joined them. They invaded
the region of what is now France, and after devastating it
for several years passed into Spain in the year 409. There
seems to have been no effective resistance, whereupon the
conquerors divided the land, giving Galicia to the Suevians
and part of the Vandals, and the southern country from
Portugal to Cartagena to the Alans and another group
of Vandals. A great part of Spain still remained subject
to the Roman Empire, even in the regions largely dominated
by the Germanic peoples. The bonds between Spain and
the empire were slight, however, for the political strife in
Italy had caused the withdrawal of troops and a general
neglect of the province, wherefore the regions not acknowledging Germanic rule tended to become semi-independent
nuclei.

The more important Visigothic invasion was not long in
coming. The Visigoths (or the Goths of the west, — to
distinguish them from their kinsmen, the Ostrogoths, or
Goths of the east) had migrated in a body from Scandinavia
in the second century to the region of the Black Sea, and in
the year 270 established themselves north of the Danube.
Pushed on by the Huns they crossed that river toward the
close of the fourth century, and entered the empire, con-
tracting with the emperors to defend it. Their long contact with the Romans had already modified their customs,
and had resulted in their acceptance of Christianity. They
had at first received the orthodox faith, but were later converted to the Arian form, which was not in accord with the
Nicene creed. After taking up their dwelling within the
empire the Visigoths got into a dispute with the emperors,
and under their great leader Alaric waged war on them in
the east. At length they invaded Italy, and in the year
410 captured and sacked the city of Rome, the first time such
an event had occurred in eight hundred years. Alaric was
succeeded by Ataulf, who led the Visigoths out of Italy into
southern France. There he made peace with the empire,
being allowed to remain as a dependent ally of Rome in the
land he had conquered. In all of these wanderings the
whole tribe, all ages and both sexes, went along. From this

*Wander-
ings of
the Visi-
goths.*

point as a base the Visigoths made a beginning of the organization which was to become a powerful independent state. There, too, in this very Roman part of the empire, they became more and more Romanized.

The Visigothic invasion. The Visigoths were somewhat troublesome allies, for they proceeded to conquer southern France for themselves. Thereupon, war broke out with the emperor, and it was in the course of this conflict that they made their first entry into Spain. This occurred in the year 414, when Ataulf crossed the Pyrenees and captured Barcelona. Not long afterward, Wallia, a successor of Ataulf, made peace with the emperor, gaining title thereby to the conquests which Ataulf had made in southern France, but renouncing those in Spain. The Visigoths also agreed to make war on the Suevians and the other Germanic peoples in Spain, on behalf of the empire. Thus the Visigoths remained in the peninsula, but down to the year 456 made no conquests on their own account. Wallia set up his capital at Toulouse, France, and it was not until the middle of the sixth century that a Spanish city became the Visigothic seat of government.

The Visigothic conquest. The Visigoths continued to be rather uncertain allies of the Romans. They did indeed conquer the Alans, and reduced the power of the Vandals until in 429 the latter people migrated anew, going to northern Africa. The Suevians were a more difficult enemy to cope with, however, consolidating their power in Galicia, and at one time they overran southern Spain, although they were soon obliged to abandon it. It was under the Visigothic king Theodoric that the definite break with the empire, in 456, took place. He not only conquered on his own account in Spain, but also extended his dominions in France. His successor, Euric (467–485), did even more. Except for the territory of the Suevians in the northwest and west centre and for various tiny states under Hispano-Roman or perhaps indigenous nobles in southern Spain and in the mountainous regions of the north, Euric conquered the entire peninsula. He extended his French holdings until they reached the river Loire. No monarch of western Europe was nearly so powerful. The Visigothic conquest, as also the conquests by the other Germanic peoples, had been marked by considerable violence, not only toward the conquered peoples of a different faith, but also in their dealings with one another. The greatest of the Visigothic kings often ascended the throne as a result of the assassination of their predecessors, who were in many cases their own brothers. Such was the case with Theodoric and with Euric, and the latter was one of the fortunate few who died a natural death. This condition of affairs was to continue throughout the Visigothic period, supplemented by other factors tending to increase the disorder and violence of the age.

The death of Euric was contemporaneous with the rise of a new power in the north of France. The Franks, under Clovis, were just beginning their career of conquest, and they coveted the Visigothic lands to the south of them. In 496 the Franks were converted to Christianity, but unlike the Visigoths they became Catholic Christians. This fact aided them against the Visigoths, for the subject population in the lands of the latter was also Catholic. Clovis was therefore enabled to take the greater part of Visigothic France, including the capital city, in 508, restricting the Visigoths to the region about Narbonne, which thenceforth became their capital. In the middle of the sixth century a Visigothic noble, Athanagild, in his ambition to become king invited the great Roman emperor Justinian (for the empire continued to exist in the east, long after its dissolution in the west in 476) to assist him. Justinian sent an army, through whose aid Athanagild attained his ambition, but at the cost of a loss of territory to the Byzantine Romans. Aided by the Hispano-Romans, who continued to form the bulk of the population, and who were attracted both by the imperial character and by the Catholic faith of the newcomers, the latter were able to occupy the greater part of southern Spain. Nevertheless, Athanagild showed himself to be an able king, and it was during his reign (554–567) that a Spanish city first became capital of the kingdom, for Athanagild fixed his residence in Toledo. The next king returned to France, leaving his brother, Leovgild, as ruler in Spain. On the death of the former in 573 Leovgild became sole ruler,

Visigothic losses to the Franks and the Byzantine Romans.

and the capital returned to Toledo to remain thereafter in Spain.

Leovgild.   Leovgild (573–586) was the greatest ruler of the Visigoths in Spain. He was surrounded by difficulties which taxed his powers to the utmost. In Spain he was confronted by the Byzantine provinces of the south, the Suevian kingdom of the west and northwest, and the Hispano-Roman and native princelets of the north. All of these elements were Catholic, for the Suevians had recently been converted to that faith, and therefore might count in some degree on the sympathy of Leovgild's Catholic subjects. Furthermore, like kings before his time and afterward, Leovgild had to contend with his own Visigothic nobles, who, though Arian in religion, resented any increase in the royal authority, lest it in some manner diminish their own. In particular the nobility were opposed to Leovgild's project of making the monarchy hereditary instead of elective; the latter had been the Visigothic practice, and was favored by the nobles because it gave them an opportunity for personal aggrandizement. The same difficulties had to be faced in France, where the Franks were the foreign enemy to be confronted. All of these problems were attacked by Leovgild with extraordinary military and diplomatic skill. While he held back the Franks in France he conquered his enemies in Spain, until nothing was left outside his power except two small strips of Byzantine territory, one in the southwest and the other in the southeast. Internal issues were complicated by the conversion of his son Hermenegild to Catholicism. Hermenegild accepted the leadership of the party in revolt against his father, and it was six years before Leovgild prevailed. The rebellious son was subsequently put to death, but there is no evidence that Leovgild was responsible.

Reccared.   Another son, Reccared (586–601), succeeded Leovgild, and to him is due the conversion of the Visigoths to Catholic Christianity. The mass of the people and the Hispano-Roman aristocracy were Catholic, and were a danger to the state, not only because of their numbers, but also because of their wealth and superior culture. Reccared therefore announced his conversion (in 587 or 589), and was followed in his change of faith by not a few of the Visigoths. This did not end internal difficulties of a religious nature, for the Arian sect, though less powerful than the Catholic, continued to be a factor to reckon with during the remainder of Visigothic rule. Reccared also did much of a juridical character to do away with the differences which separated the Visigoths and Hispano-Romans, in this respect following the initiative of his father. After the death of Reccared, followed by three brief reigns of which no notice need be taken, there came two kings who successfully completed the Visigothic conquest of the peninsula. Sisebut conquered the Byzantine province of the southeast, and Swinthila that of the southwest. Thus in 623 the Visigothic kings became sole rulers in the peninsula, — when already their career was nearing an end.

The last century of the Visigothic era was one of great internal turbulence, arising mainly from two problems: the difficulties in the way of bringing about a fusion of the races; and the conflict between the king and the nobility, centring about the question of the succession to the throne. The first of these was complicated by a third element, the Jews, who had come to Spain in great numbers, and had enjoyed high consideration down to the time of Reccared, but had been badly treated thereafter. Neither in the matter of race fusion nor in that of hereditary succession were the kings successful, despite the support of the clergy. Two kings, however, took important steps with regard to the former question. Chindaswinth established a uniform code for both Visigoths and Hispano-Romans, finding a mean between the laws of both. This was revised and improved by his son and successor, Recceswinth, and it was this code, the *Lex Visigothorum* (Law of the Visigoths), which was to exercise such an important influence in succeeding centuries under its more usual title of the *Fuero Juzgo*.[1] Nevertheless, it was this same Recceswinth who conceded

Last century of Visigothic rule.

[1] This term, characterized by Joaquín Escriche (*Diccionario razonado de legislación y jurisprudencia.* Madrid, 1847) as "barbarous," is about equivalent to "Charter of the laws."

to the nobility the right of electing the king. Internal disorder did not end, for the nobles continued to war with one another and with the king. The next king, Wamba (672–680), lent a dying splendor to the Visigothic rule by the brilliance of his military victories in the course of various civil wars. Still, the only real importance of his reign was that it foreshadowed the peril which was to overwhelm Spain a generation later. The Moslem Arabs had already extended their domain over northern Africa, and in Wamba's time they made an attack in force on the eastern coast of Spain, but were badly defeated by him. A later invasion in another reign likewise failed.

The Moslem conquest.
The last reigns of the Visigothic kings need not be chronicled, except as they relate to the entry of the Mohammedans into Spain. King Witiza endeavored to procure the throne for his son Achila without an election by the nobility, and Achila in fact succeeded, but in the ensuing civil war Roderic, the candidate of the nobility, was successful, being crowned king in the year 710. What followed has never been clearly ascertained, but it seems likely that the partisans of Achila sought aid of the Moslem power in northern Africa, and also that the Spanish Jews plotted for a Moslem invasion of Spain. At any rate the subsequent invasion found support among both of these elements. Once in 709 and again in 710 Moslem forces had effected minor landings between Algeciras and Tarifa, but in 711 the Berber chief Tarik landed with a strong army of his own people at Gibraltar,[1] and marched in the direction of Cádiz. Roderic met him at the lake of Janda,[2] and would have defeated him but for the treacherous desertion of a large body of his troops who went over to the side of Tarik. Roderic was utterly beaten, and Tarik pushed on even to the point of capturing Toledo. In the next year the Arab Musa came from Africa with another army, and took Mérida after an obstinate siege which lasted a year. Up to this time the invaders had met with little popular resistance; rather they had been welcomed. With the fall of Mérida, however, it began to be clear that

[1] Named for him, Gebel-al-Tarik, or hill of Tarik.
[2] Near Medina Sidonia and Vejer.

they had no intention of leaving the country. At the battle of Segoyuela[1] Musa and Tarik together won a complete victory, in which it is believed that Roderic was killed. Musa then proceeded to Toledo, and proclaimed the Moslem caliph as ruler of the land.

There were four principal racial elements in the peninsula in the Visigothic period : the indigenous peoples of varying grades of culture; the Germanic peoples; the western Roman, which formed a numerous body, more or less completely Romanized; and the Byzantine Roman, which influenced even beyond the Byzantine territories in Spain through the support of the clergy. The two last-named elements were the most important. The Germanic tribes, especially the Visigoths, had already become modified by contact with Rome before they reached Spain, and tended to become yet more so. The Visigoths reverted to the family in the broad sense of all descended from the same trunk as the unit of society, instead of following the individualistic basis of Rome, although individuals had considerable liberty. Members of the family were supposed to aid and protect one another, and an offence against one was held to be against all. A woman could not marry without the consent of her family, which sold her to the favored candidate for her hand. She must remain faithful to her husband and subject to his will, but *he* was allowed to have concubines. Nevertheless, she had a right to share in property earned after marriage, and to have the use of a deceased husband's estate, provided she did not marry again. A man might make a will, but must leave four-fifths of his property to his descendants. Children were subject to their parents, but the latter did not have the earlier right of life and death, and the former might acquire some property of their own.

The family in Visigothic law.

The great number of social classes at the close of the Roman period was increased under the Visigoths, and the former inequalities were accentuated, for the insecurity of the times tended to increase the grades of servitude and personal dependence. The nobility was at first a closed

Social classes in the Visigothic era.

[1] Province of Salamanca.

D

body, but later became open to anybody important enough to enter it. The kings ennobled whomsoever they chose, and this was one of the causes of the conflict between them and the older nobility. Freemen generally sank back into a condition of dependence; in the country they became serfs, being bound by inheritance both to the land and to a certain type of labor. Freemen of the city, however, were no longer required to follow the trade of their fathers. Men of a higher grade often became the retainers of some noble, pledged to aid him, and he on his part protected them. Few were completely free. The Suevians took two-thirds of the lands and half of the buildings in the regions they conquered, and it is probable that the Visigoths made some such division after Euric's conquest, although they seem to have taken less in Spain than they did in France.

Social customs. The Visigoths were not an urban people like the Romans. The tendency of this age, therefore, was for a scattering of the city populations to the country, where the fortified village or the dwelling of a Visigothic noble with his retinue of armed followers and servants formed the principal centre. The cities therefore remained Hispano-Roman in character, and their manner of life was imitated more and more by the Visigoths. There was a laxity in customs which went so far that priests openly married and brought up families, despite the prohibitions of the law.[1] Superstition was prevalent in all classes.[2] One of the popular diversions of the period seems to have been a form of bull-fighting.

Royal power under the Visigoths. Before the Visigoths reached Spain the monarchy was elective, but within a certain family. The king's authority had already increased from that of a general and chief justice to something approaching the absolutism of a Roman emperor. With the extinction of the royal family there was a long period of strife between rival aspirants for the throne.

[1] The laws themselves furnish numerous indications of the customary evils. Doctors, for example, were forbidden to cure women, unless in the presence of certain specified persons. It may be added that doctors were made responsible by law for the effect of their medicines.

[2] One curious superstitious practice was that of celebrating a mass for an enemy who was yet alive. It was believed that this would accelerate his death.

Leovgild was the first to take on all the attributes, even the ceremonial, of absolutism, and was one of many kings who tried to make the throne hereditary. Despite the support given to the kings by the clergy, who hoped for peace through enhancing the royal power, the nobles were able to procure laws for an elective monarch without limitation to a specified family; an assembly of nobles and churchmen was the electoral body. These conflicts did not modify the absolute character of the king's rule; the king had deliberative councils to assist him, but since he named the nobles who should attend, both appointed and deposed bishops, and in any event had an absolute veto, these bodies did no more than give sanction to his will. Heads of different branches of administration also assisted the king. The real limitation on absolutism was the military power of the nobles.

For a long time the Visigoths and the Hispano-Romans had different laws governing their personal relations, although in political matters the same law applied to both. In the case of litigation between Visigoths and Hispano-Romans the law of the former applied, with modifications which approximated it somewhat to the principles of the Roman law. In the eyes of the law these differences disappeared after the legislation of Chindaswinth and Recceswinth, but many of them in fact remained as a result of the force of custom and the weakness of the central authority. In general administration the Visigoths followed the Roman model from the first. The land was divided into provinces ruled by officials called dukes, while the cities were governed by counts.[1] Each had much the same authority under the king as the kings had over the land. The Roman provincial and municipal councils were retained, and their position bettered, since they were not made responsible for the taxes as in the last days of the empire. Complex as was this system and admirable as it was in theory there was little real security for justice, for in the general disorder of the times the will of the more powerful was the usual law. Taxes were less in amount than in the days of the empire, but only the Hispano-Romans were subject to them.

Visigothic administration.

[1] The word "count" was not at that time a title of nobility.

The church in Visigothic times.

The church became very influential after the time of Reccared, but lost in independence, since the kings not only appointed the higher church officers, but also intervened in matters of ecclesiastical administration, though rarely in those of doctrine. Churchmen had certain privileges, though fewer than in the last century of Roman rule and much fewer than they were to acquire at a later time. Their intervention in political affairs was very great, however, due not only to their influence with the masses, but even more to their prestige as the most learned men of the time. Monasteries increased greatly in number; at this time they were subject to the secular arm of the clergy, for the bishops gave them their rule and appointed their abbots. Religious ceremonies were celebrated by what was called the Gothic rite, and not after the fashion of Rome, although the pope was recognized as head of the church. As regards heresies the church had to oppose the powerful Arian sect throughout the period and to uproot the remnants of indigenous and pagan faiths.

Economic backwardness.

An agricultural and military people like the Visigoths, in an age of war, could not be expected to do much to develop industry and commerce. Such as there was of both was carried on by some Hispano-Romans and by Greeks and Jews. Spain dropped far behind in economic wealth in this era. Roman methods were used, however, even in the agriculture of the Visigoths.

Intellectual decline.

Spain also fell back in general culture. Public schools disappeared. The church became almost the only resort for Christians desirous of an education, but there were Jewish academies in which the teachers read from books, and commented on them, — the system adopted by the Christian universities centuries later. Latin became the dominant tongue, while Gothic speech and Gothic writing gradually disappeared. The Greek influence was notable, due to the long presence of Byzantine rule in southern Spain. The writers of the period were in the main churchmen, particularly those of Seville. Orosius of the fifth century, author of a general history of a pronouncedly anti-pagan, pro-Christian character, was one of the more notable writers of the time.

By far more important, one of the greatest writers in the history of Hispanic literature in fact, was Saint Isidore, archbishop of Seville in the early part of the seventh century. Among his numerous works were the following: a brief universal history; a history of the Visigoths, Vandals, and Suevians; lives of illustrious men; an encyclopedia of Greco-Roman knowledge; and books of thoughts, of a philosophical and juridical character. He represented very largely the ideas of the Spanish clergy, and many of the principles enunciated by him were later embodied in the *Fuero Juzgo*. He maintained that political power was of divine origin, but that the state must protect the church. He supported the ideas of hereditary succession and the prestige and inviolability of kings as the best means of securing peace.

Saint Isidore.

In architecture the Visigoths followed the Romans, but on a smaller and poorer scale. Perhaps the only matter worthy of note as regards the fine arts was the presence of Byzantine influences, especially marked in the jewelry of the period.

The fine arts.

CHAPTER V

MOSLEM SPAIN, 711–1031

Importance of the Moslem conquest.

THE Moslem period in Spanish history is the subject of a number of popular misconceptions. The Moslems are believed to have attained to a phenomenally high stage of culture and to have lived in a luxury without parallel at that time in the world. While these views are not without truth, it is also true that the conquerors never shook themselves free from their tribal instincts, and it was not until the tenth century that their civilization was well established. Even then it was more largely through the efforts of others whom they imitated than through innovations of their own that they reached their high estate, which was the natural result of their power and wealth, although its ripest fruit was reserved for a later period, when much of their political authority had passed. Nevertheless, the Moslem occupation of Spain was on other grounds fully as important for Europe as it has usually been regarded, and perhaps more important for Spain and Spanish America than has ever been stated. As to the first point, it is true that Europe, through Moslem Spain, gained a knowledge of classical and Byzantine civilization. As to the second, racial elements entered the peninsula at this time which have left a deep impress on Spanish character, especially on that of the Andalusians and through them on Spanish America. The later Spanish colonization of the Americas passed almost wholly through the ports of Seville and Cádiz, and was confined in large measure to Castilians. At that time, however, Andalusia was considered part of Castile, and it was only natural that the Andalusian "Castilians" should have

38

been the ones to go. Many present-day Spanish American peoples pronounce their language in the Andalusian way, although differing in degree of similarity and having certain practices peculiar to themselves. In other respects, too, one finds Moslem-descended Andalusian traits in the Americas.

The Arabs were a people dwelling in greatest part in that section of western Asia which bears their name. Prior to their conversion to Mohammedanism they led a tribal life, not as one great tribe but as many, some of them in settled fashion, and others in a nomadic way, but all were independent one tribe from another and all engaged in endless strife. There was no such thing as an Arabic national feeling or an Arabic political state. Early in the seventh century Mahomet began to preach the faith which he originated, a religion of extreme simplicity in its doctrinal beliefs, but based very largely on the Jewish and Christian creeds. The Mohammedans date their era from the year 622 A.D., but it was not until after that time that the Arabs were converted to the new religion. Once they did receive it they were for a long time its principal sword-bearers, since it fitted their fighting spirit and promised rewards which suited their pleasure-loving tastes. Most of them, however, were not nearly so zealous in their religious beliefs as they have at times been regarded; rather they were too sceptical and materialistic a people to be enthusiastic devotees of an abstract faith.

Conversion of the Arabs to Mohammedanism.

Nevertheless, the Arabs achieved a conquest which was remarkable alike for its extent and for its rapidity. Between 697 and 708 they overran nearly all of Syria and the entire northern coast of Africa, including Egypt. For their conquests they had formed themselves into a single state under the rule of a caliph, who was at the same time the head of the church, thus centering political and religious authority in one person. The state was divided into provinces, two of which were in northern Africa, — Egypt and northwestern Africa. This cohesion was more apparent than real, for the old tribal jealousies and strife continued, accentuated by differences both in religious zeal and in

Arabic conquests.

Elements
of dis-
sension
among the
Moslem
conquer-
ors.

interpretations of the Moslem faith. Of the Arabs who entered Spain there were two principal parties, representing at the same time religious and tribal animosities, the Sunnites, or Sunnis, who were of Yemenite race, and the Shiites, or Shiahs, of Mudarite blood. Their quarrels in Spain, as elsewhere in Moslem realms, were a factor which rendered difficult the establishment or the maintenance of a strong political state. In northwestern Africa the Arabs had encountered the Berbers, who had submitted only after opposing a determined resistance. The Berbers were by nature a devout and democratic people, and once they received the Moslem faith they took it up with fanatical enthusiasm. They never regarded their conquerors with favor, however, and their hatred was intensified by the very religious indifference of the Arabs. Here, then, was another element of dissension in Spain, for the Berbers took part in the conquest along with the Yemenite and Mudarite Arabs.

Nature of
the Mos-
lem con-
quest of
Spain.

The military conquest took seven years (711–718), for after the fall of Mérida the invaders met with vigorous, if also unorganized, resistance. In characteristic fashion the Spanish peoples fought in guerrilla bands or defended their own towns with desperate courage, but did not aid one another. Some nobles made terms whereby they were allowed to retain their estates, but the majority of them opposed the conquerors. Except for narrow strips in the mountain regions of northern Spain the entire peninsula had been overrun by the year 718, at which time the Moslem armies crossed the Pyrenees into southern France. Spain was organized as a district ruled by an emir under the governor of the province of Africa, who was in turn subject to the Moslem caliph. The bond uniting Spain to Africa was not in fact very tightly drawn, for the Spanish Moslems acted in the main with complete independence of the governor of Africa. The conquerors did not usually insist on the conversion of the Spanish peoples (although there were exceptions to the rule), preferring usually to give them the option of accepting the Mohammedan faith or of paying a poll tax in addition to the taxation on Moslems and Christians alike. Many of the Arabs opposed the conversion of the

Christians, since the continuance of the latter in their own religion meant a lighter financial burden upon the Moslems. Since, also, the conquerors were outnumbered, they often found it wise to grant the Spanish peoples a right to retain their faith. In fine the conquest was not a matter of religious propaganda, but rather was one of a more or less systematic pillage.

The lands of the Visigothic state, the Christian church, emigrating nobles, and those who resisted were confiscated, but individuals who submitted, even nobles (and in some cases monasteries), had their estates restored to them in whole or in part, subject to the usual taxation. A fifth of the confiscated lands were taken by the state, and the rest were distributed among the soldiers and the chiefs of the Moslem armies. The state holdings were re-allotted to Spanish serfs, who were required to pay a third of the produce to the government, being allowed to keep the rest for themselves. The Berbers were given lands in the north, while the Arabs took the more fertile south. These lands, too, were given over to serfs on much the same terms as those granted by the state. The mass of the people were not greatly disturbed. Indeed, the agricultural laborer advanced economically, because requirements were lighter than formerly, and, also, since the lands were divided among a great many proprietors, the evil of the vast estates which had existed formerly was for the time being corrected. Slaves profited by the conquest, in part because they were better treated, but also in that they might become free by the mere act of conversion to Mohammedanism if they were slaves of Christians or Jews. A great many Christians became Mohammedans, some of them to escape slavery, others to avoid the poll tax, and still others from sincere belief, and they came to form an important class of the Moslem world, called "Renegados," or renegades, by the Christians, and "Muladíes" by themselves. The conquest weighed more heavily on the Christian church, although, indeed, it was allowed to remain in existence. The church had to experience the curious practice of having its bishops named or deposed and its councils called by the Moslem

Division of the conquered lands.

Religious effects of the conquest.

caliph or his representative. The Jews gained more than any other element. The harsh Visigothic laws were repealed and Jews were employed in government and administration as allies of the conquerors.

Civil wars. The Moslem invasion of France was carried on with varying success for several years. In 732 occurred the so-called battle of Tours, in fact fought near Poitiers, when Charles Martel and a Frankish army defeated the Moslems. It was not this battle which caused the retreat of the invaders from France, but rather a civil war in Spain eight years later, necessitating a return to the peninsula. The Berbers of Africa had risen in revolt against their Arabic rulers, and had defeated both them and a Syrian force sent to the latter's assistance. Thereupon the Spanish Berbers rose as well. For a time they were successful, but the emir was able finally to subdue them, being aided by the Syrian army in Africa, which he had induced to come to Spain. Then followed a terrible war between the Syrians and the emir, because the promises to the former had not been fulfilled. The struggle ended with a grant of some of the state lands in southern Spain to the Syrians, who were to receive the government's third of the produce, but not the title to the lands. Shortly afterward there was another civil war, this time between the Shiite and Sunnite Arabs, caused by the harsh treatment of the former by a Sunnite governor. The war lasted eleven years, being then given a new turn by the intervention of a man who was to play an important part in the history of the period.

Coming of Abd-er-Rahman to Spain. Other parts of the Moslem world had been afflicted by the same sort of internal strife as that which was occurring in Spain. In particular there was a dynastic struggle, which resulted in the dethronement of the caliphs of the Ommayad family and in the rise to power of the Abbasside caliphs. The Ommayads were ordered to be put to death, but one of them, a youth named Abd-er-Rahman, contrived to escape. He took refuge successively in Egypt and northwestern Africa, and in 755 came to Spain with the object of establishing himself there. This he was able to do, though not without a struggle, setting himself up as emir with his capital in Cordova, and proclaiming his independence of the caliph.

The entire reign of Abd-er-Rahman I (755–788) was one of war. He had to fight the Yemenite (Sunnite) Arabs, the Berbers, and many chiefs of various tribes, as well as the governors sent out by the Abbassides, before his authority was recognized. His ideal was that of an absolute monarchy which should bring to an end the aristocratic independence and anarchy in Spain, but in order to accomplish this he had to combat Arabic tradition and pride, Berber democracy, and inter-tribal hatred. Abd-er-Rahman was at least able to subject his opponents if not to change them. It was during his reign that the Frankish king Charlemagne invaded Spain and got as far as Saragossa. Obliged by events in France to recross the Pyrenees he was attacked by the Basques in the pass of Roncesvalles, and his rearguard was completely destroyed. It was this event which gave rise to the celebrated French epic poem, the *Chanson de Roland* (Song of Roland), in which the Frankish hero Roland is supposed to combat the forces of Islam. No Mohammedan forces in fact engaged in the battle, for the Basques were Christians; they were then, as later, opposed to any foreign army which should invade their lands.

Abd-er-Rahman I

Hisham I, the next emir, was not free from wars, but his reign was more notable in its religious aspects. He was a devout Mohammedan, and enabled the religious class to attain to great power. His successor, Hakem I, was a sincere believer, but did not refrain from drinking wine, thus breaking the religious law, and he conceded less influence in the government to the church than his father had. This led to several uprisings, in which the Renegados were a principal element. Hakem subdued them, and exiled many thousands, most of them Renegados, who went to different parts of northern Africa and Egypt. Another serious revolt broke out in Toledo, which had been enjoying virtual independence, though nominally subject to the emir. The citizens of Toledo were most of them Renegados, but they were also Spanish, and were unable to forget that Toledo had once been the capital of Spain. Hakem resolved

Internal strife.

to bring them into real subjection, and was able to effect his will. Seven years later, in 829, when Abd-er-Rahman II was emir, the people of Toledo revolted again, and it took eight years to subdue them. War and disorder were also prevalent in other parts of the realm. The inhabitants of Mérida, who were Christians, rose several times; in Murcia there was a seven years' war between the Sunnites and Shiites. At this time, too, the Normans began to attack the coasts of Spain just as they were doing in other parts of Europe. They made no permanent conquest, but rendered the coasts unsafe during the greater part of the century. Toward the close of the ninth century the emirate began to break under the strain of constant war. After repeated rebellions the city of Toledo formed itself into a republic, and on the basis of an annual tribute to the emir was recognized by the latter, who had no other right there. In Aragon the Visigothic but Renegado family of Beni-Casi founded an independent kingdom. A similar kingdom sprang up in Extremadura, and another in the mountains of southern Spain. Meanwhile, the Christian kingdoms were making gains. Except for them the new states were usually made up of Renegados. They did not work together, however, or the Arabic domination might have been completely broken: rather, each little state followed a selfish policy of its own. The most important was that of Omar-ben Hafsun in the south. Omar founded his kingdom in 884, with his capital at the castle of Bobastro. In 886 the emir attacked him, and for more than thirty years thereafter there was war between Omar and the emirs of Cordova. Omar was usually successful, acquiring nearly all of Andalusia, but his political plans illustrate the lack of a truly Spanish ideal in the kingdoms carved out of the emirate. At first he planned only a tiny kingdom of his own; later he aimed to get the governor of Africa to appoint him emir of Spain; finally he became converted to Christianity, and resolved to wage a religious war, whereupon his Renegado followers abandoned him. During the same period civil wars of a racial nature broke out in other parts of Spain between the Arabic aristocracy and the Renegados, especially around the cities of Elvira and Seville. The Arabs despised the Renegados, who were at this time the principal industrial and commercial class, especially in Seville, and envied their wealth. Many Arabic chiefs also refused obedience to the emirs. For a time the aristocratic party was successful, inflicting great blows on the Renegados, and increasing their own estates, but in the reign of Abdallah, early in the ninth century, they received a check. The same Abdallah inflicted a crushing defeat on King Omar. Thus the way was prepared for Abdallah's successor, Abd-er-Rahman III, who was to establish peace in Spain after two centuries of almost continuous disorder.

Abd-er-Rahman III (912–961) was by far the greatest ruler in the history of Moslem Spain. His first problem was the establishment of the central power. Within a few years he had reduced not only the Renegado states of Toledo, Aragon, Extremadura, and Bobastro but also the aristocratic Arabs and the Berber chiefs in various parts of Spain. He then changed his title from that of emir to caliph, thus signifying his intention of maintaining a robust absolute monarchy. He also drove back the Christian kings in the north, after which he proceeded to cultivate friendly relations with them. Even the Moslem province in northwestern Africa fell under his sway. In administrative matters as well Abd-er-Rahman III proved his ability. Not only did he create a great army but he also increased the strength of the navy (which the emirs before him had already founded) until it became the most powerful fleet in the Mediterranean Sea. Spain was recognized as the greatest state in Europe, and in western Europe it was also the centre of the highest culture. Through the caliph's measures agriculture, industry, and commerce, and education, literature, and the fine arts developed to a high point, and Cordova became a city of half a million inhabitants.

Hakem II (961–976) continued his father's policy in all respects, but was able to devote even more attention to intellectual activities. In military affairs the next reign, that of Hisham II (976–1013), was particularly brilliant, but it was not the caliph who directed affairs. In the time

Abd-er-Rahman III.

Almansor.

of Hakem II a certain Mahomet-ben-Abdallah-abu-Amir had attracted the attention and won the heart of the caliph's favorite wife. Through her aid he became the chief minister of Hisham II, who was a minor at the time of his succession. Hisham was soon put aside by Mahomet, who sequestered the caliph in the palace, and ruled in the name of the virtually deposed monarch. Mahomet was principally famous for his victories, on account of which he was called Almansor, meaning "the aided of God," or "the victorious by divine favor." He reorganized the army, making it a machine which was not only efficient in a military way but also personally devoted to him. Then in repeated campaigns he defeated the Christian kings of the northwest and northeast, reducing the greater part of their territories to his authority, and making himself arbiter in the kingdoms which were allowed to exist.

Downfall of the caliphate. Almansor died in 1002, but the military supremacy of the Moslem state was sustained by his son Abdul Malik, who succeeded as chief minister and virtual ruler. The latter did not live long, however, being followed in authority by another son of Almansor, who was not so fortunate in his rule. The Moslem nobles were hostile to the military absolutism of the Almansor family, chiefly, no doubt, because of the usual intractability of the aristocracy, but also because the military element, composed of Berbers and foreigners of all descriptions, even slaves (who might be powerful generals), had become the most important in the country. Civil wars broke out, therefore, and they resulted in the fall of the Almansor family, in 1009. The wars continued, however, between the generals of Almansor's army and the various pretenders to the caliphate (even though Hisham was alive during part of the time and was believed to be living for many years after he had probably died or been put to death). In 1027, the last of the Ommayads, Hisham III, became caliph, but in 1031 was deposed. Thenceforth, no one was able to make good a claim to the throne; Moslem Spain fell apart into a number of independent units, and the caliphate came to an end.

Although the differences in social status were much the

same in Moslem Spain as in other parts of Europe, there were
added complications, owing to the differences of race and
religion. There were the usual gradations of aristocracy,
freemen, freedmen, and slaves, but the real aristocracy
was the Arabic. This was nearly destroyed in the time of
Abd-er-Rahman III, and a new aristocracy of soldiers and
merchants took its place. Prior to that time both the
Arabic and Berber nobility had gone on increasing their
holdings until they had attained vast estates, and it was
perhaps on this account that they lived for the most part
in the country, leaving the cities to the Renegados and
"Mozárabes," as the Christians living under Moslem rule
were called. The Renegados were an especially important
element in the population, both industrially and intellectually, but were despised by the other groups; indeed, many
were descendants of slaves. The Mozárabes usually lived
in a separate district, and were allowed to govern themselves
to some extent, having law courts and some administrative
officials of their own. In daily life they mixed freely with
the Moslem population. The old differences between the
Hispano-Roman and Visigothic Christians were maintained
for a time, but seem at length to have passed away. The
Mozárabes were allowed to retain their Christian worship,
and as a rule were not persecuted, although frequently insulted by lower class Moslems. Late in the ninth century,
especially in the reign of Mahomet I, there was a period of
persecution, caused very largely by the excessive zeal of
some of the Christians. The law inflicted the penalty of
death on anybody who publicly cursed the founder of the
Mohammedan faith, wherefore a number of Christians,
already exasperated by certain harsh measures of the emir,
began to seek martyrdom by cursing the prophet. A Christian church council disapproved of this practice, but it continued and was later sanctioned by the church, which
canonized many of the martyrs. The Jews were another
important element, not only in administration, but also in
commerce and in general culture. Cordova became the
world's centre for Jewish theological studies. In all of this
period the Jews were well treated.

Social
classes in
Moslem
Spain.

Status of women.

A Mohammedan was allowed to have as many as four wives and a greater number of concubines, all together forming the particular individual's harem. The wives were subject to their husbands, but were not without rights. The first wife was privileged to forbid her husband's taking concubines or additional wives without her consent, although it is doubtful if the right was generally exercised. Possibly a wife's most important powers were those having to do with property, coupled with her privilege of bringing suit at law without the previous consent of her husband. Children of legally taken concubines, even if the latter were slaves, were held to be legitimate and free. Women enjoyed more liberty than they are commonly supposed to have had, being privileged, for example, to visit freely with their relatives. The Arabs were very fond of music and dancing, and took delight in licentious poetry. Not a little of the pleasure-loving character of this race survives today in southern Spain.

Methods of warfare.

Much has been said already with regard to the general administration of the Moslem realm, which was not greatly different from that of the Visigothic kingdom preceding it. As for the Moslem armies they were not so superior in organization when they entered Spain as their rapid conquests might lead one to suppose. They were nothing more than tribal levies, each group marching with its chief as leader. Campaigns were also managed in a somewhat haphazard fashion, for the Moslem troops went forth to war when the tasks of harvest time did not require their presence at home. Many expeditions were made with no idea of military conquest; rather they were for the sake of destroying an enemy's crops or securing plunder, after which the army would return, satisfied with what it had done. The Moslem rulers gradually began to surround themselves with special troops, and, finally, Almansor abolished the tribal levy, and formed regiments without regard to tribe. As for Moslem law the Koran was at the same time a book of holy writ and one of civil law. This was supplemented by the legislation of the caliphs, but there was always more or less confusion between law and religion. There was never a formal code.

Moslem law.

Attention has already been called to the difference in Religion in the religious fervor of the Moslem tribes. Many of the Moslem Arabs even went so far as to deny the existence of God, Spain. although the vast body of them, perhaps, were indifferent-ists. The Berbers and the mass of the people generally were very enthusiastic Mohammedans, so that it was unsafe to express one's opinions contrary to the faith or even to engage openly in certain philosophical studies, for these were re-garded as heretical. Among the religious themselves there were varying interpretations of the Koran and differences of rite. Religious toleration existed to such an extent that not only were the Mozárabes allowed to retain their churches, their priesthood, and their councils, but also some of their holy days were celebrated by Christians and Moslems alike. There was one instance where the same building served as a Mohammedan mosque and a Christian church. Chris-tian clergymen from foreign lands frequently visited Moslem Spain, while native churchmen went forth from the caliphate to travel in the Christian countries, returning later to the peninsula.

In the tenth century Moslem Spain came to be one of the The richest and most populous lands in Europe. The wealth wealth of of Cordova was astounding, although some allowance has Cordova. to be made for the exaggerations of the chroniclers. At one time the Moslem capital was said to have 200,000 houses, 600 mosques, and 900 bath-houses, besides many public buildings. It was well paved, had magnificent bridges across the Guadalquivir, and contained numerous palaces of the caliphs and other great functionaries. The most famous of all was that of Az-Zahra, which was a palace and town in one, erected by Abd-er-Rahman III for one of his wives. The great mosque of Cordova, which is in use today as a Catholic cathedral, was equally luxurious. This was begun in the reign of Abd-er-Rahman I, and was con-tinued and enlarged by later Moslem rulers. It came to have nineteen aisles one way, and thirty another, with twenty-one gates, and 1293 columns of porphyry and jasper with gilded capitals. In its adornment it was a wealth of marble, silver, and precious stones. Travellers came to

E

Cordova from all parts of the world, but it is worthy of note as an evidence of the lack of complete security, even in the greatest days of the caliphate, that it was the practice to come in great bodies, for the roads were infested with bandits. One measure of the advance of Moslem Spain is in the revenues of the government, which were eighteen times greater in the reign of Abd-er-Rahman III than they were in the reign of Abd-er-Rahman I.[1] This wealth depended on economic well-being, which was especially in evidence in the tenth century. The Arabs were not innovators in agriculture, but they had already learned much from others, and they assimilated Hispano-Roman and Mozárabic methods, with the result that Spain became richer in this regard than she had ever been before. They introduced rice, sugar, and several other products which had not previously been cultivated in Spain, and made use of irrigation in Granada, Murcia, and Valencia. Stock-raising, mining, and manufacturing were also extensively carried on. As a natural result of all this activity there was a like development of commerce. The principal part of Abd-er-Rahman III's revenues proceeded from import and export duties. It is worthy of note that there was a considerable traffic not only in slaves but also in women, — such was Arabic character. Seville was perhaps the most important port. Through the medium of commerce Spain came into close contact with the Moslem East and with the Byzantine Greeks. As a result of the mathematical problems involved in trade it is believed that the Arabs introduced into Europe the very important cipher, or zero, which they on their part had received from India.

Economic prosperity.

Languages.

Not only Arabic and Latin but many other languages as well were spoken in Moslem Spain; the Berber, for example, was independent of either of the two first-named. Despite the predominatingly Latin character of the eventual Spanish tongue the Arabic influence upon it was great, — not so

[1] The figures are 300,000 and 5,408,000 dinars respectively, or roughly $700,000 and $12,600,000. It is of course impossible to reckon the comparative purchasing power of a dinar then and its equivalent today, although it was no doubt much greater then; hence, the above figures have only a relative value.

much in words as in forms and idioms of speech. There
were Moslem schools of a private character, but there was
no public school system. The caliphs often brought learned
men to their court, but it was the religious who more than
any others devoted themselves to education. There were
few Moslems who could not read or write, and in this respect Spain was in advance of the rest of western Europe.
Women, far from being excluded from education, were
taught the same branches as the men, and often became
notable both in literature and in scientific studies.

Education.

The Arabs introduced the industrially manufactured
paper of the orient instead of using the parchment or papyrus
of the Romans. This greatly lowered the cost of books, and
led to an increase in productivity, facilitating both literary
and scientific studies. Although philosophy and astronomy
were so strongly opposed by the common people and the
priestly class of the Moslems that their study was at times
forbidden by the government,[1] they were a fruitful topic in
the education and researches of the upper classes. One of
the greatest glories of Arabic civilization was the transmission of Greek culture to western Europe, for the Arabs had
become acquainted with the works of the Greeks, while
western Europe had almost completely forgotten them.
Nevertheless, Moslem Spain was to be more important in
this respect in the period following the downfall of the
caliphate. Mathematics and medicine did not meet with
popular and religious opposition, and in both of these sciences
the Arabs achieved notable results. Polite literature, however, and especially poetry, was the most favored intellectual
medium. Poetry had been cultivated by the Arabs while
they were yet in their crude tribal stage. It was not unusual
for challenges to personal combat or declarations of war to
be written in poetry. Books of science, even, made their
appearance in verse, and the improvisation of poetry was
a general practice. The most favored subject-matter illustrates a pronounced trait in Arabic character, for amorous
themes of an immoral order accorded best with Arabic

Intellec-
tual
achieve-
ments.

[1] Almansor burned great numbers of philosophical works so as
to win the favor of the Mohammedan priesthood.

The fine
arts.

taste. The Spanish Moslems were not notable in painting and sculpture, but distinguished themselves in architecture and the industrial arts. Perhaps the most important feature of their cultivation of these arts was the introduction of Byzantine influences. They made use of the dome and of the elaborate decoration of flat surfaces (especially of walls) with arabesques, so named because of their profuse employment in Arabic work. In addition they painted their buildings in brilliant and variegated colors. They rarely built in stone, preferring brick, plaster, and adobe. The mosque was the principal example of their architecture. In that and in their civil edifices they made use of one feature, not unlike that of the Roman house, which has survived in Spain, — the enclosed court, or *patio*, surrounded by arcades,

Narrow
streets.

with a fountain in the centre. Streets were narrow, both with a view to provide shade against the heat of the sun, and also because of the necessities of space, so that the city might be contained within its walls.

CHAPTER VI

ONE of the popular misconceptions of the Moslem period in the history of Spain is that the Christians began a holy war almost from the time of the Moslem invasion, and continued to gain in fervor and in power, step by step, until at length they took Granada in 1492. In fact religious enthusiasm and national conquest alike were fitful and spasmodic, and very little progress was made in the period of the emirs and caliphs.

It has usually been held, although the matter is in dispute, that the Visigoths resisted the invaders continuously at only one point in Spain, — in Asturias. In the mountains of Asturias there gathered various nobles of the centre and south of Spain, a number of bishops, and the remains of the defeated Christian armies, and, aided perhaps by the natives of that land, they prepared to make a stand against the Moslems. On the news of the death of Roderic they elected a certain Pelayo as his successor, and it is this king who is customarily regarded as the founder of the Spanish monarchy. Pelayo fixed his capital at Cangas de Onís, and is believed to have maintained amicable relations with the Moslems for a while, perhaps paying them tribute, and possibly even making a visit to Cordova. Hostilities broke out again, however, and in the year 718 Pelayo and his partisans won a victory in the valley of Covadonga. Coming as it did after several years of defeats this achievement attained to a renown which was far greater than the merits of the actual battle, and in later years legendary accounts made the combat itself assume extraordinary proportions.

Fitful character of the Christian reconquest.

The kingdom of Asturias.

Covadonga.

53

It has usually been taken as marking the beginning of the Christian reconquests, and it is said that Pelayo became king in consequence of the battle, when in fact he was elected several years before. The battle of Covadonga did secure eastern Asturias to the Christians, which was its immediate result. Aside from that tiny kingdom there is no proof that there were any independent Christian states in Spain, although it is probable that there were several in the other mountainous parts of the north.

The advance of the Asturian frontier.

Since the invaders respected the religion and customs of the conquered, the war of the Christian kingdom of Asturias against them did not at first have a religious or even a racial character. It was a war of the nobles and clergy for the reconquest of their landed estates and of the king for the restoration of his royal authority over the peninsula. The little Asturian kingdom was like the old Visigothic state in miniature; for example, there were the struggles between the nobility and the crown for precisely the same objects as formerly. For a century the history of Asturias reduced itself primarily to these quarrels. Nevertheless, the Moslem frontier tended to withdraw from the far northwest, not that the Moslems were forced out by the Christians, but possibly because their own civil wars drew them together in the centre and south, or because their numbers were not great enough to make them seek the less desirable lands in the northwest. The frontier became fixed south of the Douro along a line running through Coimbra, Coria, Talavera, Toledo, Guadalajara, and Pamplona, although the last-named place was not long retained. It cannot be said that the Christians took a conscious offensive until the eleventh century. In this period, despite the internal dissension of the Moslem state, the Christian frontier did not pass the Guadarrama Mountains even at the most favorable moments, leaving Aragon and central and southern Spain in the enemy's hands. The line of the Douro was far from being held consistently, — as witness the conquests of Abd-er-Rahman III and Almansor.

The only notable kings of Asturias in the century following the death of Pelayo (737) were Alfonso I "the Catholic"

(739–757) and Alfonso II "the Chaste" (791–842). Both made successful campaigns against the Moslems, although their principal importance was that they brought back many Mozárabes from the temporarily conquered regions, and these helped to populate the north. To assure his power Alfonso II sought an alliance with the Holy Roman Emperor, Charlemagne, and with his son, Louis the Pious. It is this which gave rise to the legend of Bernardo del Carpio, who is said to have compelled the king to forbear making treaties with foreign rulers which lowered the dignity of the Spanish people. Some writers have found in this supposed incident (for the figure of Bernardo is a later invention) an awakening sense of nationalism, but it seems rather to reflect the traditional attitude of the nobility lest the king become too strong for them, for real patriotism did not exist. The two Alfonsos did much to reorganize their kingdom internally, and Alfonso the Chaste moved the capital to Oviedo. In his reign, too, there occurred a religious event of great importance, — the finding of what was believed to be the tomb and body of the apostle Santiago (Saint James) in northwestern Galicia. The site was made the seat of a bishopric, and a village grew up there, named Santiago de Compostela. Compostela became a leading political and industrial factor in the Christian northwest, but was far more important as a holy place of the first grade, ranking with Jerusalem, Rome, and Loreto. Thenceforth, bands of pilgrims not only from Spain but also from all parts of the Christian world came to visit the site, and, through them, important outside influences began to filter into Spain. More noteworthy still was the use of the story of the miraculous discovery to fire the Christian warriors with enthusiasm in their battles against the Moslems, especially at a later period, when the war entered upon more of a crusading phase.

The people of the mountains of Navarre were of Basque race, and seem to have maintained a more or less unorganized freedom from political subjection for many years before a definite state was formed. They opposed both the Frankish kings and the Moslem emirs, and for a long time the former

Alfonso I and Alfonso II.

Santiago de Compostela.

Beginnings of Navarre and Aragon.

were their principal enemy. At length they established their independence of both. In these wars the kingdom of Navarre almost certainly had its origin, but at an uncertain date. Tradition makes Iñigo Arista one of the early kings, or chiefs, but the first name definitely to appear is that of Sancho García in the tenth century (905–925). The founding of an independent state in Aragon was due to the same causes; indeed, Aragon and Navarre were assigned a common origin in the legends of the period. Aragon was absorbed by Navarre, however, possibly toward the end of the tenth century.

Origin of the Catalan counties.
Catalonia had been overrun by the Moslems when they entered Spain, but between 785 and 811 the Frankish kings were able to reconquer that region, establishing a province there which they called the Spanish Mark. This section was at first ruled by a number of counts, independent of each other, but subject to the kings of the Franks. Catalan submission to the latter did not endure through the ninth century. Wifredo, count of Barcelona, is believed to have established his independence as early as 874, although that event is doubtful; at any rate the separation from the Frankish kingdom was not much longer delayed. Each count was lord unto himself, although the counts of Barcelona were recognized as the greatest among them. Indeed, in the entire breadth of northern Spain each unit labored for its own selfish ends. Christians fought Moslems, but also fought other Christians. Owing to the disorder of the Moslem realm, however, the Catalan counts, like the other Christian rulers, were able to make some territorial gains.

Two centuries of scant progress in Asturias.
For nearly two centuries after the death of Alfonso II, or until the fall of the Moslem caliphate, very little progress was made by the kings of Oviedo and León, which latter city had become the capital of the Christian kingdom in the northwest early in the tenth century. There was a marked opposition between the Asturian-Leonese and the Galician parts of the realm, and the Galician nobles maintained almost continuous war with the kings. Similarly the counts of the frontier often acted like petty sovereigns, or even

joined with the Moslems against their own compatriots. So, too, there were contests for the throne, and neither side hesitated to call in Moslem aid. Some kings achieved conquests of temporary moment against the Moslems; for example, Alfonso III "the Great" (866–909) added considerably to his territories in a period of marked weakness in the caliphate, but was obliged to abdicate when his sons and even his wife joined in rebellion against him; the kingdom was then divided among three sons, who took respectively León, Galicia and Lusitania, and Asturias, leaving to the king the town of Zamora alone. Then followed the caliphate of Abd-er-Rahman III, when the Christian kingdoms, except Galicia, were most of the time subject in fact to the Moslem state, although allowed to govern themselves. To the usual quarrels there was added a new separatist tendency, more serious than that of Galicia had been. This proceeded from the eastern part of the kingdom in a region which came to be called Castile because of the numerous castles there, due to its situation on the Moslem frontier. The counts of Castile, centering around Burgos, had repeatedly declined to obey the kings of Oviedo and León, — for example, when they were called to serve in the royal armies. During the reign of Ramiro II (930–950), Count Fernán González united the Castilians under his standard, and after repeated wars was able to make Castile independent of the king of León. The reign of Sancho "the Fat" is typical of the times. Sancho became king of León in 955, but was soon dethroned by his nobles, who alleged among other things that because of his corpulence he cut a ridiculous figure as a king. Sancho went to the court of Abd-er-Rahman III, and got not only a cure for fatness but also a Moslem army. Aided, too, by the Christian kingdom of Navarre he was able to regain his throne. He had promised to deliver certain cities and castles to the caliph, but did not do so until compelled to by the next caliph, Hakem. Civil wars between the nobles and the crown continued, and many of the former joined with Moslem Almansor in his victorious campaigns against their coreligionists and their king.

The independence of Castile.

Sancho the Fat.

Advance of
the Chris-
tian states
in the early
eleventh
century.
When the caliphate began to totter, following the deaths
of Almansor and Abdul Malik, the Christian kings returned
to the conquest. Alfonso V (994–1027) of León and his
uncle Sancho "the Great" (970–1035) of Navarre pushed
their frontiers southward, Alfonso crossing the Douro in
Portugal. The counts of Castile, too, now aiding one
Moslem faction, now another, now remaining neutral,
profited by each new agreement to acquire additional
territory or fortified posts. Shortly after the death of
Alfonso V, Sancho the Great intervened successfully in the
wars of the Christian kingdoms, and united Castile and
León under his authority. Since he was also king in Navarre,
Aragon, and the Basque provinces of France and Spain,
only Galicia, where the kings of León took refuge, and the
counties of Catalonia remained free from his rule in the
north. Here seemed to be an important moment in the
history of Spain, — one which might have had tremendous
consequences. But it was as yet too early, not alone for
Spanish nationalism, but even for the conception of a
Spanish state. Sancho the Great undid his own work, and
consigned himself to a place only a little short of oblivion
by dividing his kingdom among his sons. The three most
important regions resulting from this act were the kingdoms
of Navarre, Castile, and Aragon. The death of Sancho in
1035 is an important date, however, for it marks the time
when work had to be begun over again to achieve the distant
ideal of the unity of Spain. Meanwhile, the counts of
Barcelona, who had lost their territories in the days of
Almansor, regained them in the ensuing decline of the
caliphate, whether by military conquest, or by intervention
in the wars of the Moslem state in return for concessions.
The important year 1035 is notable also in Catalonia, for
at that time Ramón Berenguer I, the first outstanding figure
among the counts of Barcelona, inherited the rule of the
county.

Except in times of war, relations between the Christian
and Moslem peoples were even cordial and intimate. They
visited one another's countries, aided one another in civil
wars, engaged in commerce, and even contracted mixed

marriages, not only among people of the lower classes, but also among those of the highest rank, even to that of royalty. Mohammedan law did not require the conversion of Christian wives, but many of the latter embraced the Moslem faith, with the consent, too, of their families. Although there were instances of Mohammedan women marrying Christians, the reverse was usually the case, for the conquerors did not bring their families as had the earlier Germanic invaders. Religious differences were not an insuperable barrier in this period : there was scarcely a war confined to Christians on the one side and Mohammedans on the other; the Mozárabes were not greatly molested within the Moslem state; Christians were often employed in administrative capacities by the emirs and caliphs; and Christian mercenaries, many of them Spaniards, fought in the Moslem armies. It was only natural, therefore, that the neighboring Arabic civilization should have exercised not a little influence on Christian Spain, especially since the power and wealth of the caliphate were so much greater than in the kingdoms of the north. In intellectual aspects — for example, in philosophy and science — the Arabic influence was to be greater at a succeeding time, but in political and military matters and in language much passed over to the Christians in this period. In like manner the Spanish peoples reacted upon the invaders, but this was confined principally to the effects produced by the Renegados and Mozárabes, whose contributions were largely due to the conditions of the Moslem world in which they lived.

Christian Spain itself was far from being a unit; rather diversity was the rule. The northwest followed the Visigothic tradition, while the north centre and northeast, especially Navarre and Catalonia, while retaining much of the Visigothic institutions came into frequent contact with French peoples, who gave a new turn to their civilization. Within each section, too, there were many complex differences between one region and another. Hence the institutions of the principal areas may be taken separately.

Inter-relations of the Christian and Moslem peoples.

Diversity in Christian Spain.

Kingdoms of Asturias, León, and Castile

Social classes in the Christian northwest.

Social inequality increased in this period, due to a decline in wealth and to an accentuation of the hazards of life. The higher nobility attained to vast privileges and authority, although less than in other parts of Christian Europe. They were often, but not always, allowed to conquer lands for themselves, rule their own estates with almost absolute authority, leave the king's service for that of another monarch, and be free from taxation. The social prestige of the nobles was weakened, however, through the king's right to grant titles of nobility. The king might also deprive a noble created by himself of his titles and lands. Most of the nobility of the lower grades were in fact retainers of the greater nobles or of the king, usually rendering military service in return for protection. This state of dependence was called *encomienda* (commendation), — a term used centuries later to cover the virtual enslavement of the American Indians. Small landed proprietors and free agricultural and industrial laborers placed themselves in similar relations to the great nobles, so that the latter were about the only really free class of the time. These civilian dependents gave produce, tribute, or personal service to the lord. The various grades of servitude, from serfs attached to a piece of land and enjoying at least some of the products of their labor down to individuals held in personal slavery, continued to exist. In general the servile classes advanced in about the same degree that the free-men fell back; many of them came together to form an intermediate class in which some rights — for example, to own property and to change one's habitation freely within the same seigniorial territory — were enjoyed.

The political system.

The king's power was complete enough in theory to merit being called absolute, for in him rested supreme legislative, judicial, and administrative authority over the realm as a whole. In fact the royal authority did not extend equally over all the land. On his own properties and usually in conquered regions the king was indeed an absolute monarch, but as concerned the lands of the nobles and the church there were important limitations on his authority. On their estates the nobles enjoyed rights of an economic nature and also those of a sovereign, with almost as much power in theory and in fact as the king had in theory over all the land. They raised troops at will, and fought with one another and even against the king; they had judicial authority over most of the cases arising within their lands; and they collected taxes for themselves. The protection which they owed to all on their estates was not very faithfully accorded, but on the contrary they oppressed not only their own dependents but also those of other lords, — a practice which was a fruitful cause of private war. The nobles, too, were veritable highwaymen, robbing travellers, business men, and pilgrims, and contributing more than any other class to the lawlessness of the times. Bishops and abbots occupied a position similar to that of the great nobles. The church had acquired estates through gifts of individuals and grants of the king, and the same rights and duties attached to them as in the case of the nobles. Thus, for example, great churchmen raised troops, which at times they commanded themselves. The royal power was still further limited in fact, because of the necessity of relying upon nobles or churchmen to govern distant lands or to hold other posts of an administrative and even of a judicial nature. The rulers of administrative districts were the counts (*condes*) appointed by the king, and these individuals often gave him considerable trouble, — as witness the uprisings (at length successful) of the counts of Castile. The very necessities of civil strife obliged the kings to yield privileges to one set of nobles in order to get their aid against another. Nevertheless, great as was the nobles' authority, it was not so excessive as elsewhere in western Europe. Feudalism, the essence of which was the grant of lands in perpetuity with rights of sovereignty attached, in return for which the grantee owed fealty and some form of service, perhaps military, to the grantor, did not exist in its fullness in northwestern Spain. By special grants the king might agree to refrain from exercising his sovereign privileges, but in such cases certain limitations were usually expressed. When judicial authority was conferred on a noble, some attributes were retained, — for example, the trial of crimes of murder and the right of appeal to the royal authority from the cases in seigniorial courts.   Again, when the lords made laws for their territories they did so by special grant of the king, who frequently intervened to change the seigniorial statutes or to enact others of his own.   The difference from European feudalism, however, was perhaps more juridical than actual.

Rise of the free towns.

One element appeared in this period which was to prove a great limitation on seigniorial authority, and was to be an aid to the king in the establishment of internal good order and unity.   This was the plebeian town.   The most important type of this class was the *villa*, or *concejo*, which originated in the tenth century.   The *villas* were founded on lands conquered by the kings, and were usually in frontier districts exposed to the enemy.   On this account special privileges were granted in order to induce people to settle there.   Anybody who could contrive to reach a *villa* was declared free, even if of servile grade before.   All citizens were not equal, however; there were varying grades of rank, though all were free.   The *villas* were exempted from many duties to the state, — often from the payment of taxes.   They were also withdrawn from the jurisdiction of the counts, and were granted much political authority. Each *villa* received its own *fuero*, or charter, by a special grant, with the result that there was a great variety in the terms of different charters, although certain of them tended to become the types which were imitated in subsequent grants.   As a general rule the government of a *villa* was in the hands of the assembly of citizens, in which local laws were enacted and judges and administrative officers elected. These rights, added to a long line of exemptions, made veritable political entities of the *villas*, which were independent of all but the king, and were in great measure not subject to him.   The *villa* extended beyond its own walls to include neighboring rural districts as well.   The rise of the *villas* on royal lands compelled the nobility and the clergy to form similar settlements in order to attract people to their territories or to avoid uprisings of their dependents, although these towns did not achieve rights equal to those of the *villas*.

Since privilege was the general rule, the law in north-western Spain was very far from being uniform. The Visigothic *Fuero Juzgo* continued to be the general law, but it was often supplanted as a result of grants by the king to nobles, clergy, and *villas*, and by the nobles and clergy to yet other units under their rule. Very important, too, was the modifying effect of local customs, which in the absence of other specific law were frequently cited. These customs tended to resemble those of the Germanic invaders or even of the indigenous peoples, since the type of life at this time was similar to that of earlier unsettled periods. This era, therefore, was one of a marked falling away from Roman traditions, which had to wait several centuries before they again came into their own. Diversity and primitive character of the law.

As was natural in such an age of disorder, commerce and industry did not flourish. With the rise of the towns a beginning was made, and at least one town, Santiago de Compostela, seems to have attained to some industrial importance. Commerce was hampered by innumerable obstacles, such as the depredations of foreign enemies and robber lords, the duties which had to be paid to the king, and the tolls which were collected by the lords at highways, rivers, or bridges within their lands. Stock-raising and agriculture and the production of the bare necessities of life were the principal occupations. Even these suffered, not only from the raids of the Moslems and the nobles, but also from the extreme weight of taxation, which was all the worse in that it was levied at the caprice of the king, lord, or churchman collecting it. The state of misery was so great that it is not surprising that famine and epidemics harassed the people. Economic backwardness.

In general culture, too, there was a decline to an even lower level than that of the Visigothic period. Churches and monasteries maintained something of the old intellectual traditions, and their schools were almost the only resort for an education. Latin continued to be used in literature and in official documents, but was already acquiring the new Ignorance and superstition.

forms which were to pave the way to the various Romance tongues of later days. The age was one of superstition, which made itself manifest, as in other parts of Europe, even in judicial procedure. The tests of wager of battle (or a duel between litigants), the hot iron, and boiling water were all used to determine innocence or guilt, in the belief that God would intervene on the side of the man whose cause was just. Poverty and danger led men to live in groups, thereby introducing a fresh departure from Roman individualism. In the towns life more nearly resembled the Roman type. In architecture this period marked the introduction of the buttress in some of the churches. Naturally, it was an age of the building of castles and walls, although the materials used were perishable. Most edifices were of wood, for in that day Spain was covered with forests in regions where they no longer exist. The burning of villages in times of war, especially during the Norman invasions, led to an exchange from the wooden roof in church building to one of non-combustible material of industrial manufacture.

Innovations in architecture.

Kingdoms of Navarre, Aragon, and Catalonia

The Christian reconquest of Catalonia.

In essentials, the social organization of north central and northeastern Spain was not greatly different from that of the northwest. Navarre and Catalonia were considerably affected by French influence, — Aragon less so. The details for Navarre and Aragon are in any event obscure or lacking. The Moslem invasion caused an emigration of the people of Catalonia across the Pyrenees, with the result that most of the territory remained deserted for two centuries. By 797 Gerona had been reconquered, and by 801 Barcelona was retaken, and these dates marked the beginning of the social and political reorganization of what was to become Catalonia. Lands were allotted to the Frankish conquerors and to a number of Catalans who had either remained in that region, subject to the Moslems, or who came in at the time of the reconquest. These estates were given free of obligation, except for that of military service. The most important holders were the various counts, but there were a number of lesser proprietors beyond their jurisdiction. Many of these were converted in course of time into feudatories of the counts. The counts were at first the appointees of the French king; later they became hereditary; and finally independent. The church also acquired vast territories in Catalonia, and was allowed to enjoy immunity from obligations and an absolute dominion over its lands. The most important holdings were those of the bishop of Gerona.

From the above it appears that the feudalism of France had taken root in Catalonia, where the nobles were more absolute in their own territories and more free from the power of the king or lord to whom they were subject than was the case in northwestern Spain. The greater importance of the counts of Barcelona has already been alluded to; by the beginning of the eleventh century they were saluted with the title of prince in recognition of their sovereignty. Aside from their own estates, however, their legal authority extended little further than that of a right to inspect judicial tribunals (in order to see that their decisions were in accord with the general law of the land) and to have certain cases appealable to their courts. The *Fuero Juzgo*, in so far as it applied to the changed conditions of Catalonia, was the general law, but numerous exceptions began to appear, much as in the northwest, although the development of free towns was not nearly so great. In Navarre the administration of justice belonged to the king, but on the other hand the king could not hold court, or make war, peace, or a truce, without consulting the nobles, and he was subject in every respect to the laws which confirmed their privileges. Furthermore, he acquired his throne by election, although the choice was confined as a rule to members of a single family. Feudalism not only weakened the power of the monarchy in north central and northeastern Spain, but also tended to impair the lot of the servile classes, which were delayed in achieving emancipation in these regions much longer than in other parts of Spain.

The most important religious incident of the period was the entry of the monks of Cluny into Spain. This order

Feudalism in Catalonia and Navarre.

P

Coming of the monks of Cluny.

had taken it upon itself to combat simony (the sale of church office) and offences against the ecclesiastical law of celibacy (requiring that men who had taken holy orders should not marry), both of which practices were than very prevalent in Christendom, and to bring about a complete and effective submission of distant churches to the bishop of Rome. These monks came into Spain by way of Navarre in the reign of Sancho the Great, and by 1033 they were already in Castile. Aside from their immediate objects they produced two other important effects: they reinforced the French ideas which had preceded them ; and they accelerated the reconquest as a result of the influence which they acquired, employing it to urge on the kings in wars against the Moslems.

Backwardness of Pyrenean Spain.

In economic institutions, general culture, and the fine arts the north centre and northeast were very backward, like the northwest. It is noteworthy, however, that by the ninth century the Catalans were already beginning to engage in trade in the Mediterranean.

CHAPTER VII

ERA OF THE SPANISH CRUSADES, 1031-1276

THE period of a little more than two centuries after the downfall of the caliphate was marked by a complete change from that preceding it, and in like manner was quite independent of the next succeeding era.   Up to this time Moslem Spain had represented by far the principal element in the peninsula.   The Christian states had maintained themselves with difficulty, making occasional gains, which were not infrequently followed by equally great losses whenever the Moslem power was sufficiently united internally to present its full strength.   The civilization of the Christian kingdoms had also been notably inferior in almost every respect to that of the Moslem south.   From the eleventh to the middle of the thirteenth century, however, the region of Moslem Spain, divided against itself, could not make an effective resistance, and the Christian powers began an offensive which enabled them to reconquer all of the peninsula except for a narrow strip in southern Andalusia.   These wars partook very largely of the crusading spirit then so prevalent in Europe, and although it was not nearly so persistent, fervid, or exclusive an aim as is usually believed it seems appropriate to characterize this era as that of the Spanish crusades.   This was also a period of noteworthy advance in internal organization in Christian Spain, for although civil war and disorder were great as compared with some later eras many regions enjoyed long terms of peace, very much more complete at least than in the three preceding centuries.   The pushing back of the Moslem frontier conduced greatly to this end.   The kings gradually became more powerful than the great individual nobles, who

General characteristics of the era.

67

had been able to meet them on virtually equal terms before. The free commoners advanced both in status and in numbers. In material well-being there was a marked improvement. Finally, in general culture the same tendency appeared. In all of these respects the fund of civilization was very slight compared with what it was to become in succeeding centuries, but it was at least something, whereas the period before had represented little more than bare existence. Despite the fact that there was very little understanding of the ideal of national unity, as evidenced by the frequency with which monarchs divided their kingdoms, circumstances tended toward the accomplishment of what men could not readily grasp. Two great states emerged in Christian Spain, the kingdoms of Castile and Aragon. They were able even to act in peace and concert at times in the wars against the Moslems. A third region tended to withdraw from the current of peninsula unity, for it was in this period that the modern state of Portugal had its independent beginnings. Nevertheless, Moslem Spain, though less important than Castile and Aragon, remained the keynote of the period, not alone because of the wars against it, but also because its civilization, especially in material and intellectual aspects, was still far superior to that of Castile and Aragon. It was at this time, indeed, that the Moslem world produced its greatest scholars and the Christian states became most strongly imbued with the spirit of Moslem culture, with permanent results on Spanish character. This era was unequal in length for Castile and Aragon, closing respectively in 1252 and 1276 with the deaths of Ferdinand III and Jaime I.

Moslem Spain

The *taifa* states and the rise of Seville. With the dethronement of Hisham III in 1031 the caliphate broke up into a number of states called *taifas*, from an Arabic word meaning "tribe," or "people." Down to the close of the eleventh century there were many of these states, — twenty-three at one time, — but the most important were those of Cordova, Seville, Málaga, Granada,

Almería, Denia and the Balearic Islands, Saragossa, Toledo, and Badajoz. The rulers were usually Slavic or Berber generals of the latter-day armies of the caliphate and their descendants. Each desired to make himself sole caliph, and so an internecine strife was waged almost continuously, especially in the south. Seville soon forged ahead of its regional rivals, and was by far the most important *taifa* of the century. Like several of the others it had been founded as a republic (as early as 1023), but its skilful ruler, Abul Cassim Mohammed of the Abbadite family, soon made himself absolute, while retaining the forms of a republic. In order to overcome his most powerful neighbors he pretended that Hisham II had reappeared, availing himself of a mat-maker who resembled the dead caliph. The stratagem was so successful that Carmona, Valencia, Denia, Tortosa, and even the republic of Cordova recognized the pseudo-Hisham, whereupon the crafty Sevillian proceeded to conquer large parts of the *taifa* states of Málaga and Granada. His successors were equally fortunate, and by the end of the third quarter of the century the greater part of Moslem Spain, especially in the west and south, had acknowledged the rule of the lord of Seville. Seville, too, had become every bit as noteworthy an intellectual centre as Cordova had been under the caliphs.

The Christian kings of Castile and León had meanwhile profited by the wars of the *taifa* states to make conquests or to reduce many of the *taifas* to the payment of tribute. Even Seville was tributary to a Christian king. This inclined many of the Moslem princes, realizing their own helplessness, to invite a newly-risen Mohammedan power in northwestern Africa to come to their aid. The rulers of the *taifas* recognized that their own authority might be endangered by the entry of their coreligionists, but their feelings were well expressed in the words attributed to the ruler of Seville : "I would rather be a camel-driver in Africa than a swineherd in Castile." The African people referred to were a branch of the Berbers who had dwelt apart in the Sahara Desert. Converted at length to the Moslem faith, they became fanatically religious, taking to themselves the

Yusuf and the Almoravide conquest.

name "Almoravides" (religious men), and launching themselves forth to the conquest of all northwestern Africa. The African empire of the Almoravides was already an accomplished fact when their emperor, Yusuf, was invited to help the Spanish Moslems under a promise that he would not deprive the *taifa* rulers of their states. In 1086 Yusuf entered Spain, and encountered the army of Alfonso VI of León at Zalaca, near Badajoz. Yusuf was completely successful, and the Christian peril was rolled back, but no counter-conquests of moment were made. Yusuf himself returned to Africa. Four years later the Moslem princes had need of Yusuf, and once again he came to avert the threatening danger. By this time popular opinion, reinforced by the intrigues of the Moslem priesthood, desired the establishment of Yusuf's authority in Spain; the restoration of a single rule, it was believed, would check the Christian kings, and bring peace and prosperity. By 1091 Yusuf had reduced all of the *taifa* princes except the king of Saragossa, and the latter was subjected by Yusuf's successor. Thus the unity of Moslem Spain was again accomplished.[1]

Rise of the Almohades. The Almoravide rule rested very lightly on the Moslem population, but only for a short time. The emperors lost their religious enthusiasm, and not only did they fail to advance the conquest but they also gave themselves up to a life of luxury and dissipation. Public security declined, with the result that the people now wished to rid themselves of the sovereigns whom formerly they had desired so much. At this time there came a tremendous uprising in Africa in 1125 of the Moors of the Moroccan Atlas, an uncivilized branch of the Berber family. They had become fanatical Mohammedans, and like their Almoravide predecessors had taken a name springing from their religious faith, that of "Almohades" (unitarians). Uncultivated as they were, they were able to master the military art of that day sufficiently to overwhelm the Almoravide power in Africa, though only after a long war.

Meanwhile, a second era of *taifa* states had sprung up in Spain, but in 1146 the Almohades entered the peninsula, and

[1] Rueda continued independent, — an unimportant exception.

proceeded to reduce the *taifa* princes. By 1172 all Moslem Spain was under their sway. Spain was now formed into a province of the Almohade empire, the capital of which was in Africa. The new conquerors did more than merely garrison the peninsula, — they pursued the hated Arabs so zealously that the latter were either destroyed or absorbed. The Berbers were for many years virtually the only Mohammedan element in the peninsula except for the Renegados. The wars with the Christians were also renewed. In 1194 Alfonso VIII of Castile challenged the emperor Yacub to a battle. Yacub accepted, and the battle was fought at Alarcos (Badajoz) in 1195, ending in the rout of the Christians. The war continued, however, and in 1212 the united forces of León, Castile, Navarre, and Aragon gained a great victory at Navas de Tolosa in Andalusia. This was the turning-point in the Christian reconquest. The Almohade state soon fell to pieces, and by 1228 the *taifas* began to reappear, but one after another they were conquered by the Christian kings. A single Moslem state escaped; in 1230 it had been founded at Arjona, and presently took shape as the kingdom of Granada, establishing its capital in 1238 at the city of the same name. This tiny realm, extending at its greatest from Almería to Gibraltar, was able to maintain itself for over two centuries and a half.

The Almohades in Spain.

The Christian reconquest.

León and Castile

By the will of Sancho the Great of Navarre, Castile had become legally a kingdom in 1035. Ferdinand I (1035–1065) soon overwhelmed the king of León, uniting all northwestern Spain under his rule. Wars with Navarre followed until 1054, after which Ferdinand devoted himself with great religious zeal to campaigns against the Moslem *taifas*, making numerous conquests, and subjecting many states to the payment of tribute. Despite the lesson of his own experience he divided his realm, at death, into the three kingdoms of Castile, León, and Galicia, besides two lesser principalities. A long civil war followed, out of which there emerged Alfonso VI (1065–1109) as sole ruler of the domain

Castilian conquests.

Alfonso VI.

of his father. Alfonso VI took up the wars against the Moslems with great success, and on one occasion, in 1082, was able to ride his horse into the sea in the extreme south of Spain at Tarifa, when he is said to have exclaimed: "This is the last land in Spain, and I have trod it." The principal event of the reign was the capture of Toledo in 1085. Alfonso had promised to restore the *taifa* king of Toledo to his throne, from which he had been ousted by a rebellion, but changed his mind, and took the city for himself. From that time forward Toledo was of great military importance to the Christians, serving as the centre of the reconquest, and it was also the medium through which Moslem civilization began to produce an effect on Castile. The treaty of capitulation was not very faithfully carried out; for example, Alfonso had promised to allow the Mohammedans to retain their principal mosque for purposes of worship, but in his absence the monks of Cluny were able to persuade the queen to take over that edifice as a Christian church. The incident is illustrative of a new crusading spirit which had entered Spain with the monks of Cluny, although it had not yet become general. *Taifa* after *taifa* now humbled itself before Alfonso; Valencia was captured, and the former king of Toledo became its nominal ruler, but with a Castilian army; and Alfonso could with reason entitle himself "sovereign of the men of the two religions," a phrase which shows that Christian zeal was not altogether uncompromising. It was then that the Almoravide invasion checked the Castilian king, but although he lost Valencia he was able to maintain the principal part of his conquests.

The Cid.

It was in the reign of Alfonso VI that Rodrigo, or Ruy, Díaz of Vivar (near Burgos), better known as "the Cid," performed the achievements which have made him a famous character in literature. Until recently he was represented as a fanatically ardent, Christian crusader, ever drawing his sword against the infidel or in defence of any just and noble cause, and performing superhuman prodigies of valor. The true Cid was very far from answering to that description, and was also so typical of his age that his real career has historic value apart from literature. In the civil wars following the death of Ferdinand I, Díaz was a partisan of Sancho II of Castile, and contributed greatly to that monarch's success, — a victory which was spoiled by the assassination of his patron. Díaz then recognized Alfonso VI, and was sent by the latter to collect the tribute due from the king of Seville. On his return he was accused of having appropriated for himself certain of the funds which he was bringing to the king, and was banished from Castile; possibly Alfonso VI may still have felt resentment over Díaz's part in the victories of Sancho. Followed by only a few warriors Díaz wandered over Spain, seeking wealth and honors in return for military aid. Finally he took service with the Moslem king of Saragossa, and won fame in all the peninsula as a result of his victories not only against Moslem enemies but more than once against Christian kings; in fine, religion seems not to have entered into his program to any appreciable extent; indeed, the name Cid was applied by his Moslem soldiers, meaning "lord," or "master." In 1086 the Moslem king of Valencia, the same one who had been placed on the throne by Alfonso VI, got into difficulties with his subjects, and sought the aid of Saragossa. The Cid was sent with an army of mingled Christians and Moslems to restore the authority of the Valencian monarch. This he did, but under a contract which ignored his Saragossan master and enabled the Cid to become the virtual ruler of Valencia. In 1092 on the death of the king of Valencia the Cid converted his *de facto* into a *de jure* rule, reigning until his death in 1099. As monarch of Valencia he was selfish and cruel, like others of his time, sustaining his power by virtue of his army of Christians and Moslems against foes of whatever faith, even against Castile. He espoused one of his daughters to Ramón Berenguer III of Barcelona, and another to a prince of the royal family of Navarre. After his death his state fell before the advance of the Almoravides.

Alfonso VI was succeeded by his daughter Urraca (1109–1126), for he left no sons, and her reign was a period of anarchy. Urraca, who was a widow, was compelled by the nobles to remarry, on the ground that affairs of state

The anarchy of Urraca's reign.

needed a man's direction, while her infant son by a previous marriage, Alfonso, was brought up in Galicia, being considered king of that region. Alfonso I "the Battler" of Aragon was selected as a husband for Urraca, but the marriage was not a happy one. Urraca was so imprudent in her manner of life that the Battler saw fit to imprison her in a castle. Furthermore, he displayed a clear intention of making himself ruler in Castile as he was in Aragon, a course which the Castilian nobles were far from approving. The scene having been set the wars began. A complication entered from the side of Galicia, where Bishop Gelmírez of Santiago de Compostela proposed that the infant Alfonso should reign in León as well as in Galicia. The changes of side and fortune in these wars, not only by the three principals, but also by individual nobles, need not be followed, except to relate one incident which marked the first step toward the ultimate independence of Portugal. Teresa, a sister of Urraca, had married a French count, Henry of Lorraine, to whom (in 1095?) Alfonso VI granted territo-

The beginnings of Portugal. ries called the county of Portugal in the northern part of the land which now bears that name. These estates were held as a fief, subject to tribute and military service. Henry and later Teresa (on the former's death) profited by the civil strife to increase their holdings and acquire real strength. Urraca died in 1126, and matters were arranged by the recognition of the young Alfonso (Alfonso VII "the Emperor") as king in his grandfather's domain, while Alfonso the Battler gained some territories adjoining his kingdom of Aragon.[1]

---

[1] Less famous than the Cid, but quite as representative of his time, was the figure of Bishop Diego Gelmírez of Santiago de Compostela, who played an important part in the events of Urraca's reign. He was a vigorous, ambitious, restless, not overscrupulous man, breaking pledges and changing from one side to another with the usual facility of men of that age. He was not only ambitious for himself but was also an ardent votary of the extension of church authority. He was a fighting bishop, who engaged in military campaigns himself and encountered many vicissitudes both in the civil wars of the kingdom and in the local uprisings of his own subjects. On one occasion the citizens of Santiago besieged him in his church, and set fire to a tower in which he took refuge. Nevertheless, the bishop escaped in the guise of a beggar. In the end

The death of Urraca did not end the internal strife in Christian Spain. For ten years there were wars with Teresa and her son Affonso Enríquez of Portugal; there were wars, too, against Aragon and Navarre, following the death of Alfonso the Battler, out of which Alfonso VII procured some extensions of territory. When the century was nearly half gone Alfonso was able to turn energetically to an attack upon the Moslem states, especially between 1144 and 1147 during the second era of the *taifas*. His conquests were vast, but of brief duration, for the Almohades soon entered Spain to deprive him of what he had won. Like Ferdinand I before him Alfonso VII took the title of emperor, which then had a significance equivalent to that of sole temporal ruler of Christendom in succession to the Roman emperors. In the case of Ferdinand and Alfonso it may also have represented a protest against the like pretensions of the Holy Roman Emperors, then reigning principally in Germanic Europe. Alfonso seemed in a fair way to create a peninsula empire, for he was able to make the kings of Aragon and Navarre, the counts of Barcelona and Toulouse, various lesser princes of Spain and southern France, and some rulers of the Moslem *taifas* swear fealty to him as their feudal sovereign. The imperial confederation had no real strength, however, for the spirit of separatism was as yet too deeply rooted. Alfonso himself demonstrated this by dividing his realm at his death, in 1157, into the two kingdoms of Castile and León.

The next following reigns had their share of internal strife and one important event in the course of the Moslem wars, — the defence of Calatrava in 1158 by two Cistercian monks, who procured an army by proclaiming a crusade. Out of this event there came the founding in 1164 of the important military order of Calatrava. Alfonso VIII (1158–1214) inherited the throne of Castile while still a child. War and disorder followed until 1180, for the kings of León and

he was usually successful. He procured the erection of Santiago de Compostela into an archbishopric, and enjoyed the distinction, equally with the church of Rome, of having seven cardinals as ꝛanons. He also gained the influential post of chaplain to Alfonso VII.

Alfonso "the Emperor."

The defence of Calatrava.

Alfonso VIII and the overthrow of the Moslems.

Navarre and various nobles endeavored as usual to profit for themselves at the expense of the newly enthroned monarch. At length Alfonso VIII, who was one of the ablest rulers of this period (both in internal organization and in external conquest), directed his attention to the reconquest from the Moslems. After a rapid succession of victories he was defeated, as already noted, at the battle of Alarcos, on which occasion the kings of León and Navarre failed to accord him the aid they had promised. Wars followed against the two kings, but matters were at length adjusted and a tremendous army, including many foreigners, was raised to combat the Almohades. All seemed to be imbued with the crusading spirit, but most of the foreigners deserted before the issue presented itself. Nearly all the peoples of Christian Spain were represented in Alfonso's host, however, and together they won the great battle of Navas de Tolosa in 1212.

The independence of Portugal.

Meanwhile, the counts of Portugal had continued their policy of complete separation from León and Castile, and had also extended their frontiers southward by successful wars against the Moslems. Affonso Enríquez took the title of king, and this was recognized in 1143 by Alfonso VII, subject to the vassalage of the Portuguese monarch to León. Affonso Enríquez managed to avoid this condition by submitting his state to the sovereignty of the pope, who accepted it in 1144, though conferring only the title of duke on Affonso. A few years later Pope Alexander III recognized the Portuguese ruler as king. Thus Portugal withdrew from the current of peninsula unity, and established her independence in law and in fact.

Saint Ferdinand and the crusades in Spain.

Berenguela, daughter of Alfonso VIII of Castile, had married Alfonso IX (1188–1230) of León, by whom she had a son, Ferdinand. Pope Innocent III brought about an annulment of the marriage on the ground of consanguinity, though he recognized the legitimacy of Ferdinand. On the death of Henry I of Castile in 1217 Berenguela was proclaimed queen, but granted the throne to her son, who as Ferdinand III, later Saint Ferdinand (San Fernando), was to prove an even greater monarch than his grandfather,

Alfonso VIII. Wars with his father and with his nobles occupied the early years of his reign, but by 1225, having overcome his Christian enemies, he was able to renew the campaigns against the Moslems. City after city fell into his power; Cordova was taken in 1236; Murcia became tributary in 1241; and the culminating blow came with the siege of Seville, which surrendered to Ferdinand in 1248. Despite the fact that not a little crusading zeal entered into these campaigns and that Ferdinand himself was an ardent Christian, religious enthusiasm, even yet, was not as uncompromising as it later became. Ferdinand was an ally at one time of the Almohade emperor, whom he restored to his throne in Africa; he also accepted the alliance of the Moslem prince of Granada in the campaign against Seville; and other similar instances of his freedom from fanatical intolerance might be adduced. Nevertheless, he planned to overwhelm the Moslem authority, and would almost certainly have invaded Africa if he had lived a few years longer. His Christian spirit, however, was along practical and national lines. When Louis IX of France invited him to join in a crusade in the orient Ferdinand is said to have replied : "There is no lack of Moors in *my* land." Not only by conquests but also by internal reforms he assisted in the development of Castilian unity. One external event of capital importance was the incorporation into Castile of the kingdom of León in 1230 on the death of Alfonso IX, despite the latter's attempt to deliver his dominions to two daughters by a marriage previous to that with Berenguela. With Ferdinand's death in 1252 the era of the Castilian crusades came to an end.

Catalonia, 1035 to 1164

At the time when Ramón Berenguer I (1035–1076) became count of Barcelona, Catalonia was a federation of counties, acknowledging the ruler of Barcelona as overlord. Possessed already of Barcelona and Gerona, Ramón Berenguer soon acquired two more counties, which had been left by his father to other sons. He extended his frontiers at

The extension of the authority of the counts of Barcelona.

the expense of the Moslems, and laid the foundations of the later Catalonian power in southern France through marriage alliances with princes of that region. It was in his reign, too, that the Catalan code of the *Usáticos*, or *Usatges* (Usages, or Customs), was compiled, though at the instance of his powerful vassals, who wanted their privileges reduced to writing. By the end of his reign he had united five Catalonian counties and many other territories under his rule, including almost as much land in southern France as he possessed in Spain. No further progress was made until the reign of Ramón Berenguer III (1096–1131), who, through inheritance, without civil wars, acquired all of the Catalonian counties but two and a great part of southern France. He also waged wars against the Moslems, though perhaps the most notable thing about them was that the Pisans fought as his allies. Indeed, he established commercial and diplomatic relations with the various Italian republics, — a beginning of Spain's fateful connection with Italy. Ramón Berenguer IV (1131–1162) inherited only the Spanish portions of his father's domain, but extended his authority over Tortosa, Lérida, and other Moslem regions, being a notable warrior. In 1150 he married the daughter of the king of Aragon, and in 1164 his son by this marriage united Aragon and Catalonia under a single rule.

Aragon

The beginnings of Aragon and the union with Catalonia. The kingdom of Aragon dates from the will of Sancho the Great of Navarre in 1035. The new state was almost insignificantly small at the outset, but, by inheritances, wars with the Moslems, and the peaceful incorporation of Navarre in 1076, it already included a large portion of north central Spain by the close of the eleventh century. The era of great conquests began with Alfonso I "the Battler" (1104–1134), the same king whose marriage with Urraca of Castile had resulted so unfavorably. Better fortune awaited him on the Moslem frontier. In 1118 he captured Saragossa, an event as important in Aragon as was the acquisition of Toledo a few years before in Castile. He carried his campaigns as far south, even, as Murcia and Andalusia, but the principal result of these invasions was that he brought back ten thousand Mozárabes to settle his newly-won conquests. Having no sons he tried to leave his realm to two military orders, but this arrangement did not prove agreeable to his subjects. The nobles of Navarre elected a king of their own, withdrawing from the union with Aragon, while those of Aragon chose a brother of Alfonso, named Ramiro, who at the time of his election was a monk. The reign of Ramiro II "the Monk" (1134–1137) was exceptionally important for Spain, without any particular merit accruing therefor to the king. The pope freed him from his vows and he married. From this marriage there was born a daughter, Petronilla. Ramiro espoused her to Ramón Berenguer IV of Barcelona, and soon abdicated, returning to his monastery. Petronilla's son, Ramón Berenguer, who presently changed his name to the Aragonese-sounding Alfonso, was the first to rule in his own right over Aragon and Catalonia in what came to be called the kingdom of Aragon, although Catalonia was always the more important part.

Alfonso II inherited Catalonia in 1162, and became king of Aragon proper in 1164 on the abdication of Petronilla. Later he inherited nearly all of southern France. He was also a frequent ally of Alfonso VIII of Castile against the Moslems, gaining some territories on his own account. In 1179 these two kings made a treaty dividing Spain between them, fixing the limits of their respective present and future conquests, — a noteworthy instance of the approach toward the unification of Spain. Alfonso II was succeeded by Pedro II "the Catholic" (1196–1213) at a time when affairs were in a critical state in his French dominions. That region had been in constant turmoil, as a result both of the ambitions of the kings of France and of the comparative independence and selfish aims of the feudal lords. There was now added a new factor, — the widespread Albigensian heresy, which had been accepted by the majority of the Provençal people and even more by their lords. With matters in this state Pedro visited Rome in 1204, and, while

The act of vassalage to the pope and the French conquests in Aragonese dominions of southern France.

there, gave his dominions in vassalage to the pope, receiving them back as a fief. This act was to have important consequences at a later time, but if its immediate object was to check French pretensions to southern France, as has been supposed, it was not very successful, for the pope himself proclaimed a crusade against the Albigenses. The crusaders were French nobles, who represented a purely French invasion quite as much as they did an orthodox host. Under their leader, Simon de Montfort, they won several victories, displaying such cruelty against Catholics and heretics alike that they were censured by a famous religious at that time preaching among the Albigenses, Domingo de Guzmán. Guzmán was the Spaniard who later founded the Dominican order, named for him, and who became canonized as Saint Dominic (San Domingo). Pedro II endeavored to mediate to check the temporal designs of Montfort, but was persuaded by the pope to recognize the French leader as his vassal in the regions he had conquered. When Montfort continued in his aggressive designs Pedro II declared war against him, but was defeated in a battle which cost him his life.

Early years of the reign of Jaime "the Conqueror."

The death of Pedro II brought to the throne the greatest Aragonese monarch of the period, Jaime I "the Conqueror" (1213–1276), a worthy contemporary of Ferdinand III of Castile. At the outset of his reign he was a mere child in the dangerous possession of Simon de Montfort. On this occasion the tremendous influence of the great pope, Innocent III, was beneficial to Spain, for Montfort was constrained to surrender the boy king to his people. Then followed the usual troubles which beset the early years of a youthful monarch in that period. There were wars brought about by ambitious nobles fighting for the possession of the king, wars of the nobles among themselves, and wars of the nobles against the king. Though only a boy, Jaime took a hand in the fighting, and was many times in danger, — twice he was captured by hostile nobles, — but thanks to his courage and coolness was always able to free himself from the perils which beset him. Not until 1228 was he in full command of the situation. Meanwhile, civil wars had been taking place in southern France, resolving themselves finally into a struggle between the count of Toulouse, aided by the Catalans, and Simon de Montfort. In this war Montfort lost his life, and the French power in that region for the time being vanished.

Backed by the sentiment of most of Catalonia, which desired territorial and commercial expansion in the Mediterranean, Jaime now planned a career of conquest. Many of the Aragonese and western Catalonian nobles declined to join him in this enterprise; so he had to find means as best he could without their aid. In 1229 he entered the island of Majorca, which for centuries had been successively a pirate and Moslem stronghold. Having achieved the conquest, which proved an easy matter, Jaime distributed the lands among his Catalan followers. In 1232 Minorca was subjected, and in 1235 Ibiza, too. Thus the Balearic Islands fell into Jaime's power and received a Catalan civilization, which they still possess. The greatest prize, however, was the rich kingdom of Valencia. Although handicapped by the lukewarm support of his nobles Jaime proceeded to the conquest with such success that he won the aid of those who had previously failed to help him, and in 1238 the city of Valencia fell, — an event comparable with the capture of Seville by Ferdinand III. The rest of the kingdom was not long in falling into Jaime's power, and the lands were distributed among his nobles, but the Moslems were so numerous that they were able to rise in rebellion on two occasions before the end of the reign. On achieving the conquest of Valencia, Jaime had agreed with the king of Castile that the southern boundary of that kingdom should be the limit of the Aragonese conquest, while Murcia, which became tributary to Ferdinand III in 1241, was reserved for the ultimate definitive conquest of Castile. The unquenchable military ardor of Jaime I would not allow him to rest on his laurels, however, and he engaged to conquer Murcia for the king of Castile. This he accomplished in the years 1265 and 1266, giving the lands to his Catalan nobles, who were subjected to the Castilian king, whereupon Jaime withdrew. These relations between the

The conquests of Jaime.

G

kings of Castile and Aragon not only instanced a somewhat rare good faith, but also marked a tendency which was gradually manifesting itself toward the ultimate unity of Spain. Next, the restless warrior-king planned to go on a crusade to Palestine, but his fleet was wrecked, and he gave up the project, although some Catalan boats did reach their destination. In 1273 Jaime wanted to conquer Granada for Castile, but this time he could not persuade his Catalan nobles to follow him. He did, however, send a fleet to attack the coast of Morocco.

Other characteristics of Jaime's rule. Jaime was not only a great conqueror; he was also a great administrator. Owing to the entry of feudalism into northeastern Spain his nobles had such power that even the able Jaime was obliged often to compromise or to yield to their wishes. He took steps to reduce their power, at the cost of civil war, and in many other respects bettered the administration of his kingdom. Though deeply religious he was far from being an ascetic, as is evidenced by the many illegitimate children descended from him, and although usually magnanimous in character he was capable of acts of ferocious cruelty, — such, for example, as that of ordering the tongue of the bishop of Gerona to be torn out for the latter's having revealed to the pope a secret of the confession. In 1276 when the great king died he left a will which contradicted the policies of centralization and the aggrandizement of the kingdom which in his lifetime he had unfailingly pursued. He divided his realms, giving Aragon, Catalonia, and Valencia to his eldest son, Pedro, and Majorca and the Roussillon (southern France) to his son Jaime. The division was not to endure long, however.

Navarre

Navarre passes under French rule. There is little worth recording in the history of Navarre in this period. After the separation from Aragon in 1134 Navarre engaged periodically in civil strife and in wars with Aragon or Castile. When the throne became vacant in 1234 the French count of Champagne was elected king, and, with this, Navarre was, for many years, more involved in the history of France than in that of Spain. At length the heiress of Navarre married Philip IV of France, whereupon Navarre ceased to be a kingdom, becoming a mere dependency of the French monarch.

CHAPTER VIII

SOCIAL AND POLITICAL ORGANIZATION IN SPAIN, 1031–1276

Moslem Spain

Absolutism in government.

THE principle of absolute monarchy continued to be followed in Moslem Spain, and was even accentuated, whether in the eras of the *taifas*, or at times of a single dominion. Indeed, this was virtually the case while the *taifas* were still republics, although they soon converted themselves into confessed monarchies. In furtherance of absolutism an excess of court ceremonial was introduced, and the rulers rarely allowed their faces to be seen, holding audiences, for example, from behind a curtain. The *taifa* kings amassed great wealth, and their palaces were overflowing with luxury.

Social factors in Moslem Spain.

The most important social change was the complete overthrow of the Arabic element, leaving the Berbers and Renegados in control. Arabic influence had already done its work, however, and the passing of the contemporary members of that race did not mean the uprooting of Arabic traits in Spain. Social well-being declined, owing to the various factors of war, the development of vast landed estates (at the expense of the small proprietor), and the increase in taxation. The Jews enjoyed great consideration for a while, exercising an important influence in material, intellectual, and even political affairs. Under the Almoravides and Almohades they were severely persecuted, and many of them emigrated to Castile, where for the time being they were well received. The Mozárabes were also persecuted, and in increasing degree with the advance of the Christians, for they aided not a little in the reconquest. Many of them

were taken north by the Christian kings when they returned
from their invasions, whereupon those remaining in Moslem
territory were all the more harshly treated. The Almohades
were particularly intolerant.

León and Castile

The nobility continued to be the most important social
class, with much the same differences of grade among themselves, the same authority and privileges, and the same
tendencies to war against the king and with one another
and to commit acts of violence and robbery as in the preceding period. The conflict of the nobility as a class against
the king took definite shape, and a numerous new nobility,
the *caballeros* (knights), sprang up. The *caballeros* proceeded
from the plebeian ranks, being composed of those who could
equip themselves for war as cavalrymen. Although they
gained certain privileges, such as exemptions from taxation,
thus weakening the king's power, they served in fact as a
counterpoise to the hereditary noble class. They were much
favored by the kings, who needed well-equipped soldiers
for their wars. The clergy made distinct gains as regards
personal immunities and the freedom of their lands from
the usual obligations, especially from that of taxation.
This bettering of their position was not the result of general
laws, but rather of the accumulation of individual privileges,
granted now to one religious institution, now to another.
Their advantages in these respects were not always well
received by others, and objections were made, especially
by the popular element, through their representatives in
the national *Cortes* (Congress, or Parliament), — of which
institution presently.

The free popular element, or middle class, which had been
reborn in the preceding period with the founding of the
villas, or *concejos*, developed a much greater social importance than formerly. Many factors contributed to this end,
such as the increase in the number of the *villas*, the concession of new privileges, the material advance of Christian
Spain (agriculturally, industrially, and commercially), the

Nobles
and
clergy.

The ad-
vance of
the middle
class.

important military services of the municipal militia, and the fact that not only the *caballeros* but also the leading jurisconsults began to be recruited from the middle class. As a rule this element paid taxes, but it enjoyed not a few exemptions and privileges, — for example, a right not to be required to make unusual contributions at the mere will of the king, or in some cases a right to commute all of their **Gains of** taxes to a single tribute. At the same time, the servile **the servile** classes made striking advances, in part through their own **classes.** efforts, but aided also by an increasing sentiment in favor of manumissions, by the need for population (both as a result of the conquests and in consequence of economic development), and by the protection accorded them in the *villas.* The movement for emancipation was not uniform or free from setbacks, and this led to numerous uprisings of serfs, who joined the enemies of their masters in wars against the latter. The monks of Cluny, accustomed to the much greater subjection of the servile classes in France, represented a strong current of reaction. At Sahagún, the principal Cluniac centre, there were such limitations on liberty as those requiring that all bread must be cooked in the ovens of the monastery, and forbidding anybody to sell his wine before the monks had sold theirs, or to buy cloth, fresh fish, firewood, or other necessities before the monks had bought theirs, and there were other restrictions of a like character. By the end of the twelfth century serfs generally had gained such rights as the exact fixing of services due their lords, the abolition of the practice of selling them with the land, and the recognition of the validity of their marriages, whether consented to by their lords or not. In the thirteenth century they gained almost complete personal liberty, doing away with the *malos usos,* or bad customs, like those referred to in the case of the monastery of Sahagún.

The four Four new social classes became important at this time, **new social** principally as a result of the wars of reconquest, — the **classes.** foreigners, Jews, Mudéjares, and Mozárabes. As a general rule each group had its own law, differentiating it from the national elements. Foreigners from every prominent western European region came to León and Castile, attracted by the crusading character of the wars or by the material development of this part of Spain or perhaps fleeing from worse conditions in the lands whence they had come. For the Jews this was the happiest period they ever enjoyed in Catholic Spain, and great numbers of them entered Castile in order to escape the persecution of the Almoravides and Almohades. For a while they were on practically an equal footing socially and juridically with the Christians, and were one of the principal agencies for the diffusion of Moslem culture in León and Castile. By the opening of the thirteenth century their situation began to change with the adoption of restrictive measures, although it was not until the next period that these operated in all their harshness. As the conquests proceeded, great bodies of Moslems were incorporated into the Christian states, and they came to be called "Mudéjares." Despite the growth of intolerance with the advance in the crusading character of the wars the Mudéjares were in general very well treated. Aside from treaties of capitulation making promises to that effect, political and economic interests made it advisable both on account of the numbers of the vanquished Moslems and because of the need for population. Many of them, whether as freemen or serfs, were agricultural laborers enjoying considerable independence, including the right of publicly practising their religion. As time went on they tended to gather into the cities, although subjected to more restrictions than in the country, — such as the refusal to allow the public practice of the Moslem faith (with a number of exceptions, however) or requirements that they must wear a distinctive dress and live in a separate section of the city. If they were not greatly molested in other respects they did have to endure very heavy taxation, even including the tithe for the benefit of the Christian church. The Mozárabes, though of the same race and religion as the Leonese and Castilian population, had lived so long in contact with Moslem civilization that they represented a class apart, having their special laws differing from those of the native-born Christians. Naturally, they were well received.

Among the social traits of the era may be noted a cer-

tain moral laxity. Two forms of marriage were recognized,
that of *bendición* (blessing of the church), accompanied by
a religious ceremony, and the wedding *á yuras* (under oath),
by a simple contract between the parties concerned. A
third form of union, similar to the latter but not recognized
as lawful wedlock, was that of *barraganía* (concubinage).
The essential conditions of *barraganía* were permanence
and fidelity. Both parties were supposed to be single,
although the custom often extended to include married
men; in the latter case, but not in the former, the children
were held to be illegitimate. Many clergymen entered into
this relation, despite efforts to prevent the practice. *Barraganía* and the marriage *á yuras* have been considered to
be a Christian imitation of Moslem marital customs. Divorce was allowed for serious cause. The father was recog-

nized as the master of the family, although the wife and
children gained certain financial and personal rights which
had not formerly been accorded them. The bonds of family
were so strong, however, that individuals who were free by
law to emancipate themselves — for example, by marriage
— often continued under the parental roof. Thus great
family groups living in common were formed.

As a result of the greater economic wealth, the comparative
peace back from the frontier, and the development of the
towns the manner of life underwent a rapid change, which
may be summed up by saying that people began to live
inside the house instead of out, giving more active play to
the domestic instinct of the woman, which in its turn had
a much needed softening effect upon the man. Houses now
had hearths, although not always a chimney and as late as
the twelfth century no panes of glass in the windows. Furniture reached a degree of luxury and comfort far in advance
of what it had been since the Roman era. It was heavy and
very sober in decoration at first, but increased in adornment
later on. Beds were an object of luxury in the eleventh
century; people slept on benches or on the floor. By the
thirteenth century artisans and laborers usually had a bed,
as also a table, two chairs, and a chest. Chairs, throughout
the period, were low, and rarely had backs; those with both

arms and a back were reserved for the master of the house. Floors, even in palaces, were usually bare of cover. Habits of cleanliness were not yet very much in evidence. Clothing was customarily worn until worn out, without being changed or washed. At table it was rare for the diners to have individual plates or napkins, and the fork was not yet known. Bones and refuse were left on the table, or thrown on the floor, and the use of water for any purpose other than for drinking was unusual. The custom of public baths had some vogue in the cities, however. Men still lived much in the open, but women habitually withdrew from public view. Crimes against women, from those which were more serious down to the comparatively mild offence of pulling a woman's hair, were punished with extreme severity, — not that women enjoyed high esteem or even an equal consideration with men, for the supposed gallantry of the medieval period did not in fact exist. Men wore their hair long, and a long beard was considered as an indication of dignity, — so much so, that a heavy penalty was imposed on anybody who pulled or cut another's beard. Amusement was provided by jugglers or by dancing and singing, especially on days of religious festivals, or holidays, and during the holding of fairs. Among the great people the French sport of the tourney was much in favor. From France, too, came feudal chivalry, imposing the ideals of valor, loyalty, and dignity (to the extent that nobody should doubt another's nobility, his word, or his courage) on those professing it. This exaggerated sense of honor led to duelling, and comported ill with the real conduct of the nobles. Epidemics of leprosy and plagues (bubonic?) were frequent, resulting in the founding of hospitals and institutions of charity.

Other social customs.

Fundamentally, León and Castile had much the same political organization as before, but the popular element, as represented in the *villas* and the *Cortes*, began to be a real political force, and the kings increased their strength at the expense of the nobles, although their struggle with the nobility as a class was not to result in complete royal victory for more than two centuries yet. The throne continued elective in theory, but the tendency was for it to

Political and administrative changes.

become hereditary, although the question was not definitely settled at this time. The right of women to reign became recognized with the crowning of Berenguela. In administration many governmental districts were enlarged to include various counties, the whole being ruled by a governor appointed directly by the king, assisted by functionaries called *merinos mayores*,[1] who had charge of civil and criminal jurisdiction. An important reform was effected by removing the nobles from the post of the king's representative in the counties and substituting officials called *adelantados*, whose authority at this time was more civil than military, and therefore less dangerous.[2] Still others exercised respectively political and military authority.

Beginnings of the Cortes. For centuries the kings had been in the habit of holding councils of nobles or ecclesiastics, or both, although there was a tendency to exclude the churchmen. In 1137 a

---

[1] The word "*merino*" is an untranslatable term for an official in Spanish administration whose powers varied greatly from century to century. While the *merinos* were at times "judges of sheepwalks," as the word is often translated, they usually had much broader power as officials of the king. The *merinos mayores*, or greater *merinos*, were appointed by the king, with functions largely judicial in character and with authority extending over the greater provinces, such as Castile, León, or Galicia. *Merinos menores*, or lesser *merinos*, might be the appointees and subordinates of *merinos mayores*, or, similarly, of the *corregidores*, or rulers of districts.

[2] The term "*adelantado*" comes from the fact that the officials so-called were "advanced," or "put forward," in the place of the king, to act in his name. There is some authority to the effect that the title was in existence as early as the tenth century, but it was certainly employed by the latter part of the twelfth century. In origin the *adelantados mayores*, or greater *adelantados*, were judicial officials, hearing appeals that had formerly gone to the king. The *adelantado menor*, or lesser *adelantado*, came into existence early in the thirteenth century, at which time he was a judicial officer of higher rank than the *merinos*, but also possessed extensive administrative powers. Many of the *adelantados menores* were stationed in frontier districts, and indeed they were often called *adelantados fronterizos* (frontier *adelantados*). It was natural, therefore, that they should acquire military functions. It was the *adelantado fronterizo* of Spain who figured so prominently in the conquest of the Americas. Most of the conquerors of the sixteenth century were *adelantados*. After that the title died out. Hill, Roscoe R., *The office of adelantado*, in *Political science quarterly*, v. XXVIII, no. 4; Dec., 1913.

council of nobles at Nájera was called the *Cortes*. The popular element was first admitted in 1188, at a *Cortes* held in León, — possibly the first occasion in the history of Europe when representatives of the towns appeared in such an assembly. The first known instance in Castile occurred in 1250. For a number of years, León and Castile, though become a single kingdom, continued to have a separate *Cortes*. The kings called this body whenever they wished, although they often made promises (which they did not fulfil) to set regular intervals. None of the individuals called, whether nobles, ecclesiastics, or representatives of the *villas* (or towns), had the right to present themselves; that was left to the choice of the king, but the custom gradually became fixed that certain towns should have the privilege of being represented. Each member had one vote, but the number of representatives from the towns differed, without being subject to a general rule. The towns themselves chose who should represent them, but the methods of choice were various. The *Cortes* was allowed to make petitions to the king, each branch for itself, and to fix the sum of money that it would grant him. It had no true legislative functions, but the king sought its advice, or its approval for his laws, and its influence was such, that it was able to procure desired legislation. The king presided in person at the opening and closing sessions, and through officials of his own appointment at the other meetings. The king continued to be the principal legislative authority, and the law retained its former diversity and its fundamental basis of privilege; the variety even increased, with the introduction of the new social classes. The *Fuero Juzgo*, which was the common law, applied in but few respects. The kings did something in the way of producing greater juridical similarity, as by making dispositions of a general character at meetings of the *Cortes*, and by using certain municipal charters as types, while Ferdinand III commenced to draw up a uniform code, although he did not live to complete it. {Legislation.}

Municipal organization retained the essential features of the preceding era, such as the local assembly and the various officials, of whom the most important were the judges. The {Political life of the towns.}

latter came to be called *alcaldes* (from an Arabic term meaning "the judges"), — an example of Moslem influence.
In many cities, there were representatives of the king, called
merinos and other names. Communication with the king
was also maintained by the use of messengers, now of the
king, now of the city. The actual monarchical authority
was so slight that the towns often acted with complete independence. Like the nobles they made forays against the
Moslems on their own account, or fought one another, or
with very good reason attacked neighboring, lawless nobles.
For these wars they often formed leagues, or brotherhoods
(*hermandades*), of towns (or occasionally leagues which included some nobles), for which special ordinances were
drawn up without previously consulting the king. Some of
the towns of the north coast were so independent that they
joined in the wars between France and England, against
the latter. Often the towns changed their own charters
without royal permission, although this was not done in
open defiance of the king, but, rather, in secret and fraudu-
lently. The privileges of the towns in respect to taxation
(although, indeed, they paid the bulk of what the king received from his free, Christian subjects) have already been
mentioned.[1] Taxes were also collected within the towns for
local purposes. In addition to revenues from direct contributions the towns also imposed obligations of personal
service on their citizens, and owned lands which formed

[1] Taxes at that time were many and varied in kind, but may be
reduced to three types : regular contributions, but depending on
the happening of some event; indemnities to escape rendering
certain due services ; and fines. As examples of the first type
may be mentioned the *goyosa* (rejoicing) payable by a married man
at the birth of a child ; the *movicio* (removal) payable whenever
one changed his residence ; the *yantar*, or food supplies, for the
king and his retinue whenever he visited a town; the *servicios*
(services), or subsidies, granted by the *Cortes;* the *diezmos de mar*
(tithes of the sea), or customs duties collected at the ports. The
most notable tax of the second class was the *fonsado* (foss), payable by those who wished to escape the obligation of going on a military campaign. One of the third group was the *caloña* (fine), due from
the inhabitants of a region where a crime had been committed and
the guilty person had not been found. Gradually it became the
practice to commute these taxes for a single payment, except for
the *fonsado* and the *yantar*, which were not dispensed with.

perhaps their most important source of wealth. These lands were of two kinds, the *propios* (estates "belonging to" a municipality and utilized to assist in defraying public expenses), which were worked directly or rented by the town, and the *comunales*, or land common, for the use of all, subject to local regulations. In seigniorial towns, especially in those acknowledging an ecclesiastical lord, great progress was made toward an approximation of the rights enjoyed by the royal towns and cities. They had already gained economic independence, but now wished to attain to political freedom as well. They fought against the lord's practice of arbitrarily choosing their principal magistrates; next, they endeavored to gain for their own assembly the exclusive right of choice; then they tried to increase the powers of the locally chosen officials as compared with those appointed by the lord; and, all along, they aimed to acquire more authority for their assemblies, or for the council which came to represent them, — for example, the right to fix wages. By the opening of the thirteenth century local autonomy had been gained at Santiago de Compostela, and many other seigniorial towns (both noble and ecclesiastical) had achieved equal, or nearly equal, good fortune.

Justice belonged fundamentally to the king, but the *alcaldes* of the towns usually exercised civil jurisdiction, and often criminal as well; in some towns royal *merinos* or *adelantados* had charge of criminal jurisdiction. The king might punish local judges, however, even removing them and appointing others, but this power did not in fact enable him to check abuses. Appeals went to the king, who also had the right to try in first instance the serious crimes of murder, assault on a woman, robbery, and others. In such cases the king was assisted in administering justice by a group of men of his own appointment, called the *Cort* (not to be confused with the *Cortes*), but this body merely advised him, for the decision was left to him. As might be expected in an age of disorder, punishments were atrocious, — such, for example, as mutilation, stoning to death, throwing over a cliff, burning, burial alive, starvation, cook-

The administration of justice.

ing, stripping off the skin, drowning, and hanging; only the last-named has survived. On the other hand, composition for murder, or the payment of a sum of money, was allowable, — for men were valuable to the state, — although the murderer was not free from the private vengeance of the dead man's family. The so-called "vulgar proofs," — such as the tests of the hot iron and hot water, and the wager of battle, — besides torture, were employed (as elsewhere in western Europe) as a means for acquiring evidence, but these methods were already being looked upon with disfavor. Real justice was in fact rare; the wealthy, especially if they were nobles, were able to take matters into their own hands or to procure favorable decisions, if affairs should reach the point of litigation.

Methods of warfare. Military service was obligatory upon all, but except for a small royal guard there was no permanent army. Organization continued to be simple; the seigniorial troops were commanded by the lord or his representative, and the militia of the towns by an *alférez* (standard-bearer).[1] Large numbers of foreigners joined in the wars against the Moslems, but perhaps the most important element was that of the military orders. These orders had a mixed religious and secular character, for, while some members took the usual monastic vows, others were not required to do so. Aside from the orders of general European prominence, like that of the Templars, there were three which were confined to the peninsula, those of Calatrava, Santiago, and Alcántara, all formed in the middle of the twelfth century. Their membership became so numerous and their wealth so great that they constituted one more important force with which the kings had to reckon in the struggle for the establishment of royal authority, although the peril proved greater in its possibilities than in the fact. War was absolutely merciless, falling quite as heavily on the non-combatant as upon the opponent with arms in his hands. The enemy population might be subjected to the loss of their lands and to enslavement, unless this seemed inadvisable, and pillage was legally

[1] At the present time the word *alférez* is equivalent to "sub-lieutenant."

recognized, with a share of the booty going to the king. Such weapons as the sword, lance, and pike were still the principal types. The use of flags was introduced as a means of inciting the troops to deeds of valor, while priests were employed to provide a like stimulus. The first navy in this part of Spain was the private fleet of Bishop Gelmírez of Santiago de Compostela. Private navies were the rule. The first royal navy was formed by Ferdinand III, as a result of the important part played by the private naval levies which had assisted in the taking of Seville.

Notwithstanding the increase in privileges accorded the church, the king had always intervened in its affairs, — as by the appointment or deposition of bishops, and even by taking under his own jurisdiction certain cases on appeal from the ecclesiastical courts. The monks of Cluny, influential in so many respects, set about to uproot the dependence of the church upon the king and to bring about a closer relation of the clergy with the papacy. Aided by the piety of the kings themselves they were able to achieve their ends, although the monarchs maintained that the pope's measures should not be valid in the royal dominions without governmental consent. Thenceforth, the pope and his legates began to take the place of the king in church affairs. The same centralizing policy of the monks of Cluny and the great popes of the era was employed to bring the Castilian church into uniformity with that of Rome in matters of doctrine and rite. Some difficulty was experienced in the latter respect, for the Spanish people were attached to their form of worship, which was called the Visigothic, or Mozarabic, rite. Earlier popes had recognized this as orthodox, but Gregory VII asked Alfonso VI to abolish it. The king was willing, but the people and the clergy were not. The matter was once left to the decision of the wager of battle, and again to that of fire, but in each case the local rite came out victorious. Finally, the king rode roughshod over judicial proofs, and abolished the local rite.[1] It was in this period, therefore, that the hierarchy

The monks of Cluny and church reform.

[1] It is still allowed to exist in a chapel of the cathedral of Toledo, and in another of Salamanca.

of the church, depending on the pope, was established in Spain. At this time, too, the monasteries (and the military orders as well) became independent of the bishops, and ascended to the pope, or his legate, through the medium of their abbots (or grand masters). The increasing wealth and privileges of the church have already been sufficiently alluded to; many of the orders degenerated greatly, even that of the monks of Cluny, as a result of the luxury which their means permitted. At the moment when clerical ostentation had become greatest there came the founding of the mendicant orders, early in the thirteenth century. In the peninsula, as elsewhere, these orders (whose principal vow was poverty) achieved a great work for the church; the Franciscans went chiefly among the poor, and the Dominicans dealt more with the upper classes, but both preached the necessity for repentance and for conversion to the faith.[1] They also contributed greatly to doing away with the loose practices which had become current among the clergy in all parts of Christendom. One such practice persisted, despite their efforts, the earlier efforts of the monks of Cluny, and the continuous opposition of the kings (translated into severe laws), — that of priests entering into the form of union called *barraganía*.

Aragon proper

Social institutions in Aragon.
In institutions, Aragon proper must be distinguished, throughout this period, from the Catalonian region of the greater kingdom of Aragon. Social differences were much more marked than in León and Castile, for there was an excessively privileged feudal nobility, which had a despotic power over the servile classes; the movement for emancipation from slavery and serfdom belongs to a much later time. Lords had a right even to kill their serfs. Slavery (confined usually to Moslems) was not personal, for the slaves were attached legally to the land. What has been said for Castile as regards the church, the Jews, Mozárabes, and Mudéjares applies generally for Aragon. There were more

[1] To Saint Dominic is due the institution of the rosary.

Mudéjares than in Castile, but, although they enjoyed equality with Christians before the law, they were on a lower plane socially, and were more heavily taxed. The practice of living in communal family groups was the rule in Aragon.

The nobles had privileges of a political, as well as of a social character, being virtually sovereigns on their own estates. One noteworthy official to develop was the *Justicia* (Justice, or Justiciar), charged with hearing cases of violation of privilege and complaints generally against the authorities. The nobles tried to take the appointment of this official to themselves, but failing in this were, nevertheless, able to compel Jaime I to recognize that the functions of the *Justicia* were to be exercised in his own right, and not by delegation of the king, — for example, in cases in which the *Justicia* acted as judge, or mediator, between the nobles and the king. The free towns usually sided with the crown, as in Castile, but they were not nearly so numerous, and not equally an agency for the liberation of the servile classes. According to some writers they were represented in the *Cortes* as early as 1163 (which was earlier than in León), but others make 1274 the date of their entry. There were four estates in the Aragonese *Cortes*, — the higher nobility, the *caballeros*, the clergy, and the representatives of the towns. Aragon and Catalonia continued to have a separate *Cortes* after the union of the two states, and Valencia also received one of its own, but there were times when a general *Cortes* of the entire kingdom was held. The principal form of legislation was that of the royal charters. The same diversity of law existed as in Castile, but Jaime I did something to bring about unification by having a code drawn up. This code, called the *Compilación de Canellas* (Compilation of Canellas), for one Canellas was the compiler, embodied the traditional law of Aragon, supplemented by principles of equity. It did not do away with the charters, applying only to matters which they did not cover. The Roman law of Justinian and the canon law, both of which greatly favored the king, were beginning to be studied, but the nobility opposed the assertion of these legal principles in

Political life and administration in Aragon.

H

courts of law. Taxes fell more heavily and more vexatiously on the common people than they did in Castile, but a greater proportion went to the lords and less to the king; Jaime I had to give his note for the royal dinners, at times, and he paid his tailor by an exemption from taxation. The king was not always able to persuade his nobles to join him in war, though in other respects the military customs resembled those of Castile. The principal difference in the religious history of the two regions was that the influence of the monks of Cluny in favor of ecclesiastical dependence on the pope was much earlier accepted in Aragon; the Visigothic, or Mozarabic, rite was abolished as early as 1071. Pedro II's submission of the kingdom to the pope was not well received, however, by either the nobility or the people of both Aragon and Catalonia.

Catalonia

Social institutions in Catalonia. Different as Catalonia was from Aragon, the two regions had many features in common because of the existence of feudalism. The feudal hierarchy was composed of counts, viscounts, *valvasores* (barons), and free vassals, of whom the first three grades were noble. Underneath was the institution of serfdom, equally harsh as in Aragon, and almost equally late in advancing toward emancipation. Personal slavery (of Moslem prisoners of war, as a rule) also existed. There were not many Mozárabes or Mudéjares, but the Jews were fairly numerous. All enjoyed the same lenient treatment as that accorded in Castile and Aragon, — with a beginning of restrictive measures at the end of the period. The middle class of the cities was more important than in Aragon, especially in the coast cities or towns, where the citizens engaged in commerce. Although the communal family group was the general rule in Catalonia, this institution was considerably modified by the existence of the law of primogeniture, causing the entailment of landed properties to each successive eldest son, — a variation from the *Fuero Juzgo*. This aided in economic prosperity, because it kept estates intact, and influenced younger brothers to go forth in order to build up estates of their own. In other respects, social customs did not vary materially from those of Aragon and Castile.[1]

The only new factor of interest in general political and administrative organization was the increase in the actual authority of the counts of Barcelona (and, similarly, after they became kings of Aragon), although on the same legal basis of feudalism as before. This came about through the uniting of most of the counties in the single family of the counts of Barcelona, who therefore were able to exercise a decisive influence in Catalonian affairs. The rise in importance of Barcelona was the most notable event in municipal history. Its commerce and wealth were so great, and its prestige as capital of the county so influential, that it exercised a veritable hegemony over the other towns. Each year the general assembly elected five councillors, who in turn appointed a council of one hundred, or *Consell de Cent*, which was the principal governing body of the city. The city was allowed to coin money and to appoint consuls charged with looking after the business interests of Barcelona in foreign lands. The *Consell* also had mercantile jurisdiction. The Catalan commercial customs were to pass over in a developed form into Castile, and from there to the Americas. The Catalonian *Cortes* had but three estates, and was in other respects similar to that of Castile. The representatives of the towns were admitted in 1218, but their right to appear was not definitely affirmed until 1282. Barcelona had unusual weight in that body, for it possessed five votes. The *Usatges* (the code adopted in the reign of Ramón Berenguer I) merely expressed in writing the feudal customs which were already in vogue, and therefore it was generally observed. It did not supersede the charters, the *Fuero Juzgo*, and local customs, all of which continued in effect. The Roman and canon law, despite the resistance of the nobility, came to be regarded as supplementary to other legal sources, although not as of right until centuries later. In naval affairs Catalonia was far

Political life and administration in Catalonia.

Importance of Barcelona.

[1] A curious law of Jaime I recommended that ladies of noble rank should not offer food or lodging to jugglers, or even give them kisses.

ahead of the rest of Spain. Both a merchant and a naval marine had existed since the ninth century, and the former was encouraged by the suppression of taxes and by favorable treaties with the Italian states. The navy had become a permanent state institution by the middle of the twelfth century (in the reign of Ramón Berenguer IV). Individual lords and towns had naval vessels of their own, however. The history of the church followed the same course as in Aragon; the Roman rite was adopted in the time of Ramón Berenguer I (1035–1076).

Valencia

The royal power in the social and political life of Valencia.

When Jaime I conquered Valencia, he had an opportunity to put into effect some of his ideas with regard to strengthening the principle of monarchy, and did not fail to take advantage of it. In the distribution of lands among the nobles, the king was recognized as the only lord; furthermore, the majority of the lands were given outright, in small parcels, to middle class proprietors, subject only to the royal and the neighborhood taxes. Most of the recipients were Catalans, and thus the Catalan civilization came to predominate in Valencia. The most numerous body of the population, however, was that of the Mudéjares. Many of these were not molested in their estates and their business, and some were even granted lands, but the majority were obliged to pay heavy taxes in return for the royal protection. The Mudéjar uprisings led to the introduction of more rigorous measures. In political affairs, too, Jaime I established a system more favorable to monarchy. The nobles wished to have the Aragonese law apply, but the king introduced new legislation whereby the greater part of the authority rested with him. The Valencian Cortes, of three branches, dates from 1283.

Balearic Islands

Similarly in the Balearic Islands.

Jaime I pursued the same policy in the Balearic Islands as in Valencia, avoiding the evils of feudalism, and treating the Mudéjares well, — for here too they were in the majority.

Navarre

The extreme of feudal organization, similar to that in Aragon, existed in Navarre. French peoples were an important element in the population, and the power of the monks of Cluny was unusually great. Although the kings established hereditary succession, the nobles continued to be virtually absolute on their estates. The towns did not become as important a power as elsewhere in Spain, and it was not until the next era, possibly in the year 1300, that their representatives were admitted to the *Cortes*.

Feudalism and French influences in Navarre.

CHAPTER IX

MATERIAL AND INTELLECTUAL PROGRESS IN SPAIN, 1031–1276

Moslem Spain

Economic vicissitudes.

THE political vicissitudes of Moslem Spain could not fail to have an unfavorable effect on industry and commerce. The economic decline did not at once manifest itself and was not continuous in any event, for the periods of depression were often followed by others of great prosperity. Agriculture, industry, and the arts profited by new impulses, and trade was carried on with eastern Mediterranean lands. The Christian conquests meant an end of these commercial relations, but many of the industries survived in the hands of Moslems, now become Mudéjares.

Moslem intellectual achievements.

In intellectual culture, Moslem Spain was even greater than it had been in the days of its political power, — at least in the higher manifestations of that culture. The *taifa* kings encouraged freedom of thought and expression, even when unorthodox; yet, in literature and science the greatest heights were reached, by both Jewish and Moslem writers, in the twelfth and thirteenth centuries, during the rule of the intolerant Almoravides and Almohades. That, too, was the period of their greatest influence on the Christians. The principal service of Moslem Spain to western Europe was, as has been said, the transmission of Greek thought, although not in its purity, but with the modifications and variants of its later days, especially those of the Alexandrian school. In the twelfth and thirteenth centuries many European scholars of note visited Spain, and took back

102

with them the Greco-oriental thought which was to be the chief basis of the philosophy and science of Christendom, until the true Greek texts were discovered at the time of the Renaissance. The Moslems were further advanced in medicine than the other western European peoples, and were the first in Europe since the days of the Greeks to cultivate the study of botany. In pure mathematics and its applications, such as in astronomy and the pseudo-science of astrology, they were equally to the fore. Their greatest influence was to make itself felt, however, in the realm of philosophy, especially in the works of Averröes and Maimónides, scholars who are to be compared with Saint Isidore, both as respects the greatness of their achievements, and as concerns the breadth, almost universality, of their attainments. Averröes of Cordova (1126–1198), as commentator and propagator of the ideas of Aristotle and Plato, was perhaps the principal resort of western European scholarship for an early knowledge of Greek thought. He was also a distinguished doctor and mathematician. Maimónides (or Moisés ben Maimón), also of Cordova (1139–1205), was the founder of the rationalistic explanation of Jewish doctrine and a bitter opponent of the neoplatonism [1] of the Alexandrian school, but he was much influenced by Aristotle, whose ideas he contributed to disseminate in western Europe. He was also a celebrated physician. In addition to individual treatises on the various sciences, many encyclopedias were written inclusive of all. As might be expected, the rhetorical taste of Moslem Spain found abundant expression, in both poetry and prose, and in subject-matter of a heroic, fabulous, satirical, or amatory character. History, which at this time was more akin to literature than to science, was also much cultivated. Aben-Hayyán of Cordova wrote a history in sixty volumes, of the epoch in which he lived; and there were others almost

Averröes and Maimónides.

---

[1] Neoplatonism was a late and decadent form of the Greek philosophies. It endeavored to unite the precepts of Christian, Jewish, and oriental religions, and displayed a disregard for the empirical investigation of the universe, holding that the way to redemption lay through rising superior to the material manifestations of life.

equally prolific who dealt with different phases of the history of Moslem Spain. In the sciences, Jewish scholars followed the current of their Moslem masters, but in philosophy and literature they developed originality, inspired by their religious sentiments. Their poetry had a somewhat more elevated tone than that of the Moslems.

Architectural mediocrity.

Although the Almoravides and Almohades were great builders, this period was less important in Moslem architecture than either the preceding or the following eras. The principal characteristic seems to have been a withdrawal from Visigothic and classical forms, but the execution was less correct and in poorer taste than formerly.

León and Castile

Advance of agriculture and stock-raising.

The advance of the conquests, leaving large areas back from the frontier in the enjoyment of a measure of peace, furthered economic development. There continued to be civil wars in the interior, and personal security against abuses of the lords and the attacks of bandits was none too great, but matters were very much better than before, as a result of legislation favorable to property, the greater importance of the towns, and the emancipation of the servile classes. Agriculture was encouraged, — for example, by laws granting unbroken lands to whoever should cultivate them. The conquest made itself directly felt through the introduction of the vine and the olive of Moslem Spain into regions which had not previously cultivated them. Works of irrigation and the buildings of roads, so important for the agricultural prosperity of Spain, seem not to have been undertaken, however. Stock-raising was much more actively pursued than agriculture, due in part to the traditional importance of that occupation, and in part to the ease with which that form of wealth could be withdrawn from the hazards of war, — an advantage which agriculture, naturally, could not share. The age-long war of the stock-raisers against the farmers was usually favorable to the former, who were wont to appropriate commons for their animals and even to enter cultivated fields and damage or despoil them. Associations of stock-raisers to protect their interests were already in existence.

In the thirteenth century Castilian Spain made a beginning of industrial and commercial life, of which Santiago de Compostela had been perhaps the only representative prior to that date. Laborers united in guilds, just as in other western European lands, working together according to the laws of their guild, and living in the same street. Many of them were foreigners, Jews, or Mudéjares. An export trade of raw materials and wine developed between the towns of the north coast and the merchants of Flanders, England, and Germany, and just at the end of the period the capture of Seville added commercial wealth to Castile, through the trade of that city in the western Mediterranean. Interior commerce still encountered the difficulties which had harassed it in earlier times, but some of them were overcome through the development of fairs to facilitate exchange. Certain days in the year, usually corresponding with the feast of the patron saint of the town, were set aside by important centres for a general market, or fair, on which occasions special measures were undertaken to assure the safety of the roads and to protect all who might attend, — Moslem and Jews as well as Christians. Men naturally travelled in large groups at such times, which was an additional means of security. The season of the fair might be the only occasion in a year when a town could procure a supply of goods not produced at home, wherefore this institution assumed great importance. The increased use of coin as a medium of exchange demonstrates the commercial advance of this period over the preceding. *Industrial and commercial beginnings.*

In every branch of intellectual culture there was a vigorous awakening at this time. The classical traditions of the Spanish clergy and the Mozárabes were reinforced by western European influences coming especially from France, while the Greco-oriental culture of the Mudéjares and Mozárabes merged with the former to produce a Spanish civilization, which became marked after the conquests of the thirteenth century. In the twelfth century universities had sprung up in Italy and France, where the Roman and *The intellectual awakening.*

the canon law, theology, and philosophy were taught. In those countries the formal organization of the universities had grown naturally out of the gatherings of pupils around celebrated teachers, but Spain had no Irnerius or Abélard, wherefore the origins of the universities of the peninsula were the result of official initiative. In 1212 or 1214 Alfonso VIII founded a university at Palencia, but this institution lived only thirty-one years. About the year 1215 Alfonso IX of León made a beginning of the more celebrated University of Salamanca, the fame of which belongs, however, to the next following era. By the close of the eleventh century the Castilian language had become definitely formed, as also the Leonese and Galician variants. By the middle of the twelfth century all three had become written languages, and, by the middle of the thirteenth, Latin works were already being translated into the Romance tongues.

Romance poetry.

One of the earliest forms of Romance literature was that of popular poetry of an epic character, singing the deeds of Christian warriors. This was of French origin, coming in with French crusaders and the monks of Cluny. Two long poems of this class, both dealing with the life of the Cid, have been preserved. One, the *Poema* (Poem), is believed to date from the middle of the twelfth century, while the other, the *Crónica* (Chronicle), is probably of later origin. Both mix legend with fact, but the former is the less legendary. In the thirteenth century another type of poetry developed in Castile called *mester de clerecía* (office of the clergy), also bound up with French influences, but more erudite and formally correct and usually religious in subject-matter, a Spanish expression of European scholasticism. From the side of Aragon came the influence of southern France, in the lyrical and erotic poetry of the Provençal troubadours. Galicia was much affected by these foreign impulses, due to the journeys of pilgrims to Santiago de Compostela, and developed a notable poetry of its own. In

Beginnings of the drama.

this period, too, the Castilian theatre had its origins, in the mystery plays of the church and in the popular performances of jugglers in the streets. Whereas the former were in the nature of a religious ceremony, the latter, which were ultimately to exercise the greater influence, were of a secular character, usually satirical, and given to great liberty of expression.

In historical literature there were two names of some note in this period. Rodrigo Jiménez de Rada, archbishop of Toledo (1170–1247), reduced the early Spanish chronicles to a narrative form, embellished by erudite references which his classical knowledge enabled him to employ. He may be regarded as the father of Spanish historiography. Naturally, given the age, his works were not free from legends and errors, and do not display the critical spirit of modern times. Bishop Lucas of Tuy (died 1288), though far inferior to Jiménez de Rada in both method and criticism, wrote a life of Saint Isidore and other works which enjoyed great popularity in the thirteenth century. In scientific literature there were no great names, for this was a period of study and the translation of Arabic and western European texts, rather than one of original composition. *History and science.*

Just as the Romance tongues replaced the Latin, so Romanesque architecture took the place of the decadent classical styles. Although there was not a little variety in details, this style was characterized in León and Castile by an accentuation of the cruciform ground plan, robustness of form, heaviness in proportions, and profuse ornamentation, often of a rude type. Arches were sometimes round, and sometimes slightly pointed. Over the crossing there often appeared a polygonal dome or a tower with arcades and a cap. The wooden roof was supplanted by barrel-vaulting in stone, and this led to a strengthening of the walls, reducing the window space, and to the use of heavy piers or columns and of exterior buttresses attached to the walls. The west front, or portal, of churches was adorned in luxurious style, notably with the sculptured work of men, animals, or foliage. At the same time, new influences proceeding out of France were making themselves felt, and by the thirteenth century the so-called Gothic style of architecture was firmly established. In this the entire edifice was subordinated to the treatment of the vault, which attained to a great height through the use of the true pointed *Romanesque architecture.* *Early Gothic architecture.*

arch and of transversals to receive the weight of the vault. For this purpose the flying buttress, now free from the walls, was greatly developed. Edifices not only became higher, but also were enabled to use a large amount of space for windows, since the walls no longer had to sustain the thrust. At the same time decorative effects were increased, not only in porticoes, but also in the glass of the windows, the capitals of columns, water-spouts, pinnacles and towers, and in various forms of sculpture. The spaces between the buttresses were often filled in to form chapels. Remarkable as was the advance made in architecture, the work of this period was sober and robust when compared with the later Gothic work. Nevertheless, the development was very great, and is to be explained, very largely, by social causes, such as the advance in the population and importance of the cities and of the middle class. Greater cathedrals were therefore needed, but they were also desired from motives of vanity, which prompt new social forces to construct great monuments. The cathedrals became not only a religious centre but also a place of meeting for the discussion of business and political affairs, the heart and soul of the cities in which they were located. Gothic architecture also manifested itself in military and civil edifices. The castle was the characteristic type of the former. The material now became stone, instead of wood. As in other parts of Europe, there were the surrounding moat and the bridge, the walls with their salients and towers, the buildings inside for the artisans on the one hand, and for the lord and his soldiers on the other, and the powerfully built tower of homage to serve as a last resort. The growth of the towns gave rise to the erection of local government buildings, or town halls, and private dwellings began to have an important architec-

Mudéjar architecture.

tural character. Another style of architecture, usually called Mudéjar, existed in this period, combining Arabic with Christian elements, of which the latter were Gothic of a simplified character. The roof was of wood, but with the ornamentation of the period. The body of the edifice was of brick, which was left without covering on the outside, giving a reddish tone to the building. Sculpture had an important vogue as an adjunct of architecture. Gradually, it passed from the badly proportioned, stiff figures of the earlier years to something approaching realism and to a great variety of form. Painting was notable only for its use in the adornment of manuscripts and of windows, and in these respects the work done was of a high order. Both sculpture and painting were employed to represent sacred history or allegory. Rich tiles were much used, both in the form of azulejos, and in that of compositions of human figures, in which the usual symbolism appeared. The gold work and furniture also bore witness to the greater wealth of this period as compared with earlier times.

Sculpture, painting, and the lesser arts.

Aragon, Catalonia, and Valencia

Much that has been said about León and Castile as regards material prosperity might be repeated for Aragon, Catalonia, and Valencia. Aragon proper was the poorest part of this region, economically. Stock-raising and industries growing out of it were the principal occupations there. Catalonia, though not backward in agriculture, was not too well adapted to it, since certain crops, notably grain, could not be raised, but it had a varied industrial life and an active commerce. Valencia was the most favored region, being agriculturally wealthy, on account of the extensive use of irrigation, and, like Catalonia, having a rich industrial and commercial life. This was true also of Majorca. The Catalans had been engaged in Mediterranean commerce since the ninth century, but in this period their trade reached much greater proportions. Although Catalan boats went to every part of the Mediterranean, the principal relations were with Italy; there were frequent commercial treaties with Pisa and Genoa. Jaime I brought about the sending of commercial representatives, or consuls, to foreign countries, and was responsible for the establishment of mercantile bodies, called *consulados de mar* (commercial tribunals of the sea) in Catalan ports. A special maritime law sprang up, and was embodied in a code, called the *Libro del consulado de mar* (Book of the *consulado* of the sea).

Economic differences in the kingdom of Aragon.

Catalan commerce.

Intellectual manifestations.

The intellectual movement in Aragon and Catalonia ran along lines parallel to that in León and Castile, but with more frequent contact with French and Italian thought. Jaime I followed the custom of the era in founding universities, establishing one at Lérida and another at Valencia. One great name appeared in the literary history of this period, reaching over into the next, that of Raimundo Lulio, known to English scholars as Raymond Lull, or Lully (1232–1315), a philosopher, mystic, and poet, who wrote many books which had a noteworthy influence on European thought. Writing in the vulgar tongue and in a style adapted to the general public, he attacked the pantheistic ideals of Averröes and held that all sciences, though they have their individual principles, lead to a single all-embracing science, which, for him, was Christianity; in other words, he represented the reconcilement of Christianity with reason and science. The development of the Romance tongues followed the same course as in Castile, but the Catalan became widely separated from the other peninsular tongues, being more akin to the Provençal, or language of southern France. The Provençal influence on poetry was earlier in evidence in Catalonia than in Castile, and was more pronounced. Lyric poetry, accompanied by music, was so high in favor that great nobles and the kings themselves cultivated it. Alfonso II (1162–1196) was the first Spanish troubadour, and other kings followed, including Jaime I. History was the most important form of prose literature, and the principal work was that of Jaime I himself, a chronicle of the vicissitudes of his reign. Jaime I also compiled a collection of proverbs and the sayings of wise men.

Raymond Lull.

Architecture.

The Romanesque art of this region was less heavy and more gracefully proportioned than that of Castile, — possibly, the result of Italian influences. Catalan Gothic architecture was especially affected by Italian art, — so much so, that it lacked some of the principal elements of the Gothic.

Navarre

Attention need be called only to the profound French influence in this region.

CHAPTER X

DEVELOPMENT TOWARD NATIONAL UNITY : CASTILE, 1252–1479

AFTER the death of Ferdinand III and of Jaime I the reconquest of Spain from the Moslems came to a virtual standstill for over two centuries. Some slight accessions of territory were obtained by Castile, but no serious effort was made to acquire the only remaining enemy stronghold, the kingdom of Granada. Conditions had changed to such an extent that Moslem Spain for the first time in more than five centuries was of secondary and even minor importance. Castile and Aragon devoted their principal attention to other affairs, and both took great strides ahead in the march of civilization. In Castile the chief problems were of an internal social and political nature. On the one hand this period marked the change from a seigniorial country type of life to that of the developed town as the basis of society; on the other it witnessed the struggle of monarchy and the ideal of national unity against seigniorial anarchy and decentralization for which the lords (including many of the great churchmen) and the towns contended. As before, the king's principal opponents were the nobles, and the civil wars of this era, whatever the alleged causes, were really only the expression of the struggle just referred to. Outwardly the kings appeared to have been defeated, but in no period of the history of Spain has the external narrative been more at variance with the actual results, as shown by a study of the underlying institutions, than in this. The real victory lay with monarchy and unity, and this was to be made manifest in the reign of Ferdinand and Isabella following this era. That reign was therefore the true end

General characteristics of the era.

111

of this period, but as it was even more the beginning of modern Spain it has been left for separate treatment. The institutions of Castile from the thirteenth to the fifteenth century were therefore of more than usual importance, and particularly so since they formed the basis for the system which Spain was so soon to establish in the Americas. In almost every aspect of life, social, political, economic, and intellectual, Castile forged as far ahead over the preceding period as that had over the one before it, although it did not reach that high and intricate culture which is the product of modern times. Castile was still medieval, like nearly all of Europe, but the new age was close at hand.

Alfonso "the Learned." Alfonso X "the Learned," or "the Wise" (1252–1284), was one of the kings whose reign seemed to be a failure, but in fact it was he who sowed the seed which was to bring about an eventual victory for the principles of monarchy and national unity. Besides being a profound scholar Alfonso was a brave and skilful soldier, but his good traits were balanced by his lack of decision and will power, which caused him to be unnecessarily stubborn and extremely variable. **His foreign policy.** He engaged in a number of campaigns against the Moslems, and made some minor conquests, but these wars were of slight consequence except as they bore on his struggles with the nobles. The same thing may be said for Alfonso's European policy, which aimed not only at the aggrandizement of Castile but also at his acquisition of the title of Holy Roman Emperor. The kings of Castile had long claimed the throne of Navarre, and Alfonso now attempted to invade that realm, but desisted when it seemed that this might lead to complications with Jaime I of Aragon. He also had a legal claim to the Basque province of Gascony, which had come to the throne of Castile as the dowry of the wife of Alfonso VIII, and planned to incorporate it into a *de facto* part of the kingdom, but he renounced his rights to England upon the marriage of his sister to Prince Edward, the later Edward I, of England. In 1257 the imperial electors chose Alfonso X as Holy Roman Emperor, but many German princes supported the pretensions of an English earl of Cornwall, and on the latter's death those of Count

Rudolph of Hapsburg.   For sixteen years Alfonso endeavored to get possession of the imperial title, going to great expense in wars for that purpose, but the opposition of the popes, wars with Granada and with his own nobles, and a general lack of sympathy with the project in Castile combined to prevent him from even making a journey to Germany in order to be crowned.   In 1273 Rudolph of Hapsburg was formally chosen emperor, and Alfonso's opportunity passed.

Meanwhile, influenced by the Roman law, Alfonso had been enunciating monarchical doctrines which were at variance with the selfish and unscrupulous designs of the nobles, who fought the king at every turn.   Other causes for strife existed, but they were not fundamental.   These were, especially, the unwise measures employed by Alfonso to procure funds for his sadly depleted treasury, and on the other hand his extravagant liberality.   Alfonso reduced the tribute due from Granada, debased the coinage, increased the salaries of court officials, expended enormous sums in celebration of the marriage of his eldest son, and was responsible for other acts of a like character.   In line with his claim of absolute royal power he ceded the province of Algarve to the king of Portugal, renounced his right to homage from that king, and as already noted gave Gascony to England, all of which he did on his own authority.   These acts were alleged by the nobles, who fought him themselves, or even went so far as to join the Moslems of Granada and Morocco against him.   The most serious period of the struggle was reserved for the last years of the reign.   This was precipitated by a fresh appearance of the Moslem peril. *Causes of his strife with the nobles.*

The Almohades had been succeeded in their rule of northern Africa by the Benimerines, who were invited by the Moslems of Granada to join them in a war against Castile.   The invitation was accepted, but, although the Benimerines landed and were for a time victorious, the danger was averted. Its chief importance was that the king's eldest son, Fernando de la Cerda, was killed in battle in 1275, thereby precipitating a dynastic question.   According to the laws of succession which Alfonso had enacted the eldest son of the dead prince should have been next heir to the throne, but this did not *War of succession between Alfonso and Sancho.*

I

suit Alfonso's second son, Sancho, who alleged the superiority of his own claim. He did not fail to support his pretension by promises of favors to disaffected nobles, which procured him a backing strong enough to persuade Alfonso himself to name Sancho as his heir. Later, Alfonso decided to form a new kingdom in the territory of Jaén, though subject to Castile, for the benefit of his grandson. Sancho objected, and persisted even to the point of war, which broke out in 1281. The partisans of Sancho, who included nearly all of the nobles, the clergy, and most of the towns, held a *Cortes* in Valladolid in 1282, and deposed Alfonso. The latter soon won over some of Sancho's followers, and continued the war, but died in 1284, disinheriting Sancho, leaving Castile to his grandson and smaller kingdoms in southern Spain to two of his younger sons.

Sancho "the Brave." That the elements which supported Sancho were really fighting for their own independent jurisdiction was early made clear. In 1282 they obtained an acknowledgment from Sancho of the right of the nobles and towns to rise in insurrection against the illegal acts of the king, and to bring royal officials and judges to trial for their maladministration, being privileged to inflict the death penalty on them. With their aid he was able to set aside his father's will and become King Sancho IV (1284–1295), later styled "the Brave." Once in possession of the throne he too showed a disposition to check the turbulence of the nobles, for it was as impossible for a king to admit the arbitrary authority of the lords as it was for the latter to accept the same attribute in the king. Internal strife continued, but the pretext changed, for Sancho's opponents alleged the will of Alfonso in justification of their insurrections. Sancho was at least an energetic character, and put down his enemies with a stern hand, on one occasion having no less than four thousand partisans of his nephew put to death. His brother Juan, whom Sancho had deprived of the small kingdom which Alfonso had left him, gave him the most trouble, at one time enlisting the aid of the Benimerines, but without success.[1]

[1] The wars of Sancho and Juan gave rise to the celebrated act of heroism of Guzmán el Bueno. Guzmán was governor of Tarifa,

Ferdinand IV "the Summoned"[1] (1295–1312) was only
nine years old when his father died, wherefore the opponents
of strong monarchy seized the occasion for a new period of
civil strife which lasted fourteen years. His uncle, Juan,
and his cousin, Alfonso,[2] renewed their pretensions, furnishing an opportunity for the lords and towns to join one side
or the other, according as they could best serve their own
interests, as also affording a chance for the intervention of
Portugal, Aragon, France, and Granada with a view to
enlarging their kingdoms. Although the towns usually
supported the king, they did so at the price of such privileges
as had been exacted from Sancho in 1282, showing that they
had the same spirit of feudal independence as the lords,
despite the monarchical sentiment of the middle class and
the interest which they had in common with the king in
checking the turbulence of the lords. That the king was
able to extricate himself from these difficulties was due in
greatest measure to his mother, María de Molina, one of
the regents during his minority. By her political skill,
added to the prestige of her word and presence, she was
able to attract many towns and nobles to Ferdinand's side
and to separate the more dangerous foreign enemies from
the conflict against him. This she did not do without making concessions, but, at any rate, by the time the king had
attained his majority at the age of sixteen the most serious
perils had been overcome. Ferdinand IV showed himself

Ferdinand
"the Sum-
moned."

María de
Molina.

and had promised Sancho that he would not surrender the place.
Juan appeared before Tarifa with a Moslem army, and threatened
to kill Guzmán's infant son, whom he had in his power, unless the
fortress were delivered. Guzmán preferred to keep faith with his
king, and sent his own dagger for Juan to use in fulfilling his threat.
Juan had the boy beheaded in front of the walls of Tarifa, but
failed to take the town. The incident is illustrative of the savage
brutality of the age, and was a rather unusual instance for that
time of keeping political faith at any cost.

[1] So called from a legend respecting his death. He is said to
have ordered two men put to death for a crime which they protested they did not commit. As the sentence was being executed
they summoned Ferdinand to appear before the tribunal of God
within thirty days, and on the thirtieth day thereafter Ferdinand
was dead.

[2] The eldest son of Fernando de la Cerda, and therefore the
rightful king according to the laws of Alfonso X.

an ingrate, demanding a strict account from his mother of her use of the public funds. Not only was she able to justify her administration, but she also demonstrated her devotion to her son's interests on later occasions, causing the failure of two insurrections headed by Ferdinand's uncle, Juan. Ferdinand made several minor campaigns against the Moslems, but died while engaged in one of them, leaving as his heir a year old boy.

Able rule of Alfonso XI in domestic affairs. Alfonso XI (1312–1350) shares with Alfonso X the honor of being the greatest Castilian king of this era, and he was by far more successful than his great-grandfather had been. Naturally, civil wars broke out at the beginning of the reign; a dispute over the regency served as one of the pretexts. María de Molina came forward again, and saved her grandson as she had saved his father, although she was unable to put down the insurrections. In 1325, when he was but fourteen years old, Alfonso was declared of age, and began his reign with an act which was characteristic of the man and his time. He summoned an uncle of his, his principal opponent, to a meeting at his palace, under a pretence of coming to an agreement with him, and when the latter came had him put to death. He tried the same policy with success against other leaders, and intimidated the rest so that he soon had the situation under control. Alfonso combined a hand of iron with great diplomatic skill, both of which were necessary if a king were to succeed in that period. An exponent of the monarchical ideas of Alfonso X, he proceeded by diverse routes to his end. Thus, in dealing with the nobles he made agreements with some, deceived others, punished still others for their infractions of the law, developed a distrust of one another among them, employed them in wars against the Moslems (in order to distract their forces and their attention), destroyed their castles whenever he had a sufficient pretext, and flattered them when he had them submissive, — as by encouraging them in the practices of chivalry and by enrolling them in a new military order which he created to reward warlike services. In fine he employed all such methods as would tend to reduce the power of the nobles without stirring up unnecessary opposition.

He was strong, but was also prudent. He followed the same policy with the towns and the military orders. For example, he promised that no royal town should ever be granted to a noble (or churchman), — a promise which was not observed by his successors or even by Alfonso himself. He was also successful in getting generous grants of money from the *Cortes*, which assisted him materially in the carrying out of his policy. He won the favor of the people by correcting abuses in the administration of justice and by his willingness to hear their complaints alleging infractions of the law, whether by his own officials or by the nobles. He procured the comparative security of the roads, and in other ways interested himself in the economic betterment of his people. Meanwhile, he enhanced his own authority in local government, and always maintained that the national legislative function belonged to the king alone, not only for the making or amending of laws, but also for interpreting them.

Alfonso's great work was the political and administrative organization of the country, but there were two external events of his reign which are worth recording. In 1332 the Basque province of Álava was added to Castile, although with a recognition of the jurisdiction of the law of Álava. More important, perhaps, was a great conflict with Granada and the Benimerines of Morocco, who once more tried to emulate the successes of their coreligionists of the eighth century. The kings of Aragon and Portugal joined Alfonso to avert this peril, and a great battle was fought in 1340 at the river Salado, near Tarifa, where the Moslem forces were completely defeated. Though not yet forty at the time of his death Alfonso had already written his name in large letters on the pages of Castilian history. *The acquisition of Álava and repulse of a Moslem invasion.*

The work of Alfonso XI seemed to be rendered in vain by the civil wars of the reign of his successor, Pedro I, variously called "the Cruel" or "the Just" (1350–1369). In fact, the basis of the structure which Alfonso had reared was not destroyed, and even Pedro took some steps which tended to increase the royal power. He was not the man for the times, however, since he lacked the patience and *Pedro "the Cruel."*

diplomacy which had distinguished his father. He was, above all, impetuous and determined to procure immediate remedies for any ill which beset him, even to the point of extreme cruelty. He possessed a stern hand, energy, and courage, but he had to deal with a nobility as turbulent and unsubmissive as was the spirit of Pedro himself. The tale of his reign may be told at somewhat greater length than some of the others, — not that it was more important, but by way of illustrating the usual course of the civil wars in that time.

Civil wars of the reign of Pedro "the Cruel." Pedro I was the only legitimate son of Alfonso XI, who had left five illegitimate sons by his mistress, Leonor de Guzmán, to each of whom he had given important holdings and titles. On the death of Alfonso, his wife (Pedro's mother) procured the arrest of Leonor de Guzmán and later her assassination. Naturally, this incensed the five sons of Leonor, although all but the eldest, Count Henry of Trastamara, appeared to accept the situation. Other pretexts for internal strife were not lacking. Pedro was a mere boy, and at one time became sick and seemed about to die, whereupon the nobles began to prepare for a dynastic struggle. Pedro lived, however, but caused discontent by choosing a Portuguese, named Alburquerque, as his leading adviser and favorite; the chief basis for the objections of the nobles was that each one wished the post for himself. The resistance to Alburquerque was the rallying-cry in the early period of the wars, in which Pedro's illegitimate brothers joined against him. Pedro was successful, and it is noteworthy that he dealt leniently with his brothers, in contrast with his energetic cruelty against the other rebels. In 1353, as the result of negotiations which had been arranged by Alburquerque, Pedro married a French princess, Blanche of Bourbon. Previously, however, he had entered into relations with a handsome young lady of good family, named María de Padilla, to whom he remained ardently devoted for the rest of his life. So blindly in love with her was he that Alburquerque had to take him from the arms of María in order to have him assist at his own wedding. Three days later the youthful Pedro deserted his wife in favor of

his mistress.   Alburquerque wisely took himself away, the
Padillas were established as the favorites at court, and the
young queen was imprisoned.   The nobles could no longer
pretend that they were fighting Alburquerque; on the
contrary, they joined the very man they had assumed to
oppose, in a war against the king, with various alleged
objects, but in fact with the usual desire of seizing an opportunity for increasing their own power.   At one time they
contrived to capture Pedro, but he escaped and wreaked
a fearful vengeance on his enemies, though once again he
allowed his brothers, who as usual were against him, to submit.   Meanwhile, Pedro's marital experiences included a
new wife, for he found two bishops who declared his first
marriage null, despite the pope's efforts to get the king to
return to Blanche of Bourbon.   Pedro married Juana de
Castro, but this time was able to wait only one day before
returning to María de Padilla.   These events had their
influence in the civil wars, for many towns refrained from
giving Pedro aid or joined against him out of disgust for his
actions.

The wars were renewed from the side of Aragon, where The wars
Henry of Trastamara, who for years had been the Castilian with
monarch's principal opponent, formed an alliance with the Henry of
king of Aragon.   The ruler of Aragon at that time was Trasta-
Pedro IV, a man of the type of Alfonso XI.   Having over- mara.
come the seigniorial elements in his own realm he did not
scruple to take advantage of Pedro I's difficulties in the
same regard to seek a profit for himself, or at least to damage
a neighboring king of whom he felt suspicious.   Prior to
the outbreak of hostilities Pedro I gave himself up to a
riot of assassinations, and among his victims were three of
his half brothers and several members of their families.
His enemies were not yet able to defeat him, however, even
with the aid of Aragon, and a peace was signed in 1361.
Shortly afterward, both Blanche of Bourbon and María
de Padilla died, the latter deeply bemoaned by Pedro I.
In 1363 Henry of Trastamara and Pedro IV again formed a
league against the Castilian king, and it was at this time that
Henry first set up a claim to the crown of Castile.   To aid

them in their project they employed the celebrated "White companies," an army of military adventurers of all nations who sold their services to the highest bidder. They were at that time in southern France and (as usually happened in such cases) were regarded as unwelcome guests now that their aid was no longer required there. The pope (then resident at Avignon) gave them a vast sum of money on condition that they would go to Aragon, and Pedro IV offered them an equal amount and rights of pillage (other than in his own realm) if they would come. Therefore, led by a French knight, Bertrand du Guesclin, they entered Spain, and in 1366 procured the conquest of most of Castile for Henry, who had himself crowned king. Pedro I sought aid of his English neighbors, for England at that time possessed a great part of western France, and, in return for certain concessions which Pedro promised, Edward III of England was persuaded to give him an army under the command of the celebrated military leader, Edward, the Black Prince. It was Henry's turn to be defeated, and he fled to France. Pedro I now took cruel vengeance on his enemies, disgusting the English leader, besides which he failed to keep the promises by which he had procured his aid. The English troops therefore went back to France, at a time when a fresh insurrection was about to break out in Castile, and when Henry of Trastamara was returning with a new army. Pedro I was utterly defeated at Montiel, and was besieged in a castle where he took refuge. Captured by Henry through a trick, he engaged in a hand-to-hand struggle with his half brother, and seemed to be winning, but with the aid of one of his partisans Henry at length got the upper hand and killed Pedro, — a fitting close to a violent reign.

Difficulties of Henry II.

Henry II (1369–1379), as the victor of Montiel was now entitled to be called, did not retain his crown in peace. Despite the fact that he had gravely weakened the monarchy by his grants of lands and privileges in order to gain support, he was beset by those who were still faithful to Pedro, or who at least pretended they were, in order to operate in their own interest. Aragon, Navarre, Portugal, and England waged war on Henry, and the two last-named countries supported Pedro's illegitimate daughters by María de Padilla, Constanza and Isabel (for Pedro had no legitimate children), in their pretensions to the throne, as against the claims of Henry. The most serious demands were put forward by John of Gaunt, Duke of Lancaster and husband of Constanza, backed by Edward III of England. Henry overcame his difficulties, although at the cost of concessions to the nobles which were to be a serious obstacle to future kings.

The reign of Juan I (1379–1390) was marked by two important events. Juan married the heiress to the Portuguese throne, and the union of Spain and Portugal seemed about to take place, but this arrangement did not suit the Portuguese nobility. A new king of Portugal was chosen, and the Castilian army was completely defeated at Aljubarrota in 1385. Shortly afterward, the Duke of Lancaster landed in Spain with an English army to prosecute the claims of his wife. This matter was settled by the marriage of the Duke of Lancaster's daughter, in 1388, to Juan's heir, Prince Henry. Thus was the conflict of Pedro I and Henry II resolved. Their descendants, though tainted with illegitimacy in both cases, had joined to form the royal family of Spain. The young prince and his consort took the titles of Prince and Princess of Asturias, which have been used ever since by the heirs to the Spanish throne.

Henry III "the Sickly" (1390–1406), though already married, was only a minor when he became king, wherefore there occurred the usual troubled years of a minority. Despite the pallor of his complexion (whence his nickname) he was a spirited individual, and upon becoming of age (when fourteen years old) set about to remedy some of the evils which had been caused by the grants of favors to the nobles duirng the regency and in preceding reigns. He also adopted a vigorous policy in his relations with Portugal, Granada, and the pirates of the North African coast, and even went so far as to send two somewhat celebrated embassies to the Mogul emperor and king of Persia, Tamerlane. One event of capital importance in his reign may be taken

Juan I and the battle of Aljubarrota.

The Prince and Princess of Asturias.

Henry "the Sickly."

as the first step in the Castilian venture across the seas. In 1402 Rubín de Bracamonte and Juan de Bethencourt commenced the conquest of the Canary Islands under the patronage of Henry. The young king was also preparing to conquer Granada, when at the age of twenty-seven his life was unfortunately cut short.

Juan II and Álvaro de Luna.

It seemed likely that the opening years of the reign of Juan II (1406–1454) would witness a fresh period of civil struggle, since the king was not yet two years old. That this was not the case was due to the appearance of a man who was both able and faithful to his trust, the regent, Ferdinand of Antequera, an uncle of Juan II. In 1412, however, he left Castile to become king of Aragon, and a few years later Juan's majority was declared at fourteen years of age. Juan II was the first truly weak king of Castile. In the history of Spanish literature he occupies a prominent place, and he was fond of games of chivalry, but he lacked the decision and will-power to govern. Fortunately he had a favorite in the person of Álvaro de Luna who governed for him. On several occasions in the reign Álvaro de Luna was able to win successes against Granada, but the fruits of victory were lost because of civil discord in Castile. During most of the reign the nobles were in revolt against Álvaro de Luna, and the weak king occasionally listened to their complaints, banishing the favorite, but he could not manage affairs without him, and Álvaro de Luna would be brought back to resume his place at the head of the state. By 1445 the position of Álvaro de Luna seemed secure, when a blow fell from an unexpected quarter. He had procured a Portuguese princess as the second wife of Juan II, but she requited him by turning against him. She persuaded Juan to give an order for his arrest, and, since there was no cause for more serious charges, he was accused of having bewitched the king, and was put to death in 1453. This time Juan could not call him back; so he followed him to the grave within a year.

The evil of internal disorder which for so many years had been hanging over the Castilian monarchy came to a head in the reign of Henry IV "the Impotent" (1454–1474).

If Juan II had been weak, Henry IV was weaker still, and he had no Álvaro de Luna to lean upon. He commenced his reign with an act of characteristic flaccidity which was to serve as one of the pretexts for the insurrections against him. War was declared upon Granada, and the Castilian army reached the gates of the Moslem capital, when the king developed a humanitarianism which hardly fitted the times, declining to engage in a decisive battle lest it prove to be bloody. A more important pretext for rebellion arose out of a dynastic question. Failing to have issue by his first wife, Henry procured a divorce and married again. For six years there were no children by this marriage, wherefore the derisive name " the Impotent " was popularly applied to the king, but at length a daughter appeared, and was given the name Juana. Public opinion, especially as voiced by the nobles, proclaimed that the father was the king's favorite, Beltrán de la Cueva, on which account the young Juana became known vulgarly as "La Beltraneja." The *Cortes* acknowledged Juana, and she was also recognized as heir to the throne by the king's brothers and by his sister, Isabella, but the nobles formed a league on the basis of her supposed illegitimacy with the object of killing the favorite. They directed an insulting letter to the king, demanding that his brother, Alfonso, should be named heir. Instead of presenting a bold front against these demands, Henry was weak enough to consent to them.

Henry "the Impotent" and Juana "La Beltraneja."

The dynastic question was far from being the principal one in the eyes of the nobles. By this time it was perfectly clear that the real struggle was political, between the elements of seigniorial independence and strong monarchy. Thus the nobles and their allies had insisted that the king's guard should be disarmed and that its numbers should be fixed; that the judges in royal towns and certain other royal officials should be deprived of their office and be replaced by the appointees of the league; that the king should be subjected to a council of state formed of nobles and churchmen, which body was to intervene in the affairs formerly handled by the king himself, including even the exercise of ordinary judicial authority; that all cases against nobles

The seigniorial program and the vacillation of the king.

and churchmen should be tried by a tribunal of three nobles, three churchmen, and three representatives of the towns, and several of the members who were to compose the tribunal (all of them opponents of the king) were named in the document of these demands; and that there should be a right of insurrection against the king if he should contravene the last-named provision. After he had accepted the nobles' terms Henry realized the gravity of his act and changed his mind, declaring his agreement void. The nobles then announced the deposition of the king, and named his brother, Alfonso, in his stead, but the royal troops defeated them soon afterward, and Alfonso suddenly died. The nobles then offered the crown to Isabella, but she declined to take it while her brother was living, although consenting to do so in succession to him, thus retracting her previous recognition of Juana. On this basis the nobles offered peace to the king, and he consented, which for the second time put him in the position of acknowledging the dishonor of his wife and the illegitimacy of Juana. The queen protested, and in 1470 Henry again recanted, but at the time of his death, in 1474, he had not yet resolved the succession to the throne.

The marriage of Ferdinand and Isabella. Meanwhile Isabella had contracted a marriage of surpassing importance in the history of Spain. In 1469 she married Ferdinand, heir to the throne of Aragon, rejecting Henry IV's proposal of a marriage with the king of Portugal. Isabella was proclaimed queen on the death of her brother, but many nobles now took the other side, upholding the cause of Juana, including some who had formerly fought on the side of Isabella, — for example, the archbishop of Toledo. The hand of Juana was promised to the king of Portugal, who therefore joined in the war on her side. The forces of Isabella were victorious, and in 1479 a treaty was made whereby she was recognized as the queen. The unfortunate Juana chose to enter a convent. In the same year, 1479, Ferdinand became king of Aragon, and at last a political union of the greater part of Christian Spain had become a fact.

The union of Castile and Aragon.

CHAPTER XI

THE general remarks made with respect to Castilian General history in this period apply, with but few modifications, to character-that of the kingdom of Aragon. In Aragon the victory of istics of monarchy over seigniorial anarchy was externally clear as the era. early as the middle of the fourteenth century. The civil wars after that date (and there were very few until the last reign of the period) were due to the vast power of the city of Barcelona in conflict with the king, to the difference in interests of Aragon proper and Catalonia, and to social uprisings. Social progress in this region, but especially in Catalonia, was much more marked than in Castile, merely because there was so much more to gain, and great as were the advances made they did not bring the masses to a state of social freedom equal to that which had been attained in Castile. Of great importance to the future of Spain was the embarkation of Aragon on a career of Italian conquest. Fatal as Spain's Italian aspirations were to be in succeeding centuries, that evil was balanced, at least in part, by a contact with Renaissance influences proceeding out of Italy, and by a favorable commerce which redounded in many ways to the benefit of Spain. This was one of the periods when the advantages of the Italian connection were greater than the disadvantages.

Pedro III (1276–1285) showed in his short reign that he Pedro III was a man of his father's mould. Able as he was he had to and the yield not a little to his nobles and the oligarchical towns, as nobles. indeed had Jaime I, — as witness the case of the independent position of the *Justicia* won from Jaime I. From Pedro III

125

these elements, especially those of Aragon proper, obtained the rights embodied in a document called the "General Privilege"; by this the *Justicia* was proclaimed chief justice for all cases coming before the king, and was made to depend more closely on the nobles and allied towns. They also gained many other privileges, such as the restoration of the goods and lands taken from them by Jaime, exemption from naval service, and a reduction in the number of days of military service required of them. Yet Pedro was able to keep them sufficiently in hand to enable him to embark upon an ambitious foreign policy.

Foreign policy of Pedro III.

Pedro took the first step toward the reincorporation of the realm left by his father to Pedro's brother Jaime when he procured a recognition from the latter that he held his kingdom of Majorca as a vassal of the king of Aragon. Reaching out still farther he established a protectorate over the Moslem state of Tunis, gaining great commercial advantages at the same time. The next logical move was the conquest of the island of Sicily. Two events combined to bring Pedro III into competition for dominion there. One was his denial of vassalage to the pope, repudiating the arrangement of Pedro II, and the other was his marriage to Constance, the daughter of King Manfred of Sicily. The papacy had only recently won its struggle of several centuries against the Hohenstaufen Holy Roman Emperors, and it claimed that the territory of Naples, or southern Italy and Sicily, was at the pope's disposal. Manfred of Sicily was a member of the defeated imperial family, and would not recognize the papal claim, whereupon the pope offered the kingdom as a fief to the French prince, Charles of Anjou. Charles accepted and succeeded in conquering the island, putting Manfred to death. He then proceeded to rule in tyrannical fashion, until in 1282 he provoked the celebrated uprising known as the "Sicilian vespers," when a terrible vengeance was wreaked upon the followers of Charles. Pedro III already had a great army near by in Tunis, and when he was invited by the Sicilians to help them he accepted, alleging the claims of his wife to the Sicilian crown, and landing in Sicily in the same year, 1282.

In a short time he was master of the entire island, and through the exploits of his great admiral, Roger de Lauria, in control of not a little of the Italian coast as well, though only temporarily.

Affronted both by the denial of vassalage and by the conquest of Sicily the pope excommunicated Pedro, and declared his deposition as king of Aragon, granting the throne in his stead to Charles of Valois, second son of the king of France. He even went so far as to proclaim a crusade against Pedro, and a great French army was prepared to carry out his decision and to establish the claim of Charles of Valois. Allies were found in King Jaime of Majorca and many of Pedro's own nobles and churchmen. The French forces soon overran much of Catalonia, but when matters looked darkest a great naval victory by Roger de Lauria and an epidemic which broke out in the French army turned the tide, and the invaders were driven across the Pyrenees. In the same year Pedro died, but just before his death he offered to return Sicily to the pope, — so strong was the prestige of the papacy in that day. *The French invasion.*

Pedro's son, Alfonso III (1285–1291), had no idea of abandoning Sicily. He made it into a separate kingdom under his brother Jaime, and the strife with France and the pope went on. Alfonso was not of his father's calibre, however, and in 1291 agreed to renounce the Sicilian claim and to fight Jaime if the latter should fail to comply with this arrangement; furthermore, he agreed to pay the papal tribute of the treaty of Pedro II, including all back sums still unpaid. Before Alfonso could act on this agreement he died. His reign had not been free from struggles with the nobility, and the latter were in no small degree responsible for the weak result of his foreign policy; only an exceptionally capable monarch, such as Pedro III had been, could handle successfully the grave foreign and domestic problems of the time. The nobles and towns of Aragon proper and Valencia had banded together in a league called the Union, and they used their combined influence to exact new privileges from Alfonso. When he resisted they went so far as to conspire for the succession of the French pretender, and *Alfonso III.*

Struggles with the nobility and the Privilege of the Union.

took other extreme measures which soon decided the king to give way. In 1287 he granted the famous "Privilege of the Union." [1] By this document the king was restrained from proceeding against any member of the Union without the consent of both the *Justicia* and the *Cortes,* and a council was to be appointed to accompany him and decide with him the matters of government affecting Aragon and Valencia. If he should fail to observe the Privilege in these and other respects (for there were other articles of lesser note) the members of the Union might elect a new king. Thus, as Alfonso III put it, "There were as many kings in Aragon as there were *ricoshombres*" (great nobles). Jaime II (1291–1327), brother of the preceding, contrived to reduce some of the privileges granted by this document, although indirectly, for he recognized its legal force. He enacted laws which were in fact inconsistent with it, and in this way managed to deprive the *Justicia* of some of the vast power to which he had attained.

Jaime II and the Sicilian question. The reign of Jaime II was especially interesting from the standpoint of foreign affairs. Having been king in Sicily, Jaime was not disposed to surrender the island to the pope, and left his son, Fadrique, there to govern for him. Soon he changed his mind, and made a similar agreement to that of Alfonso III, whereby the island was to be given to the pope, and Jaime was to employ force, if necessary, to achieve this end. Jaime was soon afterward granted Sardinia and Corsica in compensation for Sicily, although they were to be held as a fief from the pope, and he was to make good his claim by conquering them. The Sicilians were not favorable to Jaime's agreement, and proceeded to elect Fadrique king, resisting Jaime's attempts to enforce his treaty. After a long war, peace was made in 1302 on terms whereby Fadrique married the daughter of the Angevin claimant, the papal candidate, and promised the succession to his father-in-law. Toward the close of Jaime's reign Sardinia

[1] This document is often rendered in English as "Privilege of Union," a phrase which is frequently misunderstood to mean, privilege to unite. The use of the article is necessary in order to give the correct connotation.

was conquered, in 1324, by the king's eldest son. It was at this time, too, that a body of Catalan mercenaries set up their rule in the duchy of Athens, thus extending Catalan influence to the eastern Mediterranean.[1]

Alfonso IV "the Benign" (1327–1335) had a brief, not very eventful reign, marked by wars with Pisa and Genoa for the possession of Sardinia, but more especially interesting as a preparation for the reign to follow. Alfonso's second wife tried to procure a kingdom for her son by a partition of the realm, thus depriving the king's eldest son, Pedro, of his full inheritance. Alfonso was willing to accede to her wishes, but the energetic character of Pedro, backed by popular sentiment, obliged him to desist from the project.

Pedro IV "the Ceremonious" (1335–1387) forms a curious parallel to his Castilian contemporaries, the great Alfonso XI and the violent Pedro I. Like the latter he was energetic,

Alfonso "the Benign."

[1] The lack of regular armies in the medieval period gave rise to the employment of mercenary troops composed of adventurers from all countries, whose presence became a danger to the state, once the purpose for which they had been hired had been achieved. Fadrique of Sicily found himself in this position at the end of the war with his father in 1302. He therefore suggested to Roger de Flor, one of his mercenary leaders, that he go to the aid of the Roman emperor of Constantinople, then in grave danger from the Turks, who had overrun Asia Minor. Roger de Flor accepted the idea, and embarked for the east with a large body of mercenaries, many of whom were Catalans. Through their aid the emperor won great successes against the Turks, and he therefore granted wealth and honors to his mercenary helpers, with the result that yet more mercenaries came to share in the prosperity of their brothers in arms. Some of the Byzantine Greek nobles became jealous of the favor accorded to Roger de Flor and his men, and planned a massacre which was so successfully executed that that leader and thousands of his followers were killed. The survivors, some 3300 in number, did not lose courage, but on the contrary resolved to avenge this treachery, and did so, so effectively that the "Catalan vengeance" has become quite as famous a term in history as the "Sicilian vespers." They defeated their enemies in several battles, and sacked and burned many towns, but at length accepted a call from the duke of Athens to assist him in his wars. They freed the duke from the danger which threatened him, but when he tried to deal with them as the Byzantine Greeks had done they dethroned him and sent a message to Fadrique of Sicily asking him to take them under his protection. Fadrique sent his son, Manfred, who established the Catalan duchy of Athens, which was destined to endure over half a century, from 1326 to 1387 or 1388.

K

Pedro
"the Cere-
monious"
and the
overthrow
of seign-
iorial
anarchy.

treacherous, and cruel, but was more hypocritical, having a great regard for appearances and standing on the letter of the law (hence his nickname). Withal, like Alfonso XI, he was the type of ruler needed at the time, and was even more successful than the great Castilian, for he definitely decided the question between the nobility and the crown. The struggle began over a dynastic issue when Pedro, who at the time had no sons, endeavored to arrange for the succession of his daughter Constance, instead of his brother Jaime. The nobles and the towns of the Aragonese and Valencian parts of the kingdom used this event as a pretext for a renewal of the activities of the Union, and in the first conflict they were too strong for Pedro. He was obliged in 1347 to acknowledge the Privilege of the Union, and in addition had to consent to a division of the kingdom into districts ruled by delegates of the Union, who had broad powers, including a right to receive the taxes, which henceforth were not to go to the king. Pedro was not a man to bow at the first defeat, and in the same year renewed the contest. It is noteworthy that the Catalonian nobles and towns were on the king's side, possibly because of their interest in Mediterranean expansion, which necessitated the backing of a strong government. In addition, certain democratic towns in Valencia and Aragon joined Pedro, as well as many individuals who resented the tyranny of the recently victorious Union. In 1348 Pedro crushed the Aragonese opposition at the battle of Épila, and then overwhelmed his opponents in Valencia, punishing them afterwards with a ruthless hand, displaying a rather vitriolic humor when he made some of his enemies drink the molten metal of which the bell for calling meetings of the Union had been composed. The legal effect of these victories was little more than the nullification of the Privilege of the Union and a reduction of the powers of the *Justicia* and of the exaggerated pretensions, social and otherwise, of the nobles, while the General Privilege and other royal charters remained in force. In fact, however, a death-blow had been struck at feudal anarchy, and the tendency henceforth was toward centralization and absolutism.

The reign of Pedro was not without note, also, in foreign affairs. Even before settling his dispute with the Union he had accomplished something for the aggrandizement of Aragon. He somewhat treacherously provoked a quarrel with the king of Majorca, and then conquered the island in 1343. Proceeding at once against the same king's possessions in southern France he incorporated them into his kingdom. Pedro had also assisted Alfonso XI of Castile against the Benimerines, contributing to the victory of the Salado in 1340. The war with Genoa and the uprisings in Sardinia which had filled the reign of his predecessor gave trouble also to Pedro, but after a campaign in Sardinia in person he was able temporarily to get the upper hand. His intervention in the civil wars of Castile has already been noted, and from these he came out with some not greatly important advantages. He also cast his eyes upon Sicily with a view to restoring it to the direct authority of the Aragonese crown, although this was not accomplished in his reign, and he encouraged commercial relations with the lands of the eastern Mediterranean. In 1381 he accepted an offer to become the sovereign of the Catalan duchy of Athens. These events were more indicative of a conscious Catalan policy of predominance in the Mediterranean than important in themselves. Pedro's successful foreign policy.

The reigns of the next two kings, Juan I (1387–1395) and Martín I (1395–1410), were more important from the standpoint of social institutions than in external political events. In the former reign occurred the loss of the duchy of Athens. In the latter, the island of Sicily, as foreseen by Pedro IV, returned to the Aragonese line when Martín of Sicily succeeded his father as king of Aragon. On the death of Martín without issue, a dispute arose as to the succession to the throne. The most prominent claimants were Ferdinand of Antequera, then regent of Castile, a son of Martín's sister, and Jaime, count of Urgel, son of a cousin of Martín. Ferdinand was supported by the Aragonese anti-pope, Benedict XIII,[1] by the ecclesiastical and popular elements Juan I and Martín I.

The dispute over the succession and the crowning of Ferdinand I.

---

[1] This was at the time of the Great Schism in the church. Benedict was an Avignon pope.

of most of Aragon proper, by various nobles, and by the political influence of the Castilian state, while Jaime counted on the popular support of Catalonia and Valencia and of part of Aragon, as well as on various noble families. Jaime had the advantage of being a native of the kingdom, while Ferdinand was looked upon as a foreigner, but as a matter of law Ferdinand had the better claim. For two years there were serious disturbances on the part of the noble families, which united their personal rivalries to the question of the dynastic succession. Finally, the matter was left to a commission of nine, three each from Aragon, Catalonia, and Valencia, and this body rendered a decision, in 1412, in favor of the Castilian claimant, who thereby became Ferdinand I of Aragon (1410–1416). Jaime resisted for a time, but was soon obliged to submit, and was imprisoned in a castle, although well treated there.

Alfonso "the Magnanimous" and Aragonese expansion into Italy.

Ferdinand was succeeded by his son, Alfonso V, called variously "the Learned" or "the Magnanimous" (1416–1458), under whom the Catalan policy of Mediterranean expansion advanced to a stage far beyond anything previously attempted. Most of his reign was passed by him in warfare in Italy. Invited by the queen of Naples, who adopted him as her heir, to assist her against the house of Anjou, Alfonso was at length able to dominate the land and to set up a brilliant court at the city of Naples. He also intervened successfully in other wars, and even thought of attempting to reconquer Constantinople from the Turks, for that city had been taken by them in 1453. Meanwhile, his absence from his Spanish dominions permitted of a revival of internal disorders, which were to come to a head in the next reign. Alfonso gave Naples (southern Italy) to his illegitimate son Ferdinand, and the rest of his domains, including Sardinia and Sicily, to his brother Juan.

Juan II, Juana Enríquez, and Charles of Viana.

Prior to his succession to the Aragonese throne Juan II (1458–1479) had married the queen of Navarre, and at her wish, consented to by their son, Charles, Prince of Viana, had continued to act as king of that land after his wife's death. He had contracted a second marriage with a Castilian lady, Juana Enríquez, and her intrigues against

Charles of Viana had already caused that prince no little trouble. In the interests of her own children (one of whom, the later great King Ferdinand, was to be a worthy exemplar of the scheming traits of his mother) she plotted to deprive him of his rights, first to the throne of Navarre, and later, after Juan had succeeded to the Aragonese crown, to that of Aragon. The Catalans took up the cause of Charles of Viana with enthusiasm, and when Juan refused to declare him his heir civil war broke out, not only in Catalonia, but also in Aragon and Navarre. Charles was at first successful, and his father consented to recognize him as his successor and to appoint him governor of Catalonia, but the agreement had hardly been signed when the young prince died. Public opinion ascribed his death to poisoning at the instigation of his step-mother, and so great was the general indignation over this event that civil war in Catalonia broke out afresh. The Catalans were at a legal disadvantage in not having a legitimate lord to set up against Juan II. They elected various individuals as count of Barcelona, and even thought of organizing a republic, but the successive deaths of their chosen rulers, and the length of the war, which had already lasted twelve years, inclined many, toward the close of the year 1470, to make peace with the king. The very misfortunes of the latter, despite the crimes which he had committed, tended to this end, for he had again become a widower, and was blind and alone, for his son, Ferdinand, had remained in Castile after his important marriage with Isabella in 1469. Finally, in 1472, a peace satisfactory to both sides was arranged. It is to be noted that this war had nothing to do with the earlier struggle of the lords against the king, but was sustained rather by the city of Barcelona and the permanent committee, or deputation, representing the *Cortes* of Catalonia, against the king, being fought mostly in Catalonia, and being involved also with the attempts of the Catalan peasant classes to shake off the social burdens which they had so long been obliged to bear. The former seigniorial stronghold of Aragon proper was in this war the most powerful royalist element. The closing years of Juan's reign were devoted

The revolt of the Catalans.

to a war against France for the reconquest of Cerdagne and the Roussillon, which had previously been granted by Juan to the French king in return for support against the former's Catalan enemies. This war was still going on when, in 1479, Juan died, and Ferdinand ascended the throne, to rule, jointly with Isabella, the entire realms of Castile and Aragon. Thus had the evil intrigues of Juana Enríquez redounded to the benefit of Spain.

Navarre

Navarre re-enters the current of peninsula history.

From 1285 to 1328 Navarre was a French province, but recovered its independence under the house of Evreux on the death of Charles IV of France without succession. The next heir after Charles of Viana was his sister Blanche, but her father, Juan II of Aragon, had her imprisoned, and a younger sister, Leonor, was enthroned in her stead.[1] Leonor and her husband, the count of Foix, established a new dynasty which was destined to be of short duration, for in 1512 Ferdinand of Aragon conquered Spanish Navarre. French Navarre remained for a time under the rule of the house of Foix, but presently became a part of the kingdom of France.

The Basque Provinces

Early history of the Basque provinces and their ultimate incorporation in the kingdom of Castile.

The three Basque provinces of Álava, Vizcaya, and Guipúzcoa had more of interest in their internal organization than in their external political history, since in the latter respect they were closely united to Navarre and Castile, which states disputed the dominion of these provinces. They were usually subject to one power or the other, although some of their towns, together with others of the Castilian north coast, formed themselves into leagues (*hermandades*), and enjoyed a certain amount of independence in their dealings with England and France.

[1] Blanche was the unfortunate queen divorced by Henry the Impotent of Castile. Shortly after her imprisonment in Navarre she died suddenly, probably poisoned by order of her sister.

A number of popular beliefs exist with regard to the history of these provinces, one of which is that they have never been conquered. It is true that no conqueror ever stamped out the indomitable spirit and the customs of the people, but the land was rarely independent. It is believed that the Moslem invasion of the eighth century did not extend to these provinces, but at a later time they did suffer from Moslem incursions. With the organization of the kingdom of Asturias, both Álava and Vizcaya seem to have been either dependent on that realm or at least in close relationship with it. At times, from the eighth to the tenth centuries, the counts of Álava were also counts of Castile. Passing into the hands of Sancho the Great of Navarre, Álava was incorporated in that kingdom until the reign of Alfonso VIII of Castile. Alfonso VIII won the battle of Vitoria, and conquered the land in 1200. Thenceforth it remained under the sovereignty of the Castilian monarch, although with an assembly, the *Cofradía* (Fraternity, or Association) of Arriaga, of its own. In 1332, in the reign of Alfonso XI, the incorporation with Castile was made complete, although with a retention of the charters and liberties of the province. Vizcaya also vacillated between Navarre and Castile as a more or less independent, protected country, until in 1370 it passed over to the Castilian crown by inheritance of the wife of Henry III. The course of events in Guipúzcoa was very similar. In 1200 the province submitted to the conqueror of Vitoria, and from that time forth the external political history of Guipúzcoa was that of Castile.

Granada

The Moslem state of Granada was of very slight political importance in this period, despite its by no means insignificant territorial extent, wealth, and population. It was a mere political accident, annoying to the Christians at times, but as a rule not worthy of serious consideration as an enemy. It was precisely because it was not greatly to be feared or very troublesome that it was permitted to maintain its independence. It is to be noted, also, that there was very

Inconsequential character of Granadine political history.

little of the crusading spirit in these centuries; if there had been, Granada would soon have been conquered. On several occasions, when the rulers of Granada called in the Benimerines and others from Africa, the Moslems were a serious peril to Christian Spain, but the battle of the Salado in 1340 proved decisive, being followed by a decline of the political strength of the Moslem states of northern Africa. After 1340 the rulers of Granada limited themselves, in their relations with the Christian states, to intervening in Castile during periods of civil war, or to asking Castilian aid at times of internal strife in Granada. Uprisings and dethronements were of frequent occurrence, but so too were Moslem raids into Castilian territory.

CHAPTER XII

SOCIAL ORGANIZATION IN SPAIN, 1252–1479

Castile

As regards social organization this period represents merely an evolution of the factors which had already appeared in the preceding era, and its chief results were the following: the end of serfdom; the advance of the middle class and its opposition to the lords, principally through its jurisconsults and the *caballeros* of the towns; an increase in the privileges of the clergy; and additional landed wealth for the nobles through the donations of the kings or private conquests. The principal social struggle was no longer that of the serfs against their lords, but rather of the middle class, as represented by the wealthier citizens of the towns, against the nobles and clergy for legal equality, especially as regards taxation and other duties to the state. The disappearance of serfdom did not bring economic well-being to the agricultural laborers; their fortunes in this regard were often as vexatious and hard to bear as their former personal dependence had been. At the same time, the poorer people of the towns became a fairly numerous class, but they were in a position of inferiority as compared with the wealthier citizens.

Through civil wars and the weakness of the kings the power of the nobles, both socially and politically, appeared to increase. They did not confine their strife to opposition to the king, but fought one another incessantly, not for any political or other ideal, but mainly for personal reasons. Such was the nature of the wars, for example, between the

137

Guzmán and Ponce families of Seville. As time went on, these intra-class struggles increased, being more numerous than ever in the fifteenth century. The nobility would have destroyed itself if the kings had known how to take advantage of the situation, but most of them failed to appreciate their opportunity. Sancho IV, Alfonso XI, Pedro I, and Henry III tried to reduce the nobles by direct attack, and Henry IV gave special attention to the development of a new nobility as a counterpoise to the old, but usually the kings dared to fight only indirectly, as by granting the petitions of the towns which involved a diminution of seigniorial authority. Two circumstances in addition to their political victories tended to secure the position of the nobles: the adoption of the law of primogeniture with regard to the succession to both their titles and their lands; and the increase in the territorial domains in the possession of the nobles. By the law of primogeniture the wealth of the family and the lustre of its name were given in charge of the eldest son, maintaining in this way the powerful position of the particular noble house. The second sons (*segundones*), in large measure disinherited, sought a career as members of the clergy or as soldiers. Henry II himself was partly responsible for the introduction of this new practice of the nobility, and he and later kings usually required that the lands granted by them to the nobles should be inalienable and subject to the law of primogeniture. The royal donations, which were especially great from the time of Henry II on, were usually of two kinds: *honores* (honors), or grants of the fiscal rights which the king had in a specifically named place; and *tierras* (lands), or grants of a fixed rent on a certain town or towns. Both forms were termed generally grants in *encomienda*. The nobles increased their holdings yet more by usurpations and private conquests. Early in the reign of Henry IV, for example, the Duke of Medina Sidonia and other nobles conquered territories of vast size from the Moslems, and these *latifundia* (broad estates) have influenced even to the present day the economic life of Andalusia.

The *caballeros* of the military orders were a notably im-

Primo-
geniture
and *lati-
fundia*.

portant element. A noble of high rank was usually chosen as grand master, and this gave him a preponderantly strong position. The vast power of these orders was the cause of their downfall, the impulse for which came from without, through the joint action of the French monarchy and the popes. The order of the Templars, the strongest of all, was abolished by the pope in 1312, and this reacted to cause a decline of the other orders. Furthermore, the reason for their existence ceased with the entry of the Turks into Europe and the cessation of the Spanish crusades. Except as concerned the military orders the nobles seemed to have reached the height of their social ambitions, conducting themselves in a lawless manner with a more or less complete lack of loyalty, high ideals, or moral sense, but (as will be pointed out in the following chapter) their authority appeared to be greater than it actually was.[1]

The personal immunities of the clergy were not only extended, but were also made applicable to a greater num- ber than formerly, and the wealth of the church was in- creased. Not only priests, but also their servants and the members of the religious orders, including even those of the lay orders, acquired the so-called "benefit of clergy,"

[1] The figure of Pedro López de Ayala (1332–1407) is typical of the nobility of the times, illustrating also the new tendency to win triumphs in court intrigues rather than in warlike pursuits. Despite the facility with which he changed from one side to another, he was able to procure a profit for himself (even out of his reverses) without scandal and under a pretence of serving the public good, being always on the border of immorality without falling openly and resolutely into it. Thus he was able to rise from untitled poverty to nobility and extraordinary wealth, and to the position of chancellor of Castile. He was also the most noted historian of his time.

A worthy successor of the preceding was Pedro Téllez Girón, grand master of Calatrava, whose achievements occupied the latter years of Juan II and most of the reign of Henry IV. As a favorite of the latter before he became king he was influential in causing the downfall of Álvaro de Luna, and profited by that event to secure honors and wealth for himself, so that in the reign of Henry IV he proved to be the most powerful of the Castilian lords. He was also one of the most turbulent and disloyal of the nobles, and knew how to procure a good price for his services in the civil wars of his time. He would have married Isabella, the successor of Henry IV, if he had lived, and in that event the history of Spain might have taken a different course.

which exempted them from certain financial obligations to the state and to the towns, and secured them the privilege of being subject judicially to the ecclesiastical courts only. Furthermore, entry into religious orders became so comparatively easy that the number of ecclesiastics proper increased greatly, although many of them continued to be business men, lawyers, administrative officers, and even jugglers and buffoons, frequently leading a licentious life. Similarly, the mendicant orders had lost their early ideals of poverty and self-sacrifice, and besides being lax at times in their mode of life were devoting themselves to the acquisition of wealth, especially by procuring inheritances. These conditions were cited in complaint after complaint of the national *Cortes*, asking the king for their redress. Finally, Henry II issued a law, confirmed by Juan I, that clergymen should contribute to the funds applied on public works, and that lands which had been tributary should continue to pay taxes after their acquisition by the church. These laws seem not to have been complied with, for the complaints were renewed in later meetings of the *Cortes;* it was charged that the clergymen excommunicated the tax collectors. On the other hand the right of the church to collect the *diezmo*, or tithe (not precisely a tenth), of the produce of lands not their own, a right which had already existed in some jurisdictions, became general. The king profited by this arrangement, since a portion called the royal thirds (*tercias reales*)[1] went to him for expenditure for public charities or pious works, such as the building of churches, although the kings did not always so employ it.[2]

Advance of the middle class. The same causes which had conduced to the development of the middle class in the preceding era were accentuated to procure a corresponding advance in this, — such as the increase in population, the growth of industry, commerce, and agriculture, the freedom of the servile classes, the prominence of the jurisconsults and secondary nobility, or

[1] Usually the "royal thirds" amounted to two-ninths. At a later time, both in Spain and the colonies, this tax was specifically called the *dos novenas* (two-ninths).

[2] The customs of the clergy will be taken up more fully in chapter XIV.

caballeros (proceeding usually from the towns, and living there allied with the middle class against the greater nobles), and the great political importance which the towns acquired. The basis of the middle class was the town, partisan of the centralizing, absolutist tendency of the kings so far as it related to the nobles and clergy, but strenuously insistent on the retention of its own local charter. The middle class had control of production and was the nerve of the state, but was virtually the only element to pay taxes, despite the fact that the great bulk of territorial wealth was in the hands of the nobility and the church. The term "middle class" began to refer more and more clearly to the wealthier, free, but untitled element, for the laboring class became more prominent in the towns, sharing in the charter privileges of their richer neighbors, but with certain limitations on their economic liberty. There was no social conflict of consequence between the two classes, however, for the laborers were not yet very numerous, and the evils of their situation were not so great as they later became, besides which, self-interest united them with the middle class against the nobles and clergy. Such strife as there was between them was of a political, and not of a social, character. The so-called popular element of the *Cortes* represented the middle class only. The practice of forming leagues (*hermandades*) of towns and *caballeros* against the abuses of the higher nobility was much indulged in, for it was not safe to rely solely on the king. The victory in the end lay with the towns, although they were far from obtaining their specific aims at this time. Nevertheless, the fourteenth century was characterized by the transformation of society from its earlier basis of chivalry and war, when the scene had been laid in the castles of the country, to the bourgeois life of the towns, devoted to industry and commerce.

The rural servile classes, which had all but won complete personal liberty in the preceding period, attained both that and nearly complete economic liberty at this time. Thus the ordinance of Valladolid, in 1325, prohibited the lords from retaining either the realty or the personalty of any man who should move from seigniorial to royal lands, preserving

Improved basis of rural society.

the owner's right to cultivate or sell his lands, and to make any use he saw fit of his personal effects. The ordinance of Alcalá, of 1348, took a step backward, limiting the owner's freedom of sale, lest the lands fall into privileged, non-taxpaying hands, and requiring him to keep somebody on the land, so that there might always be a taxpayer there. Finally, the ideal of the ordinance of Valladolid prevailed. At the same time, the old servile relation whereby the lord procured the cultivation of his own lands changed to one of landlord and tenant, based on the payment of a stipulated rent. The fact that there were no social struggles in Castile in the fourteenth and fifteenth centuries is evidence of the comparatively satisfactory condition of the rural classes. Naturally, there were abuses of an extra-legal character by the nobles, such as the forced loans exacted by them, the compulsory marriages of rich widows to members of a lord's following, and outright robbery, but the real interests of the lords called for them to use conciliatory measures to attract population, and some of them at least did follow that policy. Personal slavery still continued, but the number of slaves was very greatly diminished and gradually got smaller, — a tendency which was favored by the laws.

Slavery.

Treatment of the Mudéjares.

The free Mudéjares continued to receive lenient treatment, and their numbers increased greatly; many of the Moslem faith preferred to leave Granada and live in Christian Castile. The legislation of Alfonso X put them under the royal protection and allowed them to have their own courts and their own law. They were permitted to retain the mosques they already had, but were forbidden to build new ones; they could not worship in public in places settled chiefly by Christians, but otherwise no objection was made; the obligations of former times as regards taxation, mode of dress, and dealings with Christians were also retained; and the gathering of Mudéjares into the cities, despite the greater number of restrictions imposed upon them, went on, caused by the abuses of an unofficial character to which they were subjected at the hands of the Christian population in the country. In later reigns the restrictions were increased, but many of them were not enforced. In fact, the Mudéjares enjoyed greater prosperity in the last reign of the era than at any other time of the period, being a wealthy and important social element, represented at court even, and enjoying a number of advantages which for a long time had been denied them.

For a while the legal situation of the Jews was comparable to that of the Mudéjares, but the Christian clergy was particularly vindictive against the former, and popular sentiment was bitterly hostile to them, due not only to the influence of the church, but also in part to hatred of the Jewish tax collectors, and partly to the avarice awakened by the wealth of the Jews (fabulously exaggerated as a rule). This enmity was evidenced in more and more restrictive laws and in the open insults and violence of the Christian populace. Popular feeling began to make itself more rigorously felt from about the year 1391. In 1391 a great massacre of the Jews took place in Seville, and this was a signal for similar massacres in other parts of Spain. Shortly afterward the Jews lost their separate law courts; they were forbidden among other things to engage in commerce with Christians, to rent the taxes [1] or hold public positions, to be artisans, to carry arms, or to have intimate relations with Christians; and they were even compelled to listen to sermons preached with a view to their conversion. These laws were not always enforced, but the position of the Jews was far from equalling that of the Mudéjares. Great numbers of them were converted, but it was believed, probably with truth, that they continued to practise the Jewish faith in secret. The converts were insulted by their Christian brethren, even in the name "Marranos" (pigs) applied to them as a class. They were also envied because of their industry and wealth, and were accused of diabolical practices of which they were almost certainly not guilty. In the last years of the reign of Henry IV the massacres of Jews began to be extended to them as well as to the unconverted element.

Harsh measures against the Jews.

The Marranos.

Two forces combined to change the former type of family life: the Roman civil law (of tremendous importance); and

---

[1] It was still the practice to farm out the revenues for a fixed sum, leaving the contractor to collect them as a private venture.

Changes
in the
laws of
marriage,
the family,
and
property.

the doctrines of the church, which indeed in their judicial expression were influenced profoundly by the Roman law. They were able to strike a death-blow at the marriage *á yuras;* henceforth the law required the sanction of the church. *Barraganía* still maintained a legal though restricted standing. Cases of marriage and divorce were taken away from civil jurisdiction and turned over to the ecclesiastical courts. As an illustration of the individualistic tendencies springing from the influence of Roman jurisprudence it may be noted that up to twenty-five years of age a daughter had to have her father's consent in order to contract marriage, but could dispense with his permission after that time. The most important reform in family life was the establishment of the rule of primogeniture, a practice which rapidly became customary. The Roman law was equally influential in its effects upon property. Whereas formerly the wealth of Castile had been based on agriculture and stock-raising, with the land concentrated in few hands and cultivated by serfs, now urban lands and personalty, based on industry and commerce and adapted to Roman principles, became the more important; and despite the *latifundia* of the era a large part of the former seigniorial lands was now given over in small lots to free proprietors protected by the law. The Roman formalism appeared to some extent also in the law of property, contract, and wills, especially in the legislation of Alfonso X.

Survivals
of
medieval
col-
'ectivity.

The collectivity of medieval times had a survival in the lands common of the towns, and appeared also in the industrial guilds and the semi-religious *cofradías,* or fraternities. The latter included various classes of people organized into a group for the accomplishment of some social object, such as to perform acts of charity or hold funerary dinners, as well as to provide mutual aid; the law forbade associations for political, immoral, or illegal purposes. The guilds were far more important, and were greatly favored by the laws. At first they were closely dependent on the municipalities, which intervened to regulate the trades, even in technical respects, but at length the guilds began tc receive charters directly from the king. The new charters, too, in keeping with the practices of the era, were minute in their directions with regard to the conduct of the various industries. By the fifteenth century the guilds were paying little attention to the social matters which formerly were their most important function, — these had passed over to the *cofradías*, — and had become almost wholly economic and professional, although their members marched together in processions, and the guilds as a body rendered public service of one kind or another, — as, for example, maintaining some public charity. They were also a factor in the political life of the towns.

In general social customs, so far as they relate to the upper classes, for the practices of the humbler elements are less well known, this era was marked by great immorality, license in expression (even when referring to matters of religion), luxury, a desire for honors and noble rank (even to the point of falsely pretending to them), the mixture of an appetite for knowledge with the pursuit of superstitions, and the exaggerated practice of chivalric principles (professed more as an affectation than with sincerity). The luxury of the times manifested itself in the usual ways, and it is worthy of note that members of the middle class were now able to vie with the nobles. Women painted and powdered and used exaggerated effects in their dress, and men wore high-heeled boots, employed various devices to correct the natural defects of the body, and used perfumes. Foreign influences entered to modify clothing so that it tended more to fit the body than before, with a resulting abandonment of the flowing garments of earlier times. Men often wore stockings of different colors, a feather in their hat, and a much-adorned, variegated cape. Color, too, was equally prominent for its diversity in women's dress, but the dress itself allowed greater freedom of movement than the earlier styles had done. Superstitions were prevalent, from the alchemy and astrology of the learned, to the various forms of divination and ancient practices — such, for example, as the mass for the dead dedicated to living persons — of the common people. Jousts and tourneys and attempts to imitate the warlike feats of the heroes of fiction in such works as *Amadís de Gaula* (of which later)

General social customs.

Dress.

Superstition.

Sports.

L

formed a part of the chivalric customs of the day. Bull-fighting was clearly in existence by the time of Alfonso X, and thenceforth enjoyed great popularity.[1]

In social and political institutions Aragon proper, Catalonia, and Valencia still differed from one another sufficiently to merit separate treatment. While in many ways their customs were like those of Castile there were certain variations worthy of record.

Aragon proper

Social differences in Aragon proper.

Prior to the reign of Pedro IV the nobles increased their authority both with respect to their rights over the lower classes and in the exercise of political power, but if Pedro reduced their privileges in the latter respect neither he nor his successors did anything to prepare the emancipation of the servile classes. The nobles retained their social privileges even to the extent of procuring a law in 1451 doing away with the royal practice of granting titles of nobility of the lower grades. Feudalism continued, though in a modified form, for if the nobles could receive lands from the king and reissue them to vassals of their own they were obliged to return them to the king whenever he should ask them to do so, and were not allowed to build castles without his consent; moreover, there were various other limitations on their former nearly absolute sway. They collected taxes for themselves, and were exempt from paying them to the royal treasury, but were under the necessity of rendering military service when called upon. The clergy gained increased social importance just as it did in Castile, and the middle class became a prominent factor with the development of the towns, though far from attaining to the high place of the same element in Castile. The towns followed a divided policy, for those of the north were feudal in type and allied with the nobility, while those of the south were more democratic and royal. The condition of the servile classes was even worse than before, and no serious attempt

[1] Despite the existence of bull-fighting in much earlier times, — for example, in the Visigothic period, — there is no clear documentary reference to that game for centuries prior to the reign of Alfonso X.

was made either by them or the *Cortes* to relieve their hard lot.[1] The laws continued to recognize the lord's right to deal with them as he pleased, and even to kill them, and lands were still sold with the men and women both Christians and others who dwelt thereon. The history of the Jews and Mudéjares followed the same course that it did in Castile. Not merely in Aragon proper but in all the dominions of the crown the Jews were subjected to exceedingly harsh treatment. The Mudéjares of both Aragon and Valencia were protected by the kings and the nobles with a view to keeping their lands occupied so that they might not fail to yield rents and taxes, and in both regions the rural population was principally Mudéjar. The Roman law exercised a powerful influence in Aragon as elsewhere. Thus freedom of testament was introduced, and primogeniture attained to a predominant place. The guilds did not advance to the point reached in Castile, existing rather for purposes of mutual aid, and lacking the technical regulations of the Castilian guilds.

Catalonia

There are two prime facts in the social history of Catalonia in this period : the uprising of the serfs ; and the outstanding importance of the cities, especially Barcelona. The first marked the decline of the nobility and the appearance of a new social factor ; the second indicated the direction which modern social organization was to take. Having lost their political power the nobles concentrated their interest on getting wealth out of their lands, especially through the tributes of their serfs. In this respect they had the enormous advantage of possessing the greater part of Catalan territory.[2] The serfs were subject to a great number of annoying personal services, and (in a typical case) to as many as thirty different tributes, most of them in kind, besides the

Revolts of the serfs.

[1] The earliest recorded petition in their favor in the popular branch of the *Cortes* was in 1626 !

[2] An estimate of 1359 states that there were 25,731 dwellings on royal lands, and 57,278 on those of the lords. As late as the seventeenth century it is said that 1800 cities and towns out of 2400 belonged to the nobles or the church, or three-fourths of the total.

ordinary rental for the land. They had already won a
right to redeem themselves for money, and Juan I, Martín I,
and María (the wife and regent of Alfonso V), as well as
many jurisconsults, made some more or less ineffectual
attempts to better their condition. The plagues which
swept Europe in the fourteenth century were a greater aid,
since laborers became scarce and therefore more desirable.
By the time of Alfonso V the serfs had become sufficiently
emboldened to formulate demands, on the threat of a general
uprising. Alfonso accepted a sum of money from them,
granted what they asked, and then withdrew his promises
when the nobles also bribed him. The revolt was delayed,
however, to the year 1462 in the next reign, when it formed
one of the complications in the wars of Juan II against the
deputation of Catalonia and the city of Barcelona. Both
sides sought the aid of the serfs, but Juan was able to win
them to his support, although their military operations were
directed primarily against their own lords. The peace of
1472 did not solve the social question; so there was another
uprising in 1475, and it was still going on at Juan's death, in
1479, being left for solution to the reign of his son, Ferdinand.

Decline
of the
nobility.
As a result of these troubles the nobles declined even in
social prestige, for they had received very little in the way of
tributes from the serfs since the reign of Alfonso V, and had
aggravated the situation by their wars with one another or
against the towns. Meanwhile, the *caballeros* and others
of the secondary nobility, natural enemies of the great lords,
had advanced in importance, and in the reign of Pedro IV
had won a right to law courts of their own, free from the
jurisdiction of nobles of the upper grades. On the other
hand, the great nobles continued to receive donations of
land from the king, with more or less complete jurisdiction,
since the existing needs of the royal treasury usually seemed
greater than the ultimate evil of the grants; often the kings
gave away towns which they had previously pledged their
word never to alienate. It is to be noted that the mere
ownership of land did not entitle the lords to exercise civil
and criminal jurisdiction without a specific grant of those
powers from the king. In addition to the serfs and the kings,

the nobility had a third element against it, the very powerful bourgeoisie, or middle class, which in this period attained to the greatest splendor. The history of the Mudéjares at this time was unimportant, for there were not many in Catalonia. The Jews suffered as they did in Castile. The year 1391, which witnessed the massacre in Seville, was marked by a similar event in Barcelona, where the Jewish quarter completely disappeared. From that time on, harsh measures were taken in Catalonia, and as a result the Jews came to be regarded as sharing with slaves (of whom there were still a considerable number) the lowest level in the social hierarchy. *Persecution of the Jews.*

The modifications of family life arising from the influence of the Roman law were as notable in Catalonia as in Castile and Aragon. The guilds were developed to a point even surpassing that of Castile. As early as the fourteenth century they were already organizations for technical objects related to their trade. Every trade had its guild, from the more important associations of weavers, bakers, and the like, down to the more humble blind beggars' guilds. *Catalan guilds.*

All that has been said of Castile as regards the immorality, luxury, dress, superstition, and chivalric pursuits of the aristocracy and middle class applies generally, not only to Catalonia, but also to Aragon and Valencia. The nobles endeavored to emulate the king in extravagances, with the result that many were ruined, and their attempts to avoid paying their debts to the Jews were one cause of the massacres of the latter. The luxury in dress brought in its train the development of tailoring to such an extent that the Catalan modes were well-known even in foreign countries. In many of the amusements of the period, — dances, illuminations, pantomimes, processions, masquerades, and others, — one sees the influence of Renaissance tastes, which were to lead to modern civilization, although these same diversions were also tainted with the rudeness of earlier times.[1] In fine, the customs of the period were made *Transition from medievalism to modernity in social customs.*

[1] Thus Queen María felt it incumbent upon her to enact, in 1454, that naked men should not take part in processions of masqueraders.

up of a curious mixture of passing medievalism and coming modernity. For example, while some seigniorial castles were centres of luxury and entertainment, others retained the austere, military customs of the past. Again, at the same time that there appeared a veneer of literary and scientific culture, ideas as regards sanitation, both public and private, were still rudimentary. Laws continued to be passed forbidding people to wash clothes in public fountains, to throw water and filth in the streets, and to loose pigs therein, but they were not very generally obeyed. Even the public baths which had existed formerly fell into disuse. Thus epidemics were frequent, but aside from prayers and sequestration of cases not much was done to check their progress.

Valencia

Victory of Catalan civilization in Valencia.

The majority of the Christian settlers of Valencia were both bourgeois and Catalan, while the nobles were mostly Aragonese. Down to the time of Pedro IV, the latter exerted themselves to deprive the former of the power which Jaime I had given them, and they were successful to the point of sharing in administrative posts which had formerly been denied them, and also procured the application of the Aragonese law in the land. After their defeat by Pedro IV they declined rapidly, hastening their fall by partisan quarrels among themselves. The history of the Mudéjares and Jews followed the same course as in Aragon; here, as elsewhere, the terrible year 1391 was a time of massacres of the Jews, followed by increasingly harsh legislation. The influence of the Roman law in modifying family institutions and the development of the guilds proceeded on lines analogous to the same factors in Catalonia.

CHAPTER XIII

THE CASTILIAN STATE, 1252–1479

IN the relations of the seigniorial elements and the monarchy this was a critical period for the latter, deciding as a result of the virtual, though not at the time apparent, victory of the kings that Castile was to become a power in the world. For that very reason the evolution of political institutions in this era was important, for on the development of monarchy depended the conquest of America, but they were also important because the institutions which were set up in the new world had noteworthy antecedents at this time. Influenced largely by the principles of the Roman law the kings aspired to absolute monarchy in a centralized state, with a view to overcoming the social and political strife resulting from the diffusion of power inherent in the seigniorial system. Their most dangerous enemies were the nobles, whose spirit of independence and self-esteem and whose vast wealth in lands and fighting men made them a powerful factor in themselves. They were yet stronger because the kings had to depend on them for military service since there was no large standing army, and because they in a measure developed a class consciousness in opposition to absolutism, becoming a nobility rather than remaining a mere aggregation of nobles. While the seigniorial ideal was not lacking in the towns, they were not nearly so dangerous to the monarchy, because they were usually as hostile to the nobility as the kings were. Often, however, they fought against the kings, or exacted concessions for their services. The task for the fulfilment of royal ideals was therefore a difficult one, requiring a sagacious type of

General character and importance of the era in political institutions.

151

monarch, such as in fact rarely appeared in the period. Circumstances fought better than the kings, and nowhere does this show forth more clearly than in a review of the political institutions of the era.

Internal decline in the power of the nobles.

The external vicissitudes of the strife between the nobles and the kings have already been traced, and it would appear from them that the former gained the upper hand. In fact, however, their cause was already internally dead. One symptom of their approaching dissolution was the change in the practices of the nobles whereby they became more and more a court nobility, plotting in the shadow of the king (like the chancellor López de Ayala) instead of being semi-independent potentates on their own estates as formerly. Despite their class consciousness, parties arose within their ranks with distinct ideals, apart from personal ambition, dividing them against one another. Thus in Seville the Guzmán faction represented conservatism, while the Ponces were radical. Most important of all were the blows resulting from the social and economic changes which deprived the nobles of their serfs and created a new form of wealth in the hands of the middle class, an element better fitted than the old nobility to acquire and develop the new resources. The eagerness with which the nobles took up the practice of primogeniture, leaving their estates nearly intact to their eldest sons so that their house and their name might not be lost, showed that they realized the force of the new order of things and were taking thought for the future. In earlier times, when wealth was territorial and serfs were numerous, the land-rich nobility had been secure, but that day had passed.

The absolutist ideal of Alfonso X.

The great representative of absolutism was Alfonso X, not that he invented the idea or was the first to attempt its achievement, but because he formulated the program more clearly than any of his predecessors, embodying it in his legislation, and because he received the first shock in defence of these principles. He enacted that the legislative, judicial, and military powers and the right to coin money were fundamental, inalienable rights of the king, who could not give them away for a period longer than his own life, and declared that the lords could not exercise any judicial or other sovereign powers on their estates except those which had been granted to them by the king, or which they had enjoyed by immemorial custom. His laws also prescribed certain forms of etiquette which should be employed in treating with the king, establishing the ceremonial which has always served as such a prop for monarchy. The divine origin of royal power was asserted. Independence of the Holy Roman Emperors was specifically proclaimed, but a measure of subjection to the pope was admitted. The absolutism of Alfonso X did not pretend, even in principle, that the king might exercise arbitrary or tyrannical authority; Alfonso declared that the king was bound to observe the law and deal justly with the people, acting as their guardian and administrator, and granting them certain rights to inspect his conduct. Those who wrongly possessed themselves of the royal power, or made bad use of it, were declared to be tyrants and not legitimate kings. The people, on the other hand, owed respect, obedience, and loyalty to the legitimate king, and even a species of guardianship to prevent his non-fulfilment of obligations. Alfonso X was not able to sustain his principles in open conflict, but they remained as the ideal of future kings, even though some of them were modified by the legislation of later reigns; thus Alfonso XI declared that sovereign rights might be acquired from the crown by prescription, except the taxing power and high justice (or the hearing of cases on appeal), and that the kings could alienate any of their sovereign powers except those of high justice, coinage, and war.

Two fundamental results of the centralizing, absolutist policy of the kings were the final establishment of hereditary succession and the development of consultive and other bodies about the king, the forerunners of modern bureaucracy. The former has already been referred to. Alfonso himself was the first to break his own law in this respect, but after his reign the principle was definitely recognized. The pomp and ceremonial of royalty increased the number of officials whose principal functions were those of adding splendor to the court, — such, for example, as the king's

Establishment of hereditary succession and development of court officialdom.

cup-bearer, butler, and chamberlain. Great nobles also sent their sons to court to be educated under the protection and with the favor of the king, and these young men formed a special royal guard. In addition there began to be an infinity of servants, notaries, doctors, and others occupying posts of a less ornamental character. The most important novelty of the period was the development of the *Consejo Real*.

The *Consejo Real*.

The kings had long been surrounded by a body of nobles and prelates called the *Consejo Real*, or Royal Council, which advised them in matters of government, or sat as the *Cort*, or supreme court, in appeals from lower jurisdictions, but its membership and functions had not been very clearly established, for it dealt indiscriminately with any subject upon which the king might want advice. One important reform was the introduction of representatives of the popular element in this body. Different kings, from Sancho IV on, decreed that a certain number of the council should be "good men," — or members of the untitled, secular class, — although the practice did not become fixed. A law of Juan I in 1385 provided that the council should be composed of twelve men, of whom four should be plebeians. Two years later it was required that the last-named should be *letrados*, — that is, men learned in the law, — and shortly afterward they began to be called *oidores* (hearers of cases). Juan II divided the council into two bodies, one of government, the other of justice. It was not until the time of Ferdinand and Isabella, however, that the *Consejo Real* acquired real stability.

The hierarchy of officialdom.

There were important developments, too, in the general administrative and judicial hierarchy, although with a mixture of the two functions. The hierarchy of officialdom, from the lowest grade to the highest, with especial regard to comparative judicial authority, ran from the *alcaldes* of the towns through *merinos mayores* or the *adelantados*, the *alcalde del rey* (royal *alcalde*) of the court, and the *adelantado mayor* (or chief justice of Castile) to the king himself. In some jurisdictions cases in first instance came before *alcaldes del rey* (different from the above-named) with an appeal to *merinos menores* [1] and *merinos mayores*, or directly to the latter, and thence upward. The *merinos menores* limited themselves to jurisdiction in certain criminal cases. The *merinos mayores* were, like the *adelantados*, governors of large districts as well as judges in cases of appeal, for which latter purpose they were assisted by men acquainted with the law. They took the place of many of the former *adelantados*. The *adelantado mayor* also had administrative functions, as the superior of the *merinos* and other officials below him. Alfonso X employed the old term, *cort*, in the new and more restricted sense of a royal judicial tribunal which acted for the king. In later reigns this came to be known as the *chancillería* (chancery), or *audiencia*,[2] — which latter name was eventually transmitted to the Americas for bodies exercising similar functions.

Despite appearances, uniformity and order in the administrative and judicial organization were far from being completely established. Not only was there a great variety of jurisdictions, but there was also a great diversity in the law, for one region would differ radically from another. The towns, nobles, clergy, universities, and the great corporation of stock-raisers (the *Mesta*) all had officials of their own and exemption from royal jurisdiction. At the same time, great *hermandades*, or leagues of cities, were formed for the maintenance of public security against highwaymen or other disturbing elements, since royal activity in this regard left much to be desired, and these also had their separate jurisdictions.[3] The current toward centralization

Diversity of jurisdictions and tendencies toward centralization.

[1] See page 90, note 1.
[2] Literally "audience," or "hearing." Originally, the king gave "audience" for the decision of cases. Later, he was relieved of this duty by other officials, or bodies, and the name was applied finally to the courts referred to in this volume.
[3] The most famous of these leagues was the *Santa Real Hermandad* (Royal Holy Brotherhood) of Toledo, Talavera, and Villarreal which lasted until the nineteenth century, although with modifications of its jurisdiction and activities. The members of the league might pursue an offender as far as the borders of Portugal or Aragon. When they caught him they had a banquet, after which the criminal was tied to a post to serve as a target, and a prize was given to the one who first shot him through the heart. When the accused was already dead, a trial was held and he was sentenced.

was very strong, however, being aided by the education in the Roman law of the *letrados,* whom the king employed as his officials (for these men were pronouncedly monarchical in sentiment), and by the increase in powers to which the *adelantados* and *merinos mayores* were attaining at the expense of the semi-independent elements. The successors of Alfonso X, especially Alfonso XI, furthered this policy of centralization. Royal judges began to appear in the towns, either taking the place of the formerly elected officials, or acting concurrently with them, for the kings took advantage of one pretext or another to make an opening for their own appointees. Another important reform was the division of the *audiencia* into two sections, one of which remained in Segovia, while the other went on circuit for brief periods in Andalusia. Under Juan II there appeared in the *audiencia* the official known as the *fiscal,* who at this time was a royal prosecuting attorney, but who later was to become one of the most important all-round administrative officials in Spanish and Spanish colonial government. As an example, too, of the extension of royal jurisdiction may be mentioned the so-called recourse of *fuerza* in cases of usurpation (by force, — hence *fuerza)* of lands or jurisdiction by the clergy. The trial of these cases was ordered to be held in the royal courts.

Judicial procedure   Punishments for crime continued to be atrocious, and torture was still employed, but only in the case of persons of bad reputation or when the accused bore the evidences of crime. Privilege still obtained to modify the punishment of the upper classes. A very notable reform was the introduction of the *pesquisa,* or inquisitorial investigation, for the bringing of an indictment, or accusation, of crime. Formerly the state had intervened when one individual charged another with crime, a process which resulted to the detriment of the weak, who would not dare to accuse

This procedure helps one to visualize the real insecurity of the times, — for the same summary methods were employed which men have used both before and since when the central authority was not strong enough to guarantee public security. The California Vigilance Committees in the days of the gold rush are an instance in point.

the more powerful. The *pesquisa* not only introduced the grand jury function of an accusation by the state, without necessarily involving any individual accusers, but it also made crime partake more of the nature of a public offence than of a mere infringement of individual rights. The vulgar proofs, with one exception, were abolished, and the importance of written documents and the testimony of witnesses became more generally recognized. This also caused the rise of the lawyers, who, after a lapse of centuries, began again to be a noteworthy element in judicial affairs. The *riepto*, or duel, a special form of the wager of battle, was the only one of the vulgar proofs to remain in existence. This was a special privilege enjoyed only by those of noble blood. The duel was hedged in by a number of rules, one of which was that it must take place in the presence of the king. If the challenger were killed, the innocence of his opponent was proclaimed, but if the latter were killed, still protesting innocence, he was in this case, too, declared guiltless. The challenger could win by defeating his opponent without killing him, in which event the latter was banished, and half of his goods were granted to the king.

Although the expenses of the state were greater than formerly, the income was also greater. Many new forms of taxation were introduced: the royal monopolies on salt and mines; the *alcabala*, or tax on sales, which first became general in the reign of Alfonso XI; stamp taxes; and the *consumo*, or tax on all merchandise entering the city. These taxes fell upon goods or upon acts of individuals in connection with the state (as distinguished from the king) differing radically from the services of a feudal character, with a multitude of exceptions and privileges, which had formerly been the basis of the public income. Owing to the turbulence of the era and the excessive alienation of public wealth by grants of the kings to the nobles, receipts did not equal the royal needs, and resort was had frequently to loans, debasement of the coinage, and arbitrary confiscations of property. Even under the new system of taxation the nobles and clergy very rarely had to pay any of the numerous taxes, and privileges and exemptions were granted, much

The new system of taxation.

as before. Nevertheless, the methods employed contained the germ of a sound financial system, which was to develop in succeeding centuries. The collection of taxes was rented out as formerly, being given in charge usually of Mudéjares, Jews, or Marranos. Complaints against these collectors were so insistent that at one time churchmen were substituted for them, — without diminishing the complaints, for the fault lay in the system. There were royal financial officials for receiving the funds and examining accounts, but no organized treasury department was as yet developed.

The army and navy.

The principal military fact of the era was the increase in the number of troops sustained by the king, but in other respects there was no fundamental difference from the preceding period. Technically there were advances in the art of war, — such as the development of a greater variety in the branches of the service and the introduction of powder, — but except for cannon of not very great utility the use of firearms did not become general. Complete armor came in with the white companies. The royal navy, initiated by Ferdinand III, was continued throughout the era, and this was a period of brilliant victories against the Moslems in the Mediterranean and the English in the north; on one occasion the Castilian admiral, Pero Niño, ravaged the English coast. No results of note seem to have proceeded from these victories, however.

Greatness and decline of the towns in political authority.

This was the most flourishing epoch in the history of the free Castilian towns: their numbers and political importance increased; they received new privileges; and they made their presence felt in national affairs through their representatives in the *Cortes*. The most extreme example of municipal independence was provided by the towns of the north coast, which recognized the sovereignty of the Castilian king, but in fact governed themselves, even intervening in foreign affairs through the agency of their league. In the interior the towns were less independent politically and administratively, and in the fourteenth century their authority began to wane. The entry of royal judges into the towns has already been mentioned. In administration the kings were also able at length to exercise influence.

This came about as a result of a number of political changes, such as the substitution of a life term in office for one of a period of years, the usurpation by the *ayuntamiento* (or body of municipal officials) of powers formerly exercised by the general assembly, the limitation of the right to hold office to the *caballeros* or to specified families, the disturbances at times of election, and the corruption which occasionally manifested itself in municipal administration. In the interests of internal peace the towns themselves often sought intervention by the kings, who did not fail to profit by the situation. Under Alfonso XI some towns began to be ruled by officials appointed by the king, and that monarch also created the post of *corregidor*,[1] a royal agent placed in many towns to watch the course of local affairs and represent the king, acting with the local *alcaldes*. The *corregidores* gradually acquired considerable influence, thereby reducing the power of the popularly elected officials. Internal municipal strife continued, but now the great families fought, not for the favor of the electorate, but for that of the king, since this had become the surer route to public office. The greater towns or cities suffered through the breaking away of the villages and rural districts which had formerly been subordinate to them. These villages were desirous of local autonomy, because the municipalities on which they depended were wont to exploit them or to exclude them from a share in government. The kings granted their petitions, thus weakening the greater towns, even if they did extend the institution of chartered municipalities. It should be said, however, that this decline of the towns, with the incidents accompanying it, was not uniform, for a number of them still retained their earlier liberties, including popular election, at the end of the period. In the seigniorial towns, especially those under ecclesiastical domination, there were frequent struggles with a view to reducing the lord's intervention in local affairs, and these ended almost everywhere

Advance of the seigniorial towns.

---

[1] Literally "corrector." While the royal agent of this name might originally have been considered a "corrector" rather than an administrator, he later came to rule over areas ranging from that of a city to a province, with wide judicial and executive functions.

in a victory for the towns, which won a right to name their own officers and to possess much the same degree of liberty enjoyed by the royal towns. Here, too, the kings intervened, not only through the practice of judicial appeals to the royal courts, but also in other ways, even with armed forces, in order to reduce the power of the lords. The victory of the seigniorial towns lessened the power of the lords to an appreciable extent; the struggles of the lords with the kings were thenceforth maintained only through combinations of nobles, often with Mudéjar levies, joined at times by some of the towns.

Great age of the Castilian *Cortes*.

The institution which most clearly represented the different factors of Castilian political life, but especially that of the municipalities, was the *Cortes*, which grew in importance until the fifteenth century, when it began to show signs of decline. The *Cortes* was hardly mentioned in the legislation of Alfonso X, for it did not comport well with his theories of absolutism, but the later kings paid it great consideration, seeking the aid of the popular branch against seigniorial anarchy. Its principal function continued to be economic, rather than legislative, through the grants of subsidies by the representatives of the towns. While these were not the only source of royal revenue they were so urgently needed that the *Cortes* was able to procure legislation from the kings in response to its petitions. The fourteenth century was particularly rich in ordinances of the *Cortes*, especially those arising from the meetings of 1329 (Madrid), 1348 (Alcalá), 1351 (Valladolid), 1366 (Burgos), 1371 (Toro), 1373 (Toro), 1377 (Burgos), 1379 (Burgos), and 1380 (Soria). In most cases the kings did not put the ordinances (which should rather be considered petitions) into effect, wherefore many of them were repeated time and again, — such, for example, as the legislation requested against the Jews, against the granting of Castilian benefices by the pope, against the abuses of royal officials and renters of taxes, and against the royal donations to the lords. In a number of instances the *Cortes* got what it asked for, even in cases affecting the king's personal authority, such as a law in 1329 which prohibited the issuing of royal letters, or orders, in blank (whereby the possessor of the letter might insert anybody's name he chose, — a practice which usually served to promote unjust ends, just as in the case of the *lettres de cachet* in France prior to the French Revolution), and another of 1348 extending the prohibition to letters which the kings were in the habit of granting to individuals empowering them to marry designated persons, with or without the latter's consent. The kings also accepted petitions of a more general character, such as those asking that steps be taken for the suppression of banditry, the specification of the powers of royal officers, the correction of various abuses, the lowering of certain taxes, the regulation of disputes between the stockmen and the farmers, and the reform of judicial procedure. It was also affirmed several times, — in 1348, for example, — that there could be no new tax without a grant of the *Cortes*. The laws of Alfonso X insisted upon the king's sole right to legislate, however, and this principle was maintained by the later kings, for despite the fact that a law of 1387 declared that the ordinances of the *Cortes* were irrevocable, unless by the act of a *Cortes* itself, the kings proceeded according to their own pleasure, apparently regarding the concession of 1387 as purely theoretical. The ordinances of the various *Cortes* appeared without method or plan, and lacked the full force of law, but they demonstrated the enormous activity of this body, and were in fact a basis for much legislation, both at the time and in later years. In organization the *Cortes* followed the general practices of the preceding era. Among the comparatively few novelties may be mentioned a law of Juan II, fixing the number of representatives from a town as two, and a law of 1351 granting immunity from arrest to members of the *Cortes* while that body was in session. Up to 1301 Castile and León had a separate *Cortes*, although there were a number of joint meetings before that date. After 1301 there was but a single *Cortes* for the entire kingdom.

Not only in the ordinances of the *Cortes*, but also in the general laws of the king without intervention of the *Cortes*, in grants of municipal charters, and in the innumerable private grants (often modifying the general law) this period

M

Diversity
in the
laws and
tendencies
toward
unifica-
tion.

was exceedingly rich in legislation. The fame of the laws of Alfonso X and of Alfonso XI has obscured the legislation of other reigns, but the output of the other kings was great in quantity, if less in importance than that of the two Alfonsos. Diversity was still a leading characteristic of the legislation. For example, from Alfonso X to 1299 at least 127 local charters were granted; in the fourteenth century at least 94; and in the fifteenth, at least 5, although many were reproductions or slight modifications of certain typical charters. The *Fuero Juzgo* continued to be the general law, but there was very little of it which was not contradicted or changed by other legislation. A tendency toward unification of the laws manifested itself in many ways, however. Alfonso X issued a municipal charter in 1254, variously named, but usually called the *Fuero Real* (Royal Charter), which was a new model, more complete and systematic than those which had preceded it, but based on those already in existence and on the *Fuero Juzgo*, preserving the Visigothic and early Leonese and Castilian principles of law. The *Fuero Real* was adopted as supplementary law for use in cases of appeal to the royal courts, but was also granted as the local charter of a great many towns, being the most extensively used of the typical charters, although by no means in a majority of the municipalities. To bring about unification at one stroke it is believed that Ferdinand III and Alfonso X projected a code to apply in all the land. Ferdinand is said to have begun the drawing up of the *Setenario* (or Septenary, so-called because it was to be in seven parts), which was completed by Alfonso after the former's death. This code, if such it may be called, was never promulgated, and may rather have been intended as an encyclopedia of law. A similar compilation of the reign of Alfonso X was the *Espéculo* (or *Espejo*) *de todos los derechos* (mirror of all the laws), but it, too, never became law, although used as a reference book by jurisconsults. Yet another such compilation appeared in this reign, the famous *Leyes de las siete partidas* (laws of the seven parts), or simply the *Partidas*, and this was to attain to a very different lot from the others just named.

The *Partidas* was the work of a number of jurisconsults under the inspection, and with more or less intervention, of Alfonso himself; these men began work in 1256 and finished it in 1265.   Some of the laws and customs of Castile, — for example, the *Fuero Juzgo* and the *Fuero Real*, — were used as sources, but the preponderant influences were those of the canon law and the codes of the Roman emperor Justinian, — so much so that the *Partidas* amounted to an encyclopedia of these two sources of law, both of which were Roman in origin and very different from the customs, Visigothic and otherwise, at that time prevailing in Castile. Whether Alfonso intended that the *Partidas* should become the general law, or merely that it should serve as an encyclopedia, it was not promulgated in his day, and there were many later laws directly contradicting it.   Nevertheless, it constantly gained ground, favored especially by lawyers and university men (both of which elements were strong partisans of the Roman law), being used as a book of reference and as a text-book.   Finally the current in its favor became so strong that so far as it was not inconsistent with certain specified compilations it was declared to be law in the reign of Alfonso XI by the important ordinance of the *Cortes* of Alcalá (1348).   This set forth that the decisions of that *Cortes* should be the principal fountain of Castilian law, followed in order of precedence by the *Fuero Real*, the other municipal charters, and finally by way of supplement by the *Partidas*, which was not to be enforced in such parts as it contradicted the privileges of the nobility, for these also were confirmed.   Despite this lowly position of the *Partidas* and despite the vast quantity of later laws which took precedence of the above-mentioned hierarchy of sources, the ultimate victory of Alfonso's code was assured from the time of its official promulgation.   Without any statute to that effect it gradually became recognized, not as a mere supplementary source, but as the principal law of the land.   Reformations of its text were undertaken to make it conform with the necessities of later times, but in substance the ideas of the original remained.

Next to the state the church was the most powerful and

The code of the *Siete Partidas* and the revival of Roman principles.

influential factor in Castile. This period was one of serious internal disturbance in the Castilian church and of relaxation in discipline. Despite the efforts of the popes and some Castilian prelates, the practice of *barraganía* continued. There also occurred such incidents as competitions in beauty between the nuns of Seville and Toledo, such instances of lack of discipline as the armed resistance of the dean of Sigüenza to the pope's appointee as bishop, such turbulent intervention in politics as that of the bishops of Seville and Toledo in the time of Henry IV, and such cases of strife and violence as the attack of the monks of Melón on those of Armenteira, and that of the bishop of Mondoñedo on the Cistercians of Meyra. The disorder was enhanced owing to the appearance of the Great Schism in the church at large, in which Spanish countries were particularly interested, since several of the popes and anti-popes were of Spanish blood. On the other hand, the popes intervened

more than ever in the affairs of the Castilian church. The ideas of Gregory VII of the supremacy of the papacy over temporal rulers did not fail to produce results in Castile. In the *Partidas* of the absolutist Alfonso X it was recognized that one legitimate way of acquiring the crown was by a grant of the pope, and that the latter might also absolve Castilian subjects from obedience to the king in certain cases. The election of bishops, normally the act of the cathedral canons, provoked many disputes between the kings and the popes, for the latter frequently intervened to impose their candidate, or even to make direct appointments, while the former claimed that no election was valid until it had their approval. One of the most unpopular practices of the popes was the appointment of foreigners to Castilian benefices, and frequent protests were made against it, but usually without avail. Although the popes got rather the better of the dispute over appointments to bishoprics, the kings manifested their prerogative in other respects, as by banishing prelates who worked against royal interests, by prohibiting the publication of papal bulls which might do harm to the state, and by employing the already mentioned process of recourse of *fuerza* in cases of ecclesiastical usurpations of jurisdiction. The *Partidas* named certain cases where clergymen lost their right of resort to ecclesiastical courts, — for example, suits between clerical and lay individuals over lands and inheritances. Even Alfonso XI, who (though somewhat immoral in private life) was very pious and notably generous with churches and monasteries, was very strict in guarding the rights of the state against the intrusions of the church. On the other hand, he confirmed the jurisdiction of the church courts in spiritual and related matters, including such cases as those arising out of church taxation, marriage, births, divorce, adultery, usury, and robbery in a sacred place, as well as those of a more purely religious or ecclesiastical character. The wealth of the church in lands **Wealth** increased greatly, both as a result of royal donations, and **of the** through the gifts of individuals, especially in the fourteenth **church.** century when the terror of the plagues which were sweeping Europe caused many to seek divine favor through benefactions to the church. There were a number of protests in the *Cortes*, especially in the case of the monasteries. The objections were based on social and financial, rather than anti-clerical, grounds, since the accumulation of landed wealth in the hands of the church tended to reduce the agricultural classes to a perpetual condition of mere usufruct or rental of lands, and resulted in vast tracts remaining uncultivated. Furthermore, these lands as a rule became exempted from taxation. The *Partidas* recognized the right of the church to receive such gifts, and no effectual steps were taken to check them. It may be mentioned **Pil-** here that this was the golden age of pilgrimages to holy **grimages.** places, due to religious devotion, or in fulfilment of vows, or from pure love of travel and adventure. Naturally, Santiago de Compostela was the chief objective of pilgrims in Spain, and to that place went not only Spaniards but also many thousands of persons from all parts of western Europe.

CHAPTER XIV

THE ARAGONESE STATE, 1276–1479

Aragon proper

Victory of
the royal
authority
in Aragon
proper.

THE struggle of the kings against the seigniorial elements of Aragon and Valencia (in furtherance of their policy of absolutism and centralization) has already been traced up to the point where royalty gained the upper hand in the reign of Pedro IV. One result of Pedro's victory was the reduction of the power of the *Justicia,* no longer a creature of the nobility (to mediate between them and the king) but a royal appointee, exercising strictly judicial powers as chief justice of the realm. Even in this respect his authority was limited by the founding of a tribunal to accompany the king. Attempts continued to be made to establish the independence of the *Justicia,* and the *Cortes* declared him irremovable, but the kings compelled their appointees to give them a letter of resignation, with the date left blank, or disregarded the prohibition of the *Cortes* altogether, deposing a *Justicia* if it suited them to do so. Pedro IV enacted that no person of higher rank than that of *caballero* should be governor in Aragon, thus removing another factor which had formerly contributed to civil strife. Aside from the abolition of the Privilege of the Union and the reforms just mentioned (together with others of lesser note), the kings did not modify the political organization of Aragon, but became in fact the principal element in the state, working their will even to the point of acts at variance with the laws. Great diversity in charter rights and jurisdictions continued to exist, although a number of general compilations of legislation like those in Castile were made. These became supplements to the already-mentioned code of Jaime I.[1] Other volumes were prepared of the customs of the realm, and the agreements of the *Cortes* were also an important legislative source. The abolition of torture and of the vulgar proofs may be mentioned among the reforms in judicial procedure. The nobles remained almost wholly exempt from taxation, even with respect to the lands which they might acquire in royal territory.

The relations of the state and church in Aragon were more acute than in Castile, because of the consequences of Pedro II's act of vassalage and the wars in Italy, and because of the Great Schism, in which Aragon played a leading part, since one of the anti-popes, Benedict XIII, an Aragonese, fixed his court in Aragon for a time, causing a divided allegiance of the clergy. The matter of the election of bishops was settled early in favor of the popes when Jaime II enacted that the pope himself should appoint them. This occasioned a number of disagreeable results, especially at the time of the schism, when there were two or more popes. Some appointments were manifestly improper. Clement V appointed his nephew, a mere boy at the time, as archbishop of Saragossa, and even Benedict XIII, though a man of the highest character, made a similar appointment to the archbishopric of Toledo. In other respects the kings often insisted on the rights of the state, and intervened in matters of an ecclesiastical character. Alfonso V was the first Aragonese ruler to pronounce for the retention of papal bulls when their publication was against the interests of the monarchy, availing himself of the *pase regio* (royal permit), on which the kings based their claims to prevent documents which displeased them from being put into effect or even from reaching their intended destination. Pedro de Luna had for a long time been influential in Spain before he became Pope Benedict XIII; he it was who persuaded Juan I of Castile and Juan I of Aragon to recognize Clement VII

Relations of church and state in Aragon.

Benedict XIII.

[1] In 1283 the General Privilege was added as book eight, for there had been the usual seven parts in the code of Jaime I; in 1300 the reforms of Jaime II; in 1348 those of Pedro IV; and finally those of Juan I and Martín I.

of Avignon instead of the pope at Rome. He himself succeeded Clement VII, and because of his upright character,
piety, intellectual capacity, and Spanish blood received the
adhesion of most of the peninsula prelates. It was largely
through his support that Ferdinand of Antequera was
crowned king of Aragon instead of Jaime of Urgel. When
a general church council was called to elect a pope to replace
the three then in power, Benedict XIII alone of the three
refused to abdicate. Ferdinand, who for a time endeavored
to support him, felt obliged at last to deny him obedience.
Benedict maintained himself in the fortress of Peñíscola
until 1422 or 1423, when he died, — almost certainly poisoned
by a friar. His cardinals elected Gil Muñoz, a canon of
Barcelona, but in 1429 Muñoz renounced the title and the
schism ended.

Catalonia

Impor-
tance of
the Cata-
lan towns.
The most marked feature in the political life of Catalonia
in this period was the rise of the towns, and especially the
vast power exercised by the city of Barcelona. The towns
became veritable lords, buying jurisdictions, privileges,
immunities, castles, and lesser towns from the king, just as
the nobles were in the habit of doing. Important cities got
to be protectors of villages and towns, granting the right of
carreratge, which entitled them to be considered a street of
the city. As a rule the kings favored this increase in the
power of the municipalities, and the latter might have made
themselves an irresistible force, had it not been for their
internal party strife, and for the armed struggles of rival
cities. There began to be a certain uniformity in the organization of royal towns in the thirteenth century, and in
the fourteenth it became more marked under the influence
of the centralizing policy of Pedro IV. The general assembly
was the basis of government at first, but its place was taken
later by a council elected from the wealthy citizens; at
times, the officials themselves were the only ones to vote,
and they too chose the representatives to the *Cortes*. This
aristocratic form of government did not please the kings,

since it tended to create a force which would be hostile to them and led to social strife in the municipalities, wherefore matters were adjusted at the close of the fourteenth century by the entry of the popular element into the council. Just as in Castile, the nobles and churchmen were forced to grant privileges to their towns almost equal to those enjoyed by the royal municipalities, in order to retain the people. They still collected certain taxes, exercised judicial powers, and appointed some officials, but the greater part of local administration was in the hands of the towns themselves, which developed along lines similar to those of the royal towns.

The most accentuated representation of municipal life was to be found in the city of Barcelona. The administrative organization of the preceding era did not change fundamentally, but the power and privileges of the city increased greatly, due to the concessions of the kings. The council of five was at first composed only of *honrats*, or members of the bourgeois aristocracy, but by the year 1455 only two were of this class, a third was a merchant, a fourth an artist, and a fifth an artisan. The classes of lower grade than the *honrats* were admitted to the *Consell* in 1387, and by the end of the period the popular element had become preponderant. The five councillors, though subject to the *Consell*, formed an administrative commission for the government of the city. It was also their privilege to advise the king, something which they frequently did, and they were charged with the duty of maintaining the charter rights of the city, a matter to which they attended most zealously, even to the point of war with the king. Through purchase, annexation, royal donations, and the extensive application of the institution of *carreratge* Barcelona acquired a great part of Catalonia and other portions of the realm; the possession of Elche and other towns in Valencian territory illustrates the far-reaching authority of the great Catalan city. The subject towns had a right to protection and to the privileges and exemptions of Barcelona, in return for which the latter had more or less complete control of the administration of justice, was supposed to have their coöperation in matters

Greatness of the city of Barcelona.

of general interest, and was entitled to contributions of soldiers and the payment of certain tributes. The vast power of Barcelona was not always exercised for the best interests of the state, as in the case of the blow inflicted on the commerce of Valencia, through the influence of Barcelona, whereby no merchandise was allowed to be shipped from that port in foreign vessels. At times, the governing authorities of Barcelona equalled, or even exceeded, the power of the deputation of the *Cortes* of Catalonia, and sustained disputes with it. On the other hand, Barcelona repeatedly intervened in the struggles of *caballeros*, towns, and social classes to impose peace. The authority of the city was reflected in the pride of its aristocracy, the *honrats*. They enjoyed the right of *riepto*, or duel, the same as members of the nobility, and vigorously protested against measures which seemed to place them on a lower level than any other class of society, — for example, when the order of St. John proposed to admit only the descendants of nobles. Anybody might become an *honrat* if he combined certain prerequisites, such as wealth, with an election by the council.

Struggle between absolutism and seigniorial society in Catalonia.

The same struggle of absolutism against the seigniorial elements appeared in Catalonia as in Castile and Aragon, although the monarchy was more consistently victorious there than elsewhere. The nobles opposed the kings, though somewhat weakly, for they were more concerned with the social problems of the era. The cities and towns, especially Barcelona, also constituted a feudal element which was not always in accord with the king. Although during most of the era there was no armed conflict between these forces, there were a number of symptoms of discontent which at length broke forth in the civil wars of the reign of Juan II. Some of the causes of dissatisfaction were the following: the belief that their Castilian sovereign, Ferdinand I, and his successors had an exaggerated ideal of absolutism; the employment of foreigners in public offices, especially Castilians, by the same monarchs, — a demonstration also of the lack of Spanish national feeling; and the absence of Alfonso V in Italy and his expensive wars there, although the Catalans were as a rule partisans of the policy of Mediterranean expansion. Fundamentally, however, the strife at the end of this period was a conflict between centralized absolute monarchy and decentralization based on charter rights. Neither Juan II nor his predecessors varied the charters or the political organization of the principality, but nevertheless the blow was struck, and the downfall of the sovereign rights of the lords and towns was already at hand.

The *Cortes* continued to meet separately from that of Aragon and to be chiefly important for its grant or refusal of taxes. The third estate (representatives of the towns) endeavored to establish its right to participate with the king in legislation, but the latter made laws independently of the *Cortes* as before. When the *Cortes* was not in session, it was represented by the general deputation, or *Generalitat*, usually made up of three members, or one for each branch of the *Cortes*. In addition to keeping watch to see that the laws were strictly observed, the deputation had certain police powers, including the defence of the principality, and other less notable administrative functions. The general *Cortes* of the entire realm held occasional meetings, as did also a new *Cortes* for the Mediterranean possessions of the kingdom (Corsica, Sardinia, Sicily, and Naples).

The Catalan Cortes.

Legislation was characterized by the variety of jurisdictions of former years, but the number of grants of new municipal charters diminished greatly, and the general decrees of the kings increased. If this manifested a tendency toward unity, the citation of the principles of the Roman law did so even more. This had already proved influential in the preceding era, but it did not establish itself securely until the fifteenth century. There was a strong sentiment in its favor in Catalonia, and Pedro IV ordered its study and its use in cases at law. Finally it was established in the *Cortes* of 1409 that the Roman and canon law might be cited as supplementary law after certain other specified legal sources. Like the adoption of the *Partidas* in Castile (in 1348) this meant an ultimate, complete victory for the Roman principles. In most other respects the administration of justice in Catalonia followed the course already described for

Legislation in Catalonia.

Administration in general. Castile. In financial history the only features worthy of note were the development of a system of taxation by the deputation of Catalonia, whereby it met its own expenses and provided funds for the grants to the king, and the growth of a system of municipal finance in Barcelona on a scale in keeping with its extensive power. In both military and naval affairs the authority of the deputation was the most striking element. This body merely loaned the army and navy to the king, specifying the cases when the loan was allowable. The principal military force was that of the municipal militia, although the seigniorial levies still formed part of the army. In addition to the flotilla of the deputation there were the navies of the king, of the corporation of merchants of the city of Barcelona, and of private individuals or towns. The most persistent enemies in the Mediterranean were pirates, both the Moslems of northern Africa, and the Christians from Majorca, southern France, Italy, and Catalonia itself. Towers were built and a messenger service developed to advise of the presence of pirates, but the evil was not eliminated.

Power of the great prelates. The general relaxation in the customs and discipline of churchmen already mentioned in the case of Castile and the course of ecclesiastical history described for Aragon apply equally to the church of Catalonia. The most noteworthy characteristic in the relations of the church and state was the continuation of the feudal authority of the more powerful prelates. Principal among them were the bishops of Gerona, whose dominions and wealth in personalty were greatly increased in this period. As they were virtual monarchs on their lands, they were able to challenge the authority of neighboring nobles or of the kings themselves, and they oppressed the people. Their scant respect for the royal power was often displayed; on one occasion they compelled two of the highest officials of the kingdom to walk through the streets of Gerona in the garb of criminals, submitting all the while to a beating, and made them ascend the long stairway fronting the cathedral on their knees, wearing only a shirt, and carrying a candle. Several of the bishops were banished, and even the nobles joined the kings against the ecclesiastical lords. The Franciscans and Dominicans opposed the bishops and abbots, but although they had popular sympathy in their favor they did not have an equal political influence, since they were not represented in the *Cortes*. The power of the great churchmen was not materially diminished, but the last bishop of Gerona in the era was a strong partisan of the king.

Valencia

In some parts of Valencia the law of Aragon applied, but the usual rule, especially after the victory of Pedro IV, was the jurisdiction of the laws, or *furs*, granted by Jaime I, added to, or modified by, the grants of different kings and the ordinances of the *Cortes*. The law of Barcelona applied in a number of towns which were joined to that city by the institution of *carreratge*. In general administration the practices were much the same as those mentioned for Castile. The extreme harshness of judicial punishments, possibly surpassing other regions, may be noted. The death penalty was habitually given, and various cruel methods of execution were employed. A sentence of imprisonment was rarely inflicted. The greatness of the city of Valencia was almost as noteworthy in this part of Spain as that of Barcelona in Catalonia. Valencia put itself at the head of the Union which fought Pedro IV, only to go down in defeat.

Distinctive features in Valencian political life.

CHAPTER XV

ECONOMIC ORGANIZATION IN SPAIN, 1252–1479

Castile

General
factors of
Castilian
economic
life.

A CONTINUATION in this era of the factors which had tended in the preceding period to develop material resources brought about progress in agriculture, stock-raising, mining, industry, and commerce, although it was not great enough to cause general economic prosperity. The stock-raisers, as before, received more favors than their rivals, the farmers, and it was at this time that the powerful corporation of sheepmen, the *Mesta*, was formed. Alfonso X granted charters to various of these corporations, entitling them to elect *alcaldes* with special jurisdiction in the affairs of the *Mesta* and its disputes with the farmers. The different organizations were united in the reign of Alfonso XI to form a single Castilian *Mesta*, a body which possessed immense power. Gold, silver, quicksilver, and lead mines were worked to some extent; these, with salt mines and fisheries, constituted a royal monopoly, but were exploited by private individuals who paid rent to the kings. The advance in industry was particularly marked. Santiago de Compostela no longer enjoyed a unique position as a manufacturing centre, for every important town now had its industries devoted to supplying the needs of daily life and the exigencies of a growing artistic refinement, as evidenced by the wealth in jewelry, arms, architecture and its appurtenances, furniture, rich embroideries, and other articles far superior in quality and quantity to those of the preceding era. The towns conquered from the Moslems, especially the city of Seville, were particularly noteworthy for their industrial life. Among the principal commercial outlets for Castilian products were the ports of the Basque provinces; their exports seem to have been chiefly raw materials, but there were also such items as cloth, wine, oil, and sugar. It is probable, however, that most of the manufacturing done in the Castilian towns was for the consumption of the towns themselves and a very limited neighboring area. Distribution within Castile was not well developed, for many of the same (or similar) products as those exported were also imported. Industry and commerce were very largely in the hands of foreigners, Jews, and Mudéjares.

Legislation showed the double tendency of encouraging economic development and of checking it by laws looking to the temporary needs of the royal treasury. The *Partidas* urged the cultivation of the soil, the building of bridges and repair of roads, the prevention of frauds in customs houses, and the exemption of certain imports from the payment of duty when they seemed likely to aid in material progress, — such as farming utensils when destined for use by the importer himself and not intended for resale. Commercial treaties with foreign countries began to be made in the fourteenth century, although often by merely a portion of the kingdom, particularly the north coast ports; thus there were treaties of 1351 and 1366 with England. On the other hand there were the royal monopolies, the *alcabala*, and the rigid maintenance of customs duties, — for the exemptions, after all, were few in number. Not only was there the obstacle of different state boundaries, but also there were the duties collected by many, if not most, of the towns. No distinction was made as to the source of goods, and those of Castile paid equally with foreign products. Another hindrance to economic advance was the well-intentioned, but mistaken, policy of excessive governmental regulation of the industries. Both the state and the guilds themselves made laws fixing wages, the hours of labor, prices, methods of contract, amount of interest, and even the way in which goods should be made. These regulations were not uniform for all Castile, but varied according to the special circumstances

Legislative helps and hindrances to economic progress.

of the different regions. The municipalities also intervened to fix prices for goods of prime necessity or of general use. At times they granted an exclusive right of sale, or established municipal shops.

Progress in commerce. To facilitate commerce fairs and general markets were greatly resorted to, being established by law, or, if already in existence, favored by grants of new privileges. The insecurity of the roads and the civil wars prevented the royal grants from having their full effect, and other circumstances, such as the popular attacks on Jewish districts, the variety and uncertainty of coins and of weights and measures, the debasement of the coinage by the kings, and the prevalence of counterfeiting (despite the penalty imposed, — burning to death), tended to interfere with commerce. Nevertheless, notable progress was made. Bills of exchange first appeared in this era. Foreign merchants visited Castile, and Castilians went abroad, especially to England and Flanders; there were Castilian consuls in Bruges. The Jews figured prominently in foreign trade, as money changers and makers of loans, while their international relations due to the solidarity of their race enabled them to act as bankers.

Public works. Something, though little, was done to assist in economic betterment by the building of public works. The lords, both lay and ecclesiastical, resisted many of these projects, notably the building of bridges, since it deprived them of the tolls which they were in the habit of collecting for ferrying goods, animals, and persons across the rivers. Men travelled on horseback, or on a litter, and goods were carried by pack-animals or carts, although the latter could rarely be used because of the bad condition of the roads. Measures to improve the highways were frequently taken, however. The greater part of the revenues devoted to public works was still applied to the building or repair of fortifications.

Aragon, Catalonia, and Valencia

The economic history of this region, based on the natural differences of the three principal sections, followed much the same lines as before, but the principal note was the all-

round development in Catalonia. Grain in that region was
scarce, on which account large quantities were imported
from Aragon and from foreign countries, but some other
agricultural products, such as rice, grapes, and olives, were
cultivated with success. Stock-raising was also a prominent
occupation. The most important source of Catalan wealth
continued to be in manufacturing, especially in Barcelona.
A great variety of cloths and fabrics was made, as also pot-
tery, barrels, rope, glass, and many other articles of practical utility. Aragon was less important in commerce, as
in other respects, than the other parts of the realm. Something was done there by royal legislation to favor trade, and
enough of it existed to warrant the founding of a *consulado* in
Saragossa (1391) with mercantile jurisdiction. Catalan
commerce was so great in volume that it rivalled that of the
Italian cities. From the Scandinavian lands in the northwest to the extremes of the Mediterranean, Catalan ships
might be seen, and if there were many Italian vessels which
visited the ports of Catalonia, so too the Catalans carried
their trade to the cities of Italy, where many Catalan consuls resided. Kings, lords, and towns endeavored to build
up Catalan industry and commerce, by favorable legislation,
by extending the institution of the *consulados*, and by making
commercial treaties. Nevertheless, not a few obstacles
were also raised, largely as a result of the false economic
ideas of the era. Thus, prices were often fixed; a precise
order, or sequence, of sale might be required, — for example,
in La Bisbal the crop of the bishop had to be sold first;
the technical regulation of industries was carried to excess,
far beyond the rules established in this respect in the other
lands of the peninsula; taxes were numerous in kind, and
some were very heavy; and the policy of protection was
carried to extremes in favor of some municipalities as against
others. Furthermore there were dangers of piracy and the
insecurity of the roads. Valencia was commercially prosperous in only less degree than Catalonia. Both regions
were represented principally, in industry and commerce, by
their great capital cities.

Barcelona was easily the greatest industrial and mercantile

N

*Economic
factors in
the king-
dom of
Aragon,
especially
in Cata-
lonia.*

The indus-
trial and
mercan-
tile
system of
Barcelona.
centre in Spain, and was also the leading exponent of the
Catalan policy of protection. Foreign goods like those produced in Catalonia were either prohibited from entry or
charged with excessive duties. On the other hand, the im-
porting of goods which had no counterpart in Catalonia,
such as fine cloths, or which existed in small quantity, such
as grain, was encouraged. In the case of grain, premiums
were granted to importers, and heavy export duties were
collected, or its exportation entirely prohibited. From 1249
to 1347 the *Consell* exercised mercantile jurisdiction through
the medium of two consuls of the sea (*consules de mar*),
but in the last-named year a *consulado* was created to perform that function and to provide for the protection of commerce against pirates. Both the deputation of the *Cortes*
and the two local councils occasionally intervened, however.
The local authorities appointed the consuls to represent
Catalan interests in foreign countries. This was a post of
high consequence, and was rewarded by a grant of a certain
percentage of the purchases and sales of merchandise in the
entire realm of Aragon. The consuls acted as judges, mercantile agents, and guardians and defenders of the persons
and property of their compatriots. The councils of Barcelona concerned themselves with the introduction of new
industries, bringing in foreigners skilled in such manufactures. Financial and technical experts were maintained at
municipal expense. Not only do these facts evidence the
attention paid by the people of Barcelona to mercantile life,
but they also demonstrate a surprising modernity in point
of view. It is no wonder that the merchants of that city
were notably wealthy, proud, and given to luxury.

Economic
promi-
nence of
the city of
Valencia.
    Favored by the rich agricultural productivity of the Valen-
cian kingdom, the industrial traditions of the Moslem population, and the energy of its Catalan bourgeoisie, the city of
Valencia became a veritable rival of Barcelona in industry
and commerce, and enjoyed a wide fame in Mediterranean
lands, especially in Italy. A *consulado* was founded as early
as 1283, and the first bills of exchange known in the peninsula
(from 1376) were drawn up in Valencia. Legislation favoring
Barcelona at Valencia's expense caused a considerable

damage to the latter's commerce, although it continued to be important.

In the erection of public works this was a notable era in all the kingdom of Aragon. A number of bridges were built, and tolls were collected to provide for their preservation and repair. The Catalans were particularly mindful of improving their ports. That of Barcelona was enlarged in the fourteenth century, and in the fifteenth an artificial port was begun and completed. The fifteenth century also marked the beginning of work on the artificial port of Valencia. Old roads were improved and new ones built. A considerable advance was made in works of irrigation in all parts of the realm. In this respect Valencia took the lead, making use of the canals dating from the Moslem period, but amplifying and improving them. A mail service developed at this time. The kings and the municipalities had their separate mails, but in Catalonia there was also a private mail-carrying industry as early as the latter part of the thirteenth century.

Public works.

CHAPTER XVI

INTELLECTUAL PROGRESS IN SPAIN, 1252–1479

Castile

Beginning of Castilian intellectual superiority in the peninsula.

WITH the advance of the Christian conquest against the Moslems the political centre had passed from the northern coast to the Castilian table-land, and thence to Andalusia, where for a time the court was set up in Seville. There was a tendency, however, to return to Castile proper, since the people of that region were the principal element in the conquest and in internal political affairs. The political preponderance of the Castilian part of the realm was so clearly established that it transformed that region in many ways, and caused it to have for the first time a civilization superior to that of the coastal plains, overcoming the geographical handicaps which hitherto had held it back. The predominance of Castile in intellectual life was to become yet more marked in later centuries. In earlier times the rude Asturians and Galicians had joined with the no less rude Leonese and Castilians against the Moslems, but they had become modified by contact with the conquered people themselves and with the various foreigners who joined them in the conquest. The indigenous people did not lose their own individuality, however; rather they assimilated the new influences, and paved the way for the brilliant and original manifestation of intellectual culture of the sixteenth and seventeenth centuries. The principal characteristic of this epoch was the desire for knowledge, leading to the incorporation into indigenous civilization of many other elements. The conquest of Andalusia brought Castile into more intimate contact with Moslem civilization, which reached its

General characteristics of the era.

culminating point in science and in art in the fourteenth century. French elements continued to affect polite literature and didactic works. Especially noteworthy was the great prominence of the influences coming out of Italy, giving a new direction to Castilian literature, and substituting for the Moslem scientific element the direct study of classical texts and the use of observation and experiment as a means to knowledge. The entry of western European culture into Castile was accelerated by those Castilians who went to France and Italy at this time to study in the great schools and universities of those lands. The two capital moments of the era were the reigns of Alfonso X and Juan II.

The universities increased in number and influence to the point of being a vital factor in the intellectual life of the period. In the *Partidas*, Alfonso X distinguished between the "general studies" founded by the pope, emperor, or king, and the "particular studies," the creation of an individual or town. The former combined secondary and higher education, for the old *trivium* and *quadrivium* were retained, with the addition of the Roman and canon law.[1] Gradually the higher studies began to predominate, and associated themselves with the term "university." The "particular studies" were usually conducted by a single master with a few students, and were confined to some one or two branches of learning. Some of these subjects, when they differed from the fundamental courses of the "general studies," tended to be adopted by the latter. Thus theology was added to the university curriculum in the fifteenth century. Other subjects were also studied in the universities, even though not common to all, such as medicine and surgery at Salamanca. Primary education was neglected, although the church schools still continued and some towns or individuals founded such schools. The universities received considerable government aid, but were autonomous, and depended in part on other sources of income, such as their

University and other education.

[1] In medieval schools grammar, rhetoric, and logic (comprising the *trivium*) were the principal studies, supplemented by arithmetic, geometry, astronomy, and music (or the *quadrivium*). These subjects were almost unrecognizably unlike those of the same names today.

own fees and the gifts by individuals or corporations other than the state. The students and teachers together formed a *cofradía*, or fraternity, which elected its own rector, or president. A bishop, dean, or abbot was usually constituted a kind of guardian by royal mandate. This official was gradually replaced by the "schoolmaster of the cathedral," who came to be judge in cases affecting university students, and even arrogated to himself the right to confer degrees, rivalling the president of the university in authority. All members of the university were granted special legal privileges (approximately those of the clergy) with respect to their persons and goods. The method of teaching employed was the reading of a text by the teacher, who commented upon and explained it. Examinations were held for the granting of the bachelor's and doctor's degrees. Not only did each university possess a library, but there were also many other public and private libraries, and the trade of the copyist and the manufacture of books were markedly more prominent than before. In the universities texts were loaned (not sold) to students to enable them to correct their notes, — which shows that books were still comparatively scarce. Some time before 1475, at an uncertain date, the art of printing was introduced into Castile, — with effects which belong to the following eras.

Moslem, Jewish, and other influences on Castilian thought and science.

The oriental influence on Castilian thought and science, or rather the classical influences transmitted through Moslem and Jewish writers, advanced for a time, and continued to be preponderant until the fifteenth century, when European ideas, principally Italian, became the more important. There was a change in direction of the Moslem influence, however. Philosophy dropped back from the leading place, and was substituted by juridical and moral studies, while the physical and natural sciences, including their superstitious derivations, acquired a remarkable vogue. Christian writers imitated Moslem philosophers and moralists, or translated their works; many Castilian writers were of Moslem or Jewish origin, or still continued to belong to those peoples and faiths; many Arabic works were included in the libraries of the time; and the oriental form of scientific exposition, the encyclopedia, was frequently used. The oriental influence manifested itself especially in the natural sciences. Books of mathematics, physics, chemistry, medicine, and astronomy were almost the only ones to be translated from the Arabic, and these branches were also the ones to which Mudéjar scholars of the period most frequently devoted themselves. Moslems and Jews continued to be the most famous physicians of Castile. The deductive method and dialectic forms were still employed by them, rather than personal observation and experiment. The most marked characteristic of the cultivation of the natural sciences was in their extravagant applications with a view to a knowledge of the future or to obtain vast wealth through supernatural agencies. Thus chemistry tended toward alchemy, with the aim of finding the philosopher's stone, whereby base metals might be turned into gold, or with the object of producing mysterious elixirs endowed with wonder-working virtues. Chemists and alchemists came to be considered as practicers of magic arts in more or less intimate communion with the Devil, a belief in which the individuals themselves often shared. Men of high attainments were credulous exponents of these superstitions, — for example, Archbishop Alonso de Carrillo and the learned Enrique de Villena; the latter attained to a legendary fame which has endured even to the present day. Similarly, astronomers were at the same time astrologers. Both alchemy and astrology served a useful purpose, however, in stimulating the study of the true sciences, with a resulting advance in knowledge. The age of the Moslem and Jewish philosopher was past, and very little that was original in the realm of philosophy appeared in Castile in this period; even theological writings were not prominent, despite the study of theology in the universities and schools. Moral and political literature abounded, such as discussions of the wiles or virtues of women on the one hand, and works on the relations between church and state on the other. In the latter respect ecclesiastical writers maintained the superior authority of the pope over the king, but were in the main defenders of monarchy, although distinguishing the legitimate king from the tyrant, and sustaining the ultimate dependence of the monarch on his people. The Italian influence appeared in philosophy through translations of classical (Aristotle, Plato, Cicero, Seneca) and contemporary Italian (Colonna, Petrarch, Boccaccio) texts. The most influential manifestation of Castilian thought was in the field of jurisprudence, to which references have already been made in dealing with the *Partidas* and other legal volumes. The entire period abounded in this type of literature, not only in compilations of an official character, but also in those of private individuals, all of them greatly influenced by the legal works of Justinian.

The triumph of Castilian in polite literature.

The same factors which affected the literary history of the preceding period continued to exist in this, although occupying different positions, and in addition competing with the Classical Renaissance and Italian elements, which almost overwhelmed the others. Just as in the scientific works, so in literature, these factors were assimilated and made over to produce the original Castilian product of succeeding centuries. Castilian became the language of poetry and of didactic works, routing its Galician and Latin rivals. Latin works were translated to Castilian, and from the middle of the thirteenth century the latter began to be used instead of the former in public documents. Galician-Portuguese lyric poetry, half erudite, half popular, born of the Provençal, which it had assimilated and transformed, advanced to its highest point, and seemed to have won a victory over Castilian. About the middle of the fourteenth century it commenced to decline, and by the end of that century Castilian lyric poetry was already predominant; in the fifteenth century Galician ceased to be a literary language, and even Portuguese writers frequently used Castilian. Besides satire and even more sensuality than its Provençal prototype the Galician literature often included ethical and religious sentiments in the same poem. The Provençal influences proper also affected Castile, but did not take root as in Catalonia, because of the difference in language. When Galician poetry lost its place it was the Castilian which became its successor, manifesting in one of its forms the same curious mixture of ethics and satire. At length a satirical element of a free and sensual type prevailed, and brought about a degeneration of this kind of literature. With the fourteenth century the powerful Classical and Italian Renaissance influences made themselves felt in Castile both in poetry and in prose. Works of the classical poets (Homer, Virgil, Ovid, Lucan) and writers of prose (Livy, Sallust, Cæsar, Plutarch, and others) were translated, and served to enrich Castilian literature both in form and in content. The Italian influence proper (Dante, Petrarch, Boccaccio) was by far the greatest, however, especially that of Dante, which vanquished the former French influence in poetry, and in part the Galician, and banished the earlier Castilian literary forms. The Italian influence was most deeply felt in its effects on lyric poetry. Epic poetry and prose were not altogether uncultivated, however, and in this field French influence continued to exist. Many of the older unwritten poems were reduced to writing, and French poems of chivalry and French novels of adventure, telling of the fantastic deeds of King Arthur, Charlemagne, the magician Merlin, and others, were repeated or reconstructed in Castilian. The fabulous element became predominant, leading to the books of *caballería*, or chivalry, based on the extraordinary adventures of wandering knights (*caballeros andantes*), full of the extravagant exaggeration of unbridled imagination. The first great work of this sort in the peninsula, and the best of its kind, was a novel by Vasco de Lobeira called *Amadés de Gaula*, written originally in Portuguese, but already known in Castile in the later fourteenth century. In the fifteenth century amatory novels began to appear.

[margin: External influences upon Castilian literature.]

The advance of the preceding period in historical literature was continued in this. One of the principal names was that of Alfonso X, who was also a writer of note in other branches of literature and learning. His principal work was a history of Spain, compiled probably by a number of men under his direction, just as the *Partidas* was. Various sources were employed, Spanish, French, Latin, and Arabic, and a certain spirit of criticism, superior to that of the earlier histories, was

[margin: Historical literature.]

displayed. On the other hand the work was defective from the historiographical standpoint because of its lack of proportion, its inclusion of epic poems in the body of the narrative, and its manifestation of an ardent patriotism. Perhaps the best historian of the era was the many-sided chancellor and litterateur, López de Ayala, author among other historical works of a chronicle of the reigns of Pedro I, Henry II, Juan I, and part of that of Henry III. López de Ayala wrote in direct imitation of classical writers, especially Livy. Pérez de Guzmán, as author of a collection of biographies reaching down to the fifteenth century, made use of a psychological interpretation of human events. Dramatic literature did not change from the religious dramas and popular representations of jugglers of the preceding era, but progress was made in both of these forms, and each attained to greater favor, preparing the way for the rapidly approaching inauguration of the national theatre.

The drama.

Gothic architecture had its most brilliant expression in the early part of this period, degenerating later largely through an exaggeration of its elements. At the end of the thirteenth century Castilian Gothic may be said to have differed from that of the other European countries in the following respects: its maintenance of classical proportions, with scant difference between the length and width of an edifice, reducing the height; less development in the use of windows; greater robustness of walls, columns, and piers, diminishing the importance of buttresses; more nearly flat roofs; and the general use and ample size of cloisters in convents and churches. The structural basis and sober character of early Gothic began to be lost sight of in the fourteenth century, and, in particular, ornamentation was used without any relation to structural needs. The corruption of Gothic became more and more marked in the fifteenth century, when proportions and structural ideals were forgotten, and adornment, notably in the use of pinnacles, was employed in excessive degree. It was at this time that the choir of Spanish cathedrals was moved to the centre of the nave, in front of the high altar. This was the greatest age of Gothic civil and military art, especially of the latter.

The developed Castilian Gothic architecture.

Castles were more solidly and more richly built, with handsome towers and other exterior defences and with embattled walls. Towers and battlements also appeared on the walls of cities. Mudéjar architecture continued to develop, notably in Toledo and Seville, in both religious and civil edifices, and some of the best specimens of this art date from the fourteenth and fifteenth centuries. It was especially employed in the interior decoration of palaces and private houses, — in panelling, handsomely worked wooden roofs, painted and sculptured friezes, and the use of tiles. On the outside it appeared in eaves and beams of brightly colored woods.

Mudéjar architecture.

Sculpture remained, as before, an adjunct of architecture, but was employed more than formerly in the ornamentation of buildings. In form it became more and more affected by Italian influences. The comparative wealth and luxury of the era, as well as the needs of religion, led to an advance in metal work and the making of jewelry and rich embroideries. The illumination of manuscripts reached a higher level than before, but declined before the end of the period, partly because of the invention of printing. The painting of windows in cathedrals attained to a greater richness and variety in scene, and wall painting acquired an independent position. The Italian influence of Giotto was apparent in the fifteenth century, although it did not get beyond the point of mere copying. The Flemish influence was more important, dating from Van Eyck's visit to Spain in 1428, after which date paintings in the Flemish style abounded in Castile, especially altar-pieces. Music turned upon singing, usually of one part, although occasionally other parts were sung. Musical instruments were employed solely for accompaniments of songs and dances.

The lesser arts.

Aragon

In intellectual culture Aragon proper, Catalonia, Valencia, and Majorca may be considered together. The same general line of progress was in evidence as that already described for Castile. There was the same eagerness for learning among

General
character-
istics of
intellec-
tual cul-
ture in the
kingdom
of Aragon.

Education
and
printing.

Leading
currents in
thought
and
science.

the upper classes, the same development of educational
institutions, an analogous penetration of foreign influences
(especially French and Italian), and an identical practice of
going to other parts of Europe to study.   The landmarks in
intellectual history were the reign of Pedro IV in didactic
literature, that of Juan I for the Provençal troubadour
literature, and that of Alfonso V for the Classical Renaissance.

The most noteworthy university founded in the period
was that of Barcelona, which evolved from an academy in
the opening years of the fourteenth century to the rank of a
university in 1450, with courses in theology, civil and canon
law, philosophy, arts, and medicine.   In addition to numerous other schools similar to those of Castile there were
two more or less distinct types here : the primary school,
much more frequently met with than in other parts of the
peninsula ; and the Lulian schools (due originally to the
initiative of Raymond Lull, but carried on throughout the
era), which devoted themselves primarily to philosophy,
but also to foreign languages, especially Arabic.   Naturally
the invention of printing at the end of the period gave a
fresh impulse to intellectual culture.   The first book to be
printed in this region was published in Valencia in 1474.
In 1478, or a little before, books began to be printed in
Barcelona.

Philosophy, medicine, nautical science, cartography, and
cosmography were the studies most cultivated.   The influence of Raymond Lull continued to be felt, both in the
imitations and translations of Hebrew and Arabic philosophers, especially Averröes, and in the reaction against
them.   In the fifteenth century the Italian, and to a less
extent the French, influences began to be felt.   The Neapolitan court of Alfonso V was the great centre for the
penetration of Italian and classical thought.   Theologians
proper contributed little in this period, but there were numerous writings on ecclesiastical subjects, — works of a
controversial or moral nature, translations, and histories of
saints, mystics, ascetics, and sacred orators.   The extraordinary development of the study of medicine was due primarily to Jewish and Moslem elements.   Toward the end

of the fifteenth century a marked current of opinion against the deductive method in medicine and in favor of experimental studies became apparent.   Chemistry, the companion study of medicine, was much in favor, as also was alchemy, which counted King Juan I and Miguel Jiménez de Urrea, bishop of Tarazona, among its devotees.   The Catalans and Majorcans were famous for their knowledge of cartography and the related sciences.   To the Catalans were due the first map of the Danish peninsula and the correction of the maps of the Norwegian and Swedish coasts and the lands touching the Baltic Sea.   Jaime Ferrer, a Marrano of Majorca, was the leading nautical and geographical scholar of those whom Prince Henry attracted to Portugal to prepare the Portuguese for their rôle in the history of maritime exploration.   In addition to the kindred sciences of mathematics and astronomy the pseudo-science of astrology was also much pursued.   Just as in Castile, so in Aragon, juridical studies in both the civil and canon law had a great vogue.

At the close of the preceding era Catalan was already being employed in prose works in Catalonia, while the Provençal predominated in poetry.   In this period the Catalan, which also found support in Valencia and Majorca, invaded all types of literature.   Against this current there appeared two powerful forces which made themselves most felt in the last century of the era, — Latin and Castilian. Latin was much more firmly rooted in Catalonia than in Castile, and the Latin tradition was greatly reinforced by contact with the Classical Renaissance influences throughout the period, owing to the intimate political relations of the kings with Sicily and Naples.   These influences were at their height in the reign of Alfonso V.   Castilian had the support of Aragon proper, since the Aragonese tongue was very similar to that of Castile, and it was furthered by the Castilian dynasty of Ferdinand I, which began to rule in Aragon in 1410.   The same element appeared at the court of Alfonso V, much frequented by Castilian and Aragonese poets, and even by Catalans who chose to write in Castilian. As a result Catalan began to decline as a literary language, although it did not disappear, but on the contrary improved

Struggle of the Catalan, Latin, and Castilian languages for predominance in polite literature.

in its elements and forms. Catalan poetry of the era never completely effaced the Provençal influence, as evidenced by the subject-matter, which was predominantly amatory, although somewhat erudite, artificial, conventional, mystical, allegorical, satirical, and even moral. Catalan prose appeared principally in novels of chivalry and in history. Castilian poetry and prose also had interesting manifestations in the entire realm of Aragon. The history of dramatic literature followed the same course as in Castile, although in some of the choral representations at the court of Alfonso V an approach to the modern theatre was made.

The fine arts.
With respect to architecture, sculpture, and the related arts the general remarks about their development in Castile may be applied to the kingdom of Aragon, subject to the observation already made [1] as to the difference of Catalan Gothic from that of Castile. The Italian influences were exceptionally strong in Catalonia and Valencia, and the French were marked in regions near the Pyrenees and in Majorca. One type of edifice peculiar to the eastern coasts was the defensive tower to which the inhabitants resorted on the appearance of pirates or in times of military danger. In painting, the Italian style of Giotto was more completely assimilated than in Castile. Flemish influences were equally prevalent.

Mutual influence of Aragonese and other European civilizations.
Despite the long occupation of the duchy of Athens by Catalan rulers, who used Catalan speech and customs, the Catalan-Aragonese civilization had no noteworthy effect in Greece, and, similarly, neither the Byzantine nor the Athenian civilization reacted upon the kingdom of Aragon. In southern France, however, the Catalan-Aragonese civilization did produce effects, just as it was in turn affected. The same mutual exchange of influences was also observable between Aragon and Italy, if indeed the civilization of the latter was recognized as superior by the Spanish conquerors themselves. The principal impulse came at the time of Alfonso V and the contemporary papal reign of the Spanish pope, Alfonso Borgia, as Calixtus III (1455–1458). There was a great influx of Spaniards, especially from the realm

[1] See page 110.

of Aragon, and as they occupied the highest official posts in southern Italy, they could not but make their presence felt.   Many Spaniards left Italy upon the deaths of Alfonso V and Calixtus III, but others remained, and political relations were maintained between the two kingdoms, since the Neapolitan ruling family proceeded from the same trunk as that of Aragon, thus preparing a new period of Spanish rule and influence with the reign of Ferdinand of Aragon.

CHAPTER XVII

INSTITUTIONS OF OUTLYING HISPANIC STATES, 1252-1479

So far as they have not already been discussed, in dealing with Castile and Aragon, the institutions of Majorca, Navarre, the Basque provinces, and Granada may be dealt with here, especially in their original aspects.

Majorca

Outline of
Majorean
history.

By the will of Jaime I, Majorca and the Roussillon were constituted into a kingdom apart from Aragon, but almost immediately afterward Pedro III of Aragon compelled Jaime II of Majorca to acknowledge the overlordship of the peninsula monarch. In 1349 Pedro IV of Aragon annexed Majorca, but the political change was one of monarch only, for Majorca continued to be a separate state with a history of its own. The political life of Majorca centred about the workings of the municipal organization of Palma, its capital city (on which the government of the island was based), and was involved with social problems.

The
peculiar
social
bases of
Majorca.

After the conquest of the island by Jaime I nearly all of the great nobles who had accompanied the king returned to the peninsula, granting their lands to *caballeros* of their following, or renting them to plebeian cultivators, and Jaime I did much the same. Thus the *caballeros*, or nobility of the second grade, were virtually the only representatives of the feudal aristocracy in Majorca, and laws were passed limiting the amount of land which they might hold, so as to avoid the evil of vast estates. The *caballeros* were reinforced by a Catalan middle class element which constituted a majority of the Christians in the island in the early years following the conquest. From these two elements there emerged a new aristocracy, based on wealth, growing out of Majorcan commerce, an aristocracy open to all, given to pomp and luxury, and dwelling mostly in Palma. Some of the wealthy lived in the country, where there was also a large number of free tillers of the soil. A few of these became wealthy, but there was always a tendency for the rich to migrate to Palma. The position of the rural classes was not satisfactory at any time, but two causes appeared in the fourteenth century to make it worse. One was the increase in taxation after the reincorporation into the crown of Aragon, and the other a change in the form of wealth with the decline of Majorcan commerce in the latter fourteenth century, when the aristocracy of Palma began to buy lands and rights to collect taxes. Thus the rural districts became economically dependent on the absentee landlords at the capital, who were more zealous over the collection of their rents and taxes than in cultivating the land. Society divided itself largely on the lines of the country and the city, with the inhabitants of the former bitterly hostile to the aristocracy of the latter.

Of the despised classes the Mudéjares, as such, soon disappeared, despite their great numbers at the time of the conquest. Upon conversion to Christianity or emancipation from slavery they mixed with the lower classes of the Christians, and were completely absorbed. The history of the Jews was almost identical with that of their race in the peninsula, but was involved with the peculiar social problems of Majorca apart from race and religion. The kings collected heavy tributes from them, but protected them, allowing them the free exercise of their business and the practice of their faith, exempting them from all taxation (even municipal) except the royal tributes, aiding them in the collection of debts, and facilitating the entry of Jews and Marranos into Majorca. Numerous attacks were made on them in the fourteenth century, culminating in the sack of the Jewish quarter of the capital in 1391 (the year which was so disastrous to the Jews in other parts of Spain), when some three hundred men and women were killed. In addition to the usual animosities against them because of their

Conversion of the Mudéjares and Jews.

o

religion and the incitement of debtors this attack was in part an outgrowth of the struggle of the rural classes against the landlords, to whom the sack of the Jewish quarter was a severe financial blow, since much of their wealth depended on their relations with the Jews, with whom also they were wont to deposit their jewels. The rioters were able to obtain decrees from the royal governor-general extinguishing debts and interest due to the Jews, confirming the title of those who had taken part in the attack to the money and jewelry they had stolen, pardoning all offences committed, and ordering an immediate conversion of the Jews. The general conversion took place at once, but had to be repeated in 1435.

The municipal form of Majorcan government.

Since the outlying settlements were unimportant at the time of the conquest, the government of the city of Palma was extended over the entire island. At length the administration at the capital was organized on the basis of a magistracy of six persons (a *caballero*, two citizens, two merchants, and an artisan), who served for a year and appointed their successors. The attempt to maintain this organization after the rural population had grown to appreciable numbers was one of the causes of the social strife between the rural and city elements. Within Palma itself there were also the disputes of different social classes and of rival powerful families. By a reform of 1358 the rural population obtained some financial independence whereby their contributions were limited to those which were to be applied for expenses in which they had an interest in common with the city, and a portion was assigned to them to spend on matters of their own, for which purpose a rural organization was formed to provide for the management of their affairs. Another reform established a council subordinate to the six magistrates, in which the rural population had a minority representation, thirty in ninety-three in 1398. This did not satisfy them, for they desired a complete separation from the city government. Still other reforms were made, but they did not get at the root of the evil, for the city remained dominant over the affairs of the country, oppressing the people both economically and politically.

Shortly after the successful issue of the attack upon the

Jews in 1391 the rural levies moved against their Christian enemies in Palma. This time they failed, and a number of their chiefs were executed. No further conflict of importance occurred until 1450, when a bitter civil war broke out. Aided by the laboring classes of Palma the rural forces besieged the capital, but were unable to take it. In 1452 the insurrection was put down. In 1463 there was another uprising, and from that date to the end of the era a state of affairs bordering on anarchy prevailed, enhanced by the economic decline of Majorca, and by the disorders on the mainland which filled the reign of Juan II. In the island of Minorca a parallel situation existed throughout the era in the conflicts of the capital, Ciudadela, with the rural districts.

The social wars of Majorca and Minorca.

Majorca had an excellent climate and a fertile soil which fitted it for agricultural wealth, and the Moslems had furthered this by their use of irrigation. They had also engaged considerably in manufacturing, and had an already well-developed trade at the time of the conquest. Under Christian domination Majorca soon attained to an extraordinary commercial importance, trading in all parts of the Mediterranean and in Flanders, and having consuls and commercial exchanges in nearly all European countries. In the fourteenth century more than thirty thousand sailors resided in Palma, and many foreign merchants dwelt there. The wealthy trader was the veritable great lord in the island, with his palaces, country estates, and his display of luxury. The decline set in about the middle of the fourteenth century, due in part to the annexation of Majorca to the kingdom of Aragon. Other causes hastened the fall : disastrous plagues, earthquakes, and floods; the advance of the Turks into Europe, cutting off a rich commercial field; the increased importance of the Italian cities in the eastern Mediterranean trade; the raids of pirates; the expensive wars of Aragon; and the persistent social and political strife in Majorca itself. Nevertheless, a considerable trade remained until the middle of the fifteenth century, when a new series of misfortunes, — such as the fall of Constantinople in 1453, the prohibition of the entry of Majorcan cloths into Naples, the competition of Rhodes and Portugal in the east, and hostilities with th

Greatness and decline of Majorcan commerce.

Moslem states of northern Africa (thus cutting off that avenue of trade),— added to the continuing effect of some of the already-named evils, brought about the complete downfall of the Majorcan mercantile power. One advantage resulted, though not great enough to offset the commercial loss: a beginning was made of a more intensive cultivation of the agricultural wealth which the island was so well able to produce.

Navarre

Backwardness of Navarre. The institutions of Navarre at this time were affected by French influences, but in the main resembled those of the rest of the peninsula both in form and in their evolution, except that they displayed a backwardness which was natural in a region so thinly populated. The feudal régime persisted, although some gains were made by the servile classes, the towns, and the kings. A corporate sense of society, as manifested in the importance of the family as a whole and in the associations of neighbors and citizens (especially marked in the rural districts), still existed. The Mudéjares and Jews were comparatively numerous, and their lot was the same as in other parts of the peninsula. The marriage *á yuras* was sanctioned in Navarre longer than elsewhere, although at length it was banished. *Barraganía* (much resorted to by churchmen) survived, and received a measure of acceptance. The customs of chivalry were greatly in vogue, and bull-fighting and ball-games[1] were very popular. Agriculture, with the aid of irrigation, and stock-raising were the principal occupations. In intellectual culture and the fine arts Navarre was rather a continuation of France than a part of Spain. The country was markedly backward in

---

[1] The Basque game, with which the people of Navarre were equally familiar. This game bears no resemblance to American base-ball; rather it is more like a combination of tennis and handball. At the present time the players, three on a side, use a kind of bat, or racket, and a leather-covered, solid rubber ball. The ball is served against a side wall, and must be made to bound back over a net. The ball is thus kept in play until one side misses a return, which scores a point for the opponents. The side first making a required number of points wins the match.

these respects, however, as evidenced by the ignorance of the clergy, compared with churchmen in other regions, and by the fact that the kings rarely had any books other than those of prayer. Although Basque was the national tongue, such books as were written usually appeared in Latin or in Castilian, — one more demonstration of the intellectual predominance of central Spain. French Gothic prevailed in architecture, sculpture, gold work, and painting.

The Basque provinces

The three Basque provinces of Álava, Vizcaya, and Guipúzcoa have always been unique in their history and institutions, and are the subject of many popular legends more or less founded on fact, such as the one already discussed that the Basques have never been conquered, and another that they are all nobles. In this period they were becoming more and more Castilian in customs, but they still retained much that was indigenous.

Unique character of Basque institutions.

In general social organization Álava did not differ from other Spanish regions. It was technically a *behetría de mar á mar* (free town from sea to sea) : made up of a group of small seigniorial estates, both noble and ecclesiastical, whose rulers were free to elect a common lord without being restrained to a determinate family. The untitled inhabitants were rural laborers, who were either serfs or in a state but little removed from serfdom, and the free, popular classes of the towns, but neither of these elements exercised great influence. After the incorporation of Álava into Castile in 1332, the older type of government, based primarily on the *Cofradía* of Arriaga and the elected lord, underwent a radical change. The overlordship became fixed in the crown of Castile, and the *cofradía* disappeared, although a similar body soon developed. The king was represented at times by an *adelantado* as well as by lesser royal officials, and reserved high justice to himself, besides rights to military service and a certain few taxes. Local government was carried on by various assemblies, reaching in a hierarchy from the lesser regional institutions to the general assembly

The social and political system in Álava.

for the entire province. The general assembly was both a legislative and an administrative body, but its principal function was the inspection of royal orders to see if they conformed to the regional charters. A juridical difference existed between the towns and the country, for the former were ruled by Castilian law and the latter by ancient custom, resulting in the economic dependence of the rural laboring classes, even after serfdom had disappeared.

The social and political system in Vizcaya.
Until its consolidation with the Castilian crown by inheritance in 1370, Vizcaya was a *behetría de linaje* (free town within a family), electing its lord from a determinate family, but both before and after that date there was a marked lack of regional solidarity, for various groups were to a great degree autonomous. There were two principal types of jurisdiction: the seigniorial estates, with the usual incidents found elsewhere; and the indigenous Basque settlements, which pretended to the nobility of their inhabitants, even to the point of refusing to permit foreigners to dwell among them unless they too were of noble rank. The indigenous element was to be found in rural districts, and was ruled by customs, which were written down for the first time in 1452. The patriarchal form of family life continued to exist here, as evidenced by the requirement that lands should return to the family from which they proceeded in case of a failure of direct heirs, and by the right to leave virtually one's entire estate to a single descendant. Custom recognized a right of way over the lands of others, even when enclosed, — which would seem to indicate backwardness in the development of means of communication. In government the king was represented principally by a *corregidor*. The inhabitants of Vizcaya were exempt from any taxes of Castilian origin, but paid certain other contributions to the king, were subject to both military and naval service, and acknowledged the right of high justice in the royal officials. The general assembly of Vizcaya, like that of Álava, had a right to inspect royal decrees.

The people of Guipúzcoa claimed to be of noble rank, and this status was legally recognized for most of them by laws enacted before, during, and after this period. Nevertheless the customs of the land itself amounted to a denial of their claim, and the familiar social differences existed, even though the majority of the people were legally nobles. There was a seigniorial class of the usual variety, with dependents in a more or less servile relation. A middle class nobility existed, composed of small proprietors or the industrial laborers and merchants of the towns. This element was very insistent on its noble rank (which indeed carried with it special privileges, such as the exclusive right to hold public office and certain exemptions from taxation), and enacted laws excluding those who were not of noble blood from a right to live in the towns. These laws were not enforced, however, and a popular class grew up, composed of Guipuzcoans whose noble rank was not recognized and of foreigners, many of whom settled in the land. Politically Guipúzcoa was a *behetría* subject alternately to the kings of Navarre and Castile, until in 1200 the overlordship became fixed in the Castilian crown. At first the king was represented by an *adelantado*, who was customarily ruler at the same time of Álava or of the county of Castile; later a *corregidor* for Guipúzcoa alone was named, while there were a number of royal *merinos* as well. There was no other organization for the entire province until the fourteenth century, but each region dealt separately with the royal government. Gradually, through the formation of groups of settlements, a general league and at length a general assembly developed, with much the same powers as the assemblies of Álava and Vizcaya. The municipalities continued to be the principal centre of regional autonomy, however, especially the more important towns, which protected the lesser settlements through an institution similar to the Catalonian *carreratge*. Like the other Basque provinces Guipúzcoa enjoyed a number of privileges, of which the most prized was the exemption from general taxation, although certain specified tributes were regularly collected. More than once the province rose in arms to resist the imposition of taxes of Castilian origin.

Despite community of race and language the three provinces never formed a political unit. At times Guipúzcoa

The social and political system in Guipúzcoa.

and Álava had the same *adelantado* or held general assemblies in common, and there were some instances where the assemblies of all three provinces met to discuss matters of common interest. Alliances were made between towns of the same or different provinces, perhaps including towns in France, for such purposes as the regulation of the use of lands common. In one respect there was a certain amount of unity (in interest at least): in the conflict of the towns against the great lords and their allies, the rural population, in all three provinces. The lords were so turbulent that the kings joined with the towns in attempts to suppress them, and the lords even fought one another, wherefore their power was considerably reduced, though not entirely broken.

Granada

According to modern estimates Granada had a population of three or four millions in its last days, which bespeaks a great density, due largely to the migrations of Mudéjares from Christian lands. In social and political organization Granada was a miniature of the early caliphate. The Arabs reappeared as the principal element, and furnished the ruling family. They had the same scornful and quarrelsome aristocratic pride as in other days, and were opposed, as before, by the Berbers, who outnumbered them. The most numerous element was that of the Renegados, which was also next in importance to the Arabs. There were many thousands of Christian slaves as well. Signs of social decay were everywhere visible, especially in the passion of the wealthy for luxury and futile diversions at vast expense, while on the other hand there existed the poverty-stricken proletariat.[1] Internal political history reduced itself to a series of riots, assassinations, rebellions, acts of vengeance,

---

[1] After referring to the wealth of jewelry worn by the women of his time a Moslem writer goes on to say, "The women of Granada are beautiful, being distinguished for the symmetry of their figures, the gracefulness of their bodies, the length and waviness of their hair, the whiteness and brilliance of their teeth, the perfume of their breath, the pleasing lightness of their movements, the cleverness of their speech, and the charm of their conversation."

and exhibitions of partisan rancor.   The influence of Christian Spain was more and more intense, manifesting itself in general customs and dress; even the practices of chivalry were introduced.   Given the richness of soil and favoring climate and the great population of Granada, it was natural that there should have been a considerable measure of economic prosperity there.   This became less as the period advanced, as a result of political weakness and social decay, but Granada was still wealthy at the time (in the next era) it disappeared as a kingdom. *Economic wealth.*

In sciences and letters Granada continued the intellectual traditions of Moslem Spain, but it cannot be said that its influence was great.   In the arts, however, Granada introduced features of general importance, and especially in architecture, of which the outstanding example is the palace of the Alhambra in the city of Granada.   The most salient note in Granadine architecture was richness in ornamentation, in which it is not surpassed by any other style in the world.   The walls were adorned with relief work in stucco, and variegated azulejos tiles were also used in great profusion. The decorative motives were geometrical or floral, and the *tout ensemble* was not only brilliant in color, but also harmoniously appealing.   In structural features, too, Granadine architecture attained to great beauty. *Granadino architecture.*

CHAPTER XVIII

ERA OF THE CATHOLIC KINGS, 1479–1517

Transition
from
medieval
to modern
Spain.

THE joint reign of Ferdinand (1479–1516) and Isabella (1474–1504), known as "the Catholic Kings," witnessed the substantial fulfilment of the aims of medieval Hispanic royalty, and at the same time began in striking fashion that complexity of life and action which characterizes the modern age. On the one hand the turbulent elements which had for so long stood for decentralization and disorder as opposed to national unity and internal peace were done away with or rendered powerless; on the other, life in its various institutional phases approximated itself in a considerable degree to that of our own times, and Spain stood forth from the domestic bickerings which had formerly absorbed her attention to enter upon the career and status of a world power. The greatest single event in the period was undoubtedly the discovery of America, from which came, directly or indirectly, Spain's principal claims to the recognition of posterity. Important only in less degree were the conquest of Granada, the establishment of the Inquisition and the expulsion from Spain of the non-Catholic elements, and Spain's entry into the maelstrom of European politics on a greater scale than ever before, through the medium of Ferdinand's intervention in Italy. Measured by the success attained in their own day the Catholic Kings prospered in nearly everything they undertook, but the ultimate result, which could not have been foreseen at the time, was in many respects to prove disastrous to Spain herself, if, indeed, there were counterbalancing advantages and a glorious memory. The wealth and greatness proceeding from the conquest of the Americas were to be sacrificed in a fruitless attempt to gain a predominant place in Europe, — which, indeed, Spain might have had, much as England acquired it, if she had not pursued it so directly and insistently, but had been willing to devote her attention to her colonies. On the other hand, the Americas drained Spain of some of her best resources in manhood, while the Italian wars brought her into the current of the highest European civilization. These consequences, whatever attitude one may take with regard to them, did not become manifest until a much later time, but they had the most pronounced of their impulses, if not in all cases their origins, in the reign of the Catholic Kings.

Ferdinand's accession to the crown of Aragon and the recognition of Isabella as queen of Castile did not at that time bring about a political union of the two kingdoms, and resulted in no radical change in the separate institutions of either. They did mean the establishment of consistent policies in each (especially in international affairs) which were to bring about a more effectual union at a later day and produce the Spanish nation. The first problem of the Catholic Kings was that of the pacification of their realms. Aragon and Catalonia offered no serious difficulty, but the violence of the Castilian nobility called for repression of a vigorous type. Galicia and Andalusia were the regions where such action was most imperatively needed.

Nature of the union of Castile and Aragon.

The real weakness of the seigniorial class is well illustrated by the case of Galicia. The lawless conduct of the nobility and even of the high functionaries of the church was traditional, besides which Juana la Beltraneja had counted with many partisans there. Petty war, the oppression of individuals and towns (through the medium of illegal tributes or the collection of those belonging to the kings), and an almost complete disobedience of royal authority were the rule. Resolved to do away with such an evil state of affairs the Catholic Kings sent two delegates there in 1480, the one a soldier, Fernando de Acuña, and the other a lawyer and member of the *Consejo Real*, Garcí López de Chinchilla, accompanied by three hundred picked horsemen. Without loss of time and with praiseworthy energy they proceeded to

Overthrow of seigniorial anarchy.

carry out the royal will. Forty-six castles were demolished, the tributes which the nobles had been diverting from the king were collected once more for the royal treasury, many individuals of greater or less degree (both nobles and ordinary bandits) were put to death, and others were dominated or compelled to flee the country. Similar action was taken in Andalusia and Castile proper, wherefore within a few years the pacification of the kingdom was achieved; the seemingly hopeless anarchy of the period of Henry IV had been overcome.

The conquest of Granada. At the same time that the Catholic Kings were engaged in the establishment of good order in the realm of Castile, they were giving their attention to another problem which may well be considered as of domestic import, — the long delayed conquest of Granada. The last years of the Moslem kingdom epitomized the history of that government during its more than two centuries of existence, with the important difference that it was no longer to escape the bitter pill of conquest which its own weakness and decadent life had long rendered inevitable once a determined effort should be made. There appeared the figure of the emir, Abul Hassan, dominated by the passion which his slave girl, Zoraya, had inspired in him. Other members of his family, notably his brother, El Zagal (or Al Zagal), and his son, Abu Abdullah, best known as Boabdil, headed factions which warred with Abul Hassan or with each other. Meanwhile, the war with Castile, which had broken forth anew in 1481, was going on, and to the credit of the Moslem warrior as a fighting man was being sustained, if not with success, at least without great loss of territory. Ferdinand, to whom treachery was only a fine art of kingship, availed himself of the internal disorder of Granada to gain advantages to which his military victories in open combat did not entitle him. Twice he had Boabdil in his power as a prisoner, and on each occasion let him go, so that he might cause trouble for El Zagal, who had become emir, at the same time making promises of peace and of abstention from conquest which he disloyally failed to observe. Another time, El Zagal was similarly deceived. By these means, after ten years of war, Ferdinand was able to enter the Granadine plain and besiege the Moslem capital, courageously defended by Boabdil and his followers. The military camp of Santa Fe was founded, and for months the siege went on, signalized by deeds of valor on both sides. Overcome by hunger the defenders were at length obliged to capitulate, and on January 2, 1492, the Castilian troops occupied the Alhambra. Some time later Boabdil and his household departed for Africa. It is fitting to observe that many of the legends concerning this prince, notably those which reflect on his courage and manliness, are without foundation in fact.

The terms of surrender had included numerous articles providing for the security of the Moslem population. Virtually they amounted to a promise that the Mudéjar, or Moslem, element would not be molested in any respect, whether in Granada or elsewhere in Castile. Such a treaty could not long be enforced in the face of the religious ardor and intolerance of the age. The greatest men of the kingdom, and among them the most notable of all, the archbishop of Toledo, Ximénez de Cisneros, confessor of the queen, joined in urging a different policy. Pressure began to be exerted in direct contravention of the treaty to bring about an enforced conversion of the Mudéjares to Christianity. A Moslem uprising was the result, and this was seized upon by Ximénez as justifying a complete disregard, henceforth, of the terms of the capitulation, on the ground that the Moslems had nullified the treaty by their rebellion, — a convenient argument which did not enquire into the real causes of the outbreak. Christianization by force, not without a number of serious uprisings, now went on at a rapid rate, and was completed by a royal decree of 1502 which ordered that all Mudéjares in the Castilian domains should accept Christianity or leave the country. Many took the latter course, but the greater number remained, Christians in outward appearance if not so at heart. Officially there were no more Mudéjares in Castile except slaves. The newly converted element became known, henceforth, as "Moriscos," thus attaching them by association of ideas to their ancient faith, and since their Christianity did not in-

Forced conversion of the Mudéjares of Castile.

spire much confidence they were made subject to the dread Inquisition.

Castilian
activities
in north-
western
Africa and
the
Canary
Islands.

The discovery of America in 1492, together with other factors, directed Castilian attention to the Canary Islands and northwestern Africa, bringing the Spanish kingdom into contact and rivalry with the Portuguese, who had devoted themselves to exploration, conquest, and colonization in that region for nearly a century. It may suffice here to say that in successive treaties of 1480, 1494, and 1509 Portugal recognized Castile's claim to the Canaries and certain posts in northwestern Africa. The security of the American route was not the principal motive of Castilian interest at that time in northwestern Africa. The wars with Granada and the danger of fresh invasions, coupled with the crusading zeal which had been aroused against the Moslems, and aggravated by the activities of North African corsairs, were perhaps the leading factors affecting the policy of the Catholic Kings. In 1494 the definitive conquest of the Canary Islands was made, and at the same time a post was established on the neighboring coast of western Africa to serve as a centre for the resistance to the Moslems. Meanwhile, private attacks by Spaniards on North African ports were being made, but it was not until 1497 that the Catholic Kings formally embarked on that enterprise. Bent upon checking piracy in that region they took possession of Melilla, which thenceforth became an important Spanish post.

While Ferdinand had much to do with the events which have thus far been discussed, he and his subjects of Aragon and Catalonia were more interested in other affairs. Ferdinand aimed at nothing less than a predominant place for Spain in European affairs, to be preceded by the establishment of Aragonese supremacy in the Mediterranean. The principal stumbling-block was the power of the French kings. Ferdinand schemed, therefore, to bring about the isolation and humiliation of France. The entering wedge came through the French possession of the Catalan regions of Cerdagne and the Roussillon which had been granted to the king of France by Juan II. Charles VIII of France consented to restore the two provinces, but in return exacted

Ferdinand's promise not to interfere with the former's designs respecting the kingdom of Naples. Ferdinand readily agreed in 1493 to aid no enemy of the French king save the pope, and not to form matrimonial alliances between members of his family and those of the reigning houses of Austria, England, and Naples. With Cerdagne and the Roussillon in his possession he proceeded with characteristic duplicity to disregard the treaty. Marriage alliances were projected or arranged, some of them to be sure before 1493, not only with the ruling families of Portugal and Navarre but also with those of Austria and England. Thus Ferdinand hoped to secure considerable accesssions of territory and to avoid any interference on the part of the Holy Roman Empire and England, the only outstanding powers which might be able to hinder his plots against France. It is perhaps poetic justice that these plans, so cleverly made and executed at the time, were to have an ultimate result which was quite different from that which Ferdinand had reason to expect. Untimely deaths rendered the various Portuguese alliances of no effect; the authorities of Navarre would have nothing to do with Ferdinand's proffer; and Spanish Catherine in England was to figure in the famous divorce from Henry VIII, precipitating the English Reformation. One marriage was productive of results, that of Juana, heir of Ferdinand and Isabella, to Philip the Handsome of Burgundy. Thus the Spanish kings were brought into the line of the Hapsburg family and of imperial succession, which was to prove less a boon than a fatality.

Charles VIII wished to revive the Angevin claim to the Neapolitan territory held at the time by the illegitimate branch of Alfonso V of Aragon, related by blood to Ferdinand the Catholic. Alleging that Naples was a fief of the pope and therefore excepted from the treaty of 1493, Ferdinand resisted the pretensions of Charles, and formed an alliance with the pope, the emperor, Venice, and Milan against him. The forces of the league proving too much for him, Charles was forced in 1497 to suspend hostilities, whereupon Ferdinand agreed with him in secret to divide Naples between them, renewing the agreement with

The acquisition of Naples.

Louis XII, who ascended the French throne in 1498. The division was carried into effect, but a quarrel sprang up over a certain portion of the territory, and war broke out. Thanks to the military genius of the great Spanish leader, Gonzalo de Córdoba, Ferdinand was victorious by the year 1504, and Naples came under his authority.

In the same year, 1504, Isabella the Catholic died, leaving her throne to her elder daughter, Juana, and in case she should prove unable to govern to Ferdinand as regent until Juana's heir should become twenty years of age. Since Juana had already given evidence of that mental instability which was to earn for her the soubriquet "La Loca" (the Crazy), it was the intention of both Isabella and Ferdinand that the latter should rule, but Philip the Handsome, husband of Juana, intervened to procure the regency for himself. This was a serious set-back to the plans of Ferdinand, but fortunately for him there occurred the unexpected death of Philip in 1506. On the occasion of the latter's burial Juana gave such ample proof of her mental unfitness that it was now clear that Ferdinand would be called in as regent. In 1507 he was so installed, and he now had the resources of Spain at his back in the accomplishment of his ambitious designs. Leaving Cardinal Ximénez to effect conquests in northern Africa and to carry into execution other Castilian projects Ferdinand once again turned his attention to the aggrandizement of Aragon in Italy.

In 1508 Ferdinand joined an alliance of the pope, the emperor, and Louis XII of France against Venice, whereby he rounded out his Neapolitan possessions. Seeing that the French were gaining more than he desired he formed a new alliance, in 1511, with the pope, the emperor, Venice, and Henry VIII of England against France. The French were defeated and thrown out of Italy. Meanwhile, Ferdinand had taken advantage of the French sympathies of the ruler of Navarre and the excommunication of that king by the pope to overrun Navarre in 1512. The pope sanctioned the conquest of that part of the kingdom lying south of the Pyrenees, and it was definitely added to the Spanish domain. The French became dangerous anew with the accession of the glory-loving, ambitious Francis I in 1515. Ferdinand hastened to concert a league against him, into which entered the pope, the emperor, Milan, Florence, the Swiss states, and England, but war had hardly broken out when in 1516 Ferdinand died. For good or evil he had brought Spain into a leading place in European affairs. If his methods were questionable they were in keeping with the practices of his age; he was only worse than his rivals in that he was more successful.

Juana was still alive, but was utterly incompetent to act as head of the state. The logic of events and the will of Ferdinand pointed to her eldest son, Charles of Ghent, as the one to rule Aragon and Navarre and to act as regent of Castile (during his mother's life), although he had not attained to his twentieth year, a condition which had been exacted by the will of Isabella. Until such time as he could reach Spain, for he was then in the Low Countries, Cardinal Ximénez served as regent. With two acts of doubtful propriety Charles I, the later Charles V of the Empire, began his reign in the peninsula. He sent word to Ximénez, demanding that he be proclaimed king of Castile, despite the fact that the queen, his mother, was living. Notwithstanding the opposition of the *Cortes* and his own unwillingness Ximénez did as Charles had required. In 1517 Charles reached Spain, surrounded by a horde of Flemish courtiers. Foreseeing the difficulties likely to result from this invasion of foreign favorites Ximénez wrote to Charles, giving him advice in the matter, and hastening to meet him asked for an interview. Instead of granting this request Charles sent him a note, thanking him for his services, and giving him leave to retire to his diocese "to rest and await the reward of Heaven for his merits."

The accession of Charles I.

P

CHAPTER XIX

SOCIAL REFORMS, 1479-1517

Leading
elements
in the
social
history of
the era.

THE most important events in Spain of a social character during the period of the Catholic Kings were the expulsion of the Jews and the conversion of the Castilian Mudéjares, with the relations of the new Inquisition to both of these elements of Spanish society. Other events of more than ordinary note were the deprivation of the nobility of some of their former prestige, the settlement of the dispute between the serfs and lords of Catalonia, the purification of the Castilian clergy, and the definitive triumph of the Roman principles in private law. Greater than all of these were the problems which were to arise through the Spanish subjection of new races in the colonies overseas.

Prestige
of the
nobility,
despite
their
reverses.

Though with diminished prestige the nobility continued to be the leading social class in Castile, sharing this honor with the higher officials of the church. Much of the former economic preponderance of the nobles was gone, due to the development of personalty as a form of wealth as distinguished from land, the fruit of the commerce and industry of the Jews, Mudéjares, and middle classes. They suffered still further through Isabella's revocation of the land grants they had received at times of civil war and internal weakness in former reigns, especially in that of Henry IV. Few nobles or great churchmen, for the decree applied equally to the latter, escaped without loss of at least a portion of their rents, and some forfeited all they had. Naturally, the measure caused not a little discontent, but it was executed without any noteworthy resistance. On the other hand, through the continuance of the institution of primogeniture and through new acquisitions of land in return for

210

services in the war against Granada, the greater nobles still possessed immense wealth. The Duke of Medina Sidonia, for example, offered Philip the Handsome two thousand *caballeros* and 50,000 ducats ($750,000) if he would disembark in Andalusia. Not only in political authority but also in prestige the nobles were lowered by the measures of the Catholic Kings. Such practices as the use of a royal crown on their shields and the employment of royal insignia or ceremonial in any form were forbidden. On the other hand, the ancient privileges of the nobility, both high and low, were confirmed to them, — such, for example, as exemption from taxation and from the application in certain cases of the penalties of the law. At the same time, the Catholic Kings offered a new kind of dignity, depending for its lustre on the favor of the crown. Nobles were encouraged to appear at court and strive for the purely ornamental honors of palace officialdom. Many came, for those who remained on their estates consigned themselves to obscurity, being without power to improve their fortunes by a revolt as their ancestors had done. In Aragon and Catalonia they still displayed tendencies to engage in private war and banditry, a condition of affairs which endured throughout this period and into the next, though it was by no means so serious a problem as it had been in earlier times.

The grades of nobility remained much as before, but with a change in nomenclature. The old term of *ricoshombres* for the great nobles disappeared (though not until 1520 officially), and was substituted by that of *grandes*, or grandees. Among the grandees the title of duke (*duque*) and marquis (*marqués*) now became of more frequent usage than the formerly more general count (*conde*). In the epoch of the Catholic Kings there were fifteen grandees in Castile, but eight of them had been created, with the title of duke, by Isabella. For the nobility of the second grade, the terms *hijosdalgo* (modern *hidalgo*) and *caballero*, used in a generic sense to denote noble lineage, were employed indiscriminately. Nobles without fortune lived, as formerly, under the protection of the grandees, or took service in the military orders or even in the new royal army. Grades of nobility.

The situation of the former servile classes of Castile, aside from the slaves, had been rendered very nearly satisfactory from a juridical point of view in the previous era, but their new liberty was insecure and was not freely accorded in practice. The Catholic Kings energetically cut short the greater part of the abuses, and definitely decided that a man adscripted to the land (a *solariego*) could sell or carry away his personalty, and go wherever he willed. In Aragon proper the problem was more serious, because of the social backwardness of that region. The first step toward freedom from serfdom was taken at this time, consisting in the frequent uprisings of the serfs. Ferdinand made some attempts to modify the *malos usos*, or evil customs, of the relation of lord and serf, but found the institutions too deeply rooted in his day for remedy. In Catalonia, Ferdinand inherited the problem of the warfare of the serfs with the nobles and the high churchmen, against the latter of whom, particularly the bishop of Gerona, the wrath of the rural classes was especially directed. At the outset he attempted, as had Alfonso V and Juan II before him, to utilize the quarrel to serve his own political and financial ends, accepting bribes from both sides. Finally, an agreement was reached whereby the king was to serve as arbitrator, without appeal, between the warring elements. The Sentence of Guadalupe, so-called because the evidence was taken and the decision rendered at Guadalupe in Extremadura, in 1486, was the judgment pronounced by Ferdinand. It went to the root of the matter by abolishing the *malos usos* and declaring the freedom of the rural serfs. Furthermore, the lords were deprived of criminal jurisdiction over their vassals, this right passing to the crown, and the same privileges as that just recorded in the case of the *solariegos* of Castile was granted to the rural masses of Catalonia. On the other hand, the now freed serfs were obliged to pay a heavy ransom to their lords. The decision satisfied neither party to the issue, but was accepted, and proved in fact the solution of the evil. A rural class of small proprietors soon grew up, while many other persons occupied lands for which they paid rent instead of the former irksome services.

If a policy of benevolent assimilation had been followed by the Christians of Spain with regard to the other great elements of the population, the Mudéjar and the Jewish, it is possible that the two latter might have been made use of to the advantage of the peninsula, for they were Spanish in most of their habits, and had intermarried with Christians, even those of high rank. For centuries, however, a different practice, based primarily on religious intolerance, had tended to promote the adoption of an opposite course, and it was in the reign of the Catholic Kings that the first steps were taken to bring the matter to an issue. The measures by which the Mudéjares were compelled to emigrate from Castile or become converted as Moriscos have already been chronicled, and the same procedure was taken with regard to Navarre and the Basque provinces. Ferdinand, who was less zealous in this undertaking than his pious consort, did not go to the same lengths in Aragon. On the petition of the lords, who had many Moslem vassals and feared to lose them, he confirmed the privileges of the Mudéjares, though forbidding the erection of new mosques, and permitted of preaching to bring about their voluntary conversion.

The hatred of the Christians for the Jews was so great that the time was ripe for the final step in the measures taken against them, and early in the reign of the Catholic Kings it was decided to expel them from the peninsula. While the religious motive was the principal one, Ferdinand and Isabella were also actuated, as indeed also in the case of the Mudéjares, by their ideal of a centralized absolutism, wherefore an element which was not in sympathy with the religion of the state seemed to them to constitute a political danger. Their action was hastened, no doubt, by popular fanaticism, which expressed itself in numerous acts of violence against the hated race. With Granada conquered the Catholic Kings lost no time in promulgating a decree, dated March 31, 1492, requiring conversion or expulsion, and applicable to both Castile and Aragon. The Jews were granted four months to dispose of their affairs and leave Spain. The blow to them financially was ruinous. Forced sales, especially when there was so much to be sold, could not be expected to yield a fair return, and this was aggravated by prohibitions against carrying away any gold, silver, coin, or other kinds of personalty, except what the laws ordinarily permitted to be exported. The full effect of this harsh legislation was avoided by some through a resort to the international banking agencies which the Jews had established. A number preferred to become Christians rather than go into exile, but thousands took the latter course. Some computations hold that as many as 2,000,000 left the country, but a more careful estimate by a Jewish historian gives the following figures: emigrants, 165,000; baptized, 50,000; those who lost their lives in course of the execution of the decree, 20,000. The exiles went to Portugal, North Africa, Italy, and France, but were so harshly treated, especially in the two first-named lands, that a great many preferred to return to Spain and accept baptism. Portugal and Navarre soon followed the action of Castile and Aragon, thus completing the cycle of anti-Jewish legislation in the peninsula. In law there were no more Jews; they had become Marranos.

Activities of the Inquisition in Castile.

Not a few of the converts, both Mudéjar and Jewish, became sincere Christians, and some of them attained to high rank in the church. Hernando de Talavera, for example, at one time confessor of the queen and one of the most influential men in the kingdom, had Jewish blood in his veins. A great many, very likely the majority, remained faithful at heart to the religion of their fathers, due partly to the lack of Christian instruction, and even when they did not, they were suspected of so doing, or maliciously accused of it by those who were envious of their wealth or social position. This had led the Catholic Kings to procure a papal bull, as early as 1478, granting the monarchs a right to name certain men, whom they should choose, as inquisitors, with power to exercise the usual authority of ecclesiastical judges. This was the beginning of the modern Spanish Inquisition. Leaving aside, for the present, its formal constitution and procedure, its activities against converts may here be traced. The Inquisition began its work in Seville in 1480, with the object of uprooting heresy, especially among the Marranos. Afraid of being accused many fled, but enough remained for scores to be apprehended. In 1481 the first *auto de fe* (decision of the faith) was held, and sixteen persons were burned to death. From Seville the institution spread to other cities, and the terror became general. There is no doubt that the inquisitors displayed an excess of zeal, of which various papal documents themselves furnish ample proof. A great many were put to death, especially while Juan de Torquemada was at the head of the institution, 1485 to 1494. Some charge his inquisitorial reign with the death of 8000 persons, but more dispassionate estimates reduce the figures greatly, calculating the number to be 2000 for the reign of Isabella, ending in 1504. Very many more were either burned in effigy or put in prison, while confiscation of goods was one of the usual concomitants of a sentence involving loss of life or liberty. Books were also examined and burned or their publication or circulation forbidden, and in every way efforts were made to prevent heresy as well as to stamp it out. By far the greatest number of sufferers were the Judaizantes, or those Marranos who practised the Jewish faith in secret. It must be said that public opinion was not by any means on the side of the Inquisition; in course of time it became universally hated, as also feared, for nobody was entirely safe from accusation before the dread tribunal.

The Inquisition had existed in the kingdom of Aragon since the thirteenth century, but Ferdinand now introduced the Castilian body. In 1485 the Inquisition became a single institution for all Spain, although it was not until 1518 that this became definitive. The new organization had not been welcomed in Castile, but it found even less favor in Aragon, not only because of its excessive pretensions and rigors, but also because it superseded the traditional Aragonese Inquisition, was in the hands of Castilian "foreigners," and interfered with business. The city of Barcelona was especially resentful on this last account, because its prosperity depended not a little on the trade in the hands of Jewish converts, whom fear was driving away. On the first occa-

The Inquisition in Aragon.

sion of their appearance, in 1486, the inquisitors were obliged to leave Barcelona, and no less a personage than the bishop joined in the act of ejecting them, but in 1487 they returned to stay. The fear of the Inquisition and certain social and political disadvantages of being regarded as of Jewish or Moslem descent occasioned the introduction of documents of *limpieza de sangre* (purity of blood), attesting the Catholic ancestry of the possessors, although the development of this custom was more marked in the reign of Charles I.

Reform of the Castilian church. One of the most signal reforms of the period, to which the pious Isabella, aided by Ximénez, gave her attention, was the purification of the Castilian clergy. The church, like the great nobles, had suffered from the revocation of land grants it had gained in times of stress, and was obliged, furthermore, to restore the financial rights, such as the *alcabala* and certain rents, it had usurped from the crown. Nevertheless, its wealth was enormous. The rents of the secular church in all Spain are said to have amounted to some 4,000,000 ducats ($60,000,000), of which the archbishop of Toledo alone received 80,000 ($1,200,000). The regular clergy were equally wealthy. Vast as these sums appear, even today, their real value should be considered from the standpoint of the far greater purchasing power of money in that age than now. Whether or not the members of the clergy were softened by this wealth and by the favors they received as representatives of the church at a time of great religious zeal on the part of the Spanish people, it is certain that ignorance and immorality were prevalent among them. Despite the centuries of conflict against it, the institution of *barraganía* still had its followers, among others, Alfonso de Aragón, archbishop of Saragossa, and Cardinal Pedro de Mendoza. Laws were passed imposing fines, banishment, and the lash, — without avail. Church councils met to discuss the various evils within the church. Ximénez at length applied to the church of Castile the methods Isabella had used in suppressing seigniorial anarchy. A Franciscan himself, he proceeded to visit the convents of the order and to administer correction with a heavy hand, expelling the more recalcitrant. It is said that some four

hundred friars emigrated to Africa, and became Mohammedans, rather than submit to his rulings. From the
Franciscan order the reforms passed on to others. Isabella
intervened more particularly in the case of the secular
clergy, exercising great care in the choice of candidates for
the higher dignities, selecting them from the lower nobility
or the middle class instead of from the families of great nobles
as had formerly been the practice. At the same time, she
took steps with considerable success to prevent the appointment of foreigners by the popes to Castilian benefices. In
Aragon the same evils existed as in Castile, but the reforms
did not come at this time to modify them.

In private law, especially as regards the family, the long
struggle of the Roman principles to gain a predominant
place in Castilian jurisprudence ended in triumph. The
victory came with the legislation of the *Cortes* of Toledo in
1502, but as it was not published until the time of the *Cortes*
of Toro in 1505 it became known as the *Leyes de Toro* (Laws
of Toro). For example, the complete emancipation of children after marriage, the prohibition of the gift of all one's
possessions to other than the heirs, the increase in the for-
malities required in the case of wills, and the lengthening of
terms of years on which to base claims by prescription were
all recognized in the new laws.

Triumph of Roman principles in Castilian private law.

In immorality and luxury the reign of the Catholic Kings
differed little from the preceding era; abundant evidence
thereof appears in the literary works of this period and the
opening years of the next. The most extravagant taste
was exhibited both by men and women in matters of dress.
Clothing was made up of ruffs and puffs, ribbons and rings,
many-materialed and many-colored component parts, clothes
which dragged behind and clothes which were immodestly
short, open-work waists and cloaks which were not infrequently used to cover adventures, fancy laces, daggers,
purses, pouches, and a host of other accessories which must
have been considered ornamental, since they were only slightly
useful. Isabella herself, serious-minded and religious though
she was, liked to appear in public richly gowned and be-
jewelled. This lavish magnificence seems only to have been

General social customs.

Dress.

on display for gala occasions; at other times Spaniards lived and dressed soberly and modestly. As an Italian traveller expressed it, the Spaniard was prodigal on holidays, and lived sadly the rest of the year, for his occasional extravagances demanded more protracted economies. This was true, even in the palace, for, numerous as were the employes there, the annual expenditure was the equivalent of only about $100,000. Other social customs, such as sports, including bull-fighting, did not undergo any changes sufficient to require comment.

CHAPTER XX

POLITICAL REFORMS, 1479–1517

It has already been pointed out that the union of Castile and Aragon under the Catholic Kings lacked a real political or institutional basis. Both monarchs signed papers applicable to the two kingdoms and exercised personal influence, each with the other, but although Ferdinand assisted his consort in Castilian affairs, Isabella was clearly regarded as ruler in Castile, as Ferdinand was in Aragon. The latter's will advised Charles I to maintain the separation of the kingdoms and to conduct their affairs through native officials. Nevertheless, the long continuance of the same royal family at the head of both was bound to produce a greater unity eventually. Castile was drawn into European politics through the medium of the Aragonese wars in Italy. On the other hand, she tended to become the centre of authority and influence on account of the greater extent of her territory (especially with the addition of Granada, Navarre, and the Americas), her greater wealth, the royal practice of residing in Castile, and the more advanced social and political condition of Castile as the result of Isabella's reforms.

Both sovereigns followed the policy of centralization in their respective kingdoms. In Castile the major problem was the reduction of the oligarchical nobility, for the middle classes had already been won over in great part when Isabella ascended the throne. Her success in reducing the lawless nobles has already been discussed; it only remains to point out the significance of the act by which she completed this task, — her incorporation of the masterships of the military orders into the crown. The principal element in the three great orders of Santiago, Calatrava, and Alcántara were the

Tendency toward Spanish unity under Castile.

Masterships of the military orders incorporated into the crown.

219

segundones of great noble families and members of the lesser nobility. Not only by their military power but also by their numbers and wealth these orders constituted a potential danger to the crown unless their action could be controlled. An estimate of the year 1493 showed that there were 700,000 members and vassals in the order of Santiago, and 200,000 and 100,000 respectively in those of Calatrava and Alcántara. The first-named had annual revenues of some 60,000 ducats ($900,000), and the two last combined, some 95,000 ($1,425,000). With the masterships in royal hands the probability of civil strife was greatly lessened.

Increase of the royal authority and tendency toward unity in municipal life.

As regards the towns the Catholic Kings followed precisely the same practices which had been employed with such success in the previous era. It was rare, indeed, that they suppressed charters, but circumstances like those already recorded [1] enabled the *corregidores* and other royal officers to exercise virtual control. Meanwhile, the process of unification was going on through the ordinances of the *Cortes* and royal decrees, fortified by the unrecorded development of similarity in customs in Castilian municipal life. This was furthered by the representatives of the towns themselves, for royal and municipal interests were usually in accord. Noteworthy extensions of royal authority appeared in the subjection of local officials to the *residencia* (or trial during a number of days after the completion of a term of office, to determine the liability of an official for the wrongful acts of his administration) and in the sending of royal *pesquisidores*, or enquirers (in cases of crime), and *veedores* (inspectors), later more often called *visitadores* (visitors), to investigate matters of government, such as the accounts of financial agents and the conduct of public officers. These institutions were later transferred to the Americas, becoming an important means of sustaining the authority of the mother country. In some instances the Catholic Kings resorted to force to reduce municipalities which were too autonomous in character, notably in the case of the *hermandad* of the north coast towns, whose decadence dates from this reign.

[1] See p. 159.

The royalist ideal was manifested strikingly in the relations of the Catholic Kings with the Castilian *Cortes*. From
1475 to 1503 the *Cortes* was summoned but nine times, and
during the years 1482 to 1498, at a time when Granada was
being conquered, America discovered and occupied, the
new Inquisition instituted, and the Jews expelled, it did not
meet even once. Its decline was evidenced still further in
the increasingly respectful language employed whenever it
addressed the monarch and its growing dependence on the
Consejo Real, which body subjected the acts of the *Cortes* to
its own revision and whose president acted in a similar
capacity for the *Cortes*.

Ferdinand followed the same policy in Aragon. The
various *Cortes* of Aragon, Catalonia, and Valencia and the
general *Cortes* of all three were infrequently called; the king
acted in an arbitrary manner in his methods of raising funds,
without observing the spirit of the laws. It was in his dealings with Barcelona that he most clearly manifested the
royalist tendency, for that city was the most powerful element in the kingdom. Through his intervention the practice
of electing the five *concelleres*, or councillors, was suspended
in favor of royal appointment, and the *Consell*, or council
of a hundred, was altered so that it was no longer democratic
but represented the will of the monarch. The fact that these
changes were made without provoking resistance and almost
without protest shows how utterly dead were the political
ideals of the past.

The concentration in royal hands of so many powers
which were formerly exercised by the lords and towns made
necessary the development of a numerous and varied officialdom to assist the monarch. As the basis of the new bureaucracy in Castile the Catholic Kings had at hand the *Consejo
Real*, which with some changes was admirably adapted to
the purpose. The first step was to rid it of the great nobles.
In 1480 the untitled *letrados* became a majority in this body.
The counts, dukes, and marquises were still allowed to
attend, but were deprived of the right to vote. Shortly
afterward they were excluded altogether, and the *Consejo
Real* now responded without question to the will of the king.

It served as the head of the various branches of the bureaucratic organization, with the final decision, subject to the wishes of the king, in all matters of government. Pressure of work led to the formation of three additional councils, those of the Inquisition (*Inquisición*), the military orders, (*Órdenes Militares*), and the Americas, or Indies (*Indias*), while there were still others in the kingdom of Aragon. Particularly important among the other officials was the monarch's private secretary, who came to have a very nearly decisive influence, owing to the favor he enjoyed with the head of the state. A horde of other officers, old and new, made up the ranks of the bureaucracy. Among the older group it is to be noted that the *adelantados* were supplanted by *alcaldes mayores*, until only one of the former was left. Among newer officials the important inquisitors and *veedores*, or *visitadores*, should be noted.

Administration of justice.

A similar development to that of the executive branch was experienced in the administration of justice. The fountain-head was the *chancillería* at the capital, Valladolid, to which were subordinate in a measure the several regional *audiencias*, which were now established for the first time, besides the hierarchy of the judiciary of lower grades. In addition to unifying and regulating the judicial system the Catholic Kings gave attention to the internal purification of the courts, with a view to eliminating the unfit or undesirable and to checking abuses. The corrupt practices of those outside the courts were also attacked, especially powerful persons who attempted to overawe judges or procure a miscarriage of justice. One of the principal difficulties encountered was that of conflicts of jurisdiction, notably in the case of the church courts. Good Catholic though she was, Isabella was determined in her opposition to ecclesiastical invasions of royal jurisdiction, but despite her energetic measures the issue was far from being decided in her day. In line with the royal policy of settling disputes by law rather than by force the use of firearms was prohibited, gambling was persecuted, and the *riepto* (or judicial duel, the last survival of medieval procedure) was abolished. Good order in the present-day sense was far from existing, and this led to a revival of the medieval idea of the *her-mandades* for the punishment of crimes committed in un-inhabited places or small villages as well as for the pursuit and execution generally of those guilty of felony. The *Santa Hermandad*, with its capital at Toledo, was created as a kind of judicial body, sustained by the groups of citizens who formed part of it, employing a militia of mounted men, and making use of summary methods and extreme penalties in its procedure. Its life as an effective body was brief, although it continued to exist for many years. On the other hand the medieval *hermandad* of Toledo enjoyed a revival of life and usefulness.[1]

It is hardly necessary to trace the administrative and judicial reforms of Ferdinand in Aragon. Suffice to say that they followed the Castilian pattern much more closely, indeed, than in the matter of social organization. *Reforms in Aragon.*

The Castilian Inquisition, first created in 1478 for specific and temporary objects, underwent considerable modification when retained as a permanent body to combat heresy in general. The popes refused to allow it to be in all respects a royal instrument, and retained the right of appointing or dismissing inquisitors, permitting the kings to recommend candidates. The expansion of the institution from Seville to other cities in Spain and the creation of a supreme council of the Inquisition have already been mentioned. Ximénez, who became head of the Inquisition of Castile in 1507, ex-tended its operations to Africa and the Americas. The methods of trial were harsh, though less so if gauged by the standards of that time. Torture was used as a means of obtaining confessions. The accused was kept utterly apart from his family and friends, who did not learn what had become of him until his liberation or his appearance in an *auto de fe*. The same secrecy was employed in dealing with the prisoner, who was informed of the general charge against him, without the details and without knowing his accuser's name. He was allowed to indicate those in whom he lacked confidence, and if he should chance to hit upon an accuser that person's evidence was eliminated. Two witnesses *Procedure of the Inquisi-tion.*

[1] Cf. p. 155, n. 3.

against him were sufficient to outweigh any testimony he might give. He might have a lawyer, but could not confer with him in private. He might also object to a judge whose impartiality he had reason to suspect, and could appeal to the pope. Penalties varied from the imposition of a light penance to imprisonment or burning to death. Burning in effigy of those who escaped or burning of the remains of those who had died was also practised. The *auto de fe* represented, as the words imply, merely the decision in the given case, and not the imposition of the penalty as has often been stated. The general rule was for the executions to take place on holidays, which in Spain are indeed "holy days," or days in celebration of events in church history. A procession was held, in which the functionaries of the Inquisition took part. A public announcement of the decisions was made, and those who were condemned to death were turned over to the civil authorities, who carried out the execution in the customary place. As has already been said, the imposition of sentences was accompanied by confiscations or the levy of fines. Since the Inquisition was supported by these amercements there were numerous scandals in connection therewith. Certain royal orders implied, and complaints by men of such standing as Juan de Daza, bishop of Cordova, directly charged, that the Inquisition displayed a too great eagerness to insure its financial standing by confiscations. On one occasion it seems that the estate of a wealthy victim of the Inquisition was divided between Cardinal Carvajal, the inquisitor Lucero, the royal treasurer Morales, and Ferdinand's private secretary. The funds did not belong in law to the Inquisition. That body collected them and turned them over to the king, who granted them back again.

Financial administration.

The new Castilian and Aragonese states required greatly increased funds and a royal army, and both of these matters received the careful consideration of Ferdinand and Isabella. In financial affairs their activities were twofold: to procure more revenues; and to bring about greater economy in their collection and administration. The revocation of earlier land grants was one measure productive of income, since the taxes from them now went to the crown rather than to the lords. Two sources of revenue of a religious character were procured by papal grant. One of these was the *cruzada,* or sale of indulgences, based on the crusade (*cruzada*) against the Moslems. Designed for a temporary purpose it became an enduring element in the royal income. The other was the *diezmo,* or tithe, presumably for the same objects as the *cruzada,* although it too was diverted to other uses. Great attention was paid to the administration of the remunerative *alcabala,* and to stamp taxes and customs duties. The treasury department as a modern institution may be said to date from this era. In addition the Catholic Kings corrected abuses in the coinage of money. The final result is shown in the increase in the revenues from about 900,000 *reales* [1] in 1474 to well over 26,000,000 in 1504. Expenses were so heavy, however, that more than once a resort to loans was necessary.

The army kept pace with other institutions in the advance out of medievalism into modernity. The seigniorial levies, unequal in size and subversive of discipline as well as a potential danger, were virtually done away with after the Granadine war, although such bodies appeared occasionally even in the next era. In their place were substituted a larger royal army at state expense and the principle of universal military service. One man in every twelve of those between twenty and forty years of age was held liable, but did not take the field and was not paid except when specifically called. The glory of the new professional army attracted many who had formerly served the great lords, including a number of the nobility and the adventurous

Moderni-
zation
of the
army.

---

[1] The *real* was a former Spanish coin of elusive value. Prior to the reign of Ferdinand and Isabella it was worth slightly more than ninety *maravedís* and after that reign slightly less than eighty-nine. Today the *real* of copper (a theoretical coin) is worth thirty-four *maravedís* and the *real* of silver sixty-eight. As the *maravedí* (which is no longer coined) was worth about a sixth of a cent in present-day United States money, it will be seen that the *real* has ranged from about fifteen to five cents in value. These amounts do not, of course, represent the actual value, or purchasing power, of the *real.* That cannot be determined, but it was certainly many times greater than it would be today.

Q

element. Under the leadership of Gonzalo de Ayora and especially of the "great captain," Gonzalo de Córdoba, noteworthy reforms in tactics were made. The army was now an aggregation of equal groups, based on battalions and companies, while the larger divisions were assigned a proportionate number of infantry, cavalry, and artillery. From this period date many current military titles : colonel, captain, and others. Arms and equipment were much improved and military administration bettered. The importance of firearms was just becoming recognized; cannon, firing balls of stone, played a prominent part in the war with Granada. A similar if less pronounced development appeared in the navy. The admiral of Castile, who had enjoyed a semi-independent sinecure, now lost much of his authority, for many of his powers were taken over by the crown.

The reforms which have been chronicled were the result of a great body of legislation, most of which emanated directly from the crown, although some important laws were enacted in conjunction with the *Cortes*. Taken with the variety of legislation in preceding years it caused not a little confusion as to the precise principle governing a specific case. This led to the compilation by Alfonso Díaz de Montalvo of the *Ordenanzas Reales de Castilla* (1484?), or Royal Ordinances of Castile, commonly called the Ordinance (*Ordenamiento*) of Doctor Montalvo, in which were set forth various ordinances of the *Cortes* since that of Alcalá in 1348 and certain orders of the kings from the time of Alfonso X, together with some provisions of earlier date. In all, 1163 laws were included, of which 230 belonged to the era of the Catholic Kings. Although it is not certain, the *Ordenanzas* seems to have been promulgated as law, and in any event was very influential, running through thirteen editions down to the year 1513. The compilation was far from meeting the full requirement of the times, however. Besides being incomplete, as was only to be expected, it contained various inaccuracies of form and substance. Furthermore, with such varying elements still in effect as the *Partidas* and the medieval *fueros*, besides the unwritten

The royal navy.

The Ordinance of Montalvo and other codifications of the laws.

transformation and unification which had been going on for two centuries (as a result of royalist policies), there was need for a clear and methodical revision of Castilian legislation. Various other publications covering special phases of the laws, such as the *Ordenanzas de Alcabalas* (1491), or Ordinances of the *Alcabala*, the already mentioned *Leyes de Toro* (1505), and the privileges of the *Mesta* (1511), date from this era, while there was a similar tendency toward legislative publication in the Catalonian and Valencian parts of the kingdom of Aragon.

Although the piety of Ferdinand and Isabella earned them the sobriquet of the "Catholic Kings," particularly merited in the case of Isabella, they did not let their regard for the church interfere with their conceptions of the royal authority. Something has already been said about their resistance to the intrusions of ecclesiastical courts and their objection to appointments of foreigners to Spanish benefices. The same conflict with the pope was maintained with regard to papal appointments of Spaniards. In the case of Granada and the Americas the crown gained the *patronato real*, or royal patronage, in such degree that the monarch became the virtual administrative head of the church, but the concession for the rest of Spain was not so complete. Nevertheless, the royal nominees were usually appointed. The Catholic Kings displayed great consideration for the church when the interests of the latter did not run counter to the monarchical ideal, and in Castile the confessors of the queen obtained a certain ascendency which made them among the most powerful individuals in the state. They proved to be well deserving of their influence, however, notably cardinals Mendoza, Talavera, and Ximénez, of whom the last-named was, after the Catholic Kings, by far the most important figure of the times.

Relations of church and state.

CHAPTER XXI

MATERIAL AND INTELLECTUAL PROGRESS, 1479–1517

Economic
medieval-
ism.

THE Catholic Kings attacked the economic problems of their era with much the same zeal they had displayed in social and political reforms, but without equal success, for medievalism in material affairs was more persistent than in social, political, and intellectual institutions. The same false economic ideas of the past were still operative. Especially was this manifest in the belief that legislation and state intervention in business provided a panacea for all evils, when the real needs were the development of the wealth at hand and the modification of geographical conditions in such a way as to permit of additional productivity. Protection and excessive regulation were the keynote of the laws. As a result manufactures were stimulated on the one hand, and various cities of the two kingdoms became notable industrial centres, but on the other hand, these same industries were hindered by inspections, by laws regulating the fashion and style of goods and fixing prices, wages, and the hours of labor, and by a host of other measures which killed

Privileges
of the
Mesta.

initiative and hindered rapidity of work. In part to promote this artificial industrial life, so that raw wool might be readily procured, the Catholic Kings recognized and even extended the privileges of the great corporation of the *Mesta.* Starting from La Mancha and Extremadura in April, flocks of sheep annually ravaged Castile, returning in September to the place whence they had come. The *cañada real,* or royal sheepwalk, was set aside for their exclusive use, and a prohibition was placed on clearing, working, or enclosing any part of that strip. In fact the sheepmen ventured beyond the legal limits, and although required by law to pay damages in such cases were so powerful that they rarely did so. Withal, the stimulus to manufacturing was almost purely artificial, and the Spanish cities, even Barcelona, found competition with foreign cloths and other goods too keen. In the main, Spain continued to be a raw material land, exporting primary articles to foreign countries, in return for manufactures.

Attempts were made to encourage agriculture, but the spirit of legislative interference and the superior importance accorded the grazing industry were not conducive to progress. The menace of the *Mesta* was responsible for the almost complete destruction of forestry and agriculture in many regions which were suitable to development in those respects, while the irrigation ditches of Andalusia and other former Moslem lands were too often allowed to decay.

Lack of progress in agriculture.

The same royal solicitude appeared, to assist and to retard commerce. Interior customs lines were to some extent done away with, notably on the frontier of Castile and Aragon proper. Shipbuilding was encouraged, but favors were shown to owners of large ships, wherefore the smaller ship traffic was damaged, at the same time that the larger boats were too big for the needs of the trade. A flourishing foreign commerce developed, nevertheless, but it was in the hands of the Jews and, after their expulsion, of foreigners of Italian, Germanic, and French extraction. Many laws were passed subjecting foreigners to annoyances, lest they export precious metal or in other ways act contrary to the economic interests of the peninsula as they were then understood. It was in this period that the commerce of the Mediterranean cities of the kingdom of Aragon sank into a hopeless decline. Other factors than those of the false economic principles of the day were primarily responsible, such as the conquests of the Turks, which ended the eastern Mediterranean trade, and the Portuguese discovery of the sea-route to India, along with the Castilian voyages to America, which made the Atlantic Ocean the chief centre of sea-going traffic and closed the era of Mediterranean supremacy.

Vicissitudes of commerce.

Nevertheless, the net result of the period was a marked advance in material wealth, — in part, perhaps, because the

Advance in wealth.

false economic ideas of the Catholic Kings were shared by them with the other rulers of Europe, wherefore they did not prove so great a handicap to Spain, and, in part, because some of their measures were well calculated to prove beneficial. At this time, too, the wealth of the Americas began to pour in, although the future was to hold far more in store.

Extension of intellectual culture and the triumph of Humanism.

Brief as was the span of years embraced by the reign of the Catholic Kings it was as notable a period in intellectual progress as in other respects, bringing Spain into the current of modern life. This was due primarily to the rapid extension of printing, which had appeared in the peninsula in the closing years of the preceding period, and which now came into such general use that the works of Spanish and classical writers became available to all. Through private initiative many schools were founded which later became universities, although this activity was limited to Castile. Most notable of these institutions was that of Alcalá founded by Ximénez. This undertaking was due to the great cardinal's desire to establish a Humanist centre of learning, where Latin, Greek, Hebrew, and philology could be studied to the best advantage. The most learned Spanish Humanists assembled there, together with many foreigners, and works of note were produced, such as the famous polyglot Bible in Hebrew, Greek, Chaldean, and Latin, with accompanying grammars and vocabularies. Not a little of the advancement in intellectual manifestations was due to the encouragement of the Catholic Kings, especially Isabella. Books coming into Spain were exempted from duty; ordinances were made regulating university life, and ridding it of much of its turbulence and abuses; and the court set an example in showing favor to distinguished scholars, who were engaged as teachers of the royal children. The great nobles imitated royalty, and invited foreign savants to Spain, among whom was the Italian, Peter Martyr of Anghiera, celebrated as the author of the first history of the Americas, the *De orbe novo* (Concerning the new world). The most marked impulse to the spread of Humanist ideals came through Spaniards studying abroad, and these men returned to give Spain her leading names in intellectual production for the period. The greatest of them was Antonio de Nebrija, educated in Italy, a man of such encyclopedic attainments that he left works on theology, law, archæology, history, natural science, geography, and geodesy, although particularly noteworthy as a Latin scholar. Cardinal Ximénez is deserving of a high place in the achievements of the era for his patronage of letters, for it was through his aid that some of the most valuable work of the period was accomplished. Education was a matter for the higher classes only; people had not even begun to think, yet, of popular education.

Although the extension of intellectual culture and the triumph of Humanism were outstanding facts of the period, there were notable cultivators, too, of the sciences, moral, social, and natural, especially the last-named. Studies in geography, cosmography, and cartography received a great impulse through the discovery of America, and many scientific works along these lines were due to the scholars connected with the *Casa de Contratación* (House of Trade), or India House. Medical works were even more prominent, not a few of them on the subject of venereal disease. A number of these works were mutilated or condemned altogether by the Inquisition, in part because of their doctrines, but also because of the anatomical details which they contained, for they were considered immoral.

Progress in the sciences.

In polite literature the leading characteristics were the complete victory of the Italian influence, the predominance of Castilian, the popularity of the romances, and the beginning of the Castilian theatre. The Italian influence manifested itself both in the translation of Classical and Italian Renaissance works and in an imitation of their models and forms. Castilian was employed, not only in Castile and Aragon proper, but even in the literary works of Portuguese, Catalans, Valencians, and not a few individuals (Spaniards in the main) at the court of Naples, although Catalan and Valencian poetry still had a vogue. The poetry of the era often exhibited tendencies of a medieval character, — for example, in its use of allegory. It is curious to note also the prevalence of two somewhat opposed types of subject-matter, religious and erotic; in the latter there was a vigor-

Polite literature.

ous school which often went to the extreme of license. The romances of love and chivalry gained even greater favor than in the preceding period. The *Amadís de Gaula* (Amadis of Gaul) of Vasco de Lobeira was translated from the Portuguese by Garcí Ordóñez de Montalvo, and many other novels on the same model were written. One of these was *Las sergas de Esplandián* (The deeds of Esplandián) by Ordóñez de Montalvo himself, references in which to an "island California" as a land of fabulous wealth were to result in the naming of the present-day California, once believed to be just such an island. Much superior to the amatory or chivalric novels was a remarkable book which stood alone in its time, the *Tragicomedia de Calixto y Melibea* (The tragi-comedy of Calixtus and Melibea), better known as *La Celestina* (1499), from the name of one of the characters, believed to have been the work of Fernando de Rojas. In eloquent Spanish and with intense realism *La Celestina* dealt with people in what might be called "the under-world." This was the first of the picaresque novels (so-called because they dealt with the life of *pícaros*, or rogues), out of which was to develop the true Spanish novel. History, too, had a notable growth. The outstanding name was that of Hernando del Pulgar. His *Crónica* (Chronicle) and his *Claros varones de España* (Illustrious men of Spain), besides being well written, noteworthy for their characterizations of individuals, and influenced by classical Latin authors, showed a distinct historical sense. The already mentioned *De orbe novo* of Peter Martyr and the letters of Columbus were the chief contributions to the history of the new world. As to the theatre, while the religious mysteries continued to be played, popular representations in dialogue, some of them religious and others profane in subject-matter, began to be written and staged. The most notable writer was Juan del Enzina (1468–1534), who has been called the "father of Spanish comedy." His compositions were not represented publicly in a theatre, but only in private houses or on the occasions of royal or aristocratic feasts.

The transitional character of the age was nowhere more clear than in the various forms of art. The principal archi-

La Celestina.

History.

The theatre.

tectural style was a combination of late Gothic with early Renaissance features, which, because of its exuberantly decorative character, was called plateresque, for many of its forms resembled the work of *plateros,* or makers of plate. Structurally there was a mingling of the two above-named elements, with a superimposition of adornment marked by great profusion and richness, — such, for example, as in the façade of the convent of San Pablo of Valladolid. At the same time, edifices were still built which were more properly to be called Gothic, and there were yet others predominantly representative of the Renaissance, characterized by the restoration of the later classical structural and decorative elements, such as the slightly pointed arch, intersecting vaults, columns, entablatures, pediments, and lavish ornamentation. Sculpture displayed the same manifestations, and became in a measure independent of architecture. Noteworthy survivals are the richly carved sepulchres of the era. Gold and silver work had an extraordinary development not only in articles of luxury but also in those for popular use, and as regards luxury the same was true of work in rich embroideries and textures.

The contest between the Flemish and Italian influences on Spanish painting resolved itself decidedly in favor of the latter, although a certain eclecticism, the germ of a national school, made itself apparent in the works of Spanish artists. Characteristics of a medieval type still persisted, such as faulty drawing, color lacking in energy and richness, a sad and sober ambient, and a disregard for everything in a painting except the human figures. Like sculpture, painting began to be dissociated from architecture, and was encouraged by the purchases of the wealthy. It was not yet the custom to hang paintings on the walls; they were kept in chests or otherwise under lock and key except when brought out for temporary display. Music, employed principally in song as the accompaniment of verse, enjoyed a favor comparable with that of the plastic arts.

Plateresque architecture.

Sculpture and the lesser arts.

Advance in painting.

Music.

CHAPTER XXII

CHARLES I OF SPAIN, 1516–1556

Historical
setting of
the era of
the House
of Austria.

FROM the standpoint of European history the period of the House of Hapsburg, or Austria, covering nearly two centuries, when Spain was one of the great powers of the world, should be replete with the details of Spanish intervention in European affairs. The purposes of the present work will be served, however, by a comparatively brief treatment of this phase of Spanish history; indeed, the central idea underlying it reduces itself to this: Spain wasted her energies and expended her wealth in a fruitless attempt, first to become the dominant power in Europe, and later to maintain possessions in Italy and the Low Countries which were productive only of trouble; what she took from the Americas with the one hand, she squandered in Europe with the other. Internally there were changes which were to react on the Spanish colonial dominions, wherefore a correspondingly greater space must be accorded peninsula history than directly to the wars in Europe. The greatest feature of the period was the conquest of the Americas, accomplished in part by the spectacular expeditions of the *conquistadores*, or conquerors, and in part by the slower advance of the Spanish settlers, pushing onward the frontier of profits. Not only was this the most notable achievement when considered from the American angle, but it was, also, when taken from the standpoint of Spain, and possibly, too, from that of Europe and the world.

The Italian venture of the Aragonese kings had yielded probably more of advantage than of harm down to the time of Ferdinand, and it may be that even he did not overstep the bounds of prudence in his ambitious designs. When his policies were continued, however, in the person of Charles I, better known by his imperial title as the Emperor Charles V, the results were to prove more disastrous to Spain than beneficial. The circumstances were in fact different for the two monarchs, although their aims were much the same. Some writers have supposed that Ferdinand himself recognized the danger of a union of the Austrian, Burgundian, and Spanish dominions under one king, and they assert that he planned to make Charles' younger brother, Ferdinand, ruler of Spain and the Two Sicilies in case the former should be elected emperor. In his will, however, he respected the principle of primogeniture, and left all to Charles, eldest son of Philip the Handsome and Juana la Loca. Through his mother and Ferdinand, Charles inherited Castile, Aragon, and Navarre, the Castilian dominions in Africa and America (where the era of great conquests was just about to begin), the Roussillon and Cerdagne across the Pyrenees, and Sardinia, Sicily, and Naples in Italy; through his father he had already become possessed of the territories of the House of Burgundy, comprised of Flanders and Artois in northern France, Franche-Comté and Charolais in the east, Luxembourg, and the Low Countries. This was not all, for Charles was heir of the Emperor Maximilian, and in addition to inheriting the latter's Austrian dominions might hope to succeed to the imperial title as ruler of the Holy Roman Empire. To be sure, the system of electing the emperors by the electoral princes still obtained, but the Germanic states of the empire were almost certain to prefer a powerful Hapsburg, with such dominions as Charles had, to any other candidate, if only to serve as a counterpoise to the ambitions of France. Nevertheless, the electors did not miss the opportunity to make a profit out of the situation, and encouraged the candidacy of Henry VIII of England and especially of Francis I of France as well as that of Charles, receiving bribes and favors from all. In the end, following the death of Maximilian in 1519, they decided in favor of Charles. He was now ruler, at least in name, of one of the most vast empires in the history of the world.

The mere possession of such extensive domains inevitably

Vast empire of Charles I of Spain, the Emperor Charles V.

led to an imperialistic policy to insure their retention. Each
of the three principal elements therein, Spain, Burgundy,
and the Austrian dominions, was ambitious in itself and
especially hostile to France, and all of these aspirations and
enmities were now combined in a single monarch. Charles
himself was desirous not only of conquest but also of becoming the most powerful prince in the world, thus assuring the
Hapsburg supremacy in Europe, and making himself the
arbiter in European political affairs and the protector of
Christianity; he may even have dreamed of a world monarchy, for if he did not aspire to such a state for himself he
believed its attainment possible of realization. In the
achievement of a less vast ideal, however, Charles was certain to experience many difficulties, and at some point or
other was bound to encounter the hostility not only of France
but also of the other states of Europe. If this were not
enough there came along the unforeseen dilemma of the Reformation. Finally, his own dominions were none too strongly
held together, one with another or within themselves. They
were widely separated, some indeed entirely surrounded by
French territory, leading to a multiplicity of problems of a
military and a political nature. The imperial rank carried
little real authority in Germany, and the Burgundian realms
were not a great source of power. It appears, therefore,
that the empire was more a matter of show than of strength,
and that Spain, who already had a surfeit of responsibility,
what with her conquests in Italy, Africa, and the Americas,
must bear the burden for all. The reign of Charles would
seem to be the parting of the ways for Spain. If she could
have restricted herself to her purely Spanish inheritance,
even with the incubus of her Italian possessions, she might
have prolonged her existence as a great power indefinitely.
A century ahead of England in colonial enterprise, she had
such an opportunity as that which made the island of Britain
one of the dominant factors in the world. Even as matters
were, Spain was able to stand forth as a first rank nation for
well over a century. Whatever might have happened if a
different policy had been followed, it hardly admits of doubt
that Spain's intervention in European affairs involved too

great a strain on her resources, and proved a detriment politically and economically to the peninsula.

Charles had been brought up in Flanders, and, it is said, was unable to speak Spanish when he first entered the peninsula as king of Spain. His official reign began in 1516, but it was not until his arrival in the following year that the full effect of his measures began to be felt. Even before that time there was some inkling of what was to come in the appointments of foreigners, mostly Flemings, to political or ecclesiastical office in Castile. At length Charles reached Spain, surrounded by Flemish courtiers, who proceeded to supplant Spaniards not only in the favor but also in the patronage of the king. The new officials, more eager for personal profit than patriotic, began to sell privileges and the posts of lower grade to the highest bidders. Such practices could not fail to wound the feelings of Spaniards, besides which they contravened the laws, and many protests by individuals and towns were made, to which was joined the complaint of the *Cortes* of Valladolid in 1518. To make matters worse Chièvres, the favorite minister of the king, caused taxes to be raised. The amount of the *alcabala* was increased, and the tax was made applicable to the hitherto privileged nobility, much against their will. In like manner the opposition of the clergy was roused through a bull procured from the pope requiring ecclesiastical estates to pay a tenth of their income to the king during a period of three years. Furthermore it was commonly believed, no doubt with justice, that the Flemish office-holders were sending gold and other precious metals out of the country, despite the laws forbidding such export. Nevertheless the *Cortes* of 1518 granted a generous subsidy to the king, but this was followed by new increases in royal taxation. Opposition to these practices now began to crystallize, with the nobles of Toledo taking the lead in remonstrance against them.

Dissatisfaction over foreign favorites and increased taxation.

The situation in Castile was complicated by the question of the imperial election. Between the death of Maximilian in January, 1519, and the election of Charles in June of the same year it was necessary to pay huge bribes to the electoral princes. Once chosen, Charles accepted the imperial

Charles' manipulation of the Cortes in Galicia.

honor, and prepared to go to Germany to be crowned, an event which called for yet more expenditures of a substantial nature. So, notwithstanding the grant of 1518, it was decided to call the *Cortes* early in 1520 with a view to a fresh subsidy. Since all Castile was in a state of tumult it was deemed best that the meeting should take place at some point whence an escape from the country would be easy in case of need. Thus Santiago de Compostela in Galicia was selected, and it was there that the *Cortes* eventually met, moving to the neighboring port of Coruña after the first few days' sessions. The call for the *Cortes* provoked a storm of protest not only by Toledo but also by many other cities with which the first-named was in correspondence. Messengers were sent to the king to beg of him not to leave Spain, or, if he must do so, to place Spaniards in control of the affairs of state, and complaints were made against the practices already recounted and numerous others, such, for example, as the royal use of the title "Majesty," an unwonted term in Spain. From the first, Charles turned a deaf ear, refusing to receive the messengers of the towns, or reproving them when he did give them audience, and he even went so far as to order the arrest of the Toledan leaders. The *Cortes* at length met, and gave evidence of the widespread discontent in its demands upon the king. In accordance with their instructions most of the deputies were disinclined to take up the matter of a supply for the king until he should accede to their petitions. Under the royal eye, however, they gradually modified their demands, and when Charles took it upon himself to absolve them from the pledges they had given to their constituents they voted the subsidy without obtaining any tangible redress of grievances. The king did promise not to appoint any foreigners to Spanish benefices or political holdings during his absence, but broke his word forthwith when he named Cardinal Adrian, a foreigner, as his representative and governor during his absence. This done, Charles set out in the same year, 1520, for Germany.

Meanwhile, a riot in Toledo, promoted by the nobles whom Charles had ordered arrested, converted itself into a veritable revolt when the royal *corregidor* was expelled from the city.

This action was stated to have been taken in the name of the *Comunidad*, or community, of Toledo, and served to give a name to the uprising which now took place in all parts of Castile. Deputies to the *Cortes* who had been faithless to their trust, some of whom had accepted bribes from the king, were roughly handled upon their return home, and city after city joined Toledo in proclaiming the *Comunidad*. In July, 1520, delegates of the rebellious communities met, and formed the *Junta* of Ávila, which from that town and later from Tordesillas and Valladolid served as the executive body of the revolution. For a time the *Junta* was practically the ruling body in the state; so complete was the overturn of royal authority that Cardinal Adrian and his advisers made no attempt to put down the rebellion. Time worked to the advantage of the king, however. The revolt of Toledo had begun as a protest of the nobles and clergy against the imposition of taxes against them. The program of the *Junta* of Ávila went much further than that, going into the question of the grievances of the various social classes. At length many of the *comuneros* began to indulge in acts of violence and revenge against those by whom they regarded themselves as having been oppressed, and the movement changed from one of all the classes, including the nobles, against the royal infractions of law and privileges, to one of the popular element against the lords. Thus the middle classes, who objected to the disorder of the times as harmful to business, and the nobles, in self-defence, began to take sides with the king. City after city went over to Charles, and late in 1520 the government was strong enough to declare war on the communities still faithful to the *Junta*. Dissension, treason, and incompetent leadership furthered the decline of the popular cause, and in 1521 the revolt was crushed at the battle of Villalar. Charles promised a general pardon, but when he came to Spain in 1522 he caused a great many to be put to death. Not until 1526 did he show a disposition to clemency. Moreover he retained his Flemish advisers.

During the period of the revolt of the *Comunidades* in Castile even more bitter civil wars were going on in Valencia

War of the *Comunidades* in Castile.

(1520–1522) and Majorca (1521–1523). The contest in Valencia was a social conflict from the start, of plebeians against the lords, whereas the Castilian conflict was fundamentally political. In Majorca the strife began over pressure for financial reforms, but developed into an attempt to eliminate the nobility altogether. Both uprisings were independent of the Castilian revolt, although serving to aid the latter through the necessary diversion of troops. As in Castile, so in Valencia and Majorca, Charles took sides against the popular element, and put down the insurrections, displaying great severity toward the leaders.

Charles'
difficulties
in Ger-
many and
war with
France.

While the civil wars were at their height Charles was having more than his share of trouble in other quarters. The princes of Germany compelled him to sign a document affirming their privileges, in which appeared many paragraphs similar to those of the Castilian petitions to the king, together with one requiring Charles to maintain the empire independently of the Spanish crown. The acceptance of these principles by the emperor is an evidence of the weakness of his authority in the subject states of Germany, for not only was he a believer in the divine origin of the imperial dignity, a doctrine which would have impelled him to establish his personal and absolute rule in all of his realms if possible, but he seems also to have intended to make Spain the political centre of his dominions, because she was, after all, his strongest element of support. At the same time, a fresh difficulty appeared in Germany with the Lutheran outbreak of 1521. Charles himself favored reform in the church, but was opposed to any change in dogma. Before he could confront either the political or the religious problem in Germany, he found himself attacked on another quarter. Francis I of France had seized upon Charles' difficulties as affording him a rich opportunity to strike to advantage; so in 1521 he twice sent French armies into Spain through the western Pyrenees on the pretext of restoring the crown of Navarre to the Labrit family. With all these questions pressing for solution Charles was in an exceedingly unsatisfactory position. Thus early in the period lack of funds to prosecute European policies was chronic. Spain herself, even if there had been no civil wars, was not united internally like the compact French nation, and the other Hapsburg dominions could give but little help. Finally, Charles could not depend on the alliance of any other power, for his own realms were neighbors of all the others, and his designs were therefore generally suspected. Nevertheless, Charles brought to his many tasks an indomitable will, marked energy, a steadfast purpose, and an all-round ability which were to do much toward overcoming the obstacles that hindered him.

It is profitless, here, to relate the course of the wars with France and other European states. In the years 1521 to 1529, 1536 to 1538, and 1542 to 1544, France and Spain were at war, and at other times, down to the death of Francis I in 1547, the two countries enjoyed what was virtually no more than a truce. Meanwhile, Charles was usually in conflict with the popes, whose temporal dominions in central Italy were threatened by the growing power of Spain and the empire in the Italian peninsula. Other states in Italy fought now on Charles' side, now against him, while the princes of Germany were an equally variable quantity. England favored each side in turn, but offered little effective aid to either. As affecting the history of religion these wars gave Protestantism a chance to develop. Neither Charles nor Francis disdained the aid of Protestant princes, and the former had little opportunity to proceed against them on religious grounds. Francis even allied himself with the Moslem power of Turkey. On the whole, Charles was the victor in the wars, and could point to the occupation of Milan as a tangible evidence of his success, — about the only territorial change of consequence as a result of the many campaigns. Perhaps the most noteworthy fact as affecting the history of Spain and Spanish America was the financial drain occasioned by the fighting. Time and again lack of funds was mainly responsible for defeats or failures to follow up a victory. Spain and the Americas had to meet the bills, but, liberal as were their contributions, more were always needed.

Wars with France, the pope, the Italian states, and German princes.

The outcome.

The wars with Turkey had a special significance because of the ever impending peril from Moslem northern Africa. The pirates of the Berber, or Barbary, Coast, as the lands in

R

Wars with
the Turks
and the
Moslems
of
northern
Africa. northwestern Africa are often called, seemed to be more
than ever audacious in the early years of the reign of Charles.
Not only did they attack Spanish ships and even Spanish
ports, but they also made numerous incursions inland in
the peninsula.   Aside from the loss in captives and in economic wealth that these visitations represented, they served
to remind the authorities of the Moslem sympathies of Spanish Moriscos and of the ease with which a Moslem invasion
might be effected.   Furthermore the conquests of Isabella
and Ximénez had created Castilian interests in northern
Africa, of both a political and an economic character, which
were in need of defence against the efforts of the tributary
princes to free themselves by Turkish aid.   The situation
was aggravated by the achievements of a renegade Greek
adventurer and pirate, known best by the sobriquet "Barbarossa."   This daring corsair became so powerful that he
was able to dethrone the king of Algiers and set up his own
brother in his stead.   On the death of the latter at the hands
of the Spaniards in 1518, Barbarossa placed the kingdom of
Algiers under the protection of the sultan of Turkey, became
himself an admiral in the Turkish navy, and soon afterward
conquered the kingdom of Tunis, whence during many years
he menaced the Spanish dominions in Italy.   Charles in
person led an expedition in 1535 which was successful in de-
throning Barbarossa and in restoring the former king to the
throne, but an expedition of 1541, sent against Algiers, was
a dismal failure.   On yet another frontier, that of Hungary,
Spanish troops were called upon to meet the Turks, and there
they contributed to the checking of that people at a time
when their military power threatened Europe.   The problem
of northern Africa, however, had been little affected by the
efforts of Charles.

Charles'
failure to
stamp out
Protes-
tantism.
  Meanwhile, the religious question in Germany had all
along been considered by Charles as one of his most important problems.   The first war with France prevented any
action on his part until 1529, since he needed the support
of the Protestant princes.   The movement therefore had
time to gather headway, and it was evident that Charles
would meet with determined opposition whenever he should

decide to face the issue. Various factors entered in to complicate the matter, such, for example, as the fear on the part of many princes of the growing Hapsburg power and the belief that Charles meant to make the imperial succession hereditary in his family. A temporary adjustment of the religious situation was made by the imperial Diet held at Spires in 1526, when it was agreed that every prince should decide for himself in matters of religion. With the close of the war with France in 1529, Charles caused the Diet to meet again at Spires, on which occasion the previous decision was revoked. The princes devoted to the reform ideas protested, giving rise to the name "Protestant," but without avail. The Diet was called for the next year at Augsburg, when Charles sat in judgment between the two parties. The Protestants presented their side in a document which became known as the confession of Augsburg. The Catholic theologians replied, and Charles accepted their view, ordering the Protestant leaders to submit, and threatening to employ force unless they should do so. The international situation again operated to protect the reform movement, for the Turks became threatening, and, indeed, what with the wars with France and his numerous other difficulties Charles was unable to proceed resolutely to a solution of the religious problem until the year 1545. At last he was ready to declare war. In 1547 he won what seemed to be a decisive victory in the battle of Mühlberg, resulting in the subjection of the Protestant princes to the Roman Church. They protested anew, and, aided by the opposition to Charles on other grounds, — for example, because of his introduction of Italian and Spanish soldiery into what was regarded as a domestic quarrel, — were able to present a warlike front again. This time they were joined by Charles' former powerful ally, Maurice of Saxony, through whose assistance they successfully defended themselves. Peace was made at Passau in 1552, ratified by the Diet of Augsburg in 1555, whereby the Protestant princes obtained equal rights with the Catholic lords as to their freedom in religious beliefs.

Great as were to be the results of Charles' reign on its European side, it had nevertheless been a failure so far as

Other
failures of
Charles
and his
abdica-
tion.

Spain and Charles' own objects were concerned. Yet other disappointments were to fall to his lot. He aspired to the imperial title for his son Philip. In this he was opposed both by the Germanic nobility, who saw in it an attempt to foist upon them a Spanish-controlled absolutism, and by his brother Ferdinand, who held the Austrian dominions as a fief of the empire and aimed to become emperor himself. Unable to prevail in his own policy Charles eventually supported Ferdinand. For many years, too, he thought of establishing an independent Burgundian kingdom as a counterpoise to France, but changed his mind to take up a plan for uniting England and the Low Countries, with the same object in view. For this latter purpose he procured the hand of Queen Mary of England for his son Philip. The marriage proved childless, and Philip was both unpopular and without power in England. The death of Mary in 1558 ended this prospect. At last Charles' spirit was broken. For nearly forty years he had battled for ideals which he was unable to bring to fulfilment; so he resolved to retire from public life. In 1555 he renounced his title to the Low Countries in favor of Philip. In 1556 he abdicated in Spain, and went to live at the monastery of Yuste in Cáceres. He was unable to drop out of political life completely, however, and was wont to intervene in the affairs of Spain from his monastic retreat. In 1558 he gave up his imperial crown, to which his brother Ferdinand was elected. Thus Spain was separated from Austria, but she retained the Burgundian inheritance and the Italian possessions of Aragon. The marriage of Philip the Handsome and Juana la Loca was still to be productive of fatal consequences to Spain, for together with the Burgundian domains there remained the feeling of Hapsburg solidarity.

Greatness
of Charles
in the
history of
Spain and
Spanish
America.

Charles had failed in Europe, but in Spain and especially in the Americas he had done more than enough to compensate for his European reverses. His achievements in Spain belong to the field of institutional development rather than to that of political narrative, however. As for the Americas his reign was characterized by such a series of remarkable mainland conquests that it is often treated as a distinct epoch in American history, the era of the *conquistadores*, and Spanish America is, after all, the principal monument to the greatness of his reign.   The Emperor Charles V was a failure ; but King Charles I of Spain gave the Americas to European civilization.

Resemblance of the reign of Philip II to that of Charles I.

IN underlying essentials the reign of Philip II was a reproduction of that of Charles I. There were scattered dominions and family prestige to maintain, the enemies of the Catholic Church to combat, the dominant place of Spain in Europe to assure, the strain on Spanish resources, and, as glorious offsets to general failure in Europe, the acquisition of some European domains and the advance of the colonial conquests. Only the details varied. Philip had a more compact nation behind him than had fallen to the lot of Charles, although there was still much to be desired in that respect; France was hostile, though less powerful than formerly, but England and Philip's rebellious Protestant Netherlands more than made up for the weakness of France; issues in Germany no longer called for great attention, but family politics were not forgotten; on the other hand Philip achieved the ideal of peninsula unity through the acquisition of Portugal, carrying with it that country's colonies; and, finally, his conquests in the new world, though less spectacular than those of Charles, compared favorably with them in actual fact.

Education and character of Philip II.

Historians have often gone to extremes in their judgments of Philip II. Some have been ardently pro-Philip, while others were as bitterly condemnatory. Recently, opinions have been more moderately expressed. In addition to native ability and intelligence Philip had the benefit of an unusually good education in preparation for government. Charles himself was one of the youth's instructors, and, long before his various abdications, had given Philip political practice in various ways, — for example, by making him co-regent of Spain with Cardinal Tavera during Charles' own absence in

Germany. Philip also travelled extensively in the lands which he one day hoped to govern, — in Italy (1548), the Low Countries (1549), and Germany (1550). In 1543 he married a Portuguese princess, María, his first cousin. One son, Charles, was born of this marriage, but the mother died in childbirth. His fruitless marriage with Mary Tudor, in 1553, has already been mentioned. He remained in England until 1555, when he went to the Low Countries to be crowned, and thence to Spain, of which country he became king in 1556, being at that time twenty-nine years old. His abilities as king of Spain were offset in a measure by certain unfortunate traits and practices. He was of a vacillating type of mind; delays in his administration were often long and fatal, and more than once he let slip a golden opportunity for victory, because he could not make up his mind to strike. Of a suspicious nature, he was too little inclined to rely upon men from whose abilities he might have profited. A tremendous worker, he was too much in the habit of trying to do everything himself, with the result that greater affairs were held up, while the king of Spain worked over details. Finally, he was extremely rigorous with heretics, from motives of religion and of political policy.

The principal aim of Philip's life was the triumph of Catholicism, but this did not hinder his distinguishing clearly between the interests of the church and those of the popes as rulers of the Papal States. Thus it was not strange that Philip's reign should begin with a war against Pope Paul IV. The latter excommunicated both Charles and Philip, and procured alliances with France and, curious to relate, the sultan of Turkey, head of the Moslem world. The pope was defeated, but it was not until the accession of Pius IV, in 1559, that the bans of excommunication were raised. War with the pope.

There was a constant succession of war and peace with France throughout the reign, with the campaigns being fought more often in northern France from the vantage ground of Flanders than in Italy as in the time of Charles. In 1557 Philip might have been able to take Paris, but he hesitated, and the chance was lost. Many other times Philip's generals won victories, but attacks from other quar- Wars with France.

ters of Europe would cause a diversion, or funds would give out, or Philip himself would change his plans. France was usually on the defensive, because she was weakened during most of the period by the domestic strife between Catholics and Protestants. When in 1589 the Protestant leader became entitled to the throne as Henry IV, Philip and the uncompromising wing of the French Catholic party endeavored to prevent his actual accession to power. At one time it was planned to make Philip himself king of France, but, as this idea did not meet with favor, various others were suggested, including the proposal of Philip's daughter for the crown, or the partition of France between Philip and others. Henry IV settled the matter in 1594 by becoming a Catholic, wherefore he received the adhesion of the Catholic party. Philip was not dissatisfied, for it seemed that he had rid himself of a dangerous Protestant neighbor. Had he but known it, Henry IV was to accomplish the regeneration of a France which was to strike the decisive blow, under Louis XIV, to remove Spain from the ranks of the first-rate powers.

War with the Granadine Moriscos. While Philip had no such widespread discontent in Spain to deal with as had characterized the early years of the reign of Charles, there was one problem leading to a serious civil war in southern Spain. The Moriscos of Granada had proved to be an industrious and loyal element, supporting Charles in the war of the communities, but there was reason to doubt the sincerity of their conversion to Christianity. The populace generally and the clergy in particular were very bitter against them, and procured the passage of laws which were increasingly severe in their treatment of the Moriscos. An edict of 1526 prohibited the use of Arabic speech or dress, the taking of baths (a Moslem custom), the bearing of arms, the employment of non-Christian names, and the giving of lodging in their houses to Mohammedans whether free or slave. The Moriscos were also subjected to oppressive inspections to prevent Mohammedan religious practices; they were obliged to send their children to Christian schools; and a branch of the Inquisition was established in Granada to execute, with all the rigors of that institution, the laws against apostasy. The full effect of the edict was avoided by means of a financial gift to the king, but the Inquisition was not withdrawn. For many years the situation underwent no substantial change. The clergy, and the Christian element generally, continued to accuse the Moriscos, and the latter complained of the confiscations and severity of the Inquisition. In 1567, however, the edict of 1526 was renewed, but in harsher form, amplifying the prohibitions. When attempts were made to put the law into effect, and especially when agents came to take the Morisco children to Christian schools, by force if necessary, an uprising was not long in breaking out. The war lasted four years. The Moriscos were aided by the mountainous character of the country, and they received help from the Moslems of northern Africa and even from the Turks. The decisive campaign was fought in 1570, when Spanish troops under Philip's half-brother, Juan (or Don John) of Austria, an illegitimate son of Charles I, defeated the Moriscos, although the war dragged on to the following year. The surviving Moriscos, including those who had not taken up arms, were deported *en masse* and distributed in other parts of Castilian Spain.

The external peril from the Moslem peoples had not confined itself to the period of the Morisco war. Piracy still existed in the western Mediterranean, and the Turkish Empire continued to advance its conquests in northern Africa. Philip gained great victories, notably when he compelled the Turks to raise the siege of Malta in 1564, and especially in 1571, when he won the naval battle of Lepanto, in which nearly 80,000 Christians were engaged, most of them Spaniards. These victories were very important in their European bearings, for they broke the Turkish naval power, and perhaps saved Europe, but from the standpoint of Spain alone they were of less consequence. Philip failed to follow them up, partly because of the pressure of other affairs, and in part because of his suspicions of the victor of Lepanto, the same Juan of Austria who had just previously defeated the Moriscos. Juan of Austria was at the same time a visionary and a capable man of affairs. He was ambitious to pursue the Turks to Constantinople, capture that city, and restore the Byzantine Empire, with himself as ruler. Philip

Wars with the Turks

Juan of Austria.

withdrew his support, whereupon Juan devised a new project of a great North African empire. Juan even captured Tunis in pursuance of his plan, but Philip would give him no help, and Juan was obliged to retire, thus permitting of a Turkish reconquest. Philip was always able to offer the excuse of lack of funds, — and, indeed, the expenditures in the wars with Turkey, with all the effects they carried in their train, were the principal result to the peninsula of these campaigns.

Wars in the Low Countries. The greatest of Philip's difficulties, and one which bulked large in its importance in European history, was the warfare with his rebellious provinces in the Low Countries. Its principal bearing in Spanish history was that it caused the most continuous and very likely the heaviest drain on the royal treasury of any of Philip's problems. The war lasted the entire reign, and was to be a factor for more than a half century after Philip's death. It got to be in essence a religious struggle between the Protestants of what became the Netherlands and Philip, in which the latter was supported to a certain extent by the provinces of the Catholic Netherlands, or modern Belgium. Religion, however, was not the initial, or at any time the sole, matter in controversy. At the outset the causes were such practices as the Castilian communities had objected to in the reign of Charles, namely: the appointments of foreigners to office; the presence of foreign (Spanish) troops; measures which were regarded as the forerunner to an extension of the Spanish Inquisition to the Low Countries (against which the nobles and the clergy alike, practically all of whom were Catholic at that time, made strenuous objections); Philip's policy of centralization and absolutism; the popular aversion for Philip as a Spaniard (just as Spaniards had objected to Charles as a Fleming); and the excessive rigors employed in the suppression of heresy. The early leaders were Catholics, many of them members of the clergy, and the hotbed of rebellion was rather in the Catholic south than in the Protestant north. It was this situation which gave the Protestants a chance to strike on their own behalf. The war, or rather series of wars, was characterized by deeds of valor and by extreme cruelty. Philip was even more harsh in his instructions for dealing with heretics than his generals were in executing them. Alba (noted for his severity), Requesens (an able man who followed a more moderate policy), Juan of Austria (builder of air castles, but winner of battles), and the able Farnese, — these were the Spanish rulers of the period, all of them military men. The elder and the younger William of Orange were the principal Protestant leaders. In open combat the Spanish infantry was almost invincible, but its victories were nullified, sometimes because it was drawn away to wage war in France, but more often because money and supplies were lacking. On various occasions the troops were left unpaid for so long a time that they took matters into their own hands. Then, terrible scenes of riot and pillage were enacted, without distinction as to the religious faith of the sufferers, for even Catholic churches were sacked by the soldiery. The outcome for the Low Countries was the virtual independence of the Protestant Netherlands, although Spain did not yet acknowledge it. For Spain the result was the same as that of her other ventures in European politics, only greater in degree than most of them, — exhausting expenditures.

In the middle years of Philip's reign there was one project The annexation of Portugal. of great moment in Spanish history which he pushed to a successful conclusion, — the annexation of Portugal. While the ultimate importance of this event was to be lessened by the later separation of the two kingdoms, they were united long enough (sixty years) for notable effects to be felt in Spain and more particularly in the Americas. The desire for peninsula unity had long been an aspiration of the Castilian kings, and its consummation from the standpoint of the acquisition of Portugal had several times been attempted, though without success. The death of King Sebastián in 1578 without issue left the Portuguese throne to Cardinal Henry, who was already very old, and whom in any event the pope refused to release from his religious vows. This caused various claimants to the succession to announce themselves, among whom were the Duchess of Braganza, Antonio (the prior of Crato), and Philip. The first-named had the best hereditary claim, since she was descended from a son (the youngest) of King Manuel, a predecessor of Sebastián. Antonio of Crato was son of another of King Manuel's sons, but was of illegitimate birth; nevertheless, he was the favorite of the regular clergy, the popular classes, some nobles, and the pope, and was the only serious rival Philip had to consider. Philip's mother was the eldest daughter of the same King Manuel. With this foundation for his claim he pushed his candidacy with great ability, aided by the skilful diplomacy of his special ambassador, Cristóbal de Moura. One of the master strokes was the public announcement of Philip's proposed governmental policy in Portugal, promising among other things to respect the autonomy of the kingdom, recognizing it as a separate political entity from Spain. A Portuguese *Cortes* of 1580 voted for the succession of Philip, for the noble and ecclesiastical branches supported him, against the opposition of the third estate. A few days later King Henry died, and Philip prepared to take possession. The partisans of Antonio resisted, but Philip, who had long been in readiness for the emergency, sent an army into Portugal under the Duke of Alba, and he easily routed the forces of Antonio. In keeping with his desire to avoid giving offence to the Portuguese, Philip gave Alba the strictest orders to punish any infractions of discipline or improper acts of the soldiery against the inhabitants, and these commands were carefully complied with, — in striking contrast with the policy which had been followed while Alba was governor in the Low Countries. Thus it was that a Portuguese *Cortes* of 1581 solemnly recognized Philip as king of Portugal. Philip took oath not to appoint any Spaniards to Portuguese offices, and he kept his word to the end of his reign. Portugal had now come into the peninsula union in much the same fashion that Aragon had joined with Castile. With her came the vast area and great wealth of the Portuguese colonies of Asia, Africa, and more particularly Brazil. If only the Spanish kings might hold the country long enough, it appeared inevitable that a real amalgamation of such kindred peoples would one day take place. Furthermore, if only the kings would have, or could have, confined themselves to a Pan-Hispanic policy, embracing Spain and Portugal and their colonies, the opportunity for the continued greatness of the peninsula seemed striking. The case was a different one from that of the union of Castile and Aragon, however, for a strong feeling of Portuguese nationality had already developed, based largely on a hatred of Spaniards. This spirit had something to feed upon from the outset in the defeat of the popular Antonio of Crato and in the discontent of many nobles, who did not profit as much by Philip's accession as they had been led to expect. It was necessary to put strong garrisons in Portuguese cities and to fortify strategic points. Nevertheless, Philip experienced no serious trouble and was able to leave Portugal to his immediate successor.

Philip's relations with England, in which the outstanding event was the defeat of the Spanish Armada, had elements of importance as affecting Spanish history, especially in so far as they concerned English depredations in the Americas. They were more important to England, however, than to Spain, and the story from the English standpoint has become a familiar one. From the moment of Protestant Elizabeth's accession to the English throne in 1558, in succession to Catholic Mary, there was a constant atmosphere of impending conflict between Spain and England. Greatest of the motives in Philip's mind was that her rule meant a Protestant England, a serious break in the authority of Catholic Christianity, but there were other causes for war as well. English aid of an unofficial but substantial character was helping to sustain the Protestant Netherlands in revolt against Spain. In the Americas "beyond the line" (of Tordesillas) the two countries were virtually at war, although in the main it was a conflict of piratical attacks and the sacking of cities on the part of the English, with acts of retaliation by the Spaniards. This was the age of Drake's and Hawkins' exploits along the Spanish Main (in the Caribbean area), but it was also the age of Gilbert and Raleigh, and the first, though ineffectual, attempts of England to despoil Spain of her American dominions through the founding of colonies in the Spanish-claimed new world. Incidents of a special character served to accentuate the feeling

Causes of the war with England.

engendered by these more permanent causes, — such, for example, as Elizabeth's appropriation of the treasure which Philip was sending to the Low Countries as pay for his soldiers : the Spanish vessels took shelter in an English port to escape from pirates, whereupon Elizabeth proceeded to "borrow," as she termed it, the wealth they were carrying. Hard pressed for funds as Philip always was, this was indeed a severe blow.

Why a declaration of war was delayed.

Nevertheless, a declaration of war was postponed for nearly thirty years. English historians ascribe the delay to the diplomatic skill of their favorite queen, but, while there is no need to deny her resourcefulness in that respect, there were reasons in plenty why Philip himself was desirous of deferring hostilities, or better still, avoiding them. In view of his existing troubles with France and the Low Countries he drew back before the enormous expense that a war with England would entail, to say nothing of the military difficulties of attacking an island power. Though he received frequent invitations from the Catholics of England and Scotland to effect an invasion, these projects were too often linked with similar proposals to the kings of France, the leading European opponents of the Spanish monarch. Philip wished to break the power of Elizabeth and of Protestantism if possible, however, and gave encouragement to plots against the life of the English queen or to schemes for revolutionary uprisings in favor of Mary Stuart, a Catholic and Elizabeth's rival, but none of these designs met with success. Many Spanish leaders urged a descent upon England, among them Juan of Austria, who wished to lead the expeditionary force himself, dreaming possibly of an English crown for his reward, but it was not until 1583 that Philip viewed these proposals with favor.

Preparations for a descent upon England.

Once having decided upon an expedition Philip began to lay his plans. Mary Stuart was persuaded to disinherit her son, who was a Protestant (the later James I of England), and to make Philip her heir. The pope was induced to lend both financial and moral support to the undertaking, although it was necessary to deceive him as to Philip's intentions to acquire England for himself; the pope was told that Philip's daughter was to be made queen of England. The proposed descent upon England was no secret to Elizabeth, who made ready to resist. With a view to delaying Philip's preparations, Drake made an attack upon Cádiz in 1587, on which occasion he burned all the shipping in the bay. This only strengthened Philip's resolutions with regard to the undertaking, and tended to make him impatient for its early execution. Plans were made which proved to be in many cases ill considered. The first mistake occurred when Philip did not entertain a proposition of the Scotch and French Catholics that he should work in concert with them, thus declining an opportunity to avail himself of ports and bases of supply near the point of attack; political reasons were the foundation for his attitude in this matter. Against advice he also decided to divide the expedition into a naval and a military section, the troops to come from the Low Countries after the arrival of the fleet there to transport them. The worst error of all was that of Philip's insistence on directing the organization of the fleet himself. All details had to be passed upon by the king from his palace of the Escorial near Madrid, which necessarily involved both delay and a faulty execution of orders. Evil practices and incompetence were manifest on every hand; quantities of the supplies purchased proved to be useless; and the officers and men were badly chosen, many of the former being without naval experience. A great mistake was made in the appointment of the Duke of Medina Sidonia to lead the expedition; the principal recommendation of the duke was that of his family prestige, for he was absolutely lacking in knowledge of maritime affairs, and said as much to the king, but the latter insisted that he should take command.

At length the fleet was able to leave Lisbon, and later Coruña, in the year 1588. Because of its great size it was termed the *Armada Invencible* (the Invincible Fleet), a name which has been taken over into English as the Spanish, or the Invincible, Armada. In all there were 131 ships, with over 25,000 sailors, soldiers, and officers. The evil effect of Philip's management followed the Armada to sea. He had given detailed instructions what to do, and the com-

Defeat of the Armada.

mander-in-chief would not vary from them. Many officers
thought it would be best to make an attack on Plymouth,
to secure that port as a base of operations, but Philip had
given orders that the fleet should first go to the Low Countries to effect a junction with the troops held in readiness
there. The story of the battle with the English fleet is well
known. The contest was altogether one-sided, for the English ships were both superior in speed and equipped with
longer range artillery. Nevertheless, storms contributed
more than the enemy to the Spanish defeat. The Armada
was utterly dispersed, and many vessels were wrecked. Only
65 ships and some 10,000 men were able to return to Spain.

The decisive blow had been struck, and Spain was the
loser. The English war went on into the next reign, and
there were several spectacular military events, not all of
them unfavorable to Spanish arms, but they affected the
general situation only in that they continued the strain on
the royal exchequer. In the final analysis Philip had failed
in this as in so many other enterprises. This fact was clear,
even at the time, although the eventualities of later years
were to make the outcome appear the more decisive. Philip's
evil star did not confine its effects to his international poli-
Domestic   cies. His eldest son, Charles, proved to be of feeble body
troubles   and unbalanced mind. Getting into difficulties with his
and death   father, he was placed in prison by the latter's orders, and
of Philip.   was never seen again, dying in 1568. Charges have been
made that Philip caused his death, but he was probably
blameless, although he did plan to disinherit him. Philip
had no other son until 1571, when his eventual successor was
born, by his fourth wife. Certain other domestic troubles,
not divorced from scandal (although the evidence is in no
case conclusive), may be passed over, except to mention the
crowning grief of all. It early became clear that his son and
heir, the later Philip III, was a weak character. "God, who
has given me so many kingdoms," Philip is reported to have
said, "has denied me a son capable of ruling them." In
1598 Philip died. His last days were passed in extreme
physical suffering, which he endured with admirable resignation. Philip, like the Emperor Charles, his father, had

been indeed a great king, but he was a victim, as Charles had been, of a mistaken policy. Nevertheless, they had ruled Spain in her century of greatness, when Spain was not only the leading power in Europe, but was planting her institutions, for all time, in the vast domains of the Americas.

CHAPTER XXIV

A CENTURY OF DECLINE, 1598–1700

Spanish defeats of the sixteenth century.
THE unfortunate policies of Charles I and Philip II were continued during the seventeenth century in the reigns of Philip III, Philip IV, and Charles II, but Spain was no longer able to hold her front rank position in European affairs, especially after the buffets of fortune which fell to her lot in the reign of Philip IV. Not only that, but a decline also set in which affected Spanish civilization in all its phases. The impetus of Spain's greatness in the sixteenth century carried her along to yet loftier heights in some manifestations of her inner life, notably in art and literature, but even in these characteristics the decline was rapid and almost complete by the end of the reign of Charles II. Italy, France, and the Low Countries continued to absorb Spanish effort, but now it was Spain's turn to acknowledge defeat, while France, the great power of the century, took toll for the losses she had suffered at the hands of Charles I and Philip II. The unsuccessful Catalan revolt and the victorious war of the Portuguese for independence assisted to drain Spain of her resources, financial and otherwise, while the last-named event destroyed peninsula unity, carrying with it such of the Portuguese colonies as had not already been lost. Spain yielded the aggressive to her strongest opponent, and endeavored herself to maintain the defence. Nevertheless, great achievements were still the rule in the colonies, even if of a less showy type than formerly. Spain was still the conqueror and civilizer. On the other hand, the efforts of other nations to found colonies in lands claimed by Spain began to be successful, and this movement gathered force throughout the century,

258

together with the direct annexation of some lands which were already Spanish.

Philip III (1598–1621) was the first of three sovereigns, each of whom was weaker than his predecessor. The fifteenth-century practice of government by favorites was restored. Philip III turned over the political management of his kingdom to the Duke of Lerma, while he himself indulged in wasteful extravagances, punctuated by an equal excess in religious devotions. He had inherited wars with England and the Protestant Netherlands, but the first of these was brought to an end in 1604, shortly after the accession of James I of England. The war in the Low Countries was characterized by the same features which had marked its progress in the previous reign. Philip II had endeavored to solve the problem by making an independent kingdom of that region, under his daughter and her husband as the rulers, with a proviso for a reversion to Spain in case of a failure of the line. This measure was practically without effect, for Spanish troops and Spanish moneys continued to be the basis for the wars against the Dutch, or Protestant, element. Before the end of Philip III's reign the decision for a reversion to Spanish authority had already been made and accepted. There were two factors in the Dutch wars of the period worthy of mention. For one thing the Dutch became more bold on the seas, and began a remarkable career of maritime conquest which was to last well over half a century. As affecting Spain this new activity manifested itself mainly in piratical attacks on Spanish ships, or in descents upon Spanish coasts, but a number of Philip's Portuguese colonies were picked up by the Dutch. The Dutch wars also produced a man who was both a great soldier (a not uncommon type in that day of Spanish military importance) and a great statesman, who sensed the evil course which Spain was following in her European relations and argued against it, all to no avail. This man was Ambrosio Spínola. Spínola won victory upon victory from the Dutch, but was often obliged to rely on his personal estate for the funds with which to carry on the campaigns; so when the Dutch asked for a truce he favored the idea, and on this occasion his views

Philip III and Spanish relations with England, the Low Countries, and the Empire.

were allowed to prevail. A twelve-year truce was agreed upon in 1609, one condition of which was the recognition of the independence of the Protestant states. In 1618 the great conflict which has become known as the Thirty Years' War broke out in Germany, having its beginnings in a dispute between the Hapsburg emperor, Ferdinand, and the Protestant elector of the Palatinate. Spain entered the war on the side of Ferdinand, largely because of family reasons, but also in support of Catholicism. Spínola was sent into the Palatinate with a Spanish army, where he swept everything before him. Thus casually did Spain enter a war which was to be a thirty-nine years' conflict for her (1620–1659) and productive of her own undoing.

Relations with France, the Italian states, Turkey, and the pirates of the Barbary Coast.

Affairs with France were characterized by a bit of good fortune which postponed the evil day for Spain. Henry IV had reorganized the French kingdom until it reached a state of preparation which would have enabled it to take the offensive, a policy which Henry had in mind. The assassination of the French king, in 1610, prevented an outbreak of war between France and Spain at a time when the latter was almost certain to be defeated. Marie de Medici became regent in France, and chose to keep the peace. Italy was a constant source of trouble in this reign, due to the conflict of interests between the kings of Spain and the popes and princes of the Italian peninsula. There was a succession of petty wars or of the prospects of war, which meant that affairs were always in a disturbed condition. The Turks continued to be a peril to Europe, and their co-religionists and subjects in northern Africa were the terror of the seas. Spain rendered service to Europe by repulsing the attempts of the former to get a foothold in Italy, but could do nothing to check piratical ventures. The pirates of the Barbary Coast plied their trade both in the Mediterranean and along Spain's Atlantic coasts to their limits in the Bay of Biscay, while English and Dutch ships were active in the same pursuits.

Philip IV and Olivares.

The storm broke in the reign of Philip IV (1621–1665). Philip IV was only sixteen at the time of his accession to the throne. He had good intentions, and tried to interest himself in matters of government, but was of a frivolous and dissolute nature, unable to give consideration for any length of time to serious affairs. The result was the rule of another favorite, the Count-Duke of Olivares. Olivares was possibly the worst man who could have been chosen, precisely because he had sufficient ability to attempt the execution of his mistaken ideas. He was energetic, intelligent, and well educated, but was stubborn, proud, irascible, boastful, and insulting. He was able to make plans on a gigantic scale, and had real discernment as to the strength of Spain's enemies, but lacked the practical capacity to handle the details. The times were such as demanded a Spínola, but the counsels of Olivares prevailed, and their keynote was imperialism in Europe and a centralized absolutism in the peninsula.

The truce with the Dutch came to an end in 1621. Spínola urged that it be continued, but Olivares gave orders for the resumption of hostilities. No advantages of consequence were obtained by Spain, but the Dutch were again successful in their career on the seas. The Thirty Years' War continued to involve Spain. France, though Catholic and virtually ruled by a Catholic cardinal, Richelieu, was more intent on the development of the French state than upon the religious question, and aided the Protestants against their enemies. Richelieu did not bring France into the war until 1635, but, in the meantime, through grants of money and skilful diplomacy, he was able to make trouble for Spain in Italy and in the Low Countries. When at length it seemed as if the Catholic states might win, due largely to the effectiveness of the Spanish infantry, France entered the war on the side of the Protestant princes. Spanish troops continued to win battles, without profiting greatly because of the incessant difficulties from lack of funds. In 1643 the French, under Condé, defeated the Spaniards at Rocroy. The moral effect of this victory was tremendous, like the surrender of the ancient Spartans at the Island of Sphacteria, for it was the first time in some two centuries that the Spanish infantry had been defeated in pitched battle under nearly equal conditions. Henceforth defeats were no novelty. The tide had turned; Rocroy spelled Spain's doom as a great

Spanish losses in the Thirty Years' War.

power. The treaties of Westphalia in 1648 affected Spain only so far as concerned the war with the Protestant Netherlands. Dutch independence was reaffirmed, and the colonies which the Dutch had won, mainly from the Portuguese in the East Indies, were formally granted to them. The Catholic Netherlands remained Spanish. The war with France went on until 1659. In 1652 Cromwell offered Spain an alliance against France, but the price demanded was high; one of the conditions was that Spain should permit Englishmen to trade with the Spanish colonies, — an entering wedge for an English commercial supremacy which might easily be converted into political acquisition. Spain declined and Cromwell joined France. The English conquest of Jamaica in the ensuing war was the first great break in the solidarity of the actually occupied Spanish domain, marking a turning point in colonial history, as Rocroy had done in that of Europe. By the treaty of 1659 Spain gave up the Roussillon and Cerdagne, thus accepting the Pyrenees as the boundary between herself and France. Spain also surrendered Sardinia and large parts both of the Catholic Netherlands and of her former Burgundian possessions. The most fruitful clause in the treaty was that providing for the marriage of the Spanish princess, María Teresa, with Louis XIV of France. The former was to renounce for herself and her heirs any rights she or they might otherwise have to the Spanish throne, while a considerable dowry was to be paid by Spain on her behalf. The results of this marriage will be mentioned presently.

Catalan discontent.

Intimately related to the wars just referred to was the Catalan revolt. The Catalans had long been a nation so far as separate language and institutions go, and their traditions compared well with those of Castile, which had now come to dominate in the Spanish state. The whole course of the revolt is illustrative of the difficulties under which Spain labored in this era of European wars. The Catalans had objected for centuries, even before the union with Castile, to the policy of centralization and absolutism of the kings, alleging their charter rights which were thus contravened. Such acts as the failure of the kings to call the Catalan

Cortes, the increases in taxation, or the levying of taxes like those paid in Castile, and the introduction of the Castilian Inquisition had been unfavorably received in the past. Now came the monarchical designs of Olivares, coupled with the unavoidable exigencies of the wars, to heighten the discontent. Aside from the increased taxation there were two matters to which the Catalans were strenuously opposed on the ground that they were against their legal rights, — the maintenance of foreign troops (even Castilians and Aragonese being so regarded) in Catalonia and the enjoyment of public office by persons who were not Catalans. Furthermore they objected to the employment of Catalan troops in foreign countries, holding that their obligations were limited to defending Catalonia, and similarly they maintained that funds raised in Catalonia should not be used for wars outside that province. Philip IV tried to procure a subsidy from the Catalan *Cortes* in 1626, but the grant was denied. Another attempt was made in 1632, on which occasion Olivares imprudently followed the methods of Charles I at the time of the *Cortes* of Santiago-Coruña. He got the funds, but his action caused great dissatisfaction in the province. Meanwhile the danger of an invasion from France had led to the sending of troops to Catalonia, and constant friction followed their arrival. The imperfect military discipline of that age, together with the annoyances usually inseparable from the presence of armies, resulted in many abuses, which were resented even to the point of armed conflict; as early as 1629, eleven years before the outbreak, there was a bloody encounter between the citizens and the soldiery at Barcelona. The irksome requirement calling upon the towns to lodge the troops was also productive of ill feeling. By law the most that could be demanded was the use of a room, a bed, a table, fire, salt, vinegar, and service, while all else must be paid for. Lack of funds was such, however, that more than this was exacted. In addition to this there came an order from Madrid calling for the imposition of the *quinto,* or fifth, of the revenues of the municipalities. France took advantage of the situation to fan the flame of discontent and to win certain Catalan nobles of the frontier to her side. Nevertheless, when the French invaded the Roussillon in 1639 the Catalans rushed to arms and helped to expel them early in 1640.

Beginning of the Catalan revolt.

The questions of lodging the soldiers and of procuring additional funds continued to provoke trouble. Olivares said in an open meeting of the *Consejo Real* that the Catalans ought to be made to contribute in proportion to their wealth. Later he ordered an enforced levy of Catalan troops for use in Italy, and stated in the decree so providing that it was necessary to proceed without paying attention to "provincial pettiness" (*menudencias provinciales*). The impulse for the outbreak proceeded, however, from the conflicts between the soldiers and the peasantry of the country districts, especially on account of the excesses of the retreating royal troops at the time of the French invasion of the Roussillon. Curiously enough, the peasantry acted very largely from religious motives. Many of the soldiers were utter foreigners to the Catalans, — such, for example, as the Italians and the Irish, both of which elements were present in considerable numbers. To the ignorant peasants these strange-mannered people, who were Catholics in fact, seemed most certainly heretics. Attacks on the soldiery began in the mountain districts early in 1640, and soon extended to the cities as well. In June a serious riot occurred in Barcelona, during which the hated royal viceroy was killed. That act marked the triumph of the revolution and the beginning of the war.

The war against the Catalans.

It is possible that a policy of moderation might still have avoided the conflict, but such action was not taken. The war lasted nineteen years, and was fought bitterly until 1653. In 1640 the Catalans formed a republic, and made an alliance with France, putting themselves under the protection of the French monarchy. The republic was short-lived; in 1641 the monarchical form returned, with a recognition of the king of France as ruler. French troops aided the Catalans in many expeditions, but in this very fact lay the remedy for the grievances against Spain. The Catalans found that French officials and French soldiers committed the same abuses as those which they had objected to in the case of Castile. Coupled with a statement of Philip IV that he had never intended to interfere with the Catalan *fueros*, or charter rights (although Olivares certainly had so intended), this proved to be the turning point. Philip confirmed the charters in 1653, but the fighting went on in certain regions until 1659, when Catalonia was recognized as part of Spain in the treaty of peace with France. The war had one good result; it occasioned the dismissal of Olivares in 1643. Nevertheless, the evil had been done beyond repair, though the dispute had experienced a turn for the better, dating from Olivares' deprivation from office.

Meanwhile, Olivares had involved Spain in another direction. From the time of the acquisition of Portugal by Philip II that region had been exceedingly well treated by the Spanish kings : no public offices were given to any but Portuguese; no military or naval forces and no taxes were required for purely Spanish objects; the Portuguese colonies were left to the Portuguese, and the route around Africa to the Far East was closed to Spaniards ; Lisbon continued to be the centre of Portuguese colonial traffic, as Seville was for Spain ; and even the members of the House of Braganza, despite their dangerous claim to the throne, were allowed to remain in Portugal, and were greatly favored. Furthermore, Philip II abolished customs houses between Portugal and Castile, made advantageous administrative improvements (among other things, reforming colonial management, on the Spanish model), and attempted something in the way of public works. The annexation weighed very lightly on the country. The king was represented by a viceroy; there were a few Spanish troops in Portugal ; and some taxes were collected, though they were far from heavy in amount. Spain has been charged with the responsibility for the loss of many Portuguese colonies, on the ground that Portugal became involved in the wars against the Spanish kings, and therefore open to the attack of Spain's enemies. There is reason for believing, however, that the connection served rather as a pretext than a cause ; this was an age when the North European powers were engaging in colonial enterprises, and it is worthy of note that the Dutch, who were the principal successors to the Portuguese possessions, con-

Mildness of Spanish rule in Portugal.

tinued to make conquests from Portugal after they had formed an alliance with that country in the war of Portuguese independence from Spain. In fact, very little passed into foreign hands prior to the Portuguese separation from the Spanish crown as compared with what was lost afterward.

The im-
perialism
of Olivares
and the
uprising in
Portugal.   While the nobility and the wealthy classes favored the union with Spain, there were strong elements in the country of a contrary opinion, for whom leaders were to be found in the lower ranks of the secular clergy and especially among the Jesuits. The masses of the people still hated Spaniards; several generations were necessary before that traditional feeling could be appreciably lessened. A current of opposition manifested itself as early as the reign of Philip III, when the Duke of Lerma, the king's favorite minister, proposed to raise the prohibition maintained against the Jews forbidding them to sell their goods when emigrating, and planned to grant them civil equality with Christians. This had coincided with a slight increase in taxation to produce discontent. It was natural that the imperialistic Olivares should wish to introduce a radical change in the relations of Spain and Portugal. He early addressed the king on the advisability of bringing about a veritable amalgamation of the two countries, and suggested that Portuguese individuals should be given some offices in Castile, and Castilians in like manner awarded posts in Portugal. When this purpose became known it was used as one of the principal means of stirring up opposition to Spain, on the ground that Portugal was to be deprived of her autonomy. The renewal of legislation such as that proposed by the Duke of Lerma with respect to the Jews and an increase in taxation added to the dissatisfaction in Portugal to such an extent that there were several riots. Spain's financial difficulties arising from the European wars led Olivares to turn yet more insistently to Portugal, and in the year 1635 new and heavier taxes began to be imposed, together with the collection of certain ecclesiastical rents which had been granted to the king by the pope. This produced the first outbreak against the royal authority. A revolution was started at Évora in 1637 which soon spread to all parts of Portugal, but the nobles, the wealthy classes, and the Duke of Braganza were not in favor of the movement, and it was soon suppressed. The condition of affairs which had provoked it continued, however, and was accentuated by new burdens and fresh departures from the agreement of Philip II. Taxes became heavier still; Portuguese troops were required to serve in the Low Countries; and the Duke of Braganza, of whom Olivares was unreasonably suspicious, was appointed viceroy of Milan, with a view to getting him out of Portugal. It was this last measure which was to bring about a fresh and more determined uprising than that of 1637. The duke refused the appointment, whereupon Olivares completely changed front, possibly with a view to concealment of his real suspicions, and made Braganza military governor of Portugal, besides sending him funds with which to repair the fortifications of the kingdom. The duke would almost certainly have been satisfied with this arrangement, had it not been for his wife, whose ambitious character was not duly taken into account by Olivares. This lady was a Spaniard of the family of the dukes of Medina Sidonia, but she was desirous of being a queen, even though it should strike a blow at her native land. She conspired to bring about a Portuguese revolution headed by her husband, who should thus become king of Portugal. The Catalonian outbreak of 1640 furnished a pretext and the propitious occasion desired. The Duke of Braganza and the nobility generally were ordered to join the royal army in suppressing the Catalans. Instead, the nobles rebelled, and the revolution broke out on the first of December in the same year, 1640. Fortresses were seized, and the Duke of Braganza was proclaimed as João (or John) IV, king of Portugal.

The war lasted twenty-eight years, but, although it might well have been considered as more important than any of the problems of the time, other than the equally momentous Catalan revolt, it was not actively prosecuted by Spain. Spain was engaged in too many other wars, to which she gave perhaps an undue share of her attention, and was more than ever beset by her chronic difficulty of lack of funds. France, England, and the Protestant Netherlands gave help to Portu-

The war of Portuguese independence.

gal at different times, whereby the last-named was able to maintain herself against the weak attacks of Spain. The decisive battle was fought at Villaviciosa in 1665, but it was not until 1668, in the reign of Charles II, that peace was made. Portugal was recognized as independent, retaining such of her former colonies as had not already been taken by the Dutch, — with one exception; the post of Ceuta, in northern Africa, remained Spanish, — the only reminder of Spain's great opportunity to establish peninsula unity through the union with Portugal.

Still other difficulties arose in Italy and in Spain to harass the reign of Philip IV. There were revolts in Sicily in 1646–1647, and in Naples in 1647–1648, both of which were put down. An Aragonese plot was discovered, and there was no uprising. A similar plot in Andalusia was headed by the Duke of Medina Sidonia, captain general of the province and brother of the new queen of Portugal. This too was uncovered in time to prevent an outbreak. In Vizcaya there was a serious revolt, growing out of an alleged tampering with local privileges, but it was eventually put down. In fine, the reign had been one of disaster. Olivares had been the chief instrument to bring it about, but, after all, he only represented the prevailing opinion and traditional policies. The moment of reckoning had come.

The reign of Charles II (1665–1700) was a period of waiting for what seemed likely to be the end, unless fate should intervene to give a new turn to affairs. The king himself was doubly in need of a regent, for he was only four years old when he succeeded to the throne and was also weak and sick in mind and body. He was subject to epileptic fits, on which account he was termed Charles "the Bewitched" (*el Hechizado*), and many people believed that he was indeed possessed of a Devil. This disgusting, but pitiful, creature was expected to die at any moment, but he lived to rule, though little more than in name, for thirty-five years. The whole reign was one of plotting for the succession, since it early became clear that Charles II could have no heir. There was a pro-French party, a pro-Austrian party, and a very strong group which favored a Spaniard, Juan of Austria, illegitimate son of a Spanish king, as his predecessor of the same name had been.   Juan of Austria became virtual ruler in 1677, but died in 1679, thus eliminating the only prominent claimant in Spain.   France, at the height of her power under Louis XIV, was unwilling to wait for the death of Charles II before profiting by Spanish weakness, and therefore engaged in several wars of aggression, directed primarily against Spain's possessions in the Low Countries and against the Protestant Netherlands.   In many of these wars other powers fought on the side of Spain and the Dutch, notably the Holy Roman Emperor, many princes of Germany, and Sweden, while England and the pope joined the allies against the French military lord in the last war of the period.   Four times Spain was forced into conflict, in 1667-1668, 1672-1678, 1681-1684, and 1689-1697.   Province after province in northern Europe was wrested away, until, after the last war, when Louis XIV had achieved his greatest success, little would have remained, but for an unusual spirit of generosity on the part of the French king.   Instead of taking further lands from Spain, he restored some which he had won in this and previous wars.   The reason was that he now hoped to procure the entire dominions of Spain for his own family. French aggressions.

The leader of the party favoring the Hapsburg, or Austrian, succession in Spain was the queen-mother, María Ana, herself of the House of Austria.   After many vicissitudes she at length seemed to have achieved a victory, when she brought about the marriage of Charles II to an Austrian princess in 1689, the same year in which the king's former wife, a French princess, had died.   The situation was all the more favorable in that Louis XIV declared war against Spain in that year for the fourth time in the reign.   The very necessities of the war, added to the now chronic bad administration and the general state of misery in Spain, operated, however, to arouse discontent and to provoke opposition to the party in power.   Thus the French succession was more popular, even during the war, than that of the allied House of Austria.   After the war was over, the French propaganda was established on a solid basis, for it was evident, now, that Charles II could not long survive.   Louis XIV put forward Plottings of the Austrian and French parties for the succession.

his grandson, Philip of Anjou, as a candidate, and the Holy Roman Emperor urged the claims of his son, the Archduke Charles. Not only did Philip have the weaker hereditary claim, but he also had the renunciation of his grandmother, María Teresa, wife of Louis XIV, against him. The last-named objection was easily overcome, since Spain had never paid the promised dowry of María Teresa, wherefore Louis XIV held that the renunciation was of no effect.

Success of the French party.

The fight, after all, was a political one, and not a mere determination of legal right, and in this respect Louis XIV and his candidate, Philip, had the advantage, through skilful diplomacy. The French party in Madrid was headed by Cardinal Portocarrero, a man of great influence, assisted by Harcourt, the French ambassador. The imperial ambassador, Harrach, and Stanhope, the representative of England, worked together; the union of France and Spain under Bourbon rulers, who would probably be French-controlled, represented a serious upsetting of the balance of power, wherefore England desired the succession of the Archduke Charles, who at that time was not a probable candidate for the imperial crown. For several years Madrid was the scene of one of the most fascinating diplomatic battles in European history. The feeble-minded king did not know what to do, and asked advice on all sides, but could not make up his mind about the succession. The Austrian party had his ear, however, through his Austrian wife, and through the king's confessor, who was one of their group, but by a clever strike of Portocarrero's the king was persuaded that his wife was plotting to kill him, and was induced to change confessors, this time accepting a member of the French party. To divide his opponents Louis XIV proposed the dismemberment of Spain and her possessions among the leading claimants, assigning Spain, Flanders, and the colonies to a third candidate, the Prince of Bavaria. The French king did not intend that any such division should take place, and in any event the Bavarian prince soon died, but through measures of this type Louis XIV eventually contrived to supplant in office and in influence nearly all who opposed the Bourbon succession. Meanwhile, the unfortunate king was stirred up and worried, although possibly without evil design, so that his health was more and more broken and his mentality disordered to the point of idiocy, hastening his death. Strange medicines and exorcisms were used in order to cast out the Devil with which he was told he was possessed, exciting the king to the point of frenzy. In 1700 Louis XIV abandoned his course of dissimulation to such an extent that it became clear that he would endeavor to procure all the Spanish dominions for Philip. Henceforth it was a struggle between the two principal claimants for exclusive rule. The wretched Spanish monarch was at length obliged to go to bed by what was clearly his last illness. Even then he was not left in peace, and the plotting continued almost to the very end. On October 3, Philip was named by the dying king as sole heir to all his dominions. On November 1, Charles II died, and with him passed the rule of the House of Austria.

CHAPTER XXV

SOCIAL DEVELOPMENTS, 1516–1700

Principal events in the social history of the era.

As compared with the two preceding eras there was little in this period strikingly new in social history. In the main, society tended to become more thoroughly modern, but along lines whose origins dated farther back. The most marked novelty in Spain was the conversion of the Mudéjares of Aragon, Catalonia, and Valencia, followed less than a century later by the expulsion of the Moriscos from every part of Spain. The most remarkable phase of social history of the time, however, was the subjection, conversion, and to a certain extent the civilization of millions of Indians in the Americas. The work was thorough enough to mark those lands permanently with the impress of Spain.

Gradual approximation of the nobility to present-day society.

By a process of natural evolution from the practices current in the reign of the Catholic Kings the nobles came to exhibit characteristics very similar to those of present-day society. They now went to court if they could, or else to the nearest large city, where they became a bourgeois nobility. Those who remained on their estates were soon forgotten. Through social prestige the nobles were still able to procure not only the honorary palace posts but also the majority of the greater political and military commands. Now and then, an untitled *letrado* would attain to a viceroyalty or other high position, but these cases were the exception. In this way, the great body of the nobles were able to counteract the economic losses of their class occasioned by the new importance of mercantile and industrial wealth. Nevertheless, the wealthiest men of the times were nobles, with whom the richest of middle-class merchants could

272

hardly compare in material possessions. The more extraordinary accumulations of wealth, based on vast lands and the institution of primogeniture, were confined to a few of the greatest nobles of the land, however. The vast horde of the *segundones* and others of the lesser nobility found service as before at court, or in the train of some great noble, in the army, and in the church. The nobles retained most of the privileges they had previously enjoyed, but except in Aragon proper lost much of the political jurisdiction they had formerly exercised over their own lands. The sentiment in favor of the royal authority was now so strong that any limitation on the power of the sovereign was viewed with disapproval. The jurisdiction which the lords retained was limited by many royal rights of intervention, such as the superior authority of the king's law, or the royal institution of the *pesquisa*. Some remnants of the lords' former political and social power over their vassals existed, but in general the relation was the purely civil one of landlord and tenant. In Aragon, despite attempts to effect reforms, the lords still possessed seigniorial authority, accompanied by the irksome incidents of serfdom; required personal services of their vassals; collected tributes of a medieval character; exercised a paternal authority (such as that of permitting or refusing their vassals a right to marry); and had the power of life and death.

The hierarchy of the nobility was definitely established in this period. At the top, representing the medieval *ricos-hombres*, were the grandees (*Grandes*) and the "titles" (*Títulos*). The principal difference between the two was that the former were privileged to remain covered in the presence of the king and to be called "cousins" of the monarch, while those of the second grade might only be called "relatives," — empty honors, which were much esteemed, however, as symbolic of rank. These groups monopolized all titles such as marquis, duke, count, and prince. Below them were the *caballeros* and the *hidalgos*. The word *hidalgos* was employed to designate those nobles of inferior rank without fortune, lands, jurisdiction, or high public office. The desire for the noble rank of *hidalgo* and the

Hierarchy of the nobility.

T

Social
vanity.

vanity marked by the devising of family shields became a national disease, and resulted in fact in the increase of the *hidalgo* class. The people of Guipúzcoa claimed that they were all *hidalgos*, and received the royal recognition of their pretension. Measures were taken to check this dangerous exemplification of social pride, but on the other hand the treasury found the sale of rights of *hidalguía* a profitable source of income. In 1541 there were less than 800,000 taxpayers in Castile, but over 100,000 *hidalgos*. The nobles did not at once forget their medieval practices of duelling, private war, plotting, and violence. There were instances of these throughout the era, and in Aragon and Majorca they were almost continuous. Nevertheless, the situation did not become so serious as it had been in the past; it merely represented the deeply rooted force of noble tradition, which objected to any submission to discipline. Both the hierarchy of the nobility, with all its incidents of broad estates, jurisdictions, class pride, and vanity, and the irresponsible practices of the nobles passed over into the Americas.

Survivals
of medie-
valism
among the
nobles.

Advance
of the
plebeian
classes
through
the rise
of the
merchants
and the
letrados.

While there were many different categories of free Christian society the essential grades were those of nobles (or members of the clergy) and plebeians. There were many rich merchants of the middle class who aped the nobility in entailing their estates and in luxurious display, and there were learned men who received distinguished honors or exemptions from duties to the state, but in social prestige they could not compare with the lowest *hidalgo*. Many of them became noble by royal favor, and especially was this way open to the learned class of the *letrados*. These men provided lawyers and administrative officers for the state, and, as such, occupied positions which put them on a level, at least in authority, with the nobles. The advance of the merchants and the *letrados* represented a gain for the plebeian class as a whole, for any free Christian might get to be one or the other and even become ennobled. The economic decline of Spain in the seventeenth century was a severe blow to the merchants, while the *letrados* were unpopular with nobles and plebeians alike; nevertheless, thoughtful men agreed that the regeneration of the country must come from these two elements.

The masses were poor, as always, but their legal condition, except in Aragon, had been improved. There were many social wars in Aragon throughout the period, but the serfs, unable to act together, could not overcome their oppressors. Something was done by the kings through the incorporation into the crown of seigniorial estates where abuses were most pronounced. The same state of chronic warfare existed in Catalonia, where the rural population, though now freed from serfdom, was still subject to certain seigniorial rights. By the end of the period the victory of the plebeians was clear, and the ties which bound them to the lords were loosened. The social aspects of the civil wars in Castile, Valencia, and Majorca at the outset of the reign of Charles I have already been referred to. These revolts failed, and there were no similar great uprisings of the Christian masses in these regions, but the tendency of the nobility to go to court and the expulsion of the Moriscos were to operate to break down the survivals of seigniorial authority. *Improvement in the legal condition of the masses.*

Although objections were raised to the enslavement of the Indians in the Americas, the institution of slavery itself was generally recognized; even charitable and religious establishments possessed slaves. Moslem prisoners and negroes (acquired through war or purchase), together with their children, made up the bulk of this class, although there were some slaves of white race. Conversion to Christianity did not procure emancipation, but the slaves were allowed to earn something for themselves with which to purchase their freedom. Certain restrictions — such, for example, as the prohibition against their living in quarters inhabited by newly converted Christians, or against their entering the guilds — were placed upon them once they had become free. Only a little higher in status than the slaves were the Egipcianos, or gypsies. About the middle of the fifteenth century they had entered Spain for the first time by way of Catalonia, and, thenceforth, groups of them wandered about the peninsula, stealing and telling fortunes for a living, and having a government of their own. A law of *Slavery.* *The gypsies.*

1499 required them to settle down in towns and ply honest trades on pain of expulsion from Spain or of enslavement, but the gypsies neither left Spain nor abandoned their nomadic ways, and they were a continual problem to the kings of the House of Austria. Various royal orders provided that they must take up an occupation, although their choice was virtually limited by law to the cultivation of the soil; they were not to live in the smaller villages, were forbidden to use their native language, dress, or names, or to employ their customs in marriage and other matters, and were prohibited from dwelling in a separate quarter of their own. Fear lest the Christian population become contaminated by gypsy superstitions and a regard for public security were the guiding motives for this legislation. Severe penalties were attached, but the evil was not eradicated; similar laws had to be enacted as late as the eighteenth century.

Forced conversion of the Mudéjares of the kingdom of Aragon. After the time of the Catholic Kings there were no free Mudéjares in Castile, although there were many Moriscos, but in Aragon, Catalonia, and especially in Valencia the Mudéjares were numerous. Many elements, including the majority of the clergy (the officers of the Inquisition in particular), the king, and the Christian masses were in favor of their forcible conversion with a view to the establishment of religious unity in the country, although other reasons were alleged as well. The nobles were warmly opposed, mainly on economic grounds because the Mudéjares formed the principal element among their agricultural workers. Many of the higher clergy joined with them for the same reason, although some of them voiced their objections on the ground that compulsory baptism would only result in apostasy. During the social war in Valencia early in the reign of Charles I the popular faction had forcibly converted a number of the Mudéjares who had fought against them on the side of the lords. The question arose whether these baptisms were valid. Charles decided that they were, and ordered the children of the Mudéjares, who had thus unwillingly become Moriscos, to be baptized also. This provoked a storm of protest on the part of the lords, for the continuance of such a policy might result in emigrations or uprisings, much to their detriment. They cited the royal oath of Ferdinand and of Charles himself to the *Cortes* of Aragon not to compel the Mudéjares to abjure their faith, but this difficulty was easily overcome. The pope was persuaded to absolve Charles from his oath, and gave his consent to the forcible conversion of the free Mudéjares, on pain of perpetual enslavement or expulsion from Spain. In 1525 Charles published a decree in accordance with the terms of the papal license. The objections of the nobles and the *Cortes* were overruled, and several isolated rebellions were put down. While many Mudéjares went to Africa, thousands accepted conversion, and, although it was clear that they did not do so of their own free will, were at once made subject to the usual rules applying to converts, including the jurisdiction of the Inquisition. Soon afterward, however, Charles consented to exempt them from religious persecution for a number of years.

The problem of religious unity was now officially solved; all Spain legally had become Christian. The Moriscos were the subject of grave suspicions, however, as regards their orthodoxy, and with reason, since most of them continued to be Mohammedans in fact. The harsh legislation of other days was resurrected, and was applied with even greater severity. Prohibitions extended to the use of anything reminiscent of their former religion or customs, such as amulets, the Arabic language, Arabic names, their special form of dress, their characteristic songs and dances, and their habit of taking baths. The laws applying to Granada were particularly harsh, provoking the already mentioned war of 1568–1571. After the suppression of that rebellion and the deportation of the Granadine Moriscos to other parts of Castile, steps were taken to prevent their return and to keep them under surveillance. The Moriscos were not allowed to dwell together in a district of their own; they might not stay out overnight, or change their residence without permission; and their children were ordered to be brought up in the homes of Christians of long standing, or at any rate to be sent to Christian schools. Prohibitions

Failure of the attempts to Christianize the Moriscos.

against carrying arms and other measures designed to prevent the Moriscos from endangering the peace were general
throughout Spain. Gradually the idea arose that the best
thing to do would be to get rid of the Moriscos in some way.
In the first place the attempt to convert them had been a
failure. The Moriscos were not altogether to blame, for
no adequate steps had been taken to instruct them in the
Christian religion. Orders to do so had been issued, but for
many reasons they were difficult to execute. Such a task
would have been enormously expensive, and the funds were
not at hand; few Christian priests were competent to serve
as instructors, since not many of them knew Arabic; there
existed the serious obstacle of the hatred of the Moriscos
for the Christian religion, due to the bad treatment they had
received and their fear of the Inquisition; and the nobles
threw the weight of their influence against molesting the
Moriscos in this way as in others. In the second place, the
very hatred of the Christian masses for the Moriscos had
rendered their conversion difficult. Some of the charges
made against them would seem to indicate that prejudice
was the real foundation of this animosity. It was said that
the Moriscos ate so little meat and drank so little wine that
Christians had to pay nearly all of the *alcabala*, or the tax
on their sale; they were denounced because they monopolized
the industrial arts and trades, to the disadvantage of Christians; complaints were made that they always married,
never becoming monks, wherefore their numbers increased
more rapidly than those of the Christian population. Thus
their frugality, industry, and domesticity were made the
subject of accusations. Naturally there were more serious
grounds of complaint than these, such as the inevitable
private conflicts of old Christians and Moriscos, but differences in race, religion, and general customs were enough to
cause popular hatred in that day, when intolerance was the
rule. In the third place, it must be said in measurable
justification of Spanish policy that the Moriscos did represent a danger to the state. They were numerous, and, naturally enough, hostile to the government; time and again
they were proved to have fostered or taken part in uprisings

and to have worked in conjunction with Moslem pirates; finally, the likelihood of a fresh Moslem descent from Africa, assisted by Spanish Moriscos, was not to be disregarded.

The failure of the attempts to convert the Moriscos had long been recognized, and the question arose what to do with them. Some men proposed a general massacre, or sending them to sea and scuttling the ships. Others suggested that they be sent to the Americas to work in the mines, — a solution which might have had interesting consequences. From about 1582, however, the idea of expelling them from Spain became more and more general, and was favored by men of the highest character, — for example, by Juan de Ribera, archbishop of Valencia (canonized in the eighteenth century). The expulsion was virtually decided upon as early as 1602, but the decrees were postponed for several years. In September, 1609, the expulsion from Valencia was ordered. All Moriscos except certain specified groups were required to be at various designated ports within three days; they were allowed to carry such movable property as they could, while the rest of their possessions was to go to their lords, — a sop to the nobles, for whom the expulsion meant great economic loss; they were informed that they would be taken to Africa free of charge, but were told to carry as much food as they could. Six per cent of the Morisco men and their families were excepted by the decree, so that they might instruct the laborers who should take the place of the expelled Moriscos. Various other groups, such as slaves, small children (under certain specified conditions), and those whose conversion was regarded as unquestionably sincere, were also exempted. The Moriscos were unwilling to avail themselves of the exceptions in their favor, and a general exodus began. The decree was cruelly executed, despite the government's attempt to prevent it. Murder, robbery, and outrages against women went unpunished; even the soldiers sent to protect the Moriscos were guilty of these abuses. Many Moriscos were sold into slavery, especially children, who were taken from their parents. When news came that the peoples of northern Africa had given a harsh reception to the first of the Moriscos to disembark there,

Expulsion of the Moriscos.

many preferred to take the chances of revolt rather than submit to expulsion, but these uprisings were easily put down. Decrees for the other parts of Spain soon followed; the decree for Castile proper, Extremadura, and La Mancha came in the same year, 1609; for Granada, Andalusia, and Aragon in 1610; and for Catalonia and Murcia in 1611, although the execution of the decree for Murcia was postponed until 1614. The terms of all, while varying in details, resembled that of Valencia. More time was given, usually a month; the permission to carry away personalty was accompanied by a prohibition against the taking of money or precious metals; and in some cases all children under seven were required to remain in Spain when their parents elected to go to Africa. On this account many Moriscos made the voyage to Africa by way of France, on the pretence that they were going to the latter country, thus retaining their children.

Failure of the expulsions to stamp out the Morisco and Jewish elements in Spanish blood.
Various estimates have been made as to the number of the expelled Moriscos. It is probable that some half a million were obliged to emigrate. Many remained in Spain, forming outlaw bands in the mountains, or hiding under the protection of their lords, while thousands had long since merged with the Christian population. Almost from the start a current of re-immigration set in, for, after all, the Moriscos had in many respects become Spaniards, and they found that conditions in the lands to which they had gone were far from agreeable. Throughout the seventeenth century laws were enacted against returning Moriscos, but were of such little effect that the government virtually admitted its powerlessness in the matter. Southern Spain and the east coast below Catalonia remained strongly Moslem in blood, and the other provinces of the peninsula were not a little affected as well, but as regards religion the Morisco element was gradually merged, and this matter never became a serious problem again. Similar questions arose over returning Jews, who came back to Spain for much the same reasons the Moriscos did. They were not nearly so numerous, however, wherefore their return did not represent such a political danger as did that of the Moriscos.
The legal status of the family underwent no striking

change in this period, except that the victory of Roman principles was more and more confirmed. The decisions of the Council of Trent (1545–1563), a famous general council of the Catholic Church, prohibited divorce, clandestine marriage, and in general any kind of marital union not made according to the solemnities and forms of the church, and these principles became law in Spain, but they represented tendencies which had long before appeared in the *Partidas* and the *Leyes de Toro*. Unions lacking the sanction of the law did not disappear; rather they were one of the prominent features of the immorality of the times. It was in its economic aspects that the family experienced its most marked change, and this was due to the exceptional favor with which the institution of primogeniture had come to be viewed, keeping pace with the vanity and the furor for ennoblement of the age. The very extension of the practice was its saving grace, for not only the great nobles but also persons of lesser note, including plebeians with not too vast estates, were wont to leave their properties to the eldest son; thus accumulation in the hands of a very few was avoided. For the same reason the crown often favored the custom for the smaller holdings, but restricted it in the case of the *latifundia*, — for example, in the prohibition issued against the combining of two such great estates. The individualism and capitalism of the Roman law was most marked of all in matters of property. One interesting attempt was made to get around the laws against usury through the purchase of annuities, the *censo consignativo*. Popular opinion, reinforced by the ideas of the moralists and jurisconsults and even by a bull of the pope, opposed the practice, and it did not survive. Despite the supremacy of the Roman ideas there were many writings of a socialistic character citing the collectivism of the Peruvian Incas or other such states of society as desirable of adoption in Spain. The philosopher Luis Vives, for example, favored a redistribution of natural resources and their equal enjoyment by all.

While the law frowned upon the spirit of association, even prohibiting the founding of new *cofradías*, the guilds enjoyed

Influence of Roman principles on the institutions of the family and private property.

Evolution of the guilds.

their greatest era of prosperity. This was due in part to the intervention of the state, which supplanted the municipalities in control of the institution. State regulation, even in technical matters, went further than it had in the fifteenth century. Despite government interest, as evidenced by the according of numerous privileges, the germs of the decline of the guilds were already apparent at the close of the seventeenth century. The exclusive spirit of the guilds whereby they endeavored to keep trade in the hands of their own members and their families, without admitting others who were competent to belong, was one cause of this decline, while their loss of liberty (due to government intervention) and the strife within and without the guild were contributing factors. One novelty of the era was the growing distinction between the manual arts and the liberal professions, the latter of which rose to a higher consideration. Thus lawyers, notaries, and doctors were rated above those engaged in manual labors, while there was also a recognized hierarchy among the last-named, from the workers in gold, silver, jewelry, and rich cloths down to the drivers of mules. The great association of the *Mesta* still enjoyed wide powers, as did also that of the carriers.

Low moral tone of the era.

In laxness of morals and in luxury this period was much like the two preceding. It seems worse, but this may be due to the greater variety of materials at hand for study, such as books of travel, novels, plays, satires, letters, laws, and the frequently appearing "relations of events," which in that day took the place occupied by the modern newspaper. A Spanish writer has characterized the practices of the time in the following language: "The ideal of an exaggerated sense of honor, chivalric quixotism, religious fanaticism, and the exalted predominance of form over the essence of things ruled Spanish society of the seventeenth century, absolutely and tyrannically. Duels and stabbings at every moment to sustain the least question of etiquette or courtesy; scandalous conflicts of jurisdiction between the highest tribunals of state; absurd and ridiculous projects to make silver without silver, fomented by the leading ministers; extremely costly and showy feasts to solemnize

ordinary events, while cities, islands, provinces, and even
kingdoms were being lost through bad government and
worse administration; frequent and pompous public processions; blind belief in the miraculous virtue of some medal,
stamp, or old rag of Mother Luisa or some other impostor;
politico-religious sermons within and without the royal
palace; the most abominable and nefarious sins scattered
to an almost unbelievable extent among all classes of Madrid
society; the vice of gambling converted into a profession
by many persons; and, in fine, the censure of our court, by
those who formed part of it and by those who did not, for
its astonishing abundance and its depraved life of strumpets
and wenches. . . It is true that there were men of high
degree who preferred the coarse sackcloth of the religious
to the rich clothing of brocade and gold, and military leaders
who exchanged the sword for the monkish girdle, but these
were exceptions, which by the very fewness of their numbers
stand out the more strongly from the general stock of that
society, so accustomed to laziness, hypocrisy, routine, and
external practices as it was, removed from the true paths of
virtue, wisdom, and progress." If to these characteristics
there are added those of the misery and ignorance of the
common people, and if an exception is made of the men devoted to intellectual pursuits, the above is fairly representative of Spanish society in this period. Loose practices were
prevalent in excessive degree at Madrid, which had become
the capital in the time of Philip II. While such a state of
affairs is not unusual in all great capitals, immorality infected
all classes of society in Madrid, and little if any stigma attached in the matter. Philip IV had thirty-two illegitimate
children, and Charles I and even the somewhat sombre
Philip II were not without reproach. Much that is unspeak-
able was prevalent, and gambling was generally indulged in.
Lack of discipline also manifested itself in frequent duelling,
despite prohibitive laws, and in the turbulence of the people
on different occasions; university students were somewhat
notorious in this respect, indulging in riots which were not
free from incidents of an unsavory character. Other cities
were little better than Madrid, and those of the south and

east, where Moslem blood had been most plentiful, especially Seville and Valencia, had a yet worse reputation; Valencia had even a European notoriety for its licentious customs. These practices passed over into the Americas in an exaggerated form. The Andalusian blood of the conquerors and their adventurous life amidst subject races were not conducive to self-restraint. These evils were not to be without effect in the moulding of the Spanish American peoples. In the smaller Spanish towns and villages there was probably less vice, but there was more ignorance and greater lack of public security. Bands of robbers infested the country.

Royal extravagance.

In luxury as in immorality the example was set by the kings themselves. Some of its manifestations were meritorious (except that expenditures were out of proportion to the resources and needs of the state), especially the encouragement of art through the purchase of paintings and the construction of palaces. But if Charles I and Philip II were lavish, Philip III and Philip IV were extravagant. Both of these kings, in addition to their fondness for the theatre, bull-fighting, dancing, and hunting, were responsible for the most ostentatious display on occasions of court celebrations. When Philip III went to San Sebastián in 1615 to attend the double wedding which was to bind together the houses of Austria and Bourbon, he was accompanied by a train of 74 carriages, 174 litters, 190 state coaches, 2750 saddle mules, 374 beasts of burden (of which 128 had coverings embroidered with the royal coat of arms), 1750 mules with silver bells, and 6500 persons, besides an escort of 4000 Guipuzcoans. Equal pomp and extravagance marked the reception to the Archduchess María Ana of Austria when she came to Spain as the fiancée of Philip IV; similarly, the entertainment accorded the Prince of Wales (the later Charles I of England) and the Duke of Buckingham when they visited Spain early in the reign of Philip IV; and likewise the various masquerades during the period of Olivares, one of which is said to have cost over 300,000 ducats (nearly $5,000,000). It would seem that war was not alone responsible for the drains on the Spanish treasury. There

was a decline in expenditures in the reign of Charles II, due
principally to the fact that there was little left to spend.

Private individuals could not equal the kings in extrava- Luxury in
gance, but they did the best they could. Houses often lacked general.
comforts in the way of furniture, but made a brave showing
in tapestries and paintings. Naturally, great attention was
paid to dress. Under Charles I, just as in art, so also in dress, Dress
clothing was in a stage which may be called the transition
from the "plateresque" to the "Spanish Renaissance."
For example, influenced by German and Swiss fashions,
men wore puffs on their forearm or between the waist and
hips, variegated oblong pieces in their jackets, bright colors
generally, and a tall conical hat. In keeping with the
greater sobriety of Philip II, styles became "Herreran" in
that the puffs were abandoned, obscure colors replaced gay,
and a cap superseded its more pretentious predecessor.
Philip III inaugurated the "baroque" in dress with a return
to the styles of Charles I, but in an exaggerated form.

Men were much given to sports and outings. The duel as Sports
a sport passed out at the beginning of the era, and jousts and
and tourneys lost their vogue by the end of the sixteenth amuse-
century, but a host of new games took their place, such ments.
as equestrian contests of skill in the use of reed spears,
lances, or pikes, but, more than all, the game which has ever
since gripped Spanish interest, the bull-fight. Dances,
parties, excursions, picnics, and masquerades were also in
high favor. Dancing on the stage had a tendency to be
indecent, — so much so, that it had to be prohibited. To- General
bacco was introduced from America at this time. Bathing social
was unpopular, partly because of the stigma attaching to customs.
that hygienic practice as a result of Moslem indulgence
therein, but it was also the subject of attacks by writers on
ethics, who complained of the immoral uses to which bath-
houses were put. Public celebrations of feast days and car-
nivals were characterized by exhibitions of rough horse-play
which were far removed from modern refinement. People
considered it amusing to empty tiny baskets of ashes on
one another, to trip up passers-by with a rope across the
street, to put a lighted rag or a piece of punk in a horse's

ear, to pin an animal's tail or some other unseemly object on a woman's dress, to loose harmless snakes or rats in a crowd, to drop filthy waters on passers-by in the streets below, and to hurl egg-shells full of odorous essences at one another, varying the last-named missile with what the present-day American school-boy knows as the "spitball." These were not the acts of children, but of ladies and gentlemen! Nevertheless, there was a beginning of refinement in table manners. Napkins were introduced, first as an unnecessary luxury, and later more generally, — replacing the use of the table cloth! It also became a polite custom to wash one's hands before eating. The same progress is to be noted in another respect; Charles I indulged in the somewhat "plateresque" custom of kissing all ladies who were presented to him at court; Philip II in true "Herreran" style gave it up.

Bad care of cities. Cities were badly cared for. Barcelona, Madrid, and Seville were alone in being paved. Uncleanly human practices, despite efforts to check them, led to the accumulation of filth and odors in the streets, and this condition was not remedied, although there were officials charged with the duty of street-cleaning. No city had a lighting system worthy of the name; in Madrid the only street lights were the faintly glimmering candles or lamps which were placed before sacred images. All Europe exhibited the same social defects as those which have just been detailed, but Spain seemed reduced more than other countries to a state of poverty and misery, displaying every manifestation of mortal decay.

CHAPTER XXVI

POLITICAL INSTITUTIONS, 1516–1700

Two outstanding features marked the history of Spanish political institutions in the era of the House of Hapsburg, or Austria : the absolutism of the kings; and the development of a modern bureaucratic machinery. The Hapsburgs did not introduce absolutism into Spain, but, rather, succeeded to a system which the efforts of their predecessors, especially the Catholic Kings, had made possible. Nevertheless, it was in this period that the kings, aided by greater resources than former Spanish monarchs had possessed, by the prestige of ruling the most extensive and powerful dominions in the world, and by the predominantly royalist ideas of the age, including the theory of divine right, were able for the first time to direct the affairs of state much as they chose. To be sure, they were still supposed to respect the laws and to rule for the good of their subjects, but in practice it was left to them to interpret their own conduct. Instances have already been given of Charles I's infringements of the law, — for example, in his employment of Flemish favorites. He also introduced a system of personal rule, making himself the head and centre of all governmental action. It was Philip II, however, who carried the ideal of personal rule to the greatest extreme. Suspicion and direct intervention in state affairs were the basic principles of his government, wherefore he gave no man his full confidence, but tried to do as much as he could himself. If the methods of Philip II, the most bureaucratic king in history, often had unfortunate results, — for example, in the case of preparing the famous Armada, — those of his successors

The estab lishment of absolutism.

287

were far more disastrous. Under Philip III and Philip IV the royal authority was granted to favorites, while the power of Charles II had necessarily to be exercised most of the time by some other than the feeble-minded king himself. Thus these reigns were a period of continual intriguing by different factions for the king's confidence, in order that the victors might rule Spain for their own enrichment.

Tend-
encies
toward
centraliza-
tion.
At first sight it would seem that the kings were not successful in their policy of centralization. It was hardly to be expected that the dominions outside the peninsula could be brought under the same sytem of law and custom as governed in Castile, and the case was much the same as regards Portugal when that kingdom was added to the monarchy. With respect to the rest of the peninsula, however, Olivares expressed what was at least a desirable ideal, when he wished to bring about an amalgamation on the Castilian pattern, both in law and in common sentiment, of the dominions of the crown. Some changes were in fact made which tended to promote legal unification, but in essentials the ancient customs of Navarre, Aragon, Catalonia, Valencia, and the Basque provinces were left undisturbed. It is possible that the merger might have been attempted with safety at almost any time before 1640, when Olivares tried it, — quite probably so in the sixteenth century. That it was not undertaken may have been due to the attention given to foreign wars, but in any event the autonomy of the non-Castilian kingdoms of the monarchy was more apparent than real. The nobility and many of the people were intensely royalist, and even when they were not so in principle they supported the kings because, like them, they were profoundly Catholic. Furthermore, the organization representing the old régime had declined internally to such an extent that it was a mere shadow of its former self. Centralization had in fact been going on without process of law, and for that very reason it was easy in the next period to make it legally effective.

Submis-
siveness of
the Castil-
ian Cortes.
Nowhere was the absolutism of the kings more manifest than in their dealings with the Castilian *Cortes*. The principal functions of this body had always been to grant or withhold subsidies and to make petitions, which the kings

might, or might not, enact into law. In this period the deputies were so submissive that they never failed to grant the required subsidy, despite the exhaustion of the country, while their petitions received scant attention. Under the circumstances, since the grant of a subsidy by the representatives of the towns was now the only reason for calling a *Cortes*, the nobles and the clergy were not always summoned. Charles I encountered some resistance of the *Cortes* in the early part of his reign, but in later years the kings experienced no serious difficulty. The deputies themselves lost interest, and not infrequently sold their privilege of attendance to some individual who might even be a nonresident of the town he was to represent. The kings procured the right to appoint many of the deputies, or else issued orders to the towns, directing them how to instruct their delegates, and also gave pensions to the deputies, thus insuring the expression of their own will in the meetings of the *Cortes*. It is not strange that the *Cortes* was called frequently, — forty-four times down to 1665. In 1665 the function of granting subsidies was given directly to the towns, — with the result that no *Cortes* was held in the entire reign of Charles II. The various other *Cortes* of the peninsula were more fortunate than that of Castile. Those of the kingdom of Aragon (Aragon proper, Catalonia, and Valencia) had always participated more than that of Castile in legislation, and had been more prone to voice their grievances. The calling of a *Cortes* in these regions involved difficulties, especially in Valencia, where the king was obliged to be present, in order to constitute a legal meeting. The need for funds was such, however, that a number of *Cortes* were summoned, — seventeen in Aragon, thirteen in Catalonia, fourteen in Valencia, and seventy-three in Navarre, — but the kings did not obtain a great deal from them. Often the delegates refused to make a grant, or else gave so little that it hardly covered the expenses of the king's journey to the place of meeting. No effort was made to join these bodies with that of Castile to form a national *Cortes;* the force of particularism was as yet too strong to attempt it.

Just as in the case of the Castilian *Cortes*, so also in that

Comparative independence of the other Cortes.

u

of the towns, the absolutism of the kings made itself felt to
a marked degree, for the way had been prepared in previous
reigns, and in this instance the royal authority was equally
as noteworthy in Aragon, Catalonia, Valencia, and Majorca
as in Castile.   This was brought about principally through
the decline of the towns in political spirit, a movement which
had been going on since the fourteenth century.   As a result
the *ayuntamientos* had usurped the powers which formerly
belonged to the general assembly of citizens, and now their
functions became absorbed more and more by the kings
through their officials in the towns, such as the *corregidores*
and others.   So great was the authority of the kings that
they were able to make a profit for the treasury by the sale
in perpetuity of local offices, and when the evils which resulted became too pronounced they gave orders abolishing all
such positions acquired before 1630.   Furthermore, all local
legislation of an important character had to receive the
sanction of the *Consejo Real*.   Much the same local officials
as in the past administered the affairs of the municipalities,
and the methods of their acquisition of office continued to
be diverse, being in some towns by election, in others by lot,
in still others by inheritance, and in yet others by royal appointment; but in all of the large royal towns (*realengos*) the
king's authority was paramount.   In fine, local autonomy was
virtually dead, although the forms of the period when the
towns were a virile political factor still persisted.   In two
classes of municipalities the royal victory was not complete.
One was that of the small villages, where the system of the
medieval *villa*, or *concejo*, obtained, but since these units
were of small consequence the retention of their earlier
liberties had little or no effect on the general situation.   The
other was that of the seigniorial towns, most of them in
Aragon, Catalonia, and Navarre, where the struggles of past
eras, of the citizens against the lords, were repeated in this.

With the advance both in royal authority and in the scope
and extension of government it was inevitable that the new
bureaucracy, which had made its appearance in the modern
sense under the Catholic Kings, should increase in the number of its officials and in power until it absorbed a great part

of the functions which the kings themselves had formerly exercised in person. Aside from the royal secretaries, the governor-generals (during the absence of the king), regents, and members of the various administrative groups there were often individuals without portfolios who exercised great power as private counselors of the king. Some of the members of the *Consejo Real* were also prominent in this extra-official way. The importance of the royal secretaries, of whom there were always more than one, was notably great in this period. Whenever one of them became the favorite, the others were nevertheless retained, grouping themselves around the one who had the ear of the king. The office of the latter became a universal bureau and secretariat of state (*Secretaría de Estado y del Despacho Universal*), presiding over the others.

Meanwhile, the *Consejo Real* advanced in power, and new councils were added. The most notable reform in the *Consejo Real* was its division in 1608 into four sections, or *salas*, respectively of government (*Gobierno*), justice (*Justicia*), "fifteen hundred" (*Mil y quinientos*), and the provinces (*Provincia*). The last three had to do with affairs of justice, while the *Sala de Gobierno*, the most important of the four, was supposed to concern itself mainly with politics and administration. Nevertheless, the variety of functions which had always characterized the *Consejo* as a whole applied in like manner to each of the *salas*. Thus the *Sala de Gobierno* handled such widely divergent matters as the extirpation of vice and sin, the economic development of the country, the decision in cases of conflict of laws or jurisdictions, cases of recourse of *fuerza*, the cleaning and improvement of Madrid, questions of peace and war, together with a great number of others. Moreover, many of its functions were judicial in character. Important affairs, especially those on which the king requested advice, were taken up by the *Consejo* in full (*en pleno*), — that is, by a joint meeting of the four *salas*. While the *Consejo* had been in origin a purely consultive body, it now acquired the privilege of making suggestions to the king of its own volition and of indicating its objections to any measures he might

Power of the Consejo Real.

have taken. It was natural that the decisions, or *autos*, of the *Consejo* should have great weight, both as affecting matters of justice, and as concerned government and administration in general, since the *Consejo* might make new laws and annul or dispense with old ones, although of course consulting with the king before publishing its decision. The *autos* of the *Consejo* became, therefore, an important source of legislation, and in 1552 it was decided that they should have the same force as the laws of the king himself. Late in the sixteenth century it became customary to call the *Consejo* the *Consejo de Castilla* (Council of Castile), by which name, henceforth, it was more generally known.

Importance of the *Cámara*.
In like manner other councils were formed (in addition to those dating from the era of the Catholic Kings) which relieved the monarch of many of his responsibilities. The most important was the *Consejo de la Real Cámara* (Council of the Royal Chamber), more often called the *Cámara de Castilla*, or simply the *Cámara*. This was founded by Philip II in 1588 to assist him in handling such matters as the kings had always retained for themselves, apart from the *Consejo Real*, such as questions arising in connection with the *patronato real*, or royal patronage, of the church and appointments generally to the various councils, *audiencias*, and other important posts in Castilian administration. Men of the highest character were chosen to compose the *Cámara*, and secrecy as to their discussions was imposed upon them. In 1616 the *Cámara* advanced a step further, in that certain affairs — such as pardons for crime, authorizations for entailing estates in primogeniture, the naturalization of foreigners, and the removal of civil and political disabilities from individuals subject to them — were left for it to resolve without consulting the king. The king still intervened in the more important matters. Among the new councils of the era were those of finance (*Hacienda*), war (*Guerra*), and indulgences (*Cruzada*), all of Castilian origin.

The expansion of officialdom in the peninsula made its presence felt in the judiciary as elsewhere. The three judicial *salas* of the *Consejo Real* and in some cases the *Sala de*

Gobierno as well became the fountain-head of justice, under the king. This was especially true of the full *Consejo*, which met weekly. This body also named special judges, such as *visitadores*, both to procure information for the *Consejo* and to inspect the tribunals of lower grade. The number of *audiencias* was increased until there were five in the peninsula and one each in Majorca and the Canary Islands, besides a number in the Americas.[1] Below these was the hierarchy of the lesser officials. There were still various outstanding jurisdictions, such as those of the towns, the military orders, the Inquisition, and the church, but one of the keynotes of the era was the advance of the royal courts at the expense of the others. The administration of justice left much to be desired, however. As a result of the wars and civil conflicts and the general state of misery and lack of discipline, public security was almost non-existent. Banditry and crime went unsuppressed, and legislation served for little in the face of the corruption of officials and the lack of means to make the laws effective.

Expansion of the royal judiciary.

Frequent references have already been made to the desperate state of Spanish finances in the era of the House of Austria and to its importance as an ultimate factor affecting Spanish dominion in the Americas. Vast sums were expended for political and military ends, the only compensations for which were extensions of territory and power and a satisfaction of the desire for glory, without reflecting themselves in an increase of public wealth, the well-being of Spaniards, or even in commercial advantage; on the contrary, economic development was checked or hindered by the continual wars in which the kings engaged. Expenditures very greatly increased over what they had been before. It will be sufficient to explain this if some comment is made on two noteworthy objects to which state revenues were devoted: the maintenance of the court; and the cost of the wars. The ordinary expenses of the royal family jumped under Charles I to about 150,000 ducats ($2,250,000) a year, — more than ten times the amount required by the Catholic

Vastness of the royal expenditures.

---

[1] The two most important, those of Valladolid and Granada, were distinguished from the others by being called *chancillerías*.

Kings. To this should be added the vast sums granted to the princes; in 1550 Philip (the later Philip II) received 55,000 ducats (over $800,000) in the course of four months. The expenditures of the court constantly increased. In 1562 the ordinary court expenses amounted to 415,000 ducats (well over $6,000,000), and under Philip III they were 1,300,000 (nearly $20,000,000) annually. In addition there were the *fiestas* (festivities) and royal marriages, on which tremendous sums were squandered. As for military expenditures the war in Flanders alone consumed 37,488,565 ducats (nearly $600,000,000) in the space of eleven years, 1598 to 1609, and other campaigns were costly in proportion, — and this in spite of the fact that supplies were often not provided and salaries were left unpaid, leading to tumults on the part of the soldiery. To gain an adequate idea of the vastness of these sums one must bear in mind, not only the greater purchasing power of money in that day and the comparatively small population of the peninsula, especially the small number of taxpayers, but also the fact that the resources of the Spanish state then were as little, as compared with those of the present day, as they were great in comparison with those of medieval Spain.

Tremendous increase in taxation in Castile.
It is no wonder that the people through their representatives in the *Cortes* began to ask for peace and the termination of military adventures, even in the period when victories were frequent; the nobles also favored an end of the wars, — when the kings endeavored to get them, too, to grant a subsidy. One result of the greater financial requirements of the state was an increase in taxation, both in the collection of the existing taxes at a higher rate, and in the imposition of new ones. The grants, or *servicios*, of the Castilian *Cortes* were frequent and large in amount. In 1538 there appeared the new tax of the *millones*, so-called because it was calculated in millions of ducats. This was an excise on articles of prime necessity, — meat, wine, oil, and vinegar. It was extended soon to powder, lead, sulphur, red ochre, vermilion, sealing-wax, and playing cards, which together were called the *siete rentillas* (seven little rents). Salt, gold, silver, mercury, and many other materials were the

subject of a state monopoly, and to them were added in the reign of Philip IV the monopoly on tobacco, which was to prove an exceptionally profitable source of revenue. The *diezmo* and *cruzada* (otherwise *Bula*) continued to be collected from the church, together with several new rents which were authorized by the pope. One of these was the *subsidio de galeras* (subsidy of the galleys), or *galeras*, so-called because it was theoretically designed to assist in the expenses of the galleys used in fighting the Moslem peoples. This was granted in 1561, and consisted of an annual subsidy of 420,000 ducats (over $6,000,000). The *alcabala* and the various customs duties were increased. Stamp taxes were extended to new types of documents. The nobles were required to pay a tax called *lanzas* (lances) in lieu of military service. Various offices and titles were made subject to the *media anata* (half annates), a discount of a half year's salary, or rents, in the first year of enjoyment. The transmission of a title of nobility to one's heir was also taxed. Vanity was seized upon as likely to yield a revenue, and money was collected in return for the privilege of using the word *"Don"* before one's Christian name. In like manner illegitimate children were pronounced legitimate on payment of a specified sum. Other methods were employed to obtain ready cash which tended ultimately to dry up certain sources of revenue: the coinage was debased; portions of the government rents were disposed of; public offices and royal towns were granted in perpetuity; and the title of *hidalgo* was sold to many persons, who thereby entered the non-taxpaying class. Other ways of acquiring funds were made use of, ranging from the high-handed to the shameless. Under the name of *donativos* (gifts) the government resorted to forced loans, or even trickery, to exact money from the nobles and churchmen; confiscations of goods for offences against religion and for other delinquencies were frequently ordered; and most disgusting of all was the *limosna al rey* (alms for the king), which was collected by gentlemen of the court, each accompanied by a parish priest and a friar, in a house to house canvass of the citizens, who were asked to give what they could spare. If the kings and their favorites

thought of the most obvious way to accumulate funds, economy in expenditures, they at least did not try to put it into
practice; the court *fiestas* were held, even if the king's gentlemen had to beg the money and the nation had to starve.

Taxes in
the other
kingdoms.

The above refers to taxes collected in Castile, but the
other dominions of Spain, peninsula and otherwise, produced considerable amounts for the state. Aragon, Catalonia, and Valencia yielded much less than Castile. The
Low Countries were profitable for a time; Charles I procured 450,000 ducats a year (nearly $7,000,000) at the
outset of his reign. Under Philip II, however, they were
the scene of heavy expenditures. The Americas have often
been considered as the principal financial resort of the Spanish
kings, and although this is not certain and may even be
doubtful they did yield vast sums. Prior to the conquest of
Mexico the annual revenues were only some 70,000 ducats
(about $1,000,000), but the conquests of Cortés, followed
soon by those of Pizarro in Peru, resulted in an enormous
increase. Under Philip II they amounted annually to about
1,200,000 ($18,000,000) according to some writers, and to
as much as 2,000,000 ($30,000,000) in the opinion of
others. Castilian taxes were applied in the new world,
together with certain others arising out of the special circumstances of colonial affairs, such as the royal fifth on precious metals from the mines and the poll tax collected from
the Indians. Data are not at hand for an accurate estimate
of the entire revenues of Spain, but it seems clear that they
increased enormously in the period. They may have reached
their highest point under Philip III, when it was estimated
that they were some 24,000,000 ducats ($360,000,000) a year,
of which not more than half reached the Spanish treasury.
An estimate made toward the close of the century gave the
revenues as about 17,750,000 ($270,000,000), of which only
a third was actually available.

Growth of
the
national
debt.

Despite these relatively great sums the national debt was
a constant factor, and advanced greatly in amount under
Philip II, who is said to have left a debt of 100,000,000 ducats
($1,500,000,000). This was reduced in later reigns, but
was still 70,000,000 (well over $1,000,000,000) in 1690, —

a huge sum as national debts went then, even though creditors were frequently scaled down or not paid at all. One
of the important elements in the debt was that of the loans
made by Flemish, German, and Italian bankers, especially
those of Genoa. The frequency with which these loans
were sought and the high rate of interest required have caused
Spain to be characterized, with accuracy, as a mere bridge
over which the wealth of the Americas (and, to be sure,
that of the peninsula itself) passed to other nations as interest and part payment of the nation's debts. In 1539
this form of indebtedness amounted to about 1,000,000
ducats ($15,000,000), and in 1560, some 7,000,000 (over
$100,000,000). When the Spanish kings were unable to
pay a note that had become due, as much as $33\frac{1}{3}$ per cent
might be charged for its renewal; indeed, the ordinary rate
of interest ranged from 15 to 30 per cent. The inability
of Philip II to meet his obligations caused all but the Genoese
bankers to refuse him credit, and they joined with the others
when he suspended the payment of interest on their notes.
Unable to get funds in any other way, Philip surrendered
to the Genoese, who exacted as part payment for fresh loans
a share in various revenues of the Spanish state, such as in
that of the salt monopoly and in certain of the taxes collected
from the church, — thus belying the original object for which
the latter had been imposed. The *Cortes*, though it had
declined in other respects, was perhaps the most important
organ of public finance. It not only voted subsidies but also
collected them, a function which it had exercised in previous
eras. It had charge of several other taxes as well, such as
the productive *alcabala* and the *millones*. For these purposes special committees of the *Cortes* were formed. Nevertheless, the *Consejo de Hacienda*, founded in 1593, grew
rapidly in functions and in power, and by the close of the
seventeenth century is said to have had over 60,000 employes.
This vast number was due in part to the variety in the origin
and character of the various tributes. Without taking into
consideration the inevitable accompaniment of graft, such
a horde of officials involved the state in a heavy cost for the
collection and administration of the revenues.

The
Spanish
army in
the days
of its
greatness.
     The principal element in the Spanish army was the volun-
teer soldiery in the king's pay. Foreign mercenaries were
obtained for stated lengths of time or for specific campaigns,
but Spaniards enlisted for indefinite service, and thus became the veterans of the army. Military life was popular
during the sixteenth century and the early part of the
seventeenth, and the army abounded in *hidalgos* and others
of yet higher rank who did not disdain to serve as privates.
Later the number of Spanish recruits grew less, when the
state began to fail in its regularity of payments, and their
withdrawal marked the era when defeats became frequent.
Among the noteworthy changes in tactics was the appearance
of the regiment. Firearms had now come into general use,
and cannon were greatly improved, but it was the pikemen
of the Spanish infantry who formed the principal branch of
the army until near the close of the period. Because of the
inferiority of their weapons the troops with firearms were
regarded as a mere auxiliary to the pikemen. Armies were
small; 20,000 to 40,000 men was perhaps the usual rule.
Even in the century of Spain's greatness many lands were
left without garrison, as occurred nearly always in the case
of the Americas; one report of the period of Charles I stated
that there was not a port in the colonies which could resist
an attack of three hundred men. The worst evils in connection with the army were those of bad administration and a
lack of regularity in paying the troops and in remitting funds
for munitions and other supplies. Fraud and graft accounted
for a great deal of the money which the state did apply to the
army. These factors contributed to a lack of military discipline; it was not unusual for ragged and starving soldiers
to beg from door to door, and it is not to be wondered at that
the troops occasionally took the matter of the collection of
their wages into their own hands. It was customary for
women of bad repute to accompany the armies, and it sounds
strange today that one of the military manuals of the time
recommended that there should be eight women, who should
be common to all, for every hundred soldiers. Nevertheless,
the Spanish infantry, for more than a century, enjoyed the
reputation of being the most capable military unit in Europe.

Despite the frequency of naval warfare and the necessity of maintaining communications with the Americas, com- paratively little attention was paid to the marine establish- ment, and properly speaking there was no official navy in the entire period. The principal method employed to as- semble a fleet was by renting ships, whether from Spaniards or foreigners. In addition a few were built by the state, or purchased, and in times of stress merchant vessels were pressed into service, but this proved ruinous to commerce and ship-building alike. So long as other powers used the same methods Spain was not greatly handicapped, but with the development of national navies in England, France, and the Protestant Netherlands, she was placed at a disadvantage. Nevertheless, considerable fleets were often assembled. In 1643 a special fleet called the *Armada de Barlovento* (fleet of the Barlovento, modern Windward, Islands) was organized at colonial expense for the defence of the Americas. It was soon withdrawn, — but the tax remained. The fleet of the Catalonian deputation was maintained for a while, but disappeared early in the seventeenth century. There were also a number of private fleets, engaged principally in re- prisals against the Moslems, a kind of piracy. While privateering of this sort was forbidden by law the kings frequently granted dispensations which enabled the traffic to be carried on almost continuously. Greater strictness was employed in the Americas lest the privateers should fail to resist the temptation to pick up Spanish merchantmen, but the prohibition there was at length removed, and the Spanish boats rendered great service against pirates and national enemies. During the sixteenth century Spanish fleets were manned by volunteer forces, but this was changed in the seventeenth to compulsory service of the fishermen of the coasts. The heavier work, especially the rowing of the galleys, was done by captives in war and by criminals, who served terms in the galleys rather than in prison. During most of the period the galley, with three banks of oars, was the principal type of vessel. In ocean warfare, the *nao*, or light sailing-vessel, soon came into use, and this was gradually supplanted by heavier ships, until late in the era there developed the *fragata,* or frigate, of over two thousand tons, capable of carrying as many as 120 cannon. While the artillery was the principal arm of the fleet, Spanish tactics were at fault in depending on getting close to the enemy and boarding him, making a military action out of the combat and paying little attention to the use of cannon of long range. The same evils which have been described in connection with the army — graft, irregularity of payments, and laxity of discipline — obtained also in the navy; in the expedition of Charles I against Tunis, room on board was found for four thousand *enamoradas* (sweethearts!) of the soldiers and sailors.

Begin-
nings of
diplo-
macy.

In common with other European countries Spain developed a diplomatic service in this period. The sending of special embassies and the making of treaties had been customary since ancient times, but the practice of appointing ministers to reside at foreign courts and that of receiving those sent from abroad did not begin in Spain until the reign of Charles I. The initiative had come earlier from the Italian republics. From this time forward Spanish diplomacy, like that of other countries, took on a modern form, and ambassadors sent reports about the state of the countries to which they were accredited, strove to obtain advantages for Spain, endeavored to check the intrigues of the ambassadors of other nations, and made treaties. The use of spies as an auxiliary to ambassadorial work was general. For a time Spanish diplomacy enjoyed a high reputation for success, but in the later seventeenth century it was quite overshadowed by the French.

The
*Nueva
Recopila-
ción* and
other
codes.

The absolutism of the monarchy, its bureaucratic character, and the instinct of the *letrados* for reducing everything to rules and regulations produced an abundance of legislation, much of which was exceedingly minute in detail and casual in subject-matter. It was natural therefore that there should be a desire for a fresh codification, and this at length took shape in a compilation by Bartolomé de Arrieta in 1567 of the *Nueva Recopilación* (New Compendium, or Compilation), so-called with reference to the code of Montalvo, its predecessor, of the period of the Catholic Kings. The new collection, which was for Castile only, filled nine volumes, and amounted to little more than an elaboration of the *Ordenanzas* of Montalvo, with the addition of laws enacted since 1484. It contained the same defects, omitting many royal orders or petitions of the *Cortes* which had been granted, neglecting to eliminate obsolete laws, and failing to correct others whose text contained errors. Furthermore, in perpetuating the hierarchy of legal sources which had been established in the *Leyes de Toro* it failed to distinguish between laws in the so-called supplementary codes (such as the *Partidas*) which were indeed supplementary or obsolete and those which had in fact come to be in force as the principal law. As a result the *Nueva Recopilación* was generally discredited, and the Roman law of the *Partidas*, or even of the code of Justinian, was cited in preference. The force of government maintained the new code, however, and it ran through four more editions, — 1581, 1592, 1598, and 1640, — and in each case added legislation since the preceding publication. The zeal for codification found expression also in Aragon, Catalonia, Vizcaya, and Guipúzcoa, while the laws with regard to the Americas were gathered together, after various lesser publications had been made in earlier times, in the *Recopilación de las Leyes de Indias*, first issued in 1680. The tendency toward the legal unity of the peninsula was not systematically striven for by the kings, since the variety in private law did not greatly affect their political sovereignty. Nevertheless, something was accomplished along these lines, and within each separate unit a great deal was effected. Thus, in Castile many of the former privileges which made for a division into classes and for consequent differences in the law were done away with, and the same process, though on a smaller scale, made itself felt in the other kingdoms of the peninsula.

The submissiveness of the Spanish peoples under absolute rule has often been greatly exaggerated. In fact, neither then nor ever since were they loth to criticise the "*mal gobierno*" (bad government). Evidences are to be found on every hand of complaints against the bureaucratic organization which was absorbing a great part of the national

Under-
lying dis-
content of
the people
over the
Spanish
political
system.

wealth and of dissatisfaction with the system of government by favorites, the evils of which were only too apparent. Not a few went so far as to desire a republic. Nevertheless, as a general rule, people favored the principle of monarchy, and did not object to the reigning house, but they did desire a reform of the existing régime. The ideal of limited monarchy found strong support among political thinkers, due in a measure to the resentment of Catholics over the enforced apostasy of the subjects of Protestant princes. On this account the *Cortes* had numerous defenders, some of whom urged its participation in legislation. Many treatises also pronounced against such practices as the sale of public offices or the grant of posts in perpetuity, and against others which have been described as current in this era. In fine, Spaniards were well aware of the evils of their political system and, though patient, were keenly desirous of reform, — despite which, little attention was paid to their wishes.

CHAPTER XXVII

RELIGION AND THE CHURCH, 1516–1700

PRIOR to the era of the House of Austria it is possible to deal with the ecclesiastical institutions in Spain at the same time with other manifestations of a social, political, economic, or intellectual character, but the period of Hapsburg rule was so replete with interest on the religious side and so important in that respect in its ultimate results on the Americas that this phase of Spanish life in the sixteenth and seventeenth centuries is deserving of separate treatment. Two ideas dominated the period: the struggle for the maintenance of the Catholic faith against the inroads of Protestantism and other heretical beliefs; and the efforts of the Spanish state to acquire a virtual political supremacy over the church. Few periods of history more clearly illustrate the distinction maintained in Catholic countries between Catholicism as a religious faith and the Catholic Church as an institution, a difference which people of the United States do not readily grasp. Thus it was entirely consistent that the kings of Spain should have been almost the most ardent champions in Europe of Catholic Christianity, officers of the church not excepted, and also most persistent in their endeavors to limit the ecclesiastical authority in Spanish domains. The greatest exponent of the latter policy as well as of the former was Philip II, one of the most devout monarchs who ever occupied the Spanish throne. In both of these controversies the kings were successful. Heresy made no headway in Spain or in the colonies, and the king gained the upper hand in the management of the Spanish and American church. Meanwhile Spanish missionaries were carrying on one of the

greatest campaigns of proselytism ever waged. The thor-
oughness of the conversion of the natives in Spain's colonial
possessions has been questioned, but there is no doubt that
something of the external forms and the glamour — so much,
at least — of the Catholic religion was implanted in the
Americas in such a way that it has withstood the experiences of centuries. Spanish American peoples, like Spaniards,
were to have their conflicts with the church, — very bitter
ones in recent years, — but never, since the Franciscan,
Dominican, and Jesuit Fathers first preached their doctrine,
has favor been shown for any great length of time to the
other exotic faiths, or has any noteworthy success been met
with in the attempts, usually short-lived, at a reversion to the
earlier native creeds. The work of the Spanish missionary
was indeed a permanent factor of indisputable importance in
the new world.

Religious exaltation and the increase in the prestige and wealth of the clergy.   One of the effects of the attainment of religious unity by
the conversion or expulsion from Spain of the Jews, Mudé-
jares, and Moriscos was to exalt the feeling of religious
sentiment in the peninsula. The Protestant Reformation
and the religious wars which accompanied it tended to keep
alive these emotions among Spaniards, partly because of the
spirit of controversy they excited, and partly because of
the blows and suffering they involved, and this spirit of
religious exaltation was sustained by the increasing vigor of
the Inquisition and by the activities of the Jesuit order,
founded in this period. In consequence the power and social
influence of the clergy were materially enhanced. The
regular clergy was looked upon with especial favor, with the
result that both in riches and in membership they far surpassed the secular branch. Many new orders were founded,
while the older ones received fresh stimulus. At the beginning of the seventeenth century there were some 200,000
members of the regular clergy and over 9000 convents for
men, and in both cases the numbers increased thereafter,
while the population of the peninsula declined, — a factor
which caused political and economic writers, many of whom
were churchmen, not a little concern.[1] Despite this fact

[1] Compare the figures on population given at page 333.

the clergy enjoyed the highest social consideration, and intervened in all phases of Spanish life. This was due not only to the religious sentiment of the people but also in great measure to the superior intellectual attainments of some of the clergy. Thus they distinguished themselves on the one hand as theologians, students of the canon law, jurisconsults, men of letters, historians, and university professors, and on the other as members of state councils, or in high political positions in the Americas. The increase in the landed wealth of the church, while it was the subject of numerous unsuccessful petitions of the *Cortes* to forbid the giving of lands in mortmain, was largely responsible for the imposition of taxes on the clergy, thus diminishing the immunities they had formerly enjoyed. The church could well afford to pay, for if not the richest proprietor in Spain it was certainly among the first; toward the middle of the sixteenth century the combined rents of the clergy amounted to some 5,000,000 ducats ($75,000,000) a year, or half the total for the kingdom, four-fifths of which amount was paid to the establishments of the regular clergy. Part of the funds was expended in charities for the benefit of the poor, such as the maintenance of asylums, hospitals, and soup-kitchens, measures which (disinterested though they might be) served also to augment their popularity with the masses.

Despite the flourishing condition of the Spanish clergy and their high standing in the peninsula the state of morality among them left much to be desired. Abundant evidences on this score are at hand, not only in the form of unsympathetic attacks and satires, but also in the works of zealous and devout reformers. The fact that such writings were not condemned by the Inquisition argues the need for reproof. The practice of *barragania* was not unknown, even among bishops, some of whom entailed estates to their sons. Among the lesser churchmen, more particularly the secular clergy, the custom was more general. Solicitation by confessors and the avarice of clerical collectors of revenues were also frequently censured in the writings of the time. Nevertheless, it is but fair to consider these evils from the standpoint of that era. As compared with previous periods this

Prevalence of loose practices among the clergy.

x

age was one of marked advance in the average of clerical rectitude, and there were even writers who could claim that the Spanish clergy surpassed the churchmen of other countries in moderation and chasteness of life. Meanwhile, reforms like those instituted in the time of the Catholic Kings by Ximénez were being pushed on vigorously and effectively, and were reinforced by the decisions of the great church council of Trent (1545–1563).

Promi-
nence of
Spanish
kings and
prelates in
church
reform.

The Protestant Reformation and the Catholic Reaction, or Counter-Reformation, belong rather to European and church history than peculiarly to that of Spain, although Spain played a leading part in the events connected with them. Much in regard to them may therefore be omitted, except in so far as they affected problems in the peninsula itself and, by extension, the Spanish colonies. Charles I was an ardent partisan of church reform, but was desirous that it should be effected without change in dogma, and in this attitude he was joined by many of the greatest Catholic churchmen of the day, including some of the popes, who recognized the prevalence of abuses of which the Protestant leaders were able to make capital in the furtherance of their reforms. One of the principal policies of Charles I was the calling of a general church council for the discussion of this matter, and despite the resistance of several of the popes he labored to attain this end until he was at length successful. In 1545 there began the series of congresses which are called collectively the Council of Trent. Spanish prelates were one of the most important elements at these meetings, and in accordance with the ideas of Charles I and Philip II resisted the attempts made at a suspension of the sessions and the efforts of certain popes and other churchmen to bring about their failure. They were not only among the most frank in their references to the need for reform, but were also most rigid in their insistence upon disciplinary methods, even suggesting the application of the Spanish institution of the *residencia* to officers of the church. The eventual success of the council was due in no small degree to Spaniards, who also were among the most active in executing the corrective measures which were decided upon.

The kings of Spain combated heresy within the peninsula to the fullest extent of their ability, supported by the general opinion of Spanish Christians, who were almost unanimously opposed to the new ideas.   Measures were taken to prevent the dissemination in Spain of the works of Martin Luther or other heretical thinkers.   In 1546 Charles I caused the first *Index*, or list of prohibited works, to be published, and this was reproduced, with the addition of some other volumes, by the Inquisition.   Later the Bible was included in the *Index*, except the authorized Latin version, on the ground that the reading of the scriptures by uncultivated persons might result in misconceptions as to the true religion.   Nevertheless, Protestantism gained devotees in the various cities of Spain, more particularly in Seville and Valladolid.   The number of heretics was at no time great, but it was recruited from the highest ranks of society.   Churchmen, more often friars, were the principal element, and they found converts in not a few members of noble families.   Foreigners from northern lands frequently cast in their lot with the Protestant groups.   As was natural, proselytism on a wide scale could not be carried on; the Valladolid group numbered only about fifty and that of Seville one hundred and thirty (although there is some evidence to the effect that the latter body attained a membership of eight hundred), while those of other cities were still fewer in numbers.   The greatest name in the Sevillian movement was that of Constantino Ponce de la Fuente, whom a modern writer has ventured to compare with Martin Luther for his high qualities, within the Protestant movement.   Ponce, who was at one time the confessor of Charles I and Philip II, was the author of various heretical works.   Discovered, at length, he was imprisoned, and shortly afterward was found dead.   In the year 1559 great activity was displayed by the Inquisition in ferreting out and punishing the Protestant communities. Some individuals escaped to foreign countries, but many were condemned to die at the stake, meeting their fate, almost without exception, with admirable fortitude.   The most celebrated case was that of Bartolomé Carranza, archbishop of Toledo.   Head of the Spanish secular church

Failure of Protestantism to gain a substantial footing in Spain.

though he was, only the efforts of Pope Pius IV saved him. After more than seven years of imprisonment he was allowed to go to Rome. Some years later he was required to forswear some of his writings which had figured in the original proceedings against him in Spain, shortly after which he died. In all of this vigorous persecution of Protestantism, Charles I and Philip II took the lead. By the end of the sixteenth century the new faith was no longer a problem in Spain. Under Philip IV a degree of toleration which would not have been dreamed of in earlier years began to be allowed. By that time Catholic France was Spain's principal enemy, and this tended to soften the attitude of Spaniards toward Protestants, although the restrictions of the laws were still enforced. In 1641 a treaty was made with Denmark, permitting Protestants of that country to enter the peninsula. From this time forward Spain was to evolve toward a more lenient policy still. A discussion of Spanish Protestantism would not be complete without a reference to the numerous Spaniards who took refuge in Protestant lands, and even for a time in Italy and France. They wrote a number of works which were remarkable for the excellent literary qualities of the Castilian they employed and for the scientific value of their content. While most of their writings were of a controversial, religious type they also made translations into Castilian or even wrote volumes of a scientific character dissociated from religion. Juan de Valdés and Juan Díaz were outstanding names among them. Miguel Servet and Pedro Galés, whose heresies were equally in disfavor with Catholics and Protestants, were also men of great distinction.

The Illuminist and Quietist heresies.

Protestantism was not the only heterodoxy to menace the religious unity of the peninsula. The conversion of the Mudéjares of the eastern provinces and the expulsion of the Moriscos have already been mentioned. The Jews also gave occasional trouble. Of the other sects the most noteworthy was that of the *Iluminados* (Illuminati). The origins of this faith are obscure. Many believe it to have been purely Spanish, a conclusion to which the peculiar mystical character of the creed lends color. Others hold that it was of German extraction. In any event, though the time of its founding is not clear, it antedated the Lutheran outbreak, for it was in existence at least as early as 1512. Many of the doctrines sustained by Luther were a part of its creed, and indeed it paved the way for the entry of Protestantism into Spain. In addition it upheld the following tenets: the abdication of one's own will in that of the divine; and the capacity of the faithful, by means of ecstacies, to put themselves in personal communication with the divine essence, on which occasions it was impossible for them to commit sin. The practical result of these beliefs was an indulgence in all manner of licentious practices while in the sinless state. As in the case of Protestantism, so in this, the devotees were usually members of the clergy, especially friars and nuns. The Inquisition attacked the new faith with vigor, but found it difficult to extirpate in entirety. A notable derivation from Illuminism was that of *Quietismo* (Quietism), or *Molinismo*, founded in the seventeenth century by Miguel de Molinos, a member of the clergy. This creed, though similar even in its licentiousness to Illuminism, was not at first considered unorthodox, wherefore it gained many converts, but in the end it was condemned.

Similar in some respects to the two heretical creeds just mentioned was a peculiarly Spanish religious philosophy, that of Catholic Mysticism. It traces back through the ideas of Raymond Lull to those of the Arabic philosophers, but in the main it was a product of the Spanish religious thought of the sixteenth and seventeenth centuries. The fundamental idea was that of direct communication with God through prayer, love of God, and the renunciation of earthly things, which enabled the purified soul in a state of ecstasy to appear in the divine presence. The whole process was accompanied by miracles, but without any loss to the individual of his spiritual existence or of his intelligence for an understanding of God. At first the ecclesiastical authorities were suspicious of it, prohibiting the writings of the mystics and conducting investigations into the conduct of those who professed a belief in it. At length, however, it was accepted as orthodox, and its devotees were not molested. They produced a rich literature, in which they set forth not

Spanish Mysticism.

only the fundamental bases of their belief but also the experiences they had in journeying to God. One of the mystics, María de Jesús de Ágreda, is famous as "the Blue Lady" of the American (United States) southwest and Pacific coast, for she is said to have visited these regions while in a state of ecstacy and to have converted many of the natives, recounting her travels in her published works. She is also famous for her correspondence with Philip IV. The greatest names, however, were those of Santa Teresa de Jesús[1] and San Juan de la Cruz, the former notable in literature for the excellence of her prose, and the latter equally noteworthy as a poet. The writings of these and other mystics also displayed a profound psychological study, such, for example, as was required by their ability to distinguish between the processes of the soul on the way to communication with God, and as was evidenced by their skill in differentiating between the various elements in religious sentiment.

The Inquisition as an instrument of the kings and an agency to suppress heresy.

The two principal instruments employed to combat heresy were the Inquisition and the Jesuit order. So far as the former concerned itself with matters of the faith, it had the support of the Spanish people, who equally with the kings were desirous of the establishment and maintenance of religious unity. The Inquisition had acquired various powers and privileges, however, which were not directly connected with its principal office. Papal bulls had been procured giving it jurisdiction in cases of usury, crimes against nature, and improper solicitations of confessors; it claimed exemption for its officers and servants from the operation of the civil law courts; and its relations with these courts, made necessary by the legal incapacity of the Inquisition to execute its own sentences, often gave rise to conflicts and misunderstandings. The people of Spain were perfectly able to distinguish between the Inquisition as an instrument of the faith and the Inquisition in these extra-

[1] The addition of the name "de Jesús" to that of some of the mystics came from their assertions of a marriage with Christ, according to which fact their names, in Spanish fashion, required this indication of their marital partner.

jurisdictional phases, and protested vigorously against that body in the latter sense. The various *Cortes* of Castile, Aragon, and Catalonia presented many a petition on this score to the kings, and it was a prominent factor in the Catalan revolt of 1640. Nevertheless, the kings consistently sustained the Inquisition. When the Aragonese *Cortes* secured a papal license reducing the Inquisition to the same footing as the other ecclesiastical courts, Charles I procured the withdrawal of the license. Philip II prohibited all appeals from or complaints against the Inquisition before the *audiencias* or the *Consejo Real*. The decisions of the Inquisition thus became final, although it is true that cases of appeal and the recourse of *fuerza* (also forbidden by Philip) were occasionally allowed to go beyond that body. When there seemed to be a likelihood that the Council of Trent might deprive the Inquisition of some of its authority, Charles I used every effort to cause a failure of the project. In fact the Inquisition was virtually an instrument of the kings, who did not hesitate to direct its action as if it were legally subject to them, and who were always able to procure the appointment of members of the *Consejo Real* to the Council of the Inquisition. As regards heresy the period, naturally, was exceedingly fruitful in prosecutions and was marked by an excess of suspicion, such that individuals whose purity of faith was hardly open to question were not infrequently brought to trial, — among others, Ignacio de Loyola (Saint Ignatius), and Teresa de Jesús, who, like Loyola, was later canonized. Extreme rigor was displayed in placing the ban on unorthodox books and in expurgating those which were allowed to circulate. Charles I required all books to have the authorization of the *Consejo Real* before they could be published. Foreign books were also scrutinized carefully, and libraries were made subject to inspection. The grant of a license by the *Consejo Real* did not mean that a book might not be placed on the Inquisition's *Index* of forbidden works. It is worthy of note, too, that the Spanish *Index* and that of the Inquisition of Rome often varied from each other in their lists; thus a book condemned at Rome might circulate in Spain, and vice versa, but this of course was not the general rule. The Spanish Inquisition did not make its way to Spain's Italian possessions, but was established in the Low Countries, where it was very active, and in the Americas.

Ignacio de Loyola and the founding of the Jesuit order.

The other important agency of the Spanish Counter-Reformation, the Jesuit order, was the creation of a Spaniard, Ignacio de Loyola (1491 or 1495–1556), who became Saint Ignatius (San Ignacio) with his canonization in 1609. As a youth Loyola led the somewhat wild life of a soldier. Wounded in 1521 during the defence of Pamplona from an attack of the French, he was a long time in recovering his health, devoting the period of his convalescence to the reading of religious works. He thereupon resolved to dedicate his life to religion, and as soon as he was restored to health made a pilgrimage to Jerusalem. Upon his return he pursued religious studies at the universities of Barcelona, Alcalá, Salamanca, and Paris. While at Alcalá, where he and several companions made a practice of wearing sackcloth and preaching in the streets, he was arrested by the Inquisition, but was set free without other penalty than an order to give up his sackcloth and his preaching. A similar fate befell him in Salamanca. Eventually Loyola and his companions found their way to Rome, where they continued their street preaching, despite the opposition of the Augustinian order and some of the cardinals. They applied to themselves the name "Company of Jesus" (hence Jesuits), and in 1539 organized an order in military form, vowing implicit obedience to their superiors, — especially to the pope, — prescribing the rule of a general for life, and pledging themselves to the founding of colleges. The new order was formally approved by the pope in 1540, and Loyola became the first general.

Character-istics of the Jesuit order.

While an extended discussion of the characteristics of the Jesuit order is not necessary, some of the respects in which it differed from the others should be pointed out, in order to make clear the effect of the Jesuit appearance in Spain and the Americas. Great emphasis was placed on the military side; Loyola was wont to say that he had never ceased to be a soldier, — he had merely become a soldier of God.

Obedience to superiors and to the pope was not a new idea, but with the Jesuits it was as rigidly literal as in an army. They became one of the principal supports of the popes at a time when many church leaders were advocating the reform of the papacy with a view to limiting the powers of the head of the church. Like soldiers, they attacked the enemies of the pope, church, and the Catholic religion, and were charged with employing methods which gave rise to the term "Jesuitry" in an opprobrious sense. They did not stay in convents, but went forth among the people to fight for the principles for which they stood. There was no election of their leaders; the attainment of office came through appointment by the general, who even chose his own successor. Education was their principal weapon, — education of the high and the low. In other respects the Jesuits were at the same time more simple and more mundane in their exterior practices — at least in the beginning — than the other orders. They opposed choral singing, the wearing of a distinctive habit, participation in religious processions, the monastic life, and asceticism. They believed in the individual poverty of their members, but were willing that the order and its separate institutions should prosper in a material way. In other words they were going into the world, not away from it, and were desirous of the best equipment for the struggle which lay before them.

The influence of the new order soon made itself felt throughout the world. At first Spaniards were in the majority, and it was natural that the Jesuits should establish themselves in Spain's dominions. By 1547 they had five institutions in Spain, and by 1566 sixteen. Soon afterward they began to appear in the Americas, where they became one of the principal agencies of the Spanish crown in the conversion and subjection of the natives, being perhaps the most effective of the missionary orders. Not only as missionaries but also as theologians, scientists, and men of letters the Spanish Jesuits were among the most distinguished men of the age. They were not welcomed by their fellow-countrymen in Spain, however; rather, they had to contend against some of the most powerful elements

Spanish opposition to the Jesuits.

in the peninsula. Members of the clergy, both regular and secular, were opposed to them, — notably the Dominicans, Franciscans, Augustinians, and the officers of the Inquisition, the first named especially, — while the universities and at the outset the kings were also hostile. Melchor Cano, a Dominican and one of the most influential men of his day, charged the Jesuits with heresy, claiming that their vows savored of the doctrines of the *Iluminados*. The archbishop of Toledo, Cardinal Siliceo, forbade them to preach, confess, say mass, or administer sacraments, but was obliged by the pope to retract his decrees. Arias Montano attacked them in the preface of his polyglot Bible, asserting that the Jesuits claimed that they alone had knowledge and that they were the nearest of all men to Jesus. These are but a few instances out of many, showing the difficulties encountered by the Jesuits in establishing themselves in Spain. It seems likely that jealousy may have entered into much of the resistance to them, for they early began to outrank and even supersede other elements in teaching and in learning. Charles I and Philip II objected to them because they placed the pope ahead of the king, not acknowledging the latter's authority over them, and this was not altogether in accordance with the royal ideal of centralization. Furthermore, the Jesuits were such an aggressive factor that they were hard to manage. The Inquisition took exception among other things to the Jesuit claim of a right to absolve their own members from the charge of heresy, and imprisoned the Jesuit *provincial*, or commanding official, in Spain, together with other members of the order. Philip II took sides with the Inquisition, but the pope sustained the Jesuits. By the seventeenth century the Jesuits had succeeded in overcoming their rivals, although they never ceased to have enemies. Their success was due in the first place to the continued support of the popes; in the second to the change of heart experienced by Philip II late in life, when he began to realize that they were one of the most effective instruments for the religious unification of his dominions, and in so much furthered his ideal of centralization; in the third place to the backing of the opponents of their enemies, especially those who were hostile to the Inquisition; and, finally, and perhaps most of all, to their own superior attainments, whereby they were able to win a devoted following among all ranks of society. The successors of Philip II followed the later policy of that king, with the result that the seventeenth century was the most prosperous era in the history of the Jesuit order.

One thing Spanish kings failed to do elsewhere in Europe they achieved in Spain, — their ideal of religious unity. At the same time that they were suppressing heresy they were giving a welcome to Catholics fleeing to Spain from Protestant persecution, notably to the Irish, who came to the peninsula in great numbers. The ideal of Catholic unity was carried to an excess which transcended unity itself through an extension of the institution of *limpieza de sangre*. Certificates of *limpieza de sangre* (that is to say, sworn statements that the bearer had no Jewish, Moslem, or heretic antecedents) now began to be required for the holding of various church offices or for entry into religious orders and often also for admission to the guilds. As a matter of fact there were few families which could have withstood a close examination of their ancestry; the upper classes would almost surely have been found to contain Jewish blood, and the masses, certainly in the east and south, would have had a Moslem admixture in their veins. The attainment of religious unity and the extreme suspicion in which non-Catholics were held did not succeed in making the Spanish people respond to the moral code of their faith. Not only such licentious practices as have already been alluded to were in vogue, but also a surprising lack of reverence was displayed, as exemplified by the improper use of sacred places and sacred objects and the mixture of the human and the divine in masquerades. Nevertheless, it is not too much to say that the principal preoccupation of Spaniards in the sixteenth and the seventeenth centuries was the salvation of their souls. The worst of men would want to confess and seek absolution before they died, and many of them no doubt believed themselves to be good Catholics, even though their every-day life would not have borne inspection. One

Limpieza de sangre and the fervor of Spanish Catholicism.

notable religious manifestation of the era was the ardent insistence of Spaniards on the mystery of the Immaculate Conception at a time when Catholics of other countries were not yet ready to accept that view.

Conflict of the kings with the popes in matters of temporal import. In distinguishing between the spiritual and the temporal phases of papal authority the kings of the House of Austria followed the policy of the Catholic Kings, but surpassed the latter in their claims of the superiority, or independence, as the case might be, of the royal power. Various factors contributed to this attitude in Spain. The monarchical ideal of a centralized absolutism, now that it had triumphed over the nobility and the towns, sought out the church in its civil aspects as the next outstanding element to dominate; the interests of the Spanish kings in Italy continued to bring them into opposition to the popes as sovereigns of the Papal States; and the problems of ecclesiastical reform often found the kings and the popes widely, even bitterly, apart. Charles I had frequent conflicts with the papacy, but Philip II had even more serious contests, in which he displayed yet more unyielding resistance than his father to what he regarded as the unwarranted intrusions of the popes into the sphere of Spanish politics. When in 1556 it seemed likely that Philip would be excommunicated and his kingdom laid under an interdict, Philip created a special council to exercise in Spain such functions as were customarily in the hands of the pope. In this as in his other disputes of a political nature with the papacy he was able to count on the support of the Spanish clergy. One document reciting Philip's grievances against Pope Paul IV, applying harsh epithets to him, and expressing doubt as to the legitimacy of his election, is believed to have been written by a member of the clergy. Another document, the *Parecer*, or opinion, of Melchor Cano, a Dominican, argued the lawfulness of making war on the pope, and said that in such cases, when communication with Rome was insecure, the bishops might decide ecclesiastical questions which were ordinarily left to the pope.

To avoid such disputes and to assure Spain of an ally in Italian affairs Charles I and Philip II bent their efforts to procure the election of popes who would be favorable to

them. Charles had much to do with the choice in 1522 of
Adrian VI, who as a cardinal had been one of his principal administrative officers during his own absence from the peninsula
in the early years of his reign. Philip was successful in the
same way when in 1559 he was able to cause the elevation of
his candidate to the papal throne. This pope, Pius IV,
proceeded to annul the action of his predecessor, Paul IV,
against Charles and Philip, and condemned to death two members of the deceased pope's family, one of them a cardinal. At
the election of 1590 Philip was again fortunate, but the new
pontiff, Urban VII, lived only thirteen days. A fresh
conclave was held, at which Philip went to the extreme not
only of excluding the candidates whom he opposed but also
of naming seven Spanish churchmen as the only ones from
among whom the cardinals were to choose. One of the
seven was elected, taking the name Gregory XIV, and no
pope of the century was more unconditionally favorable to
the wishes of a Spanish king. This constant intrusion of
Philip ended by exasperating the high authorities of the
church, who a few years later under another pope condemned
Philip's practices and declared him *ipso facto* excommunicated. This proved to be a decisive blow to the influence
of the Spanish crown.

Interfer-
ence of
Charles I
and
Philip II
in papal
elections.

One of the principal struggles between the popes and the
kings was the royal claim of the *pase regio*, or the right to
examine papal bulls and pontifical letters and, if deemed
advisable, to retain them, prohibiting their publication and
therefore their execution in Spanish domains. The origin
of this claim on the part of the Spanish monarchs seems to
date from the period of the Great Schism, when Urban VI
(1378–1389) granted such a privilege to the princes allied
with him. It was not officially decreed in Spain until the
early years of Charles I, when provision for the *pase regio* in
all Spanish dominions was made in a document drawn up by
Cardinal Ximénez. According to this arrangement papal
communications were to be examined in the *Consejo Real*,
and if found to be contrary to the royal prerogative or otherwise objectionable their circulation was to be postponed
and the pope asked to change or withdraw his dispositions.

The *pase
regio* as an
aid to the
kings in
the con-
flict with
the popes.

Usually the retention of such documents took place without giving official notice to the pope, — which in the case of a hostile pontiff would have been in any event unavailing. If the popes insisted on their point of view the royal prohibitions were nevertheless continued. If any subjects of the king resisted his will in this matter, even though they were churchmen, they might incur the penalty of a loss of goods or banishment or both, and notaries or attorneys might even be condemned to death. When Paul IV excommunicated Charles I and Philip II, the latter put into effect the *pase regio*. Unable to procure the publication of his bull in Spain, Paul IV summoned to Rome two Spanish bishops who were intensely royalist in their sympathies. Philip II protected them by retaining the papal order, so that the individuals did not learn officially of the summons. Not only in serious contests of this character but also in matters of comparatively little moment the kings exercised the right of retention, — for example, in the case of a bull of Sixtus V about the dress and maintenance of the clergy. The above are only a few instances out of many. One of the most bitter conflicts was waged by Philip II in opposition to a bull of Pius V excommunicating those who retained papal dispositions. Philip II retained this bull, and punished some bishops of Spain's Italian domains who had published it within their dioceses. The pope threatened to put Spain under an interdict, but Philip declined to yield. The bull was never published in the peninsula, and the pope did not make use of the interdict.

The case of Cardinal Borja. The successors of Philip II were equally insistent upon the royal prerogative in their relations with the church. One of the most curious incidents in the disputes of the kings and the popes occurred in the reign of Philip IV. Cardinal Borja and several other Spanish cardinals were sent to Rome to present the king's grievances against the pontiff arising out of matters connected with the wars against the Protestants. Borja was roughly handled on making his protest; it is said that Cardinal San Onofre punched him in the face by direction of the pope. When this event was reported in Spain a general meeting of royal councillors was held, in which it was even discussed whether it would be lawful to challenge the pope to settle the matter by means of a duel! In this and other matters there was talk of an appeal from the pope to a church council. As the royalist attitude toward the popes was often defended in books, many of them by church-men, a practice sprang up at Rome of placing such works in the *Index* as writings which the faithful were forbidden to read, but these volumes did not appear in the *Index* of the Spanish Inquisition. Finally the attitude of superiority on the part of the monarchs made itself evident, as already indicated, in questions of the reform of the church. Charles I and Philip II labored to establish their views at the Council of Trent not only in matters of administration but also in those of doctrine. Indeed, many Catholics believed that it was the duty of the kings to remedy the evils of the church. With the conclusion of the Council of Trent, Philip II hesi-tated for a year before publishing its decisions, because of his belief that some of the provisions of the council dimin-ished, or might diminish, his royal authority. When he at length did publish them, he did so with the reservation that they were not to be considered as introducing any variation from the usual jurisdiction of the king. Consequently, various canons of the council remained without effect in Spain and her possessions.

Interfer-ence of Charles I and Philip II in matters of church reform.

The same conflict of authority between the church and the monarch manifested itself in the relations of the kings with papal nuncios, who in the reign of Charles I began to reside at the Spanish court as permanent ambassadors. In 1537 Charles I obtained a license from the pope for the creation of the tribunal of the nunciature, or court of the papal embassy in Spain. This court, composed in part at least of Spanish officials, was to hear the numerous cases in ecclesiastical law which had customarily been settled at Rome. At the same time, the nuncio was empowered to grant the benefices which formerly lay within the juris-diction of the popes. The nuncio also collected the con-siderable sums which went to the popes from ecclesiastical prebends, or livings, from the *expolios* of deceased bishops and archbishops (accretions in their benefices which they

Royal restric-tions on the powers of papal nuncios and the nuncia-ture.

had procured out of rents), and from the income of *vacantes,* or vacant benefices (that which accrued between the death of a bishop or archbishop and the appointment of his successor). Once having transferred authority from the pope to the nuncio and nunciature the kings proceeded to attack these elements near at hand so as to reduce their power of interference with the royal authority. In this they were aided by all classes. The churchmen were royalist and at the same time opposed to papal intervention in ecclesiastical administration in Spain. People generally objected to such wide jurisdiction being in the hands of a foreigner, for the nuncios were usually Italians. There were frequent complaints that the nunciature was guilty of the advocacy of lawsuits and the collection of excessive costs, with the result that the court was sustained out of Spanish funds instead of by the popes. All of these matters were the subject of criticism in both the *Cortes* and the *Consejo Real,* and the inevitable result was the employment of restrictive measures. The *pase regio* was applied to the directions by the popes to the nuncios, and the intervention of the nunciature in ecclesiastical cases in first instance was prohibited. There were times when the relations of the kings with the nuncio were indeed strained; Philip II went to the extreme of expelling a nuncio who had endeavored to publish a papal bull which the king had decided to retain; the same thing happened under Philip IV, who closed the papal embassy. Matters were arranged in 1640 by the Fachenetti concordat, or agreement of the nuncio of that name with the king. This document reduced the procedure of the nunciature and the attributes of the nuncio to writing, and although it did not remove all the causes of dispute served as the basis for diplomatic relations with the papal embassy until the middle of the eighteenth century.

The relations of the kings with the popes and nuncios formed only part of the former's royalist policy with the church. The same course was followed with the ecclesiastical organization in Spain. The gradual reduction of the clergy to a tributary state as regards payment of taxes has already been referred to. Charles I procured various grants of a financial nature from the popes, such as the right to sell certain ecclesiastical holdings (whose proceeds were to be devoted to the war with the Turks), the collection of various church rents yielding over 1,000,000 ducats (some $15,000,-000), and finally the gift of *expolios* and *vacantes*. On the other hand, despite the petitions of the *Cortes* and the opinions of leading jurisconsults, the kings declined to prevent the giving of lands in mortmain, or in other words the acquisition of estates by the church. The most serious conflicts arose over questions of immunities, growing out of the survival of ecclesiastical jurisdictions of a seigniorial character and out of the relations of the church courts to those of the king and to the royal authority in general. Many of the seigniorial groups were incorporated into the crown, especially by Philip II. As regards the legal immunity of churchmen it came to be accepted as the rule that it could be claimed only in cases within the jurisdiction of the ecclesiastical courts. This was diminished still further by royal invasions of ecclesiastical jurisdiction, as by limiting the scope of the church courts, prohibiting (under severe penalties) the intrusions of their judges in civil affairs, and intervening to correct abuses, real or alleged. The king reserved a right of inspection of the ecclesiastical courts, exercised for him by members of the *Consejo Real* or the *audiencias*, and if anybody were unduly aggrieved by a decision of the church courts he might make use of the recourse of *fuerza* to bring an appeal before the *Consejo Real*, the *Cámara*, or the *audiencias*. The effect of this was to suspend the execution of an ecclesiastical sentence, subordinating the church courts to the royal will. Many matters of a religious character were taken over into the exclusive jurisdiction of the *Consejo Real* or the *Cámara*, such as the inspections of convents of the regular clergy and the action taken as a result thereof and the execution of the decisions of the Council of Trent. Laws relative to the recourse of *fuerza* were amplified so as to prohibit ecclesiastical judges from trying cases which were considered by any of the litigants concerned as belonging to the civil law; other laws forbade the summoning of Spaniards before foreign judges;

Subjection of the ecclesiastical organization in Spain to the royal will.

Y

and still others diminished the number of appeals to Rome. Even churchmen took advantage of the recourse of *fuerza* to have their cases removed to the royal courts when it suited their convenience, despite the attempts of the popes to check the practice. In such instances, as in so many others, the *pase regio* was employed to prevent effectual action by the popes. Even in the case of the provincial councils of the Spanish church the king sent delegates, on the ground that no conventions or congresses of any sort could be held without the consent of the king and the attendance of his representatives. In 1581 Pope Gregory XIII ordered the archbishop of Toledo not to admit anybody to a council about to be held at that time who was not a member of the clergy. Philip II sent his delegate, nevertheless, and his successors followed his example. In like manner religious processions were forbidden unless authorized by the civil authorities.

The *patronato real* as a source of royal authority over the clergy.

The royal authority over the Spanish church is largely explained by the institution of the *patronato real*, or royal patronage. Charles I early gained a right to make nominations to most of the bishoprics and abbacies in Spain, although the pope had to approve before the appointment should take effect. Even in the case of benefices still reserved by the pope the kings insisted that the appointees should be Spaniards. As regards the Americas the church was yet more completely under the king's control, thus giving still other lucrative posts into his power to grant. Under these circumstances it is not surprising that the Spanish clergy should favor the king, to whom they owed their rents and dignities, rather than the pope, and should even consent to diminutions in the privileges of Spanish churchmen. Indeed, faithful service as a councillor might be the stepping-stone to a bishopric. Nevertheless the kings did not allow churchmen to intrude in political affairs without being asked, and instances of official reproof on this score were numerous, despite which fact the clergy took a prominent part in political intrigues, and were possibly the principal factor in the Portuguese war of independence from Spain. Furthermore, the solicitation of inheritances by churchmen was insistently forbidden by the king; on one occasion when accusations of this character were made against the Jesuits of Flanders the Duke of Alba annulled all testamentary dispositions to that order and provided for the inheritance of the legal heirs.

CHAPTER XXVIII

ECONOMIC FACTORS, 1516–1700

Comparative backwardness of Spain in economic development.

WHILE this era was marked by a brief period of prosperity, and while there was a noteworthy advance out of medievalism in the evolution of mercantile machinery, the keynote of the times was the failure of Spain to keep pace in material welfare with her high standing in other aspects of life. Spain continued to be a raw material country, although artificial attempts were still made to create a thriving industrial development. These efforts, when they did not fail altogether, accrued to the advantage of foreigners or resulted in establishments which were of slight consequence in comparison with those of other European lands. A combination of evils at length sank Spain to such a state of economic degradation and misery as comported ill with her political reputation in European affairs and with the opportunities she had had and failed to employ to advantage. Nevertheless, Spain's decadence, overwhelming though it was, is to be viewed from a relative standpoint. Medieval Spain at its best, except possibly during the Moslem era, did not attain to an equally flourishing state with the Spain of the seventeenth century, which marks the lowest point to which she has fallen in modern times. On the other hand, with relation to other countries in the seventeenth century and with due regard to the needs which an expanded civilization had by that time developed, Spain came to be economically about the most backward land in western Europe. This occurred, in spite of the fact that Spaniards found and developed such extraordinary wealth in their new world possessions that their colonies were the envy of Europe.

Spain did indeed get rich returns from her overseas invest-
ment, but these funds and others were squandered in the
ways which have already been pointed out.

At the outset there was a period of undoubted prosperity, *Relative
prosperity
in the
early years
of the era.* due in part to a continuation of the favoring legislation of
the era of the Catholic Kings, but more particularly to the
enormously increased demand resulting from the rapid and
extensive colonization of the Americas, whose commerce
was restricted by law to favored regions of the Spanish
kingdom. The American trade and to some extent the considerable fortunes gained in the colonies themselves pro- *The American trade.* vided capital for a yet further expansion of the industrial
wealth of the peninsula. The effects were felt principally
in Castile, but were reflected also in Aragon and Valencia.
Seville, as the sole port of the American trade, became *Industrial
wealth of
Seville.* extraordinarily rich in its industrial life, and many other
cities shared in the general prosperity. Woollen goods and
silks were manufactured on a large scale, and many other
articles, such as hats, gloves, soap, leathers, arms, and
furniture were also made. Grazing and fishing were notably *Grazing.* productive industries. When Philip II ascended the Spanish
throne in 1556, it is said that the corporation of the *Mesta*
possessed seven million sheep. Part of the wool which they
produced was supplied to Spanish manufacturers, though
other sources were also drawn upon by the makers of woollen
goods, but vast quantities of wool were sent abroad. In
1512 about 50,000 quintals were exported; in 1557 some
150,000; and in 1610 the amount had reached 180,000
quintals. The whale-fisheries off the northern and north- *Fishing.* western coasts of Spain, at that time a rich field for this
occupation, and the catching of tunny-fish in the Medi-
terranean furnished profitable employment to the people of
the coasts, who also made voyages to distant waters, even
to Newfoundland, on fishing ventures. The wars of the
reign of Philip II and the scarcity of boats soon tended to
check this phase of economic expansion. Mining produced *Mining.* but little, in part because the possessors of *latifundia* —
nobles and churchmen — did not care to develop their
estates in this respect and in part because private individuals

generally could not be certain that they would be allowed to enjoy any profit they might make. Philip II, desirous of remedying this situation, incorporated all mines into the crown, and encouraged prospecting for mineral wealth, though exacting certain tributes from those who should discover and work mines, but even under these circumstances little was done.

Relative character of Spanish industrial prosperity.

There has been a tendency to exaggerate the state of prosperity to which Spain attained and to treat it as if it suddenly collapsed. In fact Spain's industrial wealth was only great by comparison with what it once had been and with what it was presently to be in the period of decline. The manufacture of cloth in the entire kingdom in the most flourishing epoch did not equal the output of the single city of Bruges. That the growth of manufacturing was only ephemeral and did not take root in the peninsula is attested by the fact that it was usually necessary, even in the era of greatest industrial expansion, to depend upon imports to supply Spain's needs, while the considerable exports of raw materials, especially wool, show that the domestic demand could not have been great. Undoubtedly a good industrial beginning was made, which might have resulted in the economic independence of Spain. It did not continue, how-

Its duration in time.

ever, and the question arises: How long did the era of relative industrial prosperity endure? A precise answer is impossible, because some industries flourished longer than others, or the same industry prospered in one place after it had ceased to do so in another. Conflicting accounts began to appear about the middle of the reign of Charles I, and even in the first half of the seventeenth century there were documents which testified to instances of prosperity. Speaking generally, the decline may be said to have made itself felt in the reign of Philip II and to have become clearly apparent by the middle of the reign of Philip IV.

Handicaps on agriculture.

Agriculture did not advance much from its wretched state of the previous era. The economists, giving undue importance to the accumulation of specie, and obsessed by a desire to develop manufactures, did not appreciate the fundamental value of agriculture; grazing was favored at the expense of farming; agricultural labor, never plentiful, was still more scarce after the expulsion of the Moriscos; and the evil of *latifundia* tended to reduce the amount of land cultivated. The laws encouraged agriculture only when it did not interfere with what were considered the more important industries. Legislation was frequent forbidding the cultivation of lands which had ever been devoted to grazing and compelling their restoration to that industry, and the old privileges of the *Mesta* were maintained to the detriment of the farmers. The scarcity of agricultural labor caused an immigration from other countries, especially from France, and this increased after the expulsion of the Moriscos. It did not solve the problem, as the foreigners were wont to return home, after they had accumulated savings. Under the circumstances it is not surprising that agricultural production did not meet the needs of the peninsula. Something was done to protect farm laborers, and some government projects of irrigation were undertaken, but not enough was done to offset the handicaps which the state itself imposed. Intensive cultivation by small proprietors was one of the needs of the time, and one attempt to bring this about in Granada was made. Some 12,500 Castilian, Asturian, and Galician families were sent there to replace in a measure the several hundred thousand expelled Moriscos. The experiment was successful, and the colonization took root, but it was not repeated. Nevertheless, eastern and southern Spain had their period of relative prosperity, especially through the cultivation of the vine and the olive. The Americas offered a rich field for the export of wine, since the growing of vines was prohibited there, and the soil, climate, irrigation canals, and Morisco labor (prior to the expulsion) of Valencia, Granada, and Andalusia were well adapted to provide the desired supply. Even this form of agriculture suffered a serious decline in the seventeenth century, due largely to the loss of the Moriscos.

Spanish commerce had its era of splendor and its period of decline, but the former was prolonged much more than in the case of the manufacturing industry, because of Spain's

Compara-
tive pros-
perity of
Spanish
commerce.

Prosperity
of Seville
and
Medina
del
Campo.
serving as a medium for distribution between foreign countries and the Americas, and because of the continued exchange of raw materials for the foreign finished product after Spain herself had ceased to be a serious competitor in manufacturing. Seville was by far the most prosperous port in the country, since it had a monopoly of the American trade, which also necessitated the sending to that city of goods from the other parts of Spain and from foreign countries for trans-shipment overseas. Mercantile transactions on a great scale, involving the modern forms of credit and the establishment of branch houses in all parts of the world, were a natural outgrowth of Seville's great volume of trade. The wealth of the city continued until well into the seventeenth century. The transfer of the *Casa de Contratación* (which handled Spain's commerce with the Americas) from Seville to Cádiz occasioned a decline of the former and a corresponding prosperity of the latter. Possibly next in importance to Seville in mercantile affairs was the inland city of Medina del Campo, site of the greatest of Spanish fairs and, except for the east coast provinces, the contractual centre of the entire kingdom. Purchases, sales, and exchanges of goods entering or leaving the various ports of Spain were usually arranged there. Numerous other cities shared with Seville and Medina del Campo in the commercial activity of the sixteenth century, even those of the east coast, although the forces which had occasioned their decline in preceding eras were still operative and were to renew their effects before the sixteenth century had much more than passed the halfway mark. The Mediterranean trade of Spain remained largely in the hands of the Catalans, however. North European commerce, of which that with Flanders was the most important, was shared generally by Spain's Atlantic ports, although those of the north coast had in this case a natural advantage.

The *con-
sulados*
and other
mercantile
ma-
chinery.
The inevitable result of the commercial activity of the sixteenth century was the development of a mercantile machinery to handle the trade. This occurred, in Spain, on the basis of institutions already in existence, the *consulados*, merchants' exchange buildings (*lonjas*), and fairs.

To the earlier *consulados* of Valencia (1283), Barcelona (1347), Saragossa (1391), Burgos (1494), and Bilbao (1511) there were added those of Seville (1543) and Madrid (1632). Although the *consulados* of the ports differed in some respects from those of the interior the same principles applied to both, — so much so, that the ordinances of the *consulado* of Burgos were the model for that of Bilbao. The *consulado* of Burgos served as the type, indeed, upon which the ordinances of many of the later *consulados* were founded, wherefore its description may suffice for all. Strictly speaking, the *consulado* was only the tribunal of the body of merchants, who together formed the *universidad*, or association, for purposes of trade, although the term *consulado* came eventually to include both. Many cities lacked the tribunal, but did possess the *universidad* of merchants. The tribunal, or *consulado*, of Burgos exercised jurisdiction in mercantile cases, and also had charge of such important matters as maritime insurance, charter-parties, and the patronage of certain pious foundations. The *universidad* met annually to elect the officers of the *consulado*, — a prior, two consuls, and a treasurer. The jurisdiction of the *consulado* as a court was not limited to cases arising in Burgos, but extended to other towns and cities for many miles around it. There was an appeal in criminal cases to the *corregidor* of Burgos, but in civil cases the *consulado* was independent of both the royal and the municipal courts. The *consulado* of Madrid introduced some novelties, principal among which was its close attachment to the national bureaucracy through the intervention in its affairs of the *Consejo Real*. Various cities founded merchants' exchange buildings, including some which had no *consulado*. As for the fairs, the great importance of Medina del Campo has already been mentioned. Two fairs a year, in May and October, were held at that city, on which occasions merchants, bankers, and brokers from all parts of the world gathered there. By the end of the sixteenth century the fairs of Medina del Campo were already in a state of decline, and they received a death-blow when by royal mandate Burgos replaced Medina del Campo as the contractual centre of Spain.

Burgos did not greatly profit, however, for the general mercantile decadence had begun to affect all commercial institutions in the country. Mercantile machinery survived after the period of prosperity had passed, and thus it was only to be expected that a central institution should at length be founded. Such was the case, for the *Junta de Comercio y Moneda* (Junta, or Council, of Commerce and Coinage) came into existence in 1679. During the remainder of this era it was of slight consequence, however.

Medieval character and inconsistencies of mercantile legislation.

The legislation of the period reflected the prevailing economic ideas, such as the exceptional importance attached to precious metals, the insistence that the balance of trade should favor exports (lest imports should result in specie going out of the country), the favor shown toward the policy of protection, and in a measure the continuance of the medieval penchant for government regulation of industry. The state was not consistent, however, varying its laws according as the needs of the treasury or of European diplomacy or of any passing crisis might direct. Thus prohibitions against foreign goods were often maintained, while at other times the greatest freedom of entry was allowed. In the treaties of peace of the sixteenth century care to safeguard the commercial interests of Spain was employed, but in the seventeenth century they were often sacrificed through the indiscretions of ministers or for political reasons. Thus Spain's need of allies against France occasioned the grant of a right for the free entry of goods into Spain (but not into the colonies) to the Protestant Netherlands, England, Denmark, and Portugal, with reductions in duties. Treaties of 1665 and 1667 with England abolished Spain's right to inspect English boats or to search the houses of British subjects, amounting to a virtual invitation to smuggling, which was in fact the result. Smuggling in connivance with Spanish officials became so general (not altogether by Englishmen) that it was regarded as a necessary evil. The government displayed a tendency to facilitate internal commerce, — as by the suppression of interior customs lines, — but the protective and regulative spirit of the Middle Ages was too often apparent. Thus prices were fixed and exclusive rights of sale granted. A curious instance of the latter (though not out of keeping with the age) was the permit given to the religious orders of Madrid to open taverns for the sale of beverages accruing from their crops. When certain abuses and some scandal resulted the privilege was withdrawn, but was later renewed subject to certain conditions, one of which was that friars should not serve the wines to customers.

Legislation with relation to money was particularly abundant. One grave error of the past was constantly committed from the time of Philip II to the close of the era, the debasement of the coinage with a view to relieving the difficulties of the treasury, but the results were not more favorable than in former years. Despite governmental care in the matter of coinage, diversity of coins was still a problem. In addition to the national moneys there were regional pieces and numerous foreign coins. Attempts were made to fix the relation between them, but without great success. One factor which was not appreciated at the time was that of the cheapening of money through the enormous importation of precious metals from the Americas, resulting in a corresponding advance in prices. The high prices were ascribed to the exportation of precious metals from Spain, and stringent laws were passed to prevent it. It was difficult, however, to keep the gold and silver in the country. *Difficulties over coinage.*

The national record of the House of Austria in public works cannot be said to have been good. The need for more and better roads was generally recognized, but unless they suited military purposes or were to be made use of in a royal progress, or journey, the state would rarely build them. Municipalities and groups of merchants (especially the *consulados*) did something, but were hampered by the centralizing spirit of the government. A license from the *Consejo Real* was required, even though the state were not to pay. There were too few roads, and existing highways were as a general rule in a bad state of repair. Many bridges were constructed by the government in the sixteenth century, but only a few in the century following. Plans were also discussed for deepening the channels of *Scant attention to public works.*

Spain's great rivers, but that of the Tagus alone received attention, and the work to that end by Philip II was destroyed by the negligence of his successors. In like manner irrigation on a large scale was planned, but scarcely anything was accomplished. On the other hand this period marked the beginning of a mail service as an auxiliary of economic life; it was due to the state only in that the government granted a monopoly of the privilege to a private individual. Between 1580 and 1685 the extension of the service to foreign countries was brought about. Naturally the whole system was as yet defective from the modern standpoint. The government did expend moneys, however, for military objects and state buildings. Forts were built the length and breadth of the Spanish world, although many of them were allowed to decay in the seventeenth century. Royal palaces and houses of recreation and several splendid churches for royal use, all of which added to the glamor of monarchy, were built at state expense. The municipalities also erected public edifices, such as merchants' exchange buildings and city halls.

Foreigners in Spain and legislation concerning them. One of the most controversial questions of the era was that of the entry of foreigners into the economic life of the peninsula. This had begun to be a factor (without referring now to the earlier arrival of Moslem and Jewish elements) in the reign of the Catholic Kings, but it was a much more prominent issue in the period of the House of Austria. It was complicated by the fact that certain groups of foreigners might be welcomed (laborers for example), while others (merchants and manufacturers in particular) were not, but all elements would be both wanted and opposed by some class of the Spanish people at any given time. In general, popular opinion whether of rich or poor was adverse to foreigners. At times the kings yielded to the complaints of the people and passed restrictive laws, but at other times, urged on by financial needs and political aims, they took the contrary course. Dependent as they were upon foreign money-lenders the kings could not refuse to grant the privileges and monopolies which their creditors exacted as security. It would seem, however, that by far the greater number of the foreigners were engaged in the less remunerative occupations. A writer of the seventeenth century says that there were 120,000 foreigners in domestic service, and goes on to say that they also engaged in such occupations as street hawking, the keeping of retail shops of all varieties (sellers of meat, wine, cakes, etc.), and the mechanical trades, including even those of porter and vendor of water. In 1680 the French ambassador estimated that there were 77,000 of his countrymen in Spain, many of whom were farm laborers, but there were considerable numbers in various other occupations, ranging from the wealthy merchant down to the lowly shepherd or peddler. Other nationalities were also prominent. Laws were passed limiting the number of trades in which foreigners could engage, but they seem to have been without avail, for both the complaints and the legislation were often repeated. The victory of the foreign element began to be more apparent by the middle of the seventeenth century. Philip IV enacted laws to encourage immigration, because of the scarcity of labor, and permitted a foreigner who had lived for many years in Spain and married a Spanish woman to enjoy privileges little short of those of a native. Similar laws were made in the reign of Charles II.

The economic status of Spain in this era could be more clearly set forth if it were possible to have fairly reliable data as to population. In the middle of the sixteenth century there may have been about six and three quarter millions of people in Spain. By the end of the century some estimates hold that the numbers had increased to perhaps eight and a half millions, but there is ground for doubting these assertions. Figures for the seventeenth century are even more uncertain, but there is a general agreement that the population declined. One estimate makes the population of Spain 5,700,000 at the end of the era. Misery, idleness, and vagabondage were characteristic of Spanish life in the late sixteenth and throughout the seventeenth century; it has been estimated that there were 150,000 vagabonds at the close of the sixteenth century whose principal occupations were begging, thieving, and prostitution. It is true

Statistics of population.

Prevalence of vagabondage.

that a like state of affairs existed in other countries, and that many foreigners were included in this element in the peninsula, but conditions were probably worse in Spain than elsewhere in western Europe.

Causes of vaga-bondage.

Much has been written about the causes of vagabondage in Spain. The principal causes undoubtedly were economic. Foreign writers have charged it to Spanish pride and scorn of manual labor as well as to a certain native laziness. These allegations are true to some extent, flowing naturally from the circumstances of the history of Spain. Slavery had been perhaps more general and long-continuing in the peninsula than in other parts of Europe, and the slaves had usually been Moslem in faith; thus Spaniards might naturally be disinclined to do the work of slaves and infidels, and the same spirit would be present on its religious side to make them object to working in company with the questionably orthodox Moriscos. The general desire of Spaniards to be regarded as of noble blood also tended to make manual labor unpopular, since there was a strong class prejudice that nobles should not engage in such work. Finally, the ease of entry into religious orders had rendered escape from toil possible for a great number, and had increased the sentiment against laboring with one's hands. The only way out for a great many was the life of a vagabond. The sudden wealth acquired by individuals in the Americas reacted psychologically to make the necessarily slow accretions of property in Spain an irksome prospect. The exaltation of military glory had the same general effect, but as the Spanish armies were small this occupation was not open to everybody, and its perils and irregularities in pay made not a few hesitate to enter it. Furthermore, there were many contemporary writers, Cervantes among them, who pointed out that the life of a vagabond had a certain appeal for many Spaniards; young men of good family not infrequently joined bands of gypsies.

The poverty of Spain was general by the middle of the seventeenth century, and the state of the country got steadily worse thereafter. Bread riots frequently served as a reminder to the authorities, who indeed made many attempts

to remedy the situation.   Their measures to attack the root Inability
of the evil were worse than useless, however, being based on of the gov-
economic misconceptions or being discontinued (when they ernment
to cope
might have proved beneficial) if they ran counter to govern- with the
mental policies.   Direct legislation against vagabondage situation.
was frequent, but was evaded as often as enacted.   When
people were forbidden to remain in the country without
working, the vagabonds made a showing of becoming porters
or of engaging in other like occupations, under the guise of
which they continued their loose practices.   When these
occupations were limited they were to be found as theoretically in the service of the noble or wealthy, whom social
pride induced to have as many in their following as possible.
When this custom was attacked direct evasion of the laws
was rendered possible through charitable institutions,
especially through the free soup-kitchens of the religious
orders.   On the benevolent side the problem was also
approached through the founding of poor-houses, although
this method was not yet greatly developed, and through the
conversion of the former public granaries (*pósitos*), in which
stores of grain were kept to guard against the possibility of
famine, into pious institutions for the gift or loan of food
supplies to the poor.

The fact of Spain's economic decline has perhaps been Contem-
pointed out with sufficient clearness.   It is now pertinent to porary
sum up the causes which had produced it.   According to opinions as
to the
Altamira there was "a great variety of causes, accumulated causes of
upon a country which entered the modern age with weak and Spain's
incipient economic energies, a country whose governments economic
let themselves be dragged into an imperialistic policy (in decline.
great part forced upon them by problems traceable to
Ferdinand the Catholic and the fatal inheritance of Charles
I), neglecting, more for lack of means than intentionally,
those measures which could best contribute to better the
productive power and well-being of the country."   This is
an epitome not only of the causes for Spain's economic
decline in this period but also of modern Spanish history.
It places the fault where it belongs, on Spanish imperialism
with its train of costly wars, a policy which Spain might have

followed so far as the Americas were concerned, but which proved an impossible strain on her resources when carried beyond the Spanish peninsula into Europe. This was one of the principal causes assigned at the time. Some others may also be enumerated. The increase in the *alcabala* and in other taxes was often mentioned as a principal cause, although it is easy to see how this might have been a result of the warfare. In like manner another group of causes set forth at that time might well have been results of the economic decline, such as the following : emigration to the colonies ; the lack of government aid to industries ; the invasion of foreign goods and foreigners into Spain ; and the decline in population. Other causes alleged by contemporaries and deserving of prominent mention, though less important than that of the European wars, were these : the repugnance of Spaniards for manual labor ; bad financial administration by the government ; the prodigality of the kings in granting favors and exemptions ; the governmental practice of fixing the prices of agricultural products ; the evil of absentee landlordism, especially in the case of the *latifundia*, which were not developed to the extent of their resources ; waste of the means of production in luxury ; the great number of convents and monasteries ; and the exemptions enjoyed by a vast number of individuals.

Causes
assigned
by later
writers.

Later writers have put emphasis on other matters. Some present-day historians assign the expulsion of the Moriscos as the principal cause of the economic decline. It did leave many trades without hands, and temporarily depopulated whole districts, but it seems hardly accurate to regard it as anything more than one of many contributory causes. Writers of the seventeenth century were impressed by its religious and political advantages, and do not seem to have regarded it as of serious economic import. The economic effects of the conquest of the Americas have also been set forth to account for Spain's decline. That conquest induced the already-mentioned get-rich-quick spirit among Spaniards, and encouraged the false economic idea that precious metals are the basic form of wealth, leading to the assignment of an undue importance to them. More serious, perhaps, was the fact that the Americas drained Spain of some of her best and most virile blood. The number of Spaniards who went to America, however, was not excessive, — little more than the number of Englishmen who crossed the seas in the seventeenth century. Furthermore, Spain most certainly secured a vast financial profit out of the Americas, not only from precious metals, but also from commerce and the employment which thousands obtained both in Spain and in the colonies. Spanish soil was indeed not fertile enough to support a policy of European imperialism, and that argument has been put forward, but the fault was less in the land itself, which in other days had produced more richly, than in the methods (or lack of them) employed to develop its capacities. Foreign commercial vicissitudes, which are also alleged to account for Spain's economic fall, did indeed help to bring it about, — such, for example, as the disastrous consequences of the silting in of the port of Bruges, which city had been one of the best purchasers of Spain's raw materials. While it is indeed impossible to assign any single event or condition of affairs as the *sine qua non* of Spain's decadence, one factor stands out from the rest, however, as the most important, — that of the oft-mentioned policy of Spanish imperialism in Europe.

CHAPTER XXIX

THE GOLDEN AGE: EDUCATION, PHILOSOPHY, HISTORY, AND SCIENCE, 1516-1700

Causes of Spain's intellectual greatness in this era.

THE sixteenth and seventeenth centuries represent the highest point in the history of Spanish intellectual achievement in science, literature, and art. Two manifestations characterized the era: an abundant productivity which was as high in quality as it was great in amount; and the diffusion of Spanish learning in the other countries of the civilized world, so that for the first time (except for the transmission of Moslem culture) Christian Spain became a vital factor in European thought, whereas in former years she had merely received the instruction of others. The reasons for this intellectual outburst were various. For one thing the natural evolution from the past seemed to render inevitable a high degree of attainment. For another, the general effects of the Renaissance in Europe made themselves felt in Spain. In the third place, this seems to have been the era of the ripe maturity of the Spanish people, when they were at the height of their capacity in every walk of life. Finally, as has happened so many times in the history of other nations, the very fact of the establishment of a great empire was bound to react both materially and psychologically to produce an unwonted expansion intellectually. Spanish imperialism in Europe undoubtedly contributed much to the civilization of the peninsula, but it is not too much to say that the greatest influence came from Spain's conquests in the new world. These operated directly to make Spain an innovator in scientific thought, and provided the first noteworthy material for mental stimulus in the era. If the better known mani-

338

festations of polite literature and painting were not directly traceable to the attainment of a colonial empire, other achievements were, and the indirect effect of the overseas conquests should not be left out of consideration even in the case of those factors which acknowledged Italy as their principal source of inspiration.

There were many social manifestations of Spanish intellectuality, such as the eagerness with which men sought an education, the honors paid to men of letters in an age when military glory might tend to absorb attention, the encyclopedic knowledge demonstrated by scholars who were at one and the same time proficient in widely divergent fields, the circumstance that women won marked distinction (together with the fact that their achievements were well received), and the fondness of the upper classes for social functions of a literary character, — not a few of which developed from a simple gathering at some noble's house into the formation of clubs or academies of an intellectual character. This flourishing state of affairs endured a much shorter time than might have been expected from the force of its initial momentum; in a broad sense the intellectual decadence of the country accompanied, or perhaps resulted from, the political and economic decline, but just as in the case of these factors it was not equal in celerity or in completeness in all of the many-sided aspects of Spanish intellectual life. Furthermore, the fall was so rapid in some respects, and from such a high point in all, that the ultimate degradation, though deep enough, seemed by comparison to be worse than it was. At any rate, the state of intellectuality at its best was sufficiently great to deserve the title which has been applied to the period of its expression, that of the *siglo de oro* (golden century) in Spanish science, literature, and art.

Social manifestations of Spanish intellectuality and its duration in time.

A question arises as to the application of the term and the duration of the period of the *siglo de oro*. The seventeenth century has usually been regarded as the golden age, for it was then that the greatest names in polite literature and painting appeared. In fact, however, the era of intellectual brilliance dates from an early point in the sixteenth century in the reign of Charles I, lasting for about a century and a

Application and duration of the siglo de oro.

half, past the middle of the seventeenth century. The general desire for knowledge, which was so marked in the first half of the sixteenth century, had already ebbed away by the end of the reign of Philip II. The greatest achievements in didactic and scientific literature belong to the sixteenth century, and, indeed, most of the great writers and painters who won fame in the reigns of Philip III and Philip IV got their start, or at least were born, in the time of Philip II. Great results were obtained in both periods, but the stimulus came for the most part in the sixteenth century.

The universities. The aristocratic character of intellectual attainments in the *siglo de oro* was reflected in that of the institutions of learning which were founded. In addition to the eight universities existing in 1516, twenty-one were added in the sixteenth century, and five in the seventeenth, making a total of thirty-four in all. Salamanca and Alcalá stood forth as the leading universities, although outranked in legal studies by Valladolid. Salamanca had the more ample curriculum, with some sixty professorships, but Alcalá, with forty-two professorial chairs, was distinguished for the scientific labors of its faculty. Salamanca was more largely attended, having 6778 students in 1584, a number which had declined to 1955 in 1682, while Alcalá had 1949 in 1547, 2061 in 1650, and 1637 in 1700. The medieval type of internal management remained as the essential basis of university administration, characterized by the close connection between the university and the civil authorities (to which latter the former were in a measure subjected), by an intimate relationship with the cathedral or other local churches, and by the ecclesiastical origin of many of the university rents. The universities did not become religious establishments, however, even though churchmen founded the greater number of them. As time went on, the kings displayed a tendency to intervene in university life, as by the sending of *visitadores*, or by imposing their candidates for professorships upon the universities, but they did not go so far as to deprive the universities of their economic, legal, and scientific independence.

There were also various other institutions of higher education. One of them, the Estudios Reales de San Isidro of Madrid, founded early in the reign of Philip IV for the education of the sons of the greater nobility, ranked with the universities. Jesuit teachers were installed. This was not the first instance of Jesuit instruction in the peninsula. By their vows the Jesuits were obliged to found "colleges," but this term meant houses for study, only in that the members of the order living in these institutions pursued investigations there. Gradually, outside pupils began to be accepted by the Jesuits, who soon won a great reputation for their efficiency as teachers. Their teaching was markedly influenced by Renaissance ideals, for the study of classical authors formed one of the principal elements in their curriculum. They devoted themselves to the education of the wealthy classes, leaving the field of vocational preparation to the universities. Apart from the Jesuit colleges there were various schools, both religious and secular, primarily for the study of Latin. They were in essence schools of literature, at which students were given practice in the writing of poetry and the reciting of verses, both Latin and Castilian. It is said that there were more than four thousand of these institutions in 1619, although their numbers declined greatly with the advance of the century. In addition there were many schools of a purely professional character, such as those for the study of religion, war, medicine, and nautical science. The school of nautical science of the *Casa de Contratación* of Seville merits special attention. Among the manifold functions of the *Casa* in its relation to the Americas was that of the pursuit of scientific studies to facilitate overseas communication, and this was carried out to such an extent that the *Casa* was a veritable maritime university. Mathematics, cosmography, geography, cartography, navigation, the construction and use of nautical instruments, and military science (in so far as it related to artillery) were taught at the *Casa*, and in nearly all of these respects that institution not only outranked the others in Spain but was able also to add materially to the sum total of world knowledge. Primary education continued to be neglected. The current belief was that it was unnecessary unless one intended

Jesuit colleges.

Other schools of higher education.

The Casa de Contratación as a maritime university.

Neglect of primary education.

to pursue a professional career.   The education of the masses for the sake of raising the general level of culture, or even for technical advancement, was a problem which was not as yet comprehended.   Such primary schools as there were, were usually ecclesiastical or private foundations.   Reading, writing, arithmetic, and Christian doctrine were the subjects taught.   Taken as a whole it will be seen that the number of teaching establishments had vastly increased over that of the preceding eras.   An understanding of the superior facilities available for the upper classes would not be complete without a reference to the extraordinary diffu-

Great age of printing.

Beginnings of public archives.

sion of printing in this era.   Although the publication of works was subject to various conditions, printed books fairly came into their own, for the first time in the history of the peninsula.   A number of great libraries were formed.   It is worthy of mention, too, that it was at this time that care began to be taken in the accumulation of public documents in archives.   In 1558 Philip II founded an archive at Rome, and in 1563 made a beginning of the famous state archive at Simancas.

Luis Vives and Spanish originality in philosophical studies.

The revival of classical studies, which made available the writings of many Greek philosophers whose works had been unknown to the medieval scholars, and the complex movement of ideas engendered by the Protestant Reformation and the Catholic Reaction were the fundamental causes of the flourishing state of theological and philosophical studies in this period, especially in the sixteenth century.   While this was by no means confined to Spain, the peninsula furnished its quota to the great names of the period.   The philosopher Luis Vives (1492–1540) may be mentioned by way of illustration.   Vives, who spent most of his life in Flanders and in England, — in which latter country he was the teacher of Mary Tudor, the later queen of England, — was regarded by contemporaries as a philosopher of the first rank, on a plane with Erasmus.   Nearly a century before Francis Bacon (1561–1626) suggested the necessity for the observation of nature as the basis of knowledge rather than the blind following of classical texts, Vives had pronounced the same idea.   Of importance, too, were his pedagogical doctrines, which profoundly influenced Comenius. The case of Vives was not unique, for the ideas which were later to be made famous by Reid, Descartes, Montaigne, Charron, and others had already been expressed by Spaniards of the sixteenth century. The common note in all their works was that of great liberty of thought in all things other than the Catholic faith, and in particular that of a reaction against submission to consecrated authority, which brought them into opposition to the slavish acceptance of classical writings so much in vogue among the Humanists. In so doing, the Spanish philosophers were only expressing their national traits, for the Spaniards have always been able to reconcile their support of absolutism in government and of the principle of authority in religion with a degree of individualism that cannot be found in lands whose political and religious ideas have been more democratic. Partly on this account Spanish thought has not received due credit, for, though there were Spanish philosophers, there was no school of Spanish philosophy. Furthermore, sweeping originality of thought on a universal basis was precluded by the necessity of subordinating all ideas to Catholic doctrine, while the philosophers who have attained to the greatest fame in modern times expressed themselves with independence in that respect, or at least without the preoccupation of not departing from it. That Spaniards were capable of originality within the field of religion itself was proved by the development of Spanish mysticism, already alluded to.

In jurisprudence and politics Spanish writers gained an indisputable title to originality of thought, of positive influence on the civilization of other countries. This was due in part to the continuous warfare, the grave religious problems, and the many questions arising out of the conquest, colonization, and retention of the Americas, but it was also a result of a natural tendency in Spanish character to occupy itself with the practical aspects of affairs, directing philosophical thought toward its applications in actual life, — for example, in the case of matters to which the above-mentioned events gave rise. Spanish jurists achieved renown in various phases of jurisprudence, such as in international,

Important character of Spanish writings on jurisprudence, politics, and economics.

political, penal, and canonical law, in the civil law of Rome and of the Spanish peninsula, and in legal procedure. Not Grotius (1583–1645), but his Spanish predecessors of the sixteenth century laid the foundations for international law, and the great Dutch jurist more than once acknowledged his indebtedness to Spaniards, who, like Vitoria and Vázquez, had provided him with rich materials for the thesis he set forth. Among the writers on political law may be mentioned Solórzano, whose *Política indiana*, or Government of the Indies (1629–1639), was a noteworthy exposition and defence of the Spanish colonial system. In economics, too, the Spaniards were necessarily outstanding figures in their day, since the Spanish empire was the greatest and for a time the most powerful of the period. National resources, the income and expenditures of the state, and the method of the enjoyment of landed property were the three principal questions to engage the attention of the Spanish economists. When Martínez de la Mata declared that labor was the only true source of wealth, he was in so much the precursor of Adam Smith (1723–1790). Some economists expressed ideas which sound strangely like those set forth by Spencer, Wallace, Tolstoy, and others in the nineteenth and twentieth centuries, such as the following: that immovable property should be taken away from the private individuals possessing it, and be redistributed under the control of the state; and that society should be considered as having legal title to lands, giving only the user to individuals. Luis Vives was one of the representatives of these ideas. The principles of these economists found little support in practice, and cannot be said to have attained general acceptance among the Spanish writers on these subjects.

Páez de Castro and the new sense of historical content.
The advance of historical studies in this period, especially in the sixteenth century, was nothing short of remarkable. For the first time history won a right to be considered apart from polite literature. Two novelties marked the era, one of them relative to the content of history, and the other concerning the methods of investigation and composition. Formerly history had reduced itself to little more than the external political narrative, dealing with wars, kings, and

heroes, being more rhetorical in form than scientific. The new sense of content was represented principally by the philosopher Luis Vives and by the historian Páez de Castro, one-time chronicler of Charles I. Vives gave his opinion that history should deal with all the manifestations of social life. Páez de Castro stands forth, however, as the man who most clearly expressed the new ideas. According to him the history of a land should include the study of its geography, of the languages of its peoples, of the dress, laws, religions, social institutions, general customs, literature, arts, sciences, and even the aspects of nature of the land in so far as these things affected the actions of men. Páez de Castro was also a follower of Pérez de Guzmán and Hernando del Pulgar in his appreciation of the psychological element in history. The most exacting methodologists of the present day do not require more than did Páez de Castro nearly four centuries ago. Incidentally, it becomes clear that the credit ordinarily assigned to Voltaire (1694–1778) and Hume (1711–1776) as innovators in this respect belongs rather to Spaniards of the sixteenth century. Vives and Páez de Castro were not alone in their concept of history. On the other hand they were not able to put their ideas into practice, and were not followed by the majority of the writers on methodology. Nevertheless, all were agreed that the education of the historian should be encyclopedic in character, — an ideal which necessarily involved a measurable attainment of the plan of Páez de Castro.

If these concepts as to historical content were not fully realized, those with regard to the methods of investigation and criticism found a worthy representation in the majority of the historians of the era. To be sure, some of the great writers, like Florián de Ocampo and Mariana, displayed too much credulity or a disposition to imagine events for which they lacked documentary proof. Furthermore, this was a thriving period of forgeries, when writers invented classical authors, chronicles, letters, and inscriptions with which to support their narratives. Still, the evil brought about the remedy; the necessity for criticism was so great that its application became customary. In addition, men sought

Zurita and Morales and the advance in historical investigation and criticism.

documents, if only to disprove the forgeries, with the result that the employment of source material and the use of the sciences auxiliary to history were a factor in the works of the numerous great historians of the time. The highest representatives of the new sense of historical analysis were the official chroniclers of Charles I and Philip II. First in point of time was Florián de Ocampo, whose *Crónica general* (General chronicle) was published in 1543. While giving too free rein to the imagination, his *Crónica* had a fairly complete documental basis in some of its parts. Far superior was the *Anales de Aragón*, or Annals of Aragon (1562–1580), of Jerónimo Çurita, or Zurita, which in its use of archive material was the greatest historical work of the sixteenth century. Of equal rank with Zurita was Ambrosio de Morales, the continuer of Ocampo, whose *Crónica* was published in 1574–1575. Morales, who was a distinguished palæographist and archæologist, made a notable use of inscriptions, coins, manuscripts, ancient books, and other ancient evidences. While the influence of Gibbon (1737–1794) on historiography in these respects is not to be denied, it is only fair to point out the merits of his predecessors of the Spanish *siglo de oro* in precisely those qualities for which the great Englishman has won such signal fame.

The historian Mariana. The historian of this era who attained the greatest reputation, though far from equalling Vives and Páez de Castro on the one hand or Zurita and Morales on the other, was the Jesuit Mariana. In 1592–1595 he published his history of Spain in Latin (*Historia de rebus Hispaniæ*), which he brought out in Castilian in 1601 under the title *Historia general de España* (General history of Spain). This work, which is still one of the most widely read of all Spanish histories, was remarkable for its composition and style, in which respects it was superior to others of the period, though otherwise inferior to the best works of the time. It was intended to be popular, however, on which account it should not be judged too critically from the standpoint of technique. Mariana's history was an external political narrative, from the Castilian point of view, of the events which had developed the national unity of Spain. His own bias, politically and otherwise, was only too apparent, besides which he displayed the faults of credulity and imagination already alluded to. Nevertheless, Mariana made use of manuscripts and the evidence of inscriptions and coins, though not to the same degree as Zurita, Morales, and others. His style was tinged with the Humanistic ideals of the period, being strongly influenced by Livy. Many other students of history or of the sciences auxiliary to history are deserving of recognition, and at least one of them demands mention, Nicolás Antonio, the greatest bibliographer of his time. In 1672 he published his *Bibliotheca hispana* (republished in 1788 as the *Bibliotheca hispana nova*, or Catalogue of new Spanish works) of all Spanish works since 1500, and in 1696 completed his *Bibliotheca hispana vetus*, or Catalogue of old Spanish works (published in 1788), of Spanish books, manuscript and printed, prior to the sixteenth century. Deserving of special notice was a remarkable group of historians of the Americas, such as Fernando Colón (Ferdinand Columbus), Fernández de Oviedo, López de Gómara, Bernal Díaz del Castillo, Bernabé Cobos, Gutiérrez de Santa Clara, Juan de Castellanos, Acosta, Garcilaso de la Vega, Herrera, Cieza de León, Zárate, Jerez, Dorantes de Carranza, Góngora, Hevía, León Pinelo, Mendieta, Pizarro, Sahagún, Suárez de Peralta, Alvarado, Torquemada, Solís, Cortés, Las Casas, Cervantes de Salazar, López de Velasco, the already cited Solórzano, Pérez de Ribas, Tello, Florencia, Vetancurt, and many others. The works of some of these men were written in Spain as official chronicles of the Indies, while those of others were prepared independently in the Americas. Religious history was abundantly produced, as also were books of travel, especially those based on the expeditions and discoveries in the Indies. In all of the historical production of the era, not merely in the work of Mariana, the influence of classical models was marked.

If the output of Spaniards in the domain of the natural sciences was not so great as in the realm of philosophy, jurisprudence, and history, it was nevertheless distinctively original in character, — necessarily so, since the discovery of new lands and new routes, to say nothing of the effects of

The bibliographer Nicolás Antonio.

Historians of the Americas.

The conquest of the Americas and resultant Spanish achievements in natural science, geography, and cartography.

continuous warring, not only invited investigation, but also made it imperative, in order to overcome hitherto unknown difficulties. In dealing with the Americas a practice was made of gathering geographical data which for its completeness has scarcely ever been surpassed. Explorers wear required by law to make the most detailed observations as to distances, general geographical features, character of the soil, products, animals, and peoples, with a view to the collection and the study of their reports at the *Casa de Contratación*, for which purpose the post of cosmographical chronicler of the Indies was created. Equal amplitude of data was also to be found in books of travel. To enumerate the contributors to geographical knowledge it would be necessary to name the hundreds of Spanish voyages and explorations in the new world of which accounts were written by their leaders or by friars accompanying the expeditions. A noteworthy compendium of these reports has recently been published, although it was compiled in the sixteenth century, the *Geografía y descripción universal de las Indias* (Geography and general description of the Indies) for the years 1571 to 1574 by Juan López de Velasco. Something of a like nature was achieved for the peninsula itself in the reign of Philip II. As was inevitable, Spaniards were prominent in cartography. Aside from the men who accompanied the expeditions in the new world, the most famous cartographers of the time were those of the *Casa de Contratación*, many of whom made contributions to cartographical science, as well as additions to the mapping of the world. One interesting instance was the use of maps with equi-distant polar projections years before Mercator in 1569 first employed this method, which was henceforth to bear his name. Spanish innovators have not received the credit they deserve, principally because their results were in many cases deliberately kept secret by the Spanish government, which wished to retain a monopoly of the information, as well as of the trade, of the new world. Spanish achievements, it will be observed, were designed to meet practical ends, rather than to promote universal knowledge, — unfortunately for the fame of the individuals engaged in scientific production.

Naturally, these accomplishments in geography and cartography necessitated a solid foundation in the mathematical and physical sciences, and such a basis in fact existed. The leading scholars, especially those of the *Casa*, who always stood out from the rest, displayed a remarkable conjunction of theory and practice. At the same time that they were writing doctrinal treatises about cosmography, astronomy, and mathematics, they were able to make maps and nautical instruments with their own hands, and not infrequently to invent useful appliances. Problems in connection with the variations of the magnetic needle, the exact calculation of longitude, the observation of eclipses, and the perfection of the astrolabe were among those which preoccupied students of that day. The advancement of Spaniards is evidenced by the facility with which the theory of Copernicus (that the sun, and not the earth, is the centre of the solar system) was accepted in Spain, when it was rejected elsewhere. It is noteworthy, too, that when Pope Gregory XIII proposed to correct the calendar, he sought information of Spanish scholars, whose suggestions were followed. In the same year (1582) that the Gregorian calendar went into effect in Rome, it was adopted also in Spain. In nautical science, as might have been expected from the practical character of Spanish studies, Spaniards were preëminent. Among the more important names was that of Alarcón, better known for his voyage of 1540 in the Gulf of California and along the western coast of the California peninsula. Advance in naval construction accompanied that of navigation proper. The new world provided Spaniards with an opportunity, of which they did not fail to avail themselves, for progress in the sciences of physics and chemistry, always with practical ideals in mind. Theories were set forth as to such matters as cyclones, terrestrial magnetism, atmospheric pressure, and even telegraphy, while mechanical inventions were made, because these things were related to specific problems. The most remarkable example of the heights to which Spaniards attained in physics and chemistry was in the application of these sciences to metallurgy. When the mines of the Americas were first

Similarly, Spanish achievements in the mathematical and physical sciences.

exploited, it was necessary to resort to German methods, but it was not long before Spaniards easily took first rank in the world. A work by Alonso Barba, for example, published in 1640, was translated into all of the leading European languages, and served as the principal guide of metallurgists for more than a century. As engineers Spaniards lagged behind other European peoples; engineering works were not greatly involved in the colonization of the Americas. It is interesting, however, to note the numerous studies of projects by Spaniards of the sixteenth century, — among them, Cortés, Saavedra, Galván, López de Gómara, Gil González Dávila, Salcedo, Esquivel, and Mercado, — with a view to the construction of a canal at the Isthmus of Panamá to facilitate communication with the Pacific.

Progress in medicine.

Finally, the science of medicine, which had already entered upon an experimental stage in the reign of the Catholic Kings, advanced to a point which enabled it to compare, not unfavorably, with the achievements in other branches of precise knowledge. Medicine, too, had the Americas to thank for much of its progress, owing to discoveries of botanical and mineralogical specimens of a medicinal character. The universities of Salamanca, Valencia, and Barcelona took the lead in medical studies, and furnished most of the great names of the era. In the seventeenth century medical science experienced a marked decline, due among other things to a return to an imitation of classical methods. Hippocrates and other Greek writers were regarded as incapable of mistake, wherefore investigation and experiment ceased to hold the place they had won in the sixteenth century. Some men endeavored to continue the experimental tradition, but, as indeed elsewhere in Europe, they were despised by the classical element, who arrogated to themselves the honor of possessing the only real medical knowledge, charging their opponents, usually with truth, with employing experimentation because they were unable to read the accounts of classical remedies set forth in Greek and Latin. Nevertheless, it was to experimental methods, principally in the sixteenth century, that the discovery of many hitherto unknown cures was due.

CHAPTER XXX

THE GOLDEN AGE: LITERATURE AND ART, 1516–1700

THE general conditions affecting literature and art in the *siglo de oro* have already been alluded to in the preceding chapter. The influence of Humanism and the impulse of the Renaissance were more directly felt in polite literature than in didactic and scientific works. Furthermore, this type of literature was more easily understood by people at large than the more special studies, and it is not surprising that Spain's intellectual greatness should have been appreciated by the majority of the educated classes in terms of poetry, the novel, and the drama, together with the manifestations of the age in the fine arts. The very men who contributed works of a scientific character could not resist the appeal of *belles lettres,* and wrote books which not infrequently demonstrated their double right to homage. Knowledge of Latin, Greek, and various modern languages, especially Italian and French, was more or less general among the educated classes, giving an opportunity for the satisfaction of one's wishes to delve into a varied literature, and opening the way to foreign influences upon Castilian work. The day of French influence seemed for a time to have passed, however (although it returned with the decline in the later seventeenth century); rather, a current against it had set in. The effect of the other three languages was so great, however, that Castilian temporarily lost some of its prestige, which passed over especially to Latin and Italian. Most works of an erudite character now appeared in Latin, and that language was the official tongue of most of the courses in the universities. The church, too, lent its weight to Latin.

Victory of Castilian over foreign tongues in polite literature and remarkable outburst of productivity.

351

Nevertheless, Castilian was at no time in real danger. Anything intended for popular consumption found its way into Castilian, and not a few notable scientific works employed that language. Save for a few inefficacious attempts of the Humanists to use Latin, the field of polite literature was captured wholly by the native tongue. This victory for national sentiment carried with it an exuberant outburst of productivity which affected all classes. Prior to this time the clergy had provided almost the only representatives to win fame in *belles lettres;* now, they were joined and rivalled, even outdone, by laymen, both soldiers and civilians. The noble families caught the enthusiasm and made their houses centres for gatherings, and the kings themselves were carried along in the current. Charles I was exceptionally fond of the novels of chivalry, which he used to have read aloud to him; Philip II, himself little affected, tolerated the tastes of his daughters which led them to make poetry form a part of the palace distractions; but it was under Philip IV that the royal love and patronage of literature attained to its highest point. Philip IV himself wrote comedies, and filled the palace with poets, dramatists, and writers of prose. Meanwhile, the general public got its first real opportunity to attend the theatre, and bought meritorious books (which printing now rendered available), while men discussed their favorite authors with the same ardor that they might their favorite bull-fighters.

Spanish contributions to philology. One of the principal studies of the Humanists was that of grammar, Latin and Greek chiefly. The classical authors and the patristic writings of the medieval period occupied their attention, together with allied works in other languages, such as ancient Hebrew or modern Italian. The Spanish Humanists held a noteworthy place in the development of this movement in Europe. While many individuals might be named, Arias Montano was perhaps the greatest of Spain's representatives. Interest in language study carried Spaniards far afield among contemporary tongues, and in one respect led to a remarkable contribution to knowledge. As conquerors and as missionaries Spaniards came in contact with a variety of peoples hitherto unknown, or little known, to the world, from the numerous tribes of the Indians in the Americas to the Chinese and Japanese of the Far East. Many valuable data were accumulated in Spanish about these peoples and their customs, and their languages were studied and in many cases written down by Spaniards, who systematized them for the first time. Much of this material has only recently become available, but it ranks as an achievement of the *siglo de oro;* perhaps the more valuable parts were prepared in the sixteenth century. Meanwhile, the process of purifying Castilian grammar was constantly going on, and it is interesting to note the strong nationalistic tendency in favor of a phonetic spelling as opposed to the expression of the etymological form. Rhetoric was regarded as a part of grammar, and it is easy to understand that in an age of Humanism the question of style should be a favorite topic.

It was in this period that the national theatre developed, and Spaniards displayed such originality and forcefulness as to make a profound impression on the dramatic literature of the world. At the outset of the reign of Charles I, Gil Vicente and Torres Naharro were continuing the tradition of Juan del Enzina with crude farces and allegorical religious plays. Despite the fact that these were generally acted in convents, they were so frequently of a licentious character that in 1548 their publication was forbidden. Meanwhile, classical plays and compositions written in imitation of the Latin and Greek masters were proving difficult competitors to the weakly groping Spanish stage. The regeneration of the national theatre was due to Lope de Rueda of Seville, whose name first appears in 1554. The greatness of Rueda was due primarily to his own acting, which gave him an opportunity to re-introduce Spanish plays and make a success of them. While staging translations of Latin and Italian works, Rueda wrote and played short acts of a dramatic and episodical character. Others carried on the task begun by Rueda until the machinery for the Spanish theatre was fairly well prepared for the works of the great masters, — for example, the three-act comedy had developed, first employed by Francisco de Avendaño. Cervantes wrote a num-

Lope de Rueda and the development of the national theatre.

2 A

ber of plays, between 1583 and 1587, but while they were not without merit they were completely overshadowed by those of the great writers of dramatic literature.

The great masters of the Spanish theatre. First of the great masters, chronologically, was Lope de Vega (1562–1635), who was also one of the most prolific writers of all time. It is said that he wrote 1800 comedies and 400 religious, allegorical plays (one of the leading types of the era), besides many shorter dialogues, of which number 470 of the comedies and 50 of the plays have survived. His writings were not less admirable than numerous, and marked a complete break with the past. An inventive exuberance, well-sustained agreeability and charm, skill in the management of fable and in the depiction of character, the elevation of women to a leading place in the dramatical plot (a feature without precedent), an instinct for theatrical effects, intensity of emotional expression, wit, naturalness and nobility of dialogue, and realism were the most noteworthy traits of his compositions, together with a variety in subject-matter which ventured into every phase of the history and contemporary customs of Spain. His defects were traceable mainly to his facility in production, such as a lack of plan and organization as a whole, wherefore it has been said that he wrote scenes and not complete plays, although his best works are not open to this charge. In the meantime, the paraphernalia of theatrical presentation had been perfected. In 1579 the first permanent theatre was built in Madrid, followed quickly by the erection of others there and in the other large cities. Travelling companies staged plays in all parts of Spain, until the theatre became popular. If Lope de Vega profited from this situation, so also did the stage from him, for he provided it with a vehicle which fixed it in public favor at a time when the balance might have swung either way. The fame of Lope de Vega eclipsed that of his contemporaries, many of whom were deserving of high rank. In recent years one name has emerged from the crowd, that of Friar Gabriel Téllez, better known by his pseudonym, Tirso de Molina (1571–1658). In realism, depiction of character, profundity of ideas, emotion, and a sense of the dramatic he was the equal and at times the superior of Lope de Vega. The successor in fame and popularity of Lope de Vega, however, was Pedro Calderón de la Barca (1600–1681), whose compositions faithfully represented the devout Catholicism and chivalric ideals (exaggerating the fact) of his contemporaries. Calderón was above all a writer of religious, allegorical plays. In the domain of the profane his plays were too grave and rigid to adapt themselves to the comic, and they were characterized by a certain monotony and artifice, a substitution of allegory for realism, and an excess of brilliance and lyrical qualities, often tinged with rhetoric and obscure classical allusions. Not only were these three masters and a number of others great in Spain, but also they clearly influenced the dramatic literature of the world; it would be necessary to include most of the famous European playwrights of the seventeenth century and some of later times if a list were to be made of those who drew inspiration from the Spanish theatre of the *siglo de oro*.

The history of the Spanish novel in this era reduces itself to a discussion of three leading types, those of chivalry, love, and social customs, the last-named an outgrowth from the picaresque novel, and more often so-called. The novel of chivalry, descendant of *Amadís de Gaula*, was by far the most popular in the sixteenth century, having almost a monopoly of the field. Like the reprehensible "dime novel" of recent American life its popularity became almost a disease, resulting occasionally in a derangement of the mental faculties of some of its more assiduous readers. The extravagant achievements of the wandering knights ended by proving a bore to Spanish taste, and the chivalric novel was already dead when Cervantes attacked it in *Don Quixote*. Meanwhile, the amatory novel had been affected by the introduction from Italy of a pastoral basis for the story, which first appeared in the middle of the sixteenth century and endured for about a hundred years. This novel was based on an impossible situation, that of country shepherds and shepherdesses who talked like people of education and refinement. Only the high qualities of the writers were able to give it life, which was achieved by the excellence of the descriptions, the lyrical quality of the verse, and the beauty

The three types of the sixteenth century novel.

of the prose style. The true Spanish novel was to develop out of the picaresque type, which looked back to the popular *La Celestina* of 1499. About the middle of the sixteenth century and again just at its close there appeared two other works, frankly picaresque, for they dealt with the life of rogues (*pícaros*) and vagabonds. The name "picaresque" was henceforth employed for works which did not come within the exact field of these earlier volumes, except that they were realistic portrayals of contemporary life. Such was the state of affairs when Cervantes appeared.

Cervantes and *Don Quixote*. Miguel de Cervantes y Saavedra (1547–1616) had a long and varied career before his publication of the book which was to place him at a bound in the front rank of the literary men of all time. He was a pupil of the Humanist Hoyos in 1568; a chamberlain of Cardinal Acquaviva at Rome in 1569; a soldier from 1570 to 1575, taking part in the battle of Lepanto; and a captive in Algiers from 1575 to 1580. A devotee of *belles lettres* from youth, he produced many works between 1583 and 1602 in poetry, the drama, and the pastoral novel, in none of which did he attain to real eminence, though a writer of note. In 1603 he wrote the first part of the *Quixote*, and published it in 1605. The book leaped into immediate favor, ran through a number of editions, and was almost at once translated, at least in part, into all the languages of western Europe. It is easy to point out the relationship of *Don Quixote* to the many types of literature which had preceded it. There was the influence of Lucian in its audacious criticism, piquancy, and jovial and independent humor, in its satire, in fine; of Rojas' *La Celestina* or of Rueda in dialogue; of Boccaccio in style, variety, freedom, and artistic devices; of the Italian story-writers and poets of the era; even of Homer's *Odyssey;* and especially of the novels of chivalry. Nevertheless, Cervantes took all this and moulded it in his own way into something new. The case of the novel of chivalry may be taken for purposes of illustration. While pretending to annihilate that type of work, which was already dead, Cervantes in fact caught the epic spirit of idealism which the novelists had wished to represent but had drowned in a flood of extravagances and impossible happenings, raising it in the *Quixote* to a point of sublimity which revealed the eternal significance in human psychology of the knightly ideal, — and all in the genial reflection of chimerical undertakings amid the real problems of life. On this account some have said that the *Quixote* was the last and the best, the perfected novel of chivalry. Withal, it was set forth in prose of inexpressible beauty, superior to any of its models in its depth and spontaneity, its rich abundance, its irresistibly comic force, and its handling of conversation. The surprise occasioned by this totally unlooked for kind of book can in part be understood when one recalls that in the domain of the real and human, the public had had only the three picaresque novels already alluded to, before the appearance of *Don Quixote*. In his few remaining years of life Cervantes added yet other works in his inimitable style, of which the two most notable were the second part of the *Quixote* (1615), said by many to be superior to the first, and the *Novelas exemplares*, or Model tales (1612–1613), a series of short stories bearing a close relationship to the picaresque novels in their dealings with the lives of rogues, vagabonds, and profligates, but as demonstrably different from them as the *Quixote* was from the novels of chivalry, especially in that Cervantes was not satirizing, or idealizing, or even drawing a moral concerning the life he depicted, but merely telling his tale, as an artist and a poet. Well might he say that he was the first to write novels in Castilian. There were many writers of fiction after him in the era, but since the novel had reached its culminating point in its first issue, it is natural that the art did not progress, — for it could not! *The Novelas exemplares.*

While the Spanish theatre and the Spanish novel were of world-wide significance, furnishing models which affected the literature of other peoples, Spanish lyric poetry had only a national importance, but it has a special interest at this time in that it was the most noteworthy representative of the vices which were to contribute to destroy Spain's literary preëminence. In the first place, lyric poetry was an importation, for the Italian lyrics overwhelmed the native product and even imposed their form in Castilian verse. Lyric and epic poetry.

Much excellent work was done, however, notably by Garcilaso de la Vega (1503–1536). Eminent on another account was Luis de Argote y Góngora (1561–1627), commonly referred to by the name of his mother, Góngora. Góngora affected to despise popularity, declaring that he wished to write only for the cultivated classes. To attain this end he adopted the method of complicating the expression of his ideas, making violent departures from the usual order of employing words (hyperbaton), and indulging in artificial symbolism. This practice, called euphuism in English, for it was not peculiar to Spain but became general in Europe, won undying fame of a doubtfully desirable character for Góngora, in that it has ever since been termed *gongorismo* in Spanish, although the word *culteranismo* has also been applied. Similar to it was conceptism, which aimed to introduce subtleties, symbols, and obscurities into the ideas themselves. It is natural that the lyric poetry of the later seventeenth century should have reached a state of utter decline. Epic poetry did not prosper in this era; its function was supplied by romance.

Achievements in satire, panegyrics, and periodical literature. In addition to the various forms of prose writing already discussed, there were many others, and great distinction was achieved in them by the Spaniards of the *siglo de oro*. Among the many who might be mentioned was Francisco de Quevedo, especially famous as a satirist and humorist. One interesting type of literature was that of the panegyrics of Spain in answer to the Hispanophobe works of foreigners, who based their characterizations of Spaniards in no small degree, though not wholly, on the exaggerated condemnation of Spain's dealings with the American Indians by Bartolomé de Las Casas, himself a Spanish Dominican. The *Política indiana* of Solórzano belongs in this class of literature, as a refutation, though a reasoned one, of the indictment of Las Casas and others. In addition to the already-mentioned "relations of events," forerunner of the modern newspaper, it is to be noted that the *Gaceta* (Gazette), the official periodical, began to be published in the seventeenth century. With regard to the non-Castilian parts of Spain it need only be said that Castilian triumphed as the literary language, although works in the vernacular continued to be published in Catalonia, Valencia, and Majorca.

In dealing with the various phases of the *siglo de oro* much has already been said about the diffusion of Spanish thought in Europe and its influence in foreign countries. Two factors tended to bring Spanish intellectual achievements to the notice of the world. In the first place, Spanish professors were to be found in many foreign universities, while Jesuit teaching, very largely Spanish, profoundly affected Catholic Europe. In the second place, Spanish works were widely read and translated, although not equally at all times or equally in all places. In general, Italy was the centre for the dissemination of Spanish thought in the sixteenth century, though often by a double translation, from Spanish to Italian and from Italian to a third tongue, and France was the distributing point in the seventeenth century. In addition there were the works in Latin, which were equally available to all. Spanish philosophical writings were comparatively little read, abroad, but those concerning theology and religion were seized upon by friend and foe, while the offerings of the Spanish mystics were also widely translated. An even greater diffusion fell to the lot of the works on jurisprudence, politics, and international law, and the essential importance of Spanish writings in geography, cosmography, natural science, and kindred subjects has already been pointed out. The works of the historians crossed the frontiers, though more particularly those dealing with the Americas, together with the narratives of American travel. The power of Spanish arms was sufficient to induce wide reading of military writings emanating from the peninsula. Naturally, the greatest number of translations was in the field of polite literature. Every type of the Spanish novel found its way to other countries, and the novel of chivalry was almost more admired, abroad, and certainly longer-lived, than in Spain. Cervantes became a veritable cult in Germany and England, and in this special case England became the centre for the diffusion of Spanish genius. In like manner the great dramatists were famous in all of Europe. While the mere knowledge by Europeans of Spanish works would not be a

Influence of Spanish intellectual achievements upon western European thought.

sufficient basis to predicate a vital Spanish influence beyond the peninsula, such information was a condition precedent to its effectuation, and important modifications of western European thought did in fact follow. It would be possible to trace this in every branch of literature and study which has been discussed, but a number of indications have been given already, and the task is one which does not fall within the field of this volume. To those who actually produced an effect should be added the names of those who deserved to do so, but who were prevented by fortuitous circumstances from so doing; the achievements of many of these men are only now being brought to light by investigations in Spanish archives, and in some cases, — for example, in that of the anthropological group of writers about the Americas, — their works still represent contributions to universal knowledge. Toward the close of the seventeenth century Spain's hegemony in the world of letters began to be supplanted by the rising power of France.

Causes of the decline in Spanish intellectual productivity

All peoples who have had their period of intellectual greatness have sooner or later fallen from their high estate, and it was inevitable that this should occur in the case of Spain. The decline in the peninsula was so excessive in degree, however, that historians have enquired whether there were not certain special causes to induce it. The baleful effect of the Inquisition, exercising a kind of religious censorship on all works, has usually been regarded as of the first importance in this respect. Yet the Inquisition existed during the period of greatness as well as in that of decadence, and to assert that the prohibitions placed upon the expression of even such important ideas as those having a religious bearing could dry up the native independence and freedom of Spanish thought is to confess a lack of knowledge of Spanish character. The Inquisition was one of a great many factors having some influence to check production, but it was not responsible to the degree that has been charged. The same thing is true of the government censorship independent of the Inquisition. Another factor of some importance was that the manifestations of the *siglo de oro* had no solid foundation in the education of the masses, who remained as ignorant as in preceding centuries. If any set of causes can be singled out from the rest, it is probable that those having to do with the political and economic decline of the country as a whole affected, also, the intellectual output of the country. A natural aptitude in the Spanish people, together with the national expansion in resources and power, had enabled them in the sixteenth century to develop an all-round intellectual productivity, more especially of a scientific order, and when this phase of the Golden Age was already dead, private wealth, refinement, and tradition remained to encourage expression in the realm of polite literature. Even this prop was removed by the end of the seventeenth century, and the final decline became inevitable.

The general conditions affecting the history of art were the same as those already pointed out in dealing with literature. Spain produced painters whose works were to serve as among the greatest models of all time, and her attainments in other phases of art, if less inspiring, were of a distinguished order. Spanish architecture, though rarely approved by modern critics, was to become a force in the world through its transmission to the Americas. The so-called "Mission style" of California is nothing more than a reminiscence of the art forms of Spain in this period and the next. *Great era of the fine arts.*

A continuation of the evolution begun in the preceding era, from Gothic to Renaissance architecture, resulted in the banishment of the former. The Renaissance edifices were in three principal styles, which did not succeed one another rigorously in turn, but which were mixed together, or passed almost imperceptibly from one to another, although roughly representing a certain chronological order. The first of these was characterized by the predominance of Renaissance factors over those which were more properly plateresque. The façades of San Marcos of León and of the *ayuntamiento* (city hall) of Seville are good examples. By far the most noteworthy style was that of the second of this period, called variously "Greco-Roman," "second Renaissance," and "Herreran" (after Juan de Herrera, its principal exponent), and employed most largely in the second half of the *Spanish Renaissance architecture.* *The Herreran style.*

sixteenth and the first part of the seventeenth century. The edifices of this group were noteworthy for the attempt made in them to imitate the Roman architecture of the later empire through the suppression of adornment and the multiplication of flat surfaces and straight lines, achieving expression through great size and massiveness of structure, together with the use of rich materials. In the matter of embellishment the classical orders were superimposed, Doric being used in the lower story, Ionic in the next, and finally Corinthian. The pyramid capped with a ball was the favorite style of finial, while gigantic statues were also placed in niches high up in the façade. The whole effect was sombrely religious, often depressingly so. The greatest example of this type of art is the Escorial, the famous palace of Philip II, built by Juan de Herrera, possibly the most noteworthy single edifice of Christian Spanish architecture in existence, and certainly the most widely known. In the reign of Philip IV there was a pronounced reaction against the sobriety of the Herreran style, and the pendulum swung to the other extreme. Adornment and movement of line returned, but were expressed in a most extravagant way, as exemplified by the excessive employment of foliage effects and by the use of broken or twisted lines which were not structurally necessary and were not in harmony with the rest of the edifice. Variety and richness of materials were also a leading characteristic. This style, usually called "baroque," also "churrigueresque" (from Churriguera, its leading architect), has numerous examples, of which the façade of the palace of San Telmo in Seville may be taken as a type.

Sculpture developed into a vigorous art, though still employed mainly as auxiliary to architecture or in religious statuary. Gothic sculpture in both the pure and the plateresque form struggled against Italian influences until the middle of the sixteenth century, when the latter triumphed. Berruguete, Montañés, and Alonso Cano, the first-named largely responsible for the just-mentioned Italian victory and the two latter flourishing in the time of Philip IV, were the leading names of the era. A peculiarity of the Spanish sculptors was that they worked in wood, being especially

Baroque architecture.

Vigorous development of sculpture and the lesser arts.

noteworthy for the images (many crucifixions among them) which they made. The realism of the image-makers saved Spanish sculpture from the contamination of baroque art, which took root in other countries. The decline came, however, with the introduction later in the seventeenth century of the practice of dressing the images, so that only the head, hands, and feet were in fact sculptured. From this the sculptors went on to attach false hair and other false features, going even to the extreme of affixing human skin and finger nails. Other factors combined with this lack of taste to bring on the decay of the art. The excellent work in this period of the *artesonados*, or ceilings of carved woodwork, should not pass unnoticed. Meanwhile, work in gold, silver, iron, and bronze was cultivated assiduously, of which the principal manifestations of a national character were the shrines and gratings. In general, the Renaissance influences triumphed in these arts, as also in the various allied arts, such as the making of tapestry. The gold workers enjoyed an expansion of output springing naturally from the surplus wealth in secular hands, and a similar lot fell to the workers in silks and embroideries; both industries produced materials of a high artistic quality. In ceramic art Arabic tradition had one noteworthy survival in the azulejos, or varnished bricks painted by hand in blue and white and used as tiles. Renaissance factors at length appeared to change the geometric designs, reminiscent of the Moslem past, to the more prevalent classic forms. Aside from azulejos proper other tiles of many colors, often gilded, were employed.

In the early years of this period the Italian influence on Spanish painting held full sway. The leading factors were the Florentine school, headed by Raphael, and the Venetian school, of which Titian was the most prominent representative. The latter, notable for its brilliant coloring and effects of light, was by all odds the more important of the two. Spaniards went to Italy to study, and not a few Italian painters came to Spain, while many works of the Italian masters, especially those of Titian, were procured by Charles I and Philip II. Nevertheless, the signs of a

Appearance of an independent Spanish school in painting.

truly Spanish school began to appear about the middle of the sixteenth century, and before the close of Philip II's reign the era of Spanish independence in painting and the day of the great masters were at hand, to endure for over ı century. With characteristic individuality, Spaniards did not separate into well-defined local schools, but displayed a great variety, even within the same group. Still, in a general way the Andalusians may be said to have accentuated the use of light and a warm ambient, while the Castilians followed a more severe style, employing darker tones. All devoted themselves to the depiction of religious subject-matter, but with no attempt at idealism ; rather, the mundane sphere of realism, though in a religious cloak, preoccupied them, with attention, too, to expression and coloring more than to drawing and purity of form.

El Greco, first of the great masters in painting.

The era of splendor began with Domenico Theotocopuli (1545 ?–1625), better known as "El Greco." As indicated by his name this artist was not Spanish in origin, but Greek. The character of his works, however, was so original and its influences were so powerful in the formation of the Spanish school that he may truly be claimed for Spain, where he lived and worked. He established himself at Toledo in 1577, which city is still the best repository of his paintings. His early style was marked by a strong Venetian manner, with warm tones, great richness, firm drawing, and an intense sentiment of life. Toward 1581 he began to change to a use of cold, gray, shadowy tones, and the employment of a kind of caricature in his drawing, with long and narrow heads and bodies. By this method, however, he was able to attain wonderful results in portraiture. Aside from his own merits no painter so profoundly influenced the greatest of the masters, Velázquez. Chronologically next of the great painters was Ribera (1588–1656), called "Espagnoletto" in Italy, where he did most of his work in the Spanish kingdom of Naples. Naturalism, perfect technique, and the remarkable bodily energy of the figures he depicted were the leading qualities of his work. The diffusion of his paintings in Spain tended to make him influential in the Spanish school, to which his individuality, as well as his birth,

Ribera.

entitled him to belong. Zurbarán (1598–1663) was the most rigorous of the realists, including all the accessories in his paintings, even to the minute details of a person's dress. Less vigorous than Ribera he was best in his portrayal of monks, in which subject-matter his sombrely passive, exceedingly religious atmosphere found a suitable vehicle. He was nevertheless a brilliant colorist. Next in point of time came Diego Velázquez de Silva (1599–1660), greatest of Spanish masters and possibly the greatest of all painters. Velázquez had various periods and various styles, in all of which he produced admirable works. Unlike his predecessors and those who succeeded him as well, he was as diverse in subject-matter as it was possible to be, within the law, and was far less notable for his religious works than for his many others. He depicted for all time the court life of Philip III and Philip IV, including the portraits of those kings and the other leading figures of the court. Some of his greatest work appeared in these portraits, which he knew how to fit into a setting of landscape, making the central figure stand out in a way that no other painter has surpassed or perhaps equalled. He also painted common people (as in his *Los borrachos*, or Intoxicated men) and queer people (as in his paintings of dwarfs), and drew upon mythology (as in his composition entitled "the forge of Vulcan") and upon contemporary wars (as witness the famous "surrender of Breda"). Once only, during a lapse of the prohibitory law, did he paint a nude, — the celebrated Venus of the mirror, now in London, one of the greatest works of its kind. In many of his paintings he revealed himself as a wonderful landscape painter. His landscapes were characterized by the use of a pale, yet rich, pervading blue, and by effects of distance and atmosphere. No painter is more inadequately set forth by photography. To know Velázquez, one must see his works.[1] After Velázquez came Murillo (1618–1682), an Andalusian, who well represented the traits of southern Spain. His leading characteristics were a precise, energetic drawing, fresh, harmonious coloring,

[1] The best place to see them is in the Velázquez room of the Prado at Madrid.

(marginal notes) Zurbarán

Velázquez, greatest of the masters.

Murillo.

and a religious sentiment which was a remarkable combination of imaginative idealism, or even supernaturalism, of conception with realism of figures and scenes. His biblical characters were represented by the common people of the streets of Seville. Few painters have more indelibly stamped their works with their own individuality. Last of the masters was Coello (1623?–1694), who maintained the traditions of the Spanish school, though under strong Venetian influence, amidst a flood of baroque paintings which had already begun to corrupt public taste. Other names might well be included in the list of great Spanish painters in this era, such as Pacheco, Roelas, Herrera, and especially Valdés Leal and Alonso Cano. Indeed, it would be difficult to overestimate the importance of the Spanish school. It is not unthinkable that a list of the ten greatest painters in the history of the world would include the names of Velázquez, El Greco, and Murillo, with a place reserved for Goya (of the eighteenth century), and with the claims of Ribera deserving consideration.

Spanish music, though not so important in the history of the world as that of Italy or Germany, had a notable development in this period, and displayed an individuality which distinguished it from that of other lands. For the first time it came into a place of its own, apart from recitation or the merely technical presentation of medieval church ceremonial, and was characterized by a certain expressiveness, approaching sentimentality and having a flavor which has led many to assert that its roots were to be found in the song and dance of Spanish Moslems. To be sure, the influence of Italy was greatest at this time. The *siglo de oro* in Spanish music was the sixteenth century, in the time of the four great composers of the era, Morales, Guerrero, Cabezón, and Victoria. The greatest works were in the field of religious music, in which various parts were sung to the accompaniment of the organ. Music of the court occupied a half-way post between church and popular music, displaying a combination of both elements, with song to the accompaniment of the viola, which filled the rôle of the modern piano. At the close of the sixteenth

Coello.

Other notable painters.

Noteworthy character of Spanish music.

century the viola was replaced by the guitar, which became the national instrument of Spain. Popular music found its fullest expression in the theatre. It got to be the fashion for the entire company to sing as a preliminary to the play, to the music of the viola, the harp, or the violin. This song had no necessary connection with the play, but song in dialogue soon began to be employed as an integral part of one-act pieces of what might be termed a vaudeville type. In the seventeenth century, song invaded the legitimate stage, and some operas were sung in which the dialogue was entirely in music or else alternated with recitation. The last-named type, the *zarzuela*, became particularly popular. Unfortunately, none of the examples of this music which would have been most interesting, such as that employed in the *zarzuelas* of Lope de Vega and the other masters, has survived. Its true character therefore remains unknown, although its use in theatrical representation is an important fact in the history of the art.

CHAPTER XXXI

THE EARLY BOURBONS, 1700–1759

Basis and conse-
quences of
Spanish
reforms of
the eigh-
teenth
century.

THE eighteenth century in Spain was of intense import as affecting the ultimate interests of the Americas. It was an era of regeneration, of a somewhat remarkable recovery from the decadent state which Spain had reached by the time of the reign of the last Hapsburg monarch. It was accompanied, however, by Spain's engaging in a series of wars, due in some cases to unwise ambitions of an imperialistic character in European affairs and in others to unavoidable necessity as a result of the aggressions of foreign powers. It was a period when international morality with its attendant diplomatic intrigue and unprovoked attacks was in a low state, and Spain was often a sufferer thereby; indeed, many interesting parallels might be drawn between European diplomatic practices in the eighteenth century and those of William II of Germany in the twentieth. England, Austria, and France were at various times the opponents of Spain, but the first-named gradually emerged as the most persistent, aggressive, and dangerous of her enemies. If the prospects of wars were the principal motive force which induced the life-giving reforms, — so that Spain might acquire wealth and efficiency which could be converted into military strength, — the wars themselves tended to increase the needs of the state. Thus in the case of the Americas the very improvements which were introduced were to contribute to bring about the eventual separation of Spain from her colonies, in the first place because they occasioned a development in resources and capacity which gave prospects of success when the revolts should come, and in the second because

Spain drew too heavily upon the colonies in promoting European objects without giving an adequate return, wherefore discontent was fostered.   Nevertheless, her efforts were at least to have the merit of saving those colonies to themselves, thus conserving the influence of Spanish-speaking peoples in the world, with indirect effects on the history of the United States.

With the exception of Austria, whose candidate for the Spanish throne, the Archduke Charles, was unwilling to recognize the validity of the document which had chosen the grandson of Louis XIV, the European nations were disposed to view the accession of Philip V (1700–1746) with favor, especially since the French monarch consented to the conditions imposed in the will of Charles II that the crowns of France and Spain should be independent and never be united in a single person.   This seemed to insure a maintenance of the equilibrium in Europe almost more certainly than the crowning of the Archduke Charles would have done, wherefore most of the powers recognized Philip V.   It was at this time that the autocratic Louis XIV, whose many victorious wars had given him an undue confidence, made one of the serious mistakes of his life.   In certain formal letters he recognized in Philip V such rights of succession to the French throne as he would ordinarily have had but for the terms of his acquisition of Spain, and caused these documents to be recorded before the Parlement of Paris.   Other events also tended to show that Louis XIV meant to dispose of Spain as if that country belonged to him.   When he presented the Spanish ambassador at Versailles to Philip V the Castilian envoy exclaimed: "God be praised!   The Pyrenees have disappeared!   Now we are all one!"   This remark was indicative of the opinions which by that time had become current.   This new element in the situation, together with certain other impolitic acts of the French king against the interests of England and the Protestant Netherlands, caused the countries just named to join with Austria and the Holy Roman Empire in 1701 in an alliance for a war against Louis XIV and Philip V.   Austria wished to acquire the crown of Spain for the archduke, while the

Causes of the War of the Spanish Succession.

2 ʙ

English and the Dutch were primarily desirous of avoiding a Franco-Spanish union, wherefore they insisted on the dethronement of Philip V, accepting the pretensions of Charles. England was particularly inspired by a fear that her commerce and expansion in the new world would be prejudiced, or even crushed, by the joint power of France and Spain. Furthermore, the profits of contraband trade with the Spanish colonies were likely to be cut off under the energetic rule of the king of France, then the most powerful monarch in Europe, and direct indications to that effect occurred in 1701, when the *asiento* (contract), or right to introduce negro slaves into America, was granted to a French company and several South American ports were occupied by French ships.

The war in Spain. The War of the Spanish Succession, as the great conflict beginning actively in 1702 has been called, had Spain as one of its principal battle-grounds, since both Philip V and the archduke were there. The struggle was one of great vicissitudes, as evidenced by the number of times Madrid itself changed hands. Most of the people in the peninsula favored Philip V, but the Catalans early displayed a tendency toward the other side. Their resentment over the injuries received at the hands of their French allies in the revolt of 1640 had not yet cooled, and they especially objected to being governed by a king who represented the absolutist ideals of the French Bourbons, for it was logical to expect that it might mean a danger to their much cherished *fueros*, or charters. Certain conflicts with royal officials seemed to indicate that the government of Philip V intended to insist on the omnipotence of its authority, thus increasing the discontent, to which was added the encouragement to revolt arising from the greatness of the forces aligned against the Bourbons, for in addition to the powers already mentioned Savoy and Portugal had cast in their lot in 1703 and 1704. An allied attempt of 1704 to land in Catalonia having proved a failure the Bourbon officers employed rigorous measures to punish those Catalans who had aided in the movement. The principal effect was to rouse indignation to such a point that in 1705 a determined outbreak took

The Catalan espousal of the archduke's cause.

place. Henceforth, Catalonia could be counted on the side of the allies. In the same year an alliance was contracted with the English, who made promises to the Catalans which they were going to be far from fulfilling. Meanwhile, the allied failure to get a foothold in Catalonia in 1704 had been compensated by an incident of that campaign which was to be one of the most important events of the war. On its way south from Catalonia in that year the English squadron, under the command of Admiral Rooke, seized Gibraltar, which happened to be poorly defended at the time. Numerous attempts were made to recover it, but neither then nor since were the Spaniards able to wrest this guardian of the strait from English hands. In 1708 the island of Minorca was captured, to remain in the possession of England for nearly a century. In 1711 the Holy Roman Emperor died, as a result of which the archduke ascended the imperial throne as the Emperor Charles VI. This event proved to be decisive as affecting the war, for it made the candidacy of Charles for the Spanish crown almost as unwelcome as had been the earlier prospect of a Franco-Spanish union. Other factors contributed to make the former archduke's allies desirous of peace, chief of which was that Louis XIV had been so thoroughly beaten that there was no longer any danger of his insisting on the rights of Philip V to the crown of France.

The capture of Gibraltar by the English.

Events leading to peace.

England (in which country a new government representing the mercantile classes and the party of peace had just come into power) took the lead among the allies in peace negotiations, and was soon followed by all the parties engaged, except Charles VI and a few of the German princes. Between 1711 and 1714 a series of treaties was arranged, of which the principal one was that of Utrecht in 1713. As concerned Spain the most noteworthy provisions were: Philip V's renunciation for himself and his heirs of any claim to the French throne; the cession of Gibraltar and Minorca to England; the grant of the negro slave-trade *asiento* in the Americas to the English, together with accompanying rights which made this phase of the treaties a veritable entering wedge for English commerce in the Spanish colonies; and

The peace of Utrecht

the surrender of the Catholic Netherlands, Milan, Naples, and Sardinia to Austria, and of Sicily to Savoy. In 1720 Austria and Savoy exchanged the two islands which had fallen to their lot, and the latter took on the official title of the kingdom of Sardinia. On the above-named conditions Philip V was allowed to retain the Spanish dominions of the peninsula and of the Americas. If Spain could have but known it, the treaties were altogether favorable to her, but ambition was to undo their beneficial effects. One troublesome point in the various peace conferences was the so-called case of the Catalans. It had been generally believed that England in accordance with her earlier treaty with the Catalans would insist on the preservation of the much mooted *fueros* and that Philip V would make the concession, as had Philip IV before him. Philip V showed himself to be obstinate on this point, for, not once, but several times, he positively refused to yield. Furthermore, the English government, desirous of peace, the prospective advantages of which for England were already clear, repeatedly charged its ambassadors not to hold out for the Catalan *fueros*. Some attempts to secure them were made, but when they failed to overcome the persistent objections of Philip V provision was made for a general amnesty to the Catalans, who were to enjoy the same rights as the inhabitants of Castile. The rights of Castilians, however, together with the duties which were implied, were precisely what the Catalans did not want. The conduct of Charles VI was equally unmoral. He did, indeed, make repeated attempts to save the *fueros*, and declared that he would never abandon the Catalans. Yet he signed a convention withdrawing his troops from Catalonia, and left the people of that land to their fate. The latter were not disposed to yield without a struggle, and sustained a war against Philip V for more than a year. The fall of Barcelona in 1714 put an end to the unequal conflict.

One of the interesting factors of the era of the war was that of the French influence in Spain, which was to have a pronounced effect on the internal development of the country, and, by extension, on that of the colonies. Philip V

Abandonment of the Catalans by the allies.

was seventeen years of age when he ascended the throne, but, though he many times proved his valor in battle, he was in other respects a weak and irresolute character, without striking virtues or defects, fond of hunting, and exceedingly devout, — in fine, of a type such that he was inevitably bound to be led by others. These traits fitted in with the policies of Louis XIV, who fully intended to direct the affairs of Spain in his own interest. He charged Philip V never to forget that he was a Frenchman, and, indeed, with the exceptions presently to be noted, Philip was quite ready to submit to the will of his grandfather. From the first, Louis XIV surrounded the Spanish king with French councillors, some of whom occupied honorary positions only, while others filled important posts in the government of Spain, and still others, notably the French ambassadors and French generals, exercised actual authority without having any official connection with the country. One of the most important of all was Madame des Ursins, maid of honor to the queen, sent to Spain by Louis XIV because as the widow of the Duke of Braciano, a Spanish grandee, she was familiar with the customs of the country. This lady won the complete confidence of the queen, who in turn was able to dominate her husband. It may be said for Madame des Ursins that she was faithful to the interests of the Spanish monarchs, though promoting the entry of French influences, at that time much to be desired in Spain. Indeed, she not infrequently sided with Philip V against the wishes of Louis XIV, which on one occasion led to her recall by the French monarch. Finding, however, that he could not control Spanish affairs without her aid, Louis allowed her to return to Spain. Despite the enormous pressure exercised against him in favor of France, Philip V occasionally rebelled. One instance of his obstinacy has already been cited respecting the case of the Catalan *fueros*. A more important issue arose out of the presumptions of Louis XIV to dispose of Philip's crown, as an avenue of escape for himself. In every year from 1706 to 1712 Louis XIV endeavored to sacrifice the interests of Spain or of Philip V in order to propitiate the allies into a grant of

The French influence in Spain during the War of the Spanish Succession.

Madame des Ursins.

Instances of resistance by Philip V to domination by Louis XIV.

peace. In particular he was desirous of procuring the resignation of Philip from the throne of Spain in favor of the House of Austria, saving to Philip the Spanish dominions in Italy. Philip was obdurate when suggestions were made of his abandoning Spain, and more than once, even when the situation looked hopeless, declared his intention of dying at the head of his troops, rather than abdicate the throne to which he felt divinely entitled. Louis XIV was even disposed to compel him by force of arms to acquiesce, and several times withdrew his military support, but the Spanish king would not yield. Fortunately for Philip the allies played into his hands by demanding too much, with the result that Louis XIV on such occasions would renew his support of Philip. Nevertheless, it was the urgings of Louis XIV which prevailed upon Philip to surrender the Spanish dominions in Italy and the Low Countries as well as to renounce his claim to the throne of France. In all of these tribulations of the Spanish king credit should be given to María Luisa of Savoy, the spirited young queen of Spain. Not yet fourteen at the time of her marriage, in 1701, she at all times displayed a courage and ability which endeared her to the Spanish people. Though her father, the Duke of Savoy, joined the allies against France and Spain, she did not waver in her attachment to the land of her adoption. Inspired by her the Spanish people (except the Catalans) displayed an ardent spirit of nationalism for the first time in history, and were loyally devoted to the king and queen. Nevertheless, despite Spanish patriotism and Philip's obdurate resistance to Louis XIV's plans concerning the peninsula, there was the underlying truth of a profound French influence over Spain. This was best represented by men who, like Orry and Amelot, were responsible for far-reaching reforms, the effects of which will be discussed in the chapters on institutions.

The popular young queen, María Luisa of Savoy.

Unfortunately for Philip and for Spain the queen died, early in the year 1714. A young Italian abbot named Alberoni happened to be at court in that year and he suggested to Madame des Ursins that a certain Isabel Farnesio (Elizabeth Farnese) of Parma would make a suitable wife for Philip V.

According to him the sweet gentleness of her character would enable Madame des Ursins to maintain her power at the Spanish court. In December of the same year the wedding took place. Thus did the lady who has received the sobriquet, the "Termagant of Spain," become the wife of Philip V. On her first meeting with Madame des Ursins she dismissed her, and proceeded to become herself the dominant influence near the crown. Isabel Farnesio was in fact a woman of extraordinary energy and force of character, besides being so attractive as to be irresistible to the weak king, who was so violently and capriciously attached to her that he even chastised her with blows, at times, in a kind of jealous fury. Nevertheless, she submitted to anything, provided she could retain a hold on her husband, for she was ambitious for her children and for Italy, and meant to utilize Spanish power in furtherance of her aims. Early in 1715 she procured the elevation of Alberoni (soon to become a cardinal) to the direction of affairs in the Spanish state, as the instrument to procure her objects. The chief tenets in her policy were the breaking of the intimate relation with France and the recovery of the Italian possessions, based on the twofold desire of throwing the Austrians out of Italy (a patriotic Italian wish, possibly more attributable to Alberoni than to the queen) and of creating principalities for the children of her own marriage with Philip. These aims were furthered by playing upon the wishes of Philip to recover his rights to the French throne. Philip V had not willingly renounced his claim at the time Louis XIV had persuaded him to do so, and many of the events for the next few years are explained by his aspirations to obtain that crown for himself or for one of his sons. The Italian ambitions of Isabel Farnesio, however, were the enduring keynote of Spanish policy for some thirty years.

The break with France was not long in coming. In 1715 Louis XIV died, and, contrary to the expectations of Philip, not Philip V, but the Duke of Orleans, whom the Spanish king regarded as a personal opponent, was named as regent for the sickly Louis XV, who was not expected to live very long, — though in fact he was to reign for fifty-nine years.

Isabel Farnesio and the resumption of a policy of imperialism in Italy.

The breach was widened by a series of treaties between England, the Protestant Netherlands, and France in the next two years with a view to the execution of the treaty of Utrecht. To assure the peace of Europe it was necessary to procure the adhesion of Philip V and Charles VI, who alone of the parties to the War of the Spanish Succession had not made peace with each other, although no hostilities had taken place for some time. Such a peace did not fit in, however, with the plans of Isabel Farnesio, and when the emperor furnished a pretext in 1717 for the renewal of hostilities a Spanish army was suddenly dispatched to Sardinia which overran that island. England as guarantor of the neutrality of Italy protested, and endeavored to effect a peace between the two contestants by an offer to Philip of Charles' renunciation of his claims to the Spanish crown, together with a promise of the duchies of Parma and Tuscany and a vague suggestion of England's willingness to restore Gibraltar and Minorca. The English proposal was rejected, and in 1718 an expedition was sent into Sicily (then in the possession of Savoy, although the already mentioned exchange with Austria had been discussed). The Spaniards were received with enthusiasm, and soon had a mastery of the island. Meanwhile, Austria entered the triple alliance, which thereby became quadruple, on the basis of the emperor's offers to renounce his pretensions to the throne of Spain and to consent to the succession of Charles, son of Isabel Farnesio and Philip V, to the duchies of Parma, Plasencia, and Tuscany in exchange for Philip's return of Sicily and Sardinia and his renunciation of all dominion in Italy and the Low Countries. These terms were offered to Philip, who refused them, despite the English ambassador's insinuation of his country's willingness to return Gibraltar and Minorca if Philip would accept. While the British government was thus negotiating for peace through diplomatic channels it also took steps in another way to insure Spanish acquiescence in the allied proposals. An English fleet under Admiral Byng was ordered to attack the Spanish fleet without previous announcement of a warlike intent, managing the affair, if possible, so as to cast the blame on the Spanish commander. Byng found the Spanish fleet in Sicilian waters, destroyed it, and landed Austrian troops in Sicily. Several months later, in December, 1718, England declared war on Spain, which was followed in January, 1719, by a declaration of war against Philip V on the part of France. Hopelessly outnumbered, Spain nevertheless displayed a surprising capacity for resistance. Defeat was inevitable, however, and late in 1719 Alberoni, whose extraordinary web of intrigues was deemed responsible for the existing situation, was dismissed from power, a condition exacted by the allies, and in 1720 peace was made on the basis of the earlier proposals of the quadruple alliance. Philip was ready to comply with these terms, but the emperor was now unwilling to grant what had been required of him. The result was a new alliance in 1721 of England, France, and Spain, of which the most noteworthy terms were England's definite promise to restore Gibraltar to Spain and an agreement for a double matrimonial alliance between the French and Spanish courts; a Spanish princess aged three was betrothed to Louis XV, then eleven years old, while a French princess was to marry Philip's eldest son, Luis. In addition the rights of Isabel's son Charles to the Italian duchies were reaffirmed. The marriage of Luis and the French princess was duly celebrated in 1722, and the Spanish princess was sent to the French court to be educated.

For several years Philip had been expressing a desire to abdicate. In January, 1724, he carried his previously announced intention into effect, declaring that he proposed to consecrate the remainder of his life to the service of God and the important work of maintaining his own health. There has been much speculation as to whether these were his real designs, — all the more so, since the ambitious queen at no time protested against this step. Although there is no direct evidence to that effect, it is more than probable that Philip and Isabel wanted to be ready to take advantage of the situation which might arise if Louis XV should die, as was expected. At any rate Philip's eldest son was proclaimed king, as Luis I, but the reign was of brief duration. In the same year 1724 Luis contracted

Abdication of Philip V and reasons therefor.

Brief reign of Luis I and Philip's resumption of the throne.

smallpox and died. As there was a general disinclination
to the succession of Philip's second son, Ferdinand, then a
minor, the former king was asked to accept the crown again,
and despite certain compunctions he felt in the matter he
at length agreed to do so.

Ripperdá and the Austrian alliance.   The second reign of Philip V was dominated as before by
the Italian ambitions of Isabel Farnesio, with the French
aspirations of the king remaining a factor. By this time the
Baron of Ripperdá, an adventurer who had previously been
the Dutch representative at the Spanish court, had become
the agent through whom Isabel hoped to achieve her ends.
Few more unconscionable liars and intriguers are recorded
in history than this audacious courtier, who was able to
deceive even Isabel Farnesio. It occurred to the queen that
the vexed question of the Italian duchies might be settled
through an embassy to Vienna. Accordingly, Ripperdá
was sent, with the principal object of procuring the betrothal
of two Austrian archduchesses to Isabel's sons, Charles
and Philip. Ripperdá found Charles VI disinclined to
consent to the betrothals, but lied both to the emperor and
to Philip, telling each that the other accepted his petitions.
His deceptions would certainly have been unmasked, had
it not been for an unexpected turn in events. In 1725 the
French regent, fearful lest Louis XV might die without issue,
sent back the Spanish princess who had been betrothed to
him, because she was still too young to marry. The natural
consequence was a rupture between France and Spain,
facilitating a treaty between Charles VI and Philip V. The
matter of the marriage was now secondary to the political
need of support. Charles and Philip agreed to the terms
proposed to the latter in 1718 by the quadruple alliance.
In addition Philip guaranteed the Pragmatic Sanction,
whereby the succession of Charles VI's eldest daughter to
his Austrian estates was to be secured, and gave extensive
commercial privileges to Austria, particularly to the Ostend
Company of the Catholic, or Austrian, Netherlands, enabling
that company to secure trading rights in Spain and the
Americas. A defensive alliance was arranged, one feature
of which was the emperor's agreement to use his good offices

to cause England to fulfil her promised restoration of Gibraltar and Minorca to Spain. Finally, Charles VI definitely abandoned his oft-repeated demand for the recognition of the Catalan *fueros*. For his triumphs of 1725 Ripperdá was made a grandee of Spain, owing his promotion, in part at least, to his assurance that the marriage alliances were practically secure. He became first minister at the Spanish court, a post which he asked for, falsely asserting that Charles VI desired it. Such a tissue of lies could not be sustained indefinitely. His duplicity having been discovered he lost his position in 1726, and was imprisoned when he seemed to confess guilt by taking refuge in the English embassy. Escaping in 1728 he went to northern Africa, where he passed the remaining nine years of his life.

The Austrian treaties of 1725 were to have important consequences. England, France, the Protestant Netherlands, Prussia, Sweden, and Denmark immediately formed an alliance, and war seemed imminent. Spain desired it, but Austria declined to engage, much to the resentment of the Spanish court. Spain made a fruitless attempt to recapture Gibraltar, however, in 1727, but consented to peace in the same year without attaining her ends, although the definitive treaty was not signed until 1729. One factor in the agreement was the desire of Isabel Farnesio to avenge herself on Charles VI, not only for his failure to join in the recent war, but also to requite his refusal to accept the marriage projects she had proposed. Even when the emperor consented to the attainment in 1731 of Isabel's ambitions for her son concerning the three duchies of northern Italy, she did not put aside her vengeful plans. Charles of Bourbon in fact landed in Italy in that year to take possession of the duchies. A fresh step in the plans of Isabel was the treaty of 1733 with France, often called by analogy with the later treaty of 1761–1762 the "first Family Compact." The opportunity to strike at Austria, which both France and Spain desired, was now at hand, for Austria was in the meshes of a war over the Polish succession. Spain declared war on Austria late in 1733, and in the next year overran Naples and Sicily. In 1734, too, Prince Charles was brought from

The acquisition of Naples for Isabel's son Charles.

his duchies to be crowned king of Naples, or the Two Sicilies. Thus had Isabel Farnesio restored the questionably desirable Italian inheritance to Spain, but the duchies were lost. France was ready to make peace in 1735; so she calmly offered Charles VI the three duchies in exchange for a recognition of Spanish Charles as king of the Two Sicilies. Spain protested, but could do nothing more than submit. These terms were accepted in 1735, although peace was not signed until three years later. It is interesting to note that the Catalans had not yet given up hope of their *fueros*. A body of Catalan patriots visited England in 1736 to ask for the fulfilment of the earlier English promise to maintain the *fueros*, but the British government paid no attention to the petition.

The War of Jenkins' Ear. War was not long in making its reappearance on the Spanish horizon. For a long time there had been various causes of dispute with England, the most important of which arose out of the English contraband trade in the Spanish colonies. The *asiento* treaty had been used by English merchants as the entering wedge for British commerce, and their violations of the law had met with reprisals at times, especially when English smugglers were caught by the more faithful of the Spanish officials in the colonies. One Englishman, named Jenkins, brought home his ear preserved in alcohol, claiming that the Spaniards had cut it off. Such acts as this, whether of actual occurrence or not, fitted in with English conceptions of Spanish cruelty, and furnished a pretext for war to the rising party of British imperialists, headed by William Pitt. Indemnities were demanded by England and agreed to by Spain, but when the latter put in a counter-claim the British government threatened war, which was soon declared, late in 1739. This conflict, called in English histories the War of Jenkins' Ear, demonstrated that the internal reforms in Spain had not been without effect. The West Indies were the principal field of the struggle, but Spain was able to defend herself, — as witness the successful defence of Cartagena, which Admiral Vernon was so sure he was going to capture that he had commemorative medals struck off in advance. In Europe the most noteworthy events were the Spanish attempts to capture Gibraltar and Port Mahón, Minorca, both of which ended in failure. France soon came into the war on Spain's side, and the conflict became European when it merged into the great War of the Austrian Succession (1740–1748).

The various princes of Europe had guaranteed Charles VI's Pragmatic Sanction one or more times, but when the emperor died, in 1740, each of them proceeded along the line of political interest. Urged on by Isabel Farnesio, Philip V renewed his pretensions to the duchies in northern Italy and to other Italian territories in Austrian hands which had formerly belonged to Spain. France, Prussia, and other states of lesser importance also made certain claims. England's interest lay with the opponent of France and Spain, wherefore she joined with Austria. In a military way the war was very nearly indecisive, and there was a general desire for peace by the year 1746. This attitude received a fresh impulse by the accession of Ferdinand VI to the Spanish throne in that year, for he was a determined partisan of peace. The treaty of 1748 was entirely favorable to Isabel Farnesio in that she obtained the duchies of Parma, Plasencia, and Guastalla for her son Philip; Tuscany was no longer available, having been in other hands since the agreement of 1735. The dispute with England was settled by a recognition of commercial advantages in favor of that country, especially those growing out of the *asiento;* two years later the *asiento* was annulled in exchange for a heavy payment by Spain. Meanwhile, the voyage of Anson around the world, 1739–1742, had in fact dealt a blow to Spain in America, revealing the Spanish secrets of the Pacific. The peace of 1748 marked the culminating point in the aspirations of Isabel Farnesio. After more than thirty years of effort she had almost completely attained her ends. Spain had paid the bills, with little to compensate her except glory and at the cost of losses in the colonies, which though not translated into cessions of territory were to have ultimate effects to the disadvantage of Spain.

The reign of Ferdinand VI (1746–1759) looms little in external narrative, because it was an era of peace, but on

The War of the Austrian Succession and the acquisition of the North Italian duchies for Isabel's son Philip.

Impor-
tance of
the peace-
ful reign of
Ferdinand
VI.
that very account it was important in institutions. The achievements of Charles III were made possible by the policies of economic regeneration which were so strongly to the fore in the reign of Ferdinand VI. Ferdinand, who may have been deficient enough in some respects, who took very little part himself in affairs of government, and who displayed tendencies to melancholia and even insanity, was firmly of the opinion that Spain needed peace, and at a time when Europe was engaging in another great conflict, the Seven Years' War, he declined the overtures of both France and England, the leading opponents in the struggle, even when accompanied by such tempting bait as the latter's offer of the restitution of much-desired Gibraltar and Minorca. In 1759 he died without issue, and his half-brother, Charles, son of Isabel Farnesio, came to the throne of Spain, after a long experience as a ruler in Italy. Thus did the "Termagant of Spain" achieve yet a new victory to reward her maternal ambition, — and meanwhile the Two Sicilies were not lost to her line, for that kingdom passed to her grandson Ferdinand, the third son of Charles.

CHAPTER XXXII

CHARLES III AND ENGLAND, 1759–1788

UNDER Charles III, Spain reached the highest point she has attained since the sixteenth century. In many respects the internal situation was better at this time than in the great days of the *siglo de oro*, but Spain's relative authority in Europe was less, because of the striking advances which had been made by the other powers. One of them, England, was particularly dangerous, and it will be found that Spain's foreign policy in this reign was directed primarily toward meeting the possibility of war with that country. Other difficulties, such as those with Portugal and Morocco, particularly with the former, were cogent factors because of the relations which England bore, or was believed to bear, to them. Contrary to the impression usually to be derived from the histories of the American Revolution, Spain was intensely hostile to England throughout this reign. To oppose that country the Family Compact with France was formed, and continued to be the basis of Spain's foreign policy, although it early became manifest that France would honor the treaty only when it suited her purposes. In the end the policies of Charles III were crowned with success, — not so great as Spain could have wished, but sufficiently so to make this reign the most pleasingly satisfactory to Spaniards of any since the days of Isabella, next to whom Charles III has some claim to rank as the greatest Spanish monarch of modern times. This becomes the more worthy of belief when one investigates the sweeping character of and the success attained in the social, political, and economic reforms of the period. These were at the basis of Spain's

Greatness of the reign of Charles III and principal factors therein.

383

victories in European councils, for they provided the sinews of war. Nevertheless there was one drawback. The reforms in the Americas, following the precedent of nearly three centuries, were undertaken more with a view to the production of revenues for Spain than for the contented development of the colonies themselves. Spain also ran counter to a new force in world history, which she herself was obliged by circumstances to assist in establishing itself. The spirit of world democracy was born with the American Revolution, and appeared in France soon afterward. This meant that the autocratic basis of Spanish greatness was presently to be destroyed. The success of the American Revolution was to be related in no small degree to the loss of Spain's colonial empire. The failure of the French Revolution was to produce a powerful despot who was to bring Spain, under Charles IV, to the lowest point she had reached since the days of Charles II. Nevertheless, the reign of Charles III is to be considered as something more than a brilliant moment in history without ultimate effect. The internal reforms were of permanent benefit to Spain and even to the Americas, capable of utilization under the more democratic systems of the future. Finally, the part played by Spain in the successful issue of the American Revolution deserves to bulk large, even though she could not look with sympathy upon a movement which, she clearly saw, might bring about her own ruin.

Causes of Charles III's policy of opposition to England. Many writers have ascribed Charles III's policy of opposition to England to his hatred of that country, growing out of certain humiliations forced upon him by an English fleet while he was king in Naples. There is no reason to believe, however, that this feeling, if indeed it did exist in unusual degree, dominated his political action, and in fact Charles was always a partisan of peace; far from plunging into war he had rather to be convinced of its necessity. There were reasons in plenty to induce him to such a course, irrespective of any personal spite he might have felt. Prior to the reign of Charles, Spain had already engaged in four wars with England (1702–1713, 1718–1720, 1727–1729, 1739–1748) in the course of half a century, and at no time in the Bourbon

era had the two countries been on nearly cordial terms.   The
gist of the trouble lay in the British ambition to possess the
greatest colonial empire and the richest commerce in the
world.   For the realization of these aims it seemed necessary
to destroy the colonial importance of France and Spain, and
any advances in wealth or military power on the part of
either of those countries was regarded as detrimental to the
imperialistic designs of England.   With respect to Spain,
British contraband trade in the Americas under the cover
of the *asiento* treaty had tended to break down the Spanish
commercial monopoly, and the annulment of the *asiento* had
not put an end to the smuggling.   While no territories in the
Americas had been wrested from Spain under the Bourbons,
the previous century had recorded many conquests by England in the Caribbean area, principal of which was that of
Jamaica, and along the Atlantic coast strip of North America,
the southern part of which had been not only claimed but
also occupied by Spain in earlier days.   Meanwhile, the
losses of France and the aggressive character of English
foreign policy under Pitt made it appear that Spain might
expect to be deprived of her colonies whenever the opportunity to secure them should seem ripe to England.

From the outset of the reign of Charles III there occurred
many incidents to heighten Spain's suspicion or anger with
respect to England.   The exigencies of the war with France
led the English to adopt many arbitrary measures against
the as yet neutral power of Spain.   English vessels stopped
Spanish ships on the high seas, claiming a right of search, and
seized many of them, often without justification in international law ; the English government occupied a bit of Spanish
territory, and did not abandon it with a good grace ; and
there were instances when Spanish merchants in England
were treated badly.   Meanwhile, British acts of aggression
and smuggling in the Americas continued to take place ; the
English placed difficulties in the way of Spanish fishing off
the coast of Newfoundland, though beyond the territorial
waters of the British domain ; they founded establishments
in Honduras without authorization from Spain, and began
to cut the valuable dyewoods there ; and Gibraltar and

*Continu-
ance of
England's
affronts to
Spain.*

2 c

Minorca still remained in English hands, a standing affront to Spanish pride and a danger to the peninsula. Nevertheless, the underlying factor which influenced Spain was the imperialism of England, backed up as it was by her vast resources and her almost invincible navy. Charles did not wish to bring Spain into the war, but it was clear that an overwhelming defeat for France would be almost equally disadvantageous to Spain, who might expect to receive the next shock from the English arms. France had gotten much the worst of it in the Seven Years' War when Charles III ascended the Spanish throne, wherefore Charles endeavored to mediate between that power and England. The British government's arrogant rejection of his proffer tended only to make him the more disposed to consider an alliance with France. When, therefore, the French authorities approached him with the proposal for an alliance he resolved to join with them if England should refuse to meet Spain's demands relative to the release of captured Spanish ships, the free use of the Newfoundland fisheries, and the abandonment of the English settlements in Honduras. England not only refused to give satisfaction, but also asked for an explanation of the naval preparations Spain was making. Thereupon, Charles

The Family Compact and Spain's entry into the Seven Years' War.

prepared for war. Two treaties, called jointly the Family Compact, were made with the Bourbon king of France. The first of these, signed in August, 1761, was a defensive alliance against such powers as should attack either of the two crowns. The second, dated in February, 1762, was an offensive and defensive alliance directed specifically against England. War, meanwhile, had already been declared in January.

Spanish losses in the Seven Years' War.

In the ensuing campaign France and Spain were badly beaten. Manila and Havana were taken by the English, although Spain won a notable success in the capture of Sacramento, a Portuguese colony on the Río de la Plata, — for Portugal had entered the war on the side of England. Twenty-seven richly laden English boats were taken at Sacramento, — significant of the profits which the English merchants were making in contraband trade, using Sacramento as a base. In 1763 a peace which was in many respects humiliating to Spain was signed at Paris. England restored Manila and Havana, but required the cession of Florida and all other Spanish territories east of the Mississippi; Sacramento was returned to Portugal; Spain gave up all rights of her subjects to fish in Newfoundland waters; questions arising out of the English captures of Spanish ships prior to Spain's entry into the war were to be decided by the British courts of admiralty; and the English right to cut dyewoods in Honduras was acknowledged, although England agreed to the demolition of all the fortifications which British subjects might have constructed there. France, who had lost practically all her other colonies to England, now gave the scantily settled, ill-defined region of French influence west of the Mississippi, all that remained of French Louisiana, to Spain. According to the terms of the grant it was to compensate Spain for her loss of Florida, but in fact it was in order to ensure the continued alliance of Spain with France.

The peace of 1763 was looked upon by France and Spain as a truce, for if England had been dangerous before, she was doubly so now. France wished revenge and the restoration of her overseas domains, while Spain's principal motive was a desire to save her colonies from conquest by England. Both countries therefore bent their energies to preparations for another war; in Spain the next decade and a half was a period of remarkable economic reforms tending to the regeneration of the peninsula as the basis for an army and navy. Meanwhile, steps were taken to avoid the possibility of an English descent upon the Spanish West Indies, which were regarded as the principal danger-point, both because of the strength of England's position in the Caribbean area, and because that region was the key to the Spanish mainland colonies of the two Americas. Pretexts for trouble were not lacking. The English dyewood cutters of Honduras did not observe the restrictions placed upon them by the treaty of Paris, and the British government neglected to satisfy Spain's complaints in that regard; the French settlers of Louisiana refused to acknowledge their transfer to the Spanish crown, wherefore it was necessary

Prepara-tions for a renewal of the war.

Pretexts for war.

to employ force against them, and it was believed that English agents had instigated them to resist; on the other hand England repeatedly demanded the payment of a ransom which the English conquerors of Manila had exacted from that city, but Spain refused to pay the claim. The principal diplomatic interest down to 1771, however, was the so-called question of the Falkland Islands (called Malouines by the French, and Maluinas by Spaniards). This group, lying some 250 miles east of the Strait of Magellan, seems to have been discovered by Spanish navigators of the sixteenth century, for a description of the islands was in the possession of the Spanish authorities at an early time. The first English voyage to this group was that of Captain Cowley, as late as 1686, but no claim could be made on this basis, for in 1748 England formally recognized the rights of Spain. Not much attention was paid to the Falklands until after the Seven Years' War, although various navigators visited them, but in 1763 a Spanish pilot, Mathei, made the first of a series of voyages to these islands. In 1764 a French expedition under Bougainville landed at one of them, and formed a settlement, and in the next year the English captain, Biron, touched at a place called Port Egmont by him, took formal possession for England, applying the name Falkland to the group, and proceeded on his way to the Pacific Ocean and around the world. Not long afterward an English settlement was made at Port Egmont, and the governor no sooner heard of the presence of the French than he ordered their withdrawal. Meanwhile, the Spanish government had lodged a complaint at the French court against the occupation of the islands by France, and an agreement was reached, whereby the French should abandon the group and a Spanish settlement there should be formed. This was done, and the English and Spanish governors began mutually to demand each other's withdrawal, the Englishman setting a time limit of six months. The Spanish government directed the captain-general of Buenos Aires to expel the English settlers, and accordingly, though not until June, 1770, these orders were carried out. When the news reached England the British Parliament voted funds in preparation for war, and made excessive demands for reparation for what was considered an insult to England as well as for the restitution of the colony. Spain, in reliance upon the Family Compact, was not inclined to avoid the issue, and matters even went so far as the retirement of the Spanish and English ambassadors, when an unforeseen event occurred, changing the whole aspect of affairs. This was the fall of Choiseul, the French minister who had negotiated the Family Compact and who was believed by Spain to be ready to bring France into the war. It was on this occasion that Louis XV is reported to have said "My minister wanted war, but I do not," thus calmly disregarding the treaty with Spain. Consequently, Spain had to yield, and in 1771 the Spanish ambassador to London signed a declaration disapproving the removal of the English colonists and promising to restore Port Egmont, although without prejudice to Spain's claim to the islands.[1]

Spain might justly have abandoned the Family Compact after the Falkland incident, and for a time that treaty did suffer a partial eclipse. Charles III felt that in future he could count only on his own forces, but he continued to increase and equip them, for the danger from England was as great as ever. Self-interest inevitably brought Spain and France together, and with the appearance of the warlike Aranda in France, late in the year 1773, as Spanish ambassador to that court, plans with a view to meeting the common enemy were again discussed. The death of Louis XV, in May, 1774, brought matters still more to a head, for it resulted in a change of ministry in France, whereby Vergennes, believed to be an enthusiastic partisan of the Family Compact, became minister of foreign affairs. Vergennes was in fact an ardent supporter of the Franco-Spanish alliance, although his enthusiasm was tempered in moments of crisis by a clear view of what most favored France, and he did not fail to see that he might employ it as the basis for

Revival of the Family Compact as a force in European politics.

---

[1] The British settlement was abandoned in 1774, after which the Spaniards returned. Following the establishment of Argentine independence that country occupied the Falklands, and still claims them. Since 1833, however, they have been in the possession of England.

trade concessions from Spain, the better to build up the resources of France. Nevertheless, the opinion was general that Vergennes intended to adhere to the Family Compact, and consequently England planned to occupy Spain with other affairs, so as to separate her from France, or at least divert her from pursuing a common policy with the last-named country against England. Two matters were at hand, of which they might avail themselves: Spain's disputes with the sultan of Morocco; and her quarrels with Portugal over boundaries in South America.

Relations with the Moslem states of the Barbary Coast.

The never-ending wars with the Moslems of northern Africa were inherited from the preceding era, and continued to occupy Spanish troops and fleets down to the reign of Charles III. In 1767 satisfactory relations between Spain and Morocco seemed to have been reached when the latter agreed to abandon piracy and recognized Spain's title to her establishments on the North African coast. Late in 1774, however, the sultan announced that he would no longer tolerate Christian posts in his empire, and commenced a siege of Melilla. The attack was beaten off, and it was decided to strike what was hoped might be a decisive blow against the dey of Algiers, the ally of the Moroccan sultan. An expedition of some 18,000 men was prepared, and placed under the command of General O'Reilly, reformer of the Spanish army and a man of tremendous reputation, but in the ensuing operations before Algiers O'Reilly was crushingly defeated with a loss of several thousand men. Rightly or wrongly, England was believed to have instigated the Moslem rulers to attack Spain. Years later, Charles came to an understanding with the Moslem states of the Barbary Coast. Between 1782 and 1786 treaties were made, whereby the rulers of those lands agreed once again to give up piracy and also the institution of slavery, besides granting certain religious and commercial privileges to Spaniards in their lands. This was not the last of piracy and warfare in North Africa, however; the former endured for another generation, and the end of the latter, even in the restricted Spanish area, is not yet.

There was a much stronger case against England with

regard to Portugal, whose exaggerated claims were supported by the British government. The boundaries between the Spanish and Portuguese colonies in South America had been an unending source of dispute, ever since the treaty of Tordesillas in 1494, and the question was complicated by that of British and Portuguese smuggling into Spain's colonies. The principal scene of conflict was the Portuguese post of Sacramento, founded in 1679 on the eastern bank of the Río de la Plata. The Spanish-owned region of Paraguay was also a field for Portuguese aggressions. Domestic animals to the number of hundreds of thousands were driven off from the Spanish settlements, while thousands of Indian families were captured and sold into slavery. Ferdinand VI endeavored to solve these problems through a treaty which he made with Portugal, in 1750, according to which Spain acquired Sacramento in exchange for territories in the Paraguayan region. The treaty met with the spirited opposition of leading Spanish ministers, and with that of the Jesuit missionaries, the Indians, and the Spanish settlers in the regions affected, and after many vicissitudes, including a war in Paraguay, it was annulled in 1761, but the troubles on the border continued. One of the underlying difficulties was the ambition of Portugal. Under the direction of the Marquis of Pombal, Portuguese minister of state, she was desirous of making conquests in South America, for which purpose Pombal was willing to go to any length in bad faith to achieve his end, relying upon the support of England in case Spain should declare war. Pombal secretly directed the Portuguese officials in the Sacramento region to seize desirable Spanish territories, and when reports of these captures came to Europe pretended that they were false, or that they were nothing more than inconsequential affrays between the Spanish and Portuguese soldiery. He promised to order his troops to desist from such actions, and asked Charles III to do the same. The Spanish king complied with his wishes, while Pombal on the contrary continued to give orders for hostilities and to send reinforcements, hoping that the Portuguese might secure posts from which it would be impossible to dislodge them by the time his duplicity should

Disputes with Portugal over boundaries in South America.

be found out. Not only did he deceive Charles III for a while, but he also misled the English ministers, pretending that Portugal was a victim of Spanish ambition when the facts were quite the contrary. England supported Pombal with vigorous diplomatic action. By the close of the year 1775, however, England was so busily engaged in the disputes with her own colonies that she was far from desiring a war in Europe. The British Cabinet announced that it would take no part in the quarrel between Spain and Portugal, provided Charles III should make no attempts on the territorial integrity of Portugal and Brazil. Pombal now made peaceful overtures to Charles III, hoping to delay the sending of Spanish troops to South America, but the proofs of Pombal's perfidy were by this time so clear that the king of Spain would not trust him. In fact, a Portuguese fleet in South America attacked the Spanish fleet, in February, 1776, and shortly afterward the Portuguese captured the Spanish post of Santa Tecla. In November a Spanish expedition left Cádiz, and on arrival in South America put a check to the Portuguese aggressions, and captured Sacramento. Fortune played into Spain's hands in another respect when María Victoria, sister of Charles III, became regent of Portugal on the death of the king in 1777. This occasioned the dismissal of Pombal, and in October of that year a treaty was arranged between Spain and Portugal entirely favorable to the former. The much-disputed Sacramento colony was awarded to Spain, while Paraguay was retained. This treaty, supplemented by another in 1778, put an end, after nearly three centuries, to the disputes between Spain and Portugal with regard to their American boundaries.

Disputes of England with her American colonies as a factor in Spain's foreign policy.

In the midst of Spain's preparations for a war against England there loomed up a new factor, the troubles between England and her American colonies. Down to 1774 Spain had proceeded without reference to these disputes, ardently desirous of war whenever France should be ready, although Charles III himself was conservative with regard to a declaration. Until late in the year 1774 France and Spain, together with most Englishmen, believed that the colonial situation was merely a Whig device against the Tories. The first inkling of the seriousness of the situation seems to have come in a report of the French ambassador, in June, 1774, quoting a remark of the British minister, Lord Rochford, that the Boston rioters were descendants of Cromwell's Puritans, implying that they would fight. Both France and Spain welcomed the news, believing that it would keep England engaged until the Bourbon powers could get ready to strike. In December, 1774, Garnier, the French *chargé d'affaires* in London, had become convinced that the American dispute was the most important event in English history since the revolution of 1688, and he suggested that France should give secret aid to the Americans. In January, 1775, he reported that an army of 9000 men was being sent to the colonies, and sounded a warning lest they make a descent upon the French West Indies, whether in the flush of victory, or in order to gain a recompense in case of defeat. The Spanish court was informed of this opinion, and in March, 1775, received a similar message from Escarano, the Spanish minister in London, who stated that England had 11,736 soldiers in America (a great force as colonial armies went) and could easily attack Spain's possessions, both because they were near, and because the British had so many transports at hand. He was of the opinion that England could not defeat America with her "three million souls, guided by the enthusiasm of liberty, and accustomed to live in a kind of independence," a people "who had given so many proofs of valor." The danger of a return to power of William Pitt, the imperialist, now Lord Chatham, was also alluded to. Spain at once consulted with France whether it would not be advisable to break with England immediately, but Vergennes was not ready. So the matter was dropped, although a remark attributed to Lord Rochford that the Americans could be won back to allegiance by an English declaration of war against France did not tend to allay the Bourbon feeling of insecurity.

At about this time the Spanish authorities began to be impressed by the idea, first expressed by Aranda in July, 1775, that the American outbreak would endanger Spain's

Disadvantages to Spain of a victory by either the United States or England and effect on Spain's policy.

colonial empire. According to Aranda an independent America would be a menace, as her population was increasing, and consequently she needed lands, which she would be apt to seek in a region with a temperate climate like New Spain, rather than by expansion northward. Thus the Anglo-Americans might eventually dominate North America, or help Spain's colonies to become independent. On the other hand, if England should defeat the colonists, the latter would join with her in her wars as in the past, and the danger would be equally great. Thus Spain seemed to be between two horns of the dilemma. Up to this time she had been ready for a declaration of war whenever France should announce her willingness. Henceforth there was a more conservative note in Spain's attitude, while France, who had everything to gain and nothing to lose, threw off her former conservatism and became increasingly enthusiastic. Up to the close of the year 1776, however, Spain still leaned toward war, and France remained undecided as to the moment to strike. During this period Spain was influenced largely by the question with Portugal. In September, 1776, Vergennes informed Aranda that in his opinion the war ought soon to be begun, before England herself should declare it and make an attack on France and Spain. Spain's attitude was expressed by Grimaldi, the Spanish minister of state, in a letter to Aranda in October. The war was inevitable, he said, and it would be an advantage to begin it several months before England was ready to undertake it. Spain would leave it to the decision of France whether the declaration should be made at once. Incidentally, Spain hoped to conquer Portugal in course of the war. This frank statement found Vergennes less enthusiastic. Moreover, he objected to Spain's designs on Portugal, lest other European powers should be unfavorable to them. Once again the matter was dropped. Some of the higher Spanish officials were disappointed over these continued refusals by France, but Charles III said that for his part he believed the right moment had not come. Meanwhile, since June, 1776, Spain had been aiding the Americans secretly with money, arms, and ammunition, much of which was made available through shipment to New Orleans by way of Havana, and thence to destination. Nevertheless, Vergennes' refusal, in November, to begin the war marked the turning point in the attitude of both France and Spain. The disadvantages, henceforth, loomed larger and larger in the eyes of Spain, while the successful resistance of the Americans to England made the way more and more easy for France.

The new attitude of Spain was represented by both Charles III and Floridablanca, who succeeded Grimaldi early in 1777. According to Floridablanca the most immediate advantages which Spain might hope to gain from the war were the recovery of Florida and the expulsion of the English from Honduras. War ought not to be declared, however, until both France and Spain should have considerable forces in the West Indies. Furthermore, if the rebellious English colonies should establish their independence, Spain ought to contrive to keep them divided in interests, so that there might not grow up a formidable power near Spanish America. Clearly there was no enthusiasm in Spanish governmental circles on behalf of the Americans. This appears also from the cold reception accorded Arthur Lee, the American representative, who at about this time arrived in Spain, but was not received by the Spanish court. The breach between the respective courses of France and Spain was still further widened as a result of Burgoyne's surrender to the Americans at Saratoga. The British government began to make offers with a view to conciliating the colonists. France acted quickly to prevent it, for it was believed that a reconciliation would mean a loss of the commercial favors France hoped to get and perhaps a war with England in which the colonies would join on the English side. In December, 1777, therefore, France declared herself ready to enter into a treaty of commerce and alliance with the American government, specifically stating that her willingness was due partially to a desire to diminish the power of England by separating her from her colonies. In February, 1778, a treaty was signed. All of this was done, in violation of the spirit of the Family Compact, without any official notification to Spain. Spain's opinion of this procedure was voiced by Floridablanca, who

Spain's divergence from France over the American Revolution.

recommended to Charles III that Spain should continue her preparations, as if war were inevitable, but should avoid a declaration as long as possible, for under existing circumstances, one of which was the inconstancy of Spain's allies, the war could not result favorably for Spain. Henceforth, Spain pursued an independent policy. The English government was informed that Spain's attitude would depend upon England; Spain neither wished war nor feared it. France, meanwhile, had entered the conflict.

Failure of mediation and Spain's entry into the war. Charles III now began to attempt the part of a mediator, in hopes that he might get Gibraltar and Minorca as the price for bringing about peace. In May, 1778, Escarano suggested to Lord Weymouth, a member of the British ministry, that Gibraltar would be a fair equivalent for Spain's services, but was told that the price was too high, and that affairs had probably gone beyond the point where mediation would serve; England wanted no more from Spain than that she remain neutral. In making this reply Lord Weymouth rather brusquely thanked Charles III for the magnanimity of his offer, — a type of answer which was not calculated to be pleasing to the Spanish ear, as Floridablanca very plainly intimated to the English ambassador. To add to Spain's displeasure England's conduct on the sea gave cause for complaint. Nevertheless, Charles still hoped to serve as arbitrator, — all the more so, when news came of French naval victories over the English. He prevailed upon Louis XVI to submit the terms upon which he would make peace. The conditions, which included an acknowledgment of American independence and the recall of England's land and sea forces, were presented to Lord Weymouth, who haughtily rejected them. Late in the same year, 1778, Spain's proposal of a twenty-five or thirty year truce between England and her colonies was also rejected. Nothing could exceed the patience of Charles III, who then offered Weymouth an indefinite armistice, to be guaranteed by a general disarmament. Again the Spanish king's proposals were arrogantly rejected. To make matters worse, England had delayed her reply from January to March, 1779, and her ships had continued to attack those of Spain. On April 3,

Charles renewed his offer of a suspension of hostilities, this time in the form of an ultimatum. England did not answer for nearly two months, and in the meantime, seeing that war was inevitable, planned attacks on the Spanish colonies. On May 28 the ultimatum was rejected, and on June 23 war was declared.

Spain was well prepared for the war, besides which the favorable state of her relations with Portugal, and indeed with other countries, was a source of strength. France and Spain planned an invasion of England which did not materialize, but it did cause the retention of the English fleet in British waters and a diminution in the military forces sent to America, — a factor in the American war not to be overlooked. The attempts to retake Gibraltar were unsuccessful, but in 1782 Minorca fell into Spanish hands. In America, Florida was reconquered from the British, the establishments in Honduras were taken, and the English were expelled from the Bahama Islands of the West Indies. Meanwhile, England displayed great eagerness to remove Spain from the list of her enemies. Late in 1779 she offered to restore Gibraltar for the price of Spanish neutrality, and to add Florida and the right to fish in Newfoundland waters if Spain would aid her against the United States. Not only this time but also on two other occasions when England endeavored to treat separately with Spain her offers were rejected, even though they embodied favorable terms for withdrawal from the war. In an age when international faith was not very sacred, Spain preferred to remain true to France, with whom she had renewed her alliance, although to be sure England's promises never equalled Spain's hopes. It is also interesting to note, not only that the Americans had a representative in Spain (John Jay), but also that there were agents of Spain in the United States (Miralles and Rendón), besides which Bernardo de Gálvez, the conqueror of Florida, had dealings with American agents at New Orleans. The general relations of the two governments cannot be said to have been cordial, however, and at no time was there anything approaching a veritable alliance ; Bourbon Spain could not possibly approve of the democratic

The war with England and its favorable issue.

United States. By the treaty of 1783, which ended the war, Spain got Florida and Minorca, and limited the dyewood privileges of the English in Honduras to a term of years. On the other hand Spain restored the Bahamas to England. An interesting period of relations between Spain and the United States, having to do primarily with the regions of the lower Mississippi valley, began in the closing years of the reign of Charles III, but the story belongs rather to the colonial side of the history of Spain.

Death of
Charles
III.

In December, 1788, Charles III died. As will be made more clear in the chapters dealing with institutions, he had brought Spain forward to the position of a first rank power again, — even though her enjoyment of that high station was to be of brief duration.

CHAPTER XXXIII

CHARLES IV AND FRANCE, 1788–1808

IF the reign of Charles III, despite the close union of the Bourbon crowns, had been characterized mainly in its external manifestations by the hostility of Spain to England, that of Charles IV (1788–1808) was dominated by relations with France. Unaffected for a while by the principles underlying the French Revolution, Spain was toppled from her position as a first-rate power by the Emperor Napoleon, whose designs for world power and whose methods in seeking it were not unlike those followed over a century later by William II of Germany. Meanwhile, the ideas of the American and the French revolutions were permeating the Spanish colonies, and as the wars with England continued during much of this reign, shutting off effective communication between the colonies and Spain, a chance was offered for putting them into effect in the new world. The way was well prepared in the reign of Charles IV, though the outbreak was postponed until after his fall. The blow struck by Napoleon was not without its compensations, which in the long run may be considered to have outweighed the loss of prestige. Napoleon, quite without intention, gave Spain an impulse to national feeling, in the uprising against French domination, which was greater than any she had formerly experienced, and of sufficient force to endure to the present day. In the same roundabout way Napoleon gave the Spain of the *Dos de Mayo*, or Second of May (the date of the revolt against Napoleon, and the national holiday of Spain), her first opportunity to imbibe democratic ideas.

To cope with the great forces of the French Revolution

Dominating character of relations with France and their effects upon Spain.

The
Nootka
affair and
the virtual
repudia-
tion of the
Family
Compact.

and the Napoleonic Empire, Spain had to rely on the leadership of the weak, timid, vacillating Charles IV. His predecessor had left him a legacy of able ministers, but these
were not long sustained by the king. At the outset Floridablanca still ruled as first minister of state. He was liberal-
minded as concerned social and economic institutions, but
was profoundly royalist in his political ideas and an enemy
of anything which represented a diminution in the pre-
rogatives of the crown. He was alarmed by the ideas which
were being spread broadcast in France, and took steps to
prevent their introduction into Spain, becoming recognized
as an opponent of the French Revolution. In the midst of
this situation, there occurred the Nootka affair, which
obliged him for a time to change his policy. A Spanish
voyage of 1789 to the northwest coast of North America
had resulted in the discovery and capture of two English
ships at Nootka, on the western shore of Vancouver Island.
Floridablanca informed the English government of this
event, in January, 1790, complaining of the frequent usurpations of Spanish colonial territories by British subjects, and
asking for the recognition of Spain's ownership of Nootka,
which had been discovered by a Spanish voyage of 1774.
What followed was very nearly a duplicate of the Falkland
incident, twenty years before. England claimed that the
British flag had been insulted, and demanded satisfaction,
which Floridablanca refused to give, as it involved the
acknowledgment of a doubt concerning Spain's ownership
of Nootka. War seemed imminent, and the French government was invoked to stand by the Family Compact. The
National Assembly, then in actual control in France, acknowledged the obligation, but attached conditions (having to do
with the revolution) to their willingness to declare war,—with
the result that Charles IV and Floridablanca decided that it
was better to avoid a rupture with England. A series of
three treaties, from 1790 to 1794, arranged for the payment
of an indemnity by Spain, and among other matters agreed
that the ships of both nations should have a right to sail the
waters and make landings freely in regions not already
settled by either power. In effect, therefore, the lands north

of the Spanish settlements were thrown open to the entry of England. These treaties had a significance which was wider than that of the matters directly involved. They marked a new spirit in the direction of colonial affairs. In the early years of the conquest Spain had played an aggressive part, followed soon by the adoption of what might be termed an aggressive defensive, or a willingness to fight for the retention of what she had, leading also to further conquests in order to ward off foreign attack. The Nootka affair was the beginning of a spiritless, waiting kind of defensive, the inevitable outcome of which was disintegration.

The Nootka treaties left Spain free, however, to stand in opposition to the French Revolution. Louis XVI of France had written secretly to Charles IV, in 1789, that he had been compelled to agree to measures of which he did not approve. Other European monarchs were also acquainted with the perils of Louis XVI's position, and in the general interests of kingship, all desired to save him, although in the case of Spain there was the strong bond of family ties as well. In 1790 Floridablanca directed a note to the French Assembly requesting greater freedom of action for Louis XVI, making thinly veiled threats in case of a refusal to comply. This action only served to enrage the French government. In 1791 Floridablanca ordered the taking of a census of all foreigners in Spain, about half of whom were Frenchmen, compelling them to swear allegiance to the king, the laws, and the religion of the peninsula. A subsequent order prohibited the entry of any literature of a revolutionary bearing, even going so far as to forbid foreigners to receive letters. When Louis XVI accepted the constitution of 1791 Floridablanca announced that Charles IV refused to recognize that the French king had signed the document of his own free will, and asked that Louis XVI and his family be allowed to go to a neutral land, threatening war if the French government should fail to accede to Charles' wishes. Here was a direct challenge to the revolution, but instead of accepting the gauntlet France sent an agent to Spain who was able to persuade Charles IV that Floridablanca's policy was in fact contributing to the dangerous position of Louis

Florida-blanca and Spanish opposition to the French Revolution.

2 D

XVI. Floridablanca was therefore relieved from power early in 1792, and Aranda became first minister in Spain.

Brief ministry of Aranda. Aranda, who sympathized to some extent with the revolutionary ideas, placed the relations with France on a more cordial basis, although without relinquishing the efforts which were being made in company with other European sovereigns to save Louis XVI. When the news came of the revolutionary excesses of the summer of 1792 Aranda, who had not expected such a turn of affairs, became more stern, and began to consider the advisability of joint military action with Austria, Prussia, and Sardinia. Meanwhile, the French government demanded the alliance of Spain or offered the alternative of war. Induced in part by a doubt with regard to the best policy to pursue for the sake of Louis XVI, Spain hesitated, and suggested a treaty of neutrality. France imposed conditions which it was impossible for Spain to accept, among them the recognition of the French Republic, which had just been proclaimed. Before Aranda could meet the problem in a decisive manner he was dispossessed of his post as the result of a palace plot in favor of Manuel Godoy.

Godoy and the significance of his relations with the queen. At the time of his accession to the headship of the Spanish ministry in 1792 Godoy was a mere youth, twenty-five years of age. Formerly a soldier of the royal guard, he had been selected by Charles IV with the specific idea of training him to be his leading minister, for the king believed that the plebeian Godoy would, out of necessity, be devotedly attached to the royal interests. The queen, María Luisa, was influential in the choice of Godoy, for there is little doubt that she was already the mistress of this upstart youth. Godoy's abilities have perhaps been condemned too harshly. He was a man of ambition and some talent, and had studied assiduously to fit himself for his eventual post. Nevertheless, his sudden rise to high rank in the nobility (for he had been made Duke of Alcudia) and in political office, together with the notoriety of his relations with the queen, caused an indignation in Spain which was to result in the forming of a party opposed to him, — a group which the enemies of Spain were able to manipulate to advantage.

Godoy continued the efforts of his predecessors to save

Louis XVI, without more success than they, and when he declined to accede to the conditions imposed by the French Convention, then ruling in France, that body early in 1793 declared war on Spain. The war against France was joined by most of the countries of western Europe. One by one, however, the continental princes fell away, and urged Spain to do the same. The war itself, so far as Spain was concerned, was not decisive either way, although France had a little the better of it. In 1795 negotiations were undertaken which resulted in the treaty of Basle. The Pyrenean boundary was maintained, but Spain ceded that portion of the island of Hayti, or Santo Domingo, which still belonged to her, thus acknowledging the French title to the whole island.[1] The government of England, with which Spain had allied for the war with France, was exceedingly annoyed by Spain's acceptance of peace, and very soon began to act in a threatening manner. Even as an ally in the recent war England had not been altogether cordial toward Spain. On one occasion a Spanish treasure ship which had been captured by the French was retaken by the English, and retained as a prize; Englishmen had continued to engage in contraband trade, not only in Spanish America, but also in the peninsula itself; they had been responsible for encouraging separatist feelings in Spanish America, well knowing that the independence of Spain's colonies would result in advantages to British commerce; and England had refused to grant Spain a subsidy for the 1795 campaign, — a factor with a bearing on Spain's action, whatever the merits of the case. The resentment of the Spanish court was now provoked by insults which were offered to the Spanish ambassador to London and by attacks on Spanish ships, just as formerly in the reign of Charles III. The natural effect was to drive Spain into the arms of France. An alliance was formed in 1796 which was followed by a declaration of war against England. It is highly probable that Charles IV was induced to form this union by a belief, fostered perhaps by French intrigue, that the French

War with France and the treaty of Basle.

Difficulties with England and alliance with France.

---

[1] For negotiating this treaty, which certainly did not redound greatly to the advantage of Spain, Godoy won the title of Prince of the Peace.

Republic was about to collapse, in which event it seemed likely that a Spanish Bourbon might be called to the throne of France.

Unsatis-
factory
results
from the
French
alliance.
Spain's experience as an ally of France was not more happy than her previous union with England. France excluded her from representation at several conferences looking to treaties of peace between France and her enemies, and made slight efforts to secure the interests of Spain, going so far as to refuse her sanction to many of the pretensions of her Bourbon ally. Most annoying of all was the dispossession of the Duke of Parma, a relative of Charles IV by descent from Isabel Farnesio. The French government endeavored to calm Spanish feelings on this point by offering to make Godoy the Grand Master of the Knights of Malta, — an honor he was disposed to accept, subject to certain conditions, one of which was that he be absolved from the vow of chastity. In fact, however, the French authorities were suspicious of Godoy, believing that he was secretly plotting with England, because he did not insist on Portugal's refusing to allow the English fleets to remain in Portuguese ports. A French representative was sent to Spain in 1797, and the dismissal of Godoy was procured from Charles IV. Nevertheless, Godoy continued to be the principal force at the Spanish court, backed as he was by the powerful influence of the queen. The policy of truculence to France went on, however, due in part perhaps to Charles' continued hopes of acquiring the Bourbon crown, but even more, very likely, to his pusillanimity in the face of the threats of the French Directory. In 1799 his hopes were dashed when Napoleon Bonaparte overthrew the Directory and became first consul of France, a title which a few years later he converted into that of emperor.

Early
relations
with Na-
poleon and
the war
with Por-
tugal.
The change of government in France was welcomed at the Spanish court, for it was believed that Spain would receive more consideration at the hands of Napoleon than she had obtained from the Directory. Events proved that Spain was to be even more an instrument in French hands than formerly, and that Napoleon was to be more powerful and despotic and less courteous and faithful in international

affairs than the French rulers who had preceded him. One of his earliest acts was an attempt to employ the Spanish fleet to conserve French ends. When the Spanish admiral refused to carry out the wishes of Napoleon, a matter in which he was sustained by his government, the French ruler brought about the dismissal of Urquijo, at that time first minister of state in Spain, and shortly afterward the offending admiral was relieved from his command. Meanwhile, a treaty had been arranged in 1800 whereby Napoleon agreed to enlarge the dominions of the Duke of Parma (who had regained his duchy) in exchange for the recession of Louisiana to France and the gift of six ships of war. By a treaty of 1801 Tuscany was granted to the family of the Duke of Parma, whose whole domains were now called the kingdom of Etruria. It was provided that in case of a lack of succession of the reigning house a Spanish prince of the royal family should inherit the Etrurian throne, and this was to be the rule forever. Another treaty of 1801 required Spain to issue an ultimatum to Portugal demanding an abandonment of the English alliance. The name of Godoy was signed to the later treaties in the series of which the above have been mentioned. He had not ceased to be influential during his absence from power, but henceforth until 1808 he was definitely in the saddle. Though his military experience was slight he was appointed general of the Spanish army which was to invade Portugal, and when war was presently declared he entered that country. The campaign, although comparatively insignificant, resulted in victory. Portugal agreed to close her ports in return for the Spanish king's guarantee of the territorial integrity of Portugal. A celebration was held at Badajoz, at which the soldiers presented the queen with branches of orange trees taken from Portuguese groves, resulting in the application of the name "war of the oranges," — which fittingly described its inconsequential character. Napoleon was furious over such a termination of the war, and went so far as to threaten the end of the Spanish monarchy unless the campaign were pursued. At length he decided to accept the result, after Portugal had consented to increase the indemnity which she had originally agreed to pay to France. This marked a beginning, however, of the French ruler's distrust of Godoy. Shortly afterward it suited Napoleon's purposes to make peace. In 1802 a treaty was signed with England, and, naturally, Spain too made peace. Minorca, which had been occupied by the English, was restored to Spain, but the island of Trinidad was surrendered to England, — another bit chipped off Spain's colonial empire.

Godoy had emerged from the Portuguese campaign as general-in-chief of the armies of the land and sea, and was again the dominating power at court. By this time a strong opposition had grown up around Ferdinand, the eldest son of the king, directed by an ambitious canon, named Escoiquiz. Napoleon now had a political force at hand, to employ whenever he should desire it, against Godoy. Early in 1803 Napoleon was again at war with England, and proceeded to woo Spain's support by charges that she was favoring England and by threats of war. In the same year, too, he sold Louisiana to the United States, although he had promised Spain at the time of the recession that France would never transfer that region to any country other than Spain. Spain protested, but soon accepted the situation. Later in 1803 Napoleon compelled Spain to consent to a so-called treaty of neutrality, which in fact amounted to the paying of a monthly tribute to France. England objected, and followed up her complaints by capturing three Spanish frigates and stopping merchantmen, without a declaration of war. England announced that she was holding the frigates as a guarantee of Spanish neutrality. Thus courted with equal roughness by France and England, Spain was again under the necessity of choosing which of her enemies to fight. England was selected, and in 1804 war against that country was declared.

In 1805 there occurred the great battle of Trafalgar, in which the French and Spanish navies were virtually destroyed by the English under Nelson. The immediate results of this defeat as affecting Spanish action was the decision of Godoy, who had never enjoyed cordial relations with Napoleon, to seek an alliance with England. Through this agency he hoped to bolster up his own power as against the rapidly growing body of his enemies in Spain. In the midst of his plans came Napoleon's great victory over Prussia at Jena in 1806, which, following that of Austerlitz over Austria in 1805, once again made the French emperor dangerously predominant on the continent of western Europe. Godoy, who had already compromised himself, made haste to explain. Napoleon pretended to be satisfied, but decided then that he would make an end of the Bourbon monarchy. The unpopularity of Godoy and the strength of the party of Ferdinand, who was now a popular favorite, were among the means of which he availed himself; Ferdinand even wrote him letters in which he alluded freely to his mother's adulterous relations with Godoy. Meanwhile, Napoleon profited by Godoy's willingness to do anything to win the favor of the emperor by arranging for the conquest of Portugal. A partition of that territory was projected whereby the Bourbon monarch of Etruria was to have northern Portugal, Godoy (as Prince of Algarve) was to have the south, and the centre was to be exchanged for Gibraltar, Trinidad, and other colonies which England had taken from Spain. The usual ultimatum having been sent and rejected, the war began for what seemed a brilliant objective for Spain, — if Napoleon had had any intention of his keeping his word.

The campaign of 1807 resulted in a rapid, almost bloodless conquest of Portugal by the French general Junot, placing Napoleon in a position to fulfil his treaty obligations. Nothing was further from his plans, however, and, indeed, Godoy and the king had recently had cause to suspect his sincerity; action had been taken against Ferdinand and his party, resulting in the exposure of the prince's correspondence with Napoleon. Napoleon occupied Etruria, — and gave the queen of that country to understand that she need not look for compensation in Portugal. Godoy, meanwhile, remained without Algarve, although hoping against hope that he might yet get it. All this time, French troops were pouring into Spain, and through deceit were possessing themselves of the Spanish strongholds in the north. To the

Plottings of Napoleon and the abdication of Charles IV.

credit of Godoy it must be said that he divined the emperor's intentions, and favored a demand for the withdrawal of the French troops, with the alternative of war. Charles IV and his other leading advisers were opposed to this idea; the king was frightened at the very thought of fighting Napoleon. The emperor now began to unmask himself. The Spanish ambassador to France returned to Madrid as the bearer of a message from Napoleon, asking for the cession of certain Spanish provinces in the north as far as the Ebro, or else for the recognition of the emperor's title to Portugal, together with a military road thereto across Spanish territory; the ambassador added that he believed Napoleon intended to possess himself of the northern provinces and perhaps of all Spain, though possibly not until the death of Charles IV. It was now perfectly clear to Godoy and the king what Napoleon meant to do, but the party of Ferdinand, unaware of all the facts, was wedded blindly to the emperor, believing that his sole desire was to get rid of Godoy and assure the succession of Ferdinand. Charles, Godoy, and the queen thought of escaping to the Americas, and as a preliminary step moved the court from Madrid to Aranjuez. A riot followed at Aranjuez in which Godoy was captured by the followers of Ferdinand, and was with difficulty saved from death. Realizing that the army and the people were almost wholly on the side of Ferdinand, and unable to see any way out of his difficulties, Charles IV decided to abdicate, and accordingly on March 19, 1808, did so. All Spain rejoiced, for Godoy had fallen, and the idolized prince had now ascended the throne as Ferdinand VII.

Duplicity of Napoleon and the journeys of Ferdinand VII and Charles IV to Bayonne.

Napoleon was much displeased at the course of events in Spain. The flight of Charles would have fitted in with his plans, whereas the accession of Ferdinand placed him under the necessity of exposing his hand. Temporarily he saved the situation by one of the most remarkable exhibitions of successful duplicity in history. On March 23 General Murat entered Madrid with a French army, and the next day Ferdinand made his royal entry, and was received by the people with delirious joy. The foreign diplomats at once recognized him as king, — except the French ambassador.

Uncertain yet what to do, Napoleon was on the one hand giving indications of an intention to restore Charles IV, and on the other planning to set up one of his own brothers as king of Spain. Charles IV gave the emperor the opening he desired. In order to obtain some material advantages from his abdication and to save Godoy, who was still in prison, he entered into communication with Murat, and as a result secretly retracted his abdication, placing himself entirely in the hands of Napoleon. Meanwhile, Murat told Ferdinand that the emperor was coming to see him, and suggested that Ferdinand should go to Burgos to meet him. When Ferdinand decided against the journey, lest it produce a bad effect in the minds of the people, Napoleon sent General Savary with orders to bring Ferdinand whether he wanted to come or not. Savary succeeded in persuading the young prince to go to Burgos, and when Napoleon was not found there to Vitoria. Beyond this point Ferdinand was at first not disposed to go, but, urged on both by Savary and Escoiquiz, who still believed in the French emperor, the party proceeded across the boundary line to Bayonne. There indeed they found Napoleon, — and Ferdinand was informed that he must abdicate the throne. A few days later, on April 30, Charles IV, María Luisa, and Godoy arrived ; they had been easily persuaded to go there by Murat. The reunion of the royal family at Bayonne was accompanied by disgraceful quarrels of the parents and the son and by the humiliating weakness of all in the presence of Napoleon. Charles IV was again induced to abdicate, and was given a rich pension and estates in France to which he and his family, Godoy, and the royal servants might repair. Ferdinand was also granted rents and lands. To Napoleon was given the right to name a king of Spain.

Meanwhile, the French troops in Madrid and elsewhere had been conducting themselves like conquerors, and had aroused considerable hostility in the people, who were not so easily deceived and dominated as their rulers had been. After the departure of Ferdinand from Madrid the French officers did not hesitate to say that Napoleon would not recognize him, — which only increased the popular discontent. The

Uprising of the Dos de Mayo against Napoleon.

climax came when an order was received from Napoleon for the young Bourbon prince, Francisco de Paula, and for the queen of Etruria with her children to be sent to France. The departure from Madrid was set for the morning of the second of May. A crowd gathered to see the royal party off, and heard rumors which excited it to a feeling of frenzy, — for example, that the young Francisco (then only thirteen) had protested in tears against going. Insults were offered the French soldiery, and the harness of the coaches was cut. These scenes were interrupted by the appearance of a French battalion, which fired without warning into the crowd. The crowd scattered, and spread the news over the city. This was the signal for a general uprising against the French. The Spanish troops were under strict orders from the government to stay in barracks, but a number of them declined to obey. Prominent among those joining the people against the French were Captains Pedro Velarde and Luis Daoiz, the heroes of the day. When the people were driven out of the central square of the city, the Plaza del Sol, by the French artillery, Velarde hastened to the battery commanded by Daoiz. Convincing the latter that the interests of the country were superior to discipline he joined with him and a certain Lieutenant Ruiz in directing the fire against the French troops. Superior in numbers and armament, the French were successful after a battle lasting three hours in which Velarde and Daoiz were killed. The dramatic events of the *Dos de Mayo*, or the second of May, were the prelude to a national uprising against the French. Without a king or a government Spain began the war which was to usher in a new era in Spanish history, — for, just as Americans look back to the Fourth of July in 1776, so the Spaniards consider the *Dos de Mayo* of 1808 as the beginning of modern Spain.

CHAPTER XXXIV

SPANISH SOCIETY, 1700–1808

FUNDAMENTALLY, there was no change in the classes of Spanish society in this period as regards their legal and social standing, except in the case of the rural population of Aragon. One of the characteristic notes of the era was a certain democratic sentiment of a philanthropic kind, exhibiting itself vaguely in a desire for the well-being of mankind, and practically in the social, economic, and intellectual betterment of the masses, without any attempt being made to improve their juridical position. This ideal, which was not confined to Spain, became more and more widespread with the increase in influence of the French encyclopedists, and got to be a fad of high society, being encouraged by the kings themselves. Many of its manifestations will be taken up later in dealing with economic institutions, but the sentimental discussion of the ideal may be remarked upon here; this at length went so far as to result in the formulation of political doctrines of a democratic character, but they were not yet translated into law. Such social reforms as were made came for the most part in the last three reigns of the era, especially in that of Charles III.

The description of the nobility in the period of the House of Austria might almost be repeated for this era. The nobles had long since lost their political power, but the wealth of the grandees and the privileges and the prestige of all ranks of the nobility were so great that this class was a more important factor in Spanish life than it is today. Pride of noble rank continued to be almost an obsession, despite the attempts to check it; with a view to diminishing petitions for the recognition of rights of *hidalguía*, a law was passed

Social characteristics of the era.

Pride, wealth, and privileges of the nobles.

411

in 1758 calling for the payment of a large sum of money when the petitioner's title dated back to the fourth or fifth grandfather. On the other hand, the kings were responsible for acts which tended to encourage the eagerness for noble rank. Ferdinand VI officially recognized that the people of Vizcaya were all of *hidalgo* rank; Charles III created the order which bears his name, and Charles IV founded that of the "noble ladies of María Luisa"; various societies of nobles for equestrian exercises, in imitation of the military orders, were formed, and they were given certain privileges in criminal jurisdiction. To be sure, the grant of these honors was a source of revenue to the state. The recognition of the privileged character of the nobles was manifest, even in the case of the more degraded members of that class; a law of 1781 provided that nobles who were arrested as vagabonds should be sent to the army with the rank of "distinguished soldiers." The grandees and the other nobles possessed of seigniorial estates still controlled the appointment of many municipal functionaries; in 1787 there were 17 cities, 2358 *villas*, and 1818 *aldeas* and *pueblos* in seigniorial hands, in some of which the king shared jurisdiction with the lords. Similarly, the military orders had the right to appoint the clergymen of 3 cities, 402 *villas*, 119 *pueblos*, and 261 *aldeas*. Many monopolies of a medieval type still survived in favor of the lords, such as those of hunting, fishing, the baking of bread, the making of flour, and the use of streams and forests, and in some cases the lord's vassals were subject to medieval tributes and services. It is rather by comparison with matters as they are today, however, that these incidents loom large; they were but the survivals of a system which was already dead. The worst of these seigniorial rights, the Aragonese lord's power of life and death over his villeins, was abolished by Philip V. The kings did not dare to suppress all of the seigniorial privileges, but took steps to overcome them, as by submitting the rights of certain lords to rigorous proofs, by hindering sales of jurisdiction, by subjecting the appointments of the lords to the approval of the *Cámara*, by naming special royal officials for the various seigniorial holdings, and in general by facili-

Real decline of their power.

tating the reincorporation in the crown of such estates. By
this time the lesser nobility enjoyed few exemptions of a
financial character, but the great nobles still possessed such
privileges. The kings employed indirect methods to cause
them to submit to taxation. Thus payments were demanded
in lieu of military service, and the *media anata* (half annates)
was required for the recognition of the title of a successor
to landed estates; certainly the immensely wealthy grandees
were able to pay these tributes without serious economic
loss to themselves. Furthermore, the great nobles continued
to be a court nobility, and were jealously proud of the special
privileges of an empty character which marked them off
from the classes below them. For example, a grandee had
the right to keep his hat on and to sit down in the presence
of the king; to be called "cousin" by the king; to have a
private guard; to preside over the sessions of the noble
branch of the *Cortes;* to be visited and saluted by *ayuntamientos,* viceroys, and other authorities; to have a better
place than others, both indoors and out; and to be free from
imprisonment except by a special decree of the king.

There was no essential change in the composition and
character of the middle classes in this era. The working
classes of the cities attained to a little more liberty than
formerly, as a result of the decline of the guilds, while those
of the country, if they had improved their juridical position,
continued nevertheless in a state of misery and poverty.
The rural wars of past reigns were missing, however. The
evil lot of the rural classes was due more to the backwardness of agriculture, the vast extent of unworked lands common, and the widespread practice of entailing estates, than
to bonds of a social character. An interesting attempt, at
once to raise the urban laborer, and to break down the sharp
dividing line between the nobility and the plebeian classes,
was a law of 1783, which declared that the trades of artisans
— such as those of the carpenter, tailor, and shoemaker — were
to be considered honorable, and since municipal offices were
usually in the hands of the *hidalgo* class it was also enacted
that the practice of these trades did not incapacitate a man
from holding positions in the local government or even from

Slight
gains of
the work-
ing classes.

becoming an *hidalgo*. This well-meant law was not able to overcome social prejudices, however, and when an endeavor was made to interpret it in the sense that it authorized the entry of artisans into the military orders, which had always been composed only of nobles, it was decreed in 1803 that it had never been intended to raise them to that degree, for the military orders were founded on the necessity of maintaining the lustre of the nobility.

Benevolent legislation affecting gypsies, descendants of Jews, and slaves.

A spirit of racial tolerance for the despised classes made its appearance in this era. Laws placing prohibitions on the gypsies were repeatedly enacted until the time of Charles III, but in 1783 that monarch declared that the gypsies were not to be considered a tainted race, and ordered that they be admitted to the towns and to occupations on the same basis as other Spaniards, provided they would abandon their dress, language, and special customs. Similarly, in 1782 Charles III endeavored to free the descendants of Jews from the stigma of their ancestry by enacting that they should not be obliged to live in a separate quarter or wear any device indicative of their origin. A law of 1785 permitted them to serve in the army or navy, — a right which had previously been denied them. These generous laws for the gypsies and the descendants of Jews were as little capable as those just mentioned concerning artisans of overcoming social prejudices, wherefore they failed of their objects. In matters of religion the laws affecting the despised classes were more in keeping with general sentiment. In 1712 it was ordered that Moslem slaves who had been set free must leave the country; in 1802 the prohibition against Jews returning to the peninsula was reaffirmed as absolute in the case of those who retained the Jewish faith. Slavery continued to be legal, but laws were passed that slaves escaping to Spain from other lands, except from the Spanish colonies, became *ipso facto* free. The treaty of 1779 with Morocco provided that prisoners of war should not henceforth be enslaved. The institution of slavery existed on a great scale in the Americas, though Charles III alleviated the rigors of the situation by his beneficent legislation.

Legislation affecting the family aimed to tighten the bonds between parents and children, which had become loosened as a result of the increasing spirit of individualism. Thus a law of 1766 ordered that the prior consent of parents should be obtained before children could marry, although a remedy was provided for an unreasonable withholding of consent; in the preamble it was stated that the law was due to the frequent occurrence of "unequal marriages." Several later laws upheld the same principle. Legislation concerning property was characterized by the ideas of the physiocratic school of thinkers, who referred all social and economic problems to the land as the fundamental basis. Among the Spanish physiocrats (for the physiocratic ideal was widespread in western Europe) were Campomanes, Floridablanca, and Jovellanos, who were among the greatest of Spanish reformers in the reign of Charles III and the early years of Charles IV. In keeping with physiocratic views the laws tended to the release of realty from incumbrances and to the distribution of lands among many persons. The practice of entailing estates in primogeniture was one of the institutions attacked by the physiocrats. It was admitted that it was necessary in the case of the great nobles, in order to maintain the prestige of the family name, but it was held to be desirable to check the extension of the institution in other cases and to facilitate the extinction of entails. Thus a law of 1749 permitted of the sale of entailed estates for an annuity in the case of financially ruined houses; a law of 1789 prohibited the founding of new entails, and facilitated the sale of realty already so held; a law of 1795 imposed heavy taxes on existing entails; and a law of 1798 authorized the sale of entailed estates, provided the funds should be invested in a certain loan announced at that time. Still other laws were passed in this period, with the result that many entails disappeared and others were diminished in size. The nobles resisted the change, and the greater number of the entails remained in existence, although reduced in income. In the same way municipal and ecclesiastical holdings were attacked. In the case of the former (*propios*), laws were passed repeatedly — for example in 1761, 1766, 1767,

Tightening of the bonds of family.

Influence of the physiocratic school on legislation affecting property.

1768, and especially in 1770 — for the partition of the cultivable and pastoral lands and for their assignment to a number of individuals. Nevertheless, the majority of this type of municipal lands continued in the possession of the towns, for the laws were not fully executed. As concerns lands utilized for the promotion of religious objects, pious foundations were attacked, and either compelled or else permitted to sell their real property, but there was considerable hesitancy about applying the same practice to lands held in mortmain by the regular and secular clergy, although the prevailing opinion of jurisconsults was opposed to these holdings. Some steps were taken, however, to free these lands, as well as other measures to hinder the giving of realty in mortmain. In the various colonization schemes of the century it was customary to forbid the transfer of lands to ecclesiastical institutions. A law of 1763 prohibited further conveyances to the church, and a law of 1798 called for the alienation of lands owned by charitable institutions, even though they might belong to the church, and some estates accordingly were sold. The resistance of the clergy, together with a certain repugnance to laying hands on the property of the church except in case of extreme necessity, operated to prevent these laws from having their full effect. It will be noticed that all of these measures were markedly individualistic, in accord with Roman principles as opposed to those of medieval society, and favorable to the change in ownership of landed estates and to their division into small holdings. This spirit was manifested even more insistently in attacking titles of a medieval character. Thus the right of farmers to fence lands for their own use was sustained, serving as a check upon the abuses of the *Mesta*, and the various methods of tribute from vassals to a lord (*censos, foros*, etc.) were the subject of legislation tending to relieve the former from their burdens. To this epoch, also, belong laws requiring the registry of titles to land. Nevertheless, the spirit of collectivism was still alive, as expressed in doctrines favoring the condemnation of individual property and the establishment of communal inclosures with the drawing of lots for land, but the

Triumphs
of Roman
principles.

followers of Roman principles were victorious in the controversy.

The spirit of individualism appeared, also, to give a death-blow to the guilds, even though they actually increased in number; there were ninety guilds in Barcelona at the close of the eighteenth century. Among the factors contributing to the decline were the following: the continuance of the exclusive spirit of the past, making entry into the guild a difficult matter; the accentuation of social differences within the guilds, such that certain elements had special privileges based on rank in the guild, — for example, a right that their sons might enter the institution without serving as apprentices; the failure of the guilds to observe their own ordinances; the frequency of lawsuits between guilds, or even between a guild and its own members; and especially the continued intervention of the state, taking over the former municipal control of the guilds and unifying the ordinances of each trade throughout the country. The relation of the state to the guilds facilitated the application of the new economic ideas which were favorable to the freedom of labor and hostile to the guilds. Thus in 1772 foreign artisans were permitted to establish themselves, without paying a special tax and without having to undergo examinations; in 1782 a general law introduced reforms facilitating apprenticeship, freeing applicants for entry into a guild from the necessity of proving the Christian faith of their ancestry (*limpieza de sangre*), permitting of the sale of masterships, and abolishing the distinction between the sons of masters and those of the other members; in another law of the same year painters, sculptors, and architects were authorized to work independently of guilds; in 1783 the *cofradías* attached to the guilds were suppressed, and their place was taken by benefit societies (*montepíos*); in 1784 women were given a general permission to engage in any trade they wished; in 1790 it was enacted that any artisan of recognized ability could work at his trade without the need of an examination; and in 1793 a law dissolving the guilds of the silk manufacturers announced that it was neither necessary nor fitting that persons should be grouped together in guilds for carry-

Decline and fall of the guilds.

2 ᴇ

ing on such an industry. From this point it was only a step to the death of the institution. The great name in the legislation against the guilds was that of Campomanes.

Dull routine of daily life.

If the social customs of the two preceding eras may be said to have represented the virile youth of the Spanish peoples, followed by a seemingly mortal sickness resulting from a too great indulgence in "wild oats," this period stands for the recovery of the race (just as occurred in other aspects of peninsula life) in a conventional, outwardly respectable, and on the whole fairly wholesome, if also somewhat monotonous, middle age. Simplicity, regularity, and subordination to principles of authority (as represented by king, church, and parents, checking inititative and making long-established custom the guiding rule in daily life) were the dominating social characteristics. Both in the city and in the country, people arose early; the *Consejo de Castilla* met at seven in the morning from April to September, and at eight from October to March. It was the custom also to go to bed early, to perform one's daily tasks in precisely the same way each day, to hear mass daily, to have family prayers each day, to salute one's parents respectfully on the same daily recurring occasions, and to display a like respect in the presence of official personages or of clergymen. If people now and then indulged in gossip about their neighbors, they gave little thought to persons or events beyond their immediate circle; they were in no hurry to learn the news of the world, waiting tranquilly for the arrival of the mails, which were usually infrequent and meagre.

Monotony of the life at court and among the nobles.

The kings themselves helped to make this monotonous type of life fashionable. Philip V was domestically inclined, retiring, and melancholy, and from the time of his marriage with Isabel Farnesio was nearly always at the side of his wife, who even accompanied him when he received his ministers before he had arisen from bed. His daily life was passed in pious exercises and in hunting, with music to vary the monotony. Ferdinand VI, also domestic, retiring, and God-fearing, was very fond of music, with the result that the court was brightened by frequent concerts, operas, and theatrical representations, on which vast sums of money were

expended.   Charles III was a man of very simple tastes, an
enemy of the theatre and of music, but passionately devoted
to hunting.   He was so methodical that every moment of the
day within the palace was regulated by royal ordinances, and
the annual journeys and changes of residence of the royal family took place each year on the same day.   In monotonous
regularity of life Charles IV resembled his illustrious predecessor, but passion for hunting amounted in his case almost
to a disease; after having breakfast and hearing mass he
would hunt until one o'clock, and would return to that sport
after having partaken of dinner.   The sameness of court life
in this period was broken by various receptions and royal feast
days, but even these were cold and formal, following prescribed courses, although celebrated with great pomp.   In
1804 there were eight greater gala days and seventeen lesser
ones, besides those arising from unforeseen events, such as
the reception of a foreign ambassador.   Furthermore, royal
journeys necessarily involved festivities and heavy expense.
Balls, banquets, and other diversions found no place at court,
and the accession of Charles III put an end to concerts and
plays.   The ordinary life of the nobles followed that of the
kings.   Comparing it with that of France, a French duke
who came to Spain in the reign of Philip V said that it was
tiresome, almost unsociable, and lacking in comforts, despite
the fact that great sums of money were often spent for enter-
tainments of a formal nature.   Toward the close of the century the more genial practices of other European countries
began to percolate into Spain.   Godoy was one who took
pleasure in giving balls.   Others followed his example, and
the austere simplicity of Spanish life began to yield to comforts, diversions, and dissipation.   Nevertheless, the old
conventions still ruled, especially in the country districts,
where the poorer nobility resided, occupying themselves in
hunting and in local politics and intrigues.   The penurious
nobles of the *hidalgo* class continued to be found at the capital
in the train of the greater representatives of the titled element.

Some clue to the modesty of life in general may be obtained   Simplicity
from the cheapness of rents and the scantiness of furniture   of do-
in the houses of the capital.   The average annual rental   mestic life.

was 1504 *reales* ($94), and there were many houses of an inferior type to be had for 45 *reales* ($2.81) a month, although, of course, money values were much greater then than now. House decorations and furniture were poor to the point of shabbiness. Walls did not begin to be papered until the close of the eighteenth century. Usually they were whitewashed and hung with a few pictures of a religious character or with brass candlesticks. The floor was of unpolished wood, covered over in winter with mats, and there was a like simplicity in chairs. Writing-desks were often present, but were opened only when visitors were being received. Candles were employed for lighting, and the odorous, scantly warming brazier was the principal resource against cold. The same sobriety manifested itself as regards the table. The *puchero*, or *cocido*, made up primarily of chickpeas (*garbanzos*), was the basis of the meal, and usually was the only element. Inns were equally uninviting, and it was not until the close of the era that the example of foreign countries prevailed upon the Spaniards to introduce somewhat more comfortable hostelries.[1]

Struggle between the French and the native styles in dress. The simplicity and severity of Spanish customs were not maintained in matters of dress. There was a century-long conflict between the French and the native styles, the former represented by the military cut of clothing more in keeping with that of the present day, and the latter by the slouched hat and long cape, as symbolic of the indigenous modes. On grounds of morality and public safety the government opposed the native type, which lent itself too easily to the facilitation of disguise, and the methodical Charles III even considered the imposition of a national dress which should omit the traditional features. A law of 1766 ordered their abandonment and the adoption of a short cape or riding coat and the three-cornered cocked hat. The decree was the occasion of riots throughout Spain, and had to be recalled, while Squillace, the minister who had proposed it, lost his post. Aranda, his successor, achieved the desired

---

[1] Those who have lived in Spanish boarding-houses (*fondas*) in our own times will recognize that this description lacks very little of fitting contemporary Spain.

end by indirect methods. He caused the slouched hat to be made the official head-piece of the hangman, wherefore it began to lose prestige, and the French styles were soon decisively victorious. It is to be noted, however, that the three-cornered cocked hat and other French styles of the Bourbon era were retained in Spain after they were no longer in fashion in republican and imperial France. Women's dress was also reformed in a similar direction. Three outstanding features characterized the well-dressed woman: the skirt of silk or velvet; the *mantilla*, or veil, worn over the head instead of a hat; and the fan. Fans of a most luxurious type were used, with ribs of shell, mother-of-pearl, or ivory, and with ornaments of gold, while the principal part was hand-painted, often by artists of note, to represent scenes of a mythological, pastoral, or historical character. Even among the common people, especially among the so-called *majos*, or low-class dandies (both male and female) of Madrid, there were special types of elegant dress. Ladies' dress-combs of unusual size, not infrequently half a foot or more in height above the hair, may be mentioned as one phase of the *majo* styles, which stood for a reaction against French modes, though with scant knowledge or regard for ancient Spanish customs. *Majismo*, both in dress and in customs, invaded the aristocracy, and has been immortalized in some of the paintings of Goya. The common people of the country were much more conservative in maintaining the earlier styles of dress, which have survived to the present day, although the uniformity of modern life has tended to make them peculiarities, rather than the prevailing modes of the different regions in which they are found.

The monotony of Spanish life did not prevent Spaniards from being fond of diversions. On the contrary they seemed to welcome a chance to escape from the narrow course of their humdrum existence. Public feast-days were numerous and very popular; events in Christian history were the occasion of most of them. People generally, unlike the monarchs, the nobles, and their imitators among the wealthy bourgeoisie, were very fond of dancing, the theatre, and bull-fighting. Dances to the accompaniment

Fondness of the general Spanish public for diversion and sport.

of the guitar were held on every possible occasion; on Sundays they took place in the public square of the city. The days of the waltz, onestep, and other dances now in vogue in many lands (though not in Spain) had not yet come; rather, the dances were very largely national or regional, such as the *seguidillas* or *boleros*, the *fandango, guaracha, zorongo, arlequín, chacona, zarabanda*, the Aragonese *jota*, the Valencian *dansetes*, and the Catalonian *sardana*, all of which gave great play to the individual and represented harmonious action of the entire body. Many of these dances, or their derivatives, survive in Spain today. Professional dancing girls were popular favorites — and not infrequently the mistresses of the great gentlemen of the court. Charles III detested dancing, but neither he nor his successor could check it, though they did regulate it to some extent. In like manner the theatre continued to be a national passion, despite the disapproval of certain great churchmen as well as of Charles III. Three great theatres were built in Madrid in the reign of Philip V. Governmental regulations were as unavailing in this as in the case of dancing. The popularity of bull-fighting got to be greater than ever, though Philip V and Charles III disliked the sport. Ferdinand VI was a devotee, and Charles IV was not unfriendly. The repugnance felt by Philip V had the effect of causing the withdrawal of the nobles from taking part in the contests, with the result that a professional class of bull-fighters developed. Charles III went so far as to prohibit the sport in 1785, but Charles IV, in 1789, consented to its return. Godoy, however, was opposed to bull-fighting, and procured its abolition in 1805. The period from 1789 to 1805 is a famous one in the history of this game. Just as happens today, so then, the names of the favorite bull-fighters were on everybody's lips. This was a period when many of the feats of the bull-fighters which still form a part of the contest were invented. Possibly the most widely known name was that of Pepe Illo, or Hillo (great bull-fighter and writer of a treatise on the so-called art of bull-fighting), who was killed in the bull-ring at Madrid in 1801, an event which Goya reduced to canvas in one of his most famous paintings. Madrid, Aranjuez, Granada, and Seville were the only cities which had bull-rings (*plazas de toros*), but fights were held in all parts of Spain by utilizing the principal square of the city. Certain athletic exercises were very popular, among which the Basque game of ball, still played in Spain, is especially worthy of mention.[1] Performances of professional acrobats, jugglers, and magicians were frequent, as well as the playing of pantomimes.

The policing of cities for the first time became worthy of commendation. At the opening of the eighteenth century Madrid was ugly, extremely dirty, without architectural monuments, driveways, or promenades, and lacked a good water system. The great reforms of Aranda under Charles III and of Godoy in the next reign transformed the city, resulting in the opening of new streets, the organization of an efficient street-cleaning system (despite opposition on the ancient ground that the filthiness of the streets was a preventive of epidemics), the completion of the work of paving begun in the previous era, the development of a good water supply, the inauguration of a lighting system, the building of noteworthy edifices, the bettering of old promenades (*paseos*) and the opening of new ones, and the issue of numerous ordinances intended to preserve the good order and public health of the city. It was at this time, too, that the institution of the *sereno* (night-watchman in Spanish streets) was introduced from abroad; contrary to the usual opinion the *sereno* is not Spanish in origin, but of foreign importation. The walk, or drive, along the great *paseos*, just at evening before nightfall, became more popular among all classes than ever, and has remained a Spanish custom to the present day. Barcelona, Seville, and Cádiz were also much improved. *(Marked advance in the care of cities.)*

But the dances, masked balls, the theatre, evening parties, and promenades furnished occasion for vicious practices. Immorality was not so brazen and unashamed as formerly, but was very nearly as prevalent. In vain were laws passed with a view to checking the evil. The lax practices continued, and received a kind of sanction during the reign of Charles IV *(Continuance of loose practices and bad habits.)*

[1] See note at page 196.

from the example set by the queen, of which everybody except the king seemed well aware. Gambling was also the subject of restrictive legislation which failed of its design. In this respect the state was morally estopped from making complaint, because it was in this period that the national government lottery was founded. This institution, which still exists, was established, strange to say, by Charles III, in 1763, following the example of the court of Rome. Gambling, and especially the lottery, soon became the passion it has ever since remained. Smoking had long before gotten to be general among the lower classes, particularly among the already mentioned *majo* element; but the aristocracy and the bourgeoisie had been little inclined to the habit. They were soon to surrender to the influence of *majismo*, however, with the result that Spaniards and their Hispanic kinsfolk have come to be enumerated among the most inveterate smokers in the world, so far as the men are concerned. Drunkenness was not a very prevalent vice, any more than it is today, although the same could not be said with respect to the Spanish colonies.

Influence of Spanish customs on the Americas.
It only remains to add that these social practices were to be found in much the same form in the Americas. Fondness for showy feast-days was even greater there, and it is also to be noted that the improvements in Spanish cities had their counterpart in the embellishment of several of those overseas.

CHAPTER XXXV

POLITICAL INSTITUTIONS, 1700–1808

THE Bourbon kings aimed to complete the long evolution, dating from centuries before, toward the personal authority of the monarch in a pure absolutism. This movement had gone farther in other countries, although the current had set the other way in England. France under Louis XIV, if not the most extreme example of an absolute government, was certainly the most influential, and the phrase "I am the state!" attributed to the great French monarch, was (whether in fact uttered by him or not) symbolic of his ideal. It was in the atmosphere of the court of Versailles that Philip V spent his youth, wherefore it was the most natural thing in the world for him to desire the establishment in Spain of a system which he had always been accustomed to believe was the only true method of rule. Even had Philip ever doubted it, Louis XIV took care to inculcate in him the concept of absolutism. Philip showed on various occasions that he understood the French ideal of kingship, — as in his opposition to the calling of the Castilian *Cortes*, his denial of the right of the *Consejo* to share in certain governmental functions, and his habitual employment of such phrases as "for such is my will" in royal decrees. The same criterion was followed by his successors. Charles IV ordered certain laws which were inconsistent with the absolutist ideal to be stricken out of the *Novísima Recopilación*, or Latest Compilation of the Laws (1805), before he would allow that code to be published, stating that those acts (which had been incorporated in the *Nueva Recopilación* of 1567) were representative of a time when the weakness of the monarchy had compelled the kings to make concessions which were inconsistent with their sovereign authority. The laws referred

425

to concerned the intervention of the *Consejo* in royal donations, the obligation of the king to consult with the three estates of the *Cortes* in dealing with momentous affairs, and the injunction that no new taxes should be levied without the grant of a *Cortes*. In the statement of their ideal the kings met with little opposition, for this view was generally supported by all classes of society. Men who were liberal reformers in other ways were rigid in their maintenance of the principle of absolutism, and the people themselves, not only Castilians, but others as well, even including the Catalans, were intensely royalist.

Democratic manner and philanthropic rule of the Bourbons.

Nevertheless, the Bourbons were more democratic in their manner than the less autocratic kings of the House of Austria. It is said that Philip V was the first to inaugurate the practice of allowing his higher government officials to be seated while talking business with him, whereas the Hapsburg custom had been to require them to remain on their knees. The kings' advisers now became veritable ministers, with a more frank participation in government than had been the case with the secretaries and favorites of the preceding era. Furthermore, the Bourbons represented the "enlightened despotism," which had so many remarkable manifestations in eighteenth century western Europe. In keeping with this ideal the kings showed marked interest in social, economic, and intellectual reforms of a philanthropic character, without yielding an iota of their political prerogative. A great revolution took place, having a fundamental groundwork of democracy in it (which was to find expression at a later time in the field of politics), but which was accomplished wholly from above. The idea might have been expressed: "Everything *for* the people, but nothing *by* them." The only exception to this rule was the royal program whereby the popular element gained an entrance to the *ayuntamientos*, or municipal governing bodies.

Naturally, all machinery of a democratic character was viewed with suspicion, and such was the case with the *Cortes*. Only at the accession of Luis I was a *Cortes* called to swear in the new king, although that body was several times asked to acknowledge the princes of Asturias. The *Cortes* of

Castile was summoned four times by Philip V and once each by Charles III and Charles IV, but in two of the meetings under Philip not all of the elements were called, and in the dismissal of the *Cortes* of Charles IV it was made apparent that the nobles and clergy had no necessary inclusion in that body. Furthermore, the *Cortes* was called to perform some specific act, — such as the recognition of the princes above-named, the making and later the revocation of the so-called Salic law, and the approval of Philip's renunciation of his rights to the French throne, — after which it was dismissed, without having an opportunity to discuss other matters. When the *Cortes* of 1789 was retained in session to treat of certain economic questions, some of the deputies formulated petitions concerning affairs of government, — whereupon the authorities hastened to bring the sittings to a close. The *Cortes* of other regions were equally lacking in importance. The *Cortes* of Aragon met once, and that of Valencia not at all; both were incorporated into the Castilian *Cortes* in 1709. The *Cortes* of Catalonia met twice, but after 1724 it followed the course already taken in the case of Aragon and Valencia, and the same was true of the representatives from Majorca. The *Cortes* of Navarre continued to meet separately, being called eleven times, but it took no action of conspicuous importance. Nevertheless, the memory of the former power of the *Cortes* was not dead, and many persons saw in its restoration, possibly with new functions, a means for the reform of the country. In addition to having rendered the *Cortes* completely innocuous the kings took other steps to check popular intervention in national affairs. It had been the custom for the municipalities to send special commissioners to the capital to negotiate for them with the crown. This practice (which reminds one of the colonial agent of American history) was forbidden by a law of 1715 (repeated in 1804), on the alleged ground of avoiding unnecessary expense to the towns. A law of 1777 allowed the sending of special agents, however, for one purpose, — that of witnessing the births of royal children! Thus did the kings contribute both to the security and to the glamour of royalty.

Unimportance of the *Cortes* and the suppression of democratic machinery.

Royal
oppo. ition
to the
entry of
the ency-
clopedist
and revo-
lutionary
ideas from
France.

If the Spanish kings were so careful to avoid any diminution in their authority through the restoration of the former
powers of the *Cortes*, it may well be imagined that they were
alarmed over the political ideas of the French encyclopedists
of the later eighteenth century and still more so over those
of the French revolutionaries after 1789. The works of
such French writers as Diderot, Voltaire, Rousseau, Montes-
quieu, and Mirabeau, or of the Englishmen Hobbes, Locke,
Hume, and others were in many libraries of Spain, and some
of them were translated. The Encyclopedia itself found its
way into the peninsula. High Spanish officials, like Aranda,
maintained correspondence with some of the French reformers, as did also some of the great Spanish nobles, —
for example, the Duke of Alba with Rousseau, and the Marquis of Miranda with Voltaire. It was the fashion, too, for
Spaniards to get part of their education in France, or for
French professors, French laborers, and, later, French revolutionary propagandists to cross the Pyrenees. Thus the
new ideas gained a footing in Spain, where they were taken
up at educational institutions, especially at the University
of Salamanca, and by some newspapers (for that type of
periodical had begun to appear), although expressions were
naturally somewhat guarded. With the outbreak of the
French Revolution, Floridablanca sent troops to the northern
frontier to prevent the entry of political agitators. The
Inquisition issued edicts against the introduction of prohibited books, and published a new index in 1790, followed
by a supplement in 1805, for the rationalist ideas of the
French reformers were not in accord with those of the church.
The civil authorities took similar action; the Encyclopedia
was barred in 1784, and many other works at other times;
in 1792 officials were placed at customs-houses to examine
all writings, whether printed or manuscript; and in 1805
a tribunal of printing (*Juzgado de Imprenta*) was created,
independent of the *Consejo* and the Inquisition. These
measures failed to prevent the dissemination of French
literature and thought, but were successful in checking
any effective expression of democratic or republican ideals
during this period. While men of influence approved the

philanthropic side of the new ideas, very few of them accepted their political tenets. It was quite the usual thing for men to say that the contract between monarch and people was equally binding on both, or to express admiration for the freedom of thought permitted in England, while they opposed the forming of deliberative assemblies in Spain, and stood solidly behind the principle of absolutism. Some of the younger men went completely over to revolutionary ideas, and in 1795 some republican clubs were discovered, while many of the inhabitants of Guipúzcoa gave substantial aid to the French army of invasion in 1794. The reaction came quickly, as a result of the tyrannical conduct of the French military authorities. Thus the spirit of democracy in Spain seemed crushed, but it was not in fact destroyed, as was amply proved a few years later in the radical outburst of the *Cortes* of Cádiz.

Side by side with the development of absolutism there had been an effort on the part of the kings for many centuries to promote the centralization of political and administrative authority in the state as represented by the crown, and to bring about uniformity in the law. These tendencies were accelerated by the Bourbons, whose first opportunity came as a result of the War of the Spanish Succession, when Philip V was opposed by many of the non-Castilian parts of Spain. In 1707 the special statutes and privileges of Aragon and Valencia were abolished and their place taken by the laws and practices of Castile. In both regions a royally appointed *audiencia* and captain-general were set up. This action was not taken for Catalonia until 1716. In that year it was provided by the so-called decree of the "new plan" (*Nueva Planta*) that the laws and customs of Castile were to apply in Catalonia; that the Catalan language was not to be used in the administration of justice; that an *audiencia* and captain-general of royal selection were to serve as the principal governmental agencies of the region; that Catalonia was to be divided into twelve districts, over which *corregidores* named by the king should rule; and that the twenty-four *regidores* (councilmen) of the *ayuntamiento* of Barcelona, which city had been deprived

Pronounced acceleration of the tendencies toward a centralized state.

of its former type of government, should also be royally appointed. The decree of 1716 did not attempt to establish complete unification with Castile, however. Many former Catalan rights continued to exist until the nineteenth century, — such, for example, as the Catalan system of criminal law and the issue of Catalan coins. Furthermore, there was no appeal from the decisions of the *audiencia* to the central government, — an exceptional case. Nevertheless, the principles of centralization and unification had been in the main attained, and later measures tended to secure these ends still more completely. Philip's opponents in the War of the Spanish Succession were persecuted, and the royal ideas were furthered by the acts of the influential partisans of the king; in 1717 the bishop of Gerona, Taverner, summoned a provincial council with a view to "threatening with the wrath of God and the excommunication of the church" whoever should be unfaithful to Philip V and to ordering confessors to treat such infidelity as a sin. In Majorca the king placed an *audiencia* and a commandant-general, appointing also the local councillors of Palma and Alcudia, while the *audiencia* named those of the other towns. The special privileges of the Basque provinces were respected in theory, but, without apparent change in the laws, the central government gradually obtained control through the inspection or the intervention of ministers of state and the *Consejos*. Much the same course was followed with Navarre, in which the former agencies of government were left apparently undisturbed. The policy of centralization was also manifested in other respects than those of a purely regional application. Thus exemptions from military service were limited; the reversion of seigniorial rights to the king was facilitated; and, in fine, the tendency was to reduce all forms of jurisdiction, territorial or otherwise, to the king or his representatives in the central administration. Many regions continued to have at least the vestiges of their former institutions, but enough was done so that the Spanish kingdom may fairly be said to have become unitary for the first time in history.

The most notable change in the machinery of government

*c*oncerned the development of the secretariats. There got to be five of them, corresponding to the more important of the *Consejos* under the *Consejo de Castilla*, as follows: state (*Estado*); grace and justice (*Gracia y Justicia*); war and finance (*Guerra y Hacienda*); navy (*Marina*); and the Indies (*Indias*). There were variations from this arrangement at different times; for example, the navy and the Indies were often a single secretariat in the first half century of the era. Gradually it became the custom to call the secretaries ministers, and these officials began to absorb the powers formerly confided to the *Consejos*, presaging the disappearance of the latter and the development of modern ministries. As already pointed out, they also acquired a greater liberty and initiative in the performance of their duties, especially in the reigns of Ferdinand VI and Charles III. It was customary for them to consult with the king every morning, however. No new *Consejos*, or councils, were added in this period, and the *Consejo de Aragón*, last of the councils of the former crown of Aragon, was suppressed in 1707. Essentially, the *Consejos* continued to exercise the same functions as formerly, although losing ground to the rapidly advancing secretaries, or ministers. The *Consejo de Castilla* retained its importance, however, and its president, or governor, was the leading officer of state. It is to be noted that both the *Consejo* and the *Cámara*, despite their retention of the name Castile, dealt with the affairs of other regions of the peninsula, quite as much as did the councils with more general names. Except for Navarre, which continued to be a viceroyalty, the other regions of Spain apart from New Castile (Aragon, Catalonia, Valencia, Majorca, Granada, Andalusia, Old Castile, Galicia, Asturias, Extremadura, and the Canary Islands) were placed under captain-generals or commandant-generals with military and administrative powers. A number of *audiencias* were added, until now there were eleven such bodies (Valladolid, Granada, Galicia, Seville, the Canaries, Majorca, Valencia, Saragossa, Barcelona, Asturias, and Extremadura), exercising both civil and judicial functions. In 1718 the institution of the intendancies was created to take over

Changes in administrative machinery.

financial administration in the various regions, although this reform was not put into effect definitely until 1749. There were twenty-three intendants, of whom six were military. Under the captain-generals there were smaller districts ruled by *corregidores*, most of whom were civilians. The judicial functions of the *corregidor* were gradually taken over by *alcaldes mayores*, who ranked under the *corregidores*, leaving the executive power in the hands of the latter. In some cases these lesser districts were ruled over by officials called military governors. The term "province" was applied to districts of very unequal size. While there were only eight in the combined realms of Aragon, Navarre, and the Basque provinces, there were twenty-four in Castile. Charles III planned to divide Spain into a number of provinces of about the same size, but did not carry out his idea.

Increased royal control over the towns and the democratization of local political machinery.

While municipal life as a virile factor which might withstand the king had long since been dead, there was too much local authority still in existence to please the autocratic Bourbons. Furthermore, abuses in administration had developed which caused the kings to be philanthropically desirous of a remedy. To accomplish these ends they aimed at a more complete subjection of the towns to the royal authority and the democratization of the *ayuntamientos*. The principal difficulty in the way of these objectives was the fact that many municipal offices were held as a perpetual right by specific families, especially in the case of the *regidores*, — for which state of affairs the kings of the House of Austria had not infrequently been responsible by their sales of such privileges. This resulted in an aristocratic control of the municipalities, with consequent usurpations of land by the rich and the placing of the burdens of taxation on the poor. Unable to buy up these hereditary rights the royal government chose to follow what was in effect a policy of legal confiscation. This was easily accomplished for Aragon, Catalonia, Valencia, and Majorca; as already pointed out, the king took advantage of the outcome of the War of the Spanish Succession to take all of these appointments into his own hands or into those of the *audiencias*. As for Castile, laws were passed requiring the approval of the central authorities before an heir to municipal office could succeed to such an inheritance. As a result the government was enabled to refuse its assent in a number of cases. Meanwhile, the *alcaldes* continued to be appointed by the king or by the lord, according as they were royal (*realengos*) or seigniorial (*señoríos*) towns. Even the seigniorial towns were attacked, for a law of 1802 provided with regard to them that the servants or dependents of the lord could not exercise jurisdiction in his place; that the royal institution of the *residencia* was never to be dispensed with; and that the *alcaldes mayores* of the large towns must be lawyers who had been licensed to practice by the royal *consejos* or *audiencias*. No attempt was made to disturb the composition of the *ayuntamientos* of Navarre and the Basque provinces, although these regions, like the rest of Spain, were subject to laws of a general character concerning municipalities. One such general law, in 1751, required all municipalities to send their accounts annually to the *Cámara de Castilla* for inspection, and this was supplemented by a law of 1764, ordering them to deposit their surplus funds with the royal intendant of the province. Another decree, dated 1760, assigned the direction of municipal finance to the *Consejo*. Yet other laws were enacted, the total effect of which, together with those just mentioned, was to place the whole question of municipal income and expenditures in royal hands. The initiative for the democratization of the *ayuntamientos* came in the reign of Charles III. In 1766 he created the post of deputy of the common people (*diputado del común*), which official was empowered to examine the financial accounts of the towns. These officers, of whom there were to be two in the smaller towns and four in the larger, were chosen by a body of men who had previously been elected by the people. In like manner a popular syndic (*síndico*) was elected who represented the masses before the *ayuntamiento*, with a right to take part in deliberations and to propose reforms. At the same time, the office of *regidor* was thrown open to plebeians. This law was a blow at the *caballero* class of the nobility, which had monopolized the holding of municipal office. There was

2 F

much dissatisfaction over the enactment, and the Basque provinces went so far as to protest. Nevertheless, there was no outward resistance; the aristocracy of the towns limited itself to opposing the election of plebeians and to hindering their action in office.

Despite the thoroughgoing nature of the Bourbon absolutism, it is fitting for the first time to award special credit to the secretaries of state, or ministers, although the kings were responsible for their selection as well as for their acts. This was an age of great reformers. The initiative came from France on the accession of Philip V, and the first great name is that of a Frenchman, Orry. When he came to Spain, in 1701, he found that the income of the state was about 142,000,000 *reales* ($8,875,000) while expenditures were 247,000,000 ($15,437,500). The outbreak of the War of the Spanish Succession made the situation still worse. Yet he displayed such ability that national receipts actually advanced in course of the war, and were some 160,000,000 ($10,000,000) at its end. Amelot, another Frenchman, was an even more remarkable figure. He coöperated with Orry to increase the revenues, and reorganized and bettered the administration of the army. The Italian Alberoni and the Dutchman Ripperdá were less notable as reformers. With the fall of the latter in 1726 there began an era of great ministers of Spanish birth. First of these was Patiño, who, though born in Italy, was of a Galician family. He was especially prominent for his financial reforms, but was also noteworthy for his measures to develop commerce and improve the army and navy. In an age when graft was general, and in a country which has rarely been backward in this particular, Patiño was able to achieve the distinction of dying poor; his death occurred in 1736. The next notable financial reformer was Campillo, an Asturian who had been born poor, though of *hidalgo* rank. More important, however, was Somodevilla, a Castilian of very humble birth who became Marquis of Ensenada, by which name he is more generally known. The period of his power was from 1743 to 1754, and his reforms covered the same matters as those mentioned above in the case of Patiño, although he was especially remarkable in his endeavors on behalf of the Spanish navy. His fall in 1754 (as a result of his disagreement with Ferdinand VI with regard to the treaty with Portugal concerning Sacramento and Paraguay) was received with rejoicing in England; the English ambassador reported exultingly that Spain would build no more ships. Ensenada was responsible, also, for the construction of important public works, and once suggested the idea of single tax as worthy of trial in Spain.

The greatest reformers, however, belonged to the reign of Charles III and the early years of Charles IV. Earlier ministers had increased the national revenues and cut down expenses, but the deficit had not been wiped out. One of the great names of both of the above-named reigns was that of the Count of Aranda, of a distinguished Aragonese noble family. Aranda was obstinate, brutal in speech, aggressive, and energetic, but a man of vast information and clear foresight, — as witness his prediction, in 1775, of the future greatness of the yet unborn United States. Aside from his connection with Spain's foreign policies he particularly distinguished himself while president of the *Consejo de Castilla* by the reforms, already referred to, whereby Madrid became a clean and acceptable city. Yet more famous was José Moñino, son of an ecclesiastical notary of Murcia, who was ennobled as the Count of Floridablanca. An honorable man in every sense of the word, just, intelligent, and solicitous for his friends, he was hot-tempered, and unbending in his hostility to his opponents. His action made itself felt in the improvement of the means of communication in the peninsula and in his economic reforms of a commercial nature, such as the great free trade decree of 1778, which abandoned certain phases of the narrowly monopolistic policy which Spain had always followed in her trade with the colonies. Campomanes was an Asturian and, like Somodevilla, of very humble birth, but he rose to be, many hold, the greatest of the men who labored for the social and economic regeneration of Spain in the eighteenth century. He was also the most representative of his age, for, in addition to his measures to develop a better system of internal

Great reformers of the reigns of Charles III and IV.

communications and to foster industry, commerce, and technical popular education, he was a determined royalist, — the embodiment, therefore, of the ideal of the enlightened despotism. Like Aranda and Floridablanca he served for a time under Charles IV, although his greatest work belonged to the reign of Charles III. Three names deserve mention for the reign of Charles IV. Jovellanos was an Asturian of an illustrious family. He distinguished himself by his reforms in finance in conjunction with one Saavedra, but both were early deprived of their posts, as a result of the hostility of Godoy. The third name is that of Godoy, who introduced notable reforms in public instruction and in the organization of the army and navy, — whatever may be the judgment with regard to his foreign policy. The names of some of the great ministers of the Indies are also worthy of record. In addition to Patiño and Ensenada the most noteworthy were Julián de Arriaga (1750 or 1751–1776) and José de Gálvez (1776–1787), especially the former. The results, in terms of revenue, of the activities of the great ministers may serve to give some indication of the effectiveness of their work. In 1766, receipts exceeded expenditures by about 133,000,000 *reales* ($8,312,500). In 1778 revenues amounted to 630,000,000 ($39,375,000); in 1784 to 685,000,000 ($42,812,500); and in 1787 to 616,000,000 ($38,500,000). Though annual expenditures were much less, the government was never able to overcome the deficit, although the national debt reached its lowest point in the reign of Charles III. In 1791 revenues were some 800,000,000 ($50,000,000), but they fell to a general level of about 600,000,000 ($37,500,000) in the years 1793 to 1795, while expenditures, which had reached 708,000,000 ($44,250,000) in 1793, were 1,030,000,000 ($64,375,000) in 1795. Thus the deficit began to increase again, and in 1808 it was over 7,200,000,000 *reales* ($450,000,000), an enormous sum as national indebtedness went then.

Opposition of vested interests to the reforms. The efforts made by the great reformers appear the more commendable when one considers the difficulties they had to overcome. Great changes always run counter to vested interests, but this was more than usually the case in Spain.

The nobles and the church were the most powerful elements
in opposition; even though their authority was but little,
as compared with that of earlier years, they were still able
to hinder the execution of laws which damaged their interests.
Nearly everyone seemed to have an exemption from taxation,
or desired it, but the reformers set themselves resolutely
against that state of affairs. Their success against the force of
vested interests was only fair, for that element was too great
to overcome; the very bureaucracy itself displayed a weakness in this particular, for it insisted on the maintenance of
a custom which had sprung up that government officials
might buy certain articles at a fixed price, whatever the
charge to others. This calls to mind the overwhelming **Prevalence**
evil of graft, which it seemed impossible to eliminate; in- **of graft.**
deed, high officials were altogether too prone to regard it as
a more or less legitimate perquisite, and did not hesitate to
accept large gifts of money from foreign diplomats. Diffi- **Difficulties**
culties over questions of etiquette, inherent in a centralized **over ques-**
bureaucratic government, also stood in the way of the proper **tions of**
execution of the laws. For example, a serious dispute arose **etiquette**
in 1745 between the bishop of Murcia and the Inquisition, **and of**
when the latter claimed that the members of that body **juris-**
should have a better place in church than others. It was at **diction.**
length decided that they should not. In 1782 the commandant-general of Majorca complained that the wives of
the *oidores* of the *audiencia* had not called on his wife on the
occasion of the king's birthday. He was sustained, and the
regente (regent, or president) of the *audiencia* was imprisoned
for a number of months by way of punishment. Several
years later the ladies of Palma complained that the wife of
the commandant-general was in the habit of going out in
the street with an armed escort and demanding a military
salute. This time the ladies were upheld, and the escort
was prohibited. These are only a few instances out of
thousands, and if there was so much stir over such trifling
matters it can well be imagined how much more serious the
problem was in the case of disputes between officials as to
jurisdiction. Official etiquette is an important matter in all
countries, but Spaniards have always been insistent on the

letter of their rights and very sensitive over the omission of any act to which their position entitles them. Furthermore, these controversies carried in their train vast files of papers, of charges, answers and countercharges, and the evidence of witnesses. These questions had to be resolved, causing great expenditure in both time and money. No country was ever more diligent than Spain in the multiplication of state papers over affairs which ranged from those of vital importance to the most trivial incidents. The historian may have cause to rejoice over the existence of so much material, but the nation suffered, — although it is difficult to see how its contemporary accumulation could have been avoided in an absolutism like that of the Spanish Bourbons.

Improvement of the army and ineffectual attempts at additional reforms.

One of the principal objects of the reforms was the rehabilitation of the army and navy so that Spain might be in a better position in international affairs. In the army the volunteer system was employed for a while, but it was effective only in procuring contingents of foreign mercenaries and in filling the ranks of the royal guard. Gradually the idea of the draft came into favor, and it was tried several times, becoming a definitive law in the reign of Charles III. The law of Charles III provided that one man in every five — hence the term *quinta* for this institution — should become subject to military service for a term of eight years. This system was resisted in all parts of the peninsula, but was allowed to stand, although it proved impossible of enforcement. Through graft or favor, whether of the local officials charged with administering the law or of doctors who examined the individual drawn, practically nobody was required to serve except those totally lacking in influence. It was customary to seize tramps and petty criminals and send them instead of the legitimately drafted men. The government itself adopted the principle of forced levies, or impressment, of vagabonds and bad characters, but these men proved to be poor soldiers and deserted frequently. Thus the number of troops was not great, but in any event it would have been difficult to support more numerous contingents, owing to the lack of funds; even as matters were it was customary to grant a four months' furlough at the season when crops were gathered.   In times of war, rigorous methods were used to get the needed men, or else they came forward voluntarily, out of patriotism.   The reserve was formed by regional bodies of militia, which did not draw back when their services were needed in war.   At the beginning of the era it is said that there were 20,000 poorly equipped soldiers in the Spanish army; in 1737 the total of infantry and cavalry was 42,920; in 1758 the total of all arms, 108,777.   Numbers increased under Charles III, but declined under Charles IV.   In 1808, at the moment of the outbreak against Napoleon, there were from 136,000 to 147,000 but only about 100,000 effective troops, and even these were badly armed.   The situation becomes clear in the light of the expense involved; the army of 1758, in a time of peace, cost some 205,000,000 *reales* ($12,812,500), a saving of 34,000,000 ($2,125,000) over the expenditures required prior to the enactment of certain reforms by Ferdinand VI.   It will be seen that a considerable portion of the annual revenue was needed.   In this period the hierarchy of officials (from the captain-generals down through the various grades of generals, colonels, captains, and lieutenants) and of military units (such as brigades, regiments, battalions, and companies) was established in, broadly speaking, the form it has retained ever since.   The gun with the bayonet had now become the principal infantry weapon, and artillery had been developed to a high point as compared with the previous era.   Flags and uniforms varied; the latter were picturesque, but adapted more to encouraging the soldier's morale than to developing his freedom of action. A number of military schools were founded for the different branches of the service, — the infantry, cavalry, artillery, and engineers.

The eighteenth century marked the birth of a real Spanish navy.   At the outset, and during the great war which opened the era, there was virtually none at all, but in 1714 Orry took steps, which were later furthered by Alberoni, Patiño, and especially by Ensenada, to develop an effective fleet.   In 1761 there were 49 men-of-war (*navíos*), 22 frigates, and a number of smaller ships; in 1788, 64 men-of-war, 53 frigates, *Birth of a real Spanish navy, but difficulties attending its improvement.*

and 60 boats of other types, with 50,000 sailors, 20,000 infantry, 3000 artillerymen, and numerous officials of the navy department. Each war with England during the century resulted in the destruction of a considerable portion of the fleet, and the battle of Trafalgar, in 1805, destroyed it as a fighting unit, even though Spain still had 42 men-of-war, 30 frigates, and 146 other ships in 1806. The man-of-war was the principal type of vessel employed in this era, carrying from sixty to a hundred cannon, while the faster sailing frigate had from thirty to fifty cannon. Many auxiliary vessels — transports and smaller fighting ships, such as brigs and sloops of war — were used. The galley went out of service, although one was built as late as 1794. The Spanish navy suffered from a number of defects, however, which made it distinctly inferior to the English, or even to the French. The wood for the masts was fragile and the material for the sails was of bad quality, while boats were so poorly taken care of, that they deteriorated rapidly. The provision of food supplies and effects for the men was faulty, and the men on board, especially the artillerymen and the infantry, were of very poor calibre. Ensenada remarked that the Spanish navy of his day was all appearances, without substance, but set about to the best of his ability to rectify the situation. He improved shipyards, sent officers of talent abroad to study the methods employed elsewhere, gave inducements to English shipbuilders to come to Spain, built shops for the making of rigging and other equipment needed on ships of war, endeavored to improve the personnel of Spanish crews, and surrounded himself with the most competent naval men he could find. Ensenada and the other reformers did a great deal, but they could not overcome the never-ending difficulties in the way of obtaining men in sufficient numbers and of suitable quality for the requirements of the navy. The fishermen of the Spanish coasts continued to be drafted as sailors, and became less unwilling to serve than formerly when efforts were made to be punctual in payments of wages and to protect the families of the mariners. The recruiting of marine infantry and artillerymen, however, suffered from the same evil as the raising of the land forces, with one important result, which was that Spanish cannon were badly served.

Naturally, a period so rich in reforms as this was bound to have a great body of legislation. In Castile this was almost exclusively in the various forms of royal orders, recording the directions given by the king and his ministers, and the decisions of the *Consejos*. Thus the work of the *Nueva Recopilación* of 1567 got to be out of date, although five new editions were published in the eighteenth century, with the addition of some of the recent laws. Finally, a proposal for another codification was approved, and the compilation was made by Juan de la Reguera, who brought it out in twelve books, under the title of the *Novísima recopilación de las leyes de España* (Newest, or Latest, Compilation of the Laws of Spain). Reguera claimed to have solved the problem of the concentration of legal material, but in fact his work suffered from the same defects as the earlier codes of Montalvo and Arrieta. His distribution of the laws was faulty, and he failed to indicate many important acts which were still in force. Furthermore, he reproduced the ordinance of Alcalá (1348), repeated in the laws of Toro and the *Nueva Recopilación*, according to which the laws of various earlier codes, such as the *Fuero Real*, remained in effect in so far as they had not been repealed by later legislation, and the *Partidas* was valid as supplementary law. Thus the old evils of the lack of unity of the law and lack of clearness subsisted. Nobody could be certain whether a law was still in effect or not, and it remained the practice to cite textbooks and the ancient codes of Justinian on the ground that they might have a bearing as supplementary law, unless there was something clearly stated to the contrary in the *Novísima Recopilación*. In Catalonia there was a new codification in 1704, and in Navarre in 1735. In most of the formerly separate legal jurisdictions, however, the laws of Castile applied, henceforth, as a result of the changes brought about, as already mentioned, at the close of the War of the Spanish Succession.

It remains to deal with the relations of the crown and the church, to which the next chapter is devoted, and to allude

Legislation of the era and the Novísima Recopilación.

to the important reforms in the Americas. Much that was beneficial to the colonies at the time was achieved, and much else which in fact helped them to be the better prepared in the approaching combat with the mother country. In the main, however, the policies of subjection and of the development of the revenues in the supposed interests of Spain were followed, with the result that resentments were kept alive and ultimate disaster invited.

CHAPTER XXXVI

STATE AND CHURCH, 1700–1808

IF the kings of the House of Austria had displayed zeal in diminishing the range of ecclesiastical jurisdiction, the Bourbon monarchs, with their accentuated ideal of absolutism, were even more insistent in that respect. The kings were assisted by elements to which they themselves were otherwise hostile, such as the Jansenists [1] and the encyclopedists, whose partisans furnished arguments for the royal authority, because they opposed the rule of the church. Nevertheless, the monarchical ideal of the kings was sufficient to induce them to attack the church, except as concerned the purely spiritual interests of the Catholic religion, and the absolute patronage which the kings enjoyed in the Americas became the model of what they wished to establish in Spain. There were two principal angles to the problem, that of overcoming the intervention of the popes in the affairs of the Spanish church, and that of lessening the power and the privileges of the Spanish clergy. As for the intervention of the popes, they exercised the right of appointment to Spanish benefices which became vacant in any of the so-called eight "apostolic months," and also to those vacated in the four "ordinary months" (March, June, September, and December) if the death of the holder occurred at Rome; considerable sums of money were also collected for papal dispensations to marry,

Pronounced zeal of the Bourbons in subjecting the church.

The elements in controversy.

[1] The Jansenists were a sect within the Catholic Church following the teachings of Cornelis Jansen (1585–1638), who relied upon the tenets of Saint Augustine as the basis for a reform of the church. They were opposed to the doctrine of papal infallibility, and were bitter enemies of the Jesuits, besides differing from other Catholics in certain points of dogma. Their views were eventually pronounced heretical.

papal pardons, and other papal acts of an irregularly recurring character, although government officials charged that a large part of these moneys remained in the hands of Spanish and Italian intermediaries without reaching the coffers of the pope; the tribunal of the nunciature, despite the provisions of the papal brief of 1537, had come to be composed of foreign priests, and besides exercising its judicial functions independently of the royal courts administered the rents of vacant benefices (*vacantes*), which gave rise to accusations of abuses in the management of the funds; the tribunal of the *Cruzada*, for the collection of the tax of that name, was still in papal hands, although the income had frequently in the past been granted to the kings of Spain; and finally, there existed the old question of the *pase regio*, about the necessity for royal consent prior to the publication of papal bulls and briefs, or in fact even for the delivery of pontifical letters. As concerned the relations with the local clergy, the kings were preoccupied with such matters as the great numbers of churchmen (especially the regular clergy), the immunities they enjoyed, the immensity of their landed estates held in mortmain, the extent of the right of asylum in ecclesiastical edifices, and the power of the Inquisition and, far more, that of the Jesuits.

Conflict of the kings with the popes in the first half century of the era.

The conflict with the papacy began at the outset of the reign of Philip V, for the popes favored the candidacy of the Archduke Charles to the Spanish throne. Philip V expelled the nuncio, suspended the court of the nunciature, and gave orders against the circulation of papal bulls in Spain. These measures were only temporary, during the course of the war. Nevertheless, Alberoni, who restored matters to their former basis, had occasion, even though he was a cardinal himself, to banish the newly appointed nuncio. Finally, an agreement was reached in the concordat of 1737 from which the crown obtained some advantages, such as the suppression of the right of asylum in some cases and its restriction in others, the limitation of the number of churchmen with rights of personal immunity, and the giving of guarantees against false allegations with a view to extending the immunities of church estates, together with the derogation of this right for such properties as the church should acquire in future. The concordat satisfied nobody, and moreover most of its provisions were not observed. When Ferdinand VI ascended the throne, he took steps to procure a more acceptable arrangement, for though an exceedingly devout Catholic he was unbending as concerned matters affecting the royal authority. The result was a fresh concordat with the pope, dated 1753. Several important rights were gained at this time: in return for a heavy money indemnity Ferdinand obtained a recognition of the royal right of patronage in appointments to all church offices, except some fifty-two dignities and the naming of bishops to benefices vacated in the four "ordinary months"; various kinds of papal taxes were renounced in favor of Spain; the tax of the *cruzada* was granted in perpetuity to the crown; and the right of exemption from the taxation of lands held in mortmain was abolished. Nevertheless, the partisans of royalty were not yet satisfied.

Charles III was a pious Catholic, but carried the reform movement against the church further than any of his predecessors. The first step was taken as a result of a papal brief against a book written by Mesenghi, a French theologian. When the Spanish Inquisition was about to publish the condemnatory document, the king issued a decree of prohibition. This was followed by royal orders of 1761 and 1762 making the following enactments: that no papal bull, brief, or other pontifical letter should be allowed to circulate or be obeyed, whatever might be its subject-matter, unless it should previously have been presented to the king, or in certain cases of lesser moment to the *Consejo*, so that a decision might be reached whether it interfered with the royal prerogative, before a license to publish would be granted; that the Inquisition should publish only such edicts as were forwarded to it by the king; and that it should condemn no book without giving the author a chance to defend himself. Through the influence of his mother, Isabel Farnesio, Charles was persuaded to suspend these decrees, but they were put into effect in 1768 when the pope issued a bull censuring the Bourbon Duke of Parma, a relative of Charles III, for his appli-

Success of Charles III in the conflict with the popes.

cation of the *pase regio* in his domain. A further step was taken in 1771, when the pope consented to the reform of the nunciature, whereby that tribunal, henceforth called the *Rota*, was to be composed of six Spanish judges nominated by the king and appointed by the pope. A great many measures were also undertaken in this reign to subject the Spanish clergy to the royal authority, and to better economic and religious conditions. The following enactments were representative of this phase of the royal policy : the recourse of *fuerza* was frequently employed in cases of conflict of laws between the civil and the ecclesiastical courts, and the jurisdiction of the former was favored ; a law of 1766 required bishops to exercise vigilance to see that priests should say nothing against the government or the members of the royal family, and even the *alcaldes* were given authority to assist in this regard in conserving the good name of the state and its rulers ; the rights of asylum in churches and the personal immunities of churchmen were limited, as by a law of 1774, according to which such rights were not to obtain in the case of those guilty of participation in riots ; in 1780 it was ordered that the profits of vacant rural benefices should be applied to the repair of churches of the diocese or to the repopulation of abandoned districts ; bishops were prohibited by a law of 1781 from appointing vicars without the prior consent of the king ; an attempt was made in 1786 to do away with the custom of burying deceased persons in churches, but the effort was unsuccessful, owing to the opposition of the clergy ; in the same year ecclesiastical judges were forbidden to handle the temporal aspects of matrimonial cases, being restricted to decisions affecting the canonical bonds established by marriage ; and in 1787 all cases of smuggling were removed from the jurisdiction of the ecclesiastical courts, even though a churchman were involved. In the reign of Charles IV there were intervals when the church was less rigorously dealt with, but the majority of the ministers followed the tradition of their predecessors.

There had been many complaints against the Inquisition in the period of the Hapsburg kings, but they became more frequent in the far more tolerant eighteenth century, and now that the monarchs no longer regarded the danger of heresy as serious they were reinforced by the royal policy of reducing all outstanding phases of authority. The conflict with the Inquisition was fought out over the following issues: questions of jurisdiction between the civil courts and that of the Inquisition; abuse of power by the Inquisition, which was accused of using its authority in matters of religion as a political arm; decrees of the Inquisition inconsistent with those of the king, or failures to observe the royal claims of a right to apply the *pase regio;* arbitrary condemnations of books by the Inquisition; and the extraordinary amplitude of cases falling within the purview of its tribunals, such as those of usury, smuggling, the importation of coin into the kingdom, and the raising of horses, all of which were far removed from the primary objects of the institution. Not much was done until the reign of Charles III. That monarch had already shown himself hostile to the Inquisition while king of Naples, prior to his accession to the throne of Spain. One of his earliest acts as king of Spain was the banishment of the inquisitor general when the latter protested against the royal edict in the already mentioned Mesenghi case, followed by the legislation of 1761 and 1762 referred to above. When the inquisitor was allowed to return, Charles warned the other officers of the Inquisition not to disobey the king in future. In 1770 many of the cases of a secular character were removed from inquisitorial jurisdiction, and in 1784 it was ordered that all processes against grandees or the ministers or employes of the king should be submitted to the monarch. The reduction of the Inquisition was carried still further under Charles IV. Godoy, Jovellanos, and Urquijo thought of abolishing it, but fortunate turns in the political situation intervened to postpone such action. It was provided in 1799 that no subject of the king should be arrested by the Inquisition without royal authorization, and the methods of trial employed by that institution were modified in the interests of doing away with the former secrecy and the seclusion of the accused. In 1804 the king banished several members of the Inquisition who had opposed the freeing of an individual whom one of the lesser branches of

Royal action diminishing the power of the Inquisition.

that organization had pronounced guiltless. Its decline was also evidenced by the falling off in its revenues as compared with the yield of earlier times. Many of its buildings were in a state of bad repair, and its employees often died in poverty. Nevertheless, its properties were said to be worth nearly 170,000,000 *reales* (over $10,000,000) at the end of the era, and a state offer of 2,000,000 a year ($125,000), in exchange for its right to confiscate the goods of persons convicted of crimes against religion, was refused. In addition, there was the wealth of the Inquisition in the colonies; the great German traveler and naturalist, Alexander von Humboldt, estimated that the annual income of the Inquisition in New Spain alone was 800,000 *reales* ($50,000). Although the Inquisition of the eighteenth century had but a shadow of its former power, it was able to bring influential persons to trial, including great churchmen, members of the higher nobility, and ministers of state, but it did not always take effective action in these cases. Godoy was accused on three occasions, being charged with atheism, immorality, and bigamy, but the queen would not consent to his arrest, and he was able to procure the banishment of several of those who had intervened in this matter.

Increased hostility against the Jesuits.

The case of the Jesuit order was similar to that of the Inquisition, but the result of royal action was even more decisive. The hostility to the Jesuits in Catholic countries, already very great in the sixteenth and seventeenth centuries, was even more intense in the eighteenth. The other religious orders and the secular clergy were almost a unit in opposing them, for the Jesuits occupied a dominant place in church affairs, and were charged with tyrannizing over the others both in matters of theology and in questions of a temporal character. The ranks of their enemies were swelled by the continued adhesion of the universities to the Jesuit opposition and by the encyclopedists. The former complained because the youth were attending the Jesuit colleges, especially the nobility, from whom the leading ministers of state were chosen, thus continuing the Jesuit influence, while those who were more or less addicted to encyclopedist views were hostile to the order both because of its power in the

church and because of its partisanship in favor of papal jurisdiction and authority. In defending themselves the Jesuits
had the support of many royal ministers and of the kings
themselves for over half a century ; Philip V and Ferdinand
VI as well as Isabel Farnesio and the children of Charles III
had Jesuit confessors. Furthermore, the once hostile Inquisition became an instrument in Jesuit hands when that
order got control of the institution. Finally, the Jesuits
had achieved vast power as a result of their hold on the af-
fections of great numbers of the people, high and low, and
in consequence of the extraordinary wealth which they had
accumulated.

It was not until the reign of Charles III that any effective
action was taken against them. While yet king of Naples,
Charles had demonstrated his lack of cordiality toward the
Jesuit order, and had begun to feel a suspicion, in common
with other European monarchs, that the Jesuits might prove
to be a danger to the state ; in view of the actual power which
the Jesuits possessed, it is not to be wondered at that the
ultra-absolutist statesmen and kings of the eighteenth century should look upon them with disfavor. In the very
year that Charles became king of Spain they were expelled
from Portugal, and in the years 1764 to 1767 similar action
was taken in France. The accession of Charles was a blow
to the Jesuits in Spain, who now lost their influential place
at court. Four events of a political character tended to
increase the feeling of hostility toward them. One of these
occurred in the reign of Ferdinand, when the Jesuits of
Paraguay opposed the cession of that territory to Portugal
in exchange for Sacramento. The Indians of Paraguay rose
in rebellion against the transfer, and it was believed that the
Jesuits were in some way concerned. The second of the
events was the attempted assassination of the kings of Portugal and France, which was attributed to the Jesuit order
on account of the hostility of those monarchs to the Jesuits.
Many were of the opinion that Charles might be in danger
of a like fate. In the third place friction arose between
Charles and the Jesuits as a result of the former's advocacy
of the canonization of Juan de Palafox, a seventeenth century

Expulsion and suppression of the Jesuits.

2 G

bishop of Puebla de los Ángeles in New Spain. The Jesuits opposed the king in this matter, and even procured the removal from the palace of the works of Palafox which Charles had given to members of his family. The fourth matter was of far more consequence, — the riots of 1766 at the time when the proposals of Squillace with regard to the modification of Spanish dress were enacted into law. On that occasion there was grave disorder in Madrid, including an attack on the king's guards, a number of whom were cruelly put to death. The king was obliged to yield to the demands of the mob, and a few days later unexpectedly left Madrid for Aranjuez, — a virtual flight, taken as a measure of precaution. Not only in Madrid, but also in Saragossa, Cuenca, Guadalajara, Alicante, Salamanca, Daroca, Tobarra, Mombeltrán, Murcia, San Lúcar, Huesca, Borja, San Ildefonso, Azcoytia, Villena, Ciudad Real, Jumilla, Coruña, Alcaraz, Quero, Las Mesas, Aranjuez, Palencia, and Navalcarnero there were similar outbreaks, and it seemed likely that Barcelona might also give trouble. In fine, there appeared to be an organized attempt at rebellion, and Charles and his ministers believed, or at least pretended to believe, that the Jesuits were behind it. Most probably the order itself did not promote the riots, although several of its members were compromised, but late in 1766 it was formally charged with responsibility by the *Consejo*. In January, 1767, the *Consejo* proposed the expulsion of the Jesuits from Spain. The matter was submitted to a special *junta*, or council, which concurred in the recommendation of the *Consejo*, after which the decision was presented to various ecclesiastical personages, who likewise expressed their approval. It was decided, however, to say nothing of the motives, and the part of the proceedings concerning them has disappeared. Nevertheless, a document of Campomanes is at hand summing up some of the charges made at the meeting of the *Consejo*. They were the following: responsibility for the Squillace riots; the diffusion of maxims contrary to the royal and the canon law; a spirit of sedition (of which some evidence was introduced); treasonable relations with the English in the Philippine Islands; monopolization of commerce and excess of

power in the Americas; a too great pride, leading them to
support the doctrines of Rome against the king; advocacy
by many Jesuit writers of the right of tyrannicide; political
intrigues against the king; and aspiration for universal
monarchy. While the evidence in support of these charges
is no longer available, it is clear that they were exaggerated,
or even without foundation, — at least in the case of their
supposed relations with the English. On the other hand,
the intensely royalist ministers of the era of the enlightened
despotism would have felt grave concern where a more democratic age might have found no cause for worry. Some
historians claim that Charles hesitated to sign the decree,
because the Jesuit general was said to have threatened the
publication of documents purporting to show that the king
was the illegitimate son of Isabel Farnesio and Alberoni,
and others assert that Charles was given reason to believe
that the Jesuits planned to assassinate him and the members
of his family if the expulsion were promulgated. Whatever
the truth may be, he delayed only a few days, signing the
decree on February 27, 1767. The Count of Aranda was
charged with its execution, and proceeded to fulfill that duty
with great secrecy and despatch, so that the blow should fall
simultaneously and without warning in all parts of Spain's
dominions. Never was a decree more carefully carried out.
On the night of March 31 in Madrid, and on the next night
in the provinces, the Jesuits were surprised in their establishments and told that they must leave Spain. There were
at this time 2746 Spanish Jesuits in 120 institutions, scattered
through 117 towns. In the Americas the decree was carried
out later in the same year or early in 1768, and in some cases
there was popular resistance to their expulsion, although no
untoward incidents of that character had occurred in Spain.
Without consulting the pope, Charles decided to send the
Jesuits to the Papal States, although on the eve of the expulsion he informed the pope of his intention, promising also
to pay the Jesuits enough to permit them to live in a fitting
manner. Despite the pope's entire sympathy with the
Jesuits, there were reasons why he did not wish them to land
in his territory, and when the boats which were carrying

them arrived off Civita Vecchia, the port of Rome, Cardinal Torrigiani ordered them to keep away, threatening to open fire on them if they should not. Thereupon, they went to Corsica, where the Jesuits were landed, being joined later by their American brethren. Finally, the pope consented to their establishing themselves in Bologna and Ferrara, where some ten thousand from Spain and the Americas found a haven, — much against the will of the secular clergy of those places. Charles now set about to procure the dissolution of the order, and in this he was aided by the kings of Portugal, France, and Naples, from which last-named country the Jesuits had also been expelled late in 1767. In 1773 their efforts were at length successful, as a result, very largely, of the skillful diplomatic achievements of Jose Moñino, Spain's special representative at the papal court. For his work in this matter Moñino was rewarded with the title of Count of Floridablanca.

Royal attempts to reduce the financial immunities of the church. One of the leading preoccupations of the kings in dealing with the Spanish clergy was to reduce the immunities of a financial character which they enjoyed. Ever since the thirteenth century, efforts had been made with that object in view, and considerable success had been attained by the Hapsburg kings, while the attempts of the Bourbon monarchs to check the acquisition of lands by the church or to render at least a portion of them subject to taxation have already been traced in the chapter on social institutions. A great deal remained to be done, however, before the church would be reduced to the level of the bourgeois class in the payment of tributes. For a proper appreciation of this subject it is necessary to bear in mind the many sources of income of the Spanish church. In addition to the profits from their lands, cattle, and quit-rents (*censos*), churchmen received tithes (*diezmos*), first-fruits (*primicias*), fees for masses, marriages, funerals, and burials, alms for the mendicant orders, gifts, and still other forms of contributions from persons and lands not under their economic control. Their seigniorial rights were still extensive, for as late as 1787 there were 3148 towns of one type or another under their rule. To be sure, portions of these revenues were already being paid to the crown, while many former ecclesiastical earnings had altogether disappeared, or had been taken over by the state. In some places the clergy were subject to certain taxes, and in others they were not; in Castile churchmen paid part of the *alcabala;* in Catalonia they paid all the royal tributes. The laws of the century displayed a consistent intention on the part of the kings to reduce their financial immunities still further. Thus in 1721 the clergy of Castile and the Canaries were required to pay customs duties which had not previously been exacted from them; in 1737 a tax of thirty-three per cent was levied on all new landed possessions of the church in Valencia; in the concordat of the same year the pope granted that all lands thenceforth coming into the possession of ecclesiastical institutions might be taxed in the same manner as those of lay individuals, if the king should so decide; when Charles III was about to ascend the Spanish throne, Pope Benedict XIV granted him the eventual subjection of the clergy to the same tributary basis as laymen; in 1763 the clergy of the crown of Aragon were ordered to pay the *alcabala* from that time forth; in 1765 churchmen in general were made subject to the military tax of the *milicias* (militia), and in 1780 the pope authorized the king to collect up to one third of the income of benefices to which the king had the right of nomination. These provisions were not carried out in full; there would no longer have been any financial question between the kings and the church if they had been. Aside from the royal gains of a legislative character the clergy were often induced, or compelled, to make special grants to the state in times of war, and occasionally they came forward of their own free will. When the Jesuits were expelled in 1767, their properties were confiscated, although the government announced that in applying the proceeds it would bear in mind the objects of donors to the Jesuits, the interests of religion, and public utility. Nothing definite is known as to the amount of wealth this yielded to the state, although it must have been considerable. Many writers have made fanciful estimates as to the Jesuit properties, especially with regard to their holdings in the Americas, some of them exaggerating their value, and others going to the opposite extreme to make them appear inconsequential. Nevertheless, despite the progress made by the Bourbons, the church was still enormously wealthy at the end of the era; it is said that their annual income reached 1,101,753,430 *reales* (about $70,000,000).

Reduction of the number of persons in religious service.

The statesmen and economists of the Bourbon era gave considerable attention to the problems arising from the great numbers of the clergy, taking steps to prevent an increase in the membership of religious orders and to bring about a reduction in the list of benefices and chaplaincies. The reign of Charles III was especially notable in this regard, and much was achieved. Still, though there were more churchmen and religious institutions in the Hapsburg period at a time when the population was not so great, there were 2067 convents for men and 1122 for women in 1787, with 61,998 who had taken vows and 71,070 others who had not (though living at the convents), besides 70,170 members of the secular clergy. Thus there were over 200,000 persons in religious service in a total population of about 10,400,000, or one for every fifty-two persons.[1] By 1797 the numbers had been materially lessened. At that time there were 93,397 men and women connected with the institutions of the regular clergy, in 2051 convents for men and 1075 for women, and 58,833 priests. In 1808 there were eight archbishoprics and fifty-two bishoprics in Spain, sustaining 648 dignitaries, 1768 canons, 216 prebends, and 200 half prebends.

Attempts at internal reform of the church.

The question of the numbers of the clergy was closely related to the never-ending problem of reform in the internal life of the church. While matters were not so bad as they had been in earlier times, and while Spanish churchmen compared very favorably with those of some other countries, — for example, those of France, — the necessity for correction was nevertheless clear. Despite the fact that the church furnished many of the most distinguished names of the era in intellectual attainments, the mass of the lower clergy was decidedly uncultivated. There was a marked relaxation

[1] On the basis of the usual size of Spanish families, this would have meant one churchman to every five to ten adult men.

in discipline. Many churchmen absented themselves from their livings to become hangers-on at court,[1] with the result that the kings seven times in less than fifty years expelled all priests from Madrid whose parishes were not in that city. It was also deemed necessary to pass laws forbidding clergymen to wear lay dress, for it was claimed that they used it as a disguise, enabling them the more easily to indulge in immoral practices. Many clergymen were punished for improper solicitations in the confessional. Steps toward reform were taken by the popes in 1723, 1737, and 1753, — the two latter times in connection with the concordats of those years. The measures of the pope provided rules for the instruction and discipline of the clergy and sought to diminish the numbers of clergymen and of benefices and chaplaincies.

Outwardly there was little difference between this period and the one before it in the persecution of heresy and the effort to attain religious unity. Both of these ideals continued to be proclaimed in the laws, and the Inquisition made its accusations and condemnations and published its indices of prohibited books as formerly, but in fact a great change had come over the spirit in which the laws were interpreted. Such a rigorous policy to stamp out heresy as that employed by Philip II in the Low Countries was no longer thinkable, and while the Hapsburg kings had based their international policy on the re-establishment of Catholic unity, cost what it might, the Bourbons completely abandoned that idea. The treaties of Westphalia in 1648 seemed to have settled the question of religious warfare, with an acknowledgment of the right of Protestant nations to exist apart from the Catholic Church. Henceforth, wars were to be for various objects, mainly political and economic in the eighteenth century, but not for religion.

The new spirit was manifested in, and was to some extent caused by, the frequency of communications between Catholics and Protestants or between Catholics and anti-church

Diminution in the rigor of religious persecutions.

---

[1] One well-known case of clerical impropriety was that of the two ambitious priests whom Queen María Luisa employed as spies to keep her informed whether Godoy were faithful to her or not.

Inter-
relations
of the
different
religious
elements.

elements, such as the encyclopedists and Jansenists. In earlier times, such a correspondence would have been a serious religious crime which even the most prominent would have been afraid to attempt; now, it was not generally regarded as seriously reprehensible, though far from being looked upon with favor, and many churchmen themselves might have been held guilty if charges on this account had been brought. The quarrels of different factions in the church among themselves, notably the opposition to the Jesuits, and the intensely royalist policy of the kings tended in the same direction. Some evidences of the new attitude toward religion were also to be found in the laws. A treaty of 1713 with the Netherlands allowed Protestants of that country having business in Spain to reside in the peninsula, and a like privilege was granted to Spanish Catholics in the Netherlands. The *asiento* treaty with England in the same year did not, as had at first been proposed, restrict to Catholics the privileges thereby granted to Englishmen. A series of treaties with Morocco, Tripoli, Tunis, and Turkey in the reign of Charles III allowed of Catholic worship by Spaniards in those countries, and agreed that Moslems coming to Spain should be respected in their religion. A general law of 1797 provided that any foreign artist or artisan could establish himself in the peninsula, and in case he were not a Catholic he was not to be molested in his religious opinions. The Jews were excluded from the operation of the law, however. Charles III had been favorable to a policy of toleration toward them as well, and had issued a decree in 1741, when he was king of Naples, permitting of their entry into his kingdom, but public opinion was still too strongly opposed to them, and he was obliged to recall his decree. Two ministers of Charles IV, Urquijo and Varela, made a like proposal, but he did not dare to follow their advice; rather, he expressly declared in a decree of 1802 that the existing laws and practices with respect to the Jews should continue to be observed. The Inquisition directed its activities in this period to attacking the new philosophic and religious ideas and to defending itself as well as it could from the inroads of royalism, while there were still numerous processes against superstitious practices, Jewish worship, and the crimes of bigamy and notorious immorality. The number of cases before the Inquisition was not less than formerly, and not a few persons, especially Jews and Illuminati, were put to death. In general, however, greater leniency was displayed, and the Inquisition was no longer the much feared institution it once had been.

Nevertheless, both the clergy and the great majority of the people remained as intolerant as ever. Ignorance played no small part in this feeling; thus French priests expelled from their country at the time of the revolution were suspected of heresy, and the general opinion of the Spanish common people with regard to Frenchmen was that they were all not only heretics or atheists but also cannibals. The ideal of toleration hardly passed beyond the narrow circle of the upper classes, but it was they who decided the policy of the state; indeed, the attitude toward religion in this period perfectly exemplified the workings of the benevolent despotism. The very men who expressed tolerant views and framed legislation to that end were pious in their private life, furnishing numerous proofs thereof, every day. Thus Spaniards still gave a multitude of Christian names to their children, in order to procure for them the protection of many saints; they observed religious ceremonies, such as processions, baptisms, and saints' days of individuals, as the most important events of social life; they prayed daily, and at the sound of the Angelus all work stopped, even theatrical performances, and every one bowed his head in prayer; phrases with a religious turn were a part of everyday speech; sacred images and chapels were as abundant as formerly; and in a thousand ways, from the king to the lowest peasant, men continued to manifest their devotion to the Catholic faith.

Underlying spirit of intolerance and Catholic fervor.

CHAPTER XXXVII

ECONOMIC REFORMS, 1700–1808

Bases of the economic reforms of the era.

IF a review of the political and ecclesiastical institutions of this period displays the enlightened despotism on its despotic side, a study of the economic reforms effected, or tried, reveals the benevolent or enlightened attitude of the autocratic state endeavoring to improve the lot of the people. In addition to the philanthropic aspect of these attempts, they were influenced, also: by the general current of eighteenth century thought, giving attention to economic problems; by the very evident necessity for reforms in Spain, which country had found itself in a condition of utter misery at the close of the preceding era, with the result that a multitude of pamphlets had been written to explain the decline and suggest remedies; and by the desire to attain other ends, such as that of defence against the aggressions of England, which had to be based in the final analysis on the economic recovery of Spain. Not only in Spain but also in the Americas, and almost more strikingly, this was an age of economic reform, based primarily on Spain's need of the colonial markets as a factor in her own regeneration. Nevertheless, this was the period when the old monopoly utterly fell, in part because of the entry of foreigners into the colonies or their establishment in Spanish ports to take over the goods coming from the Americas, and in part as a result of a deliberate policy, throwing open the commerce of the new world, if not directly to all nations, at least indirectly through the intervention of the many Spanish cities which came to enjoy the privilege of the overseas trade. The American situation cannot be dealt with here, but it must be held in mind as one of the vital elements in Spain's economic progress.

Economic reforms in the Americas.

458

The most genuine representative of the century's political economists in Spain was Campomanes. Although a follower of the French physiocratic school, which maintained that agriculture was the principal sustain of a nation's wealth, he did not fail to recognize the importance of manufacturing, and endeavored to foster that industry through the dissemination of works of an educative character, the enactment of protective laws, and the founding of model establishments. Of equal rank with Campomanes, though not as effective in achieving reforms, was Jovellanos, while there was hardly a minister of prominence in the entire period who did not attain to some distinction as an economist. The general effect of the reforms was beneficial, making itself felt in all branches of the production, exchange, and consumption of goods, as well as in an increase in population. Thus the 5,700,000 inhabitants of Spain at the beginning of the era had nearly doubled by 1787, when the total was 10,409,879 (or 10,286,150 by another estimate), and had still further increased to 10,541,221 in 1797. The following table of occupations for these two years is interesting both as showing the economic distribution of the population and as indicating the direction of the reforms.

	1787	1797
Ecclesiastics	182,425	168,248
Nobles	480,589	402,059
Employees (of the government?) . . .	41,014	31,981
Soldiery	77,884	149,340
Students	50,994	29,812
Farmers and (farm?) laborers	1,871,768	1,677,172
Manufacturers and artisans	310,739	533,769
Servants	280,092	174,095
Merchants	No figures	25,685

The discrepancies between the two columns are in part accounted for by the fact that Spain was at peace in 1787, and at war with England in 1797. In a total of some 3,000,000 workers it is notable that the majority were devoted to agricultural pursuits (including about 100,000 engaged in pastoral labors), showing that the cultivation of the soil was the principal basis of the national life. The vast number of ecclesiastics, nobles, and servants, nearly a third of the total, is eloquent of the social problem which the government had to face. In the course of ten years they had fallen away to less than a fourth of the whole. Statistics as to density of population showed Guipúzcoa, Valencia, Asturias, Navarre, and Vizcaya in the lead, with respectively eighty, forty-eight, forty-seven, forty-three, and forty-two inhabitants to the square kilometer. Andalusia had thirty-nine, Granada and Catalonia thirty-four each, Aragon only twenty-one, while Extremadura with fourteen and La Mancha and Cuenca with thirteen each brought up the rear. In total population Galicia led with 1,345,000. Catalonia had 814,412, Valencia 783,084, Andalusia 754,293, Granada 661,661, and Aragon 623,308. Large urban groups were rare; there were fewer than forty cities with a population of 10,000, and seventeen of them were in Andalusia. The four largest cities were Madrid (156,000), Barcelona (115,000), Seville (96,000), and Valencia (80,000). Economic prosperity did not correspond exactly with these figures, for the factors of climate, soil, irrigation, and nearness to the sea entered into the situation.

Wretched state of domestic life. Despite the great body of reforms carried out, the problem was overwhelming, and much of the country was still in a backward state at the end of the era. Aragon and Old Castile were in a miserable condition, not nearly equalling their agricultural possibilities, and La Mancha was in a far worse plight. The number of large-sized towns in Andalusia gave that land an appearance of wealth and prosperity which was not borne out by the facts, if the situation of the country districts were taken into account. The character of Spanish houses at this time was also expressive of the national economic shortcomings. Cave houses and adobe huts with roofs of straw abounded in Castile. The houses of Galicia were described as having walls of unpolished stone, often without cement, reaching scarcely higher than a man's head, with great slabs of rock for a roof; the doorway and a hole in the roof served as the only means for the penetration of light and for the escape of smoke; and the domestic animals and the family made common use of the wretched house. In the Basque provinces, Navarre, and Valencia the homes were much better, besides being cleaner, although a lack of glass windows, chimneys, and furniture was quite general in all parts of Spain. Through French influences these defects were beginning to be overcome as the era approached a close. If to this miserable state of the domestic life there is added the ignorance of the people (who resisted innovations designed to benefit them), the economic inequality resulting from the concentration of vast landed estates in a few hands, the difficulty of communications, the burdens of taxation, the mismanagement of the administration (despite the efforts of enlightened ministers), the frequency of wars, and the persistence of a spirit of repugnance to labor (leading to a resort to mendicancy or vagabondage or to a reliance upon a somewhat questionably desirable charity) it becomes clear why the economic situation should have been considered perhaps the most urgent problem which the Spanish ministers had to solve, and their failure to overcome all of the difficulties can be understood. According to Campomanes there was an army of 140,000 beggars and vagabonds in Spain in his day, most of whom were able to work and might have found something to do. He and the other ministers of Charles III endeavored to solve the matter by putting the physically able women in workhouses, the men in the army and navy, and the old and infirm in homes for the aged and in hospitals, but owing to the lack of funds these projects could not be carried out in entirety.

Obstacles in the way of economic reforms.

The evils of the economic situation being clear, efforts were made, especially in the reign of Charles III, to correct them at their sources. To combat the ignorance, indifference, and in some cases the laziness and prejudice of the masses with regard to labor technical and primary schools were founded and model shops and factories established; prizes were awarded for debates and papers on various industrial subjects; printed manuals, including many translated from foreign languages, were scattered broadcast;

Construc-
tive at-
tempts of
the state
and
private in-
dividuals
to over-
come
economic
evils.

teachers and skilled laborers from foreign lands were induced to come to Spain, and Spaniards were pensioned to
go abroad to study; privileges, exemptions, and monopolies
were granted to persons distinguishing themselves by their
initiative and zeal in industry; and laws were passed to
raise the dignity of manual labor. In this campaign the
government received substantial aid from private individuals. In 1746 the first of the *Sociedades Económicas de los
Amigos del País* (economic societies of the friends of the
country) was founded. In 1766 its statutes were published,
serving thenceforth as the model for other like institutions
in Spain, all of them devoted philanthropically to the encouragement of agriculture and other phases of the economic
life of their particular district. Nobles, churchmen, and
members of the wealthy middle class formed the backbone
of these societies, of which there were sixty-two in 1804.
Many of them published periodicals, or founded schools
for the study of such subjects as agriculture, botany, chemistry, the various trades, stenography, and economics. To
promote the cultivation of the soil the state itself assisted
in schemes for the colonization of waste lands. The most
famous instance was that of the government colonies in the
Sierra Morena country of northern Andalusia. In 1766 a
certain Bavarian adventurer offered to bring six thousand
German and Flemish laborers to settle that district. Charles
III favored the project, and it was at once undertaken.
For a time it was successful; a number of settlements were
made, — there were forty-one in 1775, — and considerable
crops were raised. In the end the project failed, due to
bad administration, lack of funds, the imposition of heavy
taxes, the opposition of the clergy to the predominantly
lay spirit of the undertaking, the jealousies arising between
the Spanish and foreign elements (for many of the colonists
were Spaniards), and the failure to provide adequate means of
communication whereby the colonists could export their surplus products. Some of the towns continued to exist, however,
and the project was influential in causing private individuals
to attempt colonizations, several of which were successful.
Among other constructive governmental measures were the

removal of the legal obstacles to the sale or division of waste
lands or lands common, the restriction of the privileges of the
Mesta, the betterment of the conditions surrounding leases
(favoring the prolongation of the period of the lease, and
aiming to assist the individual who actually cultivated the
soil), and the reduction of customs duties or a grant of
complete freedom of entry in the case of certain raw materials
used in Spanish manufacturing establishments. Public
works were also undertaken, such as the construction of
irrigation canals, though many were not completed or were
made so imperfectly that they soon went to ruin; great
highways to open up the peninsula were planned, and under
Charles III much work upon them was done, though not
enough to meet the needs of the country; an efficient mail
service was developed by Floridablanca; shipbuilding was
encouraged; banditry and piracy were to a great extent
suppressed; government support was given to commercial companies; and a national bank was established by
Charles III, — which failed in the reign of Charles IV.
The government also intervened in problems of local sub-
sistence, with a view to maintaining articles of prime necessity at a low price and in sufficient quantity, but its
action in this particular did not always produce the desired
result. Finally, the government interested itself in charity.
Benevolent institutions were founded, not only with a view
to checking mendicancy and vagabondage, but also to
provide homes for unfortunate women, insane persons, and
orphans. Private individuals gave liberally for these purposes, or founded charitable organizations, which rendered
service of a somewhat remarkable character in succoring
the poor, building hospitals, and rescuing children. Mutual
benefit societies were formed, reaching into every walk of
life, and some of these, termed *montepíos* or *montes de piedad*,
were made compulsory for the employes of the government;
thus the *montepío* for soldiers, dating from 1761, served as
a pension system whereby some provision was made for the
widows and orphans of the deceased. All of these reforms
encountered the difficulties arising from ignorance, conservatism, the resistance of vested interests, graft, and

bureaucratic cumbersomeness which have already been discussed. The very immensity of the reforms projected was against their satisfactory execution, for more was tried than could be done well. Other obstacles already mentioned, such as bad administration, insufficiency of funds, and lack of persistence, contributed to the same result. Nevertheless, though plans outran accomplishment, a vast amount was done, especially in the reign of Charles III, when the spirit of the era reached its culminating point.

Obstacles to agricultural development and attempts to overcome them.

To form a correct idea of the state of agriculture in this period it is necessary to note how the lands of the peninsula were distributed. At the beginning of the nineteenth century, after a hundred years of effort directed to the release of realty, the church possessed 9,093,400 *fanegas* [1] of land, the nobles 28,306,700, and the plebeian class 17,599,000, but the greater part of the estates of both the nobles and the plebeians was entailed, and therefore impossible of alienation, closing the door to the growth of a class of small proprietors. The proportion of proprietors to population was only one in forty. In Ávila, for example, the church owned 239,591 *fanegas*, 157,092 were entailed, and only 8160 were cultivated by owners who resided in the neighborhood. The small proprietor was to be found principally in the north and east, but he was far outnumbered, even in those regions, by the lessees of lands, who were also the overwhelmingly strongest element numerically in Castile. The forms of renting were various, both as to the type of payment required and as to the length of term. Where the term was practically hereditary, conditions were much better, approximating those of the small proprietor. In Andalusia *latifundia* were the rule, cultivated in only a portion of the estate by day laborers, who were employed at certain seasons of the year, living in a state of great misery at other times. This evil was tempered in Extremadura by the utilization of lands common. Despite the sincere attempts of the government to encourage agriculture, that industry was still in an extremely backward state at the close of the era, with only a little of the cultivable ground planted,

[1] A *fanega* equals about 1.59 acres.

n insufficient development of irrigation, and a lack of fencing. Valencia and the Basque provinces were the most nearly prosperous regions; the others were in a wretched state. In addition to the governmental reforms already referred to, the following may be mentioned: several laws of Charles III forbade owners to dispossess tenants arbitrarily, and even went so far as to prohibit ejectments unless the owner should consent to reside on his lands and cultivate them; attempts were made to procure reforestation, partly with a view to conserving the water supply, but the national repugnance to trees was so great that the laws were not carried out; and the abusive privileges of the *Mesta* were attacked by Charles III, and in the next reign, in 1795, the separate jurisdiction of that organization was taken away, but as the laws did not clearly authorize the enclosure of cultivable lands the relief to agriculture was slight. Wheat was the principal crop, supplying more than enough, in normal years, for the needs of the peninsula. Grapes were also raised in large quantities, and were made into excellent wines, many of which were exported. For the rest there were fruits, vegetables, the silkworm, and other things of the sort which had always been cultivated in the peninsula. Various kinds of beans, and especially chickpeas (*garbanzos*), were grown in large quantities, and furnished an important element in the nation's food. An estimate made in 1812 calculated the total value of farm products as 72,476,189,159 *reales* (about \$4,500,000,000) yielding annually some 3,600,000,000 *reales* (about \$225,000,000).

In their efforts to revive manufacturing the kings continued during most of the period to follow the old ideal of state protection and state initiative in placing industries upon a firm foundation, intervening, also, to regulate the work on its technical side. In the second half of the century, especially in the reign of Charles III, the liberal ideas of the physiocratic school, hostile to all forms of government regulation, brought about the employment of a new system, leaving matters to the decision of the individuals concerned. Laws were now passed removing the prohibitions of earlier years. Joined with the educative measures

Revival of manufacturing.

2 H

already referred to, such as the establishment of model factories and the importation of foreign workmen, the new methods brought about a revived intensity of industrial life. Much the same things as formerly were made; the textile factories of Catalonia and Andalusia were the most prosperous. The chemical industries and those having to do with the preparation of foods did not develop equally with others. The Americas continued to be one of the principal supports of Spanish manufacturing, as a purchaser of the goods made in the peninsula. After centuries of scant productivity in mining, Spain began again to yield more nearly in accord with her natural wealth. A great variety of mineral products was mined, although very little of precious metals. On the other hand the formerly prosperous fishing industry was in a state of decline. In 1803 it was estimated that the total industrial yield for that year was 1,152,660,707 *reales* (about $72,000,000). The revival, however, was of an ephemeral character, for the social factors affecting labor were too grave a handicap. Thoroughgoing popular instruction was necessary before there could be any permanent advance; the Spanish laborer was able enough, but needed to be rescued from his abysmal ignorance. Wages were low. In 1786 the ordinary laborer of Seville earned four and a half *reales* (about $.28) a day; in Barcelona the average was eight *reales* ($.50). Agricultural laborers in Andalusia made from three and a half to five *reales* ($.22 to $.33) a day; shepherds got two pounds of bread daily and 160 *reales* ($10) a year. To be sure, money was worth more than now. Work was not always steady, with the result that famine and beggary were frequent. There was no such thing as organized labor; to go on strike was a crime. The only remedy of the laborer against his employer was an appeal to the *corregidor*, but this was so ineffectual that it was rarely tried.

Attempts were made to combat the obstacles which hindered Spanish commerce. Unable to compete with other European countries in the export trade, except as concerned small quantities of certain raw materials, Spain was hard pressed to maintain an advantage in her own domes-

Mining.

Fishing.

Unsatisfactory state of the laboring classes.

tic and American field. At the beginning of the century many of the laws tended in fact to discriminate against Spaniards, as witness the heavy export duties, which were collected according to bulk, thus operating against the type of products which Spain most frequently sent abroad. Charles III changed this system, collecting duties according to the nature of the goods as well as paying regard to weight, and charging a higher rate against foreign cargoes. Taxes were numerous in kind and heavy in amount, wherefore smuggling and graft overcame some of the beneficial effects which might have been expected from this legislation. Protective tariffs and prohibitions were also employed to encourage Spanish manufactures and trade, but particular exigencies often caused a reversal of this policy in the case of certain items of foreign make. Thus the importation of foreign muslins was forbidden in 1770, but in 1789 the prohibition was removed when it was found that local manufacture did not suffice for the country's needs. A series of decrees by Charles III endeavored also to reduce the coinage to systematic order, but the multiplicity of coins and the retention of provincial moneys militated against complete success. The prohibition against the export of coin was maintained, but licenses to take out certain quantities were granted on payment of a three per cent duty. Practically, the prohibition was a dead letter, owing to the prevalence of smuggling, and it served as a hindrance to commerce. An ineffectual attempt was made in 1801 to unify the system of weights and measures. Lack of an adequate merchant marine and an insufficiency of good ports, despite the efforts to remedy the situation in both cases, were still further obstacles to Spanish trade, whereas such an excellent port as Vigo had no suitable highway to connect it with the interior. Bands of mules continued to be used as the principal carrying agency in land commerce. Improper methods of keeping books were a handicap, but the paternalistic nature of the government made itself felt, requiring business men to employ a good method of accounting, and specifying the precise way in which they should do it. Finally, trading had usually been considered incompatible with nobility. The stigma was in a measure removed, although only in the case of business on a large scale, and some of the nobles became merchants.

Mercantile machinery found its highest official expression in the *Junta de Comercio y Moneda*. This was reorganized in 1705, at which time it was provided that the Councils of Castile, the Indies and Finance (*Hacienda*) should be represented respectively by three, five, and two members, the *Casa de Contratación* by one, and the French nation by two, besides one of the royal secretaries. The importance of the American and French trades was clearly manifested in this arrangement. This body served as a court with jurisdiction in all matters concerning trade. In 1730 it was succeeded by the *Junta de Moneda* (*Junta*, or Council, of Coinage), to which was added jurisdiction in matters concerning mines (1747), foreigners (1748), and the "five greater guilds of Madrid" (1767 and 1783). Regional *juntas* were also created. The *consulados*, though of private origin, occupied an intermediate position between the other private and the official bodies, owing to the intervention of the state and to the reorganization of the *consulados* in the middle and later eighteenth century. In addition to their functions as a mercantile court they acquired a vast number of duties of a public character, such as the care of ports and the creation of schools of navigation. Certain *consulados* had special functions, — for example, the *consulado* of Cádiz attended to supplying the province with grain and flour, and had charge of the establishment of tariffs and lotteries. The *consulados* were repaid for these services by a grant of a portion of the customs duties, a right worth 6,000,000 *reales* ($375,000) a year in Cádiz and one third of that amount in Alicante. They compromised their wealth by making loans to the crown, which brought about their ruin. At the end of the eighteenth century there were fourteen *consulados* in Spain, each differing from the others but all following rather closely the new ordinances (1737) for the *consulado* of Bilbao as a type. In the smaller cities and towns local officials were wont to appoint two men as *diputados de comercio* (commercial deputies) to act for that neighborhood in the capacity of a *consulado*. There were various other mercantile groups of a more clearly private character, and their associations were encouraged by the government. The so-called "five greater guilds of Madrid," including dealers in jewelry, silks, gold and silver ware, cloths, linens, spices (and groceries?), and drugs, was the most important of these organizations. Its business was so enormous that it extended beyond Madrid to other cities, and put up factories for the manufacture of the goods it sold. In 1777 there were 375 merchants in this corporation, with a capital of some 210,000,000 *reales* ($13,125,000). Other associations were formed for special objects, such as to buy goods in great quantities and therefore more cheaply, or to carry merchandise in their own ships. Many companies were organized specifically for trading with the Americas. In the fluctuations of commerce one fact stood out consistently: the balance of trade was heavily against Spain. In 1789 exports were valued at 289,973,980 *reales* (about $18,000,000) as against imports of 717,397,388 (nearly $45,000,000). Internal commerce amounted to an estimated 2,498,429,552 *reales* (about $156,000,000). The wars of the reign of Charles IV almost destroyed Spanish commerce. Cádiz in particular was a heavy loser.

The intervention of foreigners in the commerce of Spain, which had given so much concern in the previous era, was an even greater problem under the Bourbons. Many factors contributed to make this the case: the industrial decline of the seventeenth century, which favored the importation of foreign goods; the eighteenth century efforts for an economic revival, which led to the seeking out of foreign models and foreign teachers or workmen; the encouragement given to Frenchmen as a result of the Bourbon entry into Spain; and defeats in war, which necessitated Spain's submission to the exactions of her opponents (many of whom insisted upon commercial privileges) or the legalization of trade usurpations which they had indulged in without right. In the Americas the English were the most prominent element, but in Spain the French were. The leading

Important place of foreigners in Spanish commerce.

French merchants established themselves in Cádiz, the gateway of the Americas, whence they proceeded to absorb a great part of Spain's profits from the new world. In 1772 there were seventy-nine French wholesale houses in Cádiz, making an estimated annual profit of 4,600,000 *reales* (nearly $300,000). In 1791 there were 2701 Frenchmen in that city out of a total foreign population of 8734. Numerically, the Italians were more in evidence, for there were 5018 of them, mostly Genoese. There were some Englishmen, too, whose aggregate capital made up for their small number. In general the legislation of the era was favorable to foreigners. Their knowledge and labor were so greatly desired that they were even granted special privileges or exemptions to take up their residence in Spain, and the religious bar was ameliorated or utterly withdrawn. Popular opinion was against them, however, and the laws were not wholly free from this influence. Men complained, as formerly, that the foreigners were making immense profits and stifling Spanish competition, while the hatreds engendered by the wars with England and France and by the scant respect and haughty manners which some foreigners displayed for the laws and customs of Spain tended to increase the feeling of opposition. Foreigners were often ill-treated, although the acts were rarely official. Even the government did not recognize consuls as having any special rights or immunities differentiating them from others of their nation. A further accusation against foreigners was that they engaged in contraband trade. This was true, although as a rule it was done in complicity with corrupt Spanish officials. Foreigners justified themselves on the ground that unless they were willing to make gifts to Spaniards in authority they were obliged to suffer a thousand petty annoyances. "Money and gifts," said the French ambassador, Vaulgrenant, "have always been the most efficacious means of removing the difficulties which can be raised, on the slightest pretext, against foreign merchants. That has been the recourse to which the English have always applied themselves, with good results." The fact remains, however, that the French, English, and others had entered the commercial field in Spain and Spanish America to stay.

CHAPTER XXXVIII

INTELLECTUAL ACTIVITIES, 1700–1808

IN intellectual expression, as well as in other phases of
Spain's national life, the eighteenth century was a period
of recovery from the degradation which marked the close
of the preceding era. Spain placed herself abreast of the
times, but not as formerly in a leading position; among the
many who distinguished themselves by their achievements
there were few who attained to a European reputation, and
perhaps only one, the painter Goya, may be reckoned with
the immortals. On the other hand Spain entered more
definitely into the general current of western European
thought than at any previous time in her history; intellectual activities in France reacted almost at once in Spain,
and the influences springing out of Italy and England were
potent. The Americas began to take over the intellectual
side of their Spanish heritage much more completely than
before, and while not nearly approximating the mother
country in the amount or excellence of their contributions
furnished illustrious names in almost every branch worthy
to stand beside those of their contemporaries in Spain.
Education there became more general, more secular, and
more highly regarded than ever before. Two obstacles,
however, were a serious check upon the development of a
broad culture in the colonies: the problems of race, reducing the number of those able to participate, and lessening
the desirability of a propaganda for the ideal involved;
and the suspicions of the Spanish-controlled government,
lest ideas convert themselves into thoughts of revolution.

Cultivated Spaniards of the eighteenth century had a
clear understanding of the national problem of education,

General
character-
istics of
intellec-
tual life in
Spain and
the
Americas.

471

realizing (just as they did with regard to matters having an economic bearing) the profound ignorance of the masses and the decadent state of the institutions upon which they had to rely to combat it. The mass of the people were not only illiterate but also full of almost ineradicable superstitions and the conservatism of the undeveloped mind. In 1766 Queen Amalia, the wife of Charles III, wrote to Tanucci (one of Charles' leading ministers while he was king of Naples), "In everything (in Spain) there is something of barbarism, together with great pride." As for the women, she said, "One does not know what to talk about with them; their ignorance is beyond belief." This pessimistic view finds ample corroboration in the writings of the Benedictine Feyjóo, or Feijóo (1676–1764), and Jovellanos, both of whom devoted themselves to the struggle against the defects in Spanish mentality and its expression, leaving published works which touched upon virtually every phase of the intellectual life, or its lack, in the Iberian Peninsula. The endeavors of these men and numerous others to regenerate the country were not wholly in obedience to the national necessity or to patriotism, but responded also to the general current of humanitarianism and philanthropy characteristic of the eighteenth century. The close relationship of Spain with France during most of the era and the conditions of peace imposed by Protestant countries as a result of their military successes had favored the penetration of these ideas into Spain, where they were taken up by the well-to-do elements of the nobility, the clergy, and the wealthy middle class. The great nobles furnished few of the illustrious names of the period, although there were some exceptions (for example, the Count of Fernán-Núñez and the Count of Aranda), but they gave both financial and moral support to the efforts for intellectual reform. Some of those who held high office, notably Godoy, aided authors in the publication of their works or the continuation of their studies, giving them official employment, or subsidies, or bringing out their volumes through the royal printing estab ishment. Despite the characterization of them by Queen Amalia, the women shared in the intellectual ac-

tivities of the age. Thus there was a revival of interest
in education, but with a difference from the spirit which
had dominated the works of Vives and others of the Hapsburg era; now the ideal was that of secular education without the intervention of the clergy. Encyclopedism and
monarchism worked together to this end, while the expulsion of the Jesuits helped greatly to make its attainment
possible, although the new attitude did not go so far as to
oppose religion; indeed, that remained the basis of primary
education. All this manifested itself with especial force
beginning with the reign of Charles III, but precedents
were not lacking in earlier years. It made itself felt chiefly
in the sphere of professional training, in instruction in the
humanities, and in university education, but it did not fail
to produce effects of undoubted value on the primary schools.

Primary education, which had always received scant atten- Efforts for
tion, was the subject of some legislation under Charles III, the better-
both to expand and to better it. To make certain of the ment of
capacity of the teachers examinations were required of them and
in reading, writing, and arithmetic. In 1768 orders were secondary
given for the establishment of primary schools for girls in education.
the principal towns of Spain, and some of the confiscated
Jesuit funds were applied to this object. An important
law of 1780 went into the whole matter of primary education in the city of Madrid. In the early years of the reign
of Charles IV the *corregidores* and *alcaldes* of all towns were
ordered to inspect schools, and were requested to inquire
what towns, including those of the lords, the church, and
the military orders, lacked them or were failing to provide
sufficiently for those which they had. In 1795 the *Cortes* of
Navarre voted in favor of compulsory education. Furthermore, private individuals followed the example of the public
authorities, and founded schools. Nevertheless, the census
of 1787 showed only about a fourth of the children between
the ages of seven and sixteen attending school. Conditions were still very bad for the teachers, whose salaries
were so small that they could not live on them, while vexatious regulations were also a handicap to the free development of the schools. The teachers were imbued with the

pedagogical ideas of Rousseau, while Godoy attempted to bring about the introduction of the methods of Pestalozzi. Both Godoy and Jovellanos had extensive plans for the spread of primary education, but political exigencies interrupted the projects of the former, while the latter's brief period of rule gave hardly time enough for the execution of his ideas. The interest of the government, of individuals, and of the *Amigos del País* societies in popular technical education has already been discussed. The institutions for the study of the humanities, roughly corresponding with the modern secondary schools (at least in that they were a grade below the universities), were also reformed by the government, following the expulsion of the Jesuits. In the same year (1767) it was provided that the places of the former Jesuit teachers in the Jesuit-taught schools of nobles and in the nineteen Jesuit colleges should be filled by competitive examinations. In 1768 similar institutions were ordered to be founded in such *villas* and cities as had no university. Meanwhile, the municipal, conventual, and private schools continued to exist, as in earlier times; Ferdinand VI and Charles III enacted legislation with a view to limiting their numbers and alleviating the bad condition of some of them.

Royal attempts at reform in university education.

The twenty-four Spanish universities of this period were leading a life of languor and scant utility down to the reign of Charles III, struggling against the handicaps of a diminution in rents and students and the competition of the Jesuits. More serious still was the decline of university instruction. Studies were reduced to little more than the memorizing of books, without any attempt at scientific investigation; such little effort was made to keep abreast of the times that the great University of Alcalá had in a library of seventeen thousand volumes only some five hundred setting forth the current doctrines of other countries; and many professorships had become sinecures for indigent nobles. The reformers were eager to overcome these evils, and took the course which seemed most natural in their day, that of bringing the universities under royal control so that the benevolent state might introduce the desired changes. In 1769 Charles III appointed a director for each university, to whom the life of the particular institution was to be subject; later in the same year he gave orders for a new and better plan of studies; in 1770 a censor was added to each university by royal appointment, with the duty of watching over the program of studies and assuring himself of the correctness of the religious and political views (favoring absolutism) of prospective graduates, and at the same time the universities were asked to suggest further reforms. Most of them delayed their replies as long as possible, for the greater number of the university officers were opposed to change, but the king proceeded to make reforms, nevertheless. Between 1771 and 1787 the greater universities were subjected to such revisions of their former methods as the following: the presentation of new courses and the amplification of old ones; the provision of a better opportunity to win professorships by merit; the introduction of new texts; changes in the methods of obtaining degrees; and the virtual appointment of the rector, or president, by the *Consejo*. Godoy and Jovellanos in the next reign carried on the reforming spirit of the ministers of Charles III. In all of these reforms attempts were made to better the methods of teaching as well as the programs of study. Thus, in 1774 professors were invited to reduce their lectures to writing and make a gift of them to their university, and prizes were offered for the publication of new texts or the translation of foreign volumes. Nevertheless, the majority of the reforms produced but a slender result, for the men charged with putting them into effect were already trained in the old ideas, finding it impossible to enter into the spirit of the new.

Possibly because they realized that the universities could not be depended upon to solve the problem of higher education and scientific output, the reformers created a long series of institutions of a special character to attain these ends. Thus, schools of medicine, surgery, the physical sciences, mathematics, jurisprudence, military art, astronomy, engineering of various types, botany, mineralogy, natural history, machinery, and others were founded, while a number of royal academies, or learned societies, were established, among which may be mentioned those of the

Special institutions of learning and scientific production.

Spanish tongue (1713), history (1738), and the fine arts (1752). Many foreign teachers and scientists were brought to Spain, but since any permanent advantage had to come from the efforts of Spaniards a number of students from the peninsula were sent abroad. Similarly, the government paid the expenses of numerous expeditions, which were largely or often wholly for objects of a scientific character. As examples of this phase of the state's activity may be mentioned the visit of Juan and Ulloa to South America in 1735 with several French academicians, to measure various degrees of the meridian at the equator in order to determine the shape of the earth; that of the astronomers Doz and Medina to Baja California in 1769 in company with the Frenchman Chappe d'Auteroche, to observe the transit of Venus; and the numerous Spanish voyages to the northwest coast of North America in the last quarter of the eighteenth century, of which the best known, perhaps, is that of Malaspina, who set out in 1791 to prove the existence or non-existence of the alleged Strait of Anian through the continent of North America. This was an age, too, of official accumulation of libraries; the royal library, forerunner of the present-day Biblioteca Nacional, was thrown open to the public in 1714. Archives, also, were reorganized and their contents put in order. Such was the case with those of Simancas and the crown of Aragon, while many documents relating to the Americas were taken from the former in 1785 to make a beginning of the great Archivo General de Indias at Seville. Manuscripts were utilized, as well as merely arranged, resulting both in documented volumes and in printed collections of papers, — such, for example, as the *España sagrada*, or Sacred Spain (1747–1773), a collection of diplomas, chronicles, charters, and other old manuscripts in ecclesiastical archives, with a view to making accessible the more important materials for the history of the church; this great work, begun by Father Flórez, eventually reached fifty-one volumes. This period also marked the beginning of scientific periodical literature in Spain, occasionally as the result of private initiative, but often as a government enterprise, or at least at state expense wholly or in part. The outbreak of the French Revolution caused the royal authorities to suspend most of these periodicals, but there was a return to a more liberal policy under Godoy.

All of these efforts to rouse the nation from its intellectual lethargy encountered such obstacles as have already been mentioned in dealing with other phases of Spanish life in this period. Principal among them was the ignorance of the people. Great as were the endeavors of the reformers, they were unable to make the masses respond as quickly as could have been wished, while even on the bourgeois and upper classes the effect of the reforms was slight. Many interests directly opposed the new ideas, finding danger in them for the institutions which they represented. This was particularly true of the clergy as regards innovations in the intellectual life of the country. The state itself, prime mover in so many of the reforms, drew back when anything was suggested which seemed to impinge upon the royal prerogative. In the reign of Charles IV a distinct note of reaction began to make itself felt, coming to its full fruition at a later time under the autocratic Ferdinand VII. *Slight effect of educational reforms.*

One of the principal characteristics of the intellectual movement of the eighteenth century was the reawakened interest in the experimental sciences, representing a return to the Spanish traditions of the sixteenth century. If Spain furnished fewer great names and achievements at this time than formerly, nevertheless she made a notable recovery from the low position she held at the close of the seventeenth century, and in some respects, especially in natural science, produced men able to rank with their contemporaries in other lands. In keeping with the practical bent of Spanish character Spaniards were more famous for their applications of scientific discoveries than for their contributions to pure science. Just as in the previous era, the Americas furnished a prominent field for scientific investigations. In the realm of botany, perhaps more than in anything else, Spaniards distinguished themselves. A list of the greatest names of the period would include Mutis, Mociño, Sessé, Ruiz, Pavón, and Molina, whose works *Spanish contributions to experimental science.*

dealt with the *flora* of Bogotá, Guatemala, Mexico, Peru, and Chile, especially in their practical applications in medicine and otherwise. To their names should be added those of Cavanilles and Sarmiento, whose writings had to do with the *flora* of Valencia and Galicia. Under Philip V a botanical garden was projected, and it was founded at Madrid in the reign of Ferdinand VI. Other cities soon followed this example. Zoology and mineralogy were less prominently studied, and in the latter field Spain began to make more use of foreign specialists than in the Golden Age. A considerable impulse to the natural sciences was given by the founding, by Charles III, of the important museum at Madrid, in which existing collections were brought together and to which various specimens from the Americas were added. Another factor was the sending out of scientific expeditions, mostly in or to the Americas, in which respect, according to the testimony of Humboldt, Spain expended more than any other European government. Meritorious work in physics and chemistry was also done by Spaniards, — for example, the discoveries of Ruiz de Luzuriaga and Salvá in the realm of magnetic fluids and electricity, the discovery of tungsten by the Elhuyar brothers, and the demonstration by Antonio de Ulloa of the existence of platinum, — even though foreigners were to carry these findings still further. Medicine advanced out of the stagnation which had characterized it in the later seventeenth century, although it continued to be in a backward state in the Americas.

Mathematics and geography.

The scientific movement of the eighteenth century reached the field of mathematics and kindred branches, producing much valuable work, though usually in the field of their practical applications. In the case of mathematics the decline had even reached the point of the negation of that science as a field for study. The Jesuits reintroduced it in their colleges, but it remained for the ministers of Charles III to restore it to its earlier strong footing by creating professorships of mathematics in the universities and in the schools of higher learning devoted to special fields. Jorge Juan and Antonio de Ulloa, better known for their expedition to South America and their authorship of the *Noticias secretas*, or Secret notices (not published until 1826), about conditions there, were among those who distinguished themselves in this subject. Geographical productivity was not so great as in the preceding era, since colonial conquests were less far-reaching than before, but for the single reign of Charles III there was almost as much in the way of geographical accounts and maps as at any time in the past. The names of Pérez, Heceta, Bodega, Ayala, Arteaga, López de Haro, Elisa, and Fidalgo are only a few of the many who commanded expeditions in the new world designed in part for the acquisition of geographical information, though with political motives involved as well. In 1797 the Depósito Hidrográfico was founded in Madrid to serve as a centre for the preparation and storing of maps. This institution published many notable maps of the various parts of Spain's colonies.

Philosophical studies were influenced by the current ideas of the age. At the outset educational institutions maintained what they termed the traditional doctrine, which was in fact no more than the dry bones of the past, serving only as a hindrance to the entry of anything new, even in the field which the philosophers pretended to represent. Men ambitious of knowledge resorted to the theories which then enjoyed high repute in countries considered as leaders in the world of thought, and even churchmen, who were usually among the more conservative elements, were influenced by such of the philosophic systems as seemed least dangerous to orthodox beliefs, — such as a certain sensationalism and experimentation in philosophy, — and they were even affected by an infiltration of encyclopedic ideas. This roused orthodox thinkers to an active reaction which produced many writings of a polemic character, although there may hardly be said to have been a veritable philosophic renaissance. It is interesting to note, however, that even those who combated the new ideas showed by their works that their own views were modified by them. Only one name stands out from the rest as worthy to be ranked with the great thinkers of other lands, that of the

Philosophy.

logician Andrés Piquer. In jurisprudence this was a particularly flourishing period, for juridical studies were more in keeping with the thought and propaganda in Europe at that time. The writings of Spaniards were directed to propagating or resisting the new juridical ideas, to the jurisdictional struggle between state and church, to the questions arising concerning the government of Spain and the reforms needed, and to the preparation of manuals for the teaching of law which the introduction of fresh materials

required. The same activity was displayed in the fields of economics and politics, as has already been pointed out. The greatest names in these branches were those of ministers of state like Campillo, Ward, Ensenada, Campomanes, Floridablanca, and Jovellanos, who distinguished themselves by their writings as well as by their acts in office. In the field of economics Spanish thinkers, while strongly influenced by the current physiocratic ideas, were not so completely given over to them as the economists of other countries; they inclined toward giving an equal consideration to industrial development, thus foreshadowing the ideas which were soon to become supreme.

Many factors contributed to make this a brilliant period in Spanish historical literature. Indeed, in this field of studies more than in any other Spaniards attained to renown, even though they fell short of the glorious achievements of the historians of the preceding era. The disputes arising from the various aspects of eighteenth century thought led men to look up precedents and to cite their authorities, while the frequency with which certain writers set forth false documents necessarily sharpened the instinct for criticism. A school of critics sprang up which attacked errors and false statements wherever they found them, although the intensity of religious life and the power of the church caused most of the historians to abstain from overthrowing such legends of a sacred character as had become firmly rooted in the popular mind. Gregorio Mayáns and the Jesuit Masdeu were among the leading exponents of this school. Books or articles on historical method were frequent, and most authors of histories were wont to express their views in the preface to their volumes. These writers, in addition to their exposition of the rules for criticism and style, displayed a broad concept as to the content of history, holding that it should be expressive of the civilizations of peoples. Thus, Masdeu entitled his history *Historia crítica de España y de la cultura española* (Critical history of Spain and of Spanish culture). While these ideas had been set forth by the great writers of the sixteenth century they were now predominantly held, both in Spain and in Europe generally. This was a great age for the collection and publication of documents. The already mentioned *España sagrada* was a noteworthy example. The new Academy of History began to perform noteworthy service in this regard. Numerous copies were made and abundant notes taken by writers like Burriel (real author of the *Noticia de la California*, or Account about California, ascribed to Venegas, though a prolific writer also on subjects having nothing to do with the Americas) and Muñoz (first archivist of the Archivo General de las Indias and author of an *Historia del nuevo mundo*, or History of the new world) whose materials still remain in great part unpublished. Reprints of old editions were brought out and foreign works translated, while vast gatherings of bibliographical data (in the shape of catalogues, dictionaries of various types of subject-matter, and regional or subject bibliographies) were made. Many works of original investigation were written, like those of Masdeu and Muñoz already cited, or the *Vida de Carlos III* (Life of Charles III) of Fernán-Núñez. A special group of legal and economic historians whose writings were very important in their bearings on the times might be made up. Martínez Marina was the principal historian of this class, although Burriel, Asso, Capmany, Jovellanos, Llorente, Cornejo, and Campomanes are worthy of mention. Literary history attracted the erudite. Among the works of this group were studies concerning the origin and history of the Castilian tongue, including the first dictionary of the language, published by the Academy (1726–1739), with a statement of the authorities for the sources of each word. Many of the writings

2 x

of the historians already named, besides those of numerous others, had some reference to the Americas, but the colonies themselves were the source of a prolific historical literature. Kino, Arlegui, Mota Padilla, Espinosa, Villa-Señor, Ortega, Burriel, Alegre, Baegert, Beaumont, Palou, Clavigero, Arricivita, Revilla Gigedo, and Cavo (all dealing with New Spain, or provinces of that viceroyalty) are only a few of the writers (most of them colonials) who left volumes which serve today as a rich source of materials and as an enduring monument to the names of their authors.

Neo-classic influences upon polite literature.

The regeneration of Spain made itself felt to a certain extent in the realm of polite literature, as well as in other forms of Spanish intellectual life. Cultivated men of letters were desirous of rescuing Spanish literature from the vices which had fastened upon it at the close of the seventeenth century, and they turned to the so-called neo-classic influences then dominant in western Europe, but represented more particularly by France. Ronsard, Montaigne, Corneille, and others had already begun to affect Spanish writers of the seventeenth century, and in the period of the Spanish Bourbons the works of Corneille, Racine, Marmontel, and Voltaire were offered to Spaniards in translation. The writings of other foreigners were in like manner made accessible, such as those of Alfieri, Young, and Milton. So devoted were the Spanish neo-classicists to their trans-Pyrenean models that they were unable to see any value in the great Spanish works of the *siglo de oro*, especially those of the dramatists. They went so far as to propose the expulsion of the national drama from the Spanish stage (except such works as could be arranged according to neo-classic tastes) and the substitution of plays from the French and Italian. Among their tenets were that of the three unities (of time, place, and action) and one which required that the action should be reduced to the amount of time it took to represent it. The greatest of the neo-classicists was Ignacio de Luzán, whose *Poética*, or Poetics (1737), was the highest and most creditable example of the doctrine of his school. Naturally, if only from motives of patriotism, a group of nationalistic authors sprang up in opposition to the neo-classicists and in defence of the Spanish literature of the preceding era, but the French influence was so strong that even this group was much affected by the precepts of the new school.   The public remained faithful to the national writers of the *siglo de oro*, whose plays formed the principal element in theatrical representations.   Abroad, Spanish writers of the golden age still enjoyed a repute which their countrymen were seeking to deny them.   English and German writers continued to translate or avail themselves of the works of Cervantes and the picaresque novels, while the *Gil Blas* of the Frenchman Lesage was a clear-cut, if brilliant, imitation of Spanish models.   The expulsion of the Jesuits, who took up their residence in Italy, helped to convert Italy from the Hispanophobe attitude which in company with France she had maintained with regard to Spanish literature, for the more learned Jesuits were able to demonstrate the false basis of this feeling, both by their own works, and by their exposition of the merits of the Spanish writers of the past.   The German Humboldt and the Frenchman Beaumarchais, both of them men of wide reputation, also took up cudgels in defence of Spain.

Despite the vigorous conflict of the two schools of literature, Spain was unable to produce writers who could rank with those of the *siglo de oro*.   Epic poetry practically did not exist; oratorical literature, whether secular or religious, was of slight account; and only one notable novel appeared in the century, the *Fray Gerundio* (Brother Gerund) of the Jesuit Isla.   This work, which aimed to ridicule the sacred oratory of the times, was nevertheless defective in that it introduced much material foreign to the narrative, but it was in excellent Spanish and teeming with witty passages. Both in this work, and in his translation of Lesage's *Gil Blas*, Isla won a place along with Feyjóo as one of the best writers of the day in the handling of Spanish prose.   There were several notable lyric poets, such as Meléndez Valdés, Nicolás Fernández de Moratín (usually termed Moratín rather than Fernández), the latter's son Leandro, and Quintana.   Except for the younger Moratín all belonged to the patriotic Spanish school.   Quintana, with his philanthropic

Achieve-ments of the era in polite literature.

and liberal note, his solemn, brilliant, and pompous style, and the rigidity and coldness of his classical rhetoric, was perhaps the most typical representative of the age. The most marked achievements in the field of *belles lettres* were in the drama.   At the beginning of the century Spanish theatres had been closed as the result of a moral wave which left only the great cities, like Madrid, Barcelona, Cádiz, and Valencia, with an opportunity to attend dramatical representations.   The entry of French influences and the polemics to which they gave rise led to a revival of the drama, until it became the favorite form of literature with both the public and the writers.   Only four dramatists may be said to have displayed unquestioned merits: García de la Huerta, who employed a mixture of the old Spanish methods with the newer French; the younger Moratín, the most distinguished representative of the French school; Ramón de la Cruz, who depicted the life of the Spanish people, and for the first time placed the customs of the Madrid proletariat on the Spanish stage; and González del Castillo, a worthy rival of the last-named in the same field.   This was an era of great actors, both men and women.

Conflict between the baroque and neo-classic styles in architecture and sculpture.

The fine arts experienced the same influences and were the subject of the same conflicts as occurred in the field of polite literature.   At the outset the baroque style in an even more exaggerated form than in the preceding era was the principal basis of architecture.   This was vanquished by the classical reaction, born in Italy, and coming to Spain by way of France.   The new art, called neo-classic, or pseudo-classic, endeavored to return to Roman and what were considered Greek elements, interpreting them with an artificial and academic correctness which was entirely lacking in sentiment and warmth.   The Academy of Fine Arts (*Bellas Artes de San Fernando*), established in the reign of Ferdinand VI, became the stronghold of the neo-classic school, and was able to make its views prevail, since it was the arbiter as to the style of public buildings and the dispenser of licenses to engage in the profession of architecture.   The museum of the Prado, Madrid, the work of Juan Villanueva, may be taken as an example of the neo-classic edifices. In sculpture the traditional use of painted wood remained a dominant factor throughout most of the century, although there were evidences presaging its abandonment. While some small figures representing popular types were made, the majority of the works of statuary were for the church, which was by far the most important customer of the sculptors. Some of the most notable results were those obtained in the groups for use in the *pasos*, or floats, carried in the processions of Holy Week. Especially meritorious were those of Salcillo, greatest of the baroque sculptors. The profuse ornamentation of baroque art helped to cause a continuance of the use of stone in sculpture, since it was difficult, with wood, to procure the effects of foliage. The baroque was soon swept away, however, in favor of the neo-classic style, of which Álvarez was the most distinguished exponent. The same influences, in both architecture and sculpture, operated in the Americas as in Spain. Both arts prospered more than they had in the past.

At the close of the seventeenth century Spanish painting had fallen away, until nothing of consequence was being done. A revival commenced with the accession of Philip V, but the results were not great. The entire era was filled with the dispute between French and Italian influences. In the reign of Charles III the German painter Mengs, who represented a kind of eclecticism which endeavored to combine the virtues of the masters in the various Italian schools of the great era, became the idol of Spanish artists and the arbiter of the Academy. No Spaniard, unless possibly Bayeu and Menéndez, is even worthy of mention, — with one glorious exception. Into an age of painting which had sunk to mediocrity, when artists were endeavoring to treat their themes only according to prescribed rules and manners, came Francisco José Goya (1746–1828), the greatest painter of his time and one of the greatest of all history, deserving of a place with Velázquez, El Greco, and Murillo, perhaps ranking ahead of the two last-named in the list of superb exponents of the pictorial art whom Spain has given to the world. The keynote of his work was the free expression

Medioc-rity of Spanish painting in this era.

Greatness of Goya.

of his own personality, unhampered by convention. A thorough-going realism, both in subject-matter and in manner of treatment, was a distinctive feature of his painting, which sought to represent character, movement, and life. Even his religious pictures set forth matters as his own eyes saw them, resulting in the anachronism of scenes from sacred history in which the figures and the atmosphere were Spanish of Goya's day. He was a most prolific painter, leaving a vast number of portraits, ranging from those of members or groups of the royal family from Charles III to Ferdinand VII (notably the family of Charles IV) to persons of lesser note, some religious paintings (which are not so convincing as his other works), an exceptionally large number of scenes depicting popular customs (an invaluable collection, in which respect Goya was at his best), the stirringly patriotic pictures of the *Dos de Mayo* in 1808 and the executions of the following day, and the two remarkable *majas* (the one dressed and the other nude, each being the same person in the same attitude). Hundreds of his cartoons are still in existence, many of them exhibiting such freedom from convention and such unrestraint as to have shocked his contemporaries and many others ever since. Withal he was a most brilliant, clear, and harmonious colorist, able to get audacious effects which were extraordinary in his day, a forerunner of the modern schools. It is worthy of note that the Americas stepped forth in this period to supply several notable artists comparable with those of the age in Spain, Goya excepted.

The industrial arts. As for the various lesser arts of an industrial character, such as the making of furniture, articles of gold and silver, rich fabrics, and vases, the same succession of baroque and neo-classic styles is to be noted. Thus the furniture of the earlier years affected twisted and grotesque forms, while it was later shaped upon stiltedly correct lines. The azulejos industry remained in existence, making use of blue, yellow, green, and occasionally rose. Gold work was of scant importance, but the making of tapestries was rather notable; they were combined with the paintings of leading artists, many of which were supplied by Goya.

In the realm of music the realistic and popular indigenous type had to contend against the Italian school. The latter found favor at court and among the erudite, but the national product held its own with the people, appearing especially in the plays of dramatists of the Spanish school, such as Ramón de la Cruz. Some of the native songs were mythological or idyllic in character, but usually they were satirical or funny, interwoven with popular melodies and even with the musical cries with which street vendors called out their wares, admirably adapted to the realistic plays in which they were sung. It was to the national Spanish music that the great foreign masters looked, and this, therefore, was able to contribute notably to the progress of the art; Mozart and Rossini were among the composers affected by Spanish influences. Despite the construction at this time of magnificent organs, religious music in Spain remained in a state of corruption and decay. The guitar continued to be the favorite musical instrument.

Spanish music.

CHAPTER XXXIX

THE GROWTH OF LIBERALISM, 1808–1898

The
Spanish
American
wars of
inde-
pendence
and the
virtual
comple-
tion of
Spain's
gift to the
Americas.

WITH the outbreak of the Spanish "War of Independence" against Napoleon the interest of Spain proper as affecting the Americas almost if not wholly ceased. Her gift to the new world was by this time complete except as regards the island dependencies of the West Indies and the Philippines in the Far East. She was still to have important relations with the Americas, such as her vain endeavor to suppress the revolutions of her colonies and her relations with the United States concerning Florida and Cuba, but those matters belong to the field of Hispanic American history rather than to that of Spain as conceived in the present work. In 1808 the news of the accession of Joseph Bonaparte to the throne of Spain, after Napoleon had wrested the abdication of their rights from Charles IV and Ferdinand VII, was received in the colonies with hostile demonstrations, for the majority of Spanish Americans were loyal to Ferdinand. When in 1809 all the peninsula seemed lost, many began to hold to the view that relations with Spain, which had always been rather with the king than with the nation, were severed, and in the next year certain regions set up governments of their own, thus starting the movement for independence which ended only with the battle of Ayacucho in 1824.[1] Circumstances, skilfully directed by separatist leaders, had led the Americas to proceed out of what was at first a feeling of patriotism to the royal government to what eventually resulted in embittered wars against it. The wars were fought largely, though not wholly, by

[1] There were some relatively unimportant combats after this date. and Spain did not acknowledge defeat until 1836.

the colonists themselves, one faction supporting the newly constituted governmental machinery in the Americas, and the other following the lead of the changing national régimes in Spain, — just as if the war of the American Revolution had been a conflict of Whigs and Tories. It becomes pertinent, then, to enquire why Spain did not make a more strenuous effort to overcome the rebellions in her colonies, which she had always regarded as vital to her, and why she did not seriously attempt to reconquer them in the course of the nineteenth century. The answer lies in a statement of the internal affairs of Spain, who went through one of the most trying periods in the annals of the peninsula, characterized by an incessant recurrence of disturbances and even civil war. For Spain herself, however, it was a period of advance along Liberal lines. Spain gained, though it cost her an empire.

The years 1808 to 1814 are almost the only time in the century to which Spaniards may look back with satisfaction and pride, but the glory of their war against Napoleon may well be regarded by them as compensation for their losses and degradation in other respects. It took several weeks for the news of the treachery of Bayonne, followed by the events of the *Dos de Mayo*, to circulate throughout Spain. When at last the people comprehended what had happened, a wild outburst of rage against the French swept the peninsula. Between May 24 and June 10 every region in the country rose in arms against the invaders, each district acting independently, but all actuated by the same motives. As an English writer (Oman) has expressed it : "The movement was spontaneous, unselfish, and reckless; in its wounded pride, the nation challenged Napoleon to combat, without any thought of the consequences, without counting up its own resources or those of the enemy." *Juntas*, or governing groups, for the various provinces hastily constituted themselves and prepared for the conflict. There were some 100,000 widely scattered Spanish troops, between men of the regular army and the militia, but they were almost wholly unfit to take the field, and as events proved were badly officered. Against them were about 117,000 French soldiers

Patriotic Spanish uprising against Napoleon.

in the peninsula (including 28,000 in Portugal), and though these were far from equalling Napoleon's best military units they were vastly superior in every technical respect to the Spaniards. If it had been a mere question of armies in the field there could have been no doubt as to the outcome in the shape of a decisive French victory, but something was going on in Spain which Napoleon had never dreamed of and seemed unable to understand; in a land stirred by the furor of patriotism such as had permeated all Spain the ordinary rules of military science had to be left in abeyance. Napoleon thought that all was over, when things were just about to begin; flying patrols here and there, a species of mounted police, would be enough, he believed, in addition to the existing garrisons, to keep the peninsula under control. It was of a piece with this estimate that he should send General Dupont with a column of 13,000 men, later reinforced up to 22,000, to effect the conquest of Andalusia. Dupont found, what other French commanders were to learn after him, that the only land he could conquer was that actually occupied at a given time by his soldiers; the country in his rear rose behind him as surely as the armies before him stood ready at the first opportunity to oppose his advance. Getting into a difficult position at Baylén, he surrendered to the Spanish general, Castaños, on June 23, with 18,000 men. In less than two months the disorganized Spanish forces had been able to strike a blow such as French arms had not received for nine years. Meanwhile, Joseph Bonaparte, who had been designated by Napoleon for the crown of Spain as early as in the month of March, had been offered the throne on May 13 by the French-dominated *Junta* of the Regency, of Madrid, and on June 15 at Bayonne by a deputation of Spanish nobles who had been ordered to go there for precisely that purpose. Joseph had entered Madrid in July, but the capitulation of Baylén caused him to leave that city and retire with most of his forces behind the Ebro. Thus had the patriots won in their first trial of arms, and the moral effect of the victory made it certain, henceforth, that the Spaniards would fight to the end.

It is not necessary to go into the details of the six year

conflict, which ended only with the fall of Napoleon in 1814, although the French had been expelled from Spain by the close of the preceding year. English historians, with a pardonable pride, have been wont to make it appear that this achievement was primarily a British feat of arms under the leadership of Sir Arthur Wellesley, the later Duke of Wellington, and, to be sure, English history does not record a more brilliant series of campaigns than that of the so-called Peninsula War. It is unlikely that the Spaniards, unaided, could have driven the French from Spain, for their armies almost invariably proved unable to defeat the enemy in the open field, even though they displayed fanatical courage in the defence of their homes, — as witness the two sieges of Saragossa, desperately resisted by General Palafox, and the stubborn opposition of General Álvarez in Gerona to the French, who had to waste 20,000 men to take that post. On the other hand Wellington's victories would have been impossible but for the indirect aid of the Spanish soldiery. Speaking of the situation at the close of the year 1810 Oman says: "Enormous as was the force — over 300,000 men — which the Emperor had thrown into Spain, it was still not strong enough to hold down the conquered provinces and at the same time to attack Portugal [where the British army was stationed]. For this fact the Spaniards must receive due credit; it was their indomitable spirit of resistance which enabled Wellington, with his small Anglo-Portuguese army, to keep the field against such largely superior numbers. No sooner had the French concentrated, and abandoned a district, than there sprang up in it a local Junta and a ragged apology for an army. Even where the invaders lay thickest, along the route from Bayonne to Madrid, guerilla bands maintained themselves in the mountains, cut off couriers and escorts, and often isolated one French army from another for weeks at a time. The great partisan chiefs, such as Mina in Navarre, Julian Sanchez in Leon, and Porlier in the Cantabrian hills, kept whole brigades of the French in constant employment. Often beaten, they were never destroyed, and always reappeared to strike some daring blow at the point where they were least expected.

Half the French army was always employed in the fruitless task of guerilla-hunting. This was the secret which explains the fact that, with 300,000 men under arms, the invaders could never concentrate more than 70,000 to deal with Wellington." This is a fair statement of the general situation throughout the war. It would seem that the Spaniards accounted for rather more than half of the French troops, even when practically every province of the kingdom was theoretically occupied by the enemy. In so doing they rendered a service not only to themselves but also to Europe, for they detached enough troops from the main body of Napoleon's armies to enable the allies to swing the balance against the emperor in his northern European campaigns. Incidentally it was quite evident that Spain could give scant attention to her American colonies while fighting for her very existence as an independent nation; indeed, it was not until 1815 that Spain turned to a consideration of the American wars.

Spanish government in the early years of the war and the calling of the *Cortes*.

Meanwhile, events of a political nature had been going on in Spain which were to determine the whole course of Spanish history in the nineteenth century. It was several months after the original outbreak before the various local *juntas* were able to agree upon a supreme authority during the enforced absence of Ferdinand VII, who was regarded as the legitimate king. Late in September the somewhat unwieldy *Junta Central* of at first twenty-four, afterward thirty-five, members was created, sitting at Aranjuez. Two months later when Napoleon himself advanced upon the capital the *Junta* fled to Seville, and joining with the *junta* of that city remained in session there for over a year. It was there that the *Junta* declared, in January, 1809, that the overseas possessions of Spain were an integral part of the kingdom, refuting the colonial claim of a connection merely through the crown. Driven out again by the French the *Junta* took refuge in Cádiz, where, in January, 1810, it appointed a Regency of five men to arrange for the calling of a *Cortes* representative of Spain and the Americas. The *Junta* thereupon resigned. Fearful of the radical tone that a *Cortes* might adopt, the Regency postponed its summons as long as it could, but at last issued the call, and the *Cortes* met in September, 1810. Very little was known at the time as to the exact status and powers of the various *Cortes* of earlier centuries, but nothing was more certain than that the *Cortes* of 1810 was like no other which had ever met in the peninsula. It was a single chamber body, designed to consist of elected deputies from the towns with a traditional right of representation, from the provincial *juntas*, from groups of 50,000 population, and from the Americas. Since the American deputies could not arrive in time, and since a still greater number of Spanish deputies could not be chosen by the complicated elective machinery provided, with the land mostly in the possession of the French, their places were supplied by persons from those regions happening to be resident in Cádiz. Thus the *Cortes* came to be made up of men who did not in fact reflect the conservative temperament of the interior districts, but, rather, stood for the radical views of the people of the coast. Most of them dreamed of founding a representative body which should combine the supposed virtues of the French Revolutionary Assembly with those of the British House of Commons and the earlier *Cortes* of the peninsula kingdoms.

One of the earliest acts of the *Cortes* was to accept the resignation of the conservative Regency and to appoint a new body of three of that name responsible and subservient to the *Cortes*. Soon the *Cortes* declared itself to be the legislative power, and turned over the executive and judicial authority to the Regency, following this up by declaring itself to have sovereign power in the absence of the king. When it became clear that these measures, which were bitterly opposed by the church and the other conservative elements, were also distasteful to Ferdinand, the *Cortes* decided that all acts or agreements of the king during his captivity were to be regarded as invalid. The greatest innovation of all, however, was the famous constitution of 1812. Under a belief that they were returning to the system of the past the members of the *Cortes* broke sharply from all the precedents of Spanish history, enthroning the people through their representatives, and relegating the crown

The Liberal Cortes of 1810 and the constitution of 1812.

and the church to a secondary place in the state. Among the several hundred items of this ultra-democratic document were the following : sovereignty was declared to rest with the people, to whom, therefore, was reserved the right of legislation ; the laws were to be made through the popularly elected *Cortes;* the king was to be the executive, but was prevented from doing much on his own initiative by the requirement that his decrees should be countersigned by the ministers of state, who were responsible to the *Cortes;* all Spaniards in both hemispheres were declared a part of the Spanish nation ; all Spanish men over twenty-five years of age were entitled to vote for members of the *Cortes,* of whom there was to be one for each group of 60,000 people ; various paragraphs included a Bill of Rights, a complicated elective machinery, and the abolition of exemptions from taxation. In only one respect did a conservative tone appear in the document, — the Catholic faith was declared to be the religion of Spain, and the exercise of any other was forbidden. Nevertheless, both before and after the adoption of the constitution, the *Cortes* had shown itself to be distinctly anti-clerical, as witness its overthrow of the Inquisition, its restriction of the number of religious communities, and the expulsion of the papal nuncio when he protested against some of these laws. It was not by their workings in practice, however, that the constitution and the laws of the *Cortes* became important ; rather it was that they constituted a program which became the war-cry of the democratic faction in Spain for years to come. The constitution of 1812 eventually got to be regarded as if it would be the panacea for all the ills of mankind, and was fervently proclaimed by glib orators, who could not have stated the exact nature of its provisions.

Despotic rule of Ferdinand VII and the revolution of 1820.

Early in 1814 Ferdinand VII was freed by Napoleon, and allowed to return to Spain. It was inevitable that he should adopt a reactionary policy, toward which his own inclinations, the attitude of other continental monarchs, and the overwhelming majority of the clergy, nobles, and the people themselves of Spain impelled him. He had hardly reached the peninsula when he declared the constitution of 1812 and the decrees of the *Cortes* of no effect.   This was followed by the arrest of the Liberal deputies and by the beginning of a series of persecutions.   All might have been well, but the personal character of the rancorous, cruel, disloyal, ungrateful, and unscrupulous king and the blindness of the absolutists drove the reaction to extremes.   Ferdinand not only restored absolutism, but also attempted to undo the enlightened work of Charles III for the economic and intellectual betterment of the people.   Liberalism in every form was crushed, and in accomplishing it such ferocious severity was displayed that the government of Ferdinand was discredited both at home and abroad, even in countries where the reactionary spirit was strongest.   Back of the established forms of the restored absolutism stood the unofficial *camarilla* (small room), or "kitchen cabinet," of the king's intimate friends, but back of all was the king.   So suspicious was Ferdinand that more than thirty royal secretaries, or ministers, were dismissed from office between 1814 and 1820, and dismissal was usually accompanied by a sentence of exile or imprisonment.   Periodical literature of a political character was suppressed, although the bars began to be let down for magazines of a scientific or literary type.   Despite the rigors of the administration — in a measure because of them — there were insurrections each year from 1814 to 1817, all led by military chieftains of Liberal ideas.   They were put down, for in no case was there a popular uprising; the people were as yet little affected by the new doctrines. Meanwhile, secret plots against the government were fostered, in part as the result of Spanish American influences which desired to prevent the sending of troops to suppress the revolutions of the new world, but more largely related to the Liberal ideal in Spain.   This activity seems mainly to have been the work of societies of Freemasons, in which military men were strongly represented.   Many other elements had also become pro-Liberal by this time, including prominent representatives of the middle class, almost all of the patriots who had organized the resistance to the French in 1808, and the young men of education.   The storm broke when orders were given in 1819 for the assembling of an army at Cádiz for the extremely unpopular service of the wars in the Americas. Colonel Riego raised the standard of revolt on January 1, 1820, proclaiming the constitution of 1812. The government seemed paralyzed by the outbreak. Uncertain what to do it waited. Then late in February the example set by Riego was followed in the larger cities of northern Spain. The king at once yielded, and caused an announcement to be made that he would summon a *Cortes* immediately and would swear his adhesion to the constitution of 1812. Thus, without a battle, it seemed as if the revolution had triumphed.

In July, 1820, the *Cortes* met. Its earliest measures aimed to restore the legislation of the *Cortes* of 1810, together with other laws of a similar character. The *Cortes* of 1820 has been charged with being anti-clerical, as indeed it was, for the church was the most serious opponent of Liberalism, still able to dominate the opinions of the masses. Notwithstanding all it accomplished, the *Cortes* of 1820 satisfied nobody. Like most new-born democracies Spain found herself splitting on the rock of divergent opinions. The Liberals broke up into various well-defined groups: the Radicals felt that the *Cortes* had been too moderate and cautious; the Moderates found the new laws dangerously radical; still others wished for a reform of the constitution in the direction of yet greater moderation than most of the Moderates desired. These were only a few of the groups to spring up. Meanwhile, the king and the absolutists, who had never intended to abide by the revolution, began to turn these divisions to account. Armed bands favorable to the king were formed, while others representing other factions also came into existence, and a state of anarchy ensued. The crisis was settled from abroad, however. From the first, Ferdinand had sent appeals to the reactionary kings of Europe, representing himself to be a prisoner, much as Louis XVI had been at the outbreak of the French Revolution. At length his appeals were listened to, and France, Russia, Austria, and Prussia joined together to restore matters to the situation they were in prior to 1820. It was as a result of this decision that a French army invaded the peninsula in the spring of 1823. No effective resistance was offered; indeed, the country seemed rather to second the French efforts and to facilitate their advance. No better proof could be furnished that the revolution of 1820 did not represent the sentiment of the people; the masses were yet steeped in ignorance and weighed down by traditional influences, so that they rejected a system intended for their benefit in favor of one which had lost even the benevolent disposition of the eighteenth-century Bourbons; the intellectual elements which had promoted the revolution had shown an incapacity to face realities or to compromise with the full meed of their ideals. Thus had the revolution of 1810 been re-enacted. The example was to be many times repeated in the course of the next two generations. The constitution and the laws of the *Cortes* were abolished, and savage persecution of Liberalism began. From 1823 to 1829 the political history of Spain was a series of alternations between terrorism and a relaxation of coercive measures, according as one group or another prevailed with the king, but the dominant note was at all times that of absolutism. It is to be noted that Spain had scarcely had a moment's respite from domestic difficulties since the invasion of Napoleon in 1808. In the meantime, between 1810 and 1824, the American colonies of the mainland had seized their opportunity to separate from the mother country forever.

Reactionary as Ferdinand had shown himself to be, he did not go far enough to suit the extremists in the absolutist faction headed by the king's brother Don Carlos (Charles). This group soon formed a party, which believed that its principles could be secured only through the accession of Don Carlos to the throne, wherefore its members came to be known as Carlists. The king was childless and in feeble health, but the hopes of the Carlists received a setback when in 1829 he married again. The new queen, María Cristina of Naples, was reactionary by instinct, but was forced by Carlist opposition to lean toward the Liberal faction in order to find some element on which she could depend for support. As it soon became clear that she was about to give birth to a child, the chances of Don Carlos' succession were gone in

María Cristina and the Carlist wars.

2 κ

case the infant should prove to be a boy, but the Carlists relied upon the so-called Spanish Salic Law of Philip V to exclude the enthronement of a girl. The exigencies of the political situation in 1713 had led Philip V to declare that the male line should always succeed to the Spanish throne. In 1789 Charles IV in agreement with the *Cortes* abrogated the law, but the decision seems not to have been published. To meet every contingency Cristina persuaded Ferdinand in 1830 to publish the law of 1789. Henceforth the struggle turned on the question of the validity of the law of 1789. In October, 1830, Cristina gave birth to a daughter, María Isabel, who was crowned as Queen Isabel, or Isabella II, with her mother as regent, on the death of the king in 1833. This was the signal for the outbreak of the Carlist wars, fought principally in the north and east of Spain, where the party of Don Carlos had a strong following. Meanwhile, a Liberal policy had been inaugurated, but in the main it was of a half-hearted type, for Cristina was both illiberal by temperament and unreliable in government; she would promise reforms, only to withdraw them, and would perhaps re-enact them in the very next breath. Nevertheless, the period of her regency was one of distinct gain for the principle of limited monarchy. A wider and wider circle of the people came to believe in that ideal, the *Cortes* met frequently, Liberal legislation was passed which was not to be so lightly tossed aside as formerly, and the constitutional principle was definitely established. To be sure, the same divisions as before tore the Liberal element asunder, and even led to insurrections at the very time that the Carlist wars were in their most dangerous stage; Spain still had a long road to travel to achieve democracy. The most important piece of legislation was the constitution of 1837, overthrowing the impossible instrument of 1812, though agreeing with it in many respects, including its recognition of the sovereignty of the people, and establishing a *Cortes* of two houses, with an absolute veto by the crown, and a restricted suffrage, — a compromise between the position of the Moderates, or conservative element of the Liberals, and that of the Progressives, or radicals. Neither party was satisfied, and as

Progress of Liberalism.

a working instrument the constitution was not long-lived, but henceforth this, and not the idolized 1812 document, was to serve as a basis in constitution making. The year 1837 marked the first appearance in power of Espartero, who had distinguished himself as a general in the war against the Carlists, thus beginning an era in which successful military men were to be the virtual rulers of Spain, more or less under constitutional forms, but in reality depending upon the army as the only force which all elements would recognize. Espartero's credit reached still higher when he was able to bring the Carlist war to a close in 1840, following his negotiations with the leading enemy generals. In the same year, Cristina, who had long maintained a precarious hold on the regency as a result of her insincerity and her affiliations with the Moderates, was at length compelled to abdicate. Espartero stepped into the breach, becoming regent in 1841, and for another two years maintained himself as a veritable dictator, but proclaiming Liberal principles, fighting the Moderates, defending himself against the intrigues of Cristina, and resisting the Progressives, who were dissatisfied with his policy or jealous of his preponderance. In 1843 the storm broke, and Espartero fled to England.

Rule of Espartero.

The overthrow of Espartero had been accomplished by a combination of the extreme conservative and the radical elements, which aimed to prevent the recurrence of a regency by illegally proclaiming the thirteen-year-old Isabella II to be of age. Such widely divergent groups could not long remain harmonious, and the conservatives were soon in the saddle. The twenty-five year period of Isabella's active reign, from 1843 to 1868, was one in which reactionary forces were almost constantly in control under constitutional forms. Except for the discredited Carlists, who engaged in several minor outbreaks during these years, no party stood frankly for absolutism, although that form of government was in fact the wish of many and the virtual type of rule employed. The real master was, not the queen, but the army through its generals. The saving factor in the situation was that the latter were not united; while certain of them were ultra-reactionary, others were Liberal, though

Isabella II and the rule of the generals.

none of those who attained to power went the lengths of the radicals. In the numerous ministries of the era an occasional non-military individual was at the head of the state, — such as the reactionary González Bravo, or the clerically backed Bravo Murillo, but the terms of these and other civilian ministers were brief. The two principal rulers of the times

Narváez and O'Donnell.

were General Narváez and General O'Donnell. Narváez, who had won notoriety for his severity against the Carlists, was six times in office (1844–1846, 1846 again, 1847–1851, 1856–1857, 1864–1865, and 1866–1868). It became the habit of the queen to send for him whenever the monarchy was in danger, not only because he could control the army, but also because he invariably struck hard and successfully against Liberalism at the same time that he upheld constitutional government, though disregarding its mandates as suited his pleasure. Execution or exile followed swiftly where Narváez was displeased with an individual. Meanwhile, he made meritorious reforms which tended to restore good order and check anarchy, such as his success in stamping out brigandage and revolution. The ability of this despotic veteran was well displayed when he saved Spain from the storm which shook other European thrones in 1848. O'Donnell, who came into prominence in the temporarily successful Liberal revolution of 1854, was three times in office (1856, 1858–1863, 1865–1866), once holding power for five years. While far more liberal than Narváez he was a staunch supporter of the Bourbons. He sought to divert public attention from domestic affairs by laying stress upon foreign policy, as witness his well-advertised refusal to sell Cuba to the United States, his plans to join France in the latter's intervention in Mexico, and especially his engaging in a war with Morocco (1859–1860). The chief political result of

Rise of General Prim.

the war was to make a popular hero of General Prim, a man of Liberal tendencies and of less resolute devotion than O'Donnell to the Bourbons. Prim was the third of the great military figures who, together, explain this era. Beside them

Character of the queen.

must be considered the queen. The former regent, María Cristina, had not been free from charges of immorality, but her daughter Isabella was notorious for her bad conduct.

Furthermore, she was perfidious, selfish, superstitious, and lacking in principle. Withal she was devoutly religious. The result was that her opinions were swayed by her numerous transitory lovers or by her confessors, and ministries rose and fell according to the dictates of the *camarilla*. Even O'Donnell declared it was impossible to govern under her, for no dependence could be placed upon her word.

The character of the period was reflected in the new constitutions which were drawn up. The constitution of 1845 included the following provisions: the introduction of a property qualification, narrowing the franchise of those electing deputies to the *Cortes;* the nomination of senators by the crown; life tenure of senators; the packing of the senate with grandees, ecclesiastics, successful soldiers, and financial magnates, — reactionary elements; emphasis on the recognition of the Catholic Church as the established religion; an assent to the theory of the sovereignty of the people, but in such an attenuated form as to deprive the right of its vitality; restrictions on the freedom of the press; and the reduction of the national militia — the hope of Liberalism — to an innocuous state by making it subject to the central executive. The church was strengthened still further upon the fall of Narváez in 1851, for, reactionary though he was, he did not go far enough in ecclesiastical matters to suit the clergy. The brief term in office of their candidate, Bravo Murillo, resulted in the restoration of part of their former endowment as a result of the concordat of 1851, but their acceptance of this document was denounced by the Carlists and absolutists in general, including the pseudo-constitutional reactionaries, as a betrayal of the cause for which the churchmen had stood. Bravo Murillo proposed a constitution in 1852 which amounted to a virtual abrogation of parliamentary government, granting the crown the right to enact the budget by royal decree and to propose legislation which must be accepted or rejected by the *Cortes* without amendment, together with other provisions of a like character. It was Narváez who pointed out to the queen that the Bravo constitution would result in disaster to the government, and the instrument was only productive

Constitutional changes in the reign of Isabella II.

of its proposer's fall. During the period of Liberal control, from 1854 to 1856, at which time Espartero returned to head the ministry, a fresh constitution was presented to the *Cortes* in 1855. The former provision for life senators was abolished; financial control was vested in the *Cortes*, which was to meet at least once a year; liberty of the press was granted; and it was decided that nobody should be persecuted for his religious views contrary to the Catholic faith, provided he should not manifest them publicly. The constitution of 1855 remained an ideal only, for the *Cortes* separated without promulgating it. In the next year O'Donnell brought about a restoration of the constitution of 1845, with added enactments providing for the control of national finances by the *Cortes* and for an elected senate. When Narváez returned to power late in the same year, he caused such reform measures of the Liberals as had not already been done away with to be rescinded, and reinforced the constitution of 1845.

Revolution of General Prim and dethronement of Isabella II.

Nevertheless, very important gains were made for democracy in this period, in addition to the recognition of the constitutional principle. Most vital of all was that a large proportion of the people had now joined with the intellectual class among the civilian element in a desire for a more liberal government. The reaction had at first been welcomed as assuring the country of peace, but the promise was not fulfilled. Insurrections soon began to occur on behalf of Liberalism, and people got to believe that there would be no security from anarchy until the policies of that party triumphed. The Liberal opposition more and more directed its attacks against the queen, whose instability of character seemed to preclude the attainment, or at least the continued practice, of any political ideal. Prim at length became convinced that the dynasty must be swept away, and headed an unsuccessful revolution in 1866. The queen's position was steadily weakened, however. Radical newspapers had been founded which exposed her immorality, and the government was unable to suppress these publications. The deaths of O'Donnell in 1867 and of Narváez in 1868 were also fatal to her. The last-named was succeeded by González Bravo, who had held the leadership of the ministry from 1843 to 1844, only to lose it because he was not a soldier, and could not control the army. This time he proposed to defeat the generals, and sought to do so by banishing all of them known to hold Liberal views. But the generals returned with Prim at their head, though Serrano was the nominal leader. At last the blow had fallen, and as the year 1868 drew toward a close the long, corrupt reign of Isabella II came to an end with the dethronement of the queen. The first question now to resolve was that of the type of government to be established. This was left to the *Cortes*, which voted for a continuance of monarchy; it is significant of the advance of democratic ideas that 71 votes in a total of 285 favored the establishment of a republic. The next problem was to find a monarch. Prince after prince was approached, but it seemed as if nobody cared to be king of Spain. Leopold of Hohenzollern consented to become king, but later withdrew his candidacy, and it was this trifling incident which served as the occasion, hardly the cause, for the outbreak of war in 1870 between France and Prussia. Finally, after a search which had lasted two years, the Duke of Aosta, Amadeo of Savoy, gave a reluctant consent. On the very day when Amadeo touched Spanish soil, December 30, 1870, General Prim died of wounds received a few days before from a band of assassins. It meant that the new king (who was crowned a few days later, in January, 1871) was to lack the support of the only individual who might have saved him from the difficulties of his position.

Amadeo found himself king in a country where he had no party. At his accession there were three well-defined groups, the Alfonsists, the Republicans, and the Carlists. The first-named favored the principle of limited monarchy, under Alfonso of Bourbon, son of Isabella II. This party as yet had a meagre following, owing to the hatred of her family which Isabella had inspired among Spaniards. Republicanism was loudly proclaimed, but was untried and not trusted. The Carlist faction, standing for absolutism as well as for the accession of the heir of the earlier Don Carlos,

Troubled reign of Amadeo of Savoy.

was by all odds the strongest group of the day. Its backbone was the clergy, who were especially influential in the country districts of the north and east. They were deeply offended by the choice of a monarch from the House of Savoy, which had just occupied the last remnant of the Papal States and made the pope a "prisoner of the Vatican." They also feared that the new government might withdraw its financial support of the church, leaving them to the uncertain contributions of the faithful. Carlism was aided by the disintegration of the regular army, growing out of Prim's promise to abolish compulsory service, a policy which the Republicans included in their program, although no definite enactment to this effect was made. The morale of the army was thus destroyed, depriving the state of its only sure resort, disgusting the officers, and leading to a renewal of brigandage, anarchy, and an aggressive type of socialism. Altogether there was a recrudescence of grave disorder. There were six changes in ministry and three general elections in two years. At last Amadeo was told that he must suspend the constitution and rule with an iron hand. This he refused to do, seizing the first opportunity which offered to resign his crown, leaving the country once more without a king, in February, 1873.

The Spanish republic.

The Republicans now had their innings, but the time could hardly have been worse for the trial of their ideas. The Carlists had under arms a force of 45,000 men in 1873, which swelled to 75,000 by the close of 1875. The south received the proclamation of the republic with a resort to self-governing, jealous particularism, as if the day of democratic *taifa* states had dawned, for they were able to agree on one thing alone, — that of refusing to pay taxes to the central government. One Figueras had been proclaimed *ad interim* president until a *Cortes* could be elected, but he became terrified by the republic when he saw it, and fled before the *Cortes* could meet. There were three more presidents in 1873. Pi y Margall was a federalist who believed that the newly won freedom would provide a remedy for the prevailing disorder, — but it did not. He was therefore put aside, and Salmerón, a unitary Republican, took the helm. Salmerón initiated vigorous measures to crush the forces of disintegration, but, as he was about to succeed, drew back before the fear of militarism. Castelar was put in his place, and he revived the army. This measure strengthened the central authority, but it killed Republicanism, which had made the abolition of enforced military service one of the cardinal tenets of its creed. It was now only a question of time before the Alfonsists would take control. Carlists of constitutional leanings went over to that side as did many Republicans, since it now seemed clear that the accession of Alfonso was the only alternative to the enthronement of the Carlist representative. In December, 1874, Alfonso issued a proclamation, promising an amnesty and constitutional government. With hardly a struggle the republic fell.

The reign of Alfonso XII (1874–1885) marked the beginning of a new era, based upon the acceptance of pseudo-democracy under constitutional forms, and accompanied by a growing tendency toward internal peace. Minor outbreaks in Spain, now of Carlists, now of Republicans, continued to require military attention down to 1886, but no such disorder as had so long been the rule again prevailed. A new constitution was promulgated in 1876 which had the effect of conciliating the clergy, since it provided for state support of the church, although that institution did not receive all it had been promised; indeed, it protested bitterly against the grant of toleration to other faiths. The constitution of 1876, which with some modifications is still operative, was patterned after that of 1845, with the addition of certain of the more recent reforms. Some of its provisions were the following: the *Cortes* was to be composed of two houses, respectively the senate and the congress; the senate was to contain eighty members in their own right, such as princes of the royal family, grandees, presidents of the great councils, archbishops, and captain-generals, one hundred more by royal appointment, and one hundred and eighty elected for a term of five years by municipal and provincial assemblies, universities, and taxpayers of the highest class; congress was to be made up of 431 deputies, representing

Alfonso XII and the establishment of a conservative monarchy.

districts of 50,000 people each, chosen by an electorate which was limited by the imposition of a property qualification, — changed in 1889 by the restoration of universal manhood suffrage; legislative power was vested in the *Cortes* with the king; the king was made irresponsible, but his decrees had to be countersigned by a responsible minister; and the jury system was abolished, — although it was restored early in the next reign. The net result was a centralized monarchy in the control of the conservative elements. Many principles of the Liberal program, taken especially from the constitution of 1869 when Prim was in power, have since been added. The death of the king, who had ruined his health as the result of excesses which recalled the scandals of his mother's reign, seemed likely to raise fresh difficulties at the close of the year 1885. The queen was then pregnant, and it was not until 1886 that her son, the present Alfonso XIII, was born. The ex-queen, Isabella II, attempted to intervene, but only succeeded in strengthening the position of the queen-mother, María Cristina of Austria, who ruled henceforth as regent until Alfonso attained his majority in 1902.

The war of 1898 and disappearance of Spain as a colonial power.

It was primarily in Spain's colonial policy that the evils of the old era continued. The lesson of the Spanish American wars of independence had not taught Spain how to govern her few remaining colonies. Indeed, corrupt methods were if anything worse than before, as the opportunities for engaging in them became fewer. Spanish civilians in Cuba preyed upon the island, and political office there was reserved for those seeking reward for party service at home. A revolution broke out in 1868 which lasted ten years. The government then made promises which were not fulfilled, and a second uprising occurred, but it was severely put down. Once again there was a revolution, in 1895. This time the United States intervened, and in the brief war of 1898 Cuba became independent, and Porto Rico and the Philippines passed over to the United States. Thus was the last vestige of Spain's trans-Atlantic dominion swept away. This was the final stroke in a century of disasters. And yet the total result was one of internal progress for Spain. She had paid a heavy price in her gropings for liberty, but she had reached a stage which, while not yet satisfactory, was incomparably ahead of that with which she had begun the century.

CHAPTER XL

THE DAWN OF A NEW DAY, 1898–1917

Revival of economic prosperity.

SPANIARDS are in the habit of discussing their recent national development with reference to the year 1898, which is recognized as a turning-point in Spanish life, a change held by them to have been decidedly for the better. Nevertheless, the way had begun to be prepared with the accession of Alfonso XII to the throne; the splendid monument to that king in the Retiro at Madrid can be explained only on the ground that he symbolizes the re-establishment of good order in the peninsula, with a government based on what the Spanish people will stand, rather than on the full meed of an unworkable ideal. The country was tired of domestic strife, and asked only to be left in peace, with an opportunity to give attention to its material resources. This wish the government granted, and all Spain profited. Roads, railways, and irrigation ditches were built, and mining and the wine trade developed, while more recent times have witnessed a notable industrial growth in some of the northern cities. These matters were left very largely in the hands of foreigners, with Spaniards either wasting their blood and treasure in the colonies, or merely failing to participate in the economic enterprises of the peninsula. After 1898, however, Spaniards began to join with Englishmen, Germans, and Frenchmen in investing their capital in Spain. Many evils remained to be overcome, but the country recuperated to such an extent that its present wealth would compare favorably with that of the past at almost any stage of Spanish history, although the rate of economic progress has probably not equalled that of other countries.

On the surface the old politico-social ideas of Liberalism

508

seemed for a while to have died, and the country came
to be ruled by parties which supported the conservative
constitution of 1876, although there was a widespread
opposition in opinions if not in power. At the present time
there is a Liberal and a Conservative party, but the
difference between the two is recognized, even by many
Spaniards, as being very slight. In 1911 there was a
strike on the government-owned railways, whereupon the
authorities suspended the constitutional guarantees, on
the ground that the nation was in danger. One result
was that bodies of men could not congregate, — and
the strikers were helpless. In 1912 a general railway
strike was threatened. The premier, Canalejas, called out
the military reserves, and put them on the trains not only
as guards but also as train operatives, — for, since all Spaniards who have served their term in the active army are in
the reserves, the strikers were employed as military trainmen
to put down their own strike, — a thing which they could not
refuse to do, as they were under martial law. An early
Cortes was promised, at which the questions of increase in
wages and decrease in the hours of labor would be taken up.
The *Cortes* was called, — and the matter of the strike was
dropped. The interesting thing is that all of this took place
while a Liberal government was in power! It is also said
that the Liberals and Conservatives agreed, a few years ago,
to alternate in office, thus showing their contempt for the
spirit of representative institutions, but the Liberals did not
retire from their control of the government in 1913, wherefore not a little ill-concealed resentment was displayed by
the organs of the Conservative party. In fact, parties are
divided on lines of the allegiance of individuals to the chieftain (*cacique*) of their group. National policies and projects
of reform on the part of those in power get little beyond the
stage of rhetoric, while government is too largely given over
to the interplay of personal ambitions. To many the young
king, Alfonso XIII, has seemed the most liberal-minded of
the higher officers of the Spanish state, and in both word and
deed he has appeared, until recently at least, to merit the
characterization. Attaining to his majority at the age of

Conserva-
tive rule in
a pseudo-
Liberal
state.

sixteen, in 1902, he married the granddaughter of the English Queen Victoria in 1906, — an augury in itself of liberal views. A savage attempt was made, without success, to murder the young couple on their wedding day; on that occasion and two others when later assassinations were tried, Alfonso displayed such courage and coolness as to win for himself an immense popularity; "the valiant king" (*El rey valiente*) he is often called.

The political views of the Spanish people have been undergoing a change in recent years. Whereas the mass of the people were totally unready for the democratic constitution of 1812, or even for that of 1837, they are today becoming more and more radical in feeling. Everywhere there is discontent with the present management of state affairs, and it is customary to charge even the untoward incidents of daily life to the fault of "the bad government" (*el mal gobierno*), — for example, when a train is late, or over-crowded, both of which eventualities are of frequent occurrence. Many factors have combined to bring about this state of mind: much is traceable to social causes, to which allusion will be made presently; the very material progress of the country, resulting in a betterment of the condition of the poor, though their lot is still far from being an enviable one, has awakened desires among the masses of which their ancestors never dreamed; and the relative prosperity of many of the *indianos* (nabobs of the Indies), as returned Spanish emigrants are called, has led to a widespread belief that men can do better anywhere than under the "*mal gobierno*" of Spain. The average Spaniard of the working classes takes little interest in his right of suffrage (although this is more particularly true of the country districts than it is of the cities), for he is convinced that it makes no difference; he is helpless and hopeless in the face of a government which seems quite apart from him. Many believe, however, that there is a panacea for existing conditions, and groups have sprung up representing a variety of social, economic, and political ideas, such as single tax (*georgismo*, — from Henry George), socialism, and republicanism. The desire for a republic has grown steadily since its first public expression in 1854, and has now swept across the northern provinces of Spain, from Galicia to Catalonia, cutting through the formerly Carlist, or absolutist, country, although manifesting itself more in the cities than elsewhere. If no serious outbreak for the establishment of a republic has taken place, it is in large degree a tribute to the king. Alfonso has frequently declared himself ready to accept the wishes of the Spanish people in this matter, saying only a few years ago that if Spain should so decide he "would be the first to draw his sword in defence of the republic." Too much weight should not be given to these political gropings of the Spanish people, for the forces of conservatism, — such as the nobles and the wealthy, the clergy, and the devoutly faithful (notably in the rural districts), — are still very powerful. Even the king has recently been charged with a tendency to become reactionary. In 1917 serious internal disturbances occurred, and it is said that Alfonso did not rise to the situation in the same liberal spirit as formerly. Whether this is the mere unfounded expression of party feeling, or whether the king has in truth experienced a change of heart, it is as yet too early to say. Whatever may be the exact composition of the elements against them, there is no doubt that the majority of the people feel a deep resentment against the prevailing government. In one respect this has led to consequences of a serious character. The old regional spirit of the Catalans has reasserted itself, and a distinct Catalan national feeling, sustained by a revival of Catalan as a literary tongue, has manifested itself. One event stands out from the rest in recent times, with regard to which all elements in Spanish life have had occasion to express their political views. That is the celebrated Ferrer case.

In June, 1909, when a Conservative government was in power, with Antonio Maura at its head, credits were voted for a campaign in Morocco against some tribesmen who had attacked a railway leading to mines in the control of Spanish capitalists. There was an immediate outbreak of hostile public opinion in Spain, which in Catalonia resulted in serious riots. The strange thing about the Catalonian

The Ferrer case and the "Maura, sí !" and "Maura, no !"

manifestations, which were most pronounced in Barcelona, was that they developed into what seemed to be an organized assault, not on the government or on capitalists, but on the Catholic Church. Churches, monasteries, convents, and shrines were attacked — and nothing else. The government soon had the situation in hand, and a number of arrests were made, followed in some cases by sentences of death or imprisonment. Public attention focused itself on the case of one Ferrer. Francisco Ferrer was born in 1859, the son of a poor Catalan farmer. As a youth he was an anarchist, pronouncing bitterly against the ideal of patriotism and against the church. Having participated in a Catalonian rebellion of 1885, he fled to Paris, where he entered into relations with a Parisian spinster, who soon died and left him a fortune. Later, he returned to Barcelona, and increased his possessions as the result of successful stock speculation. He founded a number of schools, which represented his ideas, — still uncompromisingly against the church. Ferrer was also a high official of the Freemasons and other secret societies. It is not to be wondered at, either, in view of his rebellious attitude toward society, that his regard for the marriage bond and for sexual morality was clearly not in accord with prevailing views. At the time of the Catalonian outbreak of 1909 he was charged with being one of the ringleaders. A military court-martial was held, at which he was confronted with scores of witnesses, and it would seem that the prosecution established its case. Ferrer was convicted, and on October 13, 1909, was shot.[1] The case of Ferrer has been taken up internationally by various secret societies, but it has had a special significance in Spain. There, opinion has divided, not about Ferrer or the merits of his case, but with regard to the Conservative chieftain, Maura, whose government was responsible for his death. Maura is taken as the personification of the existing régime. "Maura, sí!" and "Maura, no!" ("Maura, yes!" and "Maura, no!") have come to be popular watchwords,

[1] Belloc, Hilaire, "The International," in The Dublin Review, v. CXLVI, nos. 292–293, pp. 167–181, 396–411. London. Jan. and Apr., 1910. This is an article about the Ferrer case.

indicating whether one approves of things as they are, or whether one stands for a new and liberalized, truly democratic Spain.

Spain's foreign policy since 1898 has very nearly reduced itself to three factors. First of these is the policing of a small strip of the Moroccan coast, where Ceuta and other posts are still held by Spain. This has involved the country in wars of a minor character with the traditional enemy in Moslem Northwest Africa. Of greater interest is the conscious policy of cultivating the friendship of the American countries which were once colonies of Spain, based largely on a wish to develop a market for Spanish goods, but not devoid of a sentiment which makes Spain desire to associate herself with the growing lands to which she gave the first impulse to civilization. Finally, Spain's relations with the two groups of European powers which entered upon the Great War in 1914 have occupied the attention of the country continuously in recent years, and have been an issue which has divided Spaniards. Many of the conservative elements of Spain have long been, not so much pro-German, as anti-French, and they have been supported by those parts of the masses which follow the lead of the church or else take no great interest in politics. The causes of this Francophobe feeling are numerous. The *Dos de Mayo*, Spain's national holiday, stands for an uprising against the French, followed by the glorious War of Independence, although, to be sure, this has of late exercised but little influence; many French writers have written disparagingly or in a patronizing manner of Spain, causing a natural feeling of resentment; Spanish American countries have asserted that France is their intellectual mother, not Spain, and this may have had an effect, though comparatively little, on the minds of some; mere propinquity with France, which is the only great power bordering upon the peninsula, has brought about a certain hostility which neighboring peoples so often feel with regard to each other; the affronts which Spain claims to have received at French hands in Morocco have had great weight; and the already hostile attitude of the clergy against republican France

Foreign policy of Spain since 1898 and attitude toward the Great War.

2 L

was enhanced when that country broke with the Catholic Church a few years ago. As regards England, Spain has never forgotten Gibraltar. With Germany, on the other hand, there has been little occasion for friction, and German commercial competition with England for Spanish markets has been welcomed as beneficial to the country. The radical and liberal elements, which include the intellectuals, and, generally speaking, the Liberal party have favored the *Entente* as against the Central Powers, and their position has been very greatly strengthened by the evident support of the king. In part, pro-*Entente* feeling has been a matter of political principle, because of the liberal types of government in France and England, the only two countries of the *Entente* allies (prior to American entry in the Great War) to whom Spaniards have paid attention. In large measure, however, the Spanish point of view has been the result of a certain practical, materialistic trait which is ingrained in Spanish character. Thus Spaniards have pointed out that it would be fatal for Spain to side with Germany, since her wide separation from the latter, coupled with British naval supremacy, would make it unlikely that German arms could be of any assistance to Spain. Commercial and other reasons have also been adduced to show that Spain could *gain* nothing by an alliance with Germany. These views have developed in the course of the Great War until Spain has become rather more inclined to the allies than to the Germans. It is not improbable, however, that an allied disaster might be seized upon by the pro-German military element to swing Spain the other way, for the army is still a factor to be reckoned with in Spanish politics. On the other hand, many leading Spaniards have argued that there would be no advantage for Spain if she should enter the war, whereas there has thus far been a distinct benefit for certain elements in the population, in the shape of abnormal war profits, through remaining neutral. Lately, however, great misery has been occasioned as a result of Spain's inability to procure needed supplies from the allies and the danger from the German submarines.

In no element of the national life has the well-being of

Spain since 1898 been more clearly demonstrated than in the realm of things intellectual. On the educational and scientific side (with one exception, presently to be noted), the achievement has not been great enough to attract attention, but in those branches of human knowledge which are akin to the emotions Spain has embarked upon a new *siglo de oro* which has already placed her in the forefront of the nations in the wealth and beauty of her contemporary literature and art. Many writers or artists of note did their work before 1898, while others stand athwart that year, but the most remarkable development has come in the more recent period — a growing force which is far from having run its course. Thus, before 1898, there were such poets as Becquer, Campoamor, Núñez de Arce, Rosalía de Castro, and Salvador Rueda; novelists like Alarcón, Pereda, Valera, "Clarín," Picón, Palacio Valdés, Pardo Bazán, and Pérez Galdós; dramatists including Ayala, Tamayo, Echegaray, Pérez Galdós, Guimerá, and Dicenta; critics and philologists like Milá Fontanals, Valera, "Clarín," and Menéndez y Pelayo; essayists such as Alfredo Calderón, Morote, Picavea, Ganivet, and Unamuno; painters like Pradilla, Ferrán, and Muñoz Degrain; and composers of music including Arrieta, Gastambide, Chueca, Chapí, Bretón, and Fernández Caballero. Some of the more notable of these belong also in the post-1898 group, and to them should be added, among others, the following: poets — Rubén Darío (who is included in this list, though he is a Nicaraguan, because of his influence on Spanish poetry), Villaespesa, Marquina, Ramón D. Perés, the two Machados, Mesa, Diez Canedo, Muñoz San Román, and Maragall; novelists — Blasco Ibáñez, Pío Baroja, "Azorín," Silverio Lanza, Valle Inclán, Ricardo León, Alberto Insúa, Pérez de Ayala, Martínez Sierra, Miró, and Felipe Trigo; dramatists — Benavente, Martínez Sierra, the brothers Álvarez Quintero, Carlos Arniches, Linares Rivas, Marquina, Rusiñol, and Iglesias; critics and philologists — Menéndez Pidal, Bonilla, Rodríguez Marín, Said Armesto, Américo Castro, Cejador, Alomar, Tenreiro, and González Blanco; essayists — Ortega Gasset, Maeztu, "Azorín,"

Gómez de Baquero, Manuel Bueno, Maragall, and Zulueta; painters — Zuloaga, Sorolla, the brothers Zubiaurre, Benedito, Chicharro, Villegas, Nieto, Beruete, Moreno Carbonero, Bilbao, Sotomayor, Anglada, de la Gándara, Juan Lafita, and Rusiñol; sculptors — Blay, Benlliure, Marinas, Clará, and Julio Antonio; architects — Gaudí, Puig, Velázquez, and Palacios; composers — Albéniz, Pedrell, Turina, Granados, Falla, Vives, Serrano, and Quinito Valverde; and educators — Giner de los Ríos and Cossío. Spain has also produced historians and historical scholars of note in recent years (though several of them belong in the pre-1898 group), among whom should be reckoned Cánovas del Castillo, Danvila y Collado, Hinojosa, Rafael Altamira, Colmeiro, Fidel Fita, Fernández Duro, Menéndez y Pelayo, Torres Lanzas, and Fernández Guerra. Special mention should be made of the novelists Pérez Galdós (author of the famous *Episodios nacionales*, or National episodes, — a series of historical novels from the Liberal point of view, covering the history of Spain from the time of Godoy to the present, — and esteemed by many as one of the most remarkable literary geniuses of modern times) and Blasco Ibáñez (who has used the novel as a vehicle for an attack on the old order of Spanish life); of the dramatists Jacinto Benavente (a man whom many regard as deserving to rank with the greatest names of all time in Spanish literature), Pérez Galdós (who is almost equally notable in the drama as in the novel), the brothers Álvarez Quintero (who have so clearly depicted modern Andalusian life), and Martínez Sierra (whose comedies reach to the very roots of truth and beauty); of Menéndez y Pelayo, most famous as a critic, said to have been the dominant figure of recent years in Spanish literature; of the painters Zuloaga (successor of El Greco, Velázquez, and Goya, whose works embrace both the mysticism and the austerity of the Spanish national spirit) and Sorolla (a symbolist, who has done with the brush what Blasco Ibáñez did with the pen, and whose paintings, mainly of Valencian scenes, are full of realism and naturalism, brilliant in expression and color); and of Giner de los Ríos, opponent of the church, but a man of tremendous influence on the thought of modern Spain. It is to be noted that the leading names in the realm of art are all in the post-1898 period; indeed, this form of intellectual manifestation was not in a flourishing state before that time. And in the midst of all these names one must not forget that of Santiago Ramón y Cajal, whose discoveries in histology have made him famous throughout the world. Many characterize him as the greatest Spaniard of the present day.

*   *   *   *   *   *   *

Spain clearly has entered upon a new era of her history. No man can predict, with safety, toward what goal she is tending, although there is some ground for a feeling of optimism. With the leading facts of Spanish history already before the reader, it is perhaps well at this point to give a summary account of contemporary Spanish traits and social problems, thus providing a further basis for estimates with regard to the possibilities of the future. It is best to begin with a statement of some of the things which Spaniards are *not*, — with a view to controverting certain widely circulated notions. Spaniards are *not* unusually cruel or vindictive. The notion that they *are* has arisen in various ways. Spaniards are emotional, and under the stress of excitement are capable of acts of great violence, but on the other hand they very rarely plan a crime in cold blood. The bull-fight has been charged to an innate cruelty of Spaniards, but whatever one may think of the game, the *aficionado*, or bull-fight "fan," is appealed to by the skill of the bull-fighter and the courage of the bull, rather than by the flow of blood. As regards treatment of animals, the evidence is somewhat against the Spaniard. The superficial tourist is apt to think that the majority of Spaniards in third class of the railway coaches are double-dyed brigands, for they wear wretched clothing and carry huge knives, — but the former is the result of economic necessity, and the latter is to cut bread with — and not each others' throats. The historians, however, are very largely to blame, especially those who maligned the dominant and hated Spaniards of the sixteenth century. Spaniards themselves, with their fierce party

Things which Spaniards are *not*.

spirit and rhetorical gifts, products of their emotional make-up, have provided the arguments which have been used against them, — notably in the case of Las Casas' condemnation of the Spanish treatment of the Indians. In the second place, they are *not* lazy; rather, they make excellent laborers, and work long hours without complaint. The idea that they are indolent arises in part from the fact that the titled classes still retain some of the traditional aversion to manual labor; in part from a certain lack of ambition, such that many Spaniards, notably those of the south, do not work, after they have gained enough to live on for perhaps only a little while; partly because of a lack of responsibility which many of them display, with the result that they do not do well when not under supervision; and partly, again, because histories have so described Spaniards of the past, and this time with some truth. Many of the factors which once made manual labor unpopular are not any longer operative, such as the prevalence of slaves, serfs, and Moslems in industry or agriculture, wherefore the earlier stigma attaching to those occupations has been removed. In the third place, Spaniards are not proud and arrogant to the extent of being haughty, although they do have a sense of personal pride which is rather to be commended than condemned. In the fourth place, to call a man a "Spaniard" is not a sufficient definition, for there are wide differences in blood and language as well as in feelings in the various regions of Spain; the serious-minded, progressive, European-blooded Catalan is certainly farther apart from the easy-going, pleasure-loving, improvident, part Moslem-blooded Andalusian than is the Englishman from the American, or perhaps the southern Frenchman from the North Italian. In addition to Castilian, or Spanish, there are the distinct languages of the Catalans and Basques, with a great many variants, or dialects, from the Castilian and Catalan. Nevertheless, it is true that all are "Spaniards." Castilian is generally understood, and, until the recent reappearance of Catalan, was the only literary language; the people are patriotic to the country, even though the fire of local attachments is still uncommonly strong in them; the bull-fight and the national lottery are popular in all parts of Spain; Spaniards read the same books, have the same government, and, in fine, have been brought together, though widely divergent in traits, by the circumstances of history.

The keynote to an understanding of Spanish character lies in an appreciation of the fact that Spaniards generally combine an intense individualism and marked practicality with an emotional temperament. Enough has already been intimated with regard to the two first-named traits. As for that of emotionalism it becomes more operative the farther south one goes. Some Spaniards say that the English, who are taken as representative of the northern peoples, are in the forefront of the nations as concerns matters of the *head*, but that the Spaniards lead in *heart*, and they are well content to have it that way. Yet it is far from true that Spaniards are lacking in *head;* rather, they are brilliantly intellectual, and even the man in the street often seems to have a faculty for seeing and expressing things clearly, with little or no study; their logical-mindedness is displayed in the rhetorical skill with which they set forth their opinions. It is true, however, that there is a certain lack of intellectual stamina in Spaniards; they will not use the brains with which nature has abundantly endowed them. Thus, big business and scientific discoveries (except in the practical realm of their applications) have been left to the foreigners. On the emotional, or *heart*, side one encounters numerous evidences. Spaniards are devotedly fond of children, — almost too much so, for they seem unable to refuse them anything. Thus, a child gets milk by crying, toys galore, and stays up at night until he wants to go to bed; the effects on national discipline are possibly not of the best, but the error, if such it is, springs from the heart. Spaniards, past and present, have been great in emotional expression, in the fields of literature and art. It is a novelty for Americans to find that the educated young men of Spain talk quite as easily about literature and art as they do about women, — and they move from one subject to the other without any marked change in the tenor

Intellectual and emotional traits of Spaniards.

of the conversation. Spanish crimes are usually the result of an emotional impulse. Similarly, the emotions play rather too prominent a part in the Spaniard's associations with women! Courtesy is almost universal among Spaniards, who will go to considerable personal inconvenience in order to assist a stranger; to be sure, one is not safe in reckoning on the promises to render favors later, — for by that time the impulse may have passed. The Spanish fondness for the bull-fight and the lottery also springs from the emotional stir which goes with them.

Spanish women.
The above applies principally to the men. The women should be considered apart, and this is much more necessary in dealing with Spain than it would be in treating of the United States, where women come nearer to having an equal liberty with men. Opinions differ as to the personal appearance of Spanish women, and first impressions of the foreigner are apt to be against them. This is largely because the people of the wealthy or moderately well-to-do classes do not appear in the street nearly so frequently as in the United States or in northern Europe. The women of the working classes toil harder, on the average, than do ours, — for more of them have to help earn the family living as well as bring up and take care of the children, — and they are not able to dress well, with the natural result that they are rarely prepossessing. This in part accounts also for the belief of foreigners that Spanish beauty fades, — which is not the case with those who are able to live in fairly easy circumstances any more than it is in other countries. Among Spaniards it is often said that the Valencian women are the handsomest, closely followed by the Andalusians, who rank as the most witty. It is to be noted that the Moslem element in Spanish blood is very strong in these sections. Another popular misconception as to Spanish *señoritas* (young ladies) is that they are so dainty that they would almost melt in one's hand. In fact they are unusually self-contained in manner, and if they have any pronounced defect it is one which does not go with daintiness, — that of a loud, often metallic voice. On the other hand there is most decidedly an all-pervading, unconscious grace in

Spanish women. Women other than those of the working classes find very little to do. Servants are extraordinarily cheap, — one can get a nurse-girl in Seville for about ten cents a day; so there is little occasion to do housework. Spanish women are not assiduous readers, do not even sew or knit to any marked degree, and comparatively few of them sing or play the piano. They are fond of a walk or ride in the afternoon, accompanied by the children and the nurse-girls, and enjoy social gatherings at night. In fine, their life is passed largely in pleasant conversation, with very little variety; indeed, they require little that is novel, for they are simple in their tastes, and are easily entertained. The Spanish husband is not nearly so domesticated as the American species. Instead of remaining at home at night he quite regularly goes out, — and even may occupy a different place at the theatre from the group of seats where his wife and daughter are found. This is the expected thing, and Spanish women do not appear to wish it otherwise. They seem to consider that the men have done them a great favor by marrying them, and take the attitude of desiring to repay them for the rest of their lives. The husband is devoted to his wife and the children, but he would commit suicide before he would carry a baby in the street. Despite the fact that the brains of most Spanish women may be said to lie fallow, they are often brilliant talkers, sharing with the men the intellectual potentialities of the race. They rarely travel, and know very little beyond the bounds of their home town or city and the nearest watering-place. They are usually very religious, but not in an aggressive way; in a country where there is virtually no competition with the Catholic Church there is no stimulus to make their religion anything but a purely personal matter for the individual. This helps to account for the almost complete lack of religious discussion in the Spanish circles one meets with. Young ladies rarely go into the street unless accompanied by their mother or some older person. Whenever they do appear they are stared at by the men, but the practice seems to be regarded as proper and in a measure complimentary. They are hedged around with safeguards which prevent their seeing the young man of their choice alone, except perhaps as separated by the narrow grating of a window, until the day of their marriage. According to all reports these measures fulfill their intended purpose, for the material bars are supplemented by the inherited instincts of the women themselves. Aside from prostitutes Spanish women have a nation-wide reputation for good moral conduct. Once married the size of the family depends, as many put it, "As God wills!" A family of from five to seven children is not considered large, and there are many families which are very much larger.

The aristocracy and the *latifundia*. Assuming that it would be desirable, can Spain advance any farther along the highway of democracy? If she would do so, she must contend with the aristocracy, which in fact rules the country. The modern Spanish aristocracy is composed of the nobility, their relatives, rich merchants, the clergy, and the military. The richer members of the aristocracy, especially those of central and southern Spain, control the greater part of the best Spanish lands, which they cultivate just enough to ensure wealth to themselves. Thousands of acres are given over to the raising of bulls for the bull-fights, and even the late Duke of Veragua, a descendant of Columbus, was engaged in this industry. One often wonders why Spanish towns are so far away from the railway station, especially in level tracts where it would be normal to expect a growth toward the railroad. The usual answer is that the land belongs to a personage of the realm, who would not think of selling it, and does not care to develop it himself. The agrarian problem is particularly acute in Andalusia, where the evil of *latifundia*, springing out of the later reconquests from the Moslems, is more in evidence than elsewhere.

Life of men of the better classes. The life of the men of the better classes is singularly free from care. They arise late, and go to their favorite café or club to read the newspaper. In the afternoon they frequent their club, passing the time in discussion or in general conversation. Late in the afternoon they go for a drive along the *paseo*, or driveway, the same place every day, where the principal object is to see, or be seen by, the others

who are doing the same thing. In the evening they return
to the club. Perhaps at 9:30 or 10 o'clock they go to a play,
for the theatre begins late, following this by a visit to their
favorite café and a late departure for home. The program
varies little from day to day. In the summer they go to a
watering-place, but it usually amounts only to a change of
cafés. These men rarely drink to excess, and they are the
most charming people in the world to talk to, but they
never study and, if possible to avoid it, never do any
work. Unknowingly perhaps, for they are bred to this
type of life by centuries of training, they are a drain on
the land, the most serious element in the vested interests
which stand in the way of effective reform. Those of this
class who have to work are provided with sinecures at
state expense. The social, economic, and political betterment of Spain cannot proceed very far while the aristocracy
is in control. On the other hand the experience of the
past has not demonstrated that democracy could maintain order, and this the present régime does. Furthermore,
the aristocracy is by no means an exclusive caste, but is
open to the entry of all.

In addition to the wealth and political influence of the
aristocracy other factors in Spanish life abound to aid and
abet in their maintenance of control. One of these is
emigration. Spaniards do not expect to rise from poverty
to great wealth, as men do in America, for so few of them
rarely can, under the existing system, that there is not the
stimulus of other men's successes to spur them on. The
more ambitious of the poor and moderately well-to-do,
therefore, make their way to the Americas, especially to
Argentina, and, prior to the recent era of civil war, to
Mexico. The poorest and the least ambitious, who are
less likely than the others to give trouble, remain behind.
A second aid is the lottery. The lottery, which has its
agencies in every hamlet and city of Spain, is government owned and operated, paying some of the highest
prizes offered in the world at the present time. Few
human passions are so strong as that of gambling, and
Spain has surrendered to the lottery. The poor people

Social problems of contemporary Spain.

welcome this insidious system, believing it to be almost the only avenue of advance to the envied ease of the wealthy, and invest their spare savings in a ticket. Hope and even expectation of getting a lucky number have come to be a national disease. A third abettor of the aristocracy is the bull-fight. It is not the cruelty, but rather the corrupting influence of this sport which should occupy those who protest against it. The game is so emotional, so wildly exciting, that it grips the people to the exclusion of almost every other interest; in Seville, one can almost be certain, if he hears men quarreling at the top of their voices, that they are disputing the merits of this bull-fighter or that, for that is the absorbing factor in life, every hour in the day, in every day of the year. Men who have caught the fever of the bull-fight rarely have interest in national reform; they do not want it, as it might sweep away the sport which is the major part of their life. A fourth factor would seem to be the extensive character of charitable enterprises. Thousands depend upon the unused food of the army, and line up each day to receive it. Enormous sums are also provided by the church or by charitable organizations to enable the poor to get meals free or at slight cost. The object, no doubt, is benevolent, but the result is that many men will not work. Especially is this true in the mild climate of southern Spain, where not a few contrive to exist without homes to sleep in and on the dispensations of charity. A fifth factor is the extreme poverty of the masses. Wages are unthinkably low. Men who can barely keep body and soul together are not the ones who agitate reform. A sixth aid in the maintenance of things as they are is the lack of a good public school system. Schools are inadequate and teachers poorly paid. Few Spaniards get beyond the primary grade, and many do not even go that far. The need of education is undoubtedly the *sine qua non* of any effective Spanish advancement. To change the form of government, without an accompanying or a preliminary instruction of the masses, would be, as a French writer puts it, "to change the label of a bottle, without transforming the contents." It is also necessary if any appreciable reform is to be made in the social and economic system of the country. None realizes this better than the men who, like Altamira, Azcárate, Costa, Giner de los Ríos, Posada, and Unamuno, stand for the new Spain, as distinct from the old, — for a country which shall break with the past to the extent which may be required in order to place itself in the current of modern world progress. Their ideal is not impossible of achievement, despite the forces which are against them, for the Spanish people, at bottom, are admirable material, still virile and altogether sane.

BIBLIOGRAPHICAL NOTES

The principal aim of this volume is to be of service to the general reader in English-speaking America. On this account the entries which appear below have been restricted rigidly to works in English. It was a temptation to include some of the more notable foreign works, such for example as those by Altamira, Bonilla, Cánovas del Castillo, Colmeiro, Danvila, Desdevises du Dézert, Diercks, Dozy (the *Recherches*), Fernández de Navarrete, Fernández Duro, Fernán-Núñez, Ferrer del Río, Fita, Foulché-Delbosc, Haebler, Hinojosa, Lafuente, Lembke, Mariéjol, Marvaud, Menéndez Pidal, Menéndez y Pelayo, Mignet, Morel-Fatio, Oliveira Martins, Ranke, Romey, Rosseeuw St. Hilaire, Rousseau, Salcedo, and Tapia, but the reader will be able to go to their works and to many others by using the aids which are provided here.

A complete bibliography of the works in English on the history of Spain would reach enormous proportions. It has therefore been deemed advisable to narrow the field by excluding the following classes of material: catalogues of books and manuscripts; volumes of source material; periodicals about Spain not devoted primarily to history; articles in periodicals; works on other subjects (such for example as the writings of Mommsen and other historians of the Roman Empire) which, however, contain much material on the history of Spain; works (such as those of Motley or Helps) on the activities of Spain outside the peninsula, whether in Europe or the Americas; and books which may be regarded as out of date. Works published many years ago are not omitted, however, if they are translations of important foreign works, the writings of notable historians, or volumes which are unique in their field. No attempt has been made to give an exhaustive list of all the items coming within the classes eligible for entry. Thus there might be additions to the lives of notable persons, to the histories of art and literature, or to the already long list of recent descriptive works. The plan has been rather to be representative, giving some of the works which will serve to introduce the reader to the subject. No claim is made that the works cited cover the subject of Spanish history adequately; indeed, if the most broadly inclusive basis for entry of works in English had been chosen they would not do so. They are particularly disappointing to the American reader, in that they represent the point of view of England or continental Europe rather than that of the Spanish gift to America. Furthermore, many periods are but scantily covered from any standpoint, while others, such as those of the Catholic

527

Kings and the House of Austria, have an over-supply of writings upon them. It is to be noted, however, that books of a given period have a number of preliminary chapters on the years immediately preceding it. Thus, Coppée has some two hundred pages on the Visigothic era, Plunket nearly a hundred pages on the reign of Henry IV, and most cf the histories of the nineteenth century begin with the accession of Charles IV. Concluding chapters, too, will often reach over into the next succeeding period, — as in the case of Scott, who devotes sixty-nine pages to the Moriscos under the kings of the House of Austria. Moreover, many of the volumes in the section devoted to works of travel and description, especially those dealing with particular localities, give much of their space to the record of the past, thus supplementing the writings which are more properly historical in character.

Methods of entry.   In the works selected for entry an indication is given of the dates of the first and the latest editions. In the case of translations the date of the original publication in the foreign tongue is also stated. The place of publication is not given for the latest edition if it is the same as that of the first. No attempt has been made to record minor variations in title in different editions, such for example as "Philip the Second" for "Philip II," but striking changes have been noted. The presence of bibliographical apparatus in the works cited is indicated by the abbreviation "Bib," thus enabling the reader to know what are the volumes which may take him to materials not mentioned here. Not only are the books with formal bibliographies or lists of works so characterized, but also those which have fairly ample bibliographical data in the preface. The practice has not been followed, however, where the information as to sources is confined to footnotes, although many writers, Lea for example, have valuable references scattered through their volumes.

I. BIBLIOGRAPHICAL AIDS

Aside from the partial bibliographies in the books listed below and the single periodical mentioned in this section there is no work in English on the bibliography of Spanish history. The bibliographical sections of the *Cambridge medieval history* and the *Cambridge modern history* (items 10 and 29 below) will be found particularly helpful. Three works in foreign tongues are worth noting. The bibliography in Altamira's *Historia de España* is perhaps the best general list in Spanish. The two-volume *Catalogue de l'histoire d'Espagne et de Portugal* (Paris. 1883–85) of the Bibliothèque Nationale of Paris, based on the works at the disposition of readers in the great national library at the French capital, is valuable for the older books. The sections on Spain in the German annual bibliography of historical writings, the *Jahresberichte der geschichtswissenschaft* (published at Berlin since 1880) cover publications since 1878. The only item in English follows :

1. *Hispanic American historical review.* Baltimore. 1918. Quarterly.

> This periodical begins publication in February, 1918. Will contain material on Spain and Portugal, including bibliographical notices, though primarily devoted to Hispanic America.

II. General Histories of Spain

In addition to the items of this paragraph, attention is directed to the works on special subjects, in section IX, many of which range over several or all of the various periods of Spanish history.

2. Dunham, Samuel Astley. . . . *Spain and Portugal.* 5v. London. 1832[-33]. Takes to the close of the eighteenth century.
3. Hale, Edward Everett, and Susan Hale. . . . *Spain.* New York. [c 1886].
4. Harrison, James Albert. *Spain.* Boston. [c 1881]. Republished under title *Spain in history.* New York and Akron, O. [1898].
5. Hume, Martin Andrew Sharp. *The Spanish people, their origin, growth and influence.* London and New York. 1901. 1914. Bib.
6. Mariana, Juan de. *The general history of Spain. From the first peopling of it by Tubal, till the death of King Ferdinand, who united the crowns of Castile and Aragon. With a continuation to the death of King Philip III.* Tr.[fr.the Sp.ed.of 1669 or 1670] ed.by Capt.John Stevens. London. 1699. Orig.ed.in Latin. Toledo. 1592. First Sp.ed. Toledo. 1601. Later editions have continuations, all except the first by other writers, bringing the history to the date of publication. Latest Sp.ed. Madrid. 1854.
7. Perkins, Clara Crawford. *Builders of Spain.* 2v.in 1. New York. 1911.

III. Ancient Spain, to 711

8. Bouchier, Edmund Spencer. *Spain under the Roman Empire.* Oxford. 1914. Bib.
9. Burke, Ulick Ralph. *A history of Spain, from the earliest times to the death of Ferdinand the Catholic.* 2v. London. [1894-] 1895. 1900.
10. *Cambridge medieval history.* 3v. New York. 1911-18. Bib.
11. Van Nostrand, John James. *The reorganization of Spain by Augustus.* (University of California, *Publications in history,* v.IV,no.2). Berkeley. 1916. Bib.

IV. MEDIEVAL SPAIN, 711-1479

Items 9 and 10 belong also in this section.

12. Beazley, Charles Raymond. *James the First of Aragon.* Oxford. 1890.
13. Clarke, Henry Butler. *The Cid Campeador, and the waning of the crescent in the west.* New York and London. 1902.
14. Condé, José Antonio. *History of the dominion of the Arabs in Spain.* Tr.ed.by Mrs. Jonathan Foster. 3v. London. 1854–55. Orig.Sp.ed. Madrid. 1820–21. Usually regarded as untrustworthy.
15. Coppée, Henry. *History of the conquest of Spain by the Arab-Moors.* 2v. Boston. 1881.
16. Dozy, Reinhart Pieter Anne. *Spanish Islam: a history of the Moslems in Spain.* Tr.ed.by Francis Griffin Stokes. London. 1913. Bib. Orig.Fr.ed. Leyde. 1861.
17. Drane, Augusta Theodosia. *The history of St. Dominic, founder of the Friars Preachers.* London and New York. 1891.
18. Guiraud, Jean. *Saint Dominic.* Tr.ed.by Katharine de Mattos. London. 1901. New York, Cincinnati, and Chicago. 1913. Bib. Orig.Fr.ed. Paris. 1899.
19. Ibn'Abd al-Hakām. *Ibn Abd-el-Hakem's History of the conquest of Spain.* Tr.[fr.the Arabic] ed.by John Harris Jones. Göttingen. 1858. Orig.ms.written in ninth century.
20. Lane-Poole, Stanley. . . . *The Moors in Spain.* New York and London. [1886]. New York. 1911.
21. Makkarī, Ahmed ibn Mohammed al. *The history of the Mohammedan dynasties in Spain.* Ext.and tr.[fr.ms.copies in the British Museum] ed.by Pascual de Gayangos. 2v. London. 1840–43. Orig.ms.in Arabic written early in the seventeenth century.
22. Merriman, Roger Bigelow. *The rise of the Spanish empire in the old world and the new.* 4v. New York and London. 1918–. Bib. Two volumes are announced for publication in 1918 (*The middle ages* and *The Catholic Kings*). Two more will follow (*The Emperor* and *Philip the Prudent*).
23. Miron, E. L. *The queens of Aragon, their lives and times.* London. 1913. Bib.
24. Scott, Samuel Parsons. *History of the Moorish empire in Europe.* 3v. Philadelphia and London. 1904. Bib.
25. Swift, Francis Darwin. *Life and times of James I., the conqueror, king of Aragon, Valencia, and Majorca.* Oxford. 1894.
26. Watts, Henry Edward. . . . *The Christian recovery of Spain, being the story of Spain from the Moorish conquest to the fall of Granada (711–1492 A.D.).* New York. 1901.
27. Whishaw, Bernhard and Ellen M. *Arabic Spain, sidelights on her history and art.* London. 1912. Bib.
28. Yonge, Charlotte Mary. *The story of the Christians and Moors of Spain.* London and New York. 1903.

V. Era of the Catholic Kings, 1479–1517

Items 9, 14, 15, 20–22, 24, 26, and 28 belong also in this section. Many of the items of section IX are applicable here.

29. *Cambridge modern history.* 14v. New York and London. 1902–12. Bib.
30. Hare, Christopher. *A queen of queens* [Isabella (1474–1504)] & *the making of Spain.* New York. 1906.
31. Hume, Martin Andrew Sharp. *Queens of old Spain.* New York. 1906. London. 1911.
32. Hume, Martin Andrew Sharp. *Spain, its greatness and decay (1479–1788).* Cambridge. 1898. 1913. Bib.
33. Irving, Washington. *Conquest of Granada.* New York. 1829. 1910. Bib. Orig.ed.entitled *A chronicle of the conquest of Granada.*
34. Lea, Henry Charles. *The Moriscos of Spain; their conversion and expulsion.* Philadelphia. 1901.
35. Plunket, Ierne L. *Isabel of Castile and the making of the Spanish nation, 1451–1504.* New York and London. 1915. Bib.
36. Prescott, William Hickling. *History of the reign of Ferdinand and Isabella the Catholic.* 2v.in 1. New York. 1838. 3v. Philadelphia. [1902].
37. Sabatini, Rafael. *Torquemada and the Spanish inquisition.* London. [1913]. Bib.

VI. The House of Austria, 1516–1700

Items 22, 29, 31, 32, and 34 belong also in this section. All of the items in section IX have a bearing here.

38. Armstrong, Edward. *The Emperor Charles V.* 2v. London and New York. 1902. London. 1910. Bib.
39. Calvert, Albert Frederick. *The life of Cervantes.* London and New York. 1905. Bib.
40. Calvert, Albert Frederick. *Murillo, a biography and appreciation.* London and New York. 1907.
41. Calvert, Albert Frederick, *and Mrs.* Catherine Gasquoine (Hartley) Gallichan. *El Greco; an account of his life and works.* London and New York. 1909.
42. Calvert, Albert Frederick, *and Mrs.* Catherine Gasquoine (Hartley) Gallichan. *Velazquez; an account of his life and works.* London and New York. 1908.
43. Castro y Rossi, Adolfo de. *The Spanish Protestants and their persecution by Philip II; a historical work.* Tr.ed.by T. Parker. London and Edinburgh. 1851. (*History of religious intolerance in Spain*). 1853. Orig.Sp.ed. Cádiz. 1851.
44. Coloma, Luis. *The story of Don John of Austria.* Tr.ed.by Lady Moreton. London and New York. 1912.

45. Colvill, Helen Hester. *Saint Teresa of Spain.* New York and London. 1909. Bib.
46. Dunlop, John Colin. *Memoirs of Spain during the reigns of Philip IV and Charles II, from 1621 to 1700.* 2v. 1834.
47. Fitzmaurice-Kelly, James. *The life of Miguel de Cervantes de Saavedra.* London. 1892. Bib.
48. Fitzmaurice-Kelly, James. *Miguel de Cervantes Saavedra: a memoir.* Oxford. 1913. Bib.
49. Froude, James Anthony. *The Spanish story of the Armada and other essays.* New York. 1892. London. 1901.
50. Gardiner, Samuel Rawson. *Prince Charles and the Spanish marriage.* 2v. London. 1869.
51. Gayarré, Charles Etienne Arthur. *Philip II of Spain.* New York. 1866.
52. Gómara, Francisco López de. *Annals of the Emperor Charles V.* Tr.[fr.an unpublished ms.of, probably, 1557–58] and Sp.orig.ed. by Roger Bigelow Merriman. Oxford. 1912.
53. Graham, *Mrs.* Gabriela (de La Balmondière) Cunninghame. *Santa Teresa, being some account of her life and times.* 2v. London. 1894. 1907.
54. Hughes, Thomas Aloysius. *Loyola and the educational system of the Jesuits.* New York. 1892. Bib.
55. Hume, Martin Andrew Sharp. *The court of Philip IV. Spain in decadence.* New York. 1907.
56. Hume, Martin Andrew Sharp. *Philip II. of Spain.* London. 1897. 1911. Bib.
57. Hume, Martin Andrew Sharp. *Two English queens and Philip.* London. [1898].
58. Hume, Martin Andrew Sharp. *The year after the Armada, and other historical studies.* London and New York. 1896.
59. Joly, Henri. *Saint Ignatius of Loyola.* Tr.ed.by Mildred Partridge. London. 1899. 1906. Orig.Fr.ed. Paris. 1898.
60. Justi, Karl. *Diego Velasquez and his times.* Tr.ed.by A.H. Keane. London. 1889. Orig.Ger.ed. Bonn. 1889.
61. Lovat, Alice Mary (Weld-Blundell) Fraser, *baroness.* *The life of Saint Teresa, taken from the French of "A Carmelite nun."* London. 1912.
62. Loyola, *Saint* Ignacio de. *The autobiography of St.Ignatius.* Tr.ed.by J.F.X.O'Conor. New York. 1900. Original completed in 1555.
63. Lyon, F   H. *Diego de Sarmiento de Acuña, conde de Gondomar.* Oxford. 1910.
64. McCrie, Thomas. *History of the progress and suppression of the Reformation in Spain in the sixteenth century.* Edinburgh. 1829.
65. Prescott, William Hickling. *History of the reign of Philip the Second.* 3v. Boston. 1855–58. Philadelphia. 1916.

66. Rennert, Hugo Albert. *The life of Lope de Vega* (1562–1635). Glasgow and Philadelphia. 1904. Bib.
67. Robertson, William. *The history of the reign of the Emperor Charles the Fifth.* 3v. [Philadelphia]. 1770. Philadelphia. [1902].
68. Rose, Stewart. *Ignatius Loyola and the early Jesuits.* London. 1870. 1891. Bib.
69. Sandoval, Prudencio de. *The history of Charles the vth, emperor and king of Spain, the great hero of the House of Austria : containing the most remarkable occurrences that happen'd in the world for the space of 56 years.* Tr.ed.by Capt.John Stevens. London. 1703. Orig.Sp.ed. Antwerp. 1681.
70. Stevenson, Robert Alan Mowbray. *Velasquez.* London and New York. 1899. Bib.
71. Stirling-Maxwell, *Sir* William. *The cloister life of the Emperor Charles the Fifth.* London. 1852. 1891.
72. Stirling-Maxwell, *Sir* William. *Don John of Austria; or Passages from the history of the 16th century, 1547–1578.* 2v. London. 1883.
73. Stirling-Maxwell, *Sir* William. *Velazquez and his works.* London. 1855.
74. Teresa, *Saint. Saint Theresa. The history of her foundations.* Tr.[fr.the Sp.] ed.by *Sister* Agnes Mason. Cambridge. 1909. Orig.Sp.ed. Antwerp. 1630.
75. Teresa, *Saint. The life of St. Teresa of Jesus, of the Order of Our Lady of Carmel.* Tr.ed.by David Lewis. London. 1870. 1904. Orig.Sp.ed. Salamanca. 1588.
76. Teresa, *Saint. St. Teresa of Jesus of the Order of Our Lady of Carmel, embracing the life, relations, maxims and foundations written by the saint, also, a history of St. Teresa's journeys and foundations.* Tr.ed.by John J. Burke. New York. 1911. Orig.Sp.ed.(except the *Foundations*). Salamanca. 1588. Orig. Sp.ed.of the *Foundations.* Antwerp. 1630.
77. Thompson, Francis. *Saint Ignatius Loyola.* London. 1909. 1910.
78. Watson, Robert, *and* William Thomson. *The history of the reign of Philip the Third, king of Spain.* 2v. London. 1783. 1808.

VII. The House of Bourbon, 1700–1808

Items 29 and 32 belong also in this section. Many of the items in section IX are applicable here.

79. Addison, Joseph. *Charles the Third of Spain.* Oxford. 1900.
80. Armstrong, Edward. *Elizabeth Farnese, "the Termagant of Spain."* London. 1892. Bib.
81. Calvert, Albert Frederick. *Goya, an account of his life and works.* London and New York. 1908.

82. Coxe, William. *Memoirs of the kings of Spain of the House of Bourbon, from the accession of Philip the Fifth to the death of Charles the Third.* 3v. London. 1813. 5v. 1815.
83. D'Auvergne, Edmund B. *Godoy; the queen's favorite.* Boston. [1913].
84. Hill, Constance. *Story of the Princess des Ursins in Spain.* New York. 1899.
85. Parnell, Arthur. *The war of the succession in Spain during the reign of Queen Anne, 1702-1711.* London. 1888. Bib.
86. Ripperdá, Joan Willem van. *Memoirs of the Duke de Ripperdá: 1st.* embassador from the states-general to his most catholick majesty, then duke and grandee of Spain; afterwards bashaw and prime minister to Muly Abdalla, emperor of Fez and Morocco, etc. containing account of the remarkable events . . . between 1715 and 1736. London. 1740.
87. Stokes, Hugh. *Francisco Goya; a study of the work and personality of the eighteenth century Spanish painter and satirist.* New York. 1914. Bib.

VIII. The Dawn of Liberalism, 1808 to Date

Item 29 belongs also in this section.

88. Bollaert, William. *Wars of succession of Portugal and Spain, from 1826 to 1840 : with résumé of the political history . . . to the present time.* 2v. London. 1870.
89. Challice, Rachel. *The secret history of the court of Spain during the last century.* London. 1909. Bib.
90. Clarke, Henry Butler. *Modern Spain, 1815-1898.* Cambridge. 1906. Bib.
91. D'Auvergne, Edmund B. *A queen at bay; the story of Christina and Don Carlos.* London. 1910. Bib.
92. Hannay, David. *Don Emilio Castelar.* London. 1896.
93. Hume, Martin Andrew Sharp. *. . . Modern Spain, 1788-1898.* New York and London. 1900.
94. Latimer, *Mrs.*Elizabeth (Wormeley). *Spain in the nineteenth century.* Chicago. 1897. 1898.
95. Oman, Charles William Chadwick. *A history of the peninsular war.* 5v. Oxford. 1902-14. Bib.
96. Oman, Charles William Chadwick. *Wellington's army, 1809-1814.* London. 1912. Bib.
97. Strobel, Edward Henry. *Spanish revolution, 1868-1875.* Boston. 1898.
98. White, George F. *A century of Spain and Portugal (1788-1898).* London. [1909]. Bib.
99. Whitehouse, Henry Remsen. *The sacrifice of a throne, being an account of the life of Amadeus, duke of Aosta, sometime king of Spain.* New York. 1897.

IX. Historical Works on Special Subjects

Many of the items in sections III to VIII might appropriately be entered here. Conversely, as already indicated, the items of this section have a bearing on various or all of the periods of Spanish history, but it has been deemed best to give them separate entry, because of the obviously restricted character of the subject-matter of these volumes.

100. Caffin, Charles Henry. *The story of Spanish painting.* New York. 1910.
101. Castro y Rossi, Adolfo de. *The history of the Jews in Spain, from the time of their settlement in that country till the commencement of the present century.* Tr.ed.by Edward D.G.M.Kirwan. Cambridge and London. 1851. Orig.Sp.ed. Cádiz. 1847.
102. Clarke, Henry Butler. *Spanish literature; an elementary handbook.* London. 1893. 1909. Bib.
103. Dieulafoy, Marcel Auguste. . . . *Art in Spain and Portugal.* New York. 1913.
104. Fitzmaurice-Kelly, James. *Chapters on Spanish literature.* London. 1908.
105. Fitzmaurice-Kelly, James. *A history of Spanish literature.* New York. 1898. New York and London. 1915. Bib.
106. Hume, Martin Andrew Sharp. *Spanish influence on English literature.* London. 1905.
107. Lea, Henry Charles. *Chapters from the religious history of Spain connected with the Inquisition.* Philadelphia. 1890.
108. Lea, Henry Charles. *A history of the Inquisition of Spain.* 4v. New York and London. 1906-7.
109. Lindo, Elias Hiam. *The history of the Jews of Spain and Portugal, from the earliest times to their final expulsion from those kingdoms, and their subsequent dispersion.* London. 1848.
110. Markham, *Sir* Clements Robert. *The story of Majorca and Minorca.* London. 1908.
111. Sayer, *Capt.*Frederick. *The history of Gibraltar and of its political relation to events in Europe.* London. 1862.
112. Stirling-Maxwell, *Sir* William. *Stories of the Spanish painters until Goya.* London. 1910.
113. Stirling-Maxwell, *Sir* William. *Annals of the artists of Spain.* 3v. London. 1848. Bib.
114. Ticknor, George. *History of Spanish literature.* 3v. New York. 1849. Boston. [1891].
115. Webster, Wentworth. *Gleanings in church history, chiefly in Spain and France.* London. 1903. Bib.
116. Williams, Leonard. *The arts and crafts of older Spain.* 3v. London. 1907. Bib.

X. Works of Travel and Description

Of works published prior to 1900, only those of unusual reputation, whether because of the high station of the men who wrote them or the remarkable character of the books themselves, have been included. No attempt has been made to enter all works published in English since 1900, but the list is long enough and the scope of the material covered sufficiently broad, it is believed, for the purposes of the general reader who wishes to know something about contemporary Spain.

117. Amicis, Edmondo de. *Spain and the Spaniards.* Tr.[fr.10th It.ed.]ed.by Stanley Rhoads Yarnall. 2v. Philadelphia. 1895. Orig.It.ed. Florence. 1873.

118. Andújar, Manuel. *Spain of to-day from within.* New York and Chicago. [1909].

119. Baedeker, Karl. *Spain and Portugal.* Leipsic. 1898. 1913. Bib.

120. Bates, Katharine Lee. *Spanish highways and byways.* New York and London. 1912.

121. Bell, Aubrey F   G. *The magic of Spain.* London and New York. 1912[1911].

122. Bensusan, Samuel Levy. *Home life in Spain.* New York and London. 1910.

123. Borrow, George Henry. *The Bible in Spain.* London. 1843. New York. 1908.

124. Borrow, George Henry. *Zincali; or, An account of the gypsies of Spain.* 2v. London. 1841. 1v. London and New York. [1914].

125. Boyd, *Mrs.*Mary Stuart. *The fortunate isles; life and travel in Majorca, Minorca and Iviza.* New York. 1911.

126. Browne, Edith A. . . . *Spain.* London. 1910.

127. Calvert, Albert Frederick. *The Alhambra, being a brief record of the Arabian conquest of the peninsula with a particular account of the Mohammedan architecture and decoration.* London and New York. 1907.

128. Calvert, Albert Frederick. *Catalonia & the Balearic Isles; an historical and descriptive account.* London and New York. 1910.

129. Calvert, Albert Frederick. *The Escorial; a historical and descriptive account of the Spanish royal palace, monastery and mausoleum.* London and New York. 1907.

130. Calvert, Albert Frederick. *Granada, present and bygone.* London. 1908.

131. Calvert, Albert Frederick. *Impressions of Spain.* London. 1903.

132. Calvert, Albert Frederick. *Leon, Burgos and Salamanca; a historical and descriptive account.* London and New York. 1908.

133. Calvert, Albert Frederick. *Madrid; an historical description and handbook of the Spanish capital.* London and New York. 1909.
134. Calvert, Albert Frederick. *Moorish remains in Spain; being a brief record of the Arabian conquest of the peninsula with a particular account of the Mohammedan architecture and decoration in Cordova, Seville & Toledo.* London and New York. 1906.
135. Calvert, Albert Frederick. *Royal palaces of Spain; a historical & descriptive account of the seven principal palaces of the Spanish kings.* London and New York. 1909.
136. Calvert, Albert Frederick. *Sculpture in Spain.* London and New York. 1912.
137. Calvert, Albert Frederick. *Seville; an historical and descriptive account of "the Pearl of Andalusia."* London and New York. 1907.
138. Calvert, Albert Frederick. *Southern Spain.* London. 1908.
139. Calvert, Albert Frederick. *Spanish arms and armour, being a historical and descriptive account of the royal armoury of Madrid.* London and New York. 1907.
140. Calvert, Albert Frederick. *Toledo, an historical and descriptive account of the "City of generations."* London and New York. 1907.
141. Calvert, Albert Frederick. *Valencia and Murcia, a glance at African Spain.* London and New York. 1911.
142. Calvert, Albert Frederick. *Valladolid, Oviedo, Segovia, Zamora, Ávila, & Zaragoza; an historical & descriptive account.* London and New York. 1908.
143. Calvert, Albert Frederick, *and Mrs.*Catherine Gasquoine (Hartley) Gallichan. *The Prado; a description of the principal pictures in the Madrid gallery.* London and New York. 1907.
144. Calvert, Albert Frederick, *and* Walter M.Gallichan. *Cordova, a city of the Moors.* London and New York. 1907.
145. Chapman, Abel, *and* Walter J.Buck. *Unexplored Spain.* London. 1910.
146. Chapman, Abel, *and* Walter J.Buck. *Wild Spain . . . Records of sport with rifle, rod, and gun; natural history and exploration.* London. 1893.
147. Chatfield-Taylor, Hobart Chatfield. *The land of the castanet.* Chicago. 1896. New York. 1906.
148. Clark, Keith. *The spell of Spain.* Boston. 1914. Bib.
149. Collier, William Miller. *At the court of His Catholic Majesty.* Chicago. 1912.
150. Collins, W W. *Cathedral cities of Spain.* London and New York. 1909.
151. Crockett, Samuel Rutherford. *The adventurer in Spain.* London. 1903.

152. D'Este, Margaret. *With a camera in Majorca.* New York. 1907.
153. Dickinson, Duncan. *Through Spain.* London. [1914].
154. Elliott, *Mrs.*Maud (Howe). *Sun and shadow in Spain.* Boston. 1908. 1911.
155. Ellis, Henry Havelock. *The soul of Spain.* Boston and New York. [1908].
156. Fitz-Gerald, John Driscoll. *Rambles in Spain.* New York. [1910].
157. Flitch, John Ernest Crawford. *A little journey in Spain; notes of a Goya pilgrimage.* London. 1914.
158. Flitch, John Ernest Crawford. *Mediterranean moods, footnotes of travel in the islands of Mallorca, Menorca, Ibiza, and Sardinia.* London. 1911.
159. Ford, Richard. *Gatherings from Spain.* London. 1846. London and New York. [1906]. Bib. Also issued under the title *The Spaniards and their country.*
160. Ford, Richard. *Handbook for travellers in Spain.* 2v. London. 1845. 1898.
161. Franck, Harry Alverson. *Four months afoot in Spain.* New York. 1911.
162. Gade, John Allyne. *Cathedrals of Spain.* Boston and New York. 1911. Bib.
163. Gallichan, *Mrs.*Catherine Gasquoine (Hartley). *The cathedrals of southern Spain.* London[n.d. Not earlier than 1912].
164. Gallichan, *Mrs.*Catherine Gasquoine (Hartley). *Moorish cities in Spain.* London. 1906.
165. Gallichan, *Mrs.*Catherine Gasquoine (Hartley). *Spain revisited, a summer holiday in Galicia.* London. [1911?].
166. Gallichan, *Mrs.*Catherine Gasquoine (Hartley). *The story of Santiago de Compostela.* London and New York. 1912.
167. Gallichan, Walter M. *The story of Seville.* London. 1903.
168. Gautier, Théophile. *Wanderings in Spain.* London. 1853. Orig.Fr.ed.(*Tra los montes*) Paris. 1843. 2d.Fr.ed.(*Voyage en Espagne*) Paris. 1845.
169. Hart, Jerome A. *Two Argonauts in Spain.* San Francisco. 1904[1903].
170. Hay, John. *Castilian days.* Boston. 1871. Cambridge. 1903.
171. Higgin, L. *Spanish life in town and country.* London. 1902. New York and London. [1911].
172. Howells, William Dean. *Familiar Spanish travels.* New York and London. 1913.
173. Irving, Washington. *The Alhambra.* 2v. Philadelphia. 1832. 1v. Boston and New York. [c 1915].
174. Kennedy, Bart. *A tramp in Spain, from Andalusia to Andorra.* London. 1892. 1904.

175. Llewellyn, Owen, *and* L.R.Hill. *The south-bound car.* London. 1907.
176. Lomas, John. *In Spain.* London. 1908.
177. Lowell, James Russell. *Impressions of Spain.* Boston and New York. 1899.
178. Luffmann, Charles Bogue. *Quiet days in Spain.* London. 1910.
179. Luffman, Charles Bogue. *A vagabond in Spain.* London and New York. 1895.
180. Lynch, Hannah. *Toledo, the story of an old Spanish capital.* London. 1898. 1910.
181. Marden, Philip Sanford. *Travels in Spain.* Boston and New York. 1910.
182. Marriott, Charles. *A Spanish holiday.* New York. 1908.
183. Meakin, Annette M   B. *Galicia, the Switzerland of Spain.* London. [1909]. Bib.
184. Nixon-Roulet, Mary F. *The Spaniard at home.* Chicago. 1910.
185. O'Connor, Vincent Clarence Scott. *Travels in the Pyrenees, including Andorra and the coast from Barcelona to Carcassone.* London. 1913.
186. O'Reilly, Eliza Boyle. *Heroic Spain.* New York. 1910.
187. Penfield, Edward. *Spanish sketches.* New York. 1911.
188. Rudy, Charles. *The cathedrals of northern Spain, their history and their architecture.* Boston. 1906.
189. Seymour, Frederick H   A. *Saunterings in Spain; Barcelona, Madrid, Toledo, Cordova, Seville, Granada.* London. 1906.
190. Shaw, Rafael. *Spain from within.* New York. 1910.
191. Slater, Ernest, *pseud.*Paul Gwynne. *The Guadalquivir, its personality, its people and its associations.* London. 1912.
192. Street, George Edmund. ... *Some account of Gothic architecture in Spain.* 2v. London. 1865. 1914.
193. Tyler, Royall. *Spain, a study of her life and arts.* New York. 1909. Bib.
194. Villiers-Wardell, *Mrs.*Janie. *Spain of the Spanish.* New York. 1909. 1914.
195. Ward, G   H   B. *The truth about Spain.* London, New York, Toronto, and Melbourne. 1911.
196. Wigram, Edgar T   A. *Northern Spain, painted and described.* London. 1906.
197. Williams, Leonard. *Granada, memories, adventures, studies and impressions.* Philadelphia. 1906.
198. Williams, Leonard. *The land of the Dons.* London. 1902.
199. Williams, Leonard. *Toledo and Madrid, their records and romances.* London. 1903.
200. Wood, Charles William. *Glories of Spain.* London and New York. 1901.

201. Wood, Ruth Kedzie.   *The tourist's Spain and Portugal.*   New
           York.   1913.
202. Wood, Walter.   *A corner of Spain.*   New York and London.
           1910.
203. Zimmerman, Jeremiah.   *Spain and her people.*   Philadelphia.
           1902.   London.   1906.

INDEX

2 N

FREE PRESS PAPERBACKS

A Series of Paperbound Books in the Social and Natural Sciences, Philosophy, and the Humanities

These books, chosen for their intellectual importance and editorial excellence, are printed on good quality books paper, in large and readable type, and are Smyth-sewn for enduring use. Free Press Paperbacks conform in every significant way to the high editorial and production standards maintained in the higher-priced, case-bound books published by The Free Press.

**Many of these books are available in their original cloth bindings.
A complete catalogue of all Free Press titles will be sent on request**